BMW K100 & 75
Service and Repair Manual

by Jeremy Churchill and Penny Cox

UK models covered

K75. 740cc. UK Jan '87 to Sept '96, US Feb '88 to '95
K75C. 740cc. UK Sept '85 to Dec '88, US Feb '86 to '88
K75S. 740cc. UK Jan '86 to Sept '96, US Sept '86 to '95
K75T. 740cc. US only Feb '86 to '87
K75RT. 740cc. UK Apr '91 to Dec '96, US '90 to '95
K100. 987cc. UK Oct '83 to Aug '90, US Aug '84 to '86
K100RS. 987cc. UK Nov '83 to Aug '90, US Aug '84 to '89
K100RS Special Edition. 987cc. UK and US Jun '88 to '90
K100RT. 987cc. UK and US Aug '84 to Dec '88
K100LT. 987cc. UK Jan '87 to Apr '91, US Sept '86 to '92

Also covers the UK K75S Special and K100RS Special models of 1987 and K100RS Motorsport Limited Edition of 1986
The 4-valve engined models are not covered in this manual

(1373-256-11AM7)

© Haynes Publishing 2013

ABCDE
F
2

A book in the **Haynes Service and Repair Manual Series**

All rights reserved. No part of this book may be reproduced or transmitted in any form or by any means, electronic or mechanical, including photocopying, recording or by any information storage or retrieval system, without permission in writing from the copyright holder.

ISBN **978 1 78521 305 2**

British Library Cataloguing in Publication Data
A catalogue record for this book is available from the British Library.

Library of Congress Catalog Card Number 97-75029

Printed in the UK

Haynes Publishing
Sparkford, Nr Yeovil, Somerset BA22 7JJ, England

Haynes North America, Inc
861 Lawrence Drive, Newbury Park, California 91320, USA

Contents

LIVING WITH YOUR BMW

Introduction
BMW - They did it their way	Page	0•4
Acknowledgements	Page	0•7
About this manual	Page	0•7
Identification numbers	Page	0•8
Buying spare parts	Page	0•8
Safety first!	Page	0•9

Daily (pre-ride checks)
Engine oil level	Page	0•10
Hydraulic brake checks	Page	0•11
Coolant level	Page	0•12
Suspension, steering and controls	Page	0•12
Legal and safety checks	Page	0•12
Tyre checks	Page	0•13

MAINTENANCE

Routine maintenance and servicing
Specifications	Page	1•1
Recommended lubricants and fluids	Page	1•2
Maintenance schedule	Page	1•3
Component locations	Page	1•4
Maintenance procedures	Page	1•6

Contents

REPAIRS AND OVERHAUL

Engine, transmission and associated systems

Engine	Page	**2•1**
Clutch	Page	**3•1**
Gearbox	Page	**4•1**
Cooling system	Page	**5•1**
Fuel and lubrication systems	Page	**6•1**
Ignition system	Page	**7•1**

Chassis components

Frame and front suspension	Page	**8•1**
Final drive and rear suspension	Page	**9•1**
Wheels, brakes and tyres	Page	**10•1**

Electrical system
Page **11•1**

Wiring diagrams
Page **11•14**

REFERENCE

Dimensions and Weights	Page	**REF•1**
Tools and Workshop Tips	Page	**REF•2**
Conversion factors	Page	**REF•20**
Motorcycle Chemicals and Lubricants	Page	**REF•21**
MOT Test Checks	Page	**REF•22**
Storage	Page	**REF•27**
Fault Finding	Page	**REF•30**
Fault Finding Equipment	Page	**REF•39**
Technical Terms Explained	Page	**REF•43**

Index
Page **REF•47**

Introduction

BMW – They did it their way

by Julian Ryder

BMW - Bayerische Motoren Werke

If you were looking for a theme tune for BMW's engineering philosophy you'd have to look no further than Francis Albert Sinatra's best known ditty: 'I did it my way.' The Bayerische Motoren Werke, like their countrymen at Porsche, takes precious little notice of the way anyone else does it, point this out to a factory representative and you will get a reply starting: 'We at BMW... '. The implication is clear.

It was always like that. The first BMW motorcycle, the R32, was, according to motoring sage L J K Setright: 'the first really outstanding post-War design, argued from first principles and uncorrupted by established practice. It founded a new German school of design, it established a BMW tradition destined to survive unbroken from 1923 to the present day.' That tradition was, of course, the boxer twin. The nickname 'boxer' for an opposed twin is thought to derive from the fact that the pistons travel horizontally towards and away from each other like the fists of boxers.

Before this first complete motorcycle, BMW had built a horizontally-opposed fore-and-aft boxer engine for the Victoria company of Nuremburg. It was a close copy of the British Douglas motor which the company's chief engineer Max Friz admired, a fact the company's official history confirms despite what some current devotees of the marque will claim. In fact BMW didn't really want to make motorcycles at all, originally it was an aero-engine company - a fact celebrated in the blue-and-white tank badge that is symbolic of a propeller. But in Germany after the Treaty of Versailles such potentially warlike work was forbidden to domestic companies and BMW had to diversify, albeit reluctantly.

Friz was known to have a very low opinion of motorcycles and chose the Douglas to copy simply because he saw it as fundamentally a good solution to the engineering problem of powering a two-wheeler. In the R32 the engine was arranged with the crankshaft in-line with the axis of the bike and the cylinders sticking out into the cooling airflow, giving a very low centre-of-gravity and perfect vibration-free primary balance. It wasn't just the motor's layout that departed from normal practice, the clutch was a single-plate type as used in cars, final drive was by shaft and the rear wheel could be removed quickly. The frame and suspension were equally sophisticated, but the bike was quite heavy. Most of that description could be equally well applied to any of the boxer-engined bikes BMW made in the next 70-plus years.

Development within the surprisingly flexible confines of the boxer concept was quick. The second BMW, the R37 of 1925, retained the 68 x 68 mm Douglas bore and stroke but had overhead valves in place of the side valves. In 1928 two major milestones were passed. First, BMW acquired the car manufacturer Dixi and started manufacturing a left-hand-drive version of the Austin 7 under license. Secondly, the larger engined R62 and R63 appeared, the latter being an OHV sportster that would be the basis of BMW's sporting and record-breaking exploits before the Second World War.

The 1930s was the era of speed records on land, on sea and in the air, and the name of Ernst Henne is in the record books no fewer than ten times: eight for two-wheeled exploits, twice for wheel-on-a-stick 'sidecar' world records. At first he was on the R63 with supercharging, but in 1936 he switched to the 500 cc R5, high-pushrod design reminiscent of the latest generation of BMW twins. Chain-driven camshafts operated short pushrods which opened valves with hairpin - not coil - springs. A pure racing version of this motor also appeared, this time with shaft and bevel-gear driven overhead camshafts, but with short rockers operating the valves so the engine can't be called a true DOHC design. Again with the aid of a blower, this was the motor that powered the GP 500s of the late '30s to many wins including the 1939 Senior TT. After the War, this layout would re-emerge in the immortal Rennsport.

From 1939 to 1945 BMW were fully occupied making military machinery, notably the R75 sidecar for the army. The factory didn't restart production until 1948, and then only with a lightweight single. There was a false start in 1950 and a slump in sales in 1953 that endangered the whole company, before the situation was rescued by one of the truly classic boxers. Their first post-War twin had been the R51/2, and naturally it was very close to the pre-War model although simplified to a single-camshaft layout. Nevertheless, it was still a relatively advanced OHV design not a sidevalve sidecar tug which enabled a face-lift for the 1955 models to do the marketing trick.

The 1955 models got a swinging arm - at both ends. The old plunger rear suspension was replaced by a swinging arm while

The K75C model

Introduction 0•5

The K75S model

leading-link Earles forks adorned the front. Thus were born the R50, the R60 and the R69. The European market found these new bikes far too expensive compared to British twins but America saved the day, buying most of the company's output. The car side of the company also found a product the market wanted, a small sports-car powered by a modified bike engine, thus BMW's last crisis was averted

In 1960 the Earles fork models were updated and the R69S was launched with more power, closer transmission ratios and those funny little indicators on the ends of the handlebars. Very little changed during the '60s, apart from US export models getting telescopic forks, but in 1970 everything changed...

The move to Spandau and a new line of Boxers

BMW's bike side had outgrown its site in Munich at the company's headquarters, so, taking advantage of government subsidies for enterprises that located to what was then West Berlin, surrounded by the still Communist DDR, BMW built a new motorcycle assembly plant at Spandau in Berlin. It opened in 1969, producing a completely new range of boxers, the 5-series, which begat the 6-series, which begat the 7-series.

The K100RS model

0•6 Introduction

The K100RS Special Edition model

In 1976, at the same time as the launch of the 7-series the first RS boxer appeared. It's hard to believe now, but it was the only fully faired motorcycle, and it set the pattern for all BMWs, not just boxers, to come. The RS suffix came to mean a wonderfully efficient fairing that didn't spoil a sporty riding position. More sedate types could buy the RT version with a massive but no less efficient fairing that protected a more upright rider. Both bikes could carry luggage in a civilised fashion, too, thanks to purpose-built Krauser panniers. Both the RT and RS were uncommonly civilised motorcycles for their time.

When the boxer got its next major makeover in late 1980 BMW did something no-one thought possible, they made a boxer trail bike, the R80G/S. This wasn't without precedent as various supermen had wrestled 750 cc boxers to honours in the ISDT and in '81 Hubert Auriol won the Paris-Dakar on a factory boxer. Some heretics even dared to suggest the roadgoing G/S was the best boxer ever.

The K-series

By the end of the '70s the boxer was looking more and more dated alongside the opposition, and when the motorcycle division's management was shaken up at the beginning of 1979 the team working on the boxer replacement was doubled in size. The first new bike wasn't launched until late '83, but when it was it was clear that BMW had got as far away from the boxer concept as possible.

The powerplant was an in-line water-cooled DOHC four just like all the Japanese opposition, but typically BMW did it their way by aligning the motor so its crank was parallel to the axis of the bike and lying the motor on it side. In line with their normal practice, there was a car-type clutch, shaft drive and a single-sided swinging arm. It was totally novel yet oddly familiar. And when RT and RS version were introduced to supplement the basic naked bike, the new K-series 'flying bricks' felt even more familiar.

It was clear that BMW wanted the new four, and the three-cylinder 750 that followed it, to be the mainstay of the company's production - but in a further analogy with Porsche the customers simply wouldn't let go of the old boxer. Just as Porsche were forced to keep the 911 in production so BMW had to keep the old air-cooled boxer going by pressure from their customers. It kept going until 1995, during which time the K-bikes had debuted four-valve heads and ABS. And when the latest generation of BMWs appeared in 1993 what were they? Boxers. Granted they were four-valve, fuel-injected and equipped with non-telescopic fork front ends, but they were still boxers. And that high camshaft, short pushrod layout looked remarkably similar to something that had gone before...

The K100 and K75 models

The first chance the international motorcycle press got to ride the new K100 and K100RS was at a swish launch in the south of France. We were all rather perplexed. Here was a revolutionary departure from BMW's normal practice yet the bikes - especially the naked K100 - felt very familiar. I returned home and wrote one of my better headlines: 'Strangely Strange but Oddly Normal'. Although I'd pinched the title from an obscure Manchester band's album cover, it didn't alter the fact that the K100 was underwhelming and slightly crude in the same way as the old boxers; the appellation that stuck, though, was the Flying brick, a reference to the unusual lines of the engine.

The RS was a different matter. The addition of that small fairing transformed a bike that seemed purpose-free into a genuine sports tourer. Unthinkable as it may be today, people entered them in the Isle of Man TT and recorded 100 mph lap speeds. Again this is just like the Boxers; the naked bikes were orphans, the RS was the first mass-produced bike with a fairing and was a true classic. Even when Japan started putting a fairing on everything the RS's neat little windbreaker remained the most efficient, most comfortable fitted to

The K100RT model

Introduction

any bike. A K100RS with a set of Krauser panniers with nylon inner bags (BMW options, of course) was a true gentleman's high-speed tourer.

But we had to wait a year, until late 1984, for the quintessential K100, the RT model. This was a true tourer with a barn-door of a fairing and a relaxed, upright riding position. Once again a few pieces of plastic totally altered the character of the bike and removed it even further from the basic bike. This was the model that would go on to evolve into the K100LT at the start of 1987, a bike that incorporated much of the luxury the opposition built-in without adding the bulk, weight and complexity that seemed inevitable.

If there was a valid complaint against the K100 in all its guises it was that it did what most in-line fours do, it gave off a high-frequency secondary vibration that could numb the fingers on a long journey and try and shake its rider's left foot off its rest. The answer was the three-cylinder K75. It was in all respects externally identical to the K100 except for the subtle clue of the cross-section of the exhaust pipe; on the fours it was square, on the triples it was triangular.

Internally, the same 67 x 70 mm motor had its rear cylinder lopped off and its crankshaft rearranged to space the three throws at 120°. The result was a delightful motor with much of its fun-factor liberated. The first triple, the K75C of 1985, was in mildly touring trim with a headlamp cowl, bulbous radiator surrounds and a cost-saving drum rear brake. But the 750 that really made an impression was the K75S of 1986. This model was a sports tourer but it didn't ape the K100RS, it had its own neat half-fairing and belly pan as well as, crucially, reworked front fork internals. All the other Flying Bricks followed the usual BMW pattern of impersonating a high-speed lift when the front brake was applied, but the K75S's front end was stiffened up in both the springing and damping departments.

The K100LT model

In 1987 the K75 (no suffix) appeared with lowered seat and no headlamp cowl. This model, along with the K75S and the K75RT that didn't appear until 1991, lasted right up until 1996 when the new generation of boxers took over. The K75C faded away quietly while the four-cylinder bricks started going over to four-valve heads in 1989. The triples never got updated in that way but in many ways, not least their low cost, they are still the best of the eight-valve K-series bikes. Which is probably why they lasted so long in the model range.

Acknowledgements

Our thanks are due to CW Motorcycles of Dorchester who loaned the machines on which this manual was based. We would also like to thank NGK Spark Plugs (UK) Ltd for supplying the colour spark plug condition photos and the Avon Rubber Company for supplying information on tyre fitting.

Thanks are also due to Kel Edge for supplying the rear cover transparency, and to Paul Moverley for supplying the K100RS Special Edition model on the front cover. The introduction, "BMW - They did it their way" was written by Julian Ryder.

About this Manual

The aim of this manual is to help you get the best value from your motorcycle. It can do so in several ways. It can help you decide what work must be done, even if you choose to have it done by a dealer; it provides information and procedures for routine maintenance and servicing; and it offers diagnostic and repair procedures to follow when trouble occurs.

We hope you use the manual to tackle the work yourself. For many simpler jobs, doing it yourself may be quicker than arranging an appointment to get the motorcycle into a dealer and making the trips to leave it and pick it up. More importantly, a lot of money can be saved by avoiding the expense the shop must pass on to you to cover its labour and overhead costs. An added benefit is the sense of satisfaction and accomplishment that you feel after doing the job yourself.

References to the left or right side of the motorcycle assume you are sitting on the seat, facing forward.

We take great pride in the accuracy of information given in this manual, but motorcycle manufacturers make alterations and design changes during the production run of a particular motorcycle of which they do not inform us. No liability can be accepted by the authors or publishers for loss, damage or injury caused by any errors in, or omissions from, the information given.

0•8 Identification numbers

Frame and engine numbers

The engine number is stamped into a rectangular block raised up at the rear right-hand side of the crankcase lower section, immediately in front of the bellhousing joint. The frame number is stamped into the right-hand frame tube that joins the rear suspension unit top mounting to the gearbox mounting. Note that the number is duplicated in the plate riveted to the same tube. Both of these numbers should be recorded and kept in a safe place so they can be furnished to law enforcement officials in the event of a theft.

The frame and engine numbers should also be kept in a handy place (such as with your driver's licence) so they are always available when purchasing or ordering parts for your machine.

Frame number location

Engine number location

Buying spare parts

When ordering replacement parts, it is essential to identify exactly the machine for which the parts are required. While in some cases it is sufficient to identify the machine by its title eg 'K100RS', the many modifications to most components mean that it is usually essential to identify the machine by its BMW **production** or model year eg 1986.

The BMW production year starts in September of the previous calendar year, after the annual holiday, and continues until the following August. Therefore a 1986 K100RS was **produced** at some time between September 1985 and August 1986; it may have been **sold** (to its first owner) at any time from September 1985 onwards. To avoid any further confusion, models are referred to **at all times** in this Manual by their BMW **production** or model year; to identify your own machine, record its full engine and frame numbers and take them to any BMW dealer who should have the necessary information to identify it exactly. Finally, in some cases modifications can be identified only by reference to the machine's engine or frame number; these should be noted and taken with you whenever replacement parts are required. Dates are given as precisely as possible where relevant in the text of this manual but care is usually required since some machines may well have been modified already.

To be absolutely certain of receiving the correct part, not only is it essential to have the machine's identifying title and engine and frame numbers, but it is also useful to take the old part for comparison (where possible). Note that where a modified component has superseded the original, a careful check must be made that there are no related parts which have also been modified and must be used to enable the replacement to be correctly refitted; where such a situation is found, purchase all the necessary parts and fit them, even if this means replacing apparently unworn items.

Always purchase replacement parts from an authorised BMW dealer who will either have the parts in stock or can order them quickly from the importer, and always use genuine parts to ensure the machine's performance and reliability. Pattern parts are not widely available for BMWs, being generally restricted to items such as disc brake pads, oil and air filters and exhaust system components. Unless these are of recognised quality brands which will perform as well as or better than the original, they should be avoided.

Expendable items such as lubricants, spark plugs, some electrical components, bearings, bulbs and tyres can usually be obtained at lower prices from accessory shops, motor factors or from specialists advertising in the national motorcycle press.

Safety first!

Professional mechanics are trained in safe working procedures. However enthusiastic you may be about getting on with the job at hand, take the time to ensure that your safety is not put at risk. A moment's lack of attention can result in an accident, as can failure to observe simple precautions.

There will always be new ways of having accidents, and the following is not a comprehensive list of all dangers; it is intended rather to make you aware of the risks and to encourage a safe approach to all work you carry out on your bike.

Asbestos
● Certain friction, insulating, sealing and other products - such as brake pads, clutch linings, gaskets, etc. - contain asbestos. Extreme care must be taken to avoid inhalation of dust from such products since it is hazardous to health. If in doubt, assume that they do contain asbestos.

Fire
● Remember at all times that petrol is highly flammable. Never smoke or have any kind of naked flame around, when working on the vehicle. But the risk does not end there - a spark caused by an electrical short-circuit, by two metal surfaces contacting each other, by careless use of tools, or even by static electricity built up in your body under certain conditions, can ignite petrol vapour, which in a confined space is highly explosive. Never use petrol as a cleaning solvent. Use an approved safety solvent.

● Always disconnect the battery earth terminal before working on any part of the fuel or electrical system, and never risk spilling fuel on to a hot engine or exhaust.
● It is recommended that a fire extinguisher of a type suitable for fuel and electrical fires is kept handy in the garage or workplace at all times. Never try to extinguish a fuel or electrical fire with water.

Fumes
● Certain fumes are highly toxic and can quickly cause unconsciousness and even death if inhaled to any extent. Petrol vapour comes into this category, as do the vapours from certain solvents such as trichloro-ethylene. Any draining or pouring of such volatile fluids should be done in a well ventilated area.
● When using cleaning fluids and solvents, read the instructions carefully. Never use materials from unmarked containers - they may give off poisonous vapours.
● Never run the engine of a motor vehicle in an enclosed space such as a garage. Exhaust fumes contain carbon monoxide which is extremely poisonous; if you need to run the engine, always do so in the open air or at least have the rear of the vehicle outside the workplace.

The battery
● Never cause a spark, or allow a naked light near the vehicle's battery. It will normally be giving off a certain amount of hydrogen gas, which is highly explosive.

● Always disconnect the battery ground (earth) terminal before working on the fuel or electrical systems (except where noted).
● If possible, loosen the filler plugs or cover when charging the battery from an external source. Do not charge at an excessive rate or the battery may burst.
● Take care when topping up, cleaning or carrying the battery. The acid electrolyte, evenwhen diluted, is very corrosive and should not be allowed to contact the eyes or skin. Always wear rubber gloves and goggles or a face shield. If you ever need to prepare electrolyte yourself, always add the acid slowly to the water; never add the water to the acid.

Electricity
● When using an electric power tool, inspection light etc., always ensure that the appliance is correctly connected to its plug and that, where necessary, it is properly grounded (earthed). Do not use such appliances in damp conditions and, again, beware of creating a spark or applying excessive heat in the vicinity of fuel or fuel vapour. Also ensure that the appliances meet national safety standards.
● A severe electric shock can result from touching certain parts of the electrical system, such as the spark plug wires (HT leads), when the engine is running or being cranked, particularly if components are damp or the insulation is defective. Where an electronic ignition system is used, the secondary (HT) voltage is much higher and could prove fatal.

Remember...

✗ **Don't** start the engine without first ascertaining that the transmission is in neutral.
✗ **Don't** suddenly remove the pressure cap from a hot cooling system - cover it with a cloth and release the pressure gradually first, or you may get scalded by escaping coolant.
✗ **Don't** attempt to drain oil until you are sure it has cooled sufficiently to avoid scalding you.
✗ **Don't** grasp any part of the engine or exhaust system without first ascertaining that it is cool enough not to burn you.
✗ **Don't** allow brake fluid or antifreeze to contact the machine's paintwork or plastic components.
✗ **Don't** siphon toxic liquids such as fuel, hydraulic fluid or antifreeze by mouth, or allow them to remain on your skin.
✗ **Don't** inhale dust - it may be injurious to health (see Asbestos heading).
✗ **Don't** allow any spilled oil or grease to remain on the floor - wipe it up right away, before someone slips on it.
✗ **Don't** use ill-fitting spanners or other tools which may slip and cause injury.
✗ **Don't** lift a heavy component which may be beyond your capability - get assistance.

✗ **Don't** rush to finish a job or take unverified short cuts.
✗ **Don't** allow children or animals in or around an unattended vehicle.
✗ **Don't** inflate a tyre above the recommended pressure. Apart from overstressing the carcass, in extreme cases the tyre may blow off forcibly.
✓ **Do** ensure that the machine is supported securely at all times. This is especially important when the machine is blocked up to aid wheel or fork removal.
✓ **Do** take care when attempting to loosen a stubborn nut or bolt. It is generally better to pull on a spanner, rather than push, so that if you slip, you fall away from the machine rather than onto it.
✓ **Do** wear eye protection when using power tools such as drill, sander, bench grinder etc.
✓ **Do** use a barrier cream on your hands prior to undertaking dirty jobs - it will protect your skin from infection as well as making the dirt easier to remove afterwards; but make sure your hands aren't left slippery. Note that long-term contact with used engine oil can be a health hazard.
✓ **Do** keep loose clothing (cuffs, ties etc. and long hair) well out of the way of moving mechanical parts.

✓ **Do** remove rings, wristwatch etc., before working on the vehicle - especially the electrical system.
✓ **Do** keep your work area tidy - it is only too easy to fall over articles left lying around.
✓ **Do** exercise caution when compressing springs for removal or installation. Ensure that the tension is applied and released in a controlled manner, using suitable tools which preclude the possibility of the spring escaping violently.
✓ **Do** ensure that any lifting tackle used has a safe working load rating adequate for the job.
✓ **Do** get someone to check periodically that all is well, when working alone on the vehicle.
✓ **Do** carry out work in a logical sequence and check that everything is correctly assembled and tightened afterwards.
✓ **Do** remember that your vehicle's safety affects that of yourself and others. If in doubt on any point, get professional advice.
● If in spite of following these precautions, you are unfortunate enough to injure yourself, seek medical attention as soon as possible.

0•10 Daily (pre-ride) checks

1 Engine oil level

Before you start:

✔ Place the motorcycle on the centerstand, then start the engine and allow it to reach normal operating temperature.

Caution: Do not run the engine in an enclosed space such as a garage or workshop.

✔ Stop the engine and allow the machine to sit undisturbed for a few minutes to allow the oil level to settle.

Bike care:

- If you have to add oil frequently, you should check whether you have any oil leaks. If there is no sign of oil leakage from the joints and gaskets the engine could be burning oil *(see Fault Finding)*.
- Never run the engine with the level below the oil level sight glass or above it; both conditions can lead to engine damage.
- In normal use the sight glass will be self-cleaning, but if the machine is used only in cold weather. or infrequently, or for very short journeys only, the glass will become obscured by deposits of emulsified sludge. The only way to avoid this is to take the machine regularly on a journey of sufficient length to warm it up thoroughly; this will evaporate the moisture from the oil and should clean the glass. If this is not possible, the engine oil must be changed at frequent intervals to keep it and the engine clean; note that the starter clutch may slip on early models if the sludge deposits are allowed to build up too much.

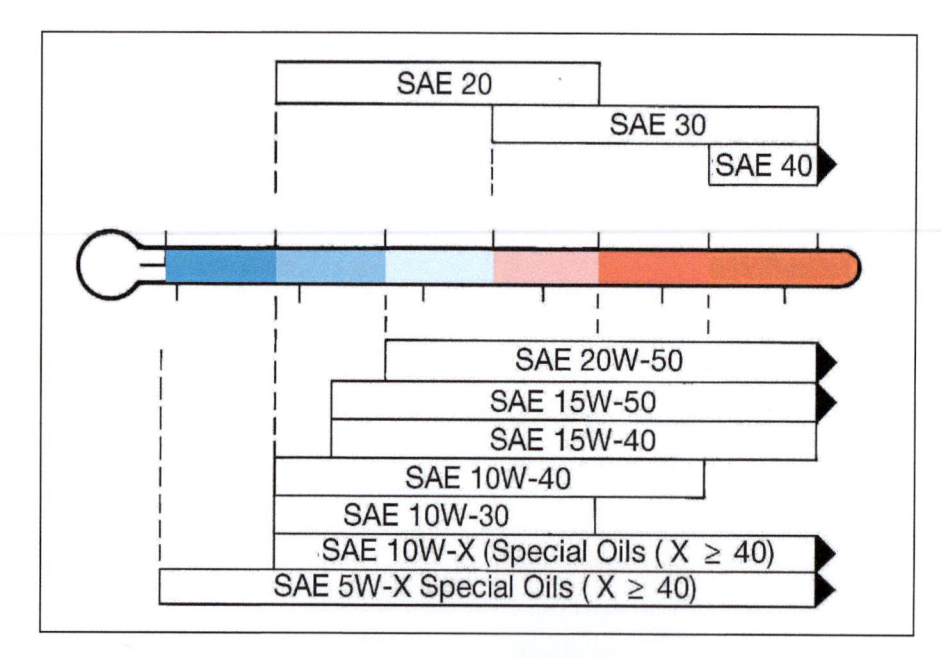

The correct oil

- Motorcycle engines place great demands on their oil. It is very important that the correct oil for your bike is used.
- Always top up with a good quality oil of the specified type and viscosity and do not overfill the engine.

Oil type	Good quality HD oil suitable for spark ignition engines. API classification SF, SG or SH
Oil viscosity	Refer to accompanying viscosity chart and select a viscosity to suit the prevailing outside temperatures. BMW recommend a medium range multigrade, eg 10W/30 is preferable to a wide range multigrade such as 10W/50. A multigrade oil is preferable to a monograde oil.

1 Check the oil level as seen in the sight glass set in the right-hand side of the crankcase lower section. The maximum and minimum level marks are indicated by imaginary horizontal lines drawn through the top and bottom of the circle marked on the glass; the oil level should be maintained between these marks; i.e. somewhere in the circle, at all times.

2 If topping-up is required, remove the filler plug from the rear end of the engine right-hand outer (crankshaft) cover and add the required amount of oil; it will take approximately 0.6 litre (1.06 Imp pint) to fill the crankcase from Minimum to Maximum. Do not overfill.

Daily (pre-ride) checks

2 Hydraulic brake checks

Before you start:

> **Warning:** Brake hydraulic fluid can harm your eyes and damage painted surfaces, so use extreme caution when handling and pouring it and cover surrounding surfaces with rag. Do not use fluid that has been standing open for some time, as it absorbs moisture from the air which can cause a dangerous loss of braking/clutch effectiveness.

✔ Use only good quality brake fluid of the recommended type (DOT 4) and ensure that it comes from a freshly opened sealed container; brake fluid is hygroscopic, which means that it absorbs moisture from the air, therefore old fluid may have become contaminated to such an extent that its boiling point has been lowered to an unsafe level.

✔ With the motorcycle held level, turn the handlebars until the top of the master cylinder is as level as possible (front brake only). On 1983 to 1987 models, the rear brake fluid reservoir is clearly visible above the right-hand footrest plate; on all 1988-on models, remove the right-hand side panel for access to the fluid reservoir.

Bike care:

● In order to ensure proper operation of the hydraulic disc brake, the fluid level in the master cylinder reservoir must be properly maintained. If the brake fluid level was low, inspect the brake system for leaks.

● Remember that while the fluid level will fall steadily as the pad friction material is used up, if the level falls below the lower level mark there is a risk of air entering the system; it is therefore sufficient to maintain the fluid level above the lower level mark, by topping-up if necessary.

● Check the operation of the hydraulic disc brakes before taking the machine on the road; if there is evidence of air in the system (spongy feel to lever or pedal), it must be bled as described in Chapter 10.

● On models with a rear drum brake, ensure that the rod linkage is lubricated and properly adjusted.

● Before removing the master cylinder cap, protect the motorcycle from brake fluid spills (which will damage the paint) and remove all dust and dirt from the area around the cap.

1 Front brake fluid reservoir level marks. Fluid must be above MIN level.

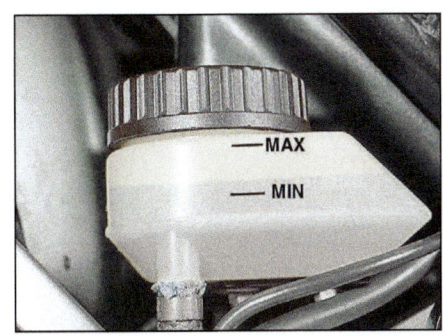

2 Rear brake fluid reservoir level marks (early models). Fluid must be above MIN level.

3 Rear brake fluid reservoir level marks (later models). Fluid must be above MIN level.

4 To top up, unscrew the cap (rear) or remove the cover screws (front). Lift out the diaphragm . . .

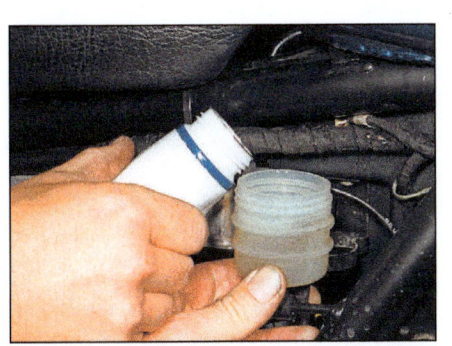

5 . . . and top up with new DOT 4 brake fluid until the level is between the MIN and MAX lines.

6 Clean and dry the diaphragm, fold it into its compressed state and fit it to the reservoir. Install the cap (rear) or cover (front).

0•12 Daily (pre-ride) checks

3 Coolant level

Before you start:
✔ Since the coolant level varies with engine temperature, it must be checked only when the engine is cold, so always perform this check before starting the engine for the first time each day.
✔ Place the motorcycle on the centerstand. Make sure the motorcycle is on level ground.

Bike care:
● Use only the specified coolant mixture (see Chapter 5). It is important that antifreeze is used in the cooling system all year round, not just during the winter months. Don't top-up with water alone, as the antifreeze will become too diluted.
● Do not overfill the coolant expansion tank. The coolant level is satisfactory if it is between the Min and Max marks on the tank. If the level tube is so discoloured that the coolant level cannot be seen, it should be renewed and the system should be refilled using the specified, nitride-free, antifreeze.
● If the coolant level seems to be consistently low, check the entire cooling system for leaks; only very small losses should occur in normal use.

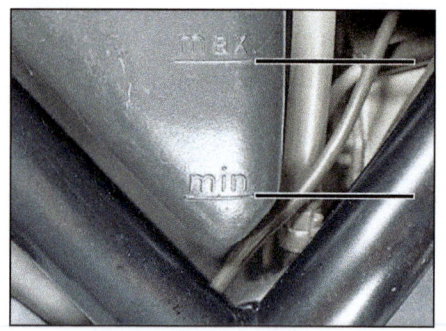

1 The expansion tank situated beneath the right-hand side panel has a level tube . . .

2 . . . or translucent area of plastic mounted on its front end with Maximum and Minimum level marks on the tank itself

3 If the level is at or below the Min mark, add the recommended coolant mixture until the Max level is reached.

4 Suspension, steering and controls

Suspension and steering:
● Make sure the steering operates smoothly, without looseness and without binding.
● Check front and rear suspension for smooth operation. Except for machines with Nivomat rear suspension, ensure that the rear suspension unit spring preload adjuster is at the correct setting for the machine's intended load.

Controls:
● Check the throttle and clutch cables and levers and the gear lever to ensure that they are adjusted correctly, functioning correctly, and that they are securely fastened. If a bolt is going to work loose, or a cable snap, it is better that it is discovered at this stage with the machine at a standstill, rather than when it is being ridden.

● Check that all fasteners are tightened securely, particularly the wheel spindle retainer and clamp bolts, the rear wheel mounting bolts and the stand, footrest and suspension unit bolts or nuts. Use the torque settings at the beginning of the following chapters if any are loose.

5 Legal and safety checks

Lighting and signalling:
● Take a minute to check that the headlamp, tail lamp, brake stop lamp and turn signals all work correctly. Check that the headlamp beam is correctly aimed - see Chapter 11 for details.
● Check that the horn sounds when the switch is operated.
● A working speedometer is a statutory requirement in the UK.

ABS check:
● On ABS-equipped models, check the system prior to riding. Once the ignition is switched on the ABS light, situated at the bottom of the speedometer, will flash on and off. At the same time the warning light (which doubles as the tail lamp warning light), situated in the central column will illuminate until the brake lever and pedal have been operated, at which point it will also flash on and off. As the machine begins to move (above 2.5 mph/4.0 kmh) and the system's checking operation is complete both lights should extinguish.

Drum brake check – K75, K75C and K75T:
● Check that the drum rear brake works effectively and without binding.
● Check that the brake rod linkage is lubricated and properly adjusted. Refer to Chapter 1 if adjustment is necessary.

Safety:
● Check that the throttle grip rotates smoothly and snaps shut when released, in all steering positions.
● Check that the engine shuts off when the kill switch is operated.

● Check that sidestand return spring holds the stand securely up when retracted. The same applies to the centerstand (where fitted).

Fuel:
● This may seem obvious, but check that you have enough fuel to complete your journey. If you notice signs of fuel leakage - rectify the cause immediately.
● Ensure you use the correct grade fuel.
● Be very careful not to allow dirt or water into the fuel tank, particularly when opening the filler cap, and never fill the tank to the brim; always leave a space at the top to allow for fuel expansion under engine heat. Owners of US models should note that the flap beneath the filler cap is fitted to prevent the tank from being overfilled; the flap must never be removed or modified - see Chapter 6 for more information.

Daily (pre-ride) checks

6 Tyre checks

Tyre care:

● Check the tyres carefully for cuts, tears, embedded nails or other sharp objects and excessive wear. Operation of the motorcycle with excessively worn tyres is extremely hazardous, as traction and handling are directly affected.

● Check the condition of the tyre valve and ensure the dust cap is in place.

● Pick out any stones or nails which may have become embedded in the tyre tread. If left, they will eventually penetrate through the casing and cause a puncture.

● If tyre damage is apparent, or unexplained loss of pressure is experienced, seek the advice of a tyre fitting specialist without delay.

Tyre tread depth:

● At the time of writing UK law requires that tread depth must be at least 1 mm over 3/4 of the tread breadth all the way around the tyre, with no bald patches. Many riders, however, consider 2 mm tread depth minimum to be a safer limit. BMW recommend a minimum tread depth of 2 mm (0.08 in) for the front tyre; for the rear tyre they recommend 2 mm (0.08 in) for speeds below 80 mph (130 km/h), and 3 mm (0.12 in) for speeds above this.

● Many tyres now incorporate wear indicators in the tread. Identify the triangular pointer on the tyre sidewall to locate the indicator bar and replace the tyre if the tread has worn down to the bar.

The correct pressures:

● The tyres must be checked when **cold**, not immediately after riding. Note that low tyre pressures may cause the tyre to slip on the rim or come off. High tyre pressures will cause abnormal tread wear and unsafe handling.

● Use an accurate pressure gauge.

● Proper air pressure will increase tyre life and provide maximum stability and ride comfort.

● The tyre pressures in the table are recommended by BMW only for the tyres fitted as standard, and should be checked by reference to the tyre information label on the machine in case different types of tyre were fitted at the factory or if the pressure recommendations have been revised.

● Check that the pressures are suited to the load the machine is carrying and the speed at which it will be travelling.

Tyre pressures	Front	Rear
75 models		
Solo	29 psi (2.00 bar)	36 psi (2.50 bar)
Pillion	34 psi (2.30 bar)	42 psi (2.90 bar)
100 models		
Solo	33 psi (2.25 bar)	36 psi (2.50 bar)
Pillion - up to 112 mph (180 km/h)	33 psi (2.25 bar)	39 psi (2.70 bar)
Pillion - above 112 mph (180 km/h)	39 psi (2.70 bar)	42 psi (2.90 bar)

1 Check the tyre pressures when the tyres are **cold** and keep them properly inflated.

2 Measure the tread depth at the centre of the tyre using a tread depth gauge.

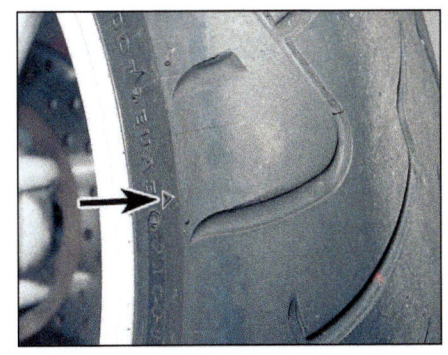

3 Tyre tread wear indicator bar location marking on the sidewall (arrow).

0•14 Daily (pre-ride) checks

Notes

Chapter 1
Routine maintenance and servicing

Contents

Air filter element - clean	8	Final inspection	10
Air filter element - renewal	15	Front fork - oil change	13
ABS - check and overhaul	4	Fuel filter - renewal	26
Battery - check	9	Fuel system - check	19
Clutch - check and adjustment	17	Gearbox - oil change	11
Controls and stand pivots - lubrication	5	Gearbox - oil level check	2
Cooling system - check	16	Spark plugs - check and adjustment	7
Disc brake fluid - renewal	21	Spark plugs - renewal	18
Disc brake pads - wear check and renewal	20	Speedometer impulse transmitter - clean	14
Drum brake - check and adjustment	22	Steering head bearings - check and adjustment	24
Engine oil and filter - change	1	Swinging arm pivot bearings - check	25
Final drive case - oil change	12	Valve clearances - check and adjustment (1983 to 1988 models)	6
Final drive case - oil level check	3	Valve clearances - check and adjustment (1989-on models)	28
Final drive shaft splines - greasing	27	Wheels and wheel bearings - check	23

Degrees of difficulty

Easy, suitable for novice with little experience
Fairly easy, suitable for beginner with some experience
Fairly difficult, suitable for competent DIY mechanic
Difficult, suitable for experienced DIY mechanic
Very difficult, suitable for expert DIY or professional

Specifications

Engine
Spark plugs ..... Bosch X5DC
Spark plug gap:
   Standard ..... 0.6 - 0.7 mm (0.024 - 0.028 in)
   Service limit ..... 0.8 mm (0.032 in)
Valve clearances - engine cold (maximum coolant temperature 20°C/68°F):
   Intake ..... 0.15 - 0.20 mm (0.006 - 0.008 in)
   Exhaust ..... 0.25 - 0.30 mm (0.010 - 0.012 in)
Idle speed ..... 950 ± 50 rpm
Throttle and 'choke' cable free play ..... 0.5 - 1.0 mm (0.02 - 0.04 in)
Clutch cable free play - at handlebar lever:
   75 models ..... 2.0 - 2.5 mm (0.08 - 0.10 in)
   100 models ..... 4.0 - 4.5 mm (0.16 - 0.18 in)
Length of clutch inner cable at gearbox end ..... 75 ± 1 mm (2.95 ± 0.04 in)

Cycle parts
Brake pad/shoe friction material minimum thickness ..... 1.5 mm (0.06 in)
ABS wheel speed sensor clearance ..... 0.35 - 0.65 mm (0.0138 - 0.0256 in)
Drum rear brake free play - at pedal tip ..... 15 - 25 mm (0.6 - 1.0 in)
Tyre pressures - tyres cold:

	Front	Rear
75 models:		
Solo	29 psi (2.00 bar)	36 psi (2.50 bar)
Pillion	34 psi (2.30 bar)	42 psi (2.90 bar)
100 models:		
Solo	33 psi (2.25 bar)	36 psi (2.50 bar)
Pillion - up to 112 mph (180 km/h)	33 psi (2.25 bar)	39 psi (2.70 bar)
Pillion - above 112 mph (180 km/h)	39 psi (2.70 bar)	42 psi (2.90 bar)

Note: *information is correct at time of writing - check with machine's handbook or label on rear mudguard for updated information. Pressures apply to original equipment tyres only - check with BMW dealer/importer or tyre manufacturer or agent if non-standard tyres are fitted - pressures may vary.*

Servicing specifications

Torque wrench settings

	Nm	lbf ft
Engine oil filter:		
1st stage	Lightly oil filter seal, screw on by hand until seal seats on machined surface	
2nd stage	Tighten through ½ turn **maximum** (10 – 12 Nm, 7.5 – 9 lbf ft)	
Engine oil pan (sump) and filter cover screws	7 ± 1	5 ± 0.5
Engine oil drain plug	32 ± 4	23.5 ± 3
Gearbox oil filler and drain plugs	20 ± 3	15 ± 2
Final drive case oil filler plug	20 ± 2	15 ± 1.5
Final drive case oil drain plug	25 ± 3	18.5 ± 2
Spark plugs	20 ± 2	15 ± 1.5
Front fork oil drain plugs:		
1985-95 75 models, all 100 models	9 ± 1	6.5 ± 0.5
1993-on 75 models	Not available	
Front fork oil filler plugs		
1985-95 75 models, all 100 models	15 ± 2	11 ± 1.5
1993-on 75 models	Not available	
Steering stem top bolt	74 ± 5	54.5 ± 4
Steering stem adjuster sleeve – late 75 models	45 ± 3	33 ± 2
Steering stem adjuster sleeve locknut – late 75 models	45 ± 3	33 ± 2
Swinging arm adjustable pivot stub	7.3 ± 0.5	5.4 ± 0.4
Swinging arm adjustable pivot stub locknut	41 ± 3	30 ± 2

Recommended lubricants

Engine
  Capacity - at oil and filter change ... 3.75 lit (6.6 Imp pint, 3.9 US qt)
  Recommended oil ... Good quality HD oil suitable for 4-stroke spark ignition engines. API classification SF, SH or SH
  Viscosity ... See chart in *Daily (pre-ride) checks*

Gearbox and final drive case
  Capacity:
    Gearbox ... 850 ± 50 cc (1.50 ± 0.09 Imp pint, 0.90 ± 0.05 US qt)
    Final drive case ... 260 cc (0.46 Imp pint, 0.28 US qt)
  Recommended oil ... Good quality hypoid gear oil of API class GL-5 or to specification MIL-L-2105 B or C
  Viscosity:
    Above 5°C (41°F) ... SAE 90
    Below 5°C (41°F) ... SAE 80
    Alternatively ... SAE 80W90

Coolant ... See Chapter 5
Fuel ... See Chapter 6

Front forks
  Capacity - per leg:
    K75 S, any model with 'S' suspension ... 280 ± 10 cc (9.86 ± 0.35 Imp fl oz, 9.47 ± 0.34 US fl oz)
    K100 all other 75 models ... 330 ± 10 cc (11.62 ± 0.35 Imp fl oz, 11.16 ± 0.34 US fl oz)
    K100 RS, K100 RT, K100 LT ... 360 ± 10 cc (12.67 ± 0.35 Imp fl oz, 12.17 ± 0.34 US fl oz)
  Recommended oil ... Use specified brands and types only - see Chapter 8

Brake fluid ... DOT 4, eg ATE 'SL'

Splined couplings and joints, ie clutch plate, gearbox input shaft, final drive shaft ... Staburags NBU 30 PTM compound, Optimol Paste PL or Uni Moly C 220 Slip Agent

Front wheel, steering head and swinging arm pivot bearings ... Good quality high melting-point lithium fibre-based grease, eg Shell Retinax A

Fluidbloc steering head damper ... Silicone grease **only** eg 'Silicone Grease 300 Heavy

All other greasing points ... As wheel bearing type

Battery terminals ... Petroleum jelly (Vaseline) or acid-free grease eg Bosch Ft 40 V1

Control cable nipples and all other pivots ... Engine oil or light machine oil

Control cables ... Nylon lined - if lubrication is considered necessary use only suitable lubricant

Maintenance schedule

Service intervals - mileage:
BMW maintenance is grouped into two parts, a minor and a major service which must be carried out at the following intervals:

Minor service every 10,000 miles (15,000 km) starting with the first 5000 miles (7500 km)
Major service every 10,000 miles (15,000 km) starting with the first 10,000 miles (15,000 km)

Therefore minor and major services should be carried out alternately at every 5000 miles (7500 km).

Service intervals - time:
If the machine is not used regularly, or does not cover a high mileage, the service intervals can be applied as follows to preserve the machine's performance and reliability.
Therefore the minor service should be carried out at least every six months, and the major service at least once annually.

Daily or before riding
- [ ] See 'Daily (pre-ride) checks' at the beginning of this Manual.

Minor service
- [ ] Engine oil and filter change (Section 1) - see Note 1
- [ ] Gearbox oil level check (Section 2)
- [ ] Final drive case oil level check (Section 3)
- [ ] Anti-lock braking system check and overhaul (Section 4)
- [ ] Controls and stand pivots lubrication (Section 5)
- [ ] Valve clearances check and adjustment - models up to 1989 (Section 6)
- [ ] Spark plugs check and adjustment (Section 7)
- [ ] Air filter element clean (Section 8) - see Note 2
- [ ] Battery check (Section 9) - see Note 3
- [ ] Final inspection (Section 10)

Major service
Perform all of the checks under the Minor service heading

- [ ] Gearbox oil change (Section 11) - see Note 4
- [ ] Final drive case oil change (Section 12) - see Note 5
- [ ] Front forks oil change (Section 13) - see Note 6
- [ ] Speedometer impulse transmitter clean (Section 14)
- [ ] Air filter element renewal (Section 15) - see Note 2
- [ ] Cooling system check (Section 16) - see Note 7
- [ ] Clutch check and adjustment (Section 17)
- [ ] Spark plugs renewal (Section 18)
- [ ] Fuel system check (Section 19)
- [ ] Disc brake pad check (Section 20)
- [ ] Disc brake fluid renewal (Section 21) - see Note 8
- [ ] Drum brake check and adjustment (Section 22)
- [ ] Wheels and wheel bearings check (Section 23) - see Note 9
- [ ] Steering head bearings check (Section 24) - see Note 9
- [ ] Swinging arm pivot bearings check (Section 25)
- [ ] Fuel filter renewal (Section 26) - see Note 10
- [ ] Final drive shaft splines grease (Section 27)
- [ ] Valve clearances check and adjustment - models from 1989 (Section 6)

Notes - Additional recommendations:
1. Engine oil - in normal use the engine oil should be changed every six months at the latest. If the machine is used in temperatures below 0°C (32°F), or for short, local journeys only, the oil should be changed every 2000 miles (3000 km) or three months at the latest.
2. Air filter - should be cleaned and renewed at more frequent intervals if the machine is used in very dusty or severe conditions.
3. Battery - should be checked at least every three months.
4. Gearbox oil - must be changed at least once annually.
5. Final drive case oil - must be changed at least once annually.
6. Front fork oil - must be changed at least once annually.
7. Coolant - must be changed every two years at least.
8. Hydraulic brake fluid - must be changed annually.
9. Wheel and steering head bearings - if conditions are very severe these bearings and the twistgrip must be cleaned and packed with new grease every 20,000 miles (30,000 km). Refer to the relevant Sections of Chapters 10 and 8.
10. Fuel filter - must be renewed every 20,000 miles (30,000 km) in normal use, ie every second major service, but if the fuel is dirty or of poor quality it must be renewed at every major service.

1•4 Component locations

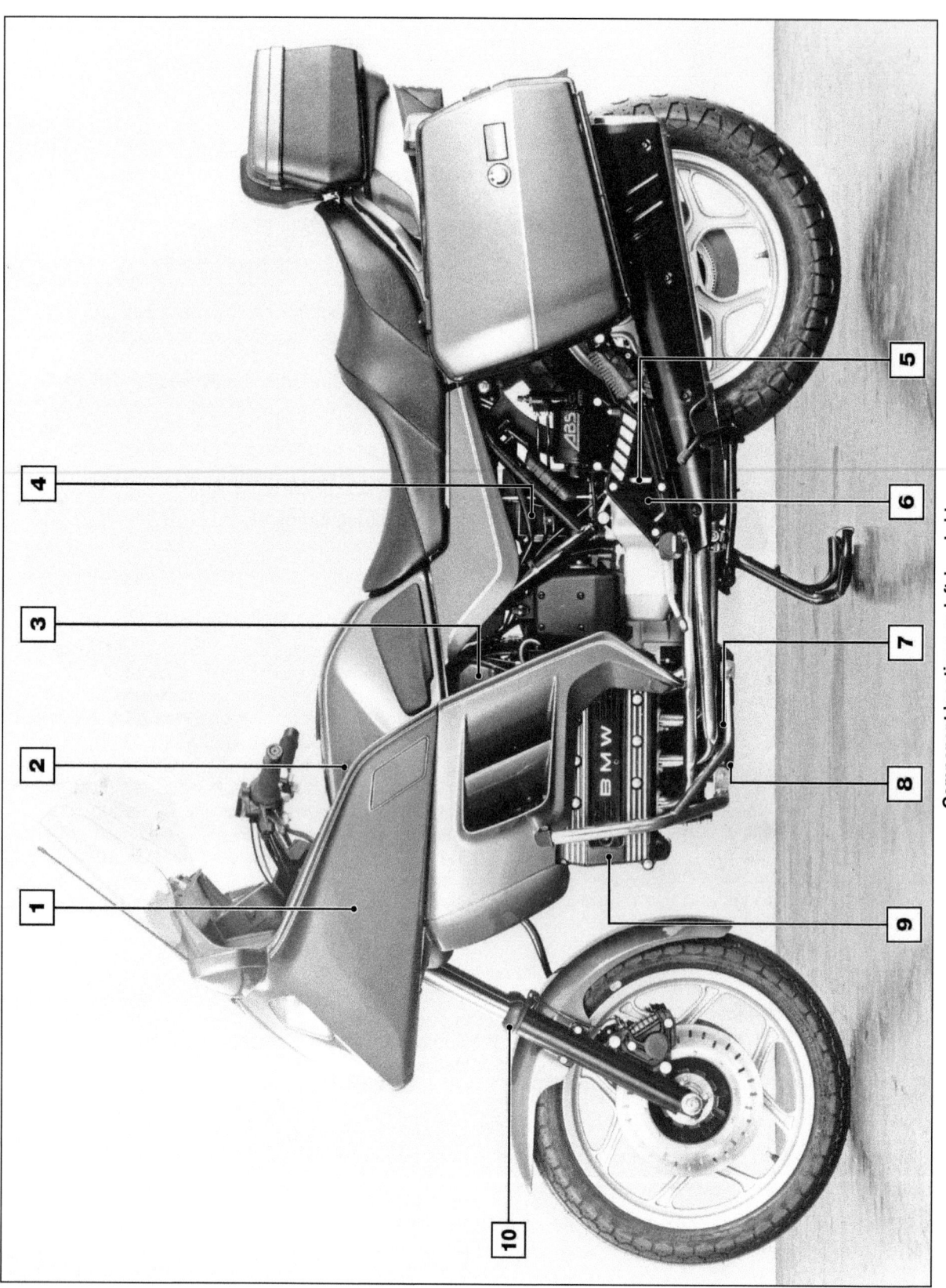

Component locations on left-hand side

1 Steering head bearings
2 Fuel filter
3 Air filter element
4 Battery
5 Clutch operating lever
6 Swinging arm adjustable pivot stub
7 Engine oil drain plug
8 Engine oil filter
9 Valves and spark plugs
10 Front fork seals

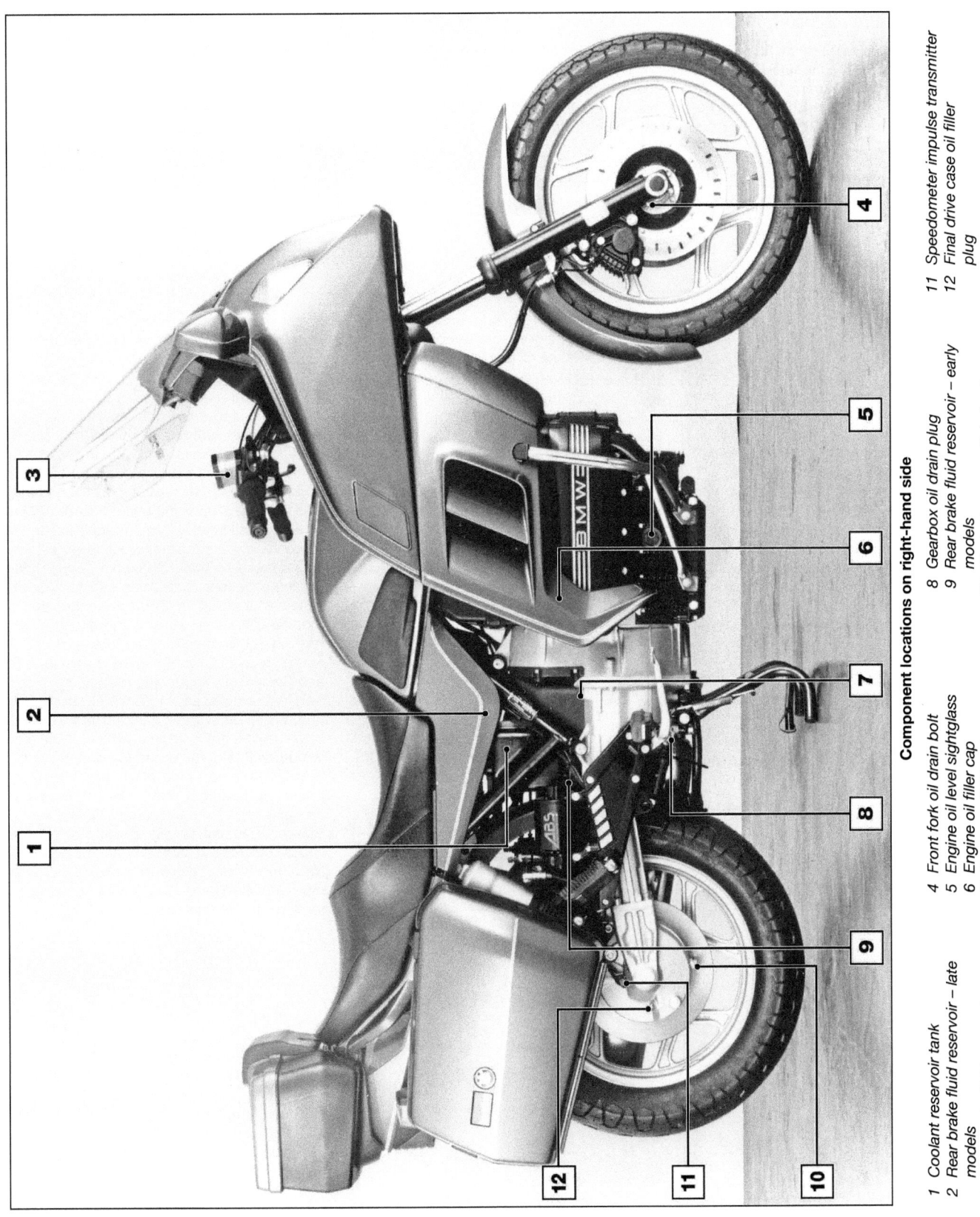

Component locations 1•5

Component locations on right-hand side

1 Coolant reservoir tank
2 Rear brake fluid reservoir – late models
3 Front brake fluid reservoir
4 Front fork oil drain bolt
5 Engine oil level sightglass
6 Engine oil filler cap
7 Gearbox oil filler plug
8 Gearbox oil drain plug
9 Rear brake fluid reservoir – early models
10 Final drive case oil drain plug
11 Speedometer impulse transmitter
12 Final drive case oil filler plug

1•6 Introduction

1 This Chapter is designed to help the home mechanic maintain his/her motorcycle for safety, economy, long life and peak performance.

2 Deciding where to start or plug into the routine maintenance schedule depends on several factors. If the warranty period on your motorcycle has just expired, and if it has been maintained according to the warranty standards, you may want to pick up routine maintenance as it coincides with the next mileage or calendar interval. If you have owned the machine for some time but have never performed any maintenance on it, then you may want to start at the nearest interval and include some additional procedures to ensure that nothing important is overlooked. If you have just had a major engine overhaul, then you may want to start the maintenance routine from the beginning. If you have a used machine and have no knowledge of its history or maintenance record, you may desire to combine all the checks into one major service initially and then settle into the maintenance schedule prescribed.

3 Before beginning any maintenance or repair, the machine should be cleaned thoroughly, especially around the oil filter, spark plugs, valve cover, etc. Cleaning will help ensure that dirt does not contaminate the engine and will allow you to detect wear and damage that could otherwise easily go unnoticed.

4 Certain maintenance information is sometimes printed on decals attached to the motorcycle. If the information on the decals differs from that included here, use the information on the decal.

Minor service

1 Engine oil and filter - change

HAYNES HiNT *Saving a little money on the difference in cost between a good oil and a cheap oil won't pay off if the engine is damaged.*

1 Oil changes will be much quicker if the machine is first ridden far enough to warm up the engine to normal operating temperature: this will thin the oil and ensure that any particles of dirt or debris will be retained in suspension in the oil and flushed out with it.

2 Place the machine on its centre stand on level ground, place a container of at least 4 litres (approx 7 Imp pints, 4 US qts) beneath the crankcase. Unscrew the filler plug from the engine right-hand outer (crankshaft) cover, then use a suitable Allen key to unscrew the drain plug from the centre of the sump (oil pan) (see illustration). While the oil is draining into the container, clean the drain plug carefully, wiping any metal particles off its magnetic insert, and renew its sealing washer if it is worn, flattened or damaged.

3 Remove the three retaining screws and withdraw the oil filter cover, noting the sealing O-ring (see illustration). Wash the cover in a high flash-point solvent and renew the O-ring if it is worn or damaged.

4 Unscrew and discard the oil filter element. On very early 100 models the element had a hexagon form moulded into its lower end to permit fitting and removal, using a suitable spanner (see illustrations). However, it was overtightened by some owners to the point where the filter cracked or its seal failed under pressure, or even the crankcase lower section was cracked. The machining of the filter sealing surface was modified on later models to lessen the risk of this happening, and a modified filter element was introduced which has no hexagon and therefore requires a special tool, BMW part number 11 4 650 to fit and unscrew it. The tool is reasonably cheap and should be easily available from any authorised BMW dealer; in fact after-market versions of it are already available. If the tool is not available, the sump (oil pan) must be withdrawn (see Chapter 6) and the filter unscrewed using a strap wrench or similar car-type filter removal tool (see illustration); if this is done the oil pump pick-up screen should be cleaned as described in Chapter 6. Note that none of the early type filters should now remain in service; all should have been replaced by the later modified type.

1.2 Unscrew drain plug from centre of sump (oil pan) to drain engine oil

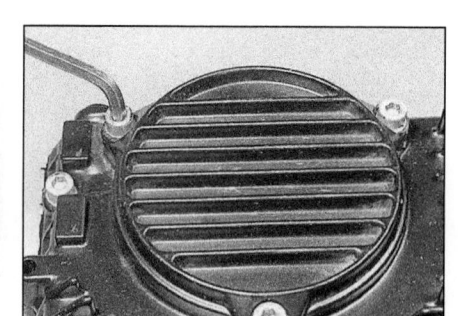

1.3 Engine oil filter is located inside separate cover bolted to sump (oil pan)

1.4a Oil filter element must be removed using a special tool which engages its shaped end . . .

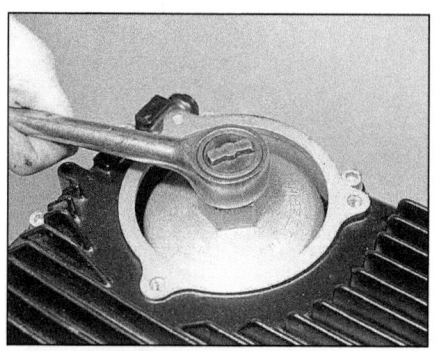

1.4b . . . and is unscrewed using a spanner or other tools as shown

1.4c If special tool is not available, filter strap wrench can be used after sump (oil pan) has been removed

Minor service 1•7

> **HAYNES HINT**: Check the old oil carefully. If the oil was drained into a clean pan, small pieces of metal or other material can be easily detected. If the oil is very metallic coloured, then the engine is experiencing wear from break-in (new engine) or from insufficient lubrication. If there are flakes or chips of metal in the oil, then something is drastically wrong internally and the engine will have to be disassembled for inspection and repair.

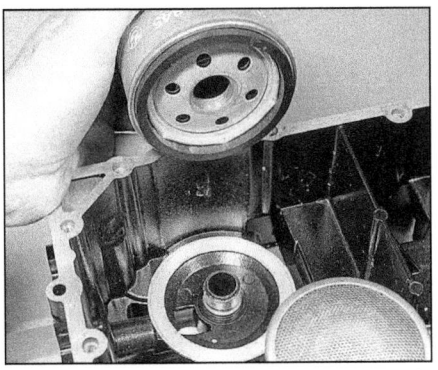

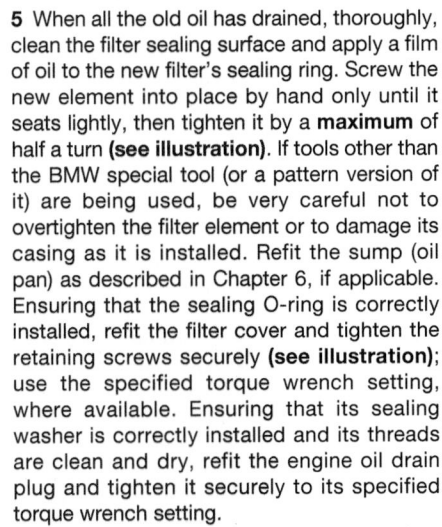

1.5a Fit filter, do not overtighten – note oil pump pick-up, which must be cleaned whenever sump is removed

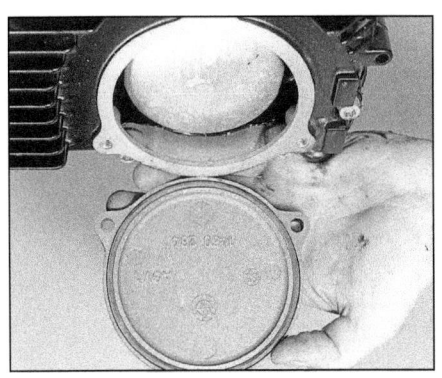

1.5b Check sealing O-ring is correctly installed when refitting filter element cover

5 When all the old oil has drained, thoroughly, clean the filter sealing surface and apply a film of oil to the new filter's sealing ring. Screw the new element into place by hand only until it seats lightly, then tighten it by a **maximum** of half a turn **(see illustration)**. If tools other than the BMW special tool (or a pattern version of it) are being used, be very careful not to overtighten the filter element or to damage its casing as it is installed. Refit the sump (oil pan) as described in Chapter 6, if applicable. Ensuring that the sealing O-ring is correctly installed, refit the filter cover and tighten the retaining screws securely **(see illustration)**; use the specified torque wrench setting, where available. Ensuring that its sealing washer is correctly installed and its threads are clean and dry, refit the engine oil drain plug and tighten it securely to its specified torque wrench setting.

6 Use only a good quality, heavy duty oil suitable for 4-stroke spark ignition engines. Refer to the oil viscosity thermometer chart in *Daily (pre-ride) checks* to decide what viscosity of oil is necessary at the prevailing outside temperatures. BMW recommend that a medium range multigrade, eg 10W30 is preferable to a wide range multigrade, such as 10W50, and that multigrades are preferable to monogrades. Fill the crankcase with the specified amount of engine oil, refit the filler plug, then start the engine and allow it to warm up to normal operating temperature to distribute the new oil fully around the engine. Stop the engine and wait a few minutes for the level to settle then check it and top up, if necessary, as described under the daily check heading. Wipe off any spilt oil, check that both filler and drain plugs (and other disturbed components) are securely and correctly refitted, and check subsequently for signs of oil leaks.

7 Note that whenever the sump (oil pan) is removed, the crankcase interior should be wiped clean with a lint-free cloth and the oil pump pick-up filter gauze should be cleaned. Refer to Chapter 6.

2 Gearbox - oil level check

1 With the machine supported upright on its centre stand on level ground, remove the gearbox oil filler plug **(see illustration)**. The C-spanner provided in the machine's toolkit is also designed to serve as a dipstick for the gearbox. If the spanner, part number 71 11 2 300 061, is not available, it can be ordered from any authorised BMW dealer or a substitute can be fabricated from the dimensions shown **(see illustration)**.

2 Insert the spanner into the gearbox filler orifice until the spanner's shoulder rests on the machined filler plug sealing surface. The oil level should be above the minimum mark formed by the spanner's bottom end, but below the maximum mark formed by the line etched across the spanner handle. Remove any surplus oil. If topping up is necessary use only good quality oil of the specified type **(see illustration)**. Renew the sealing washer if it is damaged or worn and refit the filler plug, tightening it securely, to the specified torque setting (where given). Wash off any spilt oil.

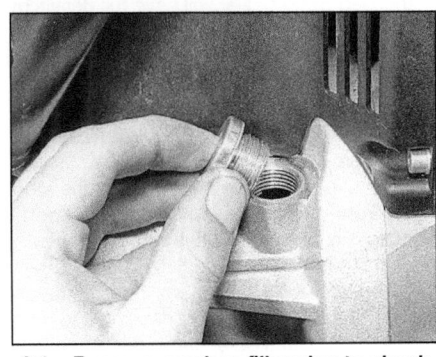

2.1a Remove gearbox filler plug to check oil level

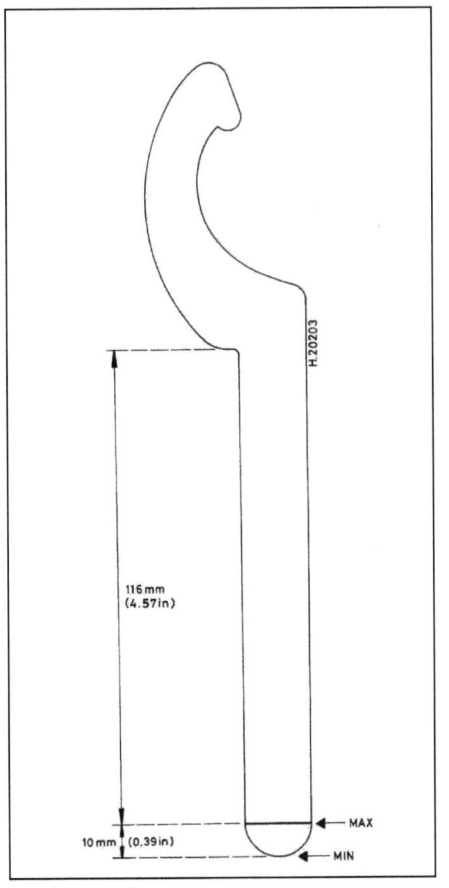

2.1b Gearbox oil level dipstick (116mm (4.57in); 10mm (0.39in) MAX/MIN)

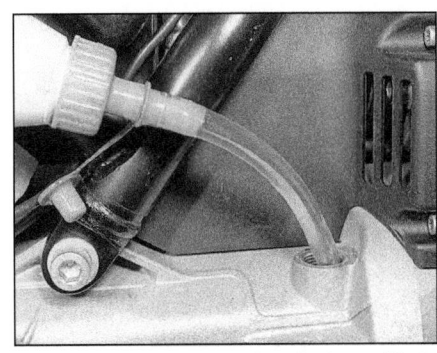

2.2 Use only good quality oil of specified type when topping up

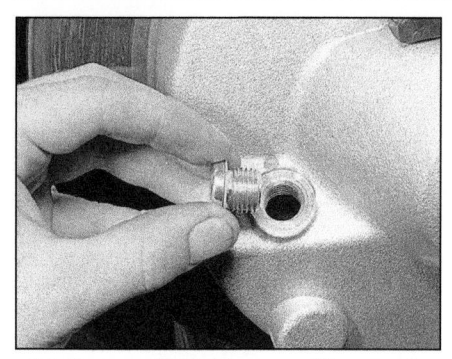

1•8 Minor service

3.1 Remove final drive case filler plug to check oil level

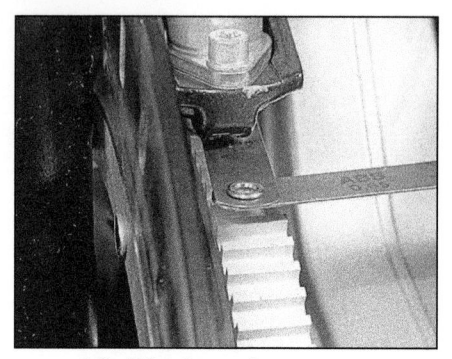

4.3a Wheel speed sensor gap measurement

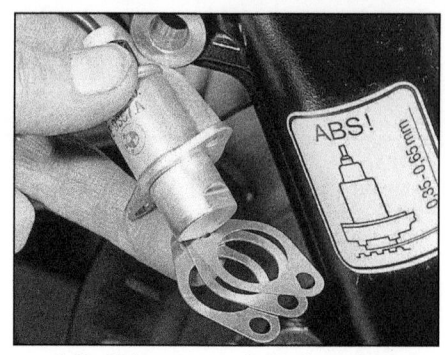

4.3b Shims are available in various thicknesses to obtain correct clearance

3 Final drive case - oil level check

1 With the machine supported on its centre stand on level ground, remove the filler plug from the final drive case **(see illustration)**. The oil level should be up to the bottom thread of the filler plug orifice ie 12 mm (0.47 in) below the machined filler plug sealing surface the filler plug must not dip into the oil. Remove any surplus oil using a syringe or similar, to prevent oil being blown on to the rear tyre or brake components via the breather.

2 If topping up is necessary, use only good quality oil of the specified type. Renew the sealing washer if it is damaged or worn and refit the filler plug, tightening it securely to the specified torque setting (where given). Wash off any spilt oil from the housing and swinging arm.

4 ABS - check and overhaul

1 Check the brake pads for wear as described in Section 20, renewing the pads as a set if they have worn to or beyond the service limit. Check the condition of the hydraulic hoses/pipes and renew any that show signs of deterioration or damage.

2 Proceed to check the brake discs for damage, wear and excessive run-out, referring to Chapter 10, Section 5 for details.

3 Using feeler gauges (or those supplied in the machine's toolkit) measure the clearance between the tip of the sensor and the corresponding tooth of the impulse gear **(see illustration)**. Take the measurement with the wheel in more than one position to take into account any deviation in the impulse gear's height. Although a tolerance of 0.2 mm is permissible, the manufacturer recommends that this be checked with the wheel in six positions, at approximately 60° intervals. If the clearance is outside the specified figure (see Specifications) the sensor's position requires adjustment. This is accomplished by inserting or deleting shims between the sensor and its holder. Shims are available from authorised BMW dealers in 0.05, 0.1. 0.2, 0.3, 0.4 and 0.5 mm thicknesses. Remove the sensor from its holder as described in Chapter 10 and insert the appropriate shim between the two components **(see illustration)**. After adjustment recheck the clearance and have the ABS system checked by an authorised BMW dealer for correct operation.

4 Complete maintenance by checking that the sensor tip and impulse gear teeth are free from any particles of grit or dust.

5 Controls and stand pivots - lubrication

Front brake and clutch levers

1 The front brake lever can be removed by unscrewing the locknut and unscrewing or tapping out (as applicable) the pivot pin or screw; withdraw the lever, noting the presence of any shims that may be fitted.

2 The clutch lever can be withdrawn similarly, after the cable adjusters have been slackened and the cable end nipples have been withdrawn from their respective levers. Note that a slotted nipple retainer is fitted at the handlebar lever (also at the gearbox end on some models); this must not be allowed to drop clear and be lost.

3 Refer to paragraph for lubrication details.

Throttle cable

4 To release the throttle cable, first remove the injector cover (where fitted), then rotate the cable pulley inwards and carefully disengage the cable end nipple from the pulley. Withdraw the cable from its stop on the throttle butterfly assembly and carefully pull it clear of the machine, noting exactly how it is routed; note particularly that the cable is routed over the top of the air filter top half/plenum chamber connecting hose.

5 Removing the handlebar cover, if necessary, first withdraw the single screw clamping the right-hand switch cluster to the twistgrip assembly, then remove its single retaining screw and withdraw the twistgrip top cover, noting how its protruding tang locates with the twistgrip drum. Disconnect the cable end nipple from the slot in the block at the chain end, then withdraw the cable.

6 On reassembly, grease liberally all twistgrip components, noting that the handlebar weights fitted to some models must be removed by slackening the screw which secures the expander bolt retaining system; be careful that the weight is not pushed so far against the twistgrip rubber on refitting that it drags and impairs free throttle movement. Before refitting the twistgrip top cover, align the mark on one of the twistgrip drum teeth with the line on the throttle pulley to ensure full throttle movement is available.

7 When refitting the throttle cable, be very careful to ensure that it is routed correctly with no kinks or sharp bends and that it does not foul or snag on any other component; check at all front fork positions. Particularly check that the outer cable does not foul the handlebar cover or any other component as it passes through the steering head area, also that there is a straight run from the outer cable stop on the throttle butterfly assembly to the cable pulley; it may be necessary to renew the stop, if this is bent out of true. Open the throttle and check that it snaps quickly and easily shut at all handlebar positions.

8 On some 1983 - 85 100 models (an authorised BMW dealer will have full details of the machines that may be affected) an additional earth wire should have been installed between the twistgrip/brake master cylinder assembly and the main frame earth point on the left-hand side of the frame top tube bracing gusset, to the rear of the steering head. If this wire is not installed and the stop lamp front switch should develop a short-circuit, since the handlebars are rubber-mounted and therefore insulated from the rest of the machine, the switch may earth through the throttle cable inner wire, causing it to heat up and drag on the outer cable. If in any doubt about the throttle operation, have the machine checked by an authorised BMW dealer.

Minor service

6.3 Cylinder is at TDC with the piston at top of bore and both valves closed – No 1 cylinder, 100 model shown

6.5 Valve clearance is measured with cam lobe pointing away from valve as shown

Choke (fast idle) cable

9 To remove the choke (fast idle) control cable slacken its locknut and unscrew the cable adjuster at its lower end, then release the cable end nipple from the butterfly operating linkage. At the handlebar end, prise off the black plastic cap and unscrew the large retaining screw to dismantle the lever. Note how the lever detent spring is fitted.

Lubrication

10 Check all lever pivot components for wear, renewing any that are damaged or worn and grease them thoroughly on refitting.
11 Check the control cable inner wires for signs of fraying, poorly-soldered nipples and other damage, and the cable outers for signs of chafing, damaged or broken covers, or frayed or damaged ends. If any cable appears to be damaged or worn, or if it is stiff and jerky in operation, it must be renewed immediately. All the cable inner wires are lined with nylon or a similar material which **must not** be lubricated with oil.

> **HAYNES HINT** *If the cables become stiff through old age, wear, or damage, they should be renewed, although the application of one of the modern 'dry' lubricants may help.*

12 Finish off control lubrication by applying a few drops of engine oil or light machine oil to all nipples and control pivots, and all adjuster threads. Apply WD40 or CRC5-56 to all locks and switches.

Pivot points

13 Working as described in the relevant Section of Chapters 2, 8 and 10, dismantle, clean and grease at regular intervals the stand pivots, the clutch release mechanism and the brake operating linkages. Check also the footrests and all return springs for security and correct operation.

6 Valve clearances - check and adjustment (1983 to 1988 models)

1 This operation is described in two subsections since while checking the clearances is within the scope of any owner, adjusting them is a different matter. Owners are advised to read the instructions to get some idea of what is involved and to then decide whether to attempt all or part of the work themselves, or whether to take the machine to a dealer. Note that while the clearances should be checked carefully at the interval, this system of valve clearance adjustment does not usually require resetting until a much greater mileage has been covered.

Checking the valve clearances

2 The engine must be cold before the valve clearances can be checked accurately. First remove the spark plugs and the engine left-hand outer (cylinder head) cover. See Chapter 2. Select top gear and rotate the crankshaft to the desired position by turning the rear wheel.
3 The valve clearances must be measured at the base circle of the cam lobe, ie with the lobe pointing directly away from the valve stem. This position is approximately just before Top Dead Centre (TDC) on the compression stroke for the exhaust cam and just after it for the intake cam. To find TDC on the compression stroke, rotate the crankshaft until the (upper) intake cam lobe for any particular cylinder has opened and closed its valve, then shine a torch down the spark plug aperture and slowly turn the rear wheel until that piston comes to the top of its stroke **(see illustration)**. It is easiest to work methodically, starting from number 1 (front, or cam chain end) cylinder and to then work backwards, ie for 100 models from number 1 cylinder at TDC a half turn of the crankshaft brings number 3 cylinder to TDC, a further half turn brings number 4 to TDC, and a final half turn brings number 2 to TDC.

4 Note that if the ignition trigger assembly cover is removed the crankshaft can also be rotated (anti-clockwise, looking at the trigger from the front of the machine) by means of an Allen key applied to the rotor retaining bolt.
5 Whichever method is used, position the cams as described and use feeler gauges to measure carefully the clearance between each cam lobe and the shim sitting on its respective cam follower recess **(see illustration)**. The correct thickness feeler gauge blade will be a tight sliding fit between the two components. Carefully record all clearances.
6 If the clearance at any valve is outside the specified range, the shim must be replaced by a thicker or thinner one, as appropriate. This procedure is described below.

Adjusting the valve clearances with service tools

7 The shims are changed by pressing down the cam follower (tappet bucket) using a specially-shaped depressor lever, BMW pan number 11 1 721, and holding it down using a spacer, BMW tool number 11 1 722 **(see illustration)**; the shims can then be extracted using a pointed instrument or a pair of large tweezers or needle-nosed pliers. If these tools are available, proceed as follows.

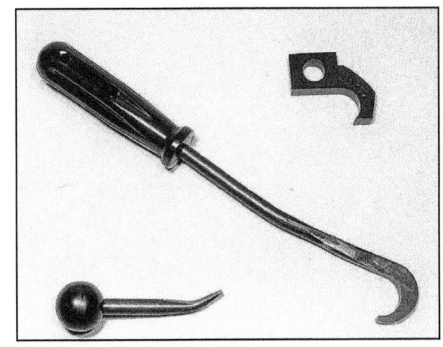

6.7 Valve clearance adjustment requires special tools if camshafts are not to be removed

1•10 Minor service

6.8a Hook depressor lever under camshaft and press lever downwards for exhaust . . .

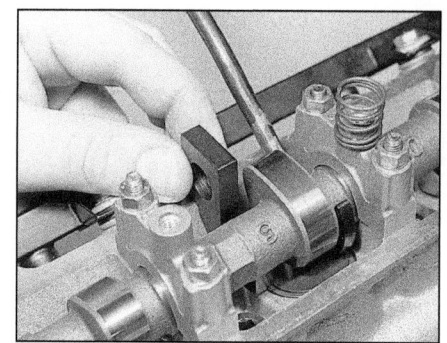

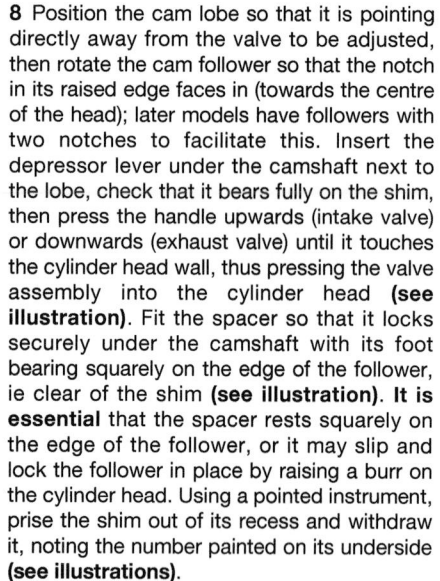

6.8b . . . or upwards for intake until valve assembly is depressed sufficiently for spacer to be fitted

6.8c Shim can be prised out via notch in cam follower rim – check spacer bears securely on follower only

8 Position the cam lobe so that it is pointing directly away from the valve to be adjusted, then rotate the cam follower so that the notch in its raised edge faces in (towards the centre of the head); later models have followers with two notches to facilitate this. Insert the depressor lever under the camshaft next to the lobe, check that it bears fully on the shim, then press the handle upwards (intake valve) or downwards (exhaust valve) until it touches the cylinder head wall, thus pressing the valve assembly into the cylinder head **(see illustration)**. Fit the spacer so that it locks securely under the camshaft with its foot bearing squarely on the edge of the follower, ie clear of the shim **(see illustration)**. **It is essential** that the spacer rests squarely on the edge of the follower, or it may slip and lock the follower in place by raising a burr on the cylinder head. Using a pointed instrument, prise the shim out of its recess and withdraw it, noting the number painted on its underside **(see illustrations)**.

9 Shims are available in increments of 0.05 mm (0.0020 in) in a range of thicknesses from 2.00 - 3.00 mm (0.0787 - 0.1181 in). To adjust a valve's clearance, note the thickness of the present shim; if the painted number has been polished away measure the shim with a micrometer or vernier caliper or similar and record it **(see illustration)**. If the measured clearance was too small, select the next size thinner shim, install it and recheck the clearance; if the clearance was too large a thicker shim must be installed. The clearance does not usually require adjusting by more than one shim size.

> **HAYNES HiNT** *It may be possible to reduce the cost by swapping shims between valves so that the smallest number of new shims has to be purchased.*

10 Refit the shims ensuring that their painted numbers are facing downwards so that they are not polished away by the cam lobe, and that each shim is seated fully in its recess **(see illustration)**. Refit the depressor lever and push down the valve assembly, withdraw the spacer and slowly move the depressor lever to release the cam follower. Rotate the follower through a full circle to ensure that the new shim is securely seated at all points, then measure the clearance again and record it. Repeat the process for all other valves.

11 When all clearances have been checked and adjusted, turn the engine over several times to settle all components (if the starter motor is used be careful to protect the ignition system components as described in Chapter 7), then recheck all clearances to ensure that none have altered through shims settling. If all is well, refit the cylinder head cover as described in Chapter 2. Note that if the clearances required significant alteration, the throttle butterfly assembly synchronisation should be checked as described in Chapter 6.

Note: *Always record the date and mileage of each check and all relevant information, ie original clearance, original shim thickness, new shim thickness and final clearance. In this way an extremely accurate picture can be obtained of the rate of wear of the valve gear, until it is almost possible to predict when a particular valve will need adjusting. Obviously if the pattern changes suddenly, the reason should be investigated before serious trouble is encountered. Note that with this system of valve clearance adjustment wear of the valve gear is minimal and it is more likely that thinner shims will be required to compensate for wear at the valve seat. Once the shims have been properly set up after running in, adjustment should be only rarely required, thus offsetting the extra expense of the system.*

Adjusting the valve clearances without service tools

12 Owners who do not have access to the service tools mentioned above should note that it is possible to adjust the clearances without them, but that this involves a much longer procedure which requires very accurate measurements of the clearances. The task is outlined below; refer to

6.8d Number painted on shim underside indicates thickness, in this case 2.05 mm

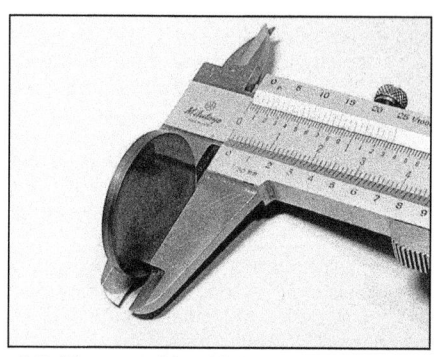

6.9 Measure shim thickness with caliper or micrometer if number is erased

6.10 Fit shims with number downwards and check that they are seated fully in their followers

Minor service 1•11

7.1a Remove spark plug cover plate from centre of cylinder head cover . . .

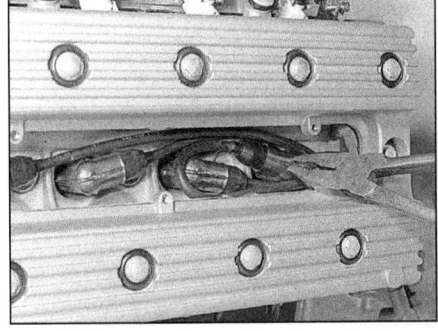

7.1b . . . and use pliers to pull off suppressor caps, noting exactly how HT leads are routed

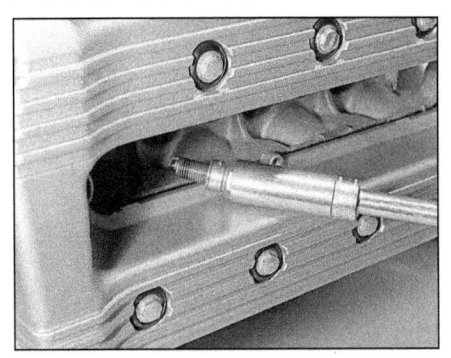

7.1c Spark plugs must be renewed as a set if any gap has worn to beyond the service limit

the relevant Sections of Chapter 2 for full details.

13 Measure and record carefully the clearances of all valves (see above). If any require adjustment, remove the engine front and right-hand outer covers and withdraw the camshafts. See Chapter 2.

14 Note that only one camshaft should be removed at a time, to avoid confusion, and that great care must be taken to avoid shims dropping clear and becoming mixed up; remove the camshaft very slowly and substitute a wooden dowel or similar to retain the shims as soon as possible.

15 Measure or note the shim thicknesses and obtain thinner or thicker shims as described above, and refit them securely to the cam follower recesses.

16 When all valves have been adjusted, refit the camshafts, set the valve timing and refit the cam chain, then re-check all valve clearances. If the work has been sufficiently accurate, the clearances will be correct; if not, repeat the procedure until all are correct. As described above, make a careful note of all relevant information so that an accurate picture can be built up of the rate of valve or valve gear wear. When adjustment is complete, refit the engine outer covers and other disturbed components. Note that if the clearances required significant alteration it will be necessary to check the synchronisation of the throttle butterfly assembly. See Chapter 6.

7 Spark plugs - check and adjustment

1 Either perform this task when the engine is cold, or take great care to prevent personal injury through burning one's hands on the hot cylinder head. Remove the three retaining Allen screws and withdraw the spark plug cover plate from the middle of the engine left-hand outer (cylinder head) cover **(see illustration)**. Noting exactly how the leads are routed, pull off each spark plug suppressor cap using a heavy pair of pliers applied to the tab protruding from each cap **(see illustration)**. Clean off any particles of dirt or other foreign matter from the spark plug channel, then unscrew the spark plugs, keeping them clearly identified by cylinder number **(see illustration)**.

2 First use feeler gauges, preferably of the wire type for accuracy, to measure the gap between the spark plug electrodes **(see illustrations)**; BMW state that the ignition system is so sensitive to spark plug condition and electrode gap that the plugs must all be renewed if the electrodes of any one spark plug have been eroded to a gap of 0.8 mm (0.032 in) or more. If this is found to be the case, or if the plugs are in any way suspect, new spark plugs of the specified make and type must be purchased and fitted. Note that if this particular make is difficult to obtain locally, the advice of an authorised BMW dealer should be sought; provided that exactly the equivalent heat range and type is obtained from a good quality brand, spark plugs of alternative makes may be used, eg NGK D7EA. Fit them as described below.

3 If the spark plugs are still serviceable, carefully compare the appearance of their electrodes with the colour section inside the rear cover and note any information which can be obtained from this. If any plug appears to show a fault, seek expert advice as soon as possible; do not forget to take the old plugs with the machine to an authorised BMW dealer. The standard grade of spark plug should prove adequate in all normal use and a change of specification (such as fitting a hotter or colder grade of plug) should not be made without expert advice.

4 Clean the electrodes by carefully scraping away the accumulated carbon deposits using a small knife blade or small files and abrasive paper; take care not to bend the centre electrode or to chip or damage the ceramic insulator. The cleaning of spark plugs on commercial sandblasting equipment is **not** recommended due to the risk of abrasive particles being jammed in the gap between the insulator and the plug metal body, only to fall clear later and drop into the engine; any plug that is so heavily fouled should be renewed.

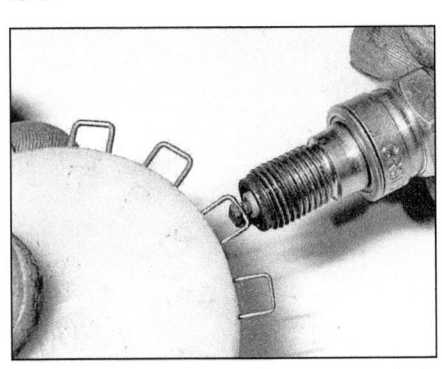

7.2a A wire type gauge is recommended to measure spark plug electrode gap

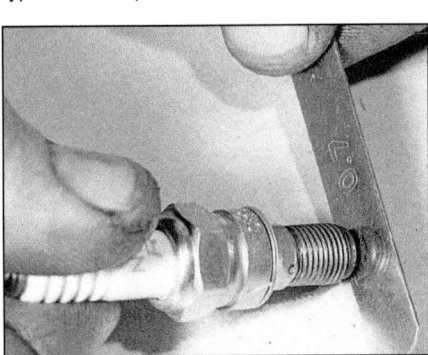

7.2b Using a feeler gauge to measure spark plug electrode gap

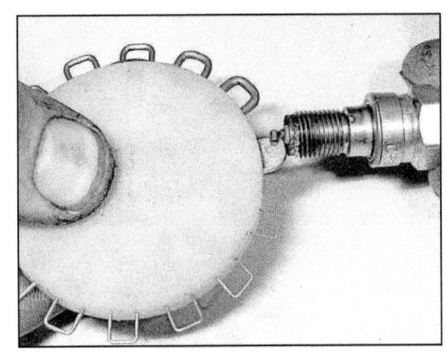

7.2c Electrode gap is adjusted by bending the side electrode

1•12 Minor service

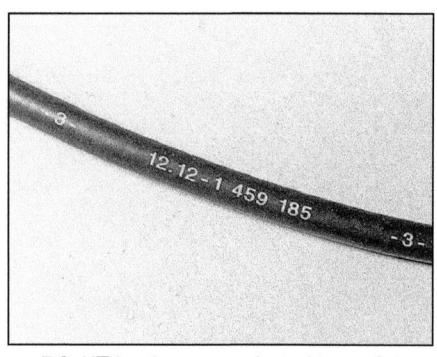

7.9 HT leads are numbered to assist identification on refitting

5 Once clean, file the opposing faces of the electrodes flat using a small fine file. A magneto file or even a nail file can be used for this purpose. Whichever method is chosen, make sure that every trace of abrasive and loose carbon is removed before the plug is refitted. If this is not done, the debris will enter the engine and can cause damage or rapid wear.

6 Whether a cleaned or new plug is to be fitted, always check the electrode gap before it is installed. Use a spark plug adjusting tool or feeler gauges to measure the gap, and if adjustment is required, bend the outer, earth electrode only. *Never* bend the centre electrode or the porcelain insulator nose will be damaged.

7 Before the plug is fitted, apply a fine coat of PBC or molybdenum disulphide grease to the threads. This will help prevent thread wear and damage. Fit the plug finger-tight, then tighten it by a further 1/4 turn only, to ensure a gas-tight seal. Beware of overtightening, and always use a plug wrench or socket of the correct size; tighten all plugs to the specified torque wrench setting, where possible.

> **HAYNES HINT** *Since the plugs are recessed, slip a short length of hose over the end of the plug to use as a tool to thread it into place. The hose will grip the plug well enough to turn it, but will start to slip if the plug begins to cross-thread in the hole - this will prevent damaged threads and the accompanying repair costs.*

8 Never overtighten a spark plug otherwise there is risk of stripping the thread from the cylinder head, especially as it is cast in light alloy. A stripped thread can be repaired without having to scrap the cylinder head by using a 'Helicoil' thread insert.

9 When refitting the spark plug suppressor caps, be careful to ensure that the HT leads

> **HAYNES HINT** *Refer to Tools and Workshop Tips in the Reference section for details of how to install a thread insert.*

are correctly routed; note that the leads are numbered as a further aid to identification **(see illustration)**.

8 Air filter element - clean

1 Remove the air filter element as described in the first part of Chapter 6, Section 14.
2 Blow through the element from the top surface downwards with a blast of compressed air and remove any large particles with a soft-bristled brush.
3 Note that if the machine has been used in particularly dusty or dirty conditions, if may be necessary to renew the element at this interval.

9 Battery - check

1 The battery must be checked regularly, at least every three months.
2 If a quick check is being made, it is only necessary to unlock and raise the seat and to remove both side panels (see Chapter 8). If the terminals are being checked or the cells topped up the storage tray and fuel injection control unit must be removed as well, as described in Chapter 6.
3 To remove the battery completely, unlock and raise the seat, remove both side panels and withdraw the storage tray and fuel

9.3 Battery (and coolant expansion tank) is retained by a single strap – unscrew securing screws to release

9.4b Battery terminals must be completely clean and securely fastened at all times

injection control unit. Disconnect the battery terminals (negative terminal first, always) and vent tube, then remove the two long screws securing the battery retaining strap to the battery tray **(see illustration)**. Withdraw the strap, noting that this will release the coolant expansion tank which must be secured out of harm's way. Tilt the battery backwards and withdraw it upwards and to the rear.

4 On refitting, insert the battery carefully, with its terminals to the front, and settle it on the rubber pads on the tray. Route the vent tube through the hole at the base of the rear mudguard and check that it is clear, with no blockages or kinks, and that it hangs down well clear of any other component particularly the rear wheel or exhaust system **(see illustration)**. Position the coolant expansion tank on its mountings and refit the battery retaining strap; tighten the retaining screws securely but do not overtighten them or the battery will be cracked. Check that the terminals are scraped clean and coated with the specified acid-free grease to prevent corrosion, then reconnect the positive (+ ve) terminal first, followed by the negative (-ve). Tighten the terminal nuts and bolts securely and refit their covers **(see illustration)**.

5 To check the electrolyte level, position the machine so that the battery is level. Where level marks are provided on the battery casing ensure that the electrolyte level is between the marks; if not the level in each cell must be between 5 - 10 mm (0.2 - 0.4 in) below the black plastic top **(see illustration)**. If topping-up is necessary, remove the battery retaining

9.4a Ensure vent tube is free from blockages or kinks on refitting

9.5 Electrolyte level must be maintained between level lines on battery casing

Minor service 1•13

strap and use a coin or similar to unscrew each cell cover plug. Use only distilled water to top up to the maximum level mark, then refit the cell cover plugs and retaining strap.

> **HAYNES HiNT** *The battery cell holes are quite small, so it may help to use a plastic squeeze bottle with a small spout to add the water*

6 Check that the vent tube is clear and that it has no kinks or blockages, also that it hangs well clear of any other component (see above). If the terminals are loose or corroded, disconnect them (negative terminal first, always) and scrape them clean. On refitting, tighten the retaining nuts and bolts securely.

> **HAYNES HiNT** *Apply a coat of petroleum jelly or acid-free grease to each battery terminal to prevent corrosion*

7 Always check that the terminals are tight and that the covers are correctly refitted, also that the fuse connections are clean and tight, that the fuses are of the correct rating and in good condition, and that spares are available on the machine should the need arise.

8 At regular intervals remove the battery and check that there is no pale grey sediment deposited at the bottom of the casing. This is caused by sulphation of the plates as a result of re-charging at too high a rate or as a result of the battery being left discharged for long periods. A good battery should have little or no sediment visible and its plates should be straight and pale grey or brown in colour. If sediment deposits are deep enough to reach the bottom of the plates, or if the plates are buckled and have whitish deposits on them, the battery is faulty and must be renewed. Remember that a poor battery will give rise to a large number of minor electrical faults.

9 If the machine is not in regular use, disconnect the battery and give it a refresher charge every month to six weeks, as described in Chapter 11.

10 Final inspection

Work methodically around the machine checking the following items:
a) Check the rear wheel mounting bolts are tightened to the specified torque setting.
b) Check the operation of the clutch and gear change mechanism.
c) Check the steering.
d) Check the wheels, brakes and tyres.
e) Check the lights and other electrical components and instruments.
f) Check the idle speed and adjust if necessary.

Major service

11 Gearbox - oil change

1 The machine must be taken on a journey of sufficient length to warm up the gearbox to normal operating temperature before the oil is drained.

2 With the machine supported on its centre stand on level ground, remove the filler and drain plugs and allow the oil to drain into a suitable container **(see illustration)**. While the oil is draining, clean the drain plug carefully, wiping any metal particles off its magnetic insert, and renew its sealing washer if it is worn, flattened or damaged. When the oil is fully drained, refit the drain plug and tighten it securely to the specified torque wrench setting, where available.

> **HAYNES HiNT** *A cardboard chute should be fabricated to direct the draining oil away from the centre stand*

3 Fill the gearbox with the correct amount of the specified type and viscosity of oil, then check the oil level as described in Section 4.

12 Final drive case - oil change

1 The machine must be taken on a journey of sufficient length to warm up the final drive to normal operating temperature before the oil is drained.

2 With the machine supported on its centre stand on level ground, remove the filler and drain plugs and allow the oil to drain into a suitable container **(see illustration)**. Use a sheet of cardboard as a chute to keep the oil off the rear wheel and tyre.

11.2 Gearbox oil drain plug is fitted with a magnetic insert – clean carefully

12.2 Final drive oil drain plug is situated on underside of final drive case

1•14 Major service

14.1 Speedometer impulse transmitter must be removed at regular intervals for cleaning

3 Renew the plug sealing washers if they are damaged or flattened, and clean both plugs; wipe any metal particles from the drain plug magnetic insert. When the oil has fully drained, refit the drain plug, tightening it to the specified torque setting and pour in the correct amount of the specified type and viscosity of oil.
4 Check the oil level as described in Section 2.

13 Front forks - oil change

1 Place a sheet of cardboard against the wheel to keep oil off the brake or tyre, place a suitable container under the fork leg and remove the drain plug which is a small hexagon-headed bolt at the rear of the fork lower leg, just above the wheel spindle.
2 Depress the forks several times to expel as much oil as possible, then repeat the process on the remaining leg. Leave the machine for a few minutes to allow any residual oil to drain to the bottom, then pump the forks again to remove it.
3 Renewing their sealing washers if worn or damaged, refit and tighten the drain plugs to the specified torque wrench settings, where given, then remove the fork leg top plastic plugs; it may be necessary to remove the handlebar cover to gain adequate working space.
4 Unscrew the Allen screw filler plugs from the centre of each fork top plug, using an open-ended spanner to hold the top plug, then lift the machine on to its centre stand on level ground and wedge a block of wood or similar under the sump so that the front wheel is clear of the ground and the forks are fully extended.
5 Fill each leg with the specified amount of one of the recommended brands of oil (see Chapter 8). BMW forks are designed to work with oils of (approximately) SAE 10 viscosity. Check the oil level by inserting a length of welding rod 1 metre (40 in) long by 5 mm (0.2 in) diameter into the fork leg; ensure that the level is the same in both fork legs. Refit the filler plugs, tightening them to the specified torque wrench setting, where given, followed by the plastic top plugs and/or any other disturbed components.
6 Push the machine off its stand, apply the front brake and pump the forks up and down 5 - 10 times until the damping effect can be felt to be fully restored.

14 Speedometer impulse transmitter - clean

1 Remove its single retaining screw and carefully prise the impulse transmitter out of the final drive case (see illustration). Renew its sealing O-ring if worn or damaged and wipe the unit clean of oil and any dirt or foreign matter. Check it for signs of damage. On refitting, tighten the retaining screw securely but do not overtighten it.

15 Air filter element - renewal

1 The element should be removed as described in Chapter 6 and discarded. Fit a new element, ensuring that it is seated correctly (see illustration). and secure the filter top half by springing the retaining clips into place (see illustration). A light application of grease around the sealing edges will help provide a good seal in very wet or dusty conditions.

16 Cooling system - check

1 With reference to Chapter 5 of this Manual, check the cooling system at regular intervals, looking for signs of leakage, damage or wear to any of the system's components.
2 Check the coolant level as described under *Daily (pre-ride) checks*.
3 Note that the coolant must be renewed at least every two years.

17 Clutch - check and adjustment

1 The clutch is adjusted correctly if there is the correct specified amount of free play in the cable measured between the handlebar lever butt end and the handlebar clamp and the clutch operates smoothly with no sign of slip or drag (see illustration).
2 To adjust the clutch, slacken the handlebar adjuster locknut then rotate the handlebar adjuster as necessary until the distance between the forward edge of the clutch operating lever on the gearbox and the rear edge of the cable outer cover on the gearbox housing (ie the exposed length of clutch cable inner wire) is 75 ± 1 mm (2.95 ± 0.04 in) (see illustrations). Tighten the handlebar adjuster locknut.
3 Slacken the locknut of the adjuster set in the clutch operating lever at the rear of the gearbox and slacken the adjuster screw by one or two full turns to check that there is no pressure on it, then screw it in until light resistance is encountered; do not overtighten

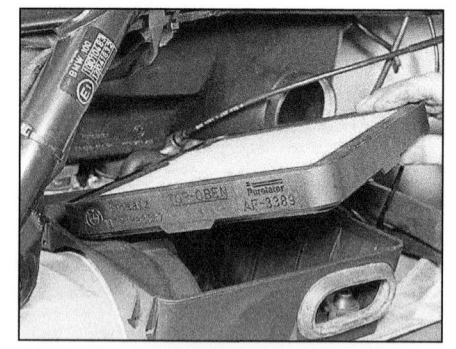

15.1a Ensure air filter element is correctly refitted to prevent entry of dirt into engine

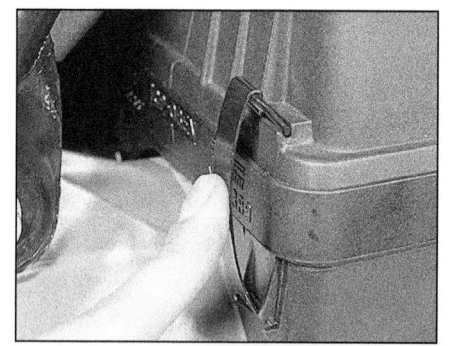

15.1b Filter casing top half is secured by spring clips

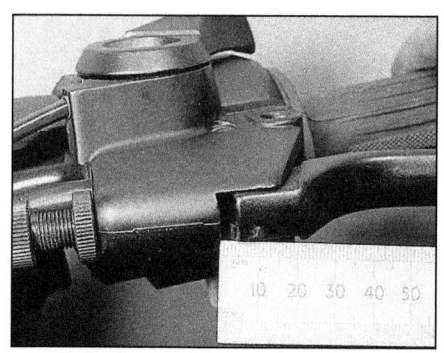

17.1 Measuring clutch cable free play – 100 model shown

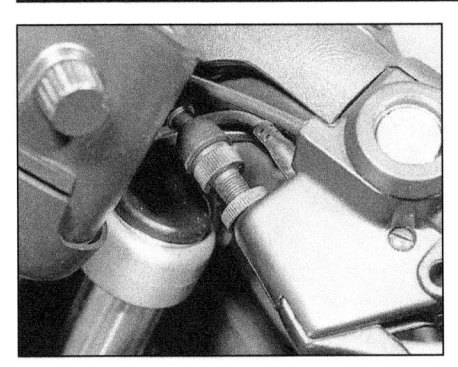

Routine Maintenance 1•15

17.2a Use cable handlebar adjuster to set...

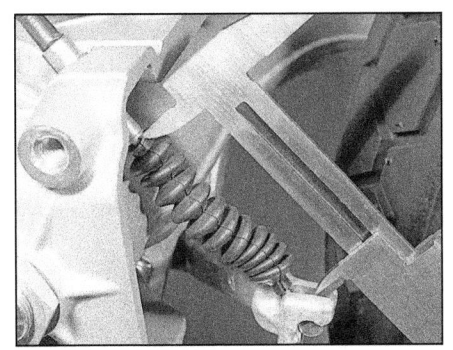

17.2b ...correct length of exposed cable inner wire, as shown

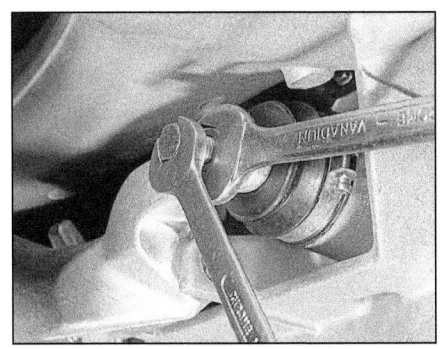

17.3a Clutch operating lever adjuster is used to set release mechanism

the screw. Hold the screw steady and tighten the adjuster locknut securely **(see illustration)**. Use the handlebar adjuster to set the specified clearance at the lever, then tighten its locknut; operate the clutch lever once or twice to settle the cable. Check that the adjustment has remained the same, resetting it if necessary. Apply a few drops of oil to all cable end nipples, adjuster threads and lever pivots. Where fitted, set the side stand retracting mechanism linkage so that free play is just eliminated with stand down **(see illustration)**.

4 If the clutch still shows signs of slipping or dragging, or if it is very sudden in action, it must be dismantled for examination. On reassembly, the components should be lubricated, (where specified) to ensure a smooth action. Refer to Chapter 3.

18 Spark plugs - renewal

1 The spark plugs should be renewed at this interval regardless of their apparent condition as they will have passed peak efficiency. Check that the new plugs are of the correct type and that they are correctly gapped before fitting them. See Section 7.

19 Fuel system - check

1 With reference to the relevant Sections of Chapter 6, check all pressure hoses for signs of leaks, check the adjustment and operation of the throttle and choke control cables and check the idle speed. Remember that if the valve clearances have been altered significantly the synchronisation of the throttle butterfly assemblies should be checked, and adjusted if necessary.
2 Note that the fuel filter must be renewed at regular intervals (see Section 26).

20 Disc brake pads - wear check and renewal

Note: *From 1989 sintered metal brake pads were fitted to the front brake caliper. It is important that the sintered metal pads are not fitted to earlier models without the modified calipers. For this reason BMW have increased the backplate thickness of the new pads, making them unsuitable for pre-1989 models.*
1 To check the degree of pad wear, prise the plastic cover off each caliper body and assess

17.3b Certain models are fitted with a side stand retracting mechanism

the amount of friction material remaining on each pad **(see illustration)**; if either is worn at any point so that the metal backing is approaching contact with the disc, both pads must be renewed immediately. If the pads are so fouled with dirt that the friction material cannot be distinguished, or if oil or grease is seen on them, they must be removed for cleaning and examination.
2 Use a suitable drift to tap out the two pad retaining pins from the inside outwards **(see illustration)**; take care not to allow the retaining spring to fly off. Remove the central pin and withdraw both pads **(see illustration)**.
3 If the pads are worn to a thickness of 1.5 mm (0.06 in) or less at any point **(see**

20.1 Prise plastic cover off caliper body to check brake pads

20.2a Use hammer and a drift to tap out pad retaining pins – do not lose retaining spring or central pin

20.2b Remove pads, noting which way round each is fitted – check for uneven wear

1•16 Major service

20.3 Pads must be renewed as a set if any is worn to service limit or less

20.5a Ensure friction material is against disc when refitting brake pads...

illustration), fouled with oil or grease, or heavily scored or damaged by dirt and debris, they must be renewed as a set; there is no satisfactory way of degreasing friction material. If the pads can be used again, clean them carefully using a fine wire brush that is completely free of oil or grease. Remove all traces of road dirt and corrosion, then use a pointed instrument to dig out any embedded particles of foreign matter. Any areas of glazing may be removed using emery cloth.

4 On reassembly, if new pads are to be fitted, the caliper pistons must now be pushed back as far as possible into the caliper bores to provide the clearance necessary to accommodate the unworn pads. It should be possible to do this with hand pressure only. If any undue stiffness is encountered the caliper assembly should be dismantled for examination as described in Chapter 10. While pushing the pistons back, maintain a careful watch on the fluid level in the reservoir. If the reservoir has been overfilled, the surplus fluid will prevent the pistons returning fully and must be removed by soaking it up with a clean cloth. Take care to prevent fluid spillage.

5 Apply a thin smear of caliper grease to the pad retaining pins. Take care to apply caliper grease to the metal backing of the pad only and not to allow grease to contaminate the friction material. Carefully fit the pads to the caliper and hold them in place while the first retaining pin (with the spring looped over it) is refitted **(see illustrations)**. Place a central pin in the pad cut-outs and press the spring over it and underneath the second retaining pin which should now be pressed into place **(see illustration)**. Refit the plastic cover.

6 Apply the brake lever gently and repeatedly to bring the pads firmly into contact with the disc until full brake pressure is restored. Be careful to watch the fluid level in the reservoir; if the pads have been re-used it will suffice to keep the level above the lower level mark, by topping-up if necessary, but if new pads have been fitted the level must be restored to the upper level line described above by topping-up or removing surplus fluid as necessary. Refit the reservoir cover or cap, gasket (where fitted) and diaphragm as described above.

7 Before taking the machine out on the road, be careful to check for fluid leaks from the system, and that the front brake is working correctly. Remember also that new pads, and to a lesser extent, cleaned pads will require a bedding-in period before they will function at peak efficiency. Where new pads are fitted use the brake gently but firmly for the first 50 - 100 miles to enable the pads to bed in fully.

21 Disc brake fluid - renewal

1 Note that hydraulic brake fluid must be changed regularly. It is necessary to renew the brake fluid at this interval to preserve maximum brake efficiency by ensuring that the fluid has not been contaminated and deteriorated to an unsafe degree.

20.5b ... insert first retaining pin with spring, then refit central pin, as shown ...

20.5c ... and tap second retaining pin into place, over spring end

Major service

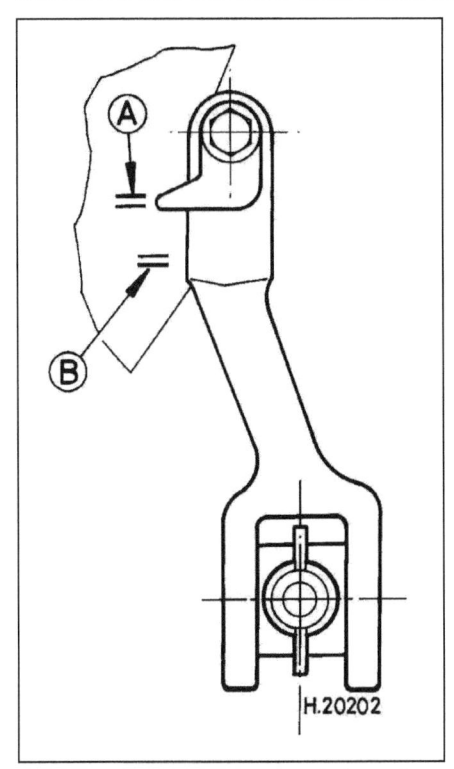

22.3 Drum rear brake wear limit marks
A Maximum friction material thickness
B Minimum friction material thickness

2 Before starting work, obtain a new, full can of the specified hydraulic fluid and read carefully the Section on brake bleeding in Chapter 10. Prepare the clear plastic tube and glass jar in the same way as for bleeding the hydraulic system, open each bleed nipple by unscrewing it 1/4 - 1/2 turn with a spanner and apply the front brake lever or rear brake pedal (as applicable) gently and repeatedly. This will pump out the old fluid. **Keep the master cylinder reservoir topped up at all times**, otherwise air may enter the system and greatly lengthen the operation.

3 Note that the manufacturer recommends that in order to ensure the complete replacement of the old brake fluid, it will first be necessary to remove the brake pads and to push the caliper pistons back as far as possible into the caliper body. Where more than one bleed nipple is fitted to a system (eg the front brake) repeat the operation on both nipples to ensure that the old fluid is completely removed. Top up the master cylinder when the operation is complete (see *Daily (pre-ride) checks*).

> **HAYNES HiNT** *The old brake fluid is invariably much darker in colour than the new, making it easier to see when it is pumped out and the new fluid has completely replaced it.*

22 Drum brake - check and adjustment

1 Note that the brake pedal height can be altered as required by setting the screw and locknut beneath the stop lamp rear switch; the pedal should be set so that it is as close as possible to the rider's foot in the normal riding position.

2 Adjustment is made by placing the machine on its centre stand with the rear wheel clear of the ground, then tightening the adjuster nut at the rear end of the brake operating rod while spinning the wheel until a rubbing sound is heard as the shoes begin to contact the drum. From this point slacken the nut by 3 - 4 turns until the rubbing sound has ceased. This should produce free play of 15 - 25 mm (0.6 - 1.0 in) at the brake pedal tip.

3 Brake shoe friction material wear can be checked by reference to the external wear indicator **(see illustration)** attached to the brake camshaft. With the brake correctly adjusted and fully applied, the pointer should align with the 'Max' line cast on the final drive case. As the shoes wear, the pointer will gradually move downwards. If it aligns with the 'Min' line at any time or extends beyond it, the brake shoes are worn out and must be renewed. See Chapter 10.

4 Note that if the rear brake appears spongy or imprecise at any time, but especially after the wheel has been disturbed, it is possible that centralising the brake components on the hub will effect an improvement. Slacken the rear wheel mounting bolts then spin the wheel and apply the rear brake firmly; maintain firm pressure while the mounting bolts are tightened securely to the specified torque setting.

5 At regular intervals check that the operating linkage is at its most efficient by ensuring that the angle formed between the brake rod and operating lever is less than 90° when the brake is firmly applied. If the angle is more than 90° at any time, the brake will not be as efficient; the operating lever must be removed from the camshaft splines, noting the position of the wear indicator pointer, and repositioned on the camshaft so that the angle is correct. This may require some trial and error to achieve the correct setting. Ensure that the operating lever is correctly refitted and securely fastened, that the wear indicator pointer is correctly aligned and that the brake is properly adjusted.

23 Wheels and wheel bearings - check

Wheels

1 Carefully check the complete wheel for cracks and chipping, particularly at the spoke roots and the edge of the rim. As a general rule a damaged wheel must be renewed as cracks will cause stress points which may lead to sudden failure under heavy load. Small nicks may be radiused carefully with a fine file and emery paper (No 600 - No 1000) to relieve the stress. If there is any doubt as to the condition of a wheel, advice should be sought from a reputable dealer or specialist repairer.

2 Each wheel is covered with a coating of lacquer or paint to prevent corrosion. If damage occurs to the wheel and the finish is penetrated, the bared aluminium alloy will soon start to corrode. A whitish grey oxide will form over the damaged area, which in itself is a protective coating. This deposit however, should be removed carefully as soon as possible and a new protective coating applied.

3 Check the lateral runout at the rim by spinning the wheel and placing a fixed pointer close to the rim edge. If the maximum run-out is greater than 0.5 mm (0.02 in) the manufacturer recommends that the wheel be renewed. If warpage was caused by impact during an accident, the safest measure it to renew the wheel complete. Worn wheel bearings may cause rim run-out. These should be renewed.

4 Note that impact damage or serious corrosion has wider implications in that it could lead to a loss of pressure from the tubeless tyres. If in any doubt as to the wheel's condition, seek professional advice.

Front wheel bearings

5 Support the machine on its centre stand on level ground so that the wheel to be examined is clear of the ground (wedge a wooden block or similar under the sump to raise the front wheel). Grasp the wheel firmly at top and bottom and attempt to rock it from side to side about its spindle; if any play is discovered, the wheel bearings must be renewed. See Chapter 10.

Rear wheel bearings

6 Support the machine on its centre stand on level ground so that the rear wheel is clear of the ground. Grasp the wheel firmly at the top and bottom and attempt to rock it from side to side about its centre. If any play is discovered the machine should be taken to a BMW dealer for the bearings in the final drive to be checked. Note that there should be no discernible endfloat (axial play) at the wheel hub.

24 Steering head bearings - check and adjustment

1 The steering head should be checked for play with the motorcycle on the centre stand and the front wheel supported clear of the ground. Grasp the fork lower legs at the bottom and alternately push and pull, feeling for any play in the bearings. The forks should

1•18 Major service

26.1 Fuel filter must be renewed at every second major service, or sooner if necessary

fall easily to either side, if moved slightly off centre. On 75 models the Fluidbloc retaining screws must first be removed.

2 If adjustment proves to be necessary, remove the handlebar cover and the fuel tank. On models fitted with frame-mounted fairings, remove the fairing inner panels if they prevent access to the fork yoke clamp bolts and to the steering head area. On all models, slacken fully the bottom yoke clamp bolts; the fork stanchions must be free to move up or down slightly in the bottom yoke.

3 On all 100 models and early 75 models slacken the steering stem top bolt and rotate the knurled, circular adjusting nut under the fork top yoke until the setting is correct, then tighten the top bolt, to its specified torque wrench setting if possible, to secure the nut. Tighten the bottom yoke pinch bolts and refit all disturbed components.

4 On later 75 models slacken the adjuster sleeve locknut and adjuster sleeve, then rotate the knurled, circular adjusting nut under the fork top yoke until the setting is correct, then tighten the adjuster sleeve to its specified torque wrench setting, followed by tightening the locknut to its torque wrench setting. Tighten the bottom yoke pinch bolts and refit all disturbed components.

5 On all models, check that all fasteners are tightened securely, to their specified torque wrench settings, if possible, then check that the forks move smoothly from lock to lock with no traces of stiffness or of free play.

25 Swinging arm pivot bearings - check

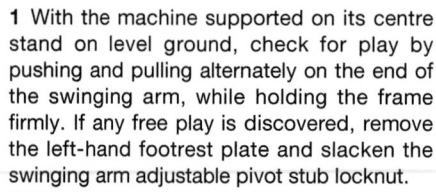

1 With the machine supported on its centre stand on level ground, check for play by pushing and pulling alternately on the end of the swinging arm, while holding the frame firmly. If any free play is discovered, remove the left-hand footrest plate and slacken the swinging arm adjustable pivot stub locknut.

2 Tighten the adjustable pivot stub as hard as possible, using hand pressure alone on an ordinary Allen key, then slacken it fully and retighten it to the specified torque wrench setting. Hold the stub in that position and tighten the locknut securely, to its specified torque wrench setting, if possible.

3 If play still exists, one or both of the pivot bearings are worn and must be renewed.

4 Note that the swinging arm must be removed (see Chapter 9) to permit the pivot bearings to be greased.

26 Fuel filter - renewal

1 Note that the full-flow filter element fitted between the fuel pump and the fuel rail must be renewed at every second service or, if the fuel used is of poor quality, at every service **(see illustration)**. Refer to Chapter 6.

27 Final drive shaft splines - greasing

1 The manufacturer recommends that the final drive assembly be disconnected from the swinging arm at this interval for greasing of the drive pinion splines which mesh with those of the drive shaft. Note that this operation is of particular importance on high mileage machines.

2 Refer to Chapter 9, Sections 2 and 4 for removal and refitting details, and the specifications in this Chapter for the recommended grease.

28 Valve clearances - check and adjustment (1989-on models)

The procedure for checking and adjusting the valve clearances remains unchanged from that detailed in Section 6 although the manufacturer recommends that this be carried out every 10 000 miles (15 000 km).

Chapter 2
Engine

Contents

Ancillary components - refitting	35
Auxiliary drive shaft and starter clutch - examination and renovation	25
Auxiliary drive shaft components and the bellhousing - refitting	33
Bearings and oil seals - examination and renovation	16
Bearings and oil seals - refitting	27
Bearings and oil seals - removal	13
Bellhousing and auxiliary drive shaft components - removal	7
Camshafts and cam chain - removal	8
Camshafts and camshaft drive mechanism - examination and renovation	17
Camshafts and setting the valve timing - refitting	32
Compression test	2
Connecting rods and big-end bearings - examination and renovation	22
Crankcase lower section and the output/balancer shaft - removal	11
Crankshaft - refitting	28
Crankshaft - removal	12
Crankshaft and main bearings - examination and renovation	23
Cylinder block - examination and renovation	20
Cylinder head - examination and renovation	18
Cylinder head - refitting	31
Cylinder head - removal	9
Dismantling the engine unit - general	3
Dismantling the engine unit - preliminaries and general procedures	5
Engine cases and covers - examination and renovation	15
Examination and renovation - general	14
Exhaust system - removal and refitting	see Chapter 6
General description	1
Oil - level check	see Daily (pre-ride) checks
Oil and filter - change	see Chapter 1
Oil pump and pressure relief valve	see Chapter 6
Outer covers - refitting	34
Outer covers - removal	6
Output/balancer shaft - examination and renovation	24
Output/balancer shaft and the crankcase lower section - refitting	29
Pistons and connecting rods - refitting	30
Pistons and connecting rods - removal	10
Pistons and piston rings - examination and renovation	21
Reassembling the engine unit - general	26
Refitting the engine unit to the frame	36
Removing the engine unit from the frame	4
Spark plugs	see Chapter 1
Starting and running the rebuilt engine	37
Taking the rebuilt machine on the road	38
Valve clearances - check and adjustment	see Chapter 1
Valves, valve seats and valve guides - examination and renovation	19

Degrees of difficulty

Easy, suitable for novice with little experience	Fairly easy, suitable for beginner with some experience	Fairly difficult, suitable for competent DIY mechanic	Difficult, suitable for experienced DIY mechanic	Very difficult, suitable for expert DIY or professional

Specifications

Engine
Bore .... 67 mm (2.64 in)
Stroke .... 70 mm (2.76 in)

	75 models	100 models
Number of cylinders	3	4
Capacity	740 cc (45 cu in)	987 cc (60 cu in)

	UK 75 models, early US 75 models	Late US 75 models*	100 models
Compression ratio	11.0 : 1	10.5 : 1	10.2 : 1
Claimed maximum power - DIN (kw/bhp @ rpm)	55/75 @ 8500	51/70 @ 8200	66/90 @ 8000
Claimed maximum torque - DIN (Nm/lbf ft @ rpm)	68/50 @ 6750	65/48 @ 6500	86/63 @ 6000

*Changeover date approximately mid-1986

Cylinder identification .... Numbered consecutively front to rear. Number 1 cylinder at front (cam chain) end

Firing order:
  75 models .... 3 - 1 - 2
  100 models .... 1 - 3 - 4 - 2
Direction of rotation .... Anti-clockwise, looking at ignition trigger from front of machine

Compression pressure - see Section 2
Good .... Over 10.0 bar (145 psi)
Normal .... 8.5 - 10.0 bar (123 - 145 psi)
Poor .... Below 8.5 bar (123 psi)

Valve timing - at 5/100 preload and 3 mm (0.12 in) lift

	UK models	US models
Intake opens	5° BTDC	5° ATDC
Intake closes	27° ABDC	27° ABDC
Exhaust opens	28° BBDC	28° BBDC
Exhaust closes	5° BTDC	5° BTDC

Valve clearances - engine cold (maximum coolant temperature 20°C/68°F)
Intake .... 0.15 - 0.20 mm (0.006 - 0.008 in)
Exhaust .... 0.25 - 0.30 mm (0.010 - 0.012 in)

Camshafts and cam followers
Camshaft bearing journal OD:
  At front (thrust) bearing .... 29.980 - 29.993 mm (1.1803 - 1.1808 in)
  At all other bearings .... 23.980 - 23.993 mm (0.9441 - 0.9446 in)
Cylinder head bearing ID:
  At front (thrust) bearing .... 30.020 - 30.041 mm (1.1819 - 1.1827 in)
  At all other bearings .... 24.020 - 24.041 mm (0.9457 - 0.9465 in)
Camshaft radial clearance .... 0.027 - 0.061 mm (0.0011 - 0.0024 in)
Camshaft base circle .... 30.000 mm (1.1811 in)
Cam lift:
  Intake .... 9.3927 mm (0.3698 in)
  Exhaust .... 9.3819 mm (0.3694 in)
Cam follower OD .... 33.475 - 33.491 mm (1.3179 - 1.3185 in)
Cylinder head bore ID .... 33.500 - 33.525 mm (1.3189 - 1.3199 in)
Cam follower/cylinder head clearance .... 0.009 - 0.050 mm (0.0004 - 0.0020 in)

Valves, guides and springs
Valve head diameter:
  Intake .... 34 mm (1.3386 in)
  Exhaust .... 30 mm (1.1811 in)
Valve head rim thickness:
  Standard .... 1.350 - 1.650 mm (0.0532 - 0.0650 in)
  Service limit .... 1.000 mm (0.0394 in)
Valve head maximum runout .... 0.030 mm (0.0012 in)
Valve overall length:
  Intake .... 111.000 mm (4.3701 in)
  Exhaust .... 110.610 - 110.810 mm (4.3547 - 4.3626 in)
Valve stem OD:
  Intake .... 6.960 - 6.975 mm (0.2740 - 0.2746 in)
  Exhaust .... 6.945 - 6.960 mm (0.2734 - 0.2740 in)
Valve guide ID .... 7.000 - 7.015 mm (0.2756 - 0.2762 in)
Valve stem/guide clearance:
  Intake - standard .... 0.025 - 0.055 mm (0.0010 - 0.0022 in)
  Exhaust - standard .... 0.040 - 0.070 mm (0.0016 - 0.0028 in)
  Intake and exhaust - service limit .... 0.150 mm (0.0059 in)
Valve guide overall length .... 45 mm (1.7717 in)
Valve guide OD .... 12.964 - 13.044 mm (0.5104 - 0.5135 in)
Cylinder head bore ID .... 13.000 - 13.018 mm (0.5118 - 0.5125 in)
Valve guide oversize available .... + 0.2 mm (+ 0.0079 in)
Valve seat angle .... 44° 10' - 44° 30'
Valve seat width .... 1.5 mm (0.0591 in)
Valve seat oversize available .... + 0.2 mm (+ 0.0079 in)
Valve spring standard free length .... 44.500 mm (1.7520 in)
Spring force at 29 mm (1.14 in) test length .... 740 - 800 N (166.36 - 179.85 lbf)

Cylinder block
Bore ID .... 66.995 - 67.005 mm (2.6376 - 2.6380 in)
Piston/cylinder clearance:
  Standard .... 0.030 - 0.040 mm (0.0012 - 0.0016 in)
  Service limit .... 0.080 mm (0.0032 in)

Engine 2•3

Pistons and gudgeon pins

	At size code A	At size code B
Piston standard OD:		
Mahle - nominal	66.970 mm (2.6366 in)	66.980 mm (2.6370 in)
Mahle - actual	66.963 - 66.977 mm (2.6363 - 2.6369 in)	66.973 - 66.987 mm (2.6367 - 2.6373 in)
KS - nominal	66.973 mm (2.6367 in)	66.983 mm (2.6371 in)
KS - actual	66.966 - 66.980 mm (2.6365 - 2.6370 in)	66.976 - 66.990 mm (2.6368 - 2.6374 in)

Piston weight group .... + or - stamped in piston crown. All pistons must be of same weight group, ie carry the same marking
Gudgeon pin OD .... 17.996 - 18.000 mm (0.7085 - 0.7087 in)
Piston bore and small-end bearing bush ID .... 18.002 - 18.006 mm (0.7088 - 0.7089 in)
Piston/gudgeon pin clearance .... 0.002 - 0.010 mm (0.0001 - 0.0004 in)

Piston rings

Top compression ring:
   Thickness .... 1.178 - 1.190 mm (0.0464 - 0.0469 in)
   End gap - installed .... 0.250 - 0.450 mm (0.0098 - 0.0177 in)
   Ring/groove side clearance - 75 models (Mahle) .... 0.050 - 0.082 mm (0.0020 - 0.0032 in)
   Ring/groove side clearance - 75 models (KS) .... 0.040 - 0.072 mm (0.0016 - 0.0028 in)
   Ring/groove side clearance - 100 models .... 0.013 - 0.027 mm (0.0005 - 0.0011 in)
Second compression ring:
   Thickness .... 1.478 - 1.490 mm (0.0582 - 0.0587 in)
   End gap - installed .... 0.250 - 0.450 mm (0.0098 - 0.0177 in)
   Ring/groove side clearance - 75 models (Mahle) .... 0.040 - 0.072 mm (0.0016 - 0.0028 in)
   Ring/groove side clearance - 75 models (KS) .... 0.030 - 0.062 mm (0.0012 - 0.0024 in)
   Ring/groove side clearance - 100 models .... 0.012 - 0.026 mm (0.0004 - 0.0010 in)
Oil scraper ring:
   Thickness .... 2.975 - 2.990 mm (0.1171 - 0.1177 in)
   End gap - installed .... 0.200 - 0.450 mm (0.0079 - 0.0177 in)
   Ring/groove side clearance .... 0.020 - 0.055 mm (0.0008 - 0.0022 in)

Connecting rods and bearings

Maximum permissible weight difference between connecting rods - without bearing shells .... ± 4 grams (0.1411 oz)
Note: all rods must always be of same weight category, ie carry the same colour coding or weight stamp
Small-end bearing bore ID - less bush .... 20.000 - 20.021 mm (0.7874 - 0.7882 in)
Big-end bearing bore ID .... 41.000 - 41.016 mm (1.6142 - 1.6148 in)
Big-end bearing width .... 21.883 - 21.935 mm (0.8615 - 0.8636 in)
Crankshaft big-end journal width .... 22.065 - 22.195 mm (0.8687 - 0.8738 in)
Connecting rod axial play (endfloat) - at big-end .... 0.130 - 0.312 mm (0.0051 - 0.0123 in)
Crankpin standard OD .... 37.976 - 38.000 mm (1.4951 - 1.4961 in)
Size groups:
   White .... 37.976 - 37.984 mm (1.4951 - 1.4954 in)
   Green .... 37.984 - 37.992 mm (1.4954 - 1.4957 in)
   Yellow .... 37.992 - 38.000 mm (1.4957 - 1.4961 in)
Big-end bearing radial clearance .... 0.030 - 0.066 mm (0.0012 - 0.0026 in)
Undersize bearing shells available:
   1st stage (1 paint mark) .... -0.25 mm (-0.0098 in)
   2nd stage (2 paint marks) .... -0.50 mm (-0.0197 in)

Crankshaft and main bearings

Crankcase bearing bore ID .... 49.000 - 49.016 mm (1.9291 - 1.9298 in)
Crankshaft endfloat .... 0.080 - 0.183 mm (0.0032 - 0.0072 in)
Thrust bearing width:
   Standard .... 23.000 mm (0.9055 in)
   At 1st stage undersize - crankshaft reground by -0.25 mm (-0.01 in) .... 23.200 mm (0.9134 in)
   At 2nd stage undersize - crankshaft reground by -0.50 mm (-0.02 in) .... 23.400 mm (0.9213 in)
Main bearing journal standard OD .... 44.976 - 45.000 mm (1.7707 - 1.7717 in)
Size groups:
   White .... 44.976 - 44.984 mm (1.7707 - 1.7710 in)
   Green .... 44.984 - 44.992 mm (1.7710 - 1.7713 in)
   Yellow .... 44 992 - 45.000 mm (1.7713 - 1.7717 in)
Main bearing radial clearance .... 0.020 - 0.056 mm (0.0008 - 0.0022 in)
Undersize bearing shells available:
   1st stage (1 paint mark) .... -0.25 mm (-0.0098 in)
   2nd stage (2 paint marks) .... -0.50 mm (-0.0197 in)

Engine

Primary drive
Reduction ratio - crankshaft to output/balancer shaft .... 1 : 1

Torque wrench settings - 75 models

	Nm	lbf ft
Cylinder head cover bolts	8 ± 1	6 ± 0.5
Crankshaft (engine right-hand) cover bolts	8 ± 1	6 ± 0.5
Cam chain (engine front) cover screws	7 ± 1	5 ± 0.5
Cam chain top guide rail Torx screws	9 ± 1	6.5 ± 0.5
Camshaft bearing cap nuts	9 ± 1	6.5 ± 0.5
Camshaft sprocket bolts	54 ± 6	40 ± 4.5
Cam chain tensioner mounting screws	9 ± 1	6.5 ± 0 5
Crankshaft sprocket and ignition rotor flange retaining bolt	50 ± 6	37 ± 4.5
Cylinder head bolts - bolt threads lightly oiled:		
1st stage	30 ± 4	22 ± 3
2nd stage - after 20 minute wait	45 ± 5	33 ± 4
Connecting rod big-end bearing cap retaining nuts:		
1st stage - to preload shells	30 ± 3	22 ± 2
2nd stage - applies to all models	Tighten (rotate) nuts through an angle of 80°	
Crankshaft main bearing cap bolts	50 ± 6	37 ± 4.5
Crankcase lower section to cylinder block:		
10 mm bolt - output shaft rear	40 ± 5	29.5 ± 4.5
8 mm bolt or screw - output shaft front	18 ± 2	13 ± 1.5.5
6 mm bolt or screw	7 ± 1	5 ± 0.5
Oil/water pump assembly mounting screws	7 ± 1	5 ± 0.5
Auxiliary drive shaft bearing retainer screws	9 ± 1	6.5 ± 0.5
Bellhousing Torx screws	9 ± 1	6.5 ± 0.5
Starter clutch body/auxiliary drive shaft - 6 mm bolts	9 ± 1	6.5 ± 0.5
Alternator drive flange/auxiliary drive shaft retaining bolt	33 ± 4	24 ± 3
Engine and transmission unit/frame mountings	40.5 ± 4	30 ± 3

Torque wrench settings - 100 models

	Nm	lbf ft
Cylinder head cover drain plugs - early models only	7	5
Cylinder head cover bolts	8 ± 1	6 ± 0.5
Crankshaft (engine right-hand) cover bolts	8 ± 1	6 ± 0.5
Cam chain (engine front) cover screws	7 ± 1	5 ± 0.5
Cam chain top guide rail Torx screws	9 ± 1	6.5 ± 0.5
Camshaft bearing cap nuts	9 ± 1	6.5 ± 0.5
Camshaft sprocket bolts	54 ± 6	40 ± 4.5
Cam chain tensioner mounting screws	9 ± 1	6.5 ± 0 5
Crankshaft sprocket and ignition rotor flange retaining bolt	50 ± 6	37 ± 4.5
Cylinder head bolts - bolt threads lightly oiled:		
1st stage	30 ± 4	22 ± 3
2nd stage - after 20 minute wait	45 ± 5	33 ± 4
Connecting rod big-end bearing cap retaining nuts:		
1st stage - to preload shells	30 ± 3	22 ± 2
2nd stage - applies to all models	Tighten (rotate) nuts through an angle of 80°	
Crankshaft main bearing cap bolts	50 ± 6	37 ± 4.5
Crankcase lower section to cylinder block:		
10 mm bolt - output shaft rear	40 ± 5	29.5 ± 4.5
8 mm bolt or screw - output shaft front	18 ± 2	13 ± 1.5.5
6 mm bolt or screw	7 ± 1	5 ± 0.5
Oil/water pump assembly mounting screws	7 ± 1	5 ± 0.5
Auxiliary drive shaft bearing retainer screws	9 ± 1	6.5 ± 0.5
Bellhousing Torx screws	9 ± 1	6.5 ± 0.5
Starter clutch body/auxiliary drive shaft:		
8 mm screws	24	18
6 mm bolts	9 ± 1	6.5 ± 0.5
Alternator drive flange/auxiliary drive shaft retaining bolt	33 ± 4	24 ± 3
Engine and transmission unit/frame mountings:		
Early (1984, 1985) models	32	23.5
Late (1986 on) models	40.5 ± 4	30 ± 3

Engine 2•5

1 General description

The engine is a liquid cooled four-stroke type, of three cylinders (75 models) or four cylinders (100 models). The cylinders are arranged in line but the crankshaft is disposed longitudinally, parallel to the machine's centre line and the cylinders are laid flat so that the cylinder head (or 'top' end) is on the machine's left and the crankshaft (or 'bottom' end) is on its right. All castings are of aluminium alloy, the main crankcase being made as light and compact as possible by the use of plated cylinder bores instead of separate (usually cast iron) liners. The pistons run in bores which are accurately machined in the crankcase and given a hard bearing surface by having a thin layer of nickel/silicon carbide ('Scanimet') deposited electrically and ground to the required tolerances. Passages for coolant are included in the cylinder head and block castings.

The forged steel crankshaft incorporates four (75 models) or five (100 models) plain main bearing journals which rotate in split shell bearings and are secured to the crankcase by large bolted-on caps. The rearmost crankshaft web is fully circular with gear teeth machined in its periphery, and a small sprocket and rotor flange are attached to the crankshaft front end to drive respectively the camshaft and ignition trigger assembly.

The connecting rods have detachable bolted on big-end caps; split shell bearings are fitted at the big-end bearing and a plain bush at the small-end bearing. The pistons are flat-topped and are fitted with two plain compression rings and one oil scraper ring.

The valves are set in deep wells in the cylinder head and are each closed by a single coil spring. An inverted bucket-type cam follower (or tappet) is fitted over each valve/spring assembly; these cam followers have a recess machined in their upper ends into which a thick steel shim is placed to permit adjustment of the valve clearances. The shims are hardened to withstand the action of the camshaft lobes which bear directly upon them.

The valve opening is controlled by two overhead camshafts which run in bearing surfaces machined directly in the cylinder head casting and are each retained by four (75 models) or five (100 models) separate bearing caps. They are driven from the crankshaft by a single-row roller chain which has plastic-faced guide blades between the camshafts and between the intake camshaft and the crankshaft, and a plastic-faced pivoting tensioner blade which is pressed against the chain 'slack' run (ie between the crankshaft and the exhaust camshaft) by a hydraulically-operated chain tensioner assembly.

Drive from the crankshaft is transmitted via the large gear on the rear web to a secondary shaft which is disposed parallel to and underneath the crankshaft along the machine's centre line. The matching gear on this secondary, or engine output, shaft is of the same size as the crankshaft gear to give a 1:1 reduction ratio but incorporates a spring-loaded anti-backlash gear to reduce noise. The shaft serves not only to transmit drive to the clutch and transmission (see Chapter 3) but also drives the combined oil/water pump assembly from its forward end. On 75 models two balancer weights are incorporated in the shaft to cancel out the rocking couple produced by the motion of the two outer pistons and thus eliminate the only vibration source inherent in any 120° triple; on 100 models drive is actually transmitted via a large housing, with vanes protruding from its inner surface, through rubber blocks to damp out transmission shocks to a vaned shock absorber inner which is splined to the output shaft. The shaft rotates in a needle roller bearing at its forward end and a ball journal bearing at its rear end, both bearings being clamped to the underside of the main crankcase/ cylinder block casting by the crankcase lower section, which also acts as the engine oil reservoir.

The fourth major engine casting is the bellhousing which is attached to the rear end of the crankcase and houses the clutch and alternator/starter motor drive components. An auxiliary drive shaft is driven via a 1.5 : 1 reduction ratio from the crankshaft gear, rotates in a needle bearing in the crankcase and a ball journal bearing set in the top of the bellhousing and has the drive flange of the alternator shock absorber bolted to its rear end. The electric starter motor drives via an idler shaft set in the bellhousing through a starter clutch mounted on the auxiliary drive shaft; a total reduction ratio of 27 : 1. Early UK only K100 and K100 RS models were fitted with a clutch containing three rollers locked by spring-loaded plungers, while later models are fitted with a sprag-type clutch containing fourteen locking elements.

Since the output/balancer shaft and the auxiliary drive shaft are gear-driven from the crankshaft they rotate in the opposite direction to it. Their combined mass, with that of the alternator and clutch, cancels out the lateral torque reaction which would otherwise be evident from the crankshaft of an engine of this layout.

2 Compression test

1 A good idea of the internal state of the engine can be gained by testing its compression as follows.
2 The engine must be fully warmed up to normal operating temperature and the battery fully charged for the test results to be accurate.
3 Remove all the spark plugs. Noting the warnings concerning servicing the ignition system given in Chapter 7. Lay the spark plugs on the cylinder head so that their metal bodies are securely earthed to the metal of the cylinder head (to prevent damage to the ignition system) and so that their electrodes are well clear of the spark plug orifices (to prevent the risk of sparks igniting any fuel/air mixture that is ejected).

⚠ **Warning: While one cylinder is being tested, place a wad of rag over each of the remaining spark plug apertures as protection against sparks igniting any fuel/air mixture that is ejected.**

4 Attach an accurate, good quality compression gauge (tester) to the cylinder head spark plug orifice, following its manufacturer's instructions. Open the throttle fully. Spin the engine over on the starter motor and note the readings recorded.
5 After one or two revolutions the pressure should build up to a maximum figure and then stabilise; note the reading and repeat the test on the remaining cylinders. There should be no discernible difference between any readings. The expected pressures are given in Specifications. If all pressures are the same and in the good or normal range then the engine is in good condition.
6 If there is a marked discrepancy between the readings, or if any is in the poor range, the appropriate cylinder must be checked carefully.
7 Note that during a normal compression test one would go on to temporarily seal the piston rings by pouring a quantity of oil into the barrel and then take a second set of readings. If the pressure increased noticeably it could then be assumed that the piston rings were worn rather than the valves. Since it would be very difficult to get a full seal from such a method in a warm flat-cylinder engine there is little point in doing this; check the pistons and rings as well as the head gasket and valves when looking for the cause of compression loss.

3 Dismantling the engine unit - general

> **HAYNES HINT**: *As a general rule, time is the primary cost of an overhaul so it doesn't pay to install worn or substandard parts.*

1 The engine unit is so designed that the only parts of it which cannot be removed easily while the main crankcase/cylinder block casting is in the frame are the auxiliary drive shaft, including the starter idler shaft and starter clutch, and the output/balancer shaft

assemblies. If the bellhousing or the crankcase lower section are to be removed to reach any of these components, the gearbox and final drive must be removed first (see Chapter 4) so that the clutch can be withdrawn (see Chapter 3) to give access to the bellhousing. The engine and frame will require very careful supporting if this procedure is adopted. See Section 7.

2 All other components can be removed with the main crankcase/cylinder block casting and the bellhousing still in the frame. Usually, components can be easily removed leaving others intact. For example, to remove the crankshaft it is possible merely to drain the coolant, to remove the engine left-hand, right-hand and front engine covers and to disconnect the cam chain before removing the big-end and main bearing caps and withdrawing the crankshaft.

3 K75 model owners should note, however, that it is necessary on reassembly to align timing marks on the crankshaft and balancer shaft gears. Since these marks may not be easily visible from the crankshaft opening it is recommended that this task be undertaken only with the engine unit removed. The amount of preliminary dismantling necessary to remove the balancer shaft with the engine in the frame means that there is in practice very little extra work to remove the entire unit and gain much improved working conditions.

4 Owners of all models should note that if a major overhaul is to be undertaken, or if more than one component requires attention at any time, the engine unit should be removed from the frame. This is a basically simple procedure which permits excellent access to all components and allows the major castings to be cleaned so that the high standards required for successful rebuilding are maintained.

5 While notes on alternative procedures are provided where necessary, this Chapter is based on the assumption that the engine/transmission unit is to be removed from the frame, that the engine will be separated from the clutch and transmission and that it will be completely overhauled.

4 Removing the engine unit from the frame

Note: *It is possible to separate the engine unit from the transmission at the bellhousing rear face and to remove the engine unit after the gearbox and final drive have first been withdrawn. (The engine cannot be removed on its own, leaving the gearbox and transmission attached to the frame, since this leads to an unacceptable risk of damage and a great deal of difficulty in aligning the clutch and gearbox input shaft and the engine mountings.)*

Since, however, the above method involves a great deal of care in aligning the gearbox input shaft and clutch release with the clutch and in supporting solidly the frame, engine and transmission components as they are separated, it is recommended that the engine and transmission are removed from the frame as a single unit and then separated; the following instructions are based on this procedure. Owners who do not wish to use the recommended method should note that procedures are similar until the final stages. Refer to Chapter 4 for more information.

1 Place the machine firmly on its centre stand so that it is standing securely and there is no likelihood that it may fall over. This is extremely important as owing to the weight of the complete machine and the engine, any instability during dismantling will probably be uncontrollable. If possible, place the machine on a raised platform. This will improve accessibility and ease engine removal. Again, owing to the weight of the machine, ensure that the platform is sufficiently strong and well supported.

2 Drain the engine oil and remove the oil filter, as described in *Routine maintenance and servicing*.

3 On K75RT, K100 RS, K100 RT and K100 LT models it should suffice to remove only the fairing knee pads and lower sections (side panels and radiator cover); owners may, however, feel it preferable to eliminate any risk of damage by removing the entire fairing. On K75 S models it is best to remove the fairing. Where fitted, remove also the engine spoiler or belly fairing. Refer to Chapter 8.

4 On all models, lift the seat, remove both side panels, remove the radiator cover panels (where fitted), then remove the fuel tank as described in Chapter 6.

5 Note that whenever any component is moved, all mounting nuts, bolts, or screws should be refitted in their original locations with their respective washers and mounting rubbers and/or spacers.

6 Disconnect and remove the fuel injection control unit and storage tray, as described in Chapter 6.

7 Remove the battery as described in *Routine maintenance and servicing* and tie the coolant expansion tank to the frame out of harm's way.

8 Remove the air intake hose.

9 Working as described in Chapter 5, drain the coolant, disconnect the radiator hoses (pull the bottom hose out of the crankcase cover) and remove the radiator.

10 Remove the exhaust system. (Chapter 6).

11 Remove the alternator cover, ignition HT coil cover **(see illustration)**, number plate bracket and the rear mudguard.

12 Working as described in Chapter 1, Section 5, disconnect and remove clear of the engine/transmission the throttle, choke and clutch cables.

13 Working methodically round the machine, disconnect all electrical wires joining the engine/transmission unit to the frame. Trace each wire from the component concerned up to the connector joining it to the main wiring loom and separate the connector; noting where each is installed. Remove the clamps or cable ties securing the wire to the frame. These wires include the alternator connector plug, the starter motor cable, the ignition HT coil low-tension wires (make a written note of exactly what colour wire is fitted to which terminal), the frame earth connection (retained by a single nut and bolt to the left-hand side of the frame top tubes, at the rear of the steering head), the speedometer impulse transmitter, the stop lamp rear switch, the gear position indicator switch, the oil pressure switch, the ignition trigger assembly, the choke warning lamp switch and the engine wiring harness **(see illustrations)**.

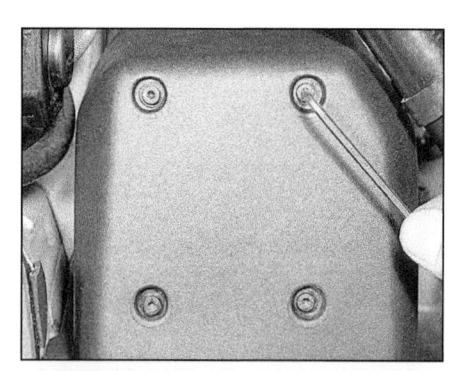

4.11 Ignition HT coil cover is retained by four Allen screws – 100 models

4.13a Make a written note of connections before disconnecting ignition HT coil leads

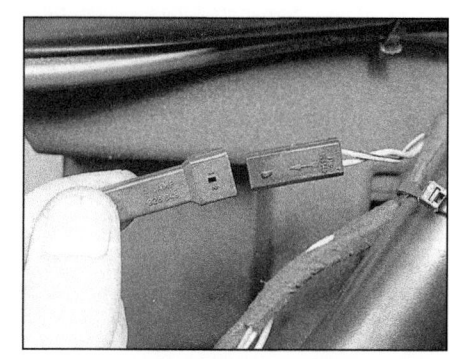

4.13b Check all wires are disconnected between engine and frame – speedometer impulse transmitter wires . . .

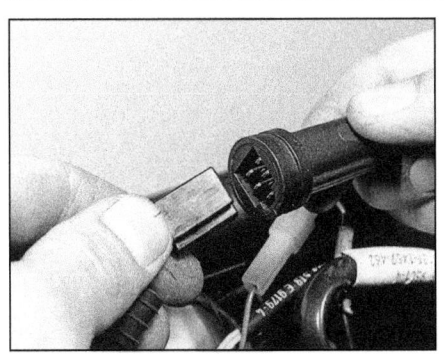

4.13c ... and ignition trigger assembly wires

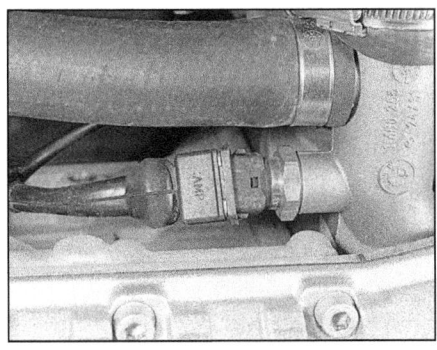

4.13d Coolant temperature sensor connector is secured by a wire clip

Caution: Be very careful to check that all wires are released and are positioned so that they will not hinder the removal of the frame from the engine/transmission unit.

14 Slacken the two engine front mounting nuts and the bolts securing the bellhousing/frame joint and the two gearbox/frame joints; also the rear suspension bottom mounting nut. If any fastener is difficult to move, apply a good quantity of penetrating fluid and allow time for it to work before proceeding further. In the case of the front mounting bolts, slacken the nuts and attempt to break the bolts free by rotating them before attempting to tap them out. Make a final check that all components have been disconnected/or removed which might hinder the removal of the frame from the engine/transmission unit; the unit should now be held only by its six mountings.

15 Enlist the aid of two or three assistants to withdraw the frame; one to 'steer' the front forks, another to lift the back of the frame and a third to help with the engine/transmission unit.

16 Place blocks of wood or similar under the sump so that the engine is securely supported and cannot fall. Place another block of wood or similar support under the final drive case; the support should be tall enough to fit closely under the casing.

17 Remove the rear suspension unit from its bottom mounting and lower the final drive case on to its support; **do not** allow the swinging arm to move too far downwards or the gaiter at its front end may be torn and **never** allow it to drop or it may crack the casing.

18 With the assistants standing ready, unscrew and remove the bellhousing mounting bolt, the engine front mountings and the gearbox mounting bolts; note carefully the presence and number of any shims that may be found at any of the mountings. The engine/transmission unit should now be supported securely on its sump support, on the centre stand and on the rear wheel/final drive support.

19 Taking care not to scratch the paintwork or damage any component, carefully lift the frame at the rear and walk it forwards clear of the engine and transmission.

20 On K100 RS, K100 RT and K100 LT models check the engine front mounting rubber bushes for cracks, splits, perishing or compaction and renew them if they show any sign of deterioration or damage.

5 Dismantling the engine unit - preliminaries and general procedures

Preliminary dismantling

1 If the engine/transmission unit has been removed as a single unit withdraw the alternator and starter motor (see Chapter 11) and separate the gearbox and final drive (see Chapter 4) from the bellhousing, noting that it will be necessary to remove the stand assembly to reach the two lowest gearbox/bellhousing retaining screws. There is no need to separate the final drive from the gearbox. Dismantle the clutch as described in Chapter 3.

2 As described in Chapter 6, remove the top half of the air filter assembly with the engine wiring harness attached to it, disconnect the loom from all other electrical components. Withdraw the air filter element and the air cleaner bottom half, the fuel rail and injectors, the plenum chamber and crankcase breather, the throttle bodies and intake stubs and the EECS pressure relief valve and hoses (where fitted).

3 Remove the coolant hose stub. See Chapter 5.

4 Remove the ignition HT coils, noting carefully where the HT leads are connected, see Chapter 7. Remove the spark plugs and HT leads as described in Chapter 1.

5 If necessary, remove the sump (oil pan) and pump pick-up as described in Chapter 6, and remove the oil/water pump assembly as described in Chapters 4 and 5.

6 Remove the ignition trigger assembly as described in Chapter 7.

General procedures

7 If any of the following operations are to be carried out with the main cylinder block still in the frame, ensure that the machine is supported firmly on the centre stand. It is less tiring if the machine can be raised off the ground on a strong, low, bench. Have blocks to hand for supporting the rear of the machine, especially if the rear wheel is to be removed.

8 Before commencing any work involving the electrical system, disconnect the battery negative (earth) lead at the terminal to prevent any risk of short circuits.

9 On K75RT, K100 RS, K100 RT and K100 LT models it will usually be necessary to remove the fairing knee pads and lower sections (side panels and radiator cover) to gain adequate access to components, refer to Chapter 8 for full details. The complete fairing can be removed to eliminate any risk of damage, if required. Where fitted, remove the belly fairing or engine spoiler. See Chapter 8.

> **HAYNES HiNT** *A clean engine will make the job easier and prevent the possibility of getting dirt into the internal areas of the engine.*

10 Before any dismantling work is undertaken, the external surfaces of the unit should be thoroughly cleaned and degreased. This will prevent the contamination of the engine internals, and will also make working a lot easier and cleaner. A high flash-point solvent, such as paraffin (kerosene) can be used. or better still, a proprietary engine degreaser such as Gunk. Use old paintbrushes and toothbrushes to work the solvent into the various recesses of the engine castings. Take care to exclude solvent or water from the electrical components and intake and exhaust ports. The use of petrol (gasoline) as a cleaning medium should be avoided, because the vapour is explosive and can be toxic if used in a confined space.

11 When clean and dry, arrange the unit on the workbench, leaving a suitable clear area for working. Gather a selection of small containers and plastic bags so that parts can be grouped together in an easily identifiable manner. Some paper and a pen should be on hand to permit notes to be made and labels attached where necessary. A supply of clean rag is also required.

12 Before commencing work, read through the appropriate section so that some idea of the necessary procedure can be gained. When removing the various engine components great force is seldom required, unless specified. In many cases, a component's reluctance to be removed is indicative of an incorrect approach or removal method. If in any doubt. recheck with the text.

13 **Note:** *All descriptions of locations, ie left, right, front and rear, refer to components as they would be if installed in the machine with the rider normally seated. Given the potential for confusion with this engine design the terms 'top end' and 'bottom end' referring respectively to the cylinder head and crankshaft assemblies, have been avoided if at*

all possible. However in some unavoidable cases, mention has been made of 'upper' or 'lower' components; these refer to the upper side, ie the intake side or top surface of the engine or to the lower side, ie the exhaust side or underneath (sump/oil pan) of the engine. Bear this in mind at all times, but particularly if the engine is supported in some unusual position on the workbench.

6 Outer covers - removal

General

1 While specific instructions are given below for each cover, the following general notes apply to all.
2 Since all are well above the level of oil there is no need to drain the engine oil before removing any of these covers but be prepared to mop up or catch the small amount of oil that will be released as the cover is removed.
3 Wipe off all traces of dirt from around the cover before removing it, so that nothing drops into the engine.
4 Take care not to stretch or damage the rubber seals fitted to the cylinder head and crankcase covers; these can be re-used many times if they are undamaged.
5 Always slacken screws by a turn at a time, working in a diagonal sequence from the outside inwards. When all pressure is released, remove the screws, tap the cover lightly once or twice with a soft-faced mallet to break the seal and pull the cover away.

Cylinder head (engine left-hand) cover

6 On K100 RT and K100 LT models remove the fairing left-hand knee pad and lower side section. Where fitted, remove the belly fairing, or engine spoiler. See Chapter 8. Remove the spark plug cover (see Chapter 1) and pack the spark plug channel with rag or similar to prevent oil from flowing into it.
7 On early K100 and K100 RS models remove the two drain plugs screwed into the cover and place the machine on its side stand so that any oil remaining in the cover can drip out. On all other models be prepared to catch the residual oil as the cover is removed.
8 Remove the ten (75 models) or twelve (100 models) bolts securing the cover and withdraw it, noting the presence of the coil spring fitted to one of the camshaft bearing caps. Mop up any spilt oil; do not allow oil to flow into the spark plug channel.

Crankshaft (engine right-hand) cover

9 On K75RT, K100 RS, K100 RT and K100 LT models remove the fairing right-hand knee pad, lower side section and radiator cover. Where fitted, remove the engine spoiler or belly fairing and the radiator cover panels. See Chapter 8.

10 Drain the coolant if not already done, then disconnect and remove the radiator bottom hose. See Chapter 5.
11 Remove the eight (75 models) or ten (100 models) bolts securing the cover and withdraw it.

Cam chain (engine front) cover

12 It is possible to remove this cover after merely slackening the crankshaft cover bolts and removing the two cylinder head cover front bolts; however this is not recommended as it is not possible to clean the sealing surfaces well enough to guarantee a leak-free joint on reassembly. Start by removing both engine side covers as described in paragraphs 6 - 11 above.
13 Remove the complete ignition trigger assembly as described in Chapter 7.
14 Disconnect the oil pressure switch wire and feed it downwards clear of the front cover, releasing the metal securing clips. Remove the horn (75 models only).
15 Remove the cover retaining screws and withdraw the cover noting the two gaskets, one along each mating surface, and the two locating dowels set in the top mating surface. Always renew the gaskets to prevent leaks.

7 Bellhousing and auxiliary drive shaft components - removal

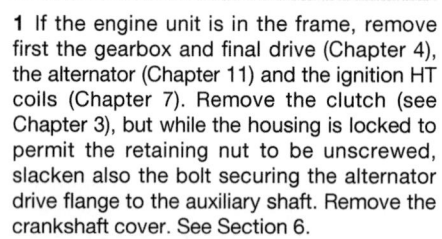

1 If the engine unit is in the frame, remove first the gearbox and final drive (Chapter 4), the alternator (Chapter 11) and the ignition HT coils (Chapter 7). Remove the clutch (see Chapter 3), but while the housing is locked to permit the retaining nut to be unscrewed, slacken also the bolt securing the alternator drive flange to the auxiliary shaft. Remove the crankshaft cover. See Section 6.
2 Owners will now have to devise some means of supporting securely the frame rear end and the engine at the same time. Note that when the frame/bellhousing mounting bolt is removed the engine will pivot, however slightly, on its two front mountings thus causing a risk of damage to other components and problems with alignment on reassembly. Only secure supports can prevent this.

7.5 Lock crankshaft to permit removal of alternator drive flange retaining bolt

3 If the frame rear end is hanging from an overhead support, as described in Chapter 7, great care must be taken not to jar the frame while the bellhousing is removed. Note that jacks should not be used to support heavy components for any length of time; they are for lifting only. Use car axle stands, blocks of wood or similar to hold the engine and frame securely at the required height.
4 When the machine is securely supported remove the bellhousing mounting bolt and any shims that may be fitted.
5 If the engine is removed from the frame temporarily refit the clutch housing and lock it as described in Chapter 3 to permit the alternator drive flange retaining bolt to be slackened **(see illustration)**. Remove the bolt and withdraw the drive flange, noting that the O-ring and thrust washer behind it may be dislodged.
6 While in practice the flange was found to be a fairly slack fit and was easily pulled away by hand, it may require a sharp tap from a hammer and a soft metal drift or a wooden dowel (to avoid damaging the shaft) on the auxiliary shaft rear end to jar it free. BMW state that a two-legged puller, with an adaptor to protect the shaft end, is required to remove the flange; it will probably be necessary to grind down the puller claws so that they will fit between the flange and the bellhousing.
7 Remove the bellhousing/crankcase retaining screws. These are Torx screws, size T30, and will require the use of a suitable key to remove and refit them **(see illustrations)**; it

7.7a Bellhousing/crankcase retaining screws are of ...

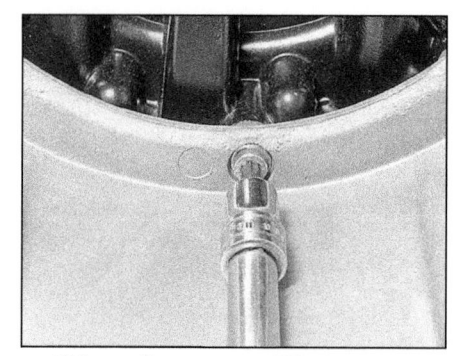

7.7b ... Torx type – a T30 size key is required for removal and refitting

7.9 Remove auxiliary drive shaft as a single unit

is useful to purchase a Torx key that is attached to a socket so that a torque wrench can be used to fasten them.

8 When all the screws are removed, tap the bellhousing sharply with a soft-faced mallet to break the seal and withdraw it, noting the presence of the two locating dowels. Check carefully that the starter idler shaft and the auxiliary drive shaft are not dislodged with the bellhousing.

9 Carefully pull the starter idler shaft out of the crankcase and note exactly how the spring behind it (if fitted on early 100 models) is fitted before removing it. Withdraw the auxiliary drive shaft as a single unit **(see illustration)**.

8 Camshafts and cam chain - removal

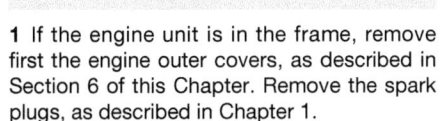

1 If the engine unit is in the frame, remove first the engine outer covers, as described in Section 6 of this Chapter. Remove the spark plugs, as described in Chapter 1.

2 Rotate the crankshaft by means of an Allen key placed in the ignition rotor retaining bolt until the camshafts are placed so that all valves are closed as far as possible, ie so that there is the minimum pressure possible exerted on the camshafts by the valve springs. On 75 models this position is close to Number 3 cylinder being at TDC on the compression stroke.

3 Remove the chain tensioner. Some early 100 models are fitted with a chain tensioner which can be locked by turning a screw as far as possible clockwise; the tensioner mounting screws are then removed and the unit can be withdrawn. The screw is to be found in that face of the tensioner opposite to the plunger/tensioner blade assembly. On 75 models and later 100 models compress the tensioner by hand, remove the mounting screws and withdraw the unit; slowly allow it to extend until the spring pressure is released.

4 Remove their retaining clips or circlips, noting the washer behind each, and withdraw the cam chain tensioner blade and chain guide **(see illustration)**. Remove its retaining screws and withdraw the chain top guide rail from between the camshafts; these are Torx screws which BMW state are size T30 but were found on the machine to be size T27 **(see illustration 8.4b overleaf)**. Owners should ensure that both sizes of key are available.

5 In some cases there may be sufficient slack in the chain, and sufficient clearance around the sprockets, to permit its removal at this stage but usually it will be necessary to withdraw the camshaft sprockets; use an open-ended spanner to hold the camshaft at the hexagon provided, remove the bolt and

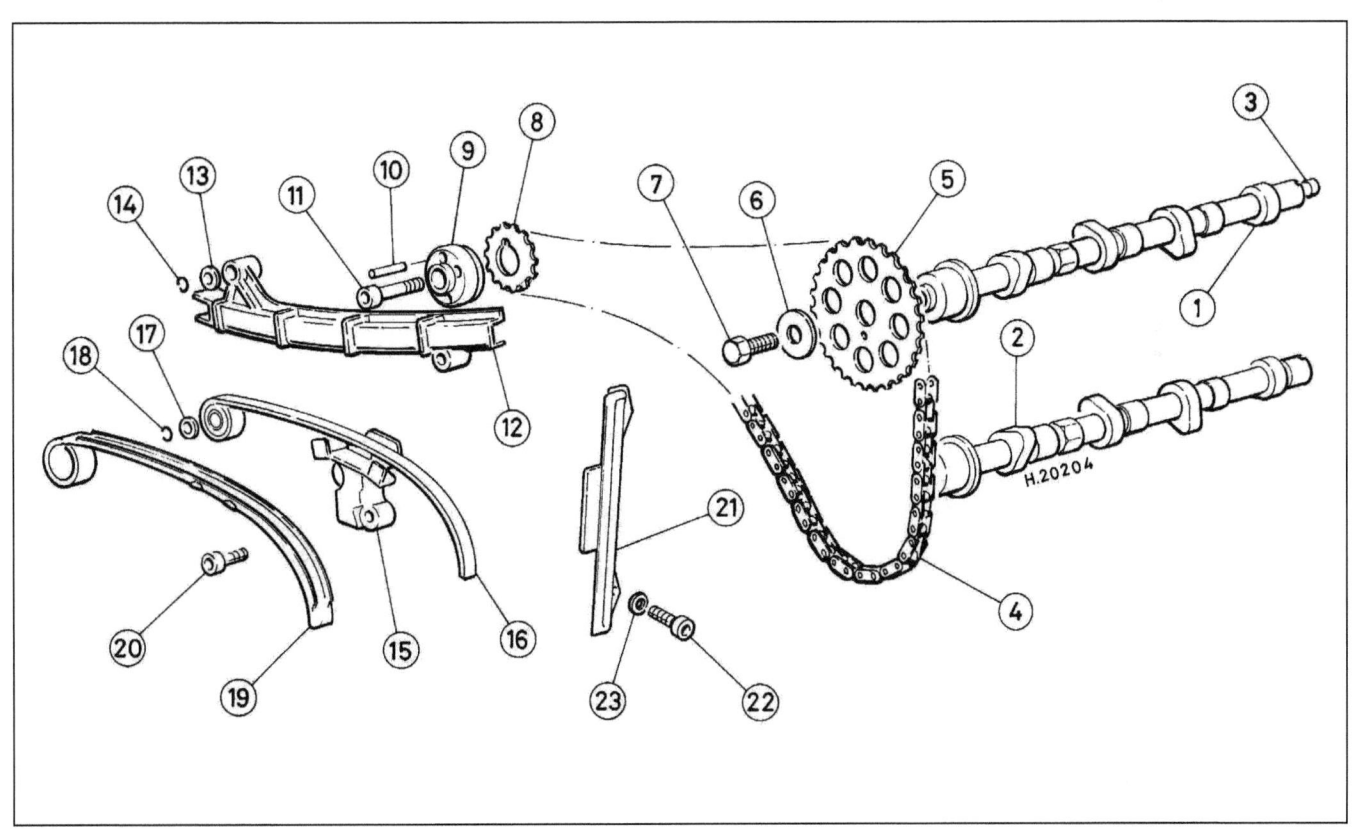

8.4a Camshafts and cam chain

1 Intake camshaft	7 Bolt – 2 off	13 Washer	19 Tensioner blade plastic face
2 Exhaust camshaft	8 Sprocket	14 Circlip	20 Screw
3 Plug – 2 off	9 Rotor	15 Tensioner	21 Chain top guide rail
4 Cam chain	10 Locating pin	16 Tensioner blade backing	22 Torx screw
5 Sprocket – 2 off	11 Bolt	17 Washer	23 Wave washer
6 Washer – 2 off	12 Chain guide	18 Circlip	

2•10 Engine

8.4b Cam chain top guide rail is retained by Torx screws – ensure correct size key is available

8.5 If sprockets are to be removed, hold camshaft as shown while retaining bolts are unscrewed

withdraw the large washer and the sprocket **(see illustration)**. While these components are the same for both intake and exhaust camshafts, it is good practice to mark them and to store them separately so that they can be refitted in their original locations. Withdraw the chain from the crankshaft sprocket.

6 If required, the ignition rotor flange and crankshaft sprocket can be withdrawn at this stage.

7 If the camshafts are to be removed, this can be done before or after the chain has been disconnected but in the former case some care will be required to avoid damaging or marking any components.

8 **Note:** *Before removing the camshafts make a careful note (using a small sketch if required), of the exact location and fitted position of the bearing caps; these are clamped to the head and line-bored in a single process on manufacture and must **not** be refitted on any other bearing, nor reversed.* The manufacturer has provided identification aids in the form of a number stamped into each bearing cap to match a number cast into the cylinder head next to the bearing pedestal; these numbers are stamped in the top of each cap above the threaded boss on the intake and below it on the exhaust and can only be read from the rear of the cylinder head looking forwards to help eliminate any possibility of their being reversed **(see illustration)**. Note that odd numbers are used for the intake and even numbers for the exhaust, except for the rear bearing on 100 models which is marked '0' indicating '10'. If necessary, make your own identifying marks, provided this does not involve scratching a cap or using a punch. It is useful to have ready some means of retaining the cam followers and shims. See paragraph 12.

9 To avoid tilting the camshafts, remove first the front or cam chain end (thrust) bearing caps. Unscrew the nuts alternately by a turn at a time so that each bearing is released evenly and remains square. Note the locating dowels fitted at each stud of these front bearing caps. Store the caps in separate, clearly marked containers.

10 With the front bearings removed, gradually and evenly slacken the nuts on the remaining bearing caps, working from the outside inwards until all valve spring pressure is released. Withdraw the caps and store them in separate clearly-marked containers. **Note:** take a great deal of time and trouble over this - if any bearing cap is cracked or damaged by careless workmanship it can only be replaced as part of a new cylinder head assembly.

11 Withdraw the camshafts **(see illustration)**. There is no need to mark them as the bearings are offset and the cams can be refitted only in the correct location.

8.8 Identify camshaft bearing caps using marks provided (arrowed) before disturbing – make notes if required

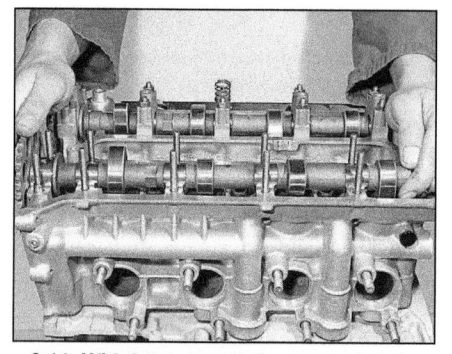

8.11 Withdraw camshafts separately to avoid mixing parts – bearings are offset, so cams cannot be interchanged

12 If the camshafts are to be removed, it is worthwhile to cut two lengths of wooden dowel, of a diameter similar to that of the camshaft rear bearings, and to fasten these lightly in place using the bearing caps. This will avoid the loss of any components and the risk of the cam followers and shims falling out and getting mixed up.

9 Cylinder head - removal

1 If the engine is in the frame a large amount of preliminary dismantling is necessary before the head can be removed. Proceed as follows, referring to Section 4 of this Chapter for information on the full procedures:

2 On K75RT, K100 RS, K100 RT and K100 LT models remove the fairing knee pads and lower side sections and radiator cover. On K75 S models, owners may wish to gain additional working space by removing the fairing. The engine spoiler or belly fairing and the radiator cover panels (where fitted) must be removed. Lift the seat, remove both side panels and disconnect the battery (negative terminal first) then remove the fuel tank and the exhaust system.

3 Remove the air intake hose, drain the cooling system and disconnect the radiator bottom hose. Remove the ignition HT coil cover and disconnect the throttle and choke cables.

4 Slacken the intake stub clips and the clips at the plenum chamber ends of the crankcase breather and air filter hoses. Disconnect the fuel rail hoses and the fuel injector wires, also all electrical leads from components on the throttle body assembly.

5 Noting that it may be necessary to gain extra working space by removing the air filter top and the element, carefully withdraw the plenum chamber/throttle body assembly, ensuring that all control cables and electrical leads are disconnected, also the fuel and vacuum hoses from the pressure regulator.

6 Disconnect the radiator top hose. The coolant and intake stubs and the fuel rail and injectors need only be removed, if required. Remove the HT leads and spark plugs.

7 Referring to Sections 6 and 8 of this Chapter, remove the engine outer covers and the camshafts and cam chain components.

8 Check that all components have been removed or disconnected which will prevent the lifting of the cylinder head, then remove the engine front left-hand mounting bolt and nut, noting the presence and number of any shims which might be fitted.

9 Working in a diagonal sequence from the outside inwards, progressively and evenly slacken the cylinder head bolts and then remove them with their washers; there are 8 bolts on 75 models, ten on 100 models.

10 Tap the head firmly at a suitably-reinforced point to break the seal without

Engine 2•11

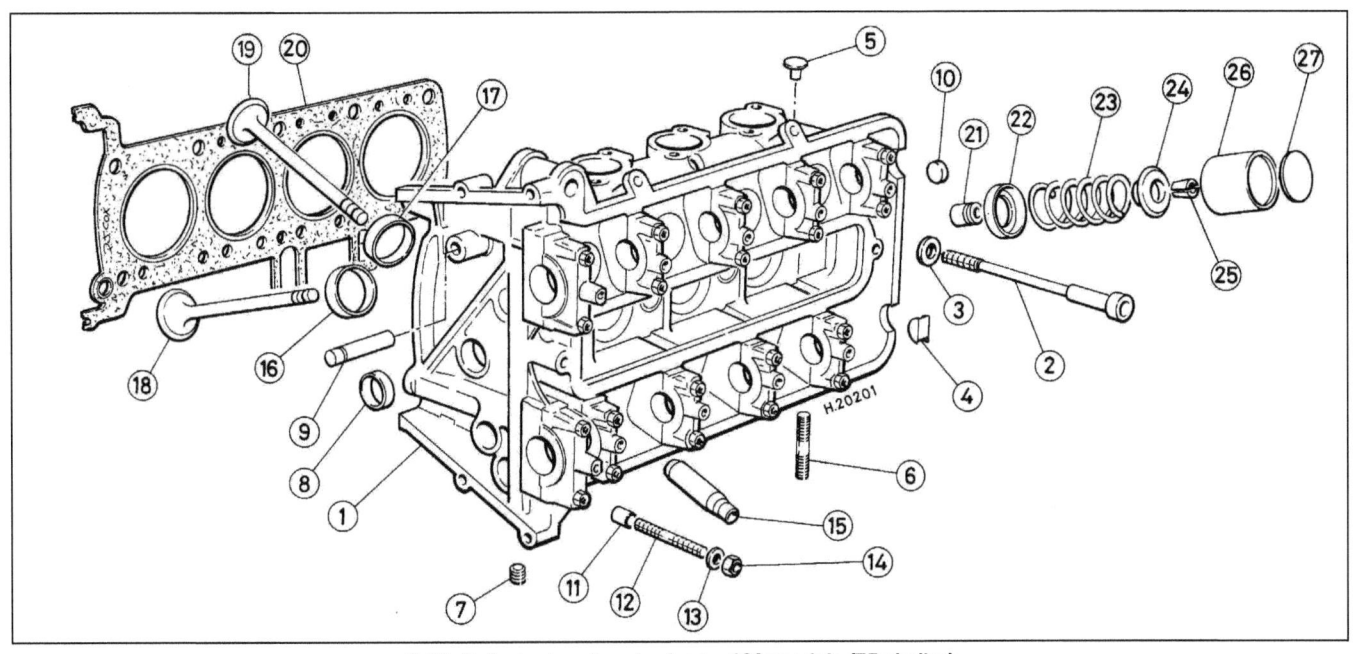

9.10 Cylinder head and valves – 100 models (75 similar)

1 Cylinder head	8 Core plug – 2 off	15 Valve guide – 8 off	22 Spring bottom seat – 8 off
2 Bolt – 10 off	9 Chain guide mounting pin	16 Intake valve seat – 4 off	23 Spring – 8 off
3 Washer – 10 off	10 Core plug – 2 off	17 Exhaust valve seat – 4 off	24 Top collar – 8 off
4 Plug – 2 off	11 Dowel – 4 off	18 Intake valve – 4 off	25 Split collet – 16 off
5 Plug – 2 off	12 Stud – 20 off	19 Exhaust valve – 4 off	26 Cam follower – 8 off
6 Stud – 8 off	13 Washer – 20 off	20 Head gasket	27 Shim – as required
7 Threaded plug	14 Nut – 20 off	21 Valve guide oil seal – 8 off	

risking damage and withdraw it **(see illustration)**.

11 Peel off the gasket and discard it. Note the two locating dowels; unless firmly fixed in the cylinder block these should be removed and stored safely.

10 Pistons and connecting rods - removal

1 If the engine is in the frame, the cylinder head must be removed first, with all the preliminary dismantling work that this entails. See Section 9.

2 Rotate the crankshaft by means of an Allen key applied to the ignition rotor flange retaining bolt. On 75 models one piston/connecting rod assembly will have to be dealt with at a time, with the crankshaft being rotated first to bottom dead centre (BDC) and then to top dead centre (TDC) as described for each assembly. On 100 models two piston/connecting rod assemblies can be removed or refitted at the same time, either the inner pair (2 and 3) or the outer pair (1 and 4).

3 Note: *Before disturbing any component, make careful written notes of exactly how each component can be identified, also how its original fitted position can be indicated* **(see illustration)**. Slowly rotate the crankshaft looking for paint spots, marks made by the

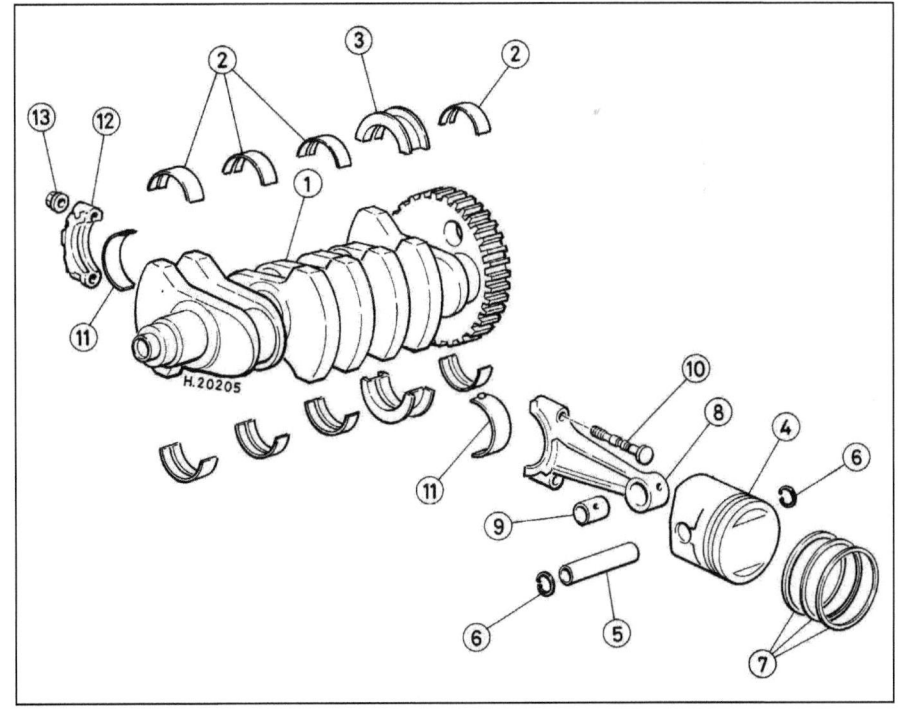

10.3 Crankshaft, connecting rods and pistons – 100 models (75 similar)

1 Crankshaft	5 Gudgeon pin	9 Small-end bearing	12 Connecting rod cap
2 Main bearing shell	6 Circlip	10 Bolt	13 Nut
3 Thrust bearing	7 Piston rings	11 Big-end bearing	
4 Piston	8 Connecting rods		

2•12 Engine

10.4 Mark connecting rods as described before removal, to ensure correct refitting

10.6 Unscrew nuts and remove big-end bearing caps, noting how shell locating tangs are positioned

10.9 Removing gudgeon pin circlips from piston – always renew disturbed circlips

manufacturer and any other identifying features; note all these and if necessary make your own.

> **HAYNES HiNT** *Obtain three or four (as appropriate) containers in which the components of each piston/connecting rod assembly can be stored separately and clearly marked.*

4 The component parts of the machine were identified as follows.
  a) *The pistons had larger valve cutaways on the intake side and an arrow stamped in the crown of each pointing towards the front (cam chain) of the engine.*
  b) *The big-end bearing caps all had red paint spots and the bearing shell lubricating channels/locating tangs were aligned against each other on the 'upper' intake side of the engine.*
  c) *The connecting rod small-end bearing oilway was also on the intake side and each connecting rod had a single spot of blue paint (indicating its weight group) on its rear face, ie towards the gearbox.*
  d) *Each rod and cap had a two-digit number etched into the flat-machined surface of its 'upper' intake side as follows: cylinder 1 marked 40, cylinder 2 marked 42, cylinder 3 marked 44, cylinder 4 marked 46. To be safe, a hammer and a small punch was used to mark the intake side of each rod and cap, making one mark on each for cylinder 1, two for 2 and so on (see illustration).* Check for similar marks on the machine being overhauled.

5 On 75 models position the crankshaft so that any piston is at the bottom of its stroke (BDC); on 100 models position the two middle pistons at BDC.

6 Working evenly, by one turn at a time, unscrew the two nuts securing each connecting rod big-end bearing cap and withdraw the cap; these will be very tight and will require a few taps from a soft-faced mallet to release them **(see illustration)**.

> **HAYNES HiNT** *When the bearing caps have been removed, it is good practice to prevent the risk of the bolt threads marking any bearing surface by slipping a length of rubber or plastic tubing over each.*

7 Rotate the crankshaft until the piston is at the top of its stroke and use a wooden dowel or similar to push the piston out of the cylinder towards the cylinder head. Store all the components of each piston/rod assembly in a separate container and mark it with the cylinder number to avoid any risk of swapping components and promoting excessive wear by mis-matching part-worn components.

8 Repeat the procedure for the remaining assemblies.

9 Before separating a piston from its connecting rod, ensure that marks are made or identified which will ensure that they are correctly refitted. For example in the case given in paragraph 4 above, the arrow indicating the direction of piston installation was pointing away from the blue paint spot on the connecting rod's rear face. Use a pointed implement to prise out the gudgeon pin retaining circlip, then press out the gudgeon pin and withdraw the piston **(see illustration)**. Discard the circlip; these should never be re-used.

> **HAYNES HiNT** *If the gudgeon pin is a very tight fit, immerse the piston in boiling water (taking care to prevent any risk of personal injury when heating components or when handling them), thus causing the aluminium alloy piston to expand faster than the steel pin.*

10 Remove the piston rings carefully, by expanding them sufficiently with the thumbs to pass over the piston. If necessary use three thin strips of metal to ease them from their grooves **(see illustration)**. The rings are very brittle, and must not be handled roughly. Note which groove each ring came out of, and which way up on each piston. The two-piece oil scraper ring must be removed in two parts; first the outer section which is removed in the same way as the compression rings, and then the coil spring-type inner section **(see illustration)**.

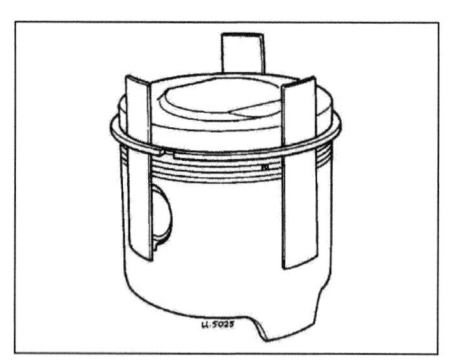

11 Crankcase lower section and the output/balancer shaft - removal

1 While these components can be removed with the main cylinder block casting still in the frame, this is not recommended. It will leave the engine unit supported precariously at its rear end and attached to the frame by two bolts (only one if the cylinder head is removed) and a few ancillary components; when one

10.10a Method of removing gummed piston rings

10.10b Oil scraper ring is two-piece design – remove in stages, as shown

Engine 2•13

11.6a Remove crankcase lower section to release output shaft . . .

11.6b . . . noting that front bearing is loose and may drop clear

realises that the frame is supported only by the front wheel and its rear end, the potential for serious damage and personal injury may be appreciated.

2 Since the removal of the engine/transmission unit complete involves so little extra work and affords so much safer working conditions and improved access, it is the only recommended method of gaining access to these components.

3 Owners who wish to carry out the work with the engine in the frame (against the above advice) should note that the gearbox and final drive must be removed (Chapters 3 and 8) the clutch must be withdrawn (Chapter 3) and the bellhousing removed (Section 7). Also the engine oil must be drained and the filter removed (Chapter 1) and the sump and oil pump pick-up removed (Chapter 6). Finally the coolant must be drained and the oil/water pump assembly must be removed (Chapter 5 and 6).

4 Remove the Allen screws along the left- and right-hand mounting surfaces of the crankcase lower section, then remove the two hexagon-headed bolts from the inside rear and the two Allen-headed bolts or screws from the inside front. Tap the lower section with a soft-faced mallet to break the joint and withdraw the lower section noting the O-rings around the oil and coolant passages and the two locating dowels, one next to each output shaft bearing. Unless the dowels are firmly fixed in the crankcase/cylinder block, they should be removed.

5 On 75 models, slowly rotate the crankshaft and balancer shaft until the timing marks can be seen. These should be in the form of a straight line on the crankshaft gear which aligns with either a dot or a V mark on the balancer gear. **Do not** disturb either shaft until the marks have been found and noted.

6 Withdraw the output/balancer shaft and its rear seal noting that its front needle roller bearing is loosely fixed and may drop clear **(see illustrations)**.

7 On some early models whose output shafts are fitted with rear bearings which have a thin (1.75 mm/0.07 in thick) locating circlip at the forward end of the bearing outer race, the bearing may be glued in place with Loctite 273, Three Bond 1110 B or similar adhesive. If any difficulty is encountered in removing such a bearing, the adhesive should be heated (maximum of 300°C/572°F) to break it down and to release the bearing.

12 Crankshaft - removal

1 As mentioned in Section 3, the crankshaft can be removed whether or not the engine unit is in the frame. It is possible, if required, to remove the crankshaft by draining the coolant and removing the engine outer covers (Section 6), removing the cam chain from the crankshaft and camshafts (Section 8), and releasing the big-end caps from the crankshaft (Section 10). If their removal is not necessary, and provided that care is taken not to allow them to touch the valves, the pistons can be left in the bores while the crankshaft is removed and refitted. This avoids the need to remove the cylinder head.

2 Owners of 75 models should check whether the crankshaft/balancer shaft marks are visible as soon as the crankshaft cover is removed. If these timing marks cannot be seen, the crankcase lower section and balancer shaft **must be removed** to permit the marks to be aligned on reassembly. See Section 11. If the cylinder head is to be removed, removing the entire engine/transmission unit involves so little extra work and produces so much better access and safer working conditions that it is strongly recommended.

3 With the preliminary dismantling operations that are described above carried out, inspect the main bearing caps, making careful written notes of how each cap can be identified and how its original fitted position can be indicated. Look for paint spots, manufacturer's stamped marks and any other identifying features; note all these and if necessary make your own **(see illustrations)**.

4 The component parts of the machine featured in the accompanying photographs were marked as follows, counting the main bearings consecutively from front to rear, number 1 being next to the cam chain; bearing caps number 1, 2 and 3 were stamped with the figure 1, 2 or 3 respectively on the 'lower' exhaust retaining bolt boss, also at the base of the cap 'lower' end. Number 4 bearing cap carried the thrust bearing and number 5 carried no identification at all; to be safe a hammer and a small punch were used to mark the sides of the 'lower' retaining bolt boss of each cap, making one mark for bearing number 1, two for 2 and so on. Check for similar marks on the machine being overhauled and note that on 75 models bearing caps numbers 1 and 2 are numbered, number 3 carries the thrust bearing and number 4 is unmarked. When the caps are removed, note that the bearing shell locating tang grooves/oilways of each cap and the crankcase are aligned against each other on the 'lower' side of each bearing.

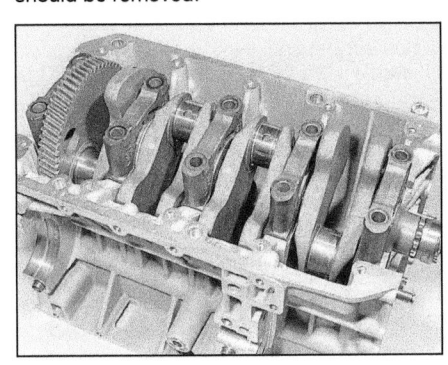

12.3a Before removing crankshaft main bearing caps . . .

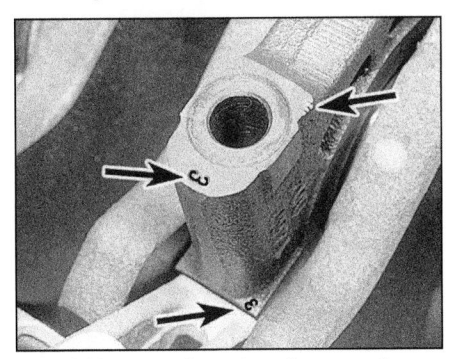

12.3b . . . make notes of any marks identifying each cap's fitted position (arrows) . . .

12.3c . . . and if necessary make your own – see text

5 Working evenly, by one turn at a time, unscrew the two bolts securing each main bearing cap, tap the cap firmly but gently with a soft-faced mallet to release it and withdraw it, noting which way round it is fitted. To ensure an even release of pressure first slacken all the bolts and then remove the caps in the following sequence:

75 models - rear bearing, front bearing (number 1), number 3, number 2

100 models - rear bearing (number 5), front bearing (number 1), number 4, number 2, number 3.

6 With all caps removed, lift out the crankshaft.

13 Bearings and oil seals - removal

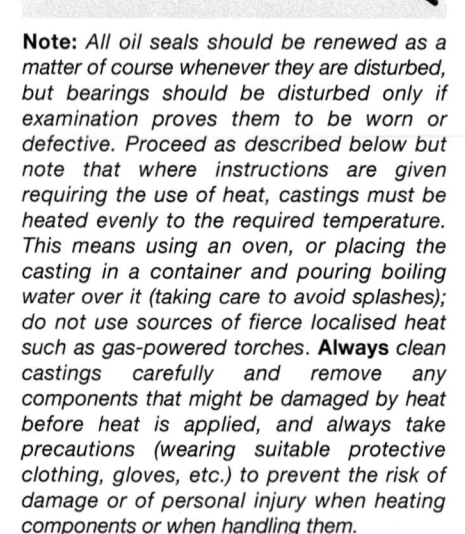

Note: *All oil seals should be renewed as a matter of course whenever they are disturbed, but bearings should be disturbed only if examination proves them to be worn or defective. Proceed as described below but note that where instructions are given requiring the use of heat, castings must be heated evenly to the required temperature. This means using an oven, or placing the casting in a container and pouring boiling water over it (taking care to avoid splashes); do not use sources of fierce localised heat such as gas-powered torches.* **Always** *clean castings carefully and remove any components that might be damaged by heat before heat is applied, and always take precautions (wearing suitable protective clothing, gloves, etc.) to prevent the risk of damage or of personal injury when heating components or when handling them.*

1 The auxiliary driveshaft rotates on a needle roller bearing at the front, in the upper rear part of the main crankcase/cylinder block casting, and on a ball bearing in the bellhousing.

2 If the needle roller bearing is to be renewed, it can be extracted using a slide-hammer with the correct internally-expanding adaptor; BMW recommend that the crankcase casting is heated evenly, in an oven or similar, to 100 - 120°C (212 - 248°F) to permit the bearing to be removed. If these tools are not available, use a hammer and a small pin punch to drive in part of the bearing outer race so that it can be gripped with pliers and drawn out; be very careful not to damage the bearing housing and to collect all the pieces of the bearing if this method is used.

3 If the rear bearing is to be removed, withdraw the retainer plate (held by three Allen screws) noting the conical spring washer behind it, and carefully lever out the oil seal (see below) before withdrawing the locating circlip. The bearing can then be driven out using a tubular drift such as a socket spanner which bears only on the bearing outer race; note that BMW recommend the bellhousing is heated evenly, in an oven or similar, to 100 - 120°C (212 - 248°F) to permit the bearing to be removed. Clean all traces of Loctite from the threads of the retainer plate screws and their tapped holes.

4 The output shaft front bearing can be pulled off the shaft front end by hand while the rear bearing will require the use of a bearing puller to withdraw it from the shaft, after the retaining circlip has been released.

5 The starter clutch gear pinion rotates on two needle roller bearings. If these are to be removed they can be driven out using a hammer and a suitable drift: take care not to damage the pinion on any surface.

6 If the output shaft rear oil seal is to be removed without separating the crankcase lower and main sections it can be levered out, providing that great care is taken not to damage the shaft, the seal housing or the crankcase around it; use only a tool with well-rounded edges and pivot it against a block of wood placed on the crankcase. Alternatively, two self-tapping screws can be screwed into the seal (as close to its outside edge as possible without marking the seal housing) to provide points which can be gripped with two pairs of pliers or similar so that the seal can be pulled out; take care not to allow the screws to touch the bearing.

7 If the auxiliary drive shaft rear seal is to be renewed with the shaft removed it can be levered out. If the shaft is still in place, the seal can be pulled out using the second of the two methods described above.

8 If the crankshaft front oil seal is to be removed from the cam chain (engine front) cover while the cover is still in place, it can be extracted using two self-tapping screws as described above. However, this seal is a tight fit and owners may find it necessary to remove the cover in order to renew the seal to prevent any risk of damage; note that refitting will be difficult with the cover in place. If the cover is removed, the seal can be tapped out using a hammer and a socket spanner or similar as a tubular drift. In exceptional circumstances heat the cover by immersing it in boiling water to loosen the seal's grip.

9 If the oil level sight glass is leaking or damaged it can be removed as follows from the crankcase lower section. Drive a sharp-edged screwdriver or similar into the sight glass centre and lever out the glass and seal, then withdraw the metal cage; this will have to be levered out, distorting it in the process, so care must be taken not to damage the housing. Use blocks of wood as pivots for the levers so that the crankcase fins are undamaged.

14 Examination and renovation - general

1 Before any component is examined, it must be cleaned thoroughly. Being careful not to mark or damage the item in question, use a blunt-edged scraper (an old kitchen knife or a broken plastic ruler can be very useful) to remove any caked-on deposits of dirt or oil, followed by a good scrub with a soft wire brush (a brass wire brush of the type sold for cleaning suede shoes is best, with an assortment of bottle-cleaning brushes for ports, coolant passages, etc).

Caution: Take care not to remove any paint code marks from internal components.

2 Soak the component in a solvent to remove the bulk of the remaining dirt or oil. If one of the proprietary engine degreasers (such as Gunk or Jizer) is not available, a high flash-point solvent such as paraffin (kerosene) should be used. The use of petrol as a cleaning agent cannot be recommended because of the fire risk. With all of the above cleaning agents take great care to prevent any drops getting into the eyes and try to avoid, prolonged skin contact. To finish off the cleaning procedure wash each component in hot soapy water (as hot as your hands can bear); this will remove a surprising amount of dirt on its own and the residual heat usually dries the component very effectively. Carefully scrape away any remaining traces of old gasket material from all joint faces.

3 Check all coolant passages and oilways for blockages, using compressed air to clear them, or implements such as pipe cleaners. Note that many of the coolant passages are sealed by core plugs. These are removed by piercing the centre with a hammer and centre punch so that a screw thread can be tapped in and a slide-hammer applied; the plugs should **never** be disturbed unless absolutely necessary **(see illustration)**. A hexagon-headed blanking plug is screwed into the underside of the cylinder head to blank off the oilways; if camshaft wear reveals a possible lubrication fault, this plug should be removed so that the oilways can be blown clear with compressed air. If it is disturbed, tighten it securely on refitting, using a drop of Loctite 242 or similar thread-locking compound on its threads.

4 If there is the slightest doubt about the lubrication system, for example if a fault appears to have been caused by a failure of

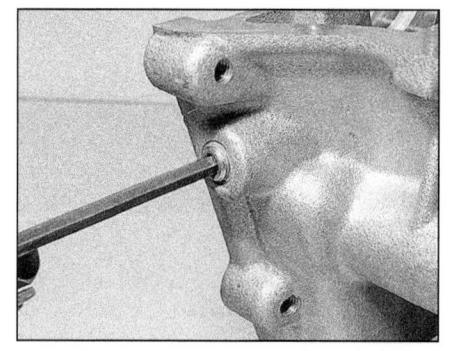

14.3 Remove blanking plug from cylinder head to clear oilways, if required

the oil supply, all components should be dismantled so that the oilways can be checked and cleared of any possible obstructions. Refer to Chapter 6 for details of the lubrication system. Always use clean, lint-free rag for cleaning and drying components to prevent the risk of small particles obstructing oilways.

5 Examine carefully each part to determine the extent of wear, checking with the tolerance figures listed in the Specifications section of this Chapter. If there is any doubt about the condition of a particular component, play safe and renew.

6 Various instruments for measuring wear are required, including a vernier gauge or external micrometer and a set of standard feeler gauges. The machine's manufacturer recommends the use of Plastigauge for measuring radial clearance between working surfaces such as shell bearings and their journals. Plastigauge consists of a fine strand of plastic material manufactured to an accurate diameter. A short length of Plastigauge is placed between the two surfaces, the clearance of which is to be measured. The surfaces are assembled in their normal working positions and the securing nuts or bolts fastened to the correct torque loading; the surfaces are then separated. The amount of compression to which the gauge material is subjected and the resultant spreading indicates the clearance. This is measured directly, across the width of the Plastigauge, using a pre-marked indicator supplied with the Plastigauge kit. If Plastigauge is not available, both an internal and external micrometer will be required to check wear limits. Additionally, although not absolutely necessary, a dial gauge and mounting bracket is invaluable for accurate measurement of endfloat, and play between components of very low diameter bores - where a micrometer cannot reach. After some experience has been gained the state of wear of many components can be determined visually or by feel and thus a decision on their suitability for continued service can be made without resorting to direct measurement.

> **HAYNES HiNT** *Refer to Tools and Workshop Tips in the Reference section for details of how to use a micrometer, vernier gauge and dial gauge.*

15 Engine cases and covers - examination and renovation

1 Small cracks or holes in aluminium castings may be repaired with an epoxy resin adhesive, such as Araldite, as a temporary expedient. Permanent repairs can be effected only by welding and a specialist will be able to advise on the availability of a proposed repair.

2 Damaged threads can be economically reclaimed by using a diamond section wire insert of the Helicoil type, which is easily fitted after drilling and re-tapping the affected thread. Most motorcycle dealers and small engineering firms offer a service of this kind.

3 Sheared studs or screws can usually be removed with screw extractors, which consist of tapered left-hand thread screws of very hard steel. These are inserted by screwing anti-clockwise into a pre-drilled hole in the stud. If any problem arises which seems to be beyond your scope it is worthwhile consulting a professional engineering firm before condemning an otherwise sound casing; many such firms advertise in the motorcycle papers.

4 If gasket or other mating surfaces are marked or damaged in any way they can be reclaimed by rubbing them on a sheet of fine abrasive paper laid on an absolutely flat surface such as a sheet of plate glass. Use a gentle figure-of-eight pattern, maintaining light but even pressure on the casting. Note that if large amounts of material are to be removed, advice should be sought as to the viability of re-using the casting in question; the internal clearances are minimal in many cases between rotating or moving components and the castings. Stop work as soon as the entire mating surface is polished by the action of the paper.

> **HAYNES HiNT** *Refer to Tools and Workshop Tips in the Reference section for thread repair methods, screw and stud extractors and gasket removal methods.*

5 Large surfaces such as the cylinder head or block gasket surface will have to be skimmed on a surface plate if warped. This is a task for a light engineering business only; be careful to warn them to remove only the minimum amount of metal necessary to true up the face. If excessive warpage is found, seek expert advice.

6 Note that the mating surface may become distorted outwards around the mounting screw holes, usually because these have been grossly overtightened. If such is the case, use a large drill bit or countersink to very lightly skim the raised lip from around the screw hole, then clean up the whole surface as described above.

7 Finally, check that all screw or bolt tapped holes are clean down to the bottom of each hole; serious damage can be caused by forcing a screw or bolt down a dirty thread and against an incorrect stop caused by the presence of dirt, oil, swarf or blobs of old jointing compound. At the very least the component concerned will be incorrectly fastened, at worst the casting could be cracked. The simplest way of cleaning such holes is to use a length of welding rod or similar to check that the hole is clean all the way to the bottom and to dig out any embedded foreign matter, then to give each hole a squirt of contact cleaner or similar solvent applied from an aerosol via the long plastic nozzle usually supplied. Be careful to wear suitable eye protection while doing this; the amount of dirt and debris that can be ejected from each hole is surprising.

16 Bearings and oil seals - examination and renovation

1 Ball bearings should be washed thoroughly to remove all traces of oil then tested as follows. Hold the outer race firmly and attempt to move the inner race up and down, then from side to side. Examine the bearing balls, cages and tracks, looking for signs of pitting or other damage. Finally spin the bearings hard; any roughness caused by wear or damage will be felt and heard immediately. If any free play, roughness or other damage is found the bearing must be removed.

2 Roller bearings are checked in much the same way, except that free play can be checked only in the up and down direction with the components concerned temporarily reassembled. Remember that if a roller bearing fails it may well mean having to replace, as well as the bearing itself, one or two components which form its inner and outer races. If in doubt about a roller bearing's condition, renew it.

3 Do not waste time checking oil seals; discard all seals and O-rings disturbed during dismantling work and fit new ones on reassembly. Considering their habit of leaking once disturbed, and the amount of time and trouble necessary to replace them, they are relatively cheap if renewed as a matter of course whenever they are disturbed.

> **HAYNES HiNT** *Refer to Tools and Workshop Tips for further information on bearings and oil seals.*

17 Camshafts and camshaft drive mechanism - examination and renovation

1 Examine the camshaft lobes for signs of wear or scoring. Wear is normally evident in the form of visual flats worn on the peak of the lobes, and this may be checked by measuring each lobe at its widest point. If any lobe is worn by a significant amount the camshaft must be renewed. Scoring or similar damage can usually be attributed to a partial failure of the lubrication system, possibly due to the oil filter element not having been renewed at the specified mileage, causing unfiltered oil to be circulated by way of the bypass valve. Before

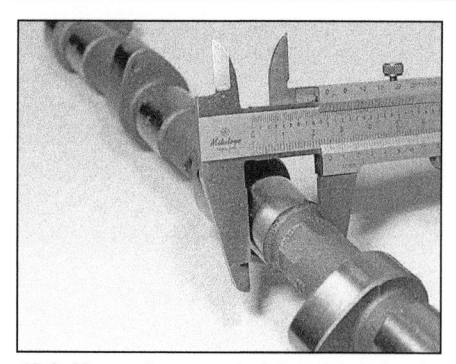

2•16 Engine

17.3 Measuring camshaft bearing journals

fitting new camshafts, examine the bearing surfaces of the camshafts, and cylinder head, and rectify the cause of the failure.

2 If the camshaft bearing surfaces are scored or excessively worn, it is likely that renewal of both the cylinder head and the camshafts will be the only solution. This is because the camshaft runs directly in the cylinder head casting, using the alloy as a bearing surface. Assemble the bearing caps and measure the internal bore using a bore micrometer. If any internal diameter exceeds that specified, it will be necessary to renew the cylinder head and bearing caps. Note that it is not possible to renew the caps alone, because they are machined together with the cylinder head and are thus matched to it. It may be possible, however, for an expert to effect a repair; many machines suffer from top-end lubrication problems and several experts offer a repair service involving (usually) the fitting of shell or needle roller bearings to rectify this. It is possible that one of these may be prepared to undertake the repair of such a basically similar design.

3 Measure the camshaft bearing journals **(see illustration)**. If any journals have worn to less than the specified outside diameter, the camshaft(s) should be renewed. The clearance between the camshafts and their bearing surfaces can be checked using Plastigauge or by direct measurement. The clearance must not exceed the specified limit.

4 Camshaft run-out can be checked by supporting each end of the shaft on V-blocks, and measuring any runout using a dial test indicator running on the bearing journals. Since no service limits are specified, expert advice must be sought if run-out appears excessive; the camshaft should be renewed, however, if warpage can be seen with the naked eye.

5 Excessive camshaft endfloat can produce a loud, regular, ticking noise noticeable mainly at idle speed. Each camshaft is located by a thrust flange which bears against a thrust face on the rear of the front bearing cap. Endfloat is measured by mounting a dial gauge on the cylinder head so that it is parallel to the camshaft, with its tip touching one end. Push the camshaft as far as possible away from the gauge, zero the gauge, then push the camshaft towards the gauge as far as possible and note the reading. Note that this will be very difficult if the valve gear is still in place; it should be removed if possible. If the reading taken appears excessive, expert advice should be sought. If excessive wear is found, it will be necessary to renew the camshaft or the cylinder head or both; repairs to reclaim such wear are extremely difficult and may be undertaken only by an engineering expert, if at all.

6 The camshaft drive chain should be checked for wear, particularly if the tensioner plunger was found to be fully extended, this latter condition being indicative that the chain is probably due for renewal. Check the chain at points all along its length, looking for cracked, broken or missing rollers or sideplates, or for any links which appear stiff or unduly sloppy; if any of these or other signs of wear or damage are found, the chain must be renewed. To check the chain for wear, lay it out on a flat surface, mark the pins at each end of a one-foot length and compress the chain endwise against a straightedge. Measure exactly the distance between the two pins, then anchor one end, draw the chain out taut and measure the stretched length between the two marked pins, repeat the test at points all along the chain's length. If the stretched measurement exceeds the compressed measurement by more than 1 - 2% (1/8 - 1/4 in per foot) at any point, the chain must be renewed.

7 The tensioner and guide blades and the tensioner assembly should be examined for wear or damage, which will normally be fairly obvious. Renew any parts which appear worn or are damaged, especially if a new chain is to be fitted. The same can be applied to the crankshaft sprocket and the two camshaft sprockets. The tensioner plunger must be smooth, unworn, free from dirt or corrosion and able to slide smoothly in the tensioner body. If the spring pressure is doubtful or if any other damage is found, the tensioner assembly must be renewed complete.

8 Note that the tensioner blade plastic face can be detached and renewed separately. The blade metal backing should be checked to ensure that the rubber bush at its bottom pivot is in good condition, also the rubber buffer which engages the tensioner plunger; otherwise it is not likely to suffer any wear. On refitting, slide the backing top fork over the locating lug on the rear of the plastic face, then insert the backing bottom end into that of the plastic face. Lastly, clip the plastic face centre to the metal backing at the tensioner plunger locating lugs **(see illustration)**.

18 Cylinder head - examination and renovation

1 Remove all traces of carbon from the cylinder head using a blunt ended scraper (the round end of an old steel rule will do). Finish by polishing with metal polish to give a smooth, shiny surface.

2 Check the condition of the spark plug threads. If the threads are worn or crossed they can be reclaimed by a Helicoil thread insert.

> **HAYNES HINT:** *Refer to Tools and Workshop Tips in the Reference section for details of how to install a thread insert*

3 Lay the cylinder head on a sheet of 1/4 inch plate glass to check for distortion. Aluminium alloy cylinder heads distort very easily,

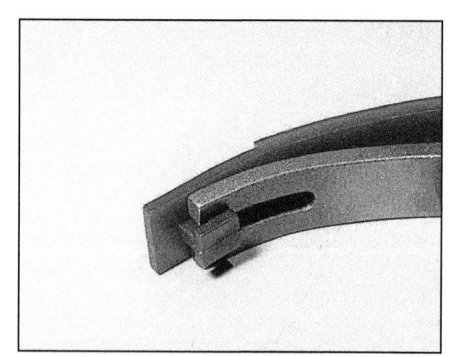

17.8a Fitting a new cam chain tensioner blade plastic face – slide metal fork over plastic locating lug . . .

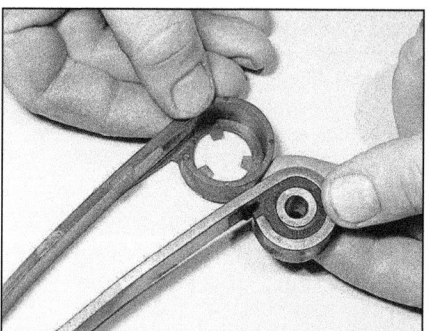

17.8b . . . and insert bottom mounting eye into recess in plastic face . . .

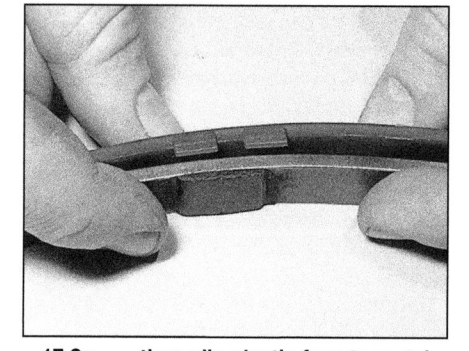

17.8c . . . then clip plastic face to metal blade at centre lugs

19.2a Use rubber sucker or magnet to extract shim and cam follower – store carefully and do not interchange

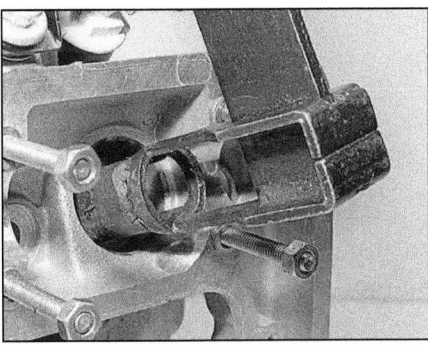

19.2b Valve spring compressor must be modified as shown to reach inside cam follower bores

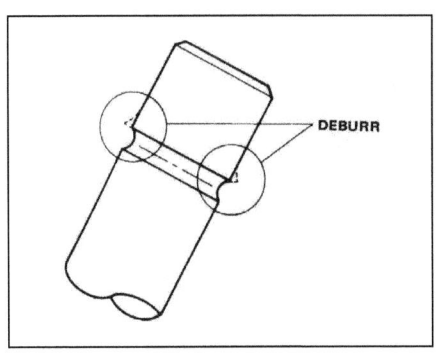

19.3 If the valve stem won't pull through the guide, deburr the area above the collet groove

especially if the cylinder head bolts are tightened down unevenly. If the amount of distortion is only slight, it is permissible to rub the head down until it is flat once again by wrapping a sheet of very fine emery cloth around the plate glass base and rubbing with a rotary motion.

4 If the cylinder head is distorted badly (one way of determining this is if the cylinder head gasket has a tendency to keep blowing), the head will have to be machined by a competent engineer experienced in this type of work. This will, of course, raise the compression of the engine, and if too much is removed can adversely affect the performance of the engine as well as to cause the valves to strike the pistons. If there is risk of this happening, the only remedy is a new replacement cylinder head.

5 Refer to Sections 17 and 19 of this Chapter for details of work concerning the camshaft bearings and valve gear respectively.

19 Valves, valve seats and valve guides - examination and renovation

1 Obtain eight suitable containers and clearly mark each one with the type and cylinder number of the valve components that will be stored in it, eg Number 1 cylinder intake. Always keep components separate and in their marked containers so that all can be refitted in their original locations.

> **HAYNES HINT**
> As far as possible work on one valve assembly at a time so that there is no risk of swapping components.

2 Use a rubber sucker or a strong magnet to remove the shim and cam follower over each valve, then compress the valve spring, using a specially-modified valve spring compressor which will fit securely over the spring top retaining collar and yet reach down inside the bores in the cylinder head without marking their walls **(see illustrations)**. Withdraw the two split collets using a slim magnetised rod (draw a permanent magnet several times down the shank of a slim screwdriver), release the compressor gradually and withdraw the top collar, the spring (noting carefully which way round it was fitted), the spring seat, the valve and the valve guide oil seal. The magnet will also be required to remove the spring seats. Store all components from each valve assembly together in their marked container.

3 If any valve is difficult to remove through its guide check for any burrs or raised edges at the collet locating groove in the stem; use fine emery paper, if necessary, to polish away any that are found until the valve stem will slide easily through the guide **(see illustration)**. Be careful to wash away all particles of abrasive material.

4 Inspect the valves for wear, overheating or burning, and replace them as necessary. Normally, the exhaust valves will need renewal more often than the inlet valves, as the latter run at relatively low temperatures. If any of the valve seating faces are badly pitted, do not attempt to cure this by grinding them, as this will invariably cause the valve seats to become pocketed. It is permissible to have the valve(s) refaced by a motorcycle specialist or small engineering works. The valve must be renewed if the head thickness (the area between the edge of the seating surface and the top of the head) is reduced to the service limit specified, if its overall length is shorter than that specified, or if its stem is bent by more than the maximum specified runout, measured at the valve head.

5 Check the valve stems and guides for wear either by direct measurement or by inserting a valve and rocking it to and fro both along the direction of cam lobe thrust and at right angles to it; any wear will be most noticeable when the valve is at the maximum lift position. Compare the original valve with a new component to check if wear is excessive. If a small bore gauge and micrometer are available, the two components can be measured at three or four points along their bearing surfaces, both in the direction of cam lobe thrust and at right angles to it. Subtract the smallest stem diameter measurement obtained from the largest guide bore diameter; if the stem/guide clearance figure thus calculated exceeds the specified service limit, one or both components must be renewed.

6 Valve guide renewal is not easy, and will require that the valve seats be recut after the guide has been fitted and reamed. It is also remarkably easy to damage the cylinder head unless great care is taken during these operations. It may, therefore, be considered better to entrust these jobs to a competent engineering company or to an authorised BMW dealer. For the more skilled and better equipped owner, the procedure is as follows:

7 Heat the cylinder head slowly and evenly, in an oven to prevent warpage, to 220 - 240°C (428 - 464°F). Using a stepped drift, tap the guide(s) lightly out of the head from the combustion chamber side, taking care not to burn yourself on the hot casting.

8 With the guide(s) removed, allow the head to cool and measure the guide bore in the cylinder head. If worn beyond the specified limits, the bore must be reamed out to the next oversize and the correspondingly oversized guide fitted.

9 To fit a valve guide, heat the cylinder head as described above and use the stepped drift to drive the guide into place from the camshaft side until it seats on the locating circlip.

10 After a new guide has been fitted it must be reamed to 7.0 mm (0.28 in) using a BMW reamer, and the seat must be re-cut to centre it on the new guide.

11 If a valve guide has been renewed, or if a valve seat face is worn or badly pitted, it must be re-cut to ensure efficient sealing. This process requires the use of the necessary cutters, with their adaptors, pilots and other equipment. It also requires some skill and experience if the cylinder head is not to be severely damaged. Accordingly, owners are strongly recommended to take the cylinder head to an authorised BMW dealer or similar expert for this sort of work to be done.

12 For those who have access to the necessary equipment and the experience, proceed as follows. Fit the appropriate cutter to the pilot bar and insert the pilot bar into the

2•18 Engine

19.18a Valve guide oil seals must be fitted to a suitable tool . . .

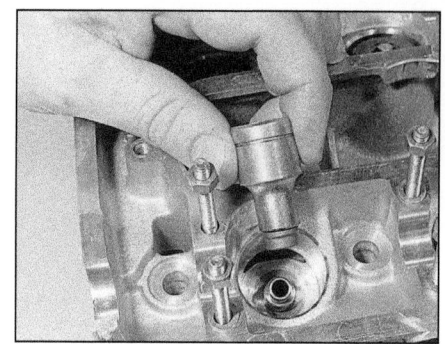

19.18b . . . so that they can be pressed correctly on to guide ends

19.18c Oil valve stems and guides liberally on reassembly

guide until the cutter makes contact with the valve seat. Using firm hand pressure, rotate the cutter through one or two full turns to clean the seat then withdraw the cutter and examine the seat. If the seat is continuous and free from pitting, proceed to the next step, but if pitting is still evident, refit the cutter and repeat the procedure until all pitting has been removed.

13 Be very careful to remove only the bare minimum of material necessary to achieve a clean surface. If valve seats become pocketed (sunk into the head) through excessive re-cutting, new valve seats must be fitted. While BMW supply separate replacement valve seats in standard size and one oversize, the removal and refitting of these seats is quite definitely a task for the expert alone who has the necessary skill, experience and equipment.
Caution: When the head is returned, be sure to clean it again very thoroughly before installation on the engine to remove any metal particles or abrasive grit that may still be present from the valve service operations. Use compressed air, if available, to blow out all the holes and passages.

14 With the seat face cleaned up check that it is 1.5 mm (0.06 in) wide at the contact area with the valve face. If it is too wide it must be narrowed, using the appropriate cutter to remove material either from the combustion chamber side or from the port side. Again, remove only the barest minimum of material.

15 The valves should be ground in, using ordinary oil-bound grinding paste, to remove any light pitting or to finish off a newly cut seat. Note that it is not normally essential to resort to using the coarse grade of paste which is supplied in dual-grade containers. Valve grinding is a simple task. Commence by smearing a trace of fine valve grinding compound (carborundum paste) on the valve seat and apply a suction tool to the head of the valve. Oil the valve stem and insert the valve in the guide so that the two surfaces to be ground in make contact with one another. With a semi-rotary motion, grind in the valve head to the seat, using a backward and forward motion. Lift the valve occasionally so that the grinding compound is distributed evenly. Repeat the application until an unbroken ring of light grey matt finish is obtained on both valve and seat. This denotes the grinding operation is now complete. Before passing to the next valve, make sure that all traces of the valve grinding compound have been removed from both the valve and its seat and that none has entered the valve guide. If this precaution is not observed, rapid wear will take place due to the highly abrasive nature of the carborundum paste.

16 If the necessary equipment is available, measure the diameter of each cam follower at several points, also the inside diameter of each respective cylinder head well. If necessary, renew any component that is found to be damaged, scored or excessively worn.

17 Examine the spring retaining collars and split collets, renewing any that are marked, worn, or damaged in any way. Measure the free length of each valve spring. If any spring has settled to a length significantly less than the nominal length specified, or if any one varies in length (check particularly the exhaust valve springs against the intakes) by a significant amount, it should be renewed. Note that while it is possible to buy the springs individually, it is considered good practice to renew them all as a set, and that many mechanics renew the springs as a matter of course to ensure good engine performance.

18 Place the spring seats over the guides and press new oil seals into place on each guide upper end **(see illustrations)**. Liberally oil the guide bore and valve stem before refitting the valves **(see illustration)**. The springs are fitted next; while new springs, being linear-wound, have no particular direction of installation, the original springs (if re-used) must be fitted as they were found **(see illustration)**. On the machine featured the spring lower end was marked by a dab of blue paint; similar markings may be found on other machines.

19 Refit the retaining collars, ensuring that the springs are correctly seated, compress the springs and refit the split collets **(see illustrations)**. Give the end of each valve stem

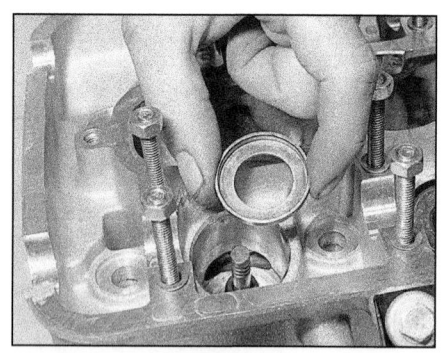

19.18d Do not forget to refit spring seat as shown . . .

19.18e . . . before inserting spring. Re-used springs must be refitted as found

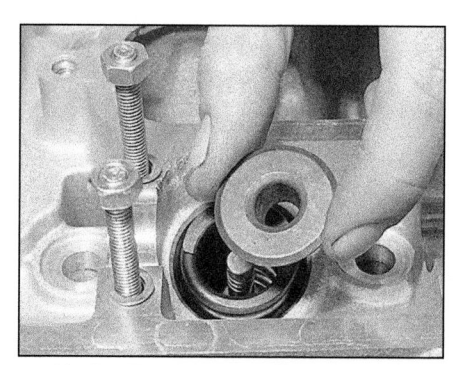

19.19a Fit spring retaining collar and compress spring . . .

Engine 2•19

19.19b ... so that split collets can be refitted to secure assembly

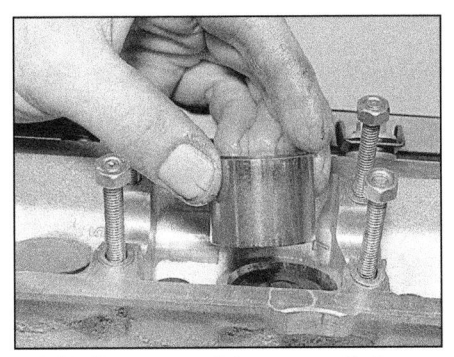

19.20 Be very careful to ensure that cam followers are square in bores on refitting

21.2 Measuring piston outside diameter – see text for measuring points

a light tap with a hammer to ensure that the collets have located correctly.

20 Refit the shims to their follower recesses, ensuring that the marked surface is downwards and using a smear of grease to retain each shim as the cam follower is oiled and refitted. Be careful to keep the followers absolutely square in their housings; the slightest tilt will jam them and make removal very difficult **(see illustration)**. Refit the dowels (if used) to retain the followers.

20 Cylinder block - examination and renovation

1 The usual indication of badly worn cylinder bores and pistons is excessive smoking from the exhausts. This usually takes the form of blue haze tending to develop into a white haze as the wear becomes more pronounced. However this must not be confused with the smoke cloud which these machines all seem to produce on starting, especially when hot or when the machine has been resting on its side stand. All K-series models do this in varying degrees and assuming that oil consumption is negligible, there is little that owners can do about it except remember to use the centre stand, or fit modified piston rings (see Section 30).

2 The other indication is piston slap, a form of metallic rattle which occurs when there is little load on the engine. if the cylinder head end of each bore is examined carefully, it will be found that there is a ridge on the thrust side, the depth of which will vary according to the rate of wear which has taken place. This marks the limit of travel of the top piston ring.

3 Measure the bore diameter just below the ridge both along the gudgeon pin axis and at right angles to it using an internal micrometer or a bore gauge. Take similar measurements at the middle and bottom of each bore. Although no service limits are specified for taper and ovality, these dimensions should not differ significantly from each other. Take the largest of these measurements to be the bore inside diameter.

4 Subtract the piston skirt diameter (see Section 21) from the bore diameter to calculate the piston/cylinder clearance; if this exceeds the specified service limit, either the pistons or the cylinder block must be renewed. Only very careful measurement can reveal whether this is necessary; in view of the expense of this solution owners are strongly advised to have their findings confirmed by an authorised BMW dealer before taking further action.

5 If sufficiently accurate measuring equipment is not available, an approximate idea of the degree of bore wear can be obtained by inserting a new piston (less rings) so that it is appropriately 3/4 inch from the top of the bore. Use feeler gauges to measure the clearance between the piston skirt and the bore at the point of greatest wear. It must be stressed that this is only approximate, to be regarded purely as a quick check before taking the cylinder block and pistons to an expert for accurate measurement.

21 Pistons and piston rings - examination and renovation

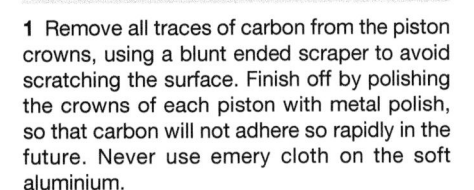

1 Remove all traces of carbon from the piston crowns, using a blunt ended scraper to avoid scratching the surface. Finish off by polishing the crowns of each piston with metal polish, so that carbon will not adhere so rapidly in the future. Never use emery cloth on the soft aluminium.

2 Piston wear usually occurs at the skirt or lower end of the piston and takes the form of vertical streaks or score marks on the thrust side of the piston. Damage of this nature will necessitate renewal and is checked by measuring the piston outside diameters at a point 12.0 mm (0.47 in) above the base of the skirt on KS pistons; on Mahle pistons the measuring points are 7.6 mm (0.30 in) on 75 models and 8.6 mm (0.34 in) on 100 models. In all cases the measurement is made at right angles to the gudgeon pin axis and the reading obtained is compared with that specified **(see illustration)**. Stamped marks in the piston crown will show the manufacturer and the size group code letter.

3 Actual piston wear limits are not given, therefore unless any piston is found to be worn to significantly less than the specified tolerances, the only way of calculating wear is to subtract the piston diameter from its respective bore's measurement (see Section 20) to calculate the piston/cylinder clearance. If this exceeds the specified service limit either the pistons or the cylinder block, or both must be renewed; only careful measurement, preferably by an authorised BMW dealer or similar expert, will indicate which.

4 Note that if any of the pistons is renewed at any time it must be of the same make and size code as the original, and must also be of the same weight group as the other pistons, ie all must carry the same weight group marking (+ or - stamped in the piston crown).

5 Check the fit of the gudgeon pin in the piston bosses; it should be a tight sliding fit with no sign of free play when installed and no trace of scoring or wear on any bearing surface. If the necessary equipment is available, the components can be checked by direct measurement. The piston and gudgeon pin should be treated as a matched pair and never interchanged.

6 Discard any gudgeon pin retaining circlips that were disturbed on dismantling and obtain new ones for refitting; these circlips should never be re-used.

7 After the engine has covered a high mileage, it is possible that the ring grooves may have become enlarged. To check this, measure the clearance between the ring and groove with a feeler gauge. A clearance in excess of the limits given will mean that the piston or rings must be renewed.

8 To measure the end gap, insert each piston ring into its cylinder bore, using the crown of the bare piston to locate it about 1 inch from the cylinder head end of the bore. Make sure it is square in the bore and insert a feeler gauge in the end gap of the ring **(see**

2•20 Engine

21.8 Measuring piston ring installed end gap

illustration). If the end gap exceeds the limits given, the ring must be renewed.

9 When fitting new piston rings, it is also necessary to check the end gap. If there is insufficient clearance, the rings will break up in the bore whilst the engine is running and cause extensive damage. The ring gap may be increased by filing the ends of the rings with a fine file. The ring should be supported on the end as much as possible to avoid breakage when filing, and should be filed square with the end. Remove only a small amount of metal at a time and keep rechecking the clearance in the bore.

22 Connecting rods and big-end bearings - examination and renovation

> **HAYNES HiNT** It is advisable to renew the bearing shells during a major overhaul as a precautionary measure. They are relatively cheap and it is false economy to re-use part worn components.

1 Examine the connecting rods for signs of cracking or distortion, renewing any rod which is not in perfect condition **(see illustration)**. Check the connecting rod side clearance, using feeler gauges. If the clearance exceeds

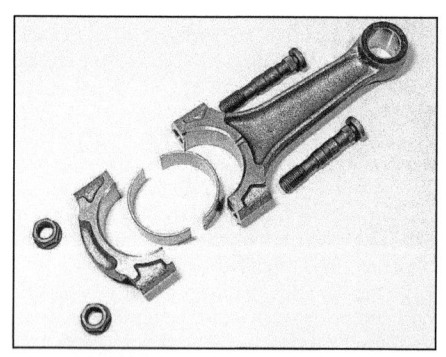

22.1 Connecting rod assembly – retaining bolts and nuts must be renewed whenever they are disturbed

the limit specified it will be necessary to renew the connecting rod or the crankshaft assembly. Connecting rod distortion, both bending and twisting, can only be measured using a great deal of special equipment and should therefore be checked only by an expert; otherwise the rods should be renewed if there is any doubt about their condition.

2 If the necessary equipment is available, the condition of the small-end assemblies can be checked by direct measurement, referring to the tolerances given in the Specifications Section of this Chapter. If the equipment is not available, it will suffice to ensure that the bearing surfaces in the connecting rod small-end bearing, in the piston bosses and over the entire gudgeon pin are smooth and unmarked by wear. The gudgeon pin should be a tight press fit in both connecting rod and piston, and there should be no free play discernible when the components are temporarily reassembled. If any wear is found, the component concerned should be renewed.

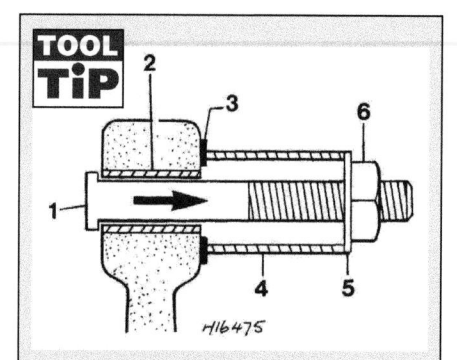

If the small-end bearing is to be renewed, it must be pressed out using a drawbolt assembly.

1 Drawbolt	4 Tube
2 Bush	5 Washer
3 Rubber washer	6 Nut

3 On fitting the new bush, align its split joint at 60° to the left or right of the connecting rod centre line and drill and deburr a new oil hole through the bush, using the connecting rod oilway as a guide to the position and size. Finally, ream the new bush to the specified size.

4 If a connecting rod is renewed at any time, it is essential that it is of the correct weight group to minimise vibration. Rods on early models are in seven weight groups each being identified by having one, two or three spots of yellow, white or blue paint. All rods must have the same paint marking, if this has been erased on all rods they must be individually weighed (less bearing shells but complete with cap, bolts and nuts) so that the weight group can be identified by an authorised BMW dealer when a new rod is ordered. The weight groups vary by 7 - 8 grams. Later models (from August 1988) have their weight in grams stamped on the rods.

5 The big-end bearing cap retaining bolts and nuts should be renewed whenever they are disturbed. The bolts are of the expansion type which are permanently stretched on tightening and must never be re-used. They are an extremely tight fit in the connecting rods, however, and great care will be required to avoid marking the rods when tapping out the old bolts and fitting new ones. If a rod is clamped in a vice for support, be careful to fit the vice with padded jaws to avoid any risk of marking the rod surfaces.

6 Examine closely the big-end bearing shells. The bearing surface should be smooth and of even texture, with no sign of scoring or streaking on its surface. If any shell is in less than perfect condition the complete set should be renewed.

> **HAYNES HiNT** Evidence of extreme heat, such as discoloration of the bearing inserts, indicates that lubrication failure has occurred. Be sure to thoroughly check the oil pump and pressure relief valve as well as all oil holes and passages before reassembling the engine.

7 The crankshaft journals should be given a close visual examination, paying particular attention where damaged bearing shells were discovered. If the journals are scored or pitted in any way, seek the advice of a good authorised BMW dealer. While undersize shells are listed, making it possible in theory to reclaim wear or damage by regrinding the crankshaft, BMW give very little information to assist the repairer and state that since the crankshaft is surface hardened it cannot be reground by normal methods.

8 To select new shells, use the manufacturer's size code system. The standard crankpin outside diameter is divided into three size groups, to allow for manufacturing tolerances. The size group of each crankpin is indicated by a dab of white, green or yellow paint on the crankshaft webs immediately adjacent to the crankpin; if the equipment is available, these marks can be checked by direct measurement **(see illustration)**. Given that the connecting rod big-end eye diameter does not vary

22.8 Measuring crankpin diameter

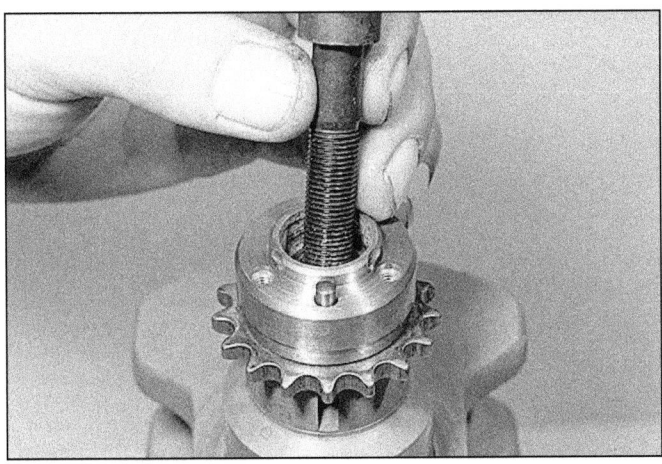

Engine 2•21

23.2a If required, unscrew retaining bolt to release ignition rotor and sprocket from crankshaft front end . . .

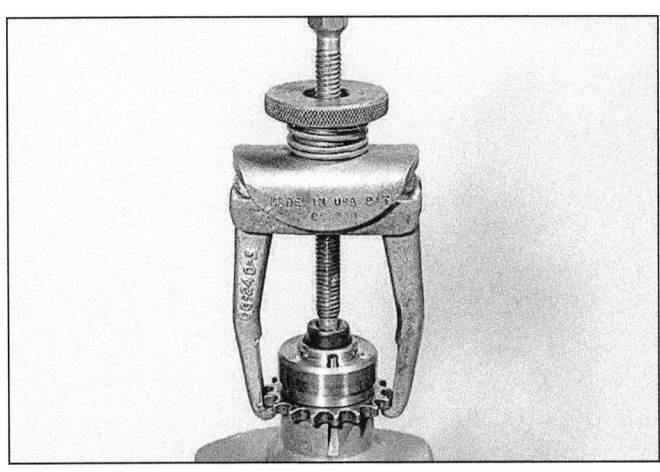

23.2b . . . noting that a puller may be required – note temporarily refitted bolt to protect crankshaft end

significantly in service, the shells, which are identified by a similar colour coding, are selected to match the crankshaft paint mark, ie a green paint mark on the crankshaft means green-ended bearing shells for that crankpin.

9 If the existing inserts are to be checked for wear with a view to re-using them, use Plastigauge to check the clearance as described in Section 14. If the clearance measured is within the specified limits, the existing shells can be re-used. If the clearance is excessive, even with new shells (of the correct size code), the crankpin is worn and expert advice must be obtained.

23 Crankshaft and main bearings - examination and renovation

1 The crankshaft should be cleaned. Be very careful to check that all oilways are completely free from dirt and other foreign matter.

2 If required, the ignition rotor flange and cam chain drive sprocket can be withdrawn. Unscrew the retaining bolt and pull the flange and sprocket off the shaft end; a puller may be required to withdraw the flange **(see illustrations)**. Note that the sprocket will fit either way round and that the locating pin set in the rotor flange passes through the sprocket to locate the two components by engaging a crankshaft keyway.

3 On reassembly, place the sprocket on the crankshaft end and refit the rotor flange, ensuring that both components are correctly located by the pin **(see illustration)**. Refit the retaining bolt and tighten it to the specified torque setting.

4 Examine the crankshaft closely. Any obvious signs of damage such as marked bearing surfaces, damaged threads, worn tapers and damaged gear teeth will mean that it must be renewed. There are, however, light engineering firms advertising in the motorcycle press who can undertake major crankshaft repairs; in view of the expense of a new component it is worth trying such firms provided they are competent.

5 Refit temporarily the crankshaft and use feeler gauges to measure the clearance between the crankcase bearing pedestals and their respective adjacent webs **(see illustration)**. Alternatively, a dial gauge can be mounted parallel to the crankshaft, and with its tip touching one end. Push the crankshaft fully away from the gauge, zero the gauge, push the crankshaft fully towards the gauge again and note the reading obtained. If the crankshaft endfloat exceeds the specified limit, the thrust bearings must be renewed. Crankshaft run-out is measured using a dial gauge with the crankshaft mounted on V-blocks at each outer main bearing journal; run-out, measured at the centre main bearing journals, must not be excessive. If any doubt arises about the amount of run-out measured, seek expert advice.

6 The procedures for examining the bearing inserts and journals, measuring the diameters of the crankshaft journals, and measuring the amount of wear on existing bearing inserts are the same as for the big-end bearings. Refer to paragraphs 6-9 of Section 22 of this Chapter. It will of course be necessary to reassemble temporarily the main bearing caps, tightening all securing bolts to the correct torque setting, when using Plastigauge to check the bearing radial clearances.

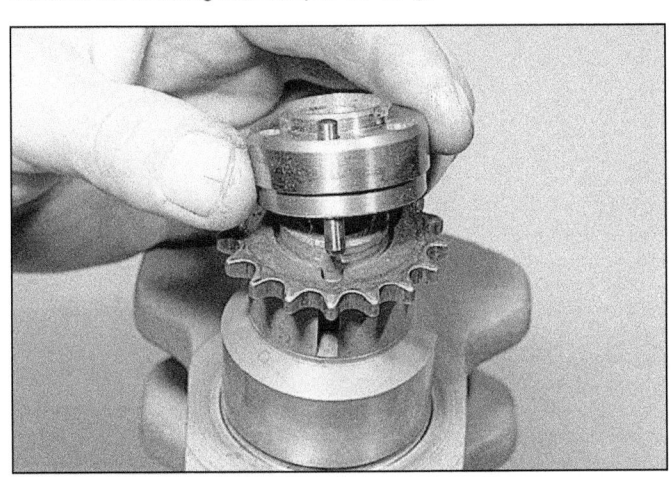

23.3 Note that locating pin locates both sprocket and rotor with crankshaft keyway

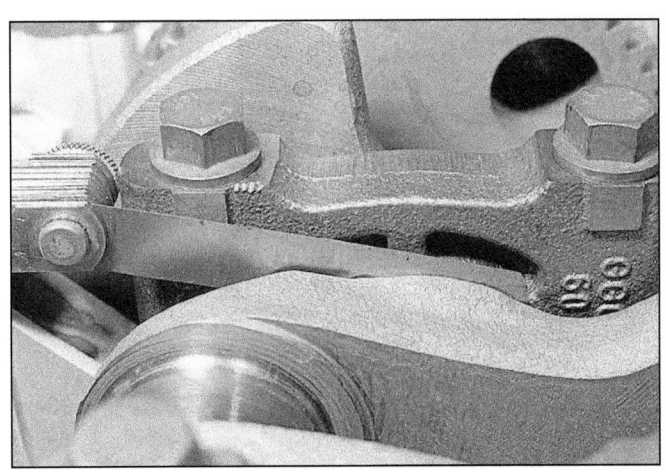

23.5 Measuring crankshaft endfloat

2•22 Engine

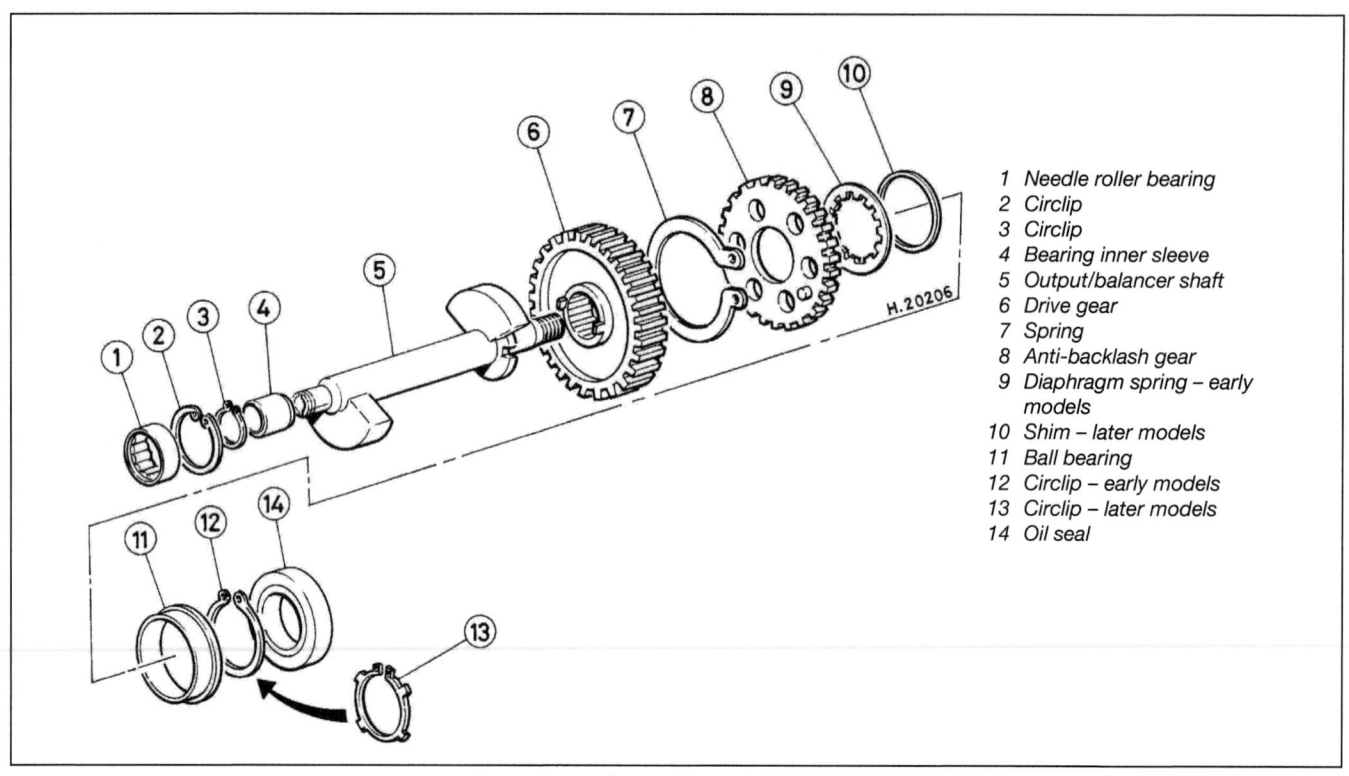

1 Needle roller bearing
2 Circlip
3 Circlip
4 Bearing inner sleeve
5 Output/balancer shaft
6 Drive gear
7 Spring
8 Anti-backlash gear
9 Diaphragm spring – early models
10 Shim – later models
11 Ball bearing
12 Circlip – early models
13 Circlip – later models
14 Oil seal

24.1a Output/balancer shaft – 75 models

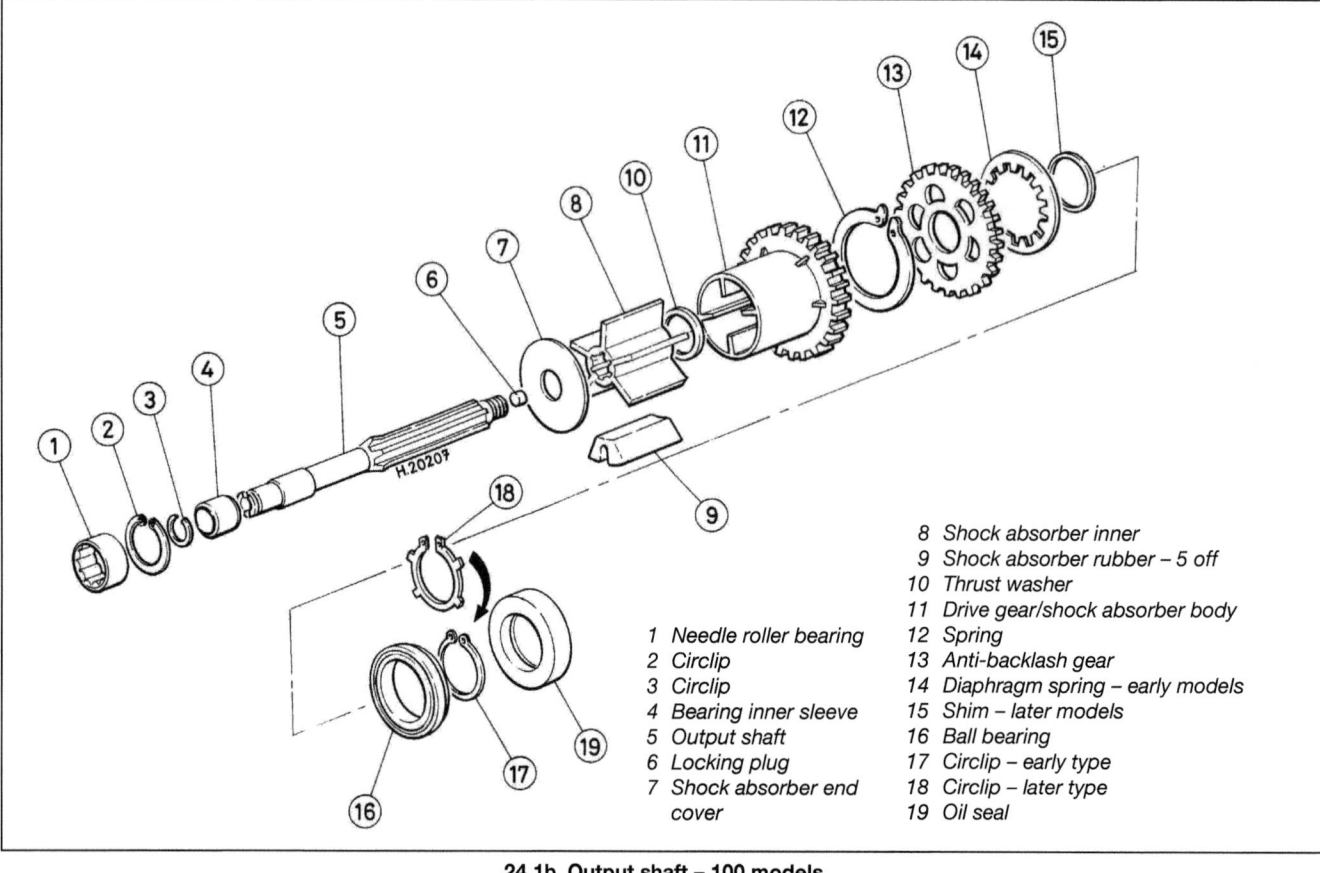

1 Needle roller bearing
2 Circlip
3 Circlip
4 Bearing inner sleeve
5 Output shaft
6 Locking plug
7 Shock absorber end cover
8 Shock absorber inner
9 Shock absorber rubber – 5 off
10 Thrust washer
11 Drive gear/shock absorber body
12 Spring
13 Anti-backlash gear
14 Diaphragm spring – early models
15 Shim – later models
16 Ball bearing
17 Circlip – early type
18 Circlip – later type
19 Oil seal

24.1b Output shaft – 100 models

Engine 2•23

24.4a Use suitable pliers to remove retaining circlip . . .

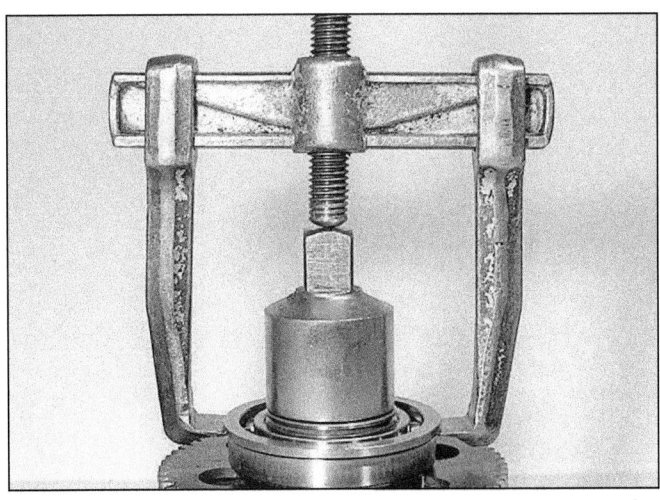

24.4b . . . before using puller as shown to draw off output shaft rear bearing

24 Output/balancer shaft - examination and renovation

1 To dismantle the output shaft assembly, remove the retaining circlip from its front end and withdraw the needle roller bearing inner sleeve (see illustrations). On 75 models, mark the drive gear front face at the point where it mates with the shaft itself, so that the shaft and drive gear can be refitted in exactly their original positions.

2 Hold the drive gear/ball bearing assembly in one hand and use a soft-faced mallet to tap the shaft out of the drive gear; do not allow the shaft to drop clear, but allow it to rest on a wadded rag or similarly soft surface.

3 On 100 models withdraw the damper rubbers from inside the shock absorber body and tap the shock absorber inner and end cover off the shaft. Note the thrust washer.

4 To dismantle the drive gear assembly, clamp the gear in a vice with soft jaw covers to prevent damage to its teeth. then remove the large retaining circlip (see illustration). Obtain a bearing puller of sufficient size and an adaptor that will bear against the drive gear boss so that the puller can exert pressure.

5 Draw off the bearing noting the diaphragm spring (early models) or the shim (late models) behind it. Discard the diaphragm spring (where fitted); this should not be re-used.

6 The anti-backlash gear should be removed using BMW tool 12 4 600 whose protruding lugs engage in the gear holes and permit it to be rotated slightly clockwise and lifted up to disengage the spring at the same time. If this tool is not available, check that the anti-backlash gear teeth are clear of the vice jaws and cover the gear with a thick layer of rag. Slip a thin-bladed knife between the two gears and gradually work the two apart until a screwdriver blade or similar can be inserted to lift the gear up and disengage it from the spring; use the thick rag to prevent any risk of personal injury caused by the gear jumping off. With the spring disengaged, withdraw the anti-backlash gear and use a pair of circlip pliers to remove the spring.

7 Check the output/balancer shaft components for any sign of wear or damage and renew any components necessary. Check particularly the gear teeth and all bearing surfaces. On 75 models, note that the drive gear and anti-backlash gear were modified from late 1987 to remedy loud gear noise in this area. For a limited period the new components were marked with a spot of blue paint on their end faces for identification purposes. The later components can be fitted to earlier 75 models. On 100 models renew the shock absorber rubbers if they are at all compacted or if they show any signs of wear or deterioration; always renew all five together, even if only one is faulty.

8 On reassembly, owners should note the following two modifications. The first was introduced on machines produced late in the 1985 model year (ie 100 models only) and consisted of a rear bearing with a thick shoulder (3.52 mm/0.14 in) integral with the bearing outer race at its rear end instead of the previous bearing which had a thin (1.75 mm/ 0.07 in) locating circlip around its outer edge. This was to improve the axial location of the output shaft. Earlier 100 models cannot be converted to the later type; their bearings must now be glued In place to ensure correct bearing location.

9 While the modified bearing was fitted to 100 models from late 1985 (model year) on and to all 75 models, a follow-up modification consisting of a retaining circlip with a conical spring cross-section was not fitted until early in the 1986 model year. The new-type circlip can be identified easily by the large square tangs protruding from it, which press firmly against the bearing inner race to ensure improved axial location of the drive gear assembly.

10 At about the same time as this subsidiary modification, the anti-backlash gear was changed and, on 100 models only the tension spring. Also the previously-fitted diaphragm spring was replaced on all models by shims to provide better anti-backlash gear retention. All these modified components can be installed in earlier machines.

11 It will be clear from the above that machines built in the late 1985 and early 1986 model years will have any one of a number of modified components. Owners of such machines should refer closely to the following text and to the accompanying illustrations; the photographs are of a late-1986 K100 RS and therefore show the fully modified assembly.

12 Clamp the drive gear in a vice with padded jaws to avoid damaging its gear teeth and fit the spring, using a pair of circlip pliers; ensure the spring fits around the drive gear boss and that its locating pin engages in the hole provided. Refit the anti-backlash gear (see illustration).

13 On 75 models it is necessary to use the special tool 12 4 600 to refit the gear unless a suitable substitute can be fabricated. Place the gear over the drive gear assembly and engage its protruding pin with the hole in the free end of the spring. Lock the tool's lugs into the holes in the gear and rotate the tool clockwise while pressing down until the anti-backlash gear centre fits over the drive gear

24.12 When refitting anti-backlash spring, anchor fixed end on locating pin (arrowed)

24.14a Refitting anti-backlash gear, 100 models – press spring free end into drive gear hole . . .

24.14b . . . then fit gear so that its locating pin engages with hole in spring free end (arrows)

24.15 Fit diaphragm spring (early models) or shim, as shown (later models) around drive gear boss

boss and its protruding pin fits through the hole in the spring free end into the hole in the drive gear; check that the anti-backlash gear is free to move against spring pressure.

14 On 100 models the tool is not necessary but care must be taken. The spring free end has a bent-over lug which can be pressed into the large hole in the drive gear so that the spring is effectively anchored at both ends. Take care that the spring does not fly off; keep a thick wad of rag over it at all times, during reassembly. Fit the anti-backlash gear, aligning its centre with the drive gear boss and engaging its protruding pin with the inner hole in the spring free end **(see illustration)**. After assembly, check the amount of gear overlap, particularly if excessive engine noise has been noted. Turn the backlash gear clockwise to take up any free play and measure the overlap between the teeth of the drive gear and output gear. This should be at least 1 mm; if less, note that adjustment of the spring lug will be necessary. Adjustment is made by grinding a calculated amount off the spring lug, details of which should be sought from an authorised BMW dealer. Note that from September 1989 (1990 models onwards) the drive gear, spring and anti-backlash gear were modified to reduce engine noise.

15 On early or unmodified models, fit a new diaphragm spring with its convex surface outwards, ie its outer edge in contact with the anti-backlash gear **(see illustration)**. On later models measure the height of the drive gear bearing locating boss above the anti-backlash gear rear face and fit shims as required to eliminate the clearance that will exist between the anti-backlash gear and the bearing (maximum remaining clearance 0.01 - 0.15 mm/0.0004 - 0.0059 in on 100 models). Shims are available in thicknesses of 1.00, 1.15, 1.30 and 1.45 mm (0.0394, 0.0453, 0.0512 and 0.0571 in) on 100 models from September 1989 and all 75 models, and 1.60, 1.75, 1.90 and 2.05 mm (0.0630, 0.0689, 0.0748 and 0.0807 in) on 100 models up to August 1989.

16 Thoroughly wash all oil from the bearing and heat it to approximately 80 - 100°C (176 - 212°F). Using suitable protective clothing drop the bearing over the drive gear boss with its thin locating circlip (early models only) towards the front (ie next to the gear) or with its thick shoulder (later models only) away from the gear (ie to the rear). Check that the diaphragm spring or shims (as applicable) are seated correctly around the drive gear boss and use a hammer and a tubular drift such as a socket spanner which bears only on the bearing inner race to drive the bearing fully on to the drive gear boss. Refit the circlip.

17 On all models **it is essential** that the circlip is seated absolutely correctly in its groove to take the high axial loads; on early models clearance between the groove and the bearing is minimal, therefore great care is required to ensure that the circlip is seated correctly **(see illustration)**. On later models with the square tang type of circlip, fit the circlip with its convex surface outwards, ie so that the square tangs around its outer edge are firmly in contact with the bearing inner race. Allow the bearing to cool, then lubricate it thoroughly.

18 On 75 models align the marks made on dismantling when refitting the shaft to the drive gear, so that the balancer weights are correctly timed. Tap the gear assembly firmly on to the shaft locating tangs.

19 On 100 models fit the end cover and shock absorber inner to the shaft, lubricate the shock absorber rubbers and refit them to the body **(see illustrations)**. Do not forget the thrust washer when refitting the shaft assembly to the shock absorber body/drive gear.

20 On all models fit the bearing inner sleeve and its locating circlip **(see illustration)**.

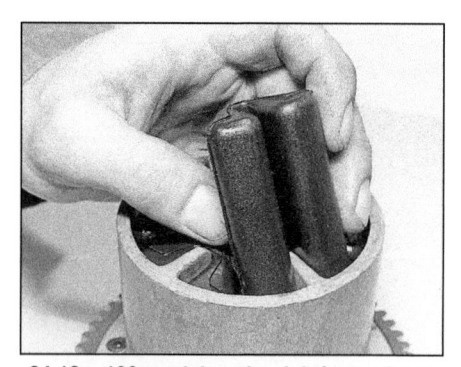

24.17 Rear bearing retaining circlip must be seated correctly – check carefully

24.19a 100 models only – lubricate shock absorber rubbers to aid reassembly . . .

24.19b . . . insert output shaft and shock absorber inner into shock absorber body, as shown

24.20 Do not omit front bearing inner sleeve and circlip from output shaft end

Engine 2•25

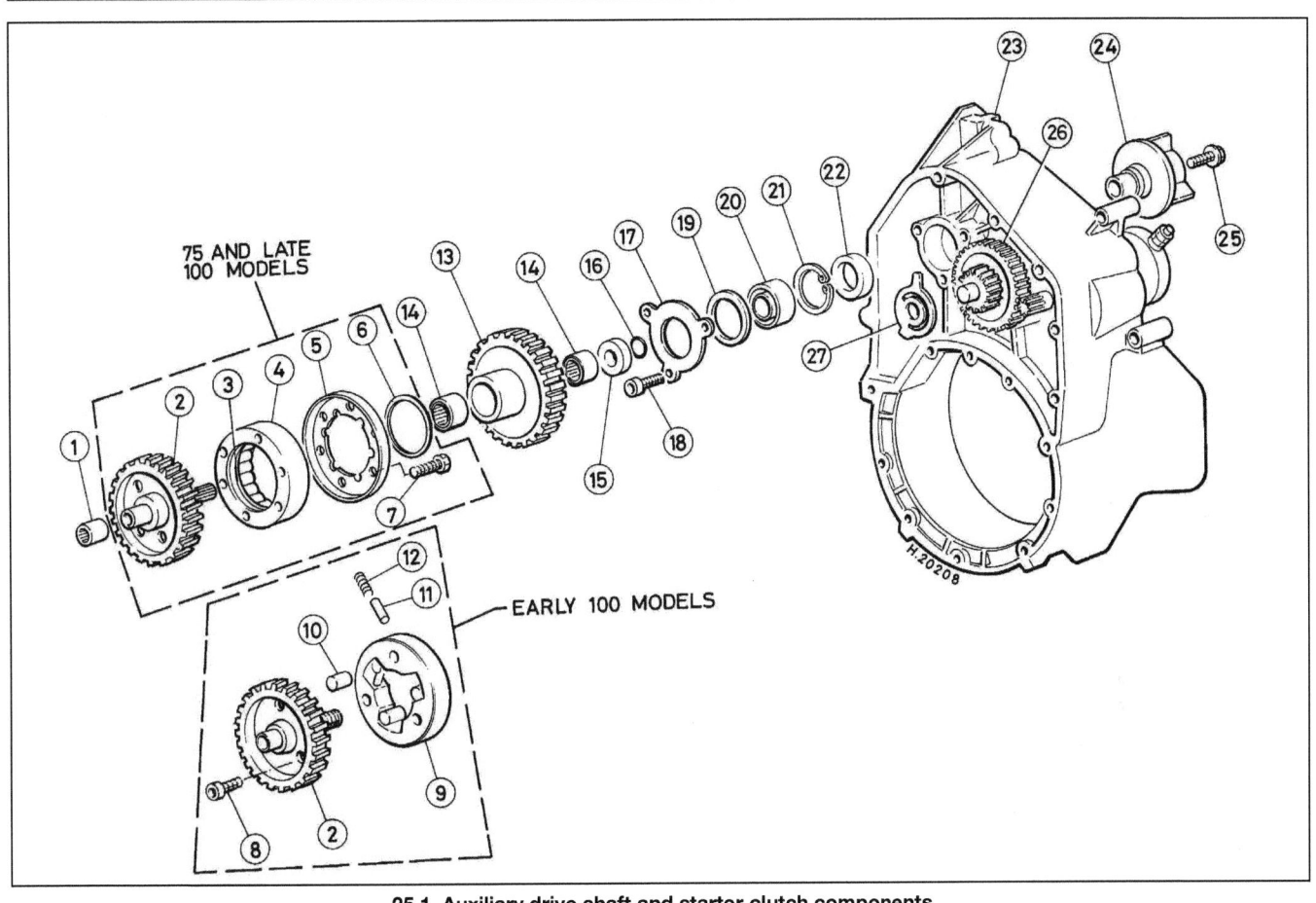

25.1 Auxiliary drive shaft and starter clutch components

1 Bearing	7 Bolt – 6 off	13 Starter clutch gear pinion
2 Auxiliary drive shaft	8 Screw – 3 off	14 Bearing – 2 off
3 Cage	9 Roller-type starter clutch	15 Thrust washer
4 Sprag-type starter clutch	10 Roller – 3 off	16 O-ring
5 End cover	11 Plunger – 3 off	17 Retainer plate
6 Conical spring washer	12 Spring – 3 off	
18 Allen bolt – 3 off	24 Alternator drive flange	
19 Conical spring washer	25 Bolt	
20 Bearing	26 Starter idler shaft	
21 Circlip	27 Spring*	
22 Oil seal	*note that this may not be fitted on early models	
23 Bellhousing		

25 Auxiliary drive shaft and starter clutch - examination and renovation

1 Remove the O-ring and thrust washer from the auxiliary drive shaft rear end, then hold the main assembly and twist the starter clutch gear pinion clockwise to release it from the locking elements so that it can be withdrawn **(see illustration)**.

2 On early 100 models remove the three rollers and the spring and plunger from behind each. Unscrew the three retaining screws and separate the clutch body from the auxiliary drive shaft.

3 On all later models remove the six bolts and withdraw the end cover, the sprag clutch assembly (noting which way round it is fitted) the clutch body and the conical spring washer. Note which way round the spring washer is fitted.

4 Thoroughly clean and degrease all components, then check each item for signs of wear or damage, looking for chipped or damaged gear teeth, worn bearing surfaces or locking elements (rollers or sprags). If any sign of wear or damage is found, the components concerned must be renewed. On the early roller-type clutch check the rollers themselves are free from pits, flats or other signs of wear and that the plungers move easily against spring pressure in the clutch body. If in doubt about the condition of the springs, they should be renewed; they can be checked only by comparison with new components. The sprag-type clutch fitted to all later models should be checked similarly and renewed as a complete assembly if worn or damaged. On both types of clutch check carefully for wear of the starter clutch gear pinion boss.

5 Above all be careful to wash thoroughly all components in a high-flash point solvent **(see illustration)**. Most problems with these components are caused by the locking elements slipping on deposits of oily sludge which build up inside the clutch assembly.

HAYNES HINT *New components must be thoroughly degreased before reassembly to remove the preservative applied at the factory.*

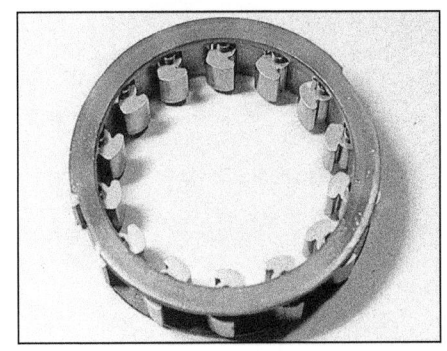

25.5 Starter clutch components must be thoroughly cleaned whenever possible

25.11a Reassembling sprag-type starter clutch – refit clutch body to drive shaft . . .

25.11b . . . and refit conical spring washer – convex face rearwards

25.11c Sprag clutch assembly is fitted with coil springs to the rear – note notches in cage showing modified type

6 Modifications to the clutch assembly are as follows: Early 100 models were fitted with a roller-type clutch. This was replaced in early 1984 by a fourteen-element sprag-type clutch. At the same time a conical spring washer 1.15 mm (0.05 in) high was fitted inside the clutch assembly to control the gear pinion endfloat and the idler shaft assembly was narrowed so that a spring could be installed, also to control endfloat. Note that the idler shaft is now 21.3 - 21.5 mm (0.84 - 0.85 in) wide, measured across the outer faces of its pinions; if a new component is any wider than this the spring must be omitted.

7 In early 1985, components of the sprag-type clutch were modified to improve the flow of oil through the unit and reduce the build-up of sludge which could otherwise render the clutch inoperative. The most important of these was the starter clutch body which had three 4 mm (0.16 in) holes drilled in it radially, at 120° intervals, to permit sludge deposits to be thrown out under centrifugal force; this should have been fitted to any machine whose owner encountered the starter clutch problem. Also modified were the clutch assembly (two flats machined in its outer diameter to improve oil flow and its components nitrided to harden them) and the conical spring washer (now 1.40 mm/0.06 in high); these latter two components need only be fitted when the originals require renewal.

8 On reassembly, thoroughly clean and degrease all components using only clean engine oil as a lubricant during rebuilding. Check that the modified components (where applicable) are available if any are to be renewed.

9 On the roller-type clutch fit the body to the auxiliary drive shaft, apply a few drops of Loctite 273 FL or similar thread-locking compound to their threads and refit the three retaining screws tightening them evenly to the specified torque setting.

10 Fit the springs and plungers together, insert each assembly into its respective bore in the clutch body and use a shim screwdriver or similar to compress the plunger into its bore while the roller is refitted.

11 On the sprag-type clutch place the clutch body on the auxiliary drive shaft and insert the conical spring washer with its convex face to the rear, ie so that its outer edge rests against the drive shaft and its raised inner edge projects rearwards, towards the starter clutch gear pinion. Fit the sprag clutch assembly with the coil springs towards the rear, followed by the end cover. Apply a few drops of Loctite 273 FL thread-locking compound or similar to their threads and refit the six retaining bolts, tightening them to their specified torque setting **(see illustration)**.

12 On both types of clutch hold still the main assembly and insert the starter clutch gear pinion with a clockwise twist to help it enter the locking elements **(see illustration)**. Refit the thrust washer and O-ring.

13 To check the operation of the clutch, hold the body and drive shaft while rotating the starter clutch gear pinion; seen from the rear, the pinion should be locked when rotated anti-clockwise and should be free to turn when rotated clockwise.

26 Reassembling the engine unit - general

1 Before reassembly of the engine unit is commenced, the various component parts should be cleaned thoroughly and placed on a sheet of clean paper, close to the working area.

2 Make sure all traces of old gaskets have been removed and that the mating surfaces

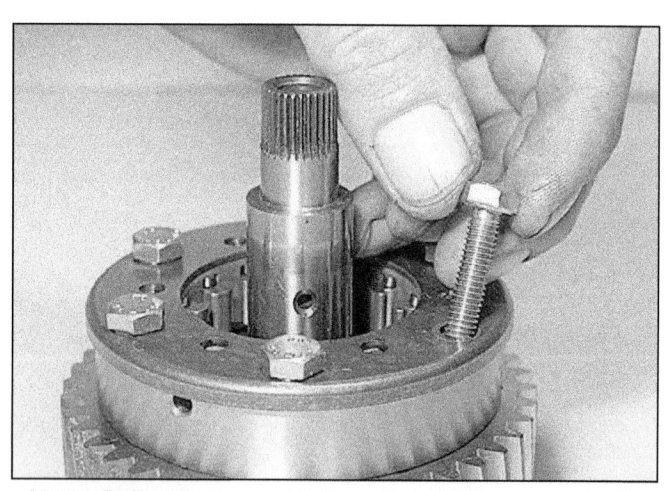

25.11d Refit end cover and bolts – secure bolts as described in text

25.12 Twist clutch gear pinion clockwise to refit to clutch assembly

are clean and undamaged. Great care should be taken when removing old gasket compound not to damage the mating surface. Most gasket compounds can be softened using a suitable solvent such as methylated spirits, acetone or cellulose thinner. The type of solvent required will depend on the type of compound used. Gasket compound of the non-hardening type can be removed using a soft brass-wire brush of the type used for cleaning suede shoes. A considerable amount of scrubbing can take place without fear of harming the mating surfaces. Some difficulty may be encountered when attempting to remove gaskets of the self-vulcanising type, the use of which is becoming widespread, particularly as cylinder head and base gaskets. The gasket should be pared from the mating surface using a scalpel or a small chisel with a finely honed edge. Do not, however, resort to scraping with a sharp instrument unless necessary.

3 Gather together all the necessary tools and have available an oil can filled with clean engine oil. Make sure that all new gaskets and oil seals are to hand, also all replacement parts required. Nothing is more frustrating than having to stop in the middle of a reassembly sequence because a vital gasket or replacement has been overlooked. As a general rule each moving engine component should be lubricated thoroughly as it is fitted into position.

4 Make sure that the reassembly area is clean and that there is adequate working space. Refer to the torque and clearance setting wherever they are given. Many of the small bolts are easily sheared if overtightened.

5 BMW now recommend the use of Three Bond 1207 B silicone sealant (formerly Loctite 574) for all mating surfaces which require the use of jointing compound and emphasise that careful work is necessary to prevent oil leaks. All mating surfaces must be cleaned of all traces of old gaskets or of old jointing compound and must be absolutely flat and unmarked. Using a clean, fluff-free cloth soaked in fresh high flash-point solvent wipe over the mating surfaces to remove all traces of old oil or grease. Apply a thin, continuous coat of sealant to the mating surfaces and assemble the parts immediately; tighten the retaining nuts, bolts or screws evenly and progressively to the specified torque settings, where available. Allow the sealant to harden for one hour before running the engine and peel off any surplus sealant from the outside of the joint.

6 Remember that if the mating surfaces are in good condition there should be no need for a thick film of sealant; the thinnest smear will usually prove sufficient to seal a joint. Sealant is wasted that is pushed out to form a bead on each side of the joint; note that while the bead on the outside is merely annoying and unsightly, proclaiming amateurish work, the bead on the inside is free to break off and block oilways or cause other similar problems.

27 Bearings and oil seals - refitting

Bearings

Note: *The refitting of bearings usually involves the use of heat. Refer to the general instructions at the beginning of Section 13.*

1 To refit the auxiliary drive shaft front bearing a stepped drift must be obtained or fabricated which fits closely inside the bearing rollers (ie of the same diameter as the shaft or 20.5 mm (0.81 in), and has a wider section of the same diameter as the bearing outer race so that the bearing is fully supported as it is driven into place. It must be fitted with the manufacturer's marks or numbers facing outwards, ie to the rear and must be driven in until it is flush with the crankcase, which must be heated to 100 - 120°C (212 - 248°F).

2 To refit the needle roller bearings to the starter clutch gear pinion a drawbolt assembly must be used. This is made up from a thick steel washer which is large enough to fit over the end of the bearing and the pinion, a smaller thick washer which is of the same outside diameter as the bearings (ie approximately 26 mm/1.02 in) so that it will fit closely inside the pinion's bearing bore, and a nut and bolt (of as large a diameter as possible) that will fit inside the washers, the pinion and one bearing **(see illustration)**.

3 Place the first bearing against the gear pinion so that it is absolutely square to the housing with the manufacturer's marks or numbers facing outwards. Place the smaller washer against the bearing and the larger washer against the opposite end of the pinion. Pass the bolt through the assembly, refit the nut and tighten it lightly. Check that the bearing is perfectly square to its housing and that the small washer is fully seated against the bearing, then tighten the nut gradually to draw the bearing into place until it is seated at a depth of 0.4 ± 0.2 mm (0.016 ± 0.008 in) inside the pinion (measured from the pinion end face to the outside edge of the bearing outer race). Dismantle the drawbolt, check

27.2 Starter clutch gear pinion bearings must be fitted to a precise depth in pinion bore

that the bearing rollers are free to rotate smoothly and easily, then lubricate the bearing. Repeat for the remaining bearing.

4 To refit the auxiliary shaft rear bearing, heat the bellhousing to approximately 100°C (212°F) and refit the locating circlip. Place the bearing squarely on its housing and tap it into place against the circlip using a hammer and a tubular drift such as a socket spanner which bears only on the bearing outer race. Install the conical spring washer so that its convex side is outwards (ie its outer edge must rest against the bearing, leaving the inner edge raised away from it). Refit the retainer plate and its retaining screws applying a few drops of Loctite 242 or similar thread-locking compound to the threads of each, tighten the screws evenly and securely, using the specified torque wrench setting, where given. Fit a new oil seal (see below).

5 The output shaft rear bearing must be heated before it can be tapped into place and the retaining circlip refitted in its groove. The front bearing is refitted during the rebuilding procedure.

Oil seals

Note: *Some oil seals have, instead of the single-lipped sprung seal described below, a lip of PTFE material (eg Teflon). These seals are not pre-shaped, but rely on elasticity for the required contact pressure. Introduced first for the auxiliary shaft rear oil seal and crankshaft front oil seal, these seals may also be found at other points on the machine. It is important that the seal is shaped for two hours prior to fitting by pressing it over the BMW service tool. Alternatively a mandrel can be used although extreme care must be taken to remove any rough edges. The manufacturer recommends the seal be installed dry, ie without lubricant.*

6 The output shaft rear oil seal fitting procedure is described in Section 29.

7 The auxiliary drive shaft rear seal and the crankshaft front seal are fitted to their respective housings in the same way. Polish away any burrs or raised edges, grease the seal inner lips and outer edge and place the seal on its housing with the manufacturer's marks or letters facing outwards, ie with the seal spring-loaded centre lips towards the fluid being retained. Using a hammer and a tubular drift such as a socket spanner which bears only on the seal hard outer edge, tap the seal into place until it is flush with its surrounding housing; note that in the case of the crankshaft seal, it must be flush with the housing rear, or inside, face.

8 If the auxiliary shaft rear oil seal is of the later (Teflon) type, observe the **Note** above when fitting. The BMW service tool No. 11.1.620 can be used to shape the seal and as a drift for its installation in the housing. If the service tool or a mandrel are not available, the seal can be shaped for two hours over the alternator drive flange boss, although extreme care must be taken to remove any rough

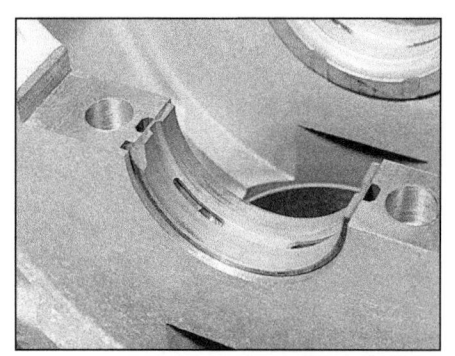

2•28 Engine

28.1a Check correct shells are refitted on reassembly – ensure locating tangs engage fully . . .

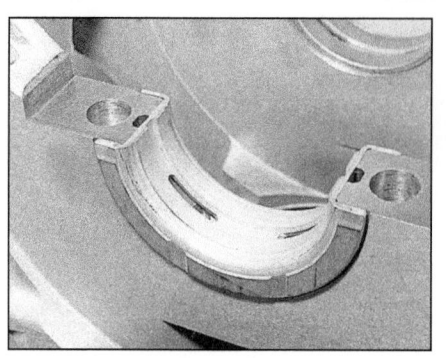

28.1b . . . except for thrust bearings

28.3a Oil all bearing surfaces liberally before refitting crankshaft

edges from the flange first and to avoid damaging the spiral on the seal's sealing lip.

Oil level sight glass

9 The oil level sight glass must be refitted, as described above, with great care. It helps to coat the outside of the sight glass with engine oil prior to installation.

28 Crankshaft - refitting

1 Check that all components are completely clean and dry. Ensuring that the correct shells are used, refit the shells to their respective recesses ensuring that the locating tangs (except thrust bearings) engage correctly in their grooves **(see illustrations)**.
2 Lubricate the crankshaft bearing journals and the bearing shells liberally with clean engine oil.
3 Lower the crankshaft carefully into place, aligning the timing marks (if possible) on 75 models, and refit the main bearing caps using the marks or notes made on dismantling to ensure that each is refitted the correct way round and on its original bearing **(see illustrations)**. Note particularly that the bearing shell locating grooves are next to each other on the 'lower' side of each bearing.
4 Tighten the bearing cap retaining bolts evenly and progressively to the specified torque setting **(see illustration)**. To apply pressure evenly work in the following sequence to tighten the caps (bearings numbered consecutively from front to rear, number 1 being at the front/cam chain end) on 75 models tighten first number 2, followed by numbers 3, 1 and 4 on 100 models tighten first number 3, followed by numbers 2, 4, 1 and 5.
5 Check after each cap is tightened that the crankshaft is able to rotate freely and with reasonable ease; some stiffness will be inevitable, especially if new shells have been fitted.
6 On 75 models, if the balancer shaft is now to be refitted, rotate the crankshaft to the position where the timing marks will align, as noted on removal.

28.3b Use identifying marks noted or made on removal to replace bearing caps correctly

29 Output/balancer shaft and the crankcase lower section - refitting

1 Check that the front bearing inner sleeve is secured in place by its circlip and fit the larger circlip, followed by the needle bearing over it **(see illustration)**. Lubricate both bearings.
2 On 75 models fit the balancer shaft to its bearing recesses ensuring that the dot or V mark aligns exactly with the straight line on the crankshaft gear, as noted on removal, and that the marks remain in alignment as the balancer shaft bearings are pressed into place **(see illustration)**. Ensure that the rear bearing shoulder fits fully into its groove and that the

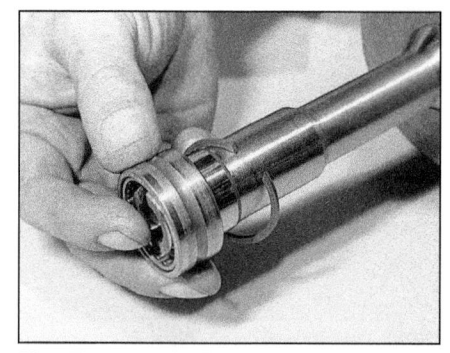

29.1 Fit larger circlip and bearing to output shaft front end

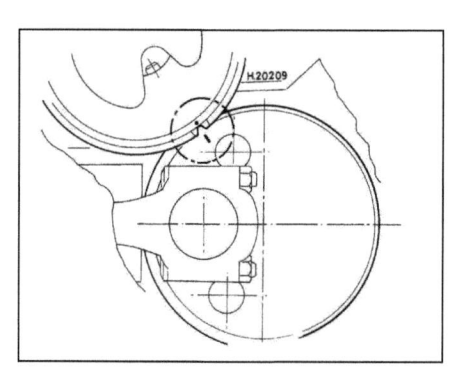

28.4 Tighten main bearing cap bolts evenly and in correct sequence – see text

front bearing locating circlip fits into its groove with its open end aligned on each side of the crankcase mating surface (ie so that the circlip compresses easily as the castings are clamped together).
3 On early 100 models - identified by the rear bearing having a thin (1.75 mm/0.07 in) locating circlip - thoroughly clean and degrease the rear bearing circlip and outside edge and the bearing recess, especially the circlip groove. Apply a thin coat of Loctite 273 or Three Bond 1110 B adhesive to the groove and refit the shaft. Press both bearings and circlips into their respective housings and grooves, ensuring that the circlip open ends are aligned on each side of the crankcase mating surface (ie so that the circlip

29.2 Crankshaft/balancer shaft timing marks – 75 models

Engine 2•29

29.4a Ensure output shaft rear bearing is settled securely in its locating groove

29.4b Position open end of front bearing locating circlip on each side of mating surface, as shown

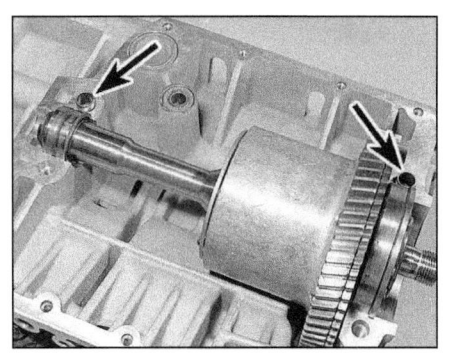

29.6a Check two locating dowels (arrowed) are pressed into locations next to bearings ...

compresses easily as the castings are clamped together).

4 On late 100 models - identified by the rear bearing having a thick (3.52 mm/0.14 in) locating shoulder at the outer race rear end - install the output shaft as described in paragraph 2 above, except that there are no timing marks to set **(see illustrations)**.

5 On all models, check that the output/balancer shaft bearings are fully seated and check that it is free to rotate with the crankshaft. On 75 models check the timing marks again after one or two revolutions.

6 Install the two locating dowels in their recesses next to each bearing and place two new O-rings in the grooves around the oil and coolant passages **(see illustrations)**.

7 Lubricate the output/balancer shaft bearings and gear teeth, check that the mating surfaces are absolutely clean, undamaged and degreased (wipe them over with a rag soaked in a suitable high flash-point solvent) and apply a thin coat of Loctite 574 or Three Bond 1207 B jointing compound following the manufacturer's instructions **(see illustrations)**.

8 Fit the crankcase lower section and its retaining bolts or screws. At first tighten evenly the four 'inside' bolts by hand until the lower section is seated securely, then tighten first the rear two hexagon headed bolts to their specified torque setting, followed by the front two Allen-headed bolts or screws to their (lower) torque setting **(see illustrations)**.

Finally refit and tighten evenly the 'outside' Allen bolts or screws to their specified torque setting **(see illustration)**.

9 Check again that the output/balancer shaft is free to rotate easily with no traces of stiffness.

10 Once the crankcase lower section is secured the output shaft rear seal may be refitted. Clean the seal outer edge, the shaft and its housing then apply a thin smear of grease to the housing, the seal outer edge and its sealing lips. Position the seal so that it is absolutely square to the housing and tap it in, until it is flush with the housing, using a hammer and a tubular drift such as a socket spanner which bears only on the seal's hard outer edge **(see illustration)**.

29.6b ... and fit new O-rings to oil and coolant passages

29.7 Apply a thin coat of sealant to mating surface as described in text

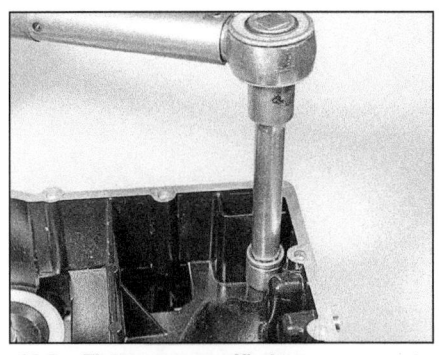

29.8a Tighten to specified torque wrench settings, the output shaft rear bolts ...

29.8b ... followed by front bolts or screws ...

29.8c ... and bolts or screws around mating surface edge

29.10 Fit output shaft rear seal as described in text

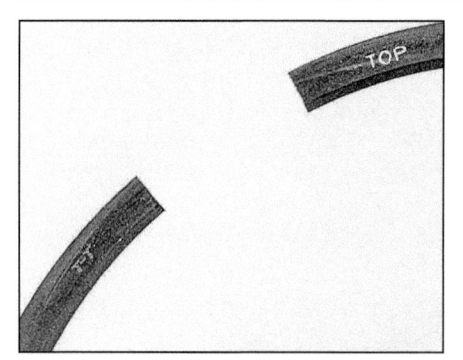

30.1 Compression ring top surfaces can be identified by markings and by cross-sections, see text

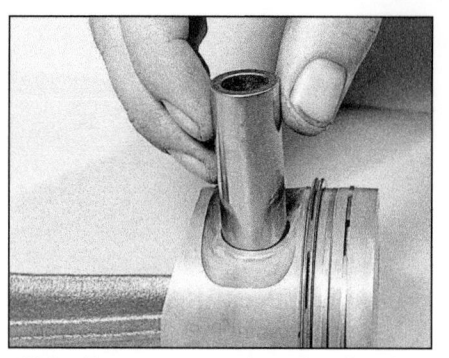

30.2a Ensure correct piston is refitted to each connecting rod piston may require heating to permit refitting

30.2b Ensure retaining circlips are correctly positioned, as shown

30 Pistons and connecting rods - refitting

Note: *From 1989-on modified pistons and rings were fitted to overcome the problem of excessive exhaust smoke on starting after the machine has stood on its side stand for a while. The second compression ring is pegged in place. This prevents rotation of the ring in use, and ensures that the ring end gaps do not align with each other and allow engine oil to pass up into the combustion chamber. If required, similarly modified piston/ring assemblies can be obtained for pre-1989 models.*

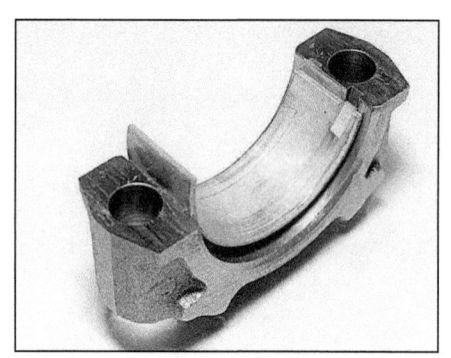

1 Fit the oil scraper ring inner section to its groove in each of the pistons followed by the outer section; their end gaps should be 180° apart. The second (lower) compression ring has a tapered inner edge on its top surface; this surface may also have the word TOP etched in it **(see illustration)**; on later models (1989-on) ensure that the ring ends locate each side of the peg in the ring groove. The top compression ring is a plain rectangular cross-section which has the word TOP etched into its top surface and was found to be chrome-plated. Fit the two compression rings as indicated by their markings and identified by their cross-sections, space their end gaps at 120° from the scraper ring outer section end gap and from each other.

2 Fit each piston to its connecting rod and refit the gudgeon pin, warming the piston if necessary to permit this **(see illustration)**. Fit new gudgeon pin circlip(s) ensuring that they are settled fully in their grooves with the open ends well away from the slot provided for removal **(see illustration)**. Use the marks or notes made on dismantling (see Section 10) to ensure that the piston is positioned correctly on the rod; if a new rod is being fitted note that it's 'upper' or intake surface is indicated by the slots for the bearing shell locating tangs or oilways. From this can be found the connecting rod's front (cam chain) face which is to be aligned with the arrow in the piston crown.

3 Fit the bearing shells to the connecting rod and cap ensuring that each shell is pressed firmly into place with its locating tang fitted into the slot in the rod or cap **(see illustration)**. Try to avoid touching the bearing surface, and lubricate the shells and crankpins liberally with clean oil, then liberally oil the cylinder bore, piston and rings.

4 Position the crankshaft at BDC for the assembly being refitted and slip the lengths of protective tubing over the threads of the connecting rod bolts. Fit a piston ring compressor (use any suitably-sized car-type compressor available from most auto accessory shops) to the piston, checking first that the rings are correctly arranged as described above. Checking that the piston/rod assembly is the correct one for that cylinder and that it is refitted the correct way round - arrow stamped in the piston crown facing towards the front (cam chain) end of the engine, connecting rod bearing shell locating tangs/oilways upwards (intake side) - insert the assembly into the bore from the cylinder head side.

5 Carefully insert the piston into the bore until the ring compressor is seated, then tap the piston gently but firmly through the compressor until it is fully in the bore. At the same time, guide the connecting rod big-end over the crankpin.

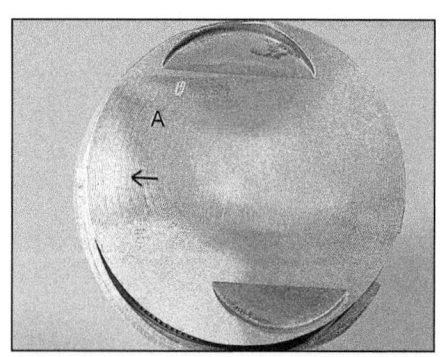

30.3 Bearing shell locating tangs must engage with cap or rod grooves – oil liberally

30.4a Arrow on piston points to front (cam chain) end of engine – note larger (intake) valve cutaway uppermost

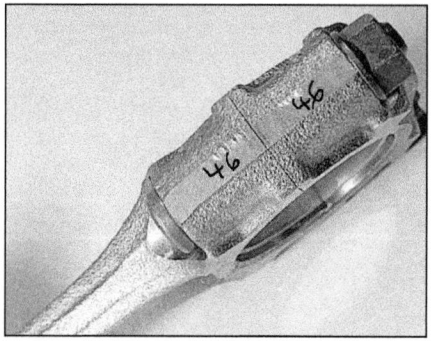

30.4b Marks on connecting rod and cap should ensure correct refitting of all components

30.5 Use car-type ring compressor when refitting piston/rod assemblies

Engine 2•31

30.6 Oil liberally bearing surfaces before refitting bearing caps

30.7a Tightening big-end bearing cap retaining nuts – first stage is by torque wrench . . .

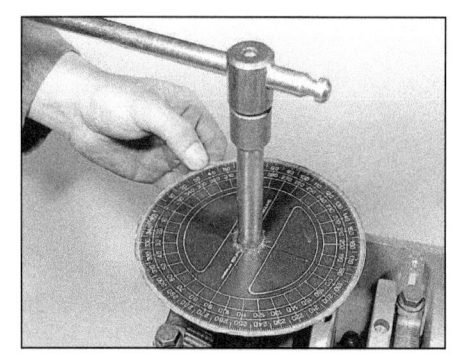

30.7b . . . second stage is by degrees of rotation – see text

6 Again lubricate the bearing surfaces, remove the tubing from the bolts, then refit the big-end bearing cap ensuring that its shell is correctly seated and that the locating tang/oilway is uppermost **(see illustration)**. Tighten the cap retaining nuts evenly until the cap is seated, then tighten them to the specified amount.

7 The big-end bearing cap retaining nuts are tightened in two stages. The first, to preload the bearing shells, is carried out using an ordinary torque wrench set to the specified pressure **(see illustration)**. The second stage is carried out using a method not yet in common use in the motorcycle world, ie to tighten the nuts by rotating them further through a specified angle **(see illustration)**. To measure this either use a degree disc, or cut a circular piece of cardboard, pierce a hole in its centre and mark a heavy zero line from the centre to the edge along the true radius, then use a protractor to mark exactly the required angle anti-clockwise from the zero line. Fit the disc to the tightening tool as shown and align the zero line with any convenient fixed point on the engine unit, then tighten the nut until the 80° mark aligns with the fixed point. Hold the engine unit steady (an assistant would be useful) and be very careful not to move the card on the tool during tightening or the angle measurement will be lost. **Note**: This method is very precise and effective in tightening fasteners but must be used with great care and accuracy if the nuts are to be correctly tightened; the pressures involved are quite high and the permissible tolerances minimal.

8 Repeat this procedure to refit the remaining assemblies. Check for free crankshaft rotation at each stage; some stiffness will be inevitable, especially if the bearing shells have been renewed, but the crankshaft should be able to rotate with reasonable ease.

9 Refit the cylinder head as described in the following Section.

31 Cylinder head - refitting

1 Check that the sealing faces of the cylinder head and block are completely clean and free from dirt, oil, grease, corrosion or old gasket material, also that they are undamaged.

2 Check that the tapped holes for the head retaining bolts are clean right to the bottom and free from oil. A quick squirt of aerosol-applied contact cleaner will clear any oil from each hole. Carefully clean the bolts, particularly the threads.

3 Fit the two locating dowels to their recesses in the cylinder block and fit the new gasket over them **(see illustration)**. No jointing compound should be used but a smear of grease will help the gasket to settle and will hold it in place. Note that the gasket will fit correctly only one way; check that all coolant passages, bolt holes, oilways and oil drain passages are clear. Lightly oil the threads and under the heads of the cylinder head bolts and check that all are fitted with their flat washers **(see illustration)**.

4 Refit the cylinder head, positioning it over the locating dowels, and fit the retaining bolts. Tighten them lightly at first, until all are in place and the head is settled.

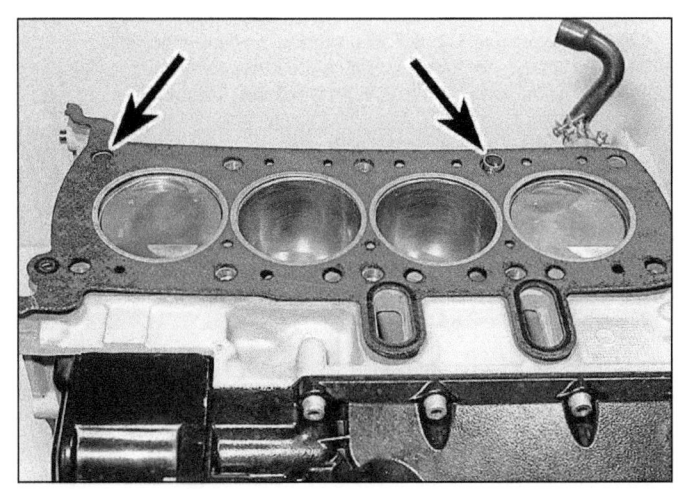

31.3a Fit new head gasket over two locating dowels (arrowed)

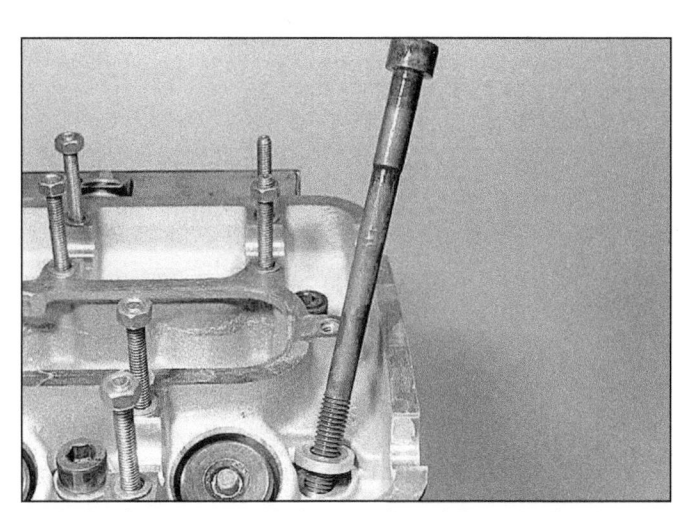

31.3b Clean threaded holes and oil retaining bolts lightly as described before refitting

2•32 Engine

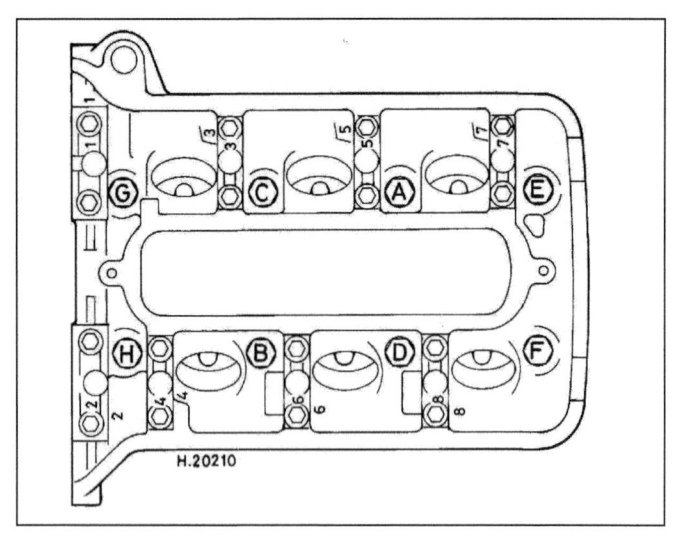

31.5a Cylinder head bolt tightening sequence – 75 models

A to H – head bolt tightening sequence*
1 to 8 – camshaft cap location numbering
*reverse for slackening

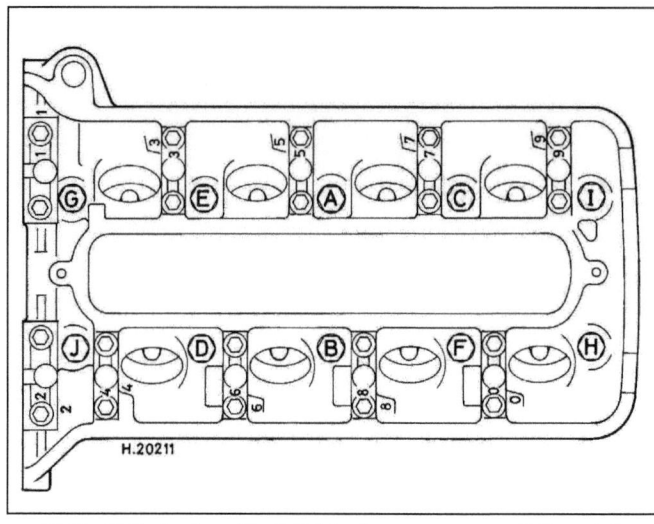

31.5b Cylinder head bolt tightening sequence – 100 models

A to J – head bolt tightening sequence*
0 to 9 – camshaft cap location numbering
*reverse for slackening

5 Working in the sequence shown **(see illustrations)** tighten the bolts evenly, in gradual stages, to the 1st stage torque wrench settings specified; this seats the gasket **(see illustration)**.

6 After a 20-minute wait, repeat this procedure but tighten the bolts to the higher 2nd stage torque wrench setting specified. As can be seen, the bolts can be tightened (but not all can be removed and refitted) with the camshaft in place **(see illustration)**; therefore this second stage tightening need not hold up reassembly work.

7 Where appropriate, refit the engine front left-hand mounting bolt and nut; do not forget to refit any shims that were found on removal.

32 Camshafts and setting the valve timing - refitting

1 Remove the wooden dowels (if used) from the camshaft locations. Lay out all the bearing caps with their nuts and washers, keeping separate intake and exhaust components and remove all traces of dirt from the bearing surfaces and cam followers. Refit all four dowel pins to the cylinder head.

2 Remove each cam follower bucket in turn and check that the adjustment shim is correctly seated with its marked face downwards. These shims are easily displaced and can cause a lot of trouble if not checked at this stage. If work has been done on the valve gear, making it necessary to check the valve clearances, do not forget to do this at the appropriate time, the work necessary being described in Chapter 1.

3 Check that number 3 cylinder (75 models) or number 1 cylinder (100 models) is at top dead centre (TDC). Pack the spark plug channel with clean rag or similar so that oil cannot enter, and check that the blanking plug is securely fixed in the rear end of each camshaft **(see illustration)**.

4 Positioning the camshaft so that its lobes are pointing away from all valves as much as possible, copiously oil the bearing surfaces of the cylinder head, caps and camshaft and offer up the first camshaft, refit the rear bearing caps (ie not yet the front thrust bearing caps) and, when possible, the retaining nuts and washers. **Ensure that the number in each bearing cap matches the number cast into the cylinder head next to the bearing pedestal and that the number is above (intake) or below (exhaust) the threaded boss and can be read only from the rear**; this ensures that the caps are installed in exactly the same way as they were originally fitted. See illustrations 8.8, 31.5a and 31.5b for details.

5 Working evenly and gradually, by a turn at a time, tighten the nuts of the inner bearing caps first (ie first and second from the front on 75 models, second and third from the front on 100 models) in a diagonal sequence. As the camshaft is tightened on to its bearings against valve spring pressure prevent any risk of its tilting by lightly tightening the nuts of the outer bearing caps. When the inner bearing caps are seated securely on the cylinder head, tighten the outer cap retaining nuts until all rear caps are seated, then lubricate and fit

31.5c Tighten cylinder head retaining bolts evenly to first stage torque setting . . .

31.6 . . . then to second stage setting after specified time – note tool used with camshafts in place

32.3 Check that blanking plug is securely fixed in each camshaft rear end

Engine 2•33

32.8a Note position of cam lobes when cylinder is at TDC – number 1 cylinder, 100 models shown

32.8b Align locating pin on sprocket rear face with camshaft keyway . . .

32.8c . . . and fit large washer with recessed face against sprocket

the front (thrust) bearing cap. When all caps are seated, tighten their retaining nuts in the same sequence to the specified torque wrench setting; be careful to maintain the same even application of pressure. **Note:** *Take a great deal of time and trouble over this - if any bearing cap is cracked or damaged by careless workmanship it can only be replaced as part of a new cylinder head assembly.*
6 Copiously lubricate its bearing surfaces and refit the second camshaft as described above.
7 Slowly and carefully rotate each camshaft using an open-ended spanner on the hexagon provided, until the lobe for number 3 cylinder (75 models) or number 1 cylinder (100 models) is pointing away from its valve but is inclined slightly inwards towards the opposite camshaft. If resistance is encountered at any point stop and turn the crankshaft backwards so that there is sufficient clearance between the piston and valve for the camshaft to continue rotating. **Do not** apply any extra force other than that normally required to rotate the camshaft; there is a risk of damaging the valves or pistons if they are forced against each other.
8 When both camshafts and the crankshaft are thus positioned approximately so that number 3 or 1 cylinder (as appropriate) is at TDC on the compression stroke (both valves closed) refit the camshaft sprockets **(see illustration)**. If the cam chain can be removed and refitted with the sprockets in place they

can be fully secured at this stage; if not they should be refitted loosely as they will have to be removed and refitted during the valve timing procedure. To fit the sprockets, place each one on its respective camshaft, aligning the locating pin protruding from the sprocket rear face with the camshaft keyway, then refit the large washer with its recessed face against the sprocket **(see illustrations)**. Refit the sprocket retaining bolt and, holding the camshaft by applying an open-ended spanner to the hexagon provided, tighten the bolt to the specified torque setting **(see illustration)**.
9 Rotate the camshafts until the marks on the sprockets are aligned exactly with the cylinder head top (ie left-hand, when installed) machined surface, ie the joint between the head and the front (thrust) bearing caps **(see illustration)**. Rotate the crankshaft until the ignition rotor flange locating pin aligns exactly with the centre rib cast in the cylinder block/crankcase **(see illustration)**; later models have a more precise mark cast on the crankcase wall, closer to the flange for easier alignment (OT is the German equivalent of TDC). These are the valve timing marks, with number 3 or 1 cylinder exactly at TDC on the compression stroke; check regularly that all are aligned **exactly** as the chain 15 refitted.
10 Engage the cam chain on the sprockets so that the runs between the crankshaft and intake camshaft and the two camshafts are as taut as possible while all three shafts are

32.8d Tighten sprocket retaining bolts to specified torque wrench setting

aligned with their marks **(see illustration)**. In some cases, as previously noted, this will require the removal and refitting of the camshaft sprockets; proceed as described in paragraph 8 above.
11 To ensure that the chain runs are absolutely taut, it may be necessary to rotate the driven sprocket slightly towards the driving sprocket, ie intake cam sprocket towards crankshaft, exhaust cam sprocket towards intake, so that the chain can be fitted and the driven sprocket can be rotated forwards again until its timing mark aligns. However, depending on the degree of wear in the chain this may not be possible and some error will be inevitable as the chain wears. If

32.9a Rotate camshafts until notches in sprockets align exactly with bearing cap/cylinder head joints (arrowed)

32.9b Rotate crankshaft until ignition rotor pin aligns with crankcase mark when appropriate piston is at TDC

32.10 Refit the cam chain without disturbing timing mark alignment and so that chain runs are taut, see text

2•34 Engine

32.12 Fit chain tensioner blade and rotate engine to check valve timing ...

32.13 ... if correct, secure blade with large washer and retaining clip, as shown

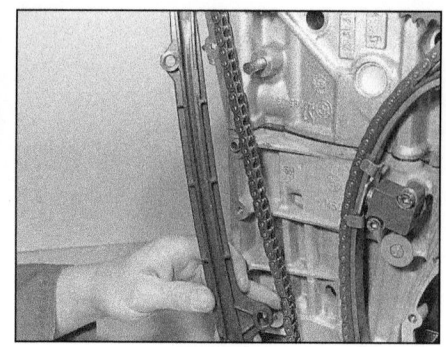

32.14a Chain guide blade is fitted over chain ...

the marks are no more than one tooth out they are as close as production tolerances will permit.

12 Fit the chain tensioner blade to its pivot and press it hard, by hand, against the chain lower run to take up any slack (see illustration). Applying an Allen key to the ignition rotor flange retaining bolt, rotate the crankshaft slowly forwards (anti-clockwise, looking at the rotor flange from the front of the machine) through a full cycle until number 3 (75 models) or 1 (100 models) cylinder is again at TDC on the compression stroke and the timing marks are all aligned. If resistance is encountered, **stop immediately** and find out the cause. If a valve is touching a piston the valve timing is incorrect and the procedure must be repeated until the error is found and rectified.

13 If the timing marks align exactly (or so closely that the error cannot be corrected by moving even one tooth at the driven sprocket) the valve timing is correctly set. Secure the chain tensioner blade by refitting its washer and retaining clip **(see illustration)**.

14 Refit the chain guide blade noting the washer under each retaining clip or circlip **(see illustrations)**. Refit the chain top guide rail and tighten securely its retaining Torx screws; use the torque wrench setting, where specified.

15 Rebuild the chain tensioner assembly **(see illustration)**. On the later type, without a locking screw, insert the plunger ratchet into the tensioner body, and place the spring inside the ratchet bore. Ensuring that the spring does not snag on the plunger guide pin, insert the plunger into the tensioner body, over the ratchet, until the guide pin engages with the curved slot in the ratchet. Press the plunger fully into the tensioner body, allowing it to twist as its guide pin follows the ratchet slot. When it is seated fully in the tensioner body, rotate the plunger clockwise until its head is square to the tensioner body with the two small tangs on the outside. Hold the assembly compressed while it is placed on the crankcase. noting that the plunger tangs match with the moulded extensions from the tensioner blade plastic face so that there is no metal-to-metal contact between the plunger and blade **(see illustration)**. Refit and tighten securely the tensioner mounting screws; use the torque wrench setting, where specified **(see illustration)**. Press the blade firmly against the chain run; the tensioner should extend to take up the slack.

16 On the early type of tensioner, fit the assembly exactly as described above but note that the plunger will not extend until the locking screw has been turned fully anti-clockwise to release it.

17 Refit the engine outer covers and the spark plugs.

33 Auxiliary drive shaft components and the bellhousing - refitting

1 Lubricate the crankcase bearings. Ensuring that it has been thoroughly cleaned and degreased, and assembled with clean engine oil, fit as a single unit the auxiliary drive shaft.

2 Position the starter idler shaft spring (where fitted, early 100 models) around the crankcase webs with the narrower of its two protruding ears upwards; the spring outer diameter should bear against the starter clutch gear pinion, as should be shown by the wear marks **(see**

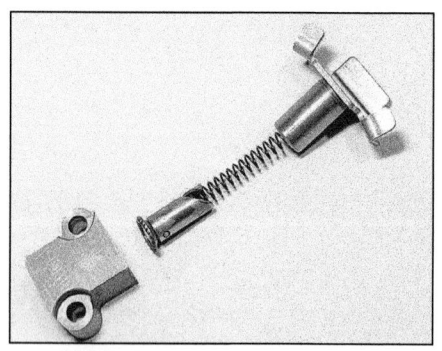

32.14b ... and is secured with a washer and retaining clip at each mounting

32.15a Reassemble tensioner as described in text – later type shown ...

32.15b ... and refit, ensuring that plunger tangs engage on plastic lugs

32.15c Tighten tensioner retaining screws securely

Engine 2•35

33.2a Fit auxiliary drive shaft, followed by (where fitted) idler shaft spring, as shown

33.2b Fit starter idler shaft – note thrust washer and O-ring on auxiliary drive shaft rear end

illustration). Refit the idler shaft and place the thrust washer and a new sealing O-ring on the auxiliary drive shaft rear end, using a dab of grease to retain them **(see illustration)**.

3 Check that the two locating dowels are firmly fixed in the crankcase mating surface; each must protrude by 6.5 - 7.0 mm (0.26 - 0.28 in). Apply a thin film of jointing compound to the mating surface **(see illustration)**.

4 Lubricate the bearing in the bellhousing and make a final check that the starter clutch is operating correctly; it should lock when the gear pinion is rotated anti-clockwise but rotate freely when it is turned clockwise. Refit the bellhousing and tighten securely and evenly its retaining Torx screws; use the torque wrench setting where specified. Refit and tighten the frame/bellhousing mounting bolt to the specified torque setting.

5 Check that the two large locating dowels and the clutch housing rubber fillet are firmly fixed in place in the bellhousing rear mating surface; each of the dowels must protrude by 6.5 - 7.0 mm (0.26 - 0.28 in).

6 Check that the new O-ring and the thrust washer are in place on the auxiliary drive shaft rear end then fit the alternator drive flange. Apply a few drops of Loctite 273 FL or similar thread-locking compound to the threads of its retaining bolt and temporarily refit the clutch housing and locking device to prevent rotation while the bolt is screwed in and tightened to

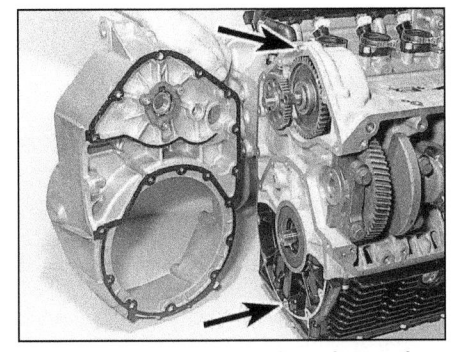

33.3 Apply sealant to bellhousing mating surface – note two locating dowels (arrowed)

the specified torque wrench setting **(see illustration)**. Refit the crankshaft cover, as described in the next Section.

7 Refit the clutch (Chapter 3) and the gearbox and final drive (Chapter 4). Refit the alternator (Chapter 11) and ignition HT coils (Chapter 7).

34 Outer covers - refitting

General

1 Before refitting any of the covers, check that the mating surfaces are free from dirt, oil,

33.6 Tighten alternator drive flange retaining bolt – note gearbox locating dowels (arrowed) and rubber fillet

grease or old jointing compound and that they are flat and undamaged.

2 The rubber seals at the crankshaft and cylinder head covers should be checked for damage; they can be re-used many times if they are not torn, stretched, or distorted. Soak a rag in suitable high flash-point solvent and wipe over the sealing surfaces and seals to remove all traces of grease; do not forget the conical seals around the retaining bolts. Apply a very thin smear of jointing compound to the moulded inner edges of the cover seals and use this to stick the seal in place in the cover groove **(see illustrations)**. The only jointing compound required on the actual mating

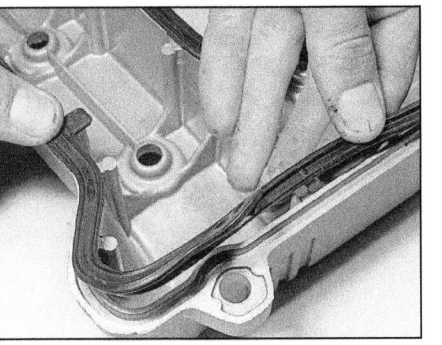

34.2a Engine cover rubber seals can be re-used if undamaged – check carefully

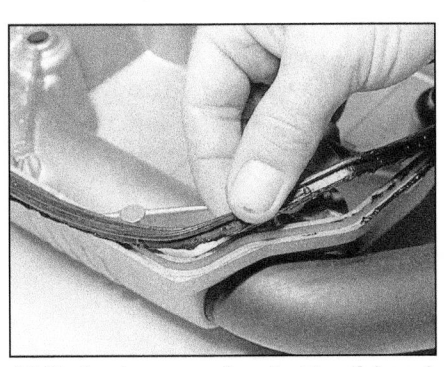

34.2b Apply smear of sealant to stick seal in cover groove

34.2c Sealant is required only at points mentioned in text

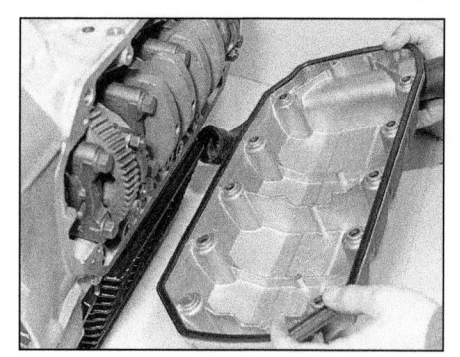

34.2d Hold seal securely in place as cover is refitted

34.2e Tighten bolts securely and evenly – do not overtighten

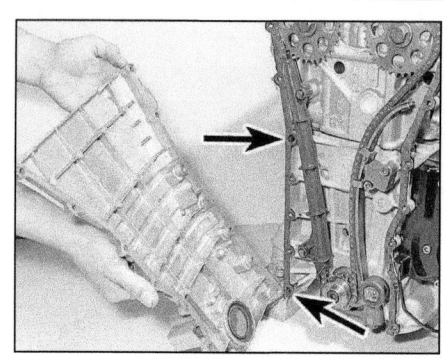

34.3 Cam chain cover upper gasket fits over two locating dowels (arrowed)

surface is a thin smear at the joint between the crankcase and bellhousing or crankcase and cam chain cover (crankshaft cover) and between the cam chain cover and cylinder head (cylinder head cover); the coating should extend approximately 10 mm (0.4 in) on each side of the joint **(see illustration)**. Fit the cover and hold it in place while the bolts are refitted; do not forget a smear of jointing compound around the bolt seals **(see illustration)**. Tighten the bolts securely but do not overtighten them or the seals will be distorted; use the specified torque wrench settings, where given, and tighten the bolts in a diagonal sequence working from the centre outwards.

Cam chain (engine front) cover

3 Apply a thin smear of jointing compound to both mating surfaces, fit the new gaskets noting the two locating dowels set in the top surface and offer up the cover **(see illustration)**. Pass the oil pressure switch lead through the cover passage and keep it taut as the cover is refitted so that a loop of wire does not become trapped.

4 Smear grease over the lips of the crankshaft front oil seal and carefully ease the cover into place, ensuring that it fits over the locating dowels and that the seal lips are not damaged as they fit over the ignition rotor flange. Fit the retaining screws and tighten them evenly to the specified torque wrench setting working from the centre outwards in a diagonal sequence.

5 Feed the oil pressure switch lead up through the cover passage and secure it with the metal clips **(see illustration)**. On 75 models only, refit the horn.

6 Fit the ignition trigger assembly as described in Chapter 7 and set the ignition timing as accurately as possible.

7 Refit the engine 'side' covers as described below.

Crankshaft (engine right-hand) cover

8 This cover is refitted as described in the general notes above (paragraphs 1 and 2).

9 Refit the radiator bottom hose and refill the cooling system. See Chapter 5.

10 Refit the cover panels or fairing components disturbed on dismantling.

Cylinder head (engine left-hand cover)

11 This cover is refitted as described in the general notes above (paragraphs 1 and 2) but note that the half-moon seals at the camshaft rear ends will require special care to ensure that they are properly seated, and that the coil spring must not be forgotten that is fitted to one of the camshaft bearing caps **(see illustration)**.

12 The spring is fitted to provide an earth return from the cylinder head cover (which is otherwise totally insulated, being rubber mounted) so that static charges caused by the spark plugs are dispersed; otherwise the static charges might build up and jump the gap to the crankcase, thus producing a stray spark which might well interfere with the ignition system components **(see illustration)**. On models with black-painted engine castings, ensure that the paint is scraped away from the inside of the cover so that the spring makes a good metal-to-metal contact.

13 Refit the oil drain plugs (where fitted), tightening them to the specified torque wrench setting, then refit the spark plug cover. See Chapter 1.

14 Refit the fairing components disturbed on dismantling.

35 Ancillary components - refitting

1 Refit the ignition trigger assembly and set the ignition timing as carefully as possible. See Chapter 7. Remember to take the machine to a good BMW authorised dealer for the timing to be checked as soon as possible.

2 Refit the oil/water pump assembly (see Chapters 4 and 5), and the pump pick-up and sump (oil pan) as described in Chapter 6.

3 Ensuring that the HT leads are refitted to their correct terminals refit the spark plugs and HT leads and connect the leads to the coils. Refit the spark plug cover. See Chapters 1 and 7.

4 Refit the coolant hose stub. See Chapter 5.

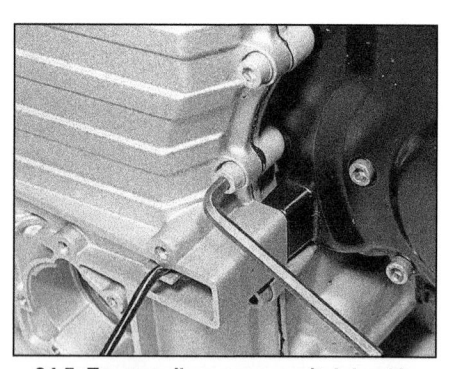

34.5 Ensure oil pressure switch lead is correctly routed on refitting cover

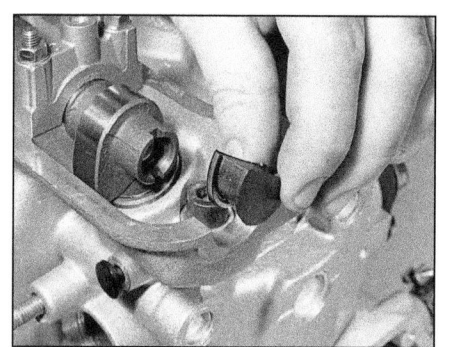

34.11 Half-moon seals require special care on refitting cylinder head cover

34.12 Do not omit coil spring – ignition system may be damaged

Engine 2•37

5 Working as described in Chapter 6, refit the EECS valve and hose (where fitted), the intake stubs and throttle bodies, the plenum chamber and crankcase breather, the fuel rail and injectors and the air filter assembly. Ensure that the engine wiring harness is routed correctly and secured by any clamps or ties provided.
6 Refit the clutch. See Chapter 3.
7 Refit the gearbox (Chapter 4) with the stand assembly, then refit the alternator and starter motor (Chapter 11). Assemble the swinging arm, drive shaft, final drive case, rear brake components and rear wheel as described in Chapter 9.
8 Check that all components have been refitted which have been disturbed and that the frame and engine/transmission unit are now ready to be assembled.

36 Refitting the engine unit to the frame

1 First check that the frame paint has been scraped away and the metal cleaned at the frame earth point and the bellhousing mounting point **(see illustrations)**. Apply a thin smear of silicone grease at both points to prevent corrosion but to ensure good electrical contact. Many different electrical faults can be caused by a poor earth contact at these two points on these machines.
2 Next check that all mounting bolts and nuts are completely clean and free from dirt or corrosion, and that the bolt shanks are well greased to aid refitting and to prevent corrosion. Enlist the aid of two or three assistants to ensure safe refitting.
3 The installation procedure varies slightly according to model. Early (ie 1984 and 1985) 100 models, which have a frame/bellhousing mounting bracket 70 mm (2.7 in) wide, must have both front mountings shimmed. All 75 models and 1986-on 100 models, which have a frame/bellhousing mounting bracket 100 mm (3.9 in) wide, must have shims at the bellhousing mounting and for rubber-mounted frames, at the front left-hand engine mounting. Proceed as described in the relevant subsection below.

Early 100 models

4 Lower the frame over the engine/transmission unit and refit loosely the mounting bolts, including the rear suspension mounting. While specific mounting points require careful attention on these models, the fit of the frame to the engine/transmission unit should always be checked and corrected if necessary with shims at all points; remember that vibration will be greatly increased if stresses are trapped in a frame member which is distorted by being clamped on to an engine mounting.
5 Check the fit of the frame/gearbox mountings and of the frame/bellhousing mounting. If significant clearance is found at any point, it must be eliminated using shims of the required thickness placed between the frame and the mounting lug. Note that at the gearbox mountings two thin shims of equal thickness must be used, one on each side, rather than one thick shim, to ensure that the gearbox is exactly central in the frame.
6 Tighten the rear suspension mounting firmly, the gearbox mountings and the bellhousing mounting. Note that BMW recommend a thin coat of copper-based anti-seize compound such as Copaslip or Never-Seize for this latter bolt, to prevent corrosion and aid electrical contact.
7 Check with feeler gauges the gap between each frame lug and its respective engine front mounting boss and install shims of the required thickness to remove it as closely as possible. Shims are available from BMW dealers in 0.25 mm (0.01 in) increments from 1.00 mm (0.04 in) to 5.50 mm (0.22 in) thick. Again, note that rather than use one thick shim to take up all the clearance, two thinner shims of equivalent total thickness should be used, one on each side, to ensure that the engine unit is exactly central in the frame.
8 When the frame is closely fitted and is seated securely but without stress on all mountings, tighten the mounting bolts or nuts to their specified torque settings.

All other models

9 Lower the frame over the engine/transmission unit and refit loosely the mounting bolts, including the rear suspension mounting but not yet the engine front left-hand bolt. While specific mounting points require careful attention on these models, the fit of the frame to the engine/transmission unit should always be checked and corrected, if necessary, with shims at all points; remember that vibration will be greatly increased if stresses are trapped in a frame member which is distorted by being clamped onto an engine mounting.
10 Check the fit of the frame/gearbox mountings **(see illustration)**. If significant clearance is found it must be eliminated using shims of the required thickness placed between the frame lugs and the gearbox mounting bosses. Rather than use one thick shim to take up all the clearance, two thinner shims of equivalent total thickness should be used, one on each side, to ensure that the gearbox is exactly central in the frame.
11 Tighten to the specified torque setting the engine front right-hand mounting bolt and the gearbox right-hand mounting bolt.
12 Use feeler gauges to measure the gap between the frame bracket and the bellhousing and insert shims of the required thickness to eliminate the gap as much as possible; the maximum permissible clearance remaining after shimming is 0.25 mm (0.01 in). A range of shims is available from BMW dealers in thicknesses from 1.00 mm (0.04 in) to 5.50 mm (0.22 in) in 0.25 mm (0.01 in) increments. With the gap closed by shims, check that there is clean metal-to-metal contact across the shims between the bellhousing and frame bracket (paint scraped away) and apply a smear of silicone grease to prevent corrosion. Smear the bolt with a thin coat of copper-based anti-seize compound such as Copaslip or Never Seize, refit it and tighten it to the specified torque setting.
13 Tighten to the specified torque wrench settings the gearbox left-hand mounting bolt and the rear suspension unit bottom mounting nut.
14 On all 75 models and K100 models (ie those with rigid engine front mountings) clearance between the frame lug and the engine left-hand front mounting should have been eliminated and the mounting bolt and nut can be refitted and tightened to the

36.1a Carefully clean away paint at frame earth point . . .

36.1b . . . and bellhousing mounting to ensure good earth contact

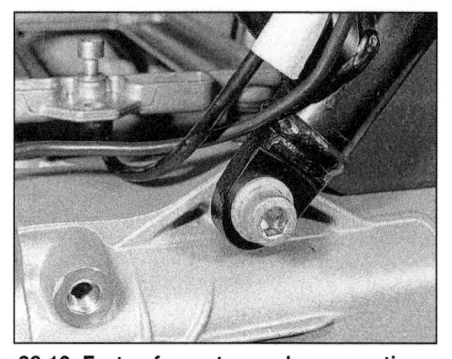

36.10 Fasten frame to gearbox mountings as described

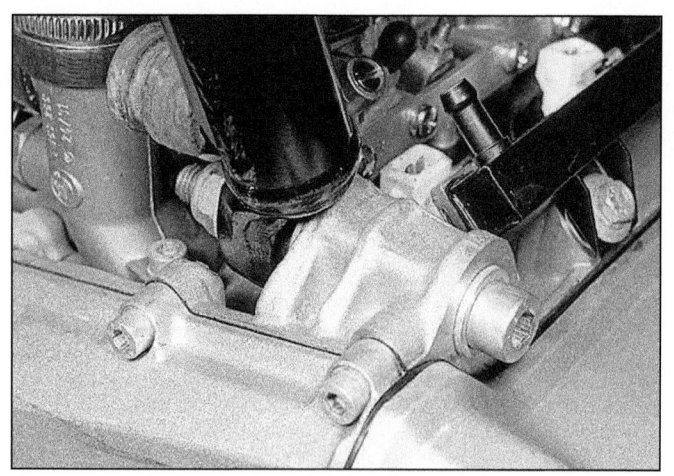

36.14 On machines with rigid front mountings shims should not be required...

36.15 ...but gap must be eliminated using shims on rubber-mounted engines

specified torque setting **(see illustration)**. However, if a significant gap is found on any machine it should be closed with shims (as described in paragraph 12 above) before the bolt is fitted and tightened.

15 On K100 RS, K100 RT and K100 LT models (ie those with rubber bushes at the engine front mountings) the clearance between the frame lug and the engine mounting boss must be measured with feeler gauges and closed as much as possible, using shims of the required thickness; the maximum permissible clearance remaining after shimming is 0.25 mm (0.01 in) **(see illustration)**. When the gap has been closed as far as possible refit the mounting bolt and nut and tighten them to the specified torque setting.

All models

16 Check that the engine/transmission unit is refitted securely and without strain to the frame mountings and that all fasteners are secured to their specified torque wrench settings. Check also that no other components are trapped or distorted, and that the machine is now supported securely on the front wheel and centre stand so that it cannot fall.

17 Ensuring they are correctly routed and secured neatly out of harm's way by any clamps or ties provided, reconnect to the main wiring loom all electrical components **(see illustrations)**. Use the notes made on dismantling to ensure that components such as the ignition HT coils are correctly re-connected.

18 Working as described in Chapter 1 connect the throttle, choke and clutch cables again and adjust them correctly.

19 Refit the rear mudguard and number plate bracket and the alternator and ignition HT coil covers. Refit the exhaust system as described in Chapter 6.

20 Refit the radiator, check that the drain plug is securely fastened and all cooling system components are correctly refitted. Fill the system with coolant (see Chapter 5) and check for leaks. Do not forget to recheck the coolant level after the engine has first been started; accordingly do not fit the radiator cap until this has been done.

21 Refit the battery (see Chapter 1) and install the coolant expansion tank. Refit the fuel injection control unit and storage tray. See Chapter 6. Refit the air intake hose and fasten its single mounting bolt.

22 Working as described in Chapter 1, fit a new oil filter element and refill the crankcase with oil. Note that a larger amount than usual will be required if the engine has been dismantled.

23 On those machines so equipped, refit the fairing. See Chapter 8.

24 Make a final check that all components have been correctly refitted and are correctly adjusted and working properly, where applicable. Refit the fuel tank, the radiator cover panels (where fitted), the side panels and the seat, but remember that the coolant and engine oil levels must be checked after the engine has been run, also that the ignition timing may have to be checked. It will be necessary for example to remove the fuel tank again to check the coolant level at the radiator.

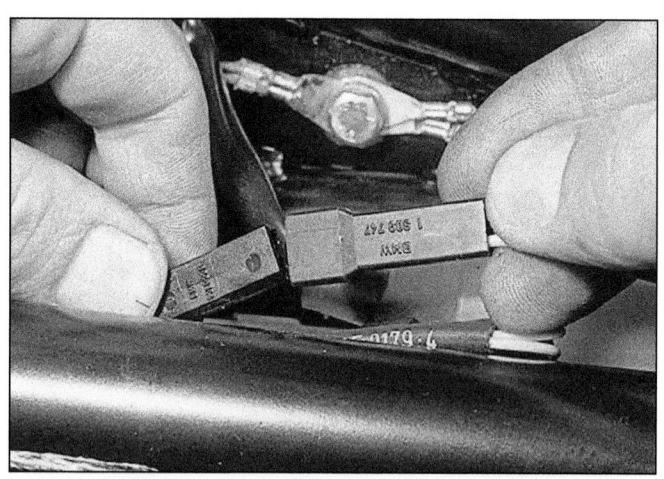

36.17a Ensure that all electrical components are connected to wiring loom...

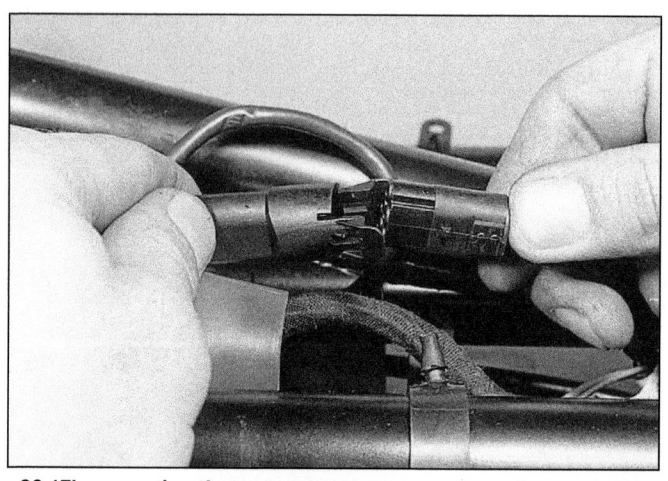

36.17b ...noting that some connectors can be refitted only the correct way

37 Starting and running the rebuilt engine

1 Start the engine using the usual procedure adopted for a cold engine. Do not be disillusioned if there is no sign of life initially. A certain amount of perseverance may prove necessary to coax the engine into activity even if new parts have not been fitted. Should the engine persist in not starting, check that the spark plugs have not become fouled by the oil used during reassembly. Failing this go through the fault finding charts and work out what the problem is methodically.

2 When the engine does start, keep it running as slowly as possible to allow the oil to circulate. The oil warning light should go out almost immediately the engine has started, although in certain instances a very short delay can occur whilst the oilways fill and the pressure builds up. If the light does not go out, the engine should be stopped before damage can occur, and the cause determined. Open the choke as soon as the engine will run without it. During the initial running, a certain amount of smoke may be in evidence due to the oil used in the reassembly sequence being burnt away. The resulting smoke should gradually subside.

3 Check the engine for blowing gaskets and oil leaks. Before using the machine on the road, check that all the gears select properly, and that the controls function correctly.

4 When the machine has reached normal operating temperature, check the coolant level at the radiator filler neck. Top up if necessary (see Chapter 5) and fit the cap, then check the expansion tank level.

5 If the ignition trigger assembly was disturbed and the ignition timing is still to be checked, ride the machine slowly and carefully to the nearest BMW dealer for the work to be done as soon as possible.

6 Finally, check the engine oil level and top up if necessary, as described in *Daily (pre-ride) checks*.

38 Taking the rebuilt machine on the road

1 Any rebuilt machine will need time to settle down, even if parts have been replaced in their original order. For this reason it is highly advisable to treat the machine gently for the first few miles to ensure oil has circulated throughout the lubrication system and that any new parts fitted have begun to bed down.

2 Even greater care is necessary if the engine has been rebored or if a new crankshaft has been fitted. In the case of a rebore, the engine will have to be run-in again, as if the machine were new. This means greater use of the gearbox and a restraining hand on the throttle until at least 500 miles (800 km) have been covered. There is no point in keeping to any set speed limit; the main requirement is to keep a light loading on the engine and to gradually work up performance until the 500 mile (800 km) mark is reached. Experience is the best guide since it is easy to tell when an engine is running freely.

3 If at any time a lubrication failure is suspected, stop the engine immediately, and investigate the cause. If any engine is run without oil, even for a short period, irreparable engine damage is inevitable.

4 When the engine has cooled down completely after the initial run recheck the various settings, especially the valve clearances. During the run most of the engine components will have settled into their normal working locations. Check the various oil levels, particularly that of the engine as it may have dropped slightly now that the various passages and recesses have filled.

Notes

Chapter 3
Clutch

Contents

Clutch - check and adjustment .... see Chapter 1
Clutch - dismantling 3
Clutch - examination and renovation 4
Clutch - reassembly 5
Clutch - removal 2
Clutch release mechanism - removal, examination and
  reassembly 6
General description 1

Degrees of difficulty

Easy, suitable for novice with little experience	Fairly easy, suitable for beginner with some experience	Fairly difficult, suitable for competent DIY mechanic	Difficult, suitable for experienced DIY mechanic	Very difficult, suitable for expert DIY or professional

Specifications

Clutch friction plate
Diameter:
   75 models .... 165 ± 1 mm (6.50 ± 0.04 in)
   100 models .... 180 ± 1 mm (7.09 ± 0.04 in)
Thickness:
   Standard .... 5.05 - 5.55 mm (0.1988 - 0.2185 in)
   Service limit .... 4.50 mm (0.1772 in)

Torque wrench settings - 75 models	**Nm**	**lbf ft**
Clutch housing/engine output shaft retaining nut	140 ± 5	103 ± 4
Cover plate/housing bolts or screws	19 ± 2	14 ± 1.5

Torque wrench settings - 100 models	**Nm**	**lbf ft**
Clutch housing/engine output shaft retaining nut:		
1st stage	140 ± 5	103 ± 4
2nd stage release, then tighten to	90 - 114	66 - 84
Cover plate/housing bolts or screws	19 ± 2	14 ± 1.5

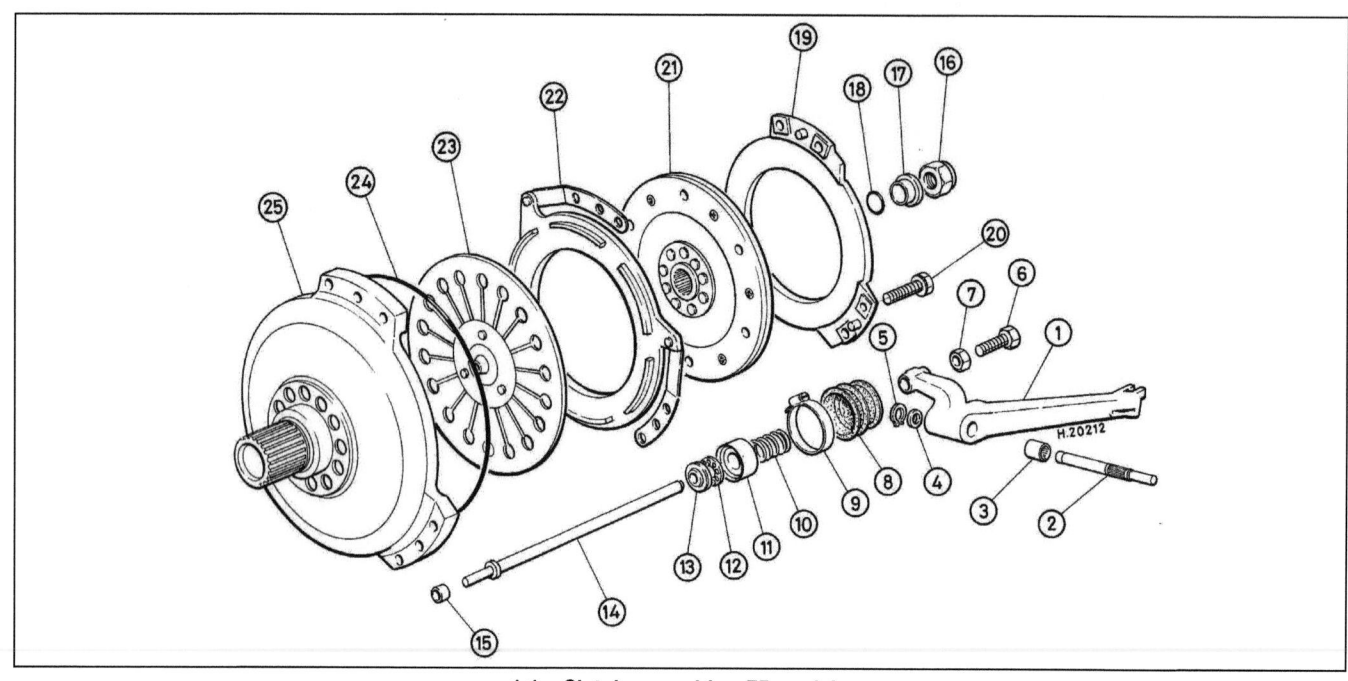

3•2 Clutch

1.1a Clutch assembly – 75 models

1 Release lever	7 Adjuster locknut	12 Thrust bearing	16 Nut	21 Friction plate
2 Pivot pin	8 Rubber boot	13 Thrust bearing front race	17 Shouldered spacer	22 Pressure plate
3 Needle roller bearing	9 Clamp	14 Pushrod	18 O-ring	23 Diaphragm spring
4 Washer – 2 off	10 Coil spring	15 Pilot bearing bush	19 Cover plate	24 Wire ring
5 Circlip – 2 off	11 Thrust piston		20 Bolt	25 Housing
6 Adjuster bolt				

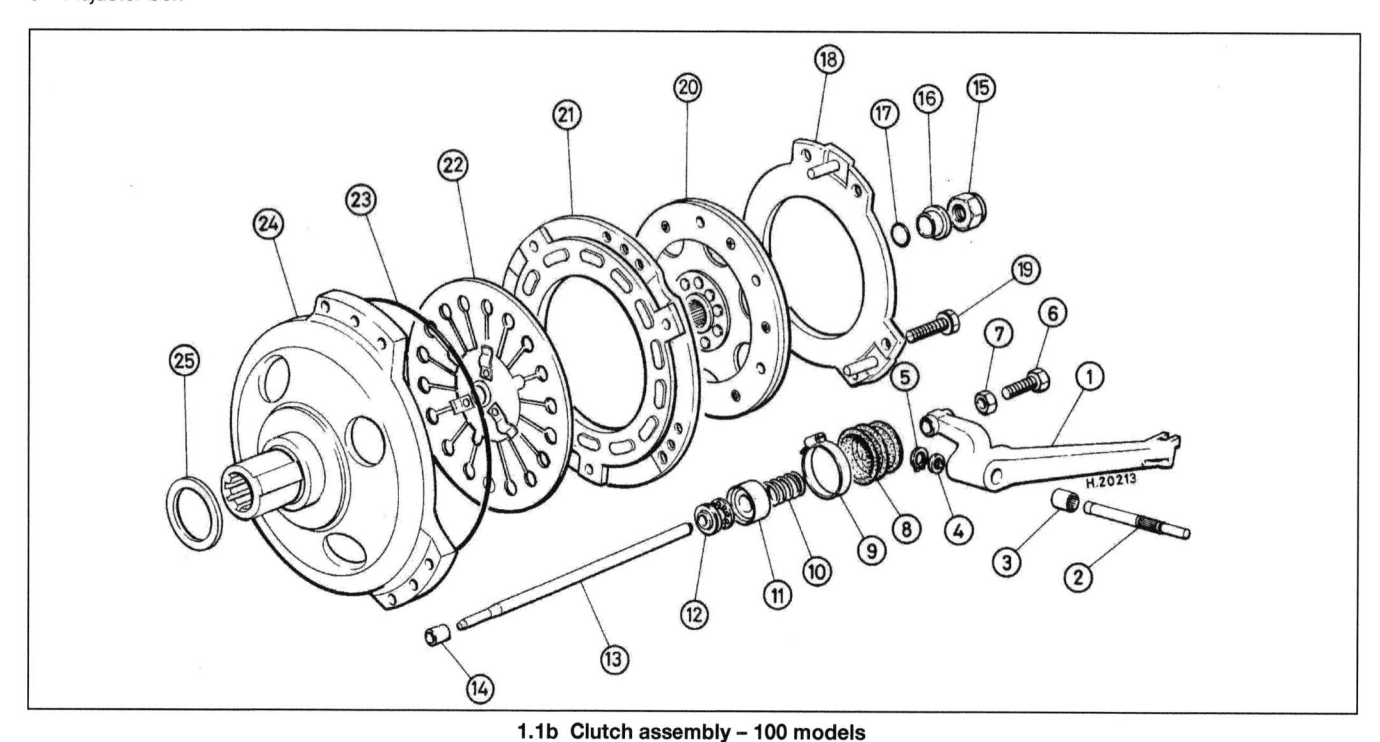

1.1b Clutch assembly – 100 models

1 Release lever	6 Adjuster bolt	11 Thrust piston	16 Shouldered spacer	21 Pressure plate
2 Pivot pin	7 Adjuster locknut	12 Thrust bearing	17 O-ring	22 Diaphragm spring
3 Needle roller bearing	8 Rubber boot	13 Pushrod	18 Cover plate	23 Wire ring
4 Washer – 2 off	9 Clamp	14 Pilot bearing bush	19 Bolt	24 Housing
5 Circlip – 2 off	10 Coil spring	15 Nut	20 Friction plate	25 Thrust washer

Clutch 3•3

1 General description

The clutch is of the dry single plate type mounted in a light alloy housing which is bolted to the engine output/balancer shaft rear end. A diaphragm spring, seated on a wire ring in the housing, forces a pressure plate to clamp the friction plate firmly against the cover plate which is bolted securely to the housing **(see illustrations)**. Since the friction plate is mounted on the gearbox input shaft, drive is thus transmitted from the engine to the gearbox.

The release mechanism is operated by cable from the handlebar lever and acts on a pushrod, via a thrust bearing, that is situated in the gearbox input shaft. The pushrod front end is held in a pilot bearing set in the engine output shaft rear end; when the release mechanism is operated a shoulder on the pushrod forces the diaphragm spring to deform and relax the clamping force it exerts on the pressure and friction plates. Clutch adjustment is described in Chapter 1.

Note that BMW recommend that the clutch be dismantled once a year so that the gearbox input shaft and clutch friction plate centre splines can be degreased, checked for wear and lubricated on reassembly. This is to preserve the clutch's smooth action and reliability.

2 Clutch - removal

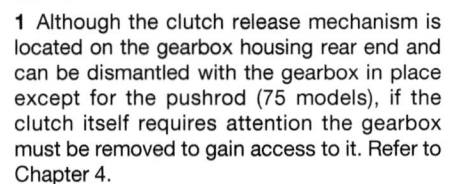

1 Although the clutch release mechanism is located on the gearbox housing rear end and can be dismantled with the gearbox in place except for the pushrod (75 models), if the clutch itself requires attention the gearbox must be removed to gain access to it. Refer to Chapter 4.

2 The clutch can be serviced with the engine in the frame, or it can be removed with the engine and dismantled on the bench. Refer to Chapter 2 for details of engine removal.

3 Check the gearbox input shaft and clutch friction plate centre splines whenever the gearbox is removed, lubricating them on reassembly, and also take the opportunity to overhaul the clutch operating mechanism.

4 Note also the two large locating dowels protruding from the bellhousing rear surface: these should be checked whenever the gearbox is removed. See Section 4.

3 Clutch - dismantling

1 Before starting dismantling work check the clutch components for balancing marks; there should be a yellow- or white-painted mark on the cover plate, pressure plate and housing, which should be spaced at 120° to each other. If no marks can be seen, make your own. Using paint or a thick-nibbed felt marker, draw a line across the housing, pressure plate and cover plate so that these three components can be refitted in their original position by aligning their marks.

> **HAYNES HiNT** *Remember that the clutch components represent a significant proportion of the engine's rotating mass and, if unbalanced, may produce severe vibration.*

2 Note also which way round the clutch friction plate is fitted; the longer extended part of the centre boss usually faces towards the gearbox. It is advisable to mark the outer (rearmost) face of the clutch friction plate with paint or a felt marker to ensure that this is not fitted the wrong way round on reassembly.

3 Slacken the six bolts or screws around the periphery of the cover, then, working in a diagonal sequence, slacken each bolt or screw by one turn at a time to release spring pressure smoothly and evenly **(see illustration)**. When spring pressure is released, remove the six bolts or screws and their lock washers.

4 Remove the cover plate, clutch friction plate, pressure plate (checking the balancing marks) and diaphragm spring, noting which way round the latter is fitted. If the cover plate is very tight on its three locating dowels it must be carefully levered away; take care not to let it fly off under spring pressure. The wire ring can be prised out of the housing if desired.

5 The housing must be locked to prevent rotation while the retaining nut is slackened. On 100 models pass a large wooden rod (a hammer handle or similar) through one of the holes in the housing and lock it against the crankcase webs.

6 On 75 models obtain a short but thick strip of metal with an 8 mm (0.32 in) hole drilled in one end. Attach this to the housing using one of the cover plate bolts or screws and wedge it against a strongly-reinforced part of the bellhousing so that the housing cannot rotate anti-clockwise.

7 Both of the above methods are an alternative to the use of the BMW service tool number 11 2 800 which is meant to bolt to the housing so that it will lock against the bellhousing wall. The tool would not fit the housing of the machine featured, however, and required some modification. If owners wish to fabricate such a tool the basic dimensions are given **(see illustration)**; the standard item is constructed of metal strip 6 mm (0.24 in) thick and may need to be shortened to approximately 220 mm (8.66 in) to fit inside the bellhousing.

8 With the housing securely locked, unscrew the retaining nut and withdraw the shouldered spacer behind it. Grasp the housing in both hands and work it backwards and forwards along the shaft splines until the O-ring can be reached and removed with a pointed

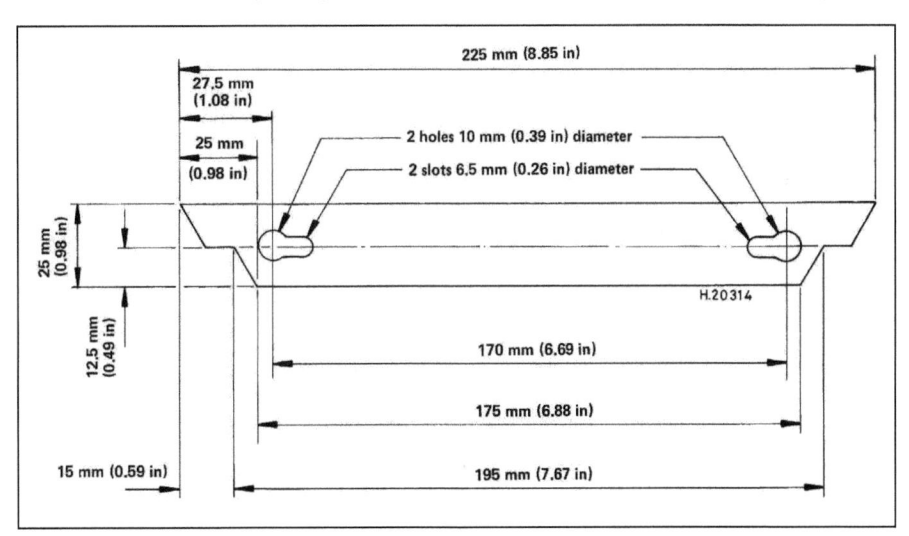

3.3 Note balancing marks and installed direction of friction plate before dismantling clutch

3.7 Clutch housing locking tool

3•4 Clutch

3.8 Removing O-ring from centre of clutch housing

4.1 Measuring clutch friction plate thickness

5.1 100 models only – fit thrust washer to clutch housing front boss

instrument **(see illustration)**. Withdraw the housing, noting the thrust washer fitted to it (100 models only).

9 If it is to be renewed, the pushrod pilot bearing can be extracted by cutting a thread on its inside (6 mm/0.24 in dia) using a suitable tap and then screwing in a bolt or screw which can be gripped to provide purchase for removal; do not screw the tap or extracting tool in too far as the locking plug (100 models only) may be damaged. Do not disturb the pilot bearing unless necessary.

4 Clutch - examination and renovation

1 If the clutch friction plate is damaged in any way, or if the friction material is worn to the rivets, fouled with grease or oil, or glazed, it must be renewed as a matter of course. If it appears to be in good condition measure the thickness of the friction material at several points; if the plate is worn to 4.5 mm (0.1772 in) or less at any point, it must be renewed **(see illustration)**.

2 Check carefully the condition of the friction plate centre splines and check for signs of cracking or splitting around the centre; if any damage is found the plate must be renewed.

3 Check the friction and pressure plates for distortion and the spring pressure of the diaphragm spring; renew any component that is found to be damaged, worn or otherwise faulty.

4 If the clutch action has become sudden, with grabbing or snatching in evidence, first check the release mechanism (see Section 6). If this is in good condition check closely the gearbox input shaft and friction plate centre splines; renew either component if excessive wear is found. Lastly check the preload of the input shaft. See Chapter 4.

5 If the clutch has been slipping and the plate friction material is found to be in good condition, the clutch cover plate should be checked very carefully and renewed.

6 If oil has found its way into the clutch housing, thoroughly degrease all clutch components and wash all traces of oil off the crankcase and gearbox castings. Check the seals at the output shaft rear end and the gearbox input shaft front and rear. Check carefully that the housing has not been rubbing on the output shaft seal, renewing the seal if traces of this are found.

7 Note that the clutch housing retaining nut is of the self-locking type and must be renewed whenever it is disturbed; also the housing O-ring.

8 If severe damage to clutch components or excessive wear of the splines is found, check that the locating dowels are fitted to align correctly the engine, bellhousing and gearbox castings. There are two large locating dowels set in each of the bellhousing front and rear faces; always ensure that these are refitted whenever the bellhousing joints are disturbed.

5 Clutch - reassembly

1 On 100 models only, fit the thrust washer to the front of the clutch housing **(see illustration)**. On all models, tap the new pilot bearing (if disturbed) into the output shaft rear end. Apply a smear of the specified lubricant to the bearing.

2 Insert the housing into the output shaft and press it fully into place. Fit the new O-ring and the shouldered spacer (spacer flange outwards, towards the gearbox) followed by the new retaining nut **(see illustrations)**. Lock the housing by the method used on dismantling.

3 On 100 models tighten the nut to the first stage torque wrench setting to settle the housing and O-ring then slacken it fully and tighten it again to the (final) second stage setting **(see illustration)**. On 75 models tighten the nut to the setting specified.

5.2a Fit new O-ring, followed by shouldered spacer – fit as shown

5.2b Housing nut is self-locking type – renew whenever disturbed

5.3a Note method used to lock housing (100 models only) to tighten or slacken retaining nut

Clutch 3•5

5.3b Fit wire ring to clutch housing and smear with specified lubricant

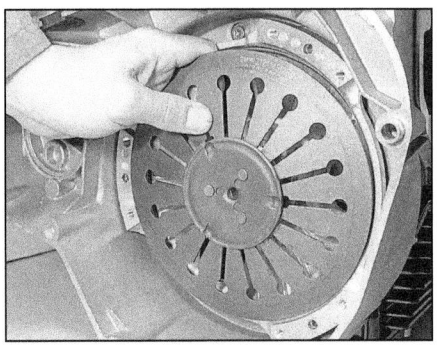

5.5a Fit clutch spring as shown – pressure plate wear marks confirm direction of installation

5.5b Lubricate points of spring contact when refitting pressure plate – note balancing mark

5.6 Friction plate centre boss extends towards gearbox

5.7a Lubricate locating dowels when refitting cover plate – note balancing mark

5.7b BMW service tool locates on bellhousing dowels to centre clutch components

Refit the wire ring to the housing **(see illustration)**.

4 For the next part of the operation have an assistant hold each component in place while the next is fitted. Some lubricant will be required; BMW recommend Optimol Paste PL, Staburags NBU 30 PTM compound, or Uni Moly C220 Slip Agent. If these cannot be obtained locally, seek the advice of a BMW dealer. Degrease all components carefully before applying new lubricant and apply only thin smears; do not allow any lubricant on to the friction material.

5 Fit the diaphragm spring to the housing wire ring applying a smear of lubricant to all points of contact between the two and to the three support arms securing the spring centre **(see illustrations)**. Ensure that the spring is the correct way round; refer to the illustrations to check this, or examine the spring closely, looking for polished wear marks where the spring contacts the pressure plate. With the spring the correct way round refit the pressure plate. Ensure that the balancing marks are correctly aligned; if BMW's own marks are used, the pressure plate mark must be 120° away from that on the housing. If your own marks were made as recommended, align the pressure plate mark with that of the housing. Apply a smear of lubricant to all points of contact between the spring and pressure plate.

6 Fit the friction plate to the pressure plate, ensuring that it is fitted the correct way round;

the centre boss extended end should face the gearbox **(see illustration)**.

7 Refit the cover plate, aligning the balancing mark as described above. Apply a smear of lubricant to the cover dowels to prevent corrosion **(see illustration)**. Before the screws are fully tightened, the friction plate must be centred. The easiest way of doing

this is to push the gearbox input shaft into the clutch assembly and to line it up with the dowels protruding from the rear of the bellhousing. If this is not possible it will be necessary to acquire the BMW centring tool No. 21 2 670 or to make up a substitute for it **(see illustrations)**. Insert the tool into the friction plate centre splines, passing the long

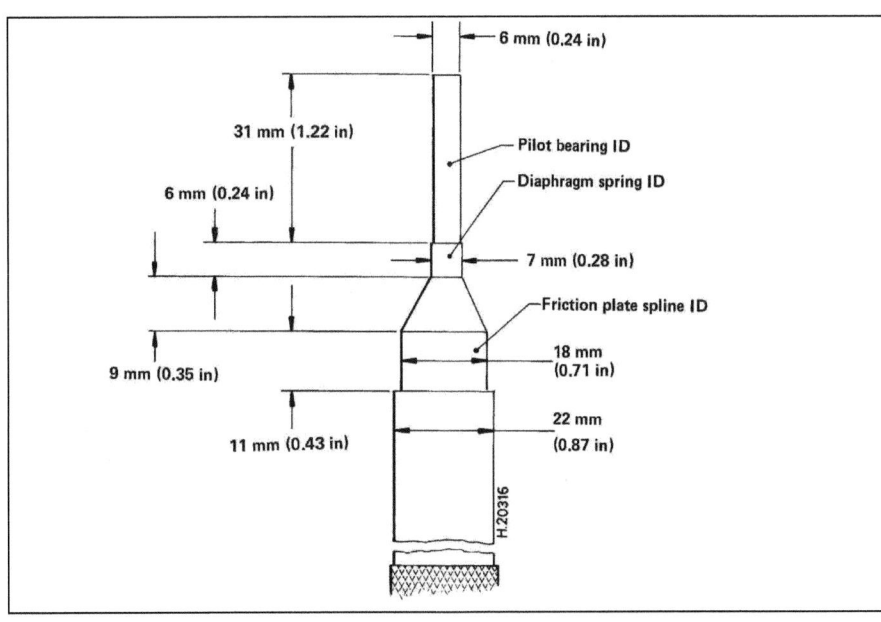

5.7c Clutch friction plate centring tool

3•6 Clutch

nose into the output shaft pilot bearing. The BMW tool now incorporates a bridge which fits on the bellhousing locating dowels to ensure perfect alignment. With the friction plate aligned, tighten the cover plate bolts or screws evenly and in a diagonal sequence to the specified torque wrench setting **(see illustration)**.

8 Apply a smear of lubricant to the pushrod and pilot bearing and to the splines of the gearbox input shaft and friction plate centre before refitting the gearbox.

6 Clutch release mechanism - removal, examination and reassembly

1 Slacken the handlebar adjuster locknut, screw in the adjuster to gain the maximum cable free play and disconnect the cable from the operating lever on the gearbox.

2 The lever pivot pin is retained by a circlip at each end; remove the right-hand circlip and plain washer and pull the pivot pin out to the left **(see illustration)**. On models fitted with the side stand retracting mechanism the link rod nut must first be unscrewed so that the lever return spring pressure is released; the lever and spring can then be withdrawn with the pivot pin **(see illustrations)**.

3 Slacken the clamp screw securing the rubber boot to the gearbox cover and withdraw the lever assembly, followed by the coil spring, the thrust piston and the thrust bearing (piston and bearing combined on later models) **(see illustration)**. On 100 models only, withdraw the clutch pushrod. These last three items can be removed using a suitable pair of pliers or similar, but if they prove to be awkward a piece of hooked wire or a strong magnet (the aluminium alloy pushrod has a steel cap and head) should be able to extract them. If they are bent or stuck fast; the gearbox must be removed to release them. Note that the rear wheel must be removed (100 models) only to permit the pushrod to be completely withdrawn.

4 On 75 models the pushrod has a raised flange at its front end which bears against the clutch spring; it is therefore necessary to remove the gearbox (see Chapter 4) before the pushrod can be withdrawn. Remove the clutch release components as described above, then tap the pushrod forwards out of the thrust bearing front race and pull it forwards out of the input shaft. On refitting, grease it thoroughly and push it very carefully backwards through the input shaft rear seal; a very thin layer of insulating tape wrapped around its tip would also help to protect the seal lips as the pushrod end passes through them. Hold the pushrod in place when it is

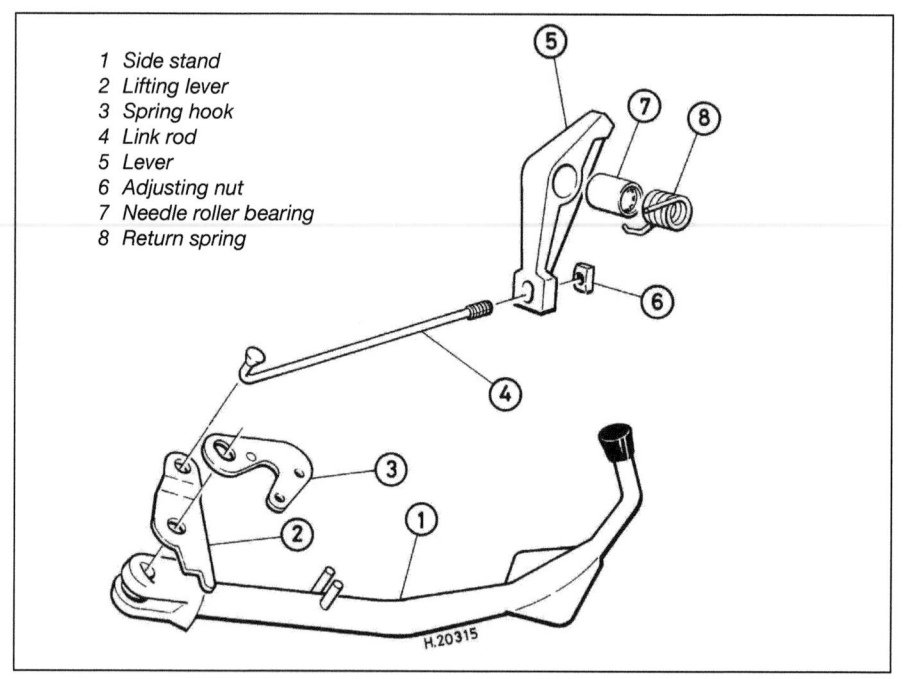

5.7d Tighten clutch cover bolts or screws evenly to specified torque setting

6.2a Withdraw circlip and washer, then tap clutch release pivot out to left

1 Side stand
2 Lifting lever
3 Spring hook
4 Link rod
5 Lever
6 Adjusting nut
7 Needle roller bearing
8 Return spring

6.2b Side stand retracting mechanism – late models

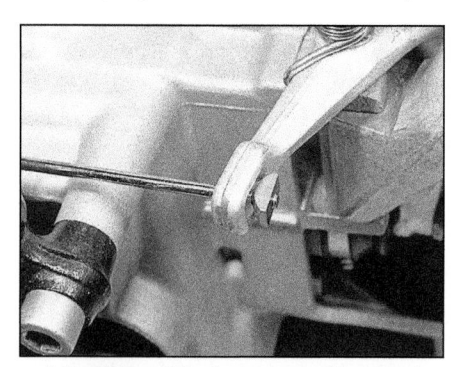

6.2c Where fitted, unscrew side stand retracting mechanism link rod nut

6.2d Withdraw retracting mechanism lever with release lever pivot pin

6.3 Slacken clamp to release rubber boot and lever

Clutch 3•7

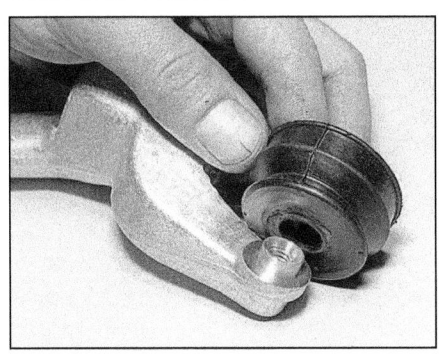

6.5 Check rubber boot for splits or tears – renew if leaking

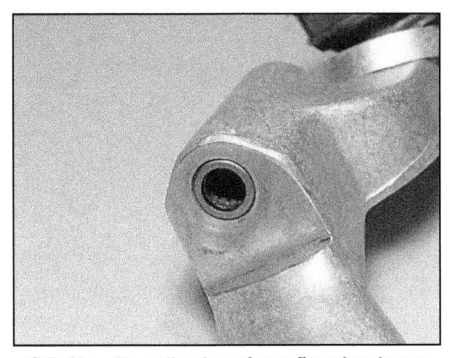

6.7 Needle roller bearings fitted to lever pivots – pack with grease on refitting

6.9a Pushrod can be withdrawn to rear on 100 models – gearbox must be removed first on 75 models

fully inserted, remove the tape (if used) and use a hammer and a tubular drift such as a socket spanner to tap the bearing race on to its rear end. Lubricate the pushrod front end and clutch plate splines before refitting the gearbox.

5 Check all components, cleaning them thoroughly. The pushrod must be straight; roll it on a flat surface such as a sheet of plate glass to check for any signs of warpage. Check that the rubber boot is undamaged and that the thrust bearing and piston are undamaged and in good condition **(see illustration)**. If any signs of wear or damage are found on any component it must be renewed.

6 Check that the thrust piston is able to move freely in the casting, if it has distorted so that the maximum outside diameter of 28.7 mm (1.13 in) is exceeded there is danger of the piston tying in the casting and preventing smooth clutch operation; from June 1988 a combined thrust bearing and piston was fitted.

7 Check the lever pivot bearings, if these are worn or corroded they must be driven out and renewed. Immerse the alloy lever in boiling water (taking due care to prevent any risk of injury) to ease the task of removal and refitting. Pack the lever bores with grease on reassembly **(see illustration)**.

8 Whenever the gearbox is removed, examine the condition of the pilot bearing bush in the engine output shaft rear end. This carries the front end of the pushrod; if the pushrod is a slack fit at any time, or if the bearing is otherwise damaged. it must be renewed. Lubricate it whenever the opportunity arises.

9 Reassembly is the reverse of the dismantling procedure. On 75 models fit the clutch pushrod as described above, then refit the gearbox (see Chapter 4). On 100 models pack a small amount of lubricant via the seal into the input shaft; grease or oil the pushrod and refit it **(see illustration)**. On all models, oil the release bearing, the thrust piston and coil spring with gearbox oil as they are refitted **(see illustrations)**. Note that from June 1988 a combined thrust bearing and piston was fitted.

10 Refit the rear wheel, if disturbed (100 models only). Connect the clutch cable and adjust the clutch as described in Chapter 1.

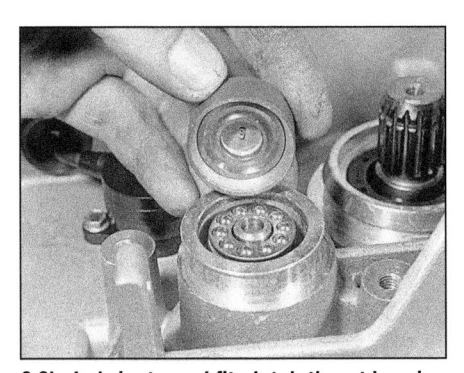

6.9b Lubricate and fit clutch thrust bearing as shown, followed by thrust piston (early models) . . .

6.9c . . . coil spring and release lever assembly

6.9d Retracting mechanism lever return spring fits as shown

Notes

Chapter 4
Gearbox

Contents

Bearings and seals - removing and refitting	4	General description	1
Gearbox - dismantling	3	Refitting the gearbox to the frame	9
Gearbox - examination and renovation	6	Removing the gearbox from the frame	2
Gearbox - reassembly	8	Shafts - dismantling and reassembly	5
Gearbox - oil change	see Chapter 1	Shafts endfloat and preload - checking and resetting	7
Gearbox - oil level check	see Chapter 1		

Degrees of difficulty

Easy, suitable for novice with little experience	Fairly easy, suitable for beginner with some experience	Fairly difficult, suitable for competent DIY mechanic	Difficult, suitable for experienced DIY mechanic	Very difficult, suitable for expert DIY or professional

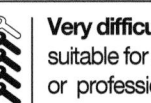

Specifications

Gearbox

Reduction ratios - inclusive of input shaft/layshaft reduction of 1.944 : 1 (35/18T):
- 1st . . . . 4.497 : 1
- 2nd . . . . 2.959 : 1
- 3rd . . . . 2.304 : 1
- 4th . . . . 1.879 : 1
- 5th . . . . 1.666 : 1

Layshaft and output shaft standard endfloat . . . . 0.050 - 0.150 mm (0.0019 - 0.0059 in)

Input shaft preload:
- Tolerance . . . . 0.030 - 0.080 mm (0.0012 - 0.0032 in)
- Approximate equivalents of preload values, expressed in friction values:
  - 0.030 mm (0.0012 in) preload . . . . 0.19 ± 0.02 Nm (0.14 ± 0.01 lbf ft)
  - 0.055 mm (0.0022 in) preload . . . . 0.34 ± 0.02 Nm (0.25 ± 0.01 lbf ft)
  - 0.080 mm (0.0032 in) preload . . . . 0.50 ± 0.02 Nm (0.37 ± 0.01 lbf ft)

Gearbox lubrication

Recommended oil . . . . Good quality hypoid gear oil of API class GL-5 or to specification MIL-L-2105 B or C

Viscosity:
- Above 5°C (41°F) . . . . SAE 90
- Below 5°C (41°F) . . . . SAE 80
- Alternatively . . . . SAE 80W90

Capacity . . . . 850 ± 50 cc (1.50 ± 0.09 Imp pint, 0.90 ± 0.05 US qt)

Torque wrench settings

	Nm	lbf ft
Selector lever/gearchange pedal shaft grub screw	17 ± 2	12.5 ± 1.5
Neutral detent assembly plug	13 ± 2	9.5 ± 1.5
Front cover retaining screws	9 ± 1	6.5 ± 0.5
Gearbox/bellhousing retaining screws	16 ± 1	12 ± 0.5
Engine and transmission unit/frame mountings:		
Early (1984, 1985) 100 models	32	23.5
Late (1986 on) 100 models, all 75 models	40.5 ± 4	30 ± 3
Filler and drain plugs	20 ± 3	15 ± 2

4•2 Gearbox

1 General description

The gearbox is a separate unit bolted on to the rear face of the engine unit and carries the clutch friction plate on its input shaft. Developed with and built for BMW by Getrag, the gearbox is a five-speed constant-mesh type which differs from general motorcycle practice in being all indirect, with a three shaft layout.

The input shaft rotates on taper roller bearings which are preloaded in service by the addition of shims between the front bearing and a collar on the shaft. The shaft carries a two lobe face-cam shock absorber tensioned by a single coil spring to damp out transmission shock loads and transmits drive from the clutch to the output shaft via the layshaft.

These latter two shafts rotate in ball journal bearings and apart from the helical-cut top gear pinions, use straight-cut gears. The different gear ratios are selected by moving two pinions on the output shaft and one on the layshaft. These pinions are splined on to their respective shafts and have integral dogs which lock into corresponding dogs or slots in their neighbouring pinions, thus locking the second pinion to the shaft to transmit the drive. The sliding pinions are controlled by selector forks which are guided by slots machined in a selector drum. The drum is rotated by a claw mechanism operated from the gearchange pedal and fitted with a spring-loaded positive stop roller arm, or detent arm. and a limiting pawl on the selector claw arm which rotates the drum to prevent overselection. A spring-loaded ball provides the neutral detent mechanism and a switch on the outside of the rear cover transmits information about the selector drum position to the instrument panel where a green lamp lights when neutral is selected (ignition switched on) and a liquid-crystal display (LCD) panel in the tachometer (rev counter) face indicates which gear is selected.

2 Removing the gearbox from the frame

Note: *It is possible to remove the engine and transmission as a single unit from the frame, and then to separate the unit into its major components. If this course is preferred, refer to Chapter 2 for details of the procedure. Given below are instructions on removing the transmission from the frame, leaving the clutch and engine in place.*

1 If the gearbox is to be overhauled, drain the oil (see *Routine maintenance and servicing*).
2 Lift the seat and remove both side panels, then disconnect the fuel injection control unit and withdraw it with the storage tray. See Chapter 6.
3 Remove the battery as described in *Routine maintenance and servicing*, then secure the coolant expansion tank to the frame seat tube out of harm's way. Remove their retaining screws and withdraw the ignition HT coil and alternator covers.
4 Remove the exhaust, as described in Chapter 6.
5 On K75, K75 C and K75 T models unscrew the adjusting nut to disconnect the rear brake operating rod. On all models, disconnect the wires from the speedometer impulse transmitter, the stop lamp rear switch and the gear position indicator switch.
6 Remove the rear wheel. See Chapter 10. Remove its four mounting nuts and withdraw the rear mudguard.
7 Working as described in Chapter 9, remove both footrest plates and the rear brake system components, disconnect the rear suspension unit bottom mounting and withdraw the final drive case, dismantle the swinging arm and withdraw the final drive shaft.
8 Disconnect the clutch cable from the release lever and remove it from the gearbox. See Chapter 1. Working as described in Chapter 3, remove the clutch release mechanism components.
9 Unscrew the starter motor mounting bolts and withdraw the starter motor. Enlist the aid of two assistants for the next stage.
10 Place a jack under the engine, with a block of wood positioned to protect the sump fins and raise the machine until the centre stand is clear of the ground; be very careful that the machine does not topple. Place blocks of wood or similar supports underneath the sump and in front of the front wheel. If a suitable support can be obtained, the frame rear end should be secured at the necessary height. If work is being carried out in a building with strong enough roof timbers a satisfactory support could be obtained by hanging the frame rear end from one of these timbers using a length of strong rope or a strong webbing strap. If all else fails have your assistants support the frame rear end while the gearbox is removed.
11 When the machine is securely supported, unscrew the four mounting bolts and withdraw the stand assembly **(see illustration)**. Unscrew the six gearbox/bellhousing Allen screws **(see illustrations)**.
12 Remove the two gearbox/frame mounting Allen bolts and pull the gearbox backwards off the clutch splines. There should be no difficulty in separating the gearbox from the engine. but if any problems are encountered first check that the starter motor and all the gearbox/bellhousing retaining screws have been removed, also any other component which might prevent separation. If the gearbox is still stuck in place it is probably because one of the locating dowels is corroded. Apply a good quantity of penetrating fluid to the affected area, allow time for it to work, then tap the gearbox backwards with a few firm blows of a

2.11a Remove the stand assembly ...

2.11b ... to permit the removal of all gearbox/bellhousing retaining screws

Gearbox 4•3

2.11c Gearbox housing

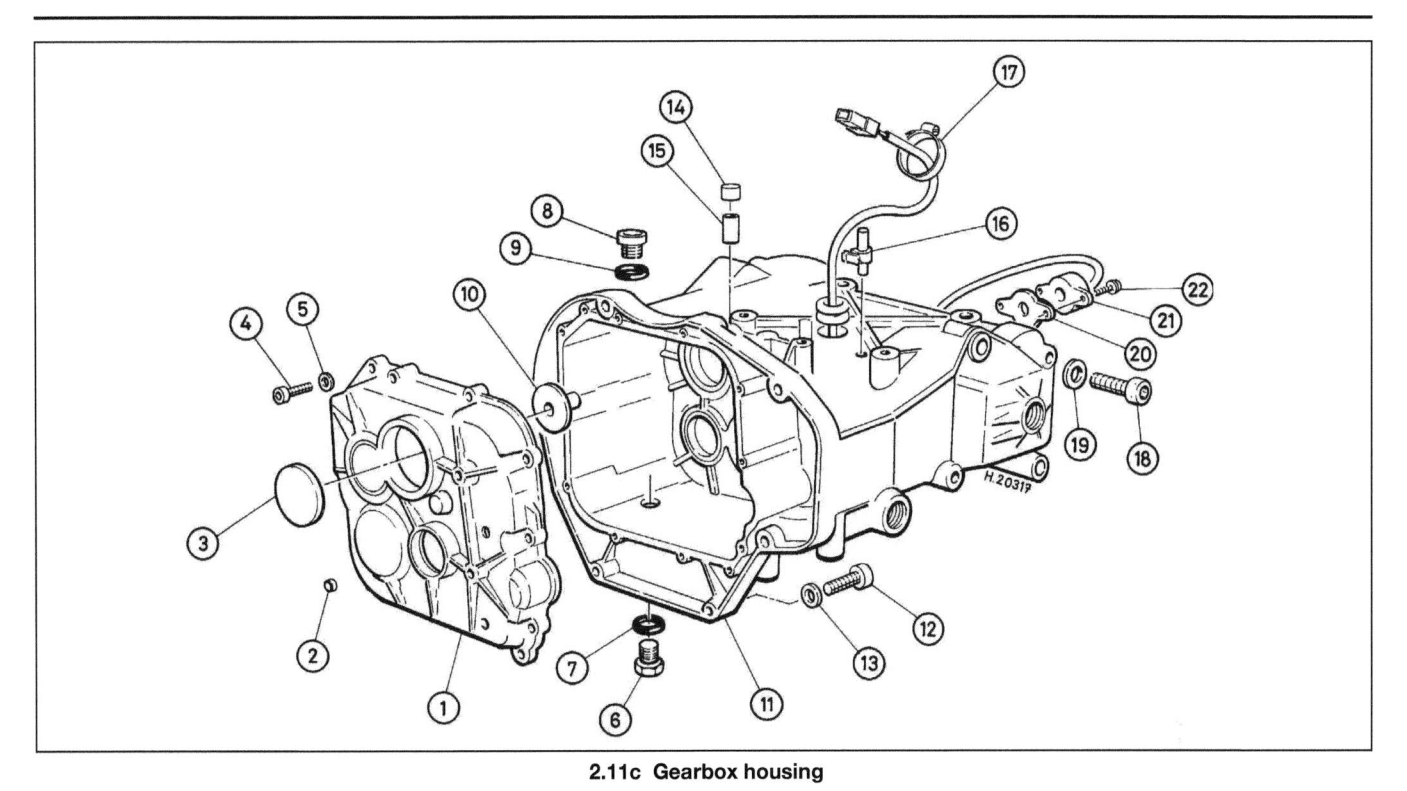

1 Front cover
2 Locking plug
3 Sealing plug
4 Screw – 10 off
5 Wave washer
6 Drain plug
7 Sealing washer
8 Filler plug
9 Sealing washer
10 Oil guide
11 Gearbox housing
12 Screw – 6 off
13 Washer – 6 off
14 Cap
15 Breather sleeve
16 Clamp
17 Cable clamp
18 Gearbox/frame mounting bolt – 2 off
19 Washer – 2 off
20 Gasket
21 Neutral switch
22 Bolt – 2 off

soft-faced mallet on the swinging arm pivot or frame mounting lugs.

13 Note the two large locating dowels protruding from the mating surface of the bellhousing rear face; it is essential that these are present and firmly fixed at all times to ensure that the gearbox is correctly aligned on the bellhousing. If this is not the case, the clutch action will be heavy and the clutch will suffer excessive spline wear and even serious damage. Note also the rubber fillet sealing the clutch housing, underneath the starter motor; check that this is securely installed.

14 On 75 models, and on 100 models if necessary, withdraw the clutch pushrod from the input shaft.

3 Gearbox - dismantling

> **HAYNES HiNT** When disassembling the transmission shafts, place the parts on a long rod or thread a wire through them to keep them in order and facing the proper direction. A large rubber band will keep them from being disturbed

1 Unscrew the neutral detent plug and tip out the coil spring and ball behind it (see illustration).The gear position indicator switch can be removed from the gearbox housing if required, but note that this is not essential for removal of the gearbox shafts and selector assembly.

2 Unscrew the front cover retaining screws, then withdraw the front cover; a loud click will be heard as the detent roller arm slips off the selector cam. BMW recommend that the cover is heated evenly, in an oven or similar to 100°C (212°F) to permit removal but it was found in practice that this was not necessary; although the cover was a tight fit, as soon as the retaining screws were removed a few taps on the input and output shaft ends with a soft-faced mallet broke the seal so that the cover could then be pulled off with the aid of a few further taps. Note the provision of a leverage point at the bottom right-hand (gearbox in position on the machine) 'corner' of the front cover; this is provided so that a screwdriver can be inserted to exert sufficient leverage to break the initial seal. Do not force the screwdriver (or any other tool) between the machined sealing surfaces, and do not exert excessive pressure to release a stubborn cover or it may crack.

3 As soon as the cover is removed, check inside the bearing locations and note exactly the presence and number of any shims that may be fitted. These shims must be clearly labelled so that they can be returned to their original locations on reassembly. Note also the two locating dowels in the mating surface.

4 Withdraw the selector fork shafts and place them in separate, clearly-marked containers; while they are identical when new they must not be confused when part-worn or the mismatching of part-worn components will cause greatly accelerated wear. Rotate all three selector forks away from their drum tracks.

5 Press back the selector claw arm and lift out the selector drum; a very light tap on its rear end with a soft-faced mallet will dislodge it if it proves stubborn. The cam and pins can be withdrawn from the drum if required.

6 Noting the presence of the separate rollers around their guide pins, remove and place in

3.1 Unscrew detent plug to release neutral detent assembly

separate, clearly-marked containers the selector forks. As each fork is removed use a spirit-based felt marker or similar to mark its top (or front surface).
7 Holding them together as a single unit, pull out the layshaft and output shaft. BMW recommend that the housing is heated evenly, in an oven or similar, to approximately 100°C (212°F) to permit shaft removal but again this was found not to be necessary in practice; a firm tap on the output shaft rear end from a soft-faced mallet proved sufficient to dislodge both shafts. With these removed the input shaft can be withdrawn. Check that there are no shims fitted at the shaft rear bearings.
8 To dismantle the selector mechanism, first prise off the black plastic cap from the gearbox breather then use a hammer and a suitable drift to tap out the breather sleeve from the inside; take care not to deform the sleeve.
9 Withdraw the circlip from the claw arm mounting guide rod and push the guide rod upwards and out through the breather orifice. Withdraw the claw arm and mounting; if desired the two can be separated by removing the retaining circlip from the claw arm pivot. Note how the spacer fits inside the loop of the claw arm spring.
10 Unscrew the tapered grub screw from the gearchange pedal shaft and withdraw the shaft: note the shim between the return spring and the housing wall. Displace the two circlips and withdraw the locating plate with the selector lever and return spring and the shim. If the gearchange pedal is to be removed from the shaft, first mark the shaft end next to the split in the lever so that the lever can be refitted in the same position.
11 The detent roller arm can be withdrawn from the front cover by lifting its return spring straight end over the cover stop lug to release the spring pressure and then removing the retaining circlip to release the arm. The roller can be removed and refitted after its retaining circlip has been withdrawn. Drive out from the inside the small plug which seals the passage next to the detent roller arm.

4 Bearings and seals - removing and refitting

1 All oil seals should be renewed as a matter of course whenever they are disturbed and especially if they show any signs of leakage or of damage **(see illustration)**.
2 Using a socket or similar as a drift, tap out the seal from the inside outwards; note first which way round the seal is fitted and at exactly what depth. In the case of the output shaft front sealing plug, this will mean that the oil guide must be removed as well; do not forget to clean it and install it with the protruding spout projecting inwards (to the rear) before fitting a new sealing plug **(see illustration)**. Where seals cannot be driven out from behind, eg input shaft rear end seal or gearchange shaft seal, they must be levered out using a tool with rounded edges, taking great care not to scratch or damage the seal housing **(see illustration)**.
3 To fit new seals, find a socket spanner or similar tube which bears only on the seals hard outer edge and use this to position the seal squarely in the mouth of its housing **(see illustration)**. Apply a thin smear of grease to the seal outside edge and tap it into place until it is flush with its surrounding housing or, in cases such as the output shaft rear seal, until it seats on a locating shoulder. Seals should be installed with the manufacturer's marks facing outwards, ie with the spring-loaded centre lip towards the fluid or gas being sealed. Note that the shaft rear seal, therefore is installed with the centre lip outwards, ie to the rear. If rotation arrows are found, the seal must be installed so that these face in the normal direction of rotation of the shaft.
4 All gearbox ball bearings should be easily removed with their shafts. If this is not the case, or if taper roller bearing outer races are to be removed, heat the casting evenly in an oven or similar to 100°C (212°F) and tap it firmly down on to a clean, flat wooden surface; this should dislodge the bearings or bearing outer races easily. Take great care to prevent any risk of personal injury when heating components or handling heated components. Note carefully the presence and number of any shims behind any of the bearings. Remember also to renew any seals that may have been left in place; the heat will almost certainly damage them.
5 If any of the shafts or bearings are renewed, or if the tolerances are found to be incorrect, the shim thicknesses must be adjusted. Before any bearings or seals are refitted, refer to Section 7 of this Chapter.
6 Ball bearings are refitted to their shafts using a hammer and a tubular drift such as a socket spanner, which bears only on the bearing inner race. Drive each bearing down its shaft until the inner race contacts the locating shoulder or other component against which it must rest.
7 Input shaft taper roller bearings are fitted in a similar manner but must be heated first to approximately 80°C (176°F) before they can be fitted The front bearing must be driven down to rest against shims placed against the shaft front flange and the rear bearing must be driven along the shaft until the retaining circlip can be refitted in its groove; the bearing must then be pulled back against the circlip to locate it.

4.1 Oil seals should be renewed as a matter of course – remove and refit as described in text

4.2a Note correct fitted position of output shaft oil guide

4.2b Be careful not to damage seal housing when levering seals out . . .

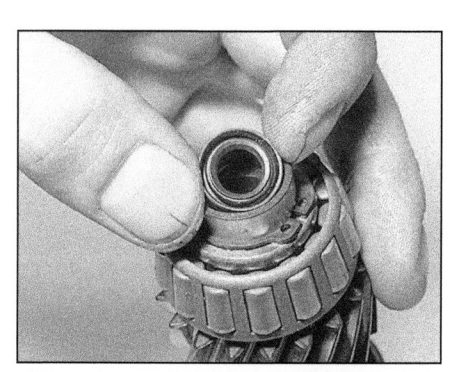

4.3 . . . and note how seal is fitted so that the new component can be correctly installed

Gearbox

5.1 Note method used to compress shock absorber spring before removing or refitting input shaft rear bearing

5.3 Input shaft shock absorber can be easily dismantled once rear bearing is removed

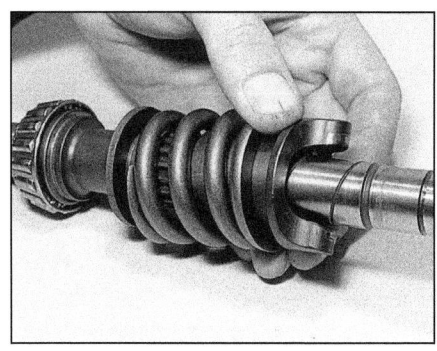

5.4 Fit spring seat, spring and shock absorber as shown – note shoulder and circlip groove on shaft rear end

5 Shafts - dismantling and reassembly

Input shaft

1 Before the input shaft can be dismantled some means must be devised of compressing safely the shock absorber spring. On the machine featured, a knife-edged bearing puller was assembled on the shaft rear end with its edges pulling against the shock absorber front cam (see illustration). This relieved spring pressure enough for the retaining circlip to be removed and the shaft rear bearing to be drawn off using another puller.

2 Gradually release spring pressure by unscrewing the compressing tool until the spring is at full extension (43 mm/1.7 in on the machine featured) and its pressure is released.

3 Dismantle the compressor and withdraw the rear cam, the front cam, the spring and the spring seat (see illustration). If the front bearing is to be renewed, draw it off using one of the pullers and note the presence and number of any shims fitted between it and the shaft collar. Do not forget to renew the bearing outer race at the same time. See Section 4.

4 On reassembly, lubricate the shaft splines and fit the spring seat, the spring, the front cam and the rear cam (see illustration). Clamp the shaft front end in a vice with soft jaws so that the shaft is held securely upright but cannot be marked or damaged. Obtain a new circlip as a safety measure; re-used circlips can occasionally fail in service.

5 BMW recommend that the bearing is heated to approximately 100°C (212°F) to permit refitting but this was found in practise to be unnecessary. Although the bearing was a tight fit it was possible to refit it using a hammer and a long tubular drift which bore only on the inner race. Drive the bearing down until it contacts the shoulder, at which point the circlip groove should be exposed. Fit the new circlip and use a bearing puller to draw the bearing back into contact with it (see illustration). Note, there must be no clearance between the bearing inner race and the circlip or the preload setting will be incorrect.

6 BMW recommend the input shaft front bearing be heated to approximately 80°C (176°F) before it can be installed. Whether this actually proves necessary or not it is essential that the correct size shim is placed against the shaft collar and that the bearing is driven down the shaft, using a tubular drift which bears only on its inner race, to rest firmly against the shim and collar. See Section 7.

Layshaft

7 If it is necessary to renew the layshaft bearings they can be removed and refitted using respectively a knife-edged bearing puller and a hammer and tubular drift of suitable size, as described above. If it is found to be faulty in any other way, the shaft must be renewed complete.

Output shaft

8 Use a knife-edged bearing puller or similar to remove the bearing from each end of the shaft, then remove the various gear pinions with their bushes or needle roller bearings, using circlip pliers to release the retaining circlips, where fitted (see illustration).

9 BMW recommend that the 1st gear pinion centre bush must be heated to approximately 80°C (176°F) to permit removal, using a puller bearing on the 4th gear pinion; in practice the bush was found to be a fairly slack fit and could be pulled off by hand.

10 Ensure that all components are stored exactly as they are removed so that they can be refitted the same way round and in the original sequence. If in doubt, refer to the photographs and illustration accompanying the text.

11 On reassembly, lubricate all components, and renew any circlips which appear to be distorted, damaged or worn. The accompanying illustrations show the rebuilding of an output shaft assembly; use this if in any doubt about the fitting or location of any component (see illustrations).

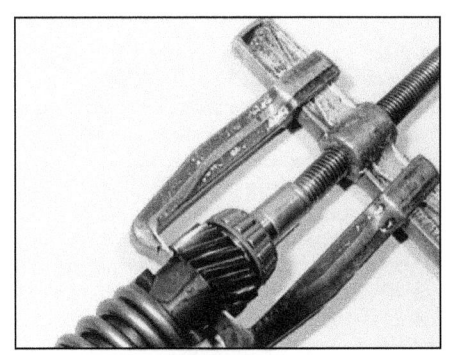

5.5 Bearing should be tapped down until circlip can be fitted, and then drawn back against circlip

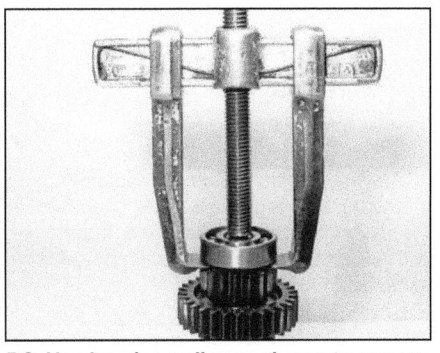

5.8 Use bearing puller as shown to remove shaft bearings

5.11a Fit shim and 5th gear pinion centre bush to output shaft as shown . . .

4•6 Gearbox

5.11b . . . followed by the 5th gear pinion and a second shim, and the rear bearing . . .

5.11c . . . which is fitted as shown to rest against the centre bush and shim

5.11d Fit the 3rd gear pinion as shown over the shaft front end followed by a circlip and a splined thrust washer

5.11e 2nd gear pinion rotates on a split-cage needle roller bearing

5.11f Fit the 2nd gear pinion as shown . . .

5.11g . . . pinion is located by a splined thrust washer and secured by a circlip

5.11h Fit 4th gear pinion as shown, followed by shim and 1st gear pinion centre bush

5.11i Fit 1st gear pinion as shown, followed by . . .

5.11j . . . shim and shaft front bearing

5.11k Note method used to refit gearbox bearings to shafts

6 Gearbox - examination and renovation

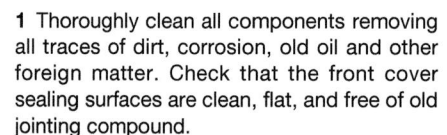

1 Thoroughly clean all components removing all traces of dirt, corrosion, old oil and other foreign matter. Check that the front cover sealing surfaces are clean, flat, and free of old jointing compound.
2 Check the housing and front cover for cracks, damage or other faults such as damaged threads. Most faults of this sort can be repaired but such work is usually for the expert, a good authorised BMW dealer should be able to recommend such an expert, depending on the nature of the fault.
3 Examine each of the gear pinions to ensure there are no chipped, rounded or broken teeth and that the dogs on the ends of the pinions are not rounded **(see illustration)**. Worn dogs are a frequent cause of jumping out of gear; renewal of the pinions concerned is the only effective remedy. Check that the inner splines are in good condition and the pinions are not slack on the shafts. Bushed pinions require special attention in this respect, since wear will cause them to rock.
4 Check both the input and the output shafts for worn splines, damaged threads and other

Gearbox 4•7

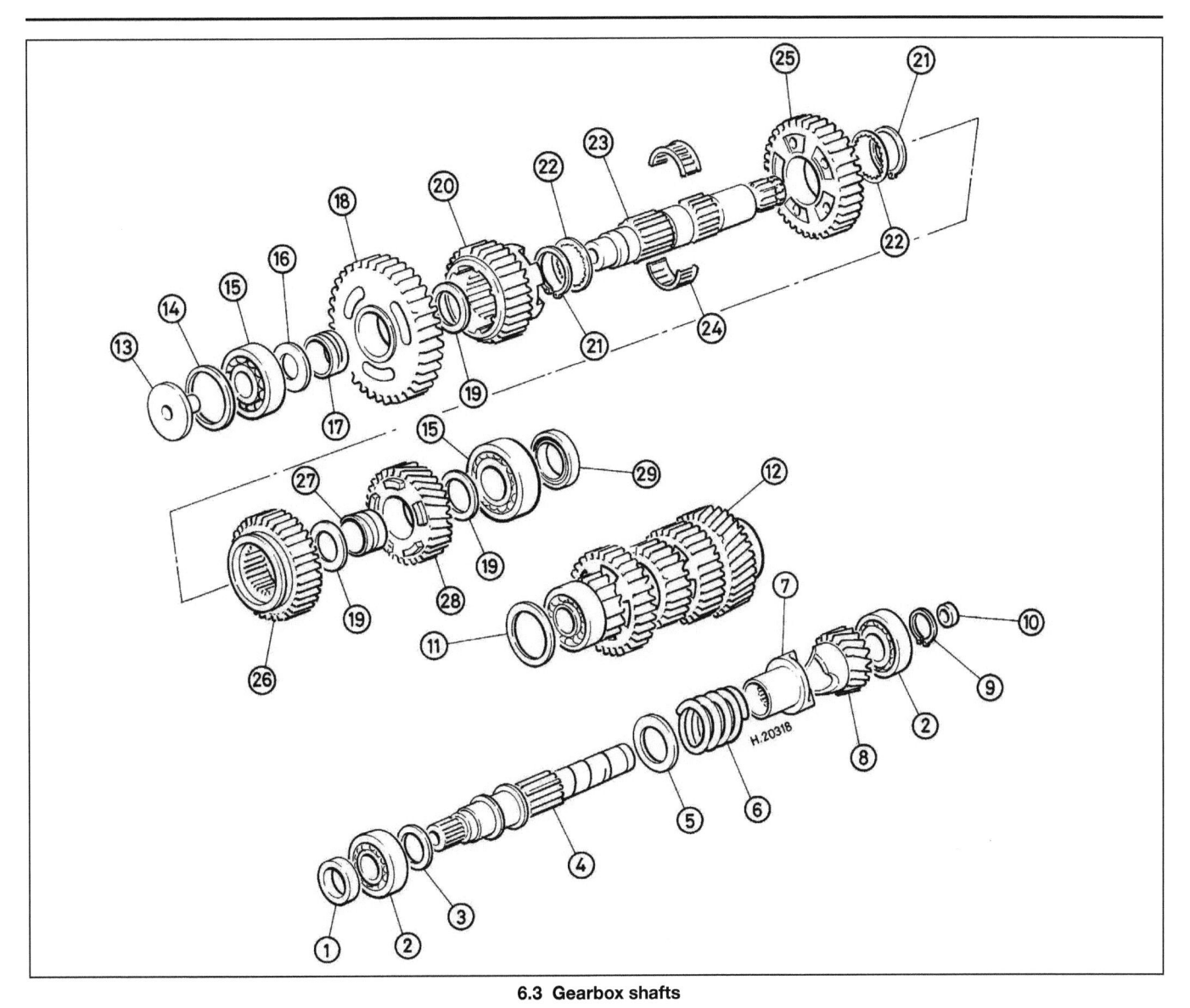

6.3 Gearbox shafts

1 Oil seal	7 Shock absorber front cam	12 Layshaft assembly	19 Shim – 3 off
2 Taper roller bearing – 2 off	8 Shock absorber rear cam/drive gear	13 Oil guide	20 4th gear pinion
3 Shim – as required	9 Circlip	14 Shim – as required	21 Circlip – 2 off
4 Input shaft	10 Oil seal	15 Ball bearing – 2 off	22 Splined thrust washer – 2 off
5 Spring seat	11 Shim – as required	16 Shim	23 Output shaft
6 Coil spring		17 Bush	24 Split needle roller bearing
		18 1st gear pinion	25 2nd gear pinion
			26 3rd gear pinion
			27 Bush
			28 5th gear pinion
			29 Oil seal

points at which wear may occur, such as the extremities which pass through the bearings. If signs of binding or local overheating are evident. check both shafts for straightness.

5 Examine the selector forks to ensure they are not twisted or badly worn. Wear at the fork end will immediately be obvious; check each claw end in conjunction with the groove with which it normally engages. Do not overlook the roller which engages with the selector drum groove; this is subject to wear.

6 Check the remaining selector components for damage or wear. Check that all are straight and that there is little or no wear at the various points of contact. Renew any worn or damaged component.

7 As previously stated, all oil seals should be renewed as a matter of course whenever they are disturbed.

8 Wash the bearings thoroughly in a high flash-point solvent. Do not pull bearings off their shafts if they can be cleaned and checked in place. Do not 'spin' a dry bearing. If any radial play is evident, or if the bearing feels rough when turned, it should be renewed. Examine the inner and outer races and the balls or rollers for damage. Renew any bearing that is showing the least sign of pitting or discoloration on any of its tracks or elements.

> **HAYNES HiNT** *If any wear or damage is found on the selector drum, selector forks or the gearchange pedal arm, do not attempt any sort of repairs involving the use of heat. These components are made from a special light alloy which may well react strongly if heated excessively. It is recommended that all of these components are renewed if they are found to be worn or damaged.*

4•8 Gearbox

9 Any circlips that were disturbed during the course of dismantling should be examined closely and renewed if there is the slightest doubt about their condition. If any are a slack fit on their shafts they must be renewed as a matter of course.
10 Similarly the various springs in the selector mechanism should be renewed if there is any doubt about their condition. Unless they are actually damaged, in which case renewal should be automatic, it is difficult to assess whether springs are fatigued or not.

7 Shafts endfloat and preload - checking and resetting

1 If any of the gearbox shafts are renewed, or if any of their bearings are renewed, the fit of the shafts in the gearbox must be checked and adjusted, if necessary, using shims.

Layshaft and output shaft

2 With the gearbox housing stripped and heated evenly, in an oven or similar, to approximately 100°C (212°F), check that each shaft is completely rebuilt and that its bearings are pressed as far on to the shaft as possible, then mesh the two together and install them in the housing. Tap each shaft firmly into place with a soft-faced mallet; the heated casing should ensure that the shaft rear bearings are fully and correctly seated.
3 Lay a straightedge across the housing mating surface next to the shafts and using a vernier caliper depth gauge or similarly accurate measuring device, measure the distance from the front edge of each shaft's front bearing outer race to the straightedge, ie the total amount each shaft projects beyond the gearbox housing mating surface; let this measurement be called dimension A.
4 Record this measurement for both shafts, then lay the straightedge across the front cover over the shaft front bearing housings. Measure the distance from the straightedge to the shoulder in each shaft's bearing housing against which the bearing outer race will locate; let this measurement be called dimension B.
5 For each shaft, subtract dimension A from dimension B to give the total amount of endfloat available for that shaft. Subtract the specified standard endfloat tolerance from this total to give the required thickness of shims.
6 Shims are available from BMW dealers in thicknesses of 0.30, 0.40 and 0.50 mm (0.0118, 0.0158 and 0.0197 in); use whatever number and combination of these that will reduce the endfloat as much as possible within the specified limits. Store the shims carefully with their respective shafts until reassembly.

Input shaft

7 Assemble the input shaft as described in Section 5 but do not yet fit the front bearing. Check that the rear bearing is correctly positioned against the circlip and that its outer race is pressed fully into the gearbox housing, then heat the front cover evenly, in an oven or similar, to approximately 100°C (212°F) and fit the front bearing outer race, ensuring that it is driven squarely into its housing to rest against the locating shoulder. Allow the cover to cool.
8 Fit the input shaft into the stripped housing and lay a straightedge across the housing mating surface next to the shaft. Use a vernier caliper depth gauge or similarly accurate measuring device to measure the distance from the straightedge to the shaft collar (the locating flange against which the shims and bearing will be fitted); let this measurement be dimension A.
9 Place the straightedge across the front cover mating surface over the shaft front bearing outer race and measure the distance from the straightedge to the rear edge of the outer race; let this measurement be dimension B.
10 Subtract dimension A from dimension B to give the total amount of endfloat available for the input shaft; let this be dimension C. However, since the input shaft must be **preloaded** (ie slightly compressed when the front cover is fitted) the required shim thickness is C **plus** the specified preload tolerance.
11 Shims are available from BMW dealers in thicknesses of 0.30, 0.40, 0.50, 1.42, 1.44, 1.46, 1.48 and 1.50 mm (0.0118, 0.0158, 0.0197, 0.0559, 0.0567, 0.0575, 0.0583 and 0.0591 in); use whatever number and combination of these that will preload the shaft as closely as possible within the specified limits. Fit the selected shims to the shaft and drive the bearing into place against them **(see illustration)**.
12 To check the preloading, assemble the shaft into the housing, lubricating its bearings with the specified oil, and refit the front cover, tightening its retaining screws to the specified torque wrench setting. The shaft oil seals must not be fitted yet or their drag may produce a false reading.
13 The amount of effort required to rotate the shaft can be measured with a friction gauge or with an extremely accurate spring balance attached to the end of a lever of known length from the shaft centre, ie the setting is correct if the pull required is in the range 0.13 - 0.38 lb measured at the end of a lever 1 ft from the shaft centre. If the setting proves to be incorrect, the measurements or calculations must have been faulty at some point and the operation must be repeated until the setting is correct.

8 Gearbox - reassembly

1 All components should be completely clean and renewed or repaired as necessary. All bearings or bearing inner races should be installed correctly on their respective shafts and all oil seals, oil guides and taper roller bearing outer races should be installed in the housing or front cover, as appropriate.
2 Refit the detent roller arm and secure it with its circlip, ensuring that its spring is fitted as shown **(see illustrations)**
3 Refit the gearchange pedal to the shaft using the mark made on removal to ensure

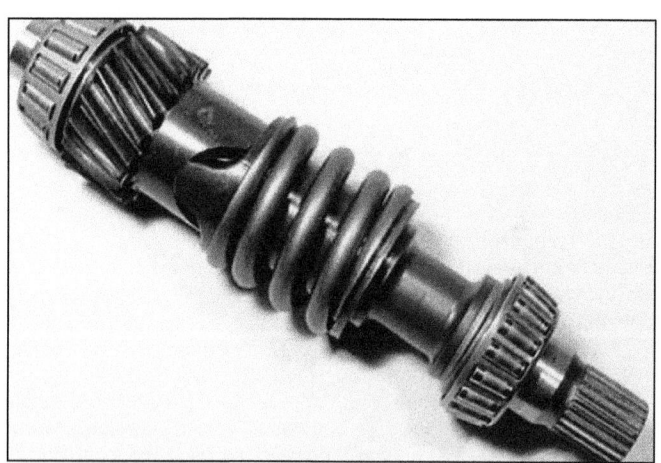

7.11 Input shaft preload shims are fitted between bearing and shaft collar

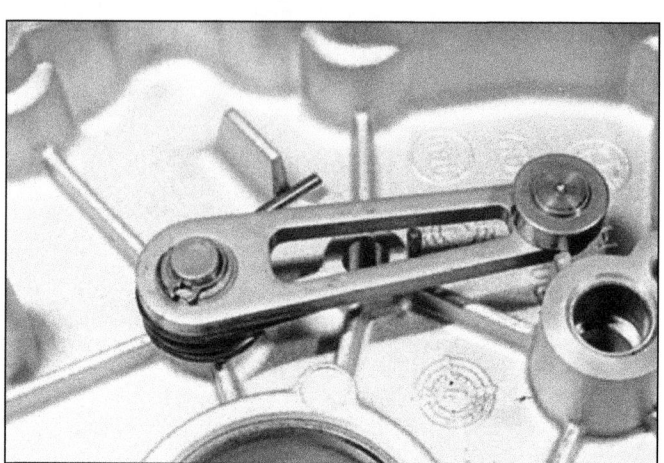

8.2a Refit detent roller arm with return spring as shown

Gearbox 4•9

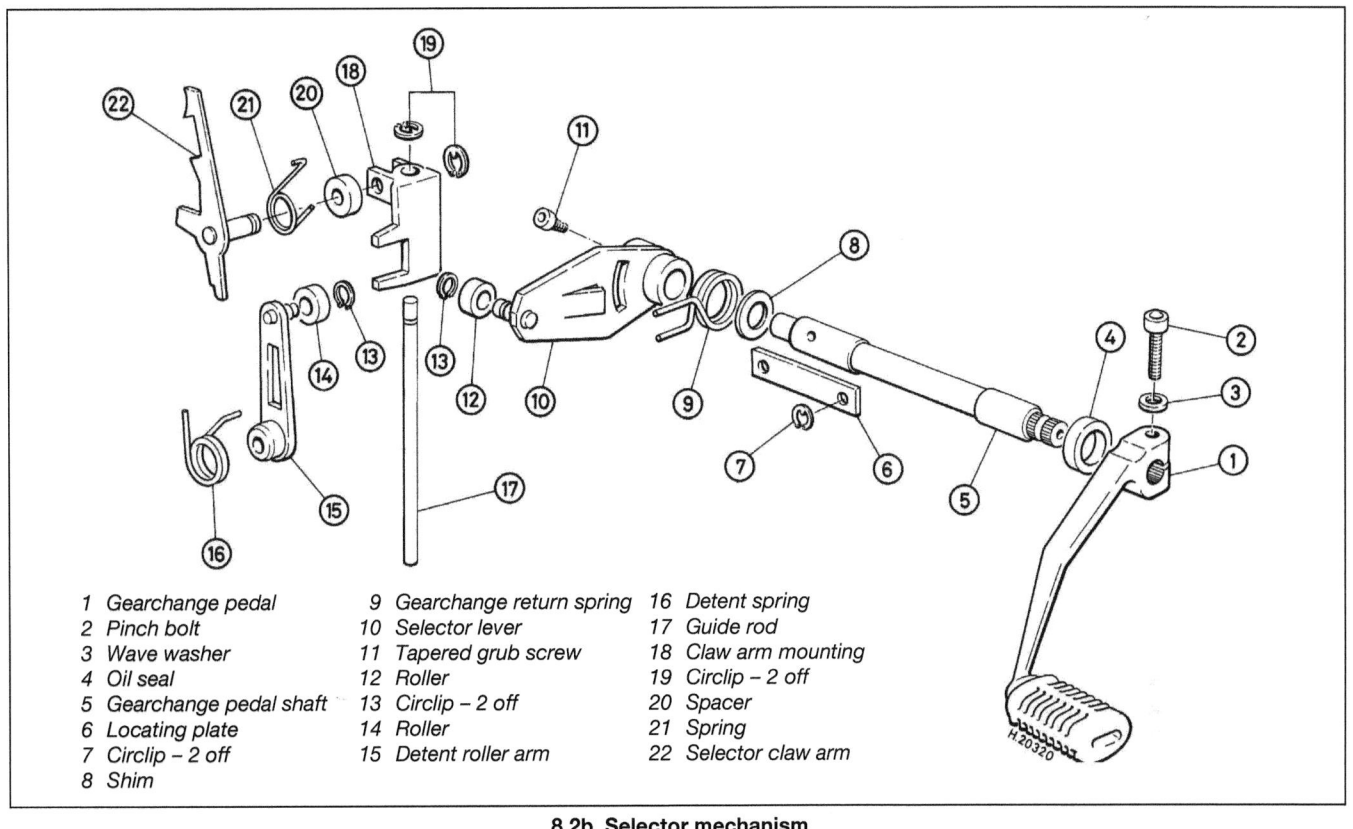

8.2b Selector mechanism

1. Gearchange pedal
2. Pinch bolt
3. Wave washer
4. Oil seal
5. Gearchange pedal shaft
6. Locating plate
7. Circlip – 2 off
8. Shim
9. Gearchange return spring
10. Selector lever
11. Tapered grub screw
12. Roller
13. Circlip – 2 off
14. Roller
15. Detent roller arm
16. Detent spring
17. Guide rod
18. Claw arm mounting
19. Circlip – 2 off
20. Spacer
21. Spring
22. Selector claw arm

that the pedal is correctly positioned **(see illustration)**. Tighten the pinch bolt securely.

4 Fit the return spring and the locating plate to the selector lever as shown **(see illustration)** and fit the assembly to the housing; do not forget the shim between the spring and the housing wall **(see illustration)**. Refit the two retaining circlips. Grease the gearchange pedal shaft and refit it, taking care not to damage the lips of the shaft oil seal. The shaft will fit only one way if the tapered grub screw is to lock it correctly to the selector lever; ensure that the two are correctly aligned, apply a few drops of Loctite 242 or similar thread-locking compound to the screw threads and refit it, tightening it securely **(see illustrations)**. Use the torque wrench setting, where specified.

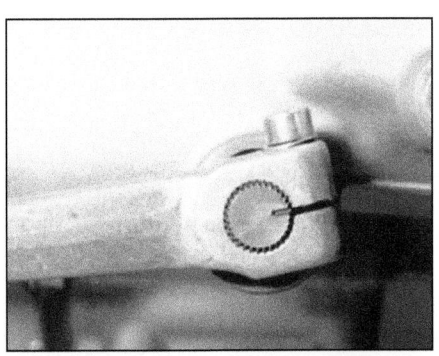

8.3 Mark made before removal will ensure gearchange pedal is refitted correctly to shaft

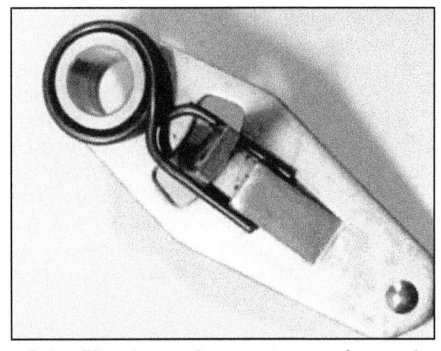

8.4a Fit selector lever return spring and locating plate to selector lever as shown

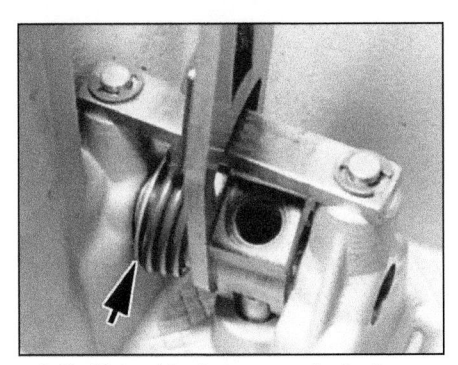

8.4b Note shim between selector lever assembly and housing wall

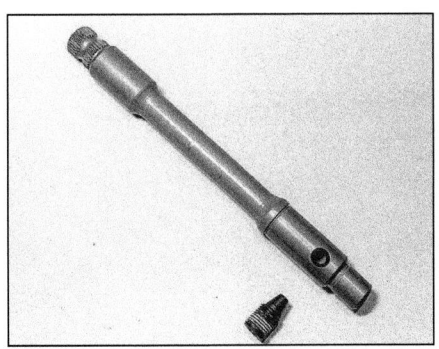

8.4c Gearchange pedal shaft will fit only one way – note tapered grub screw

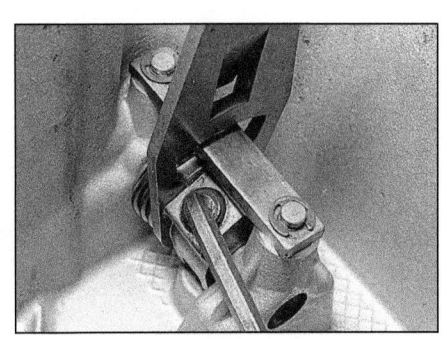

8.4d Tighten grub screw securely to retain gearchange pedal shaft use thread locking compound

4•10 Gearbox

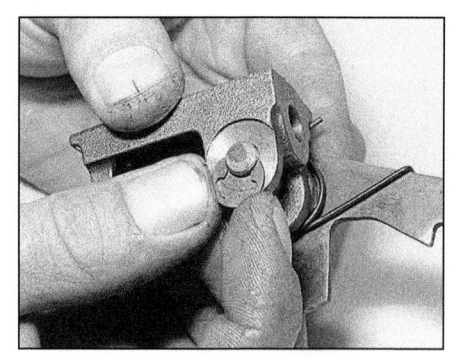

8.5a Fit claw arm spring and spacer to claw arm – refit pivot retaining circlip to secure to claw arm mounting

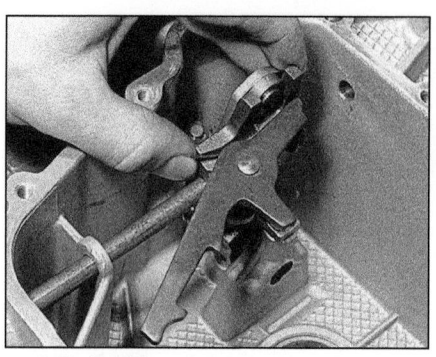

8.5b Position claw arm mounting as shown and refit guide rod . . .

8.5c . . . which is secured by a circlip

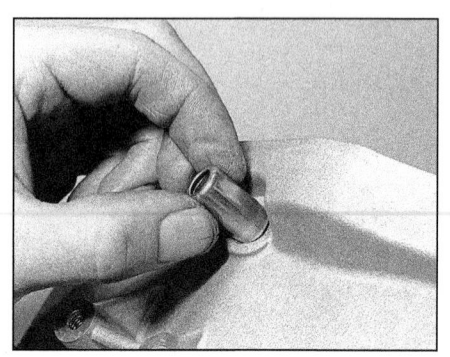

8.5d Breather sleeve must be carefully installed – see text . . .

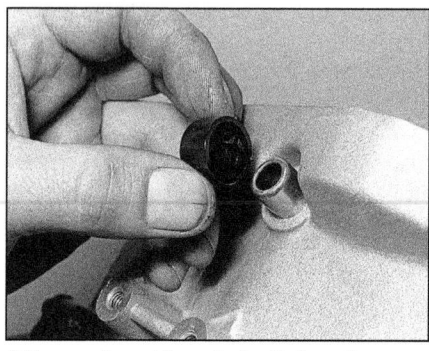

8.5e . . . do not forget plastic breather cap

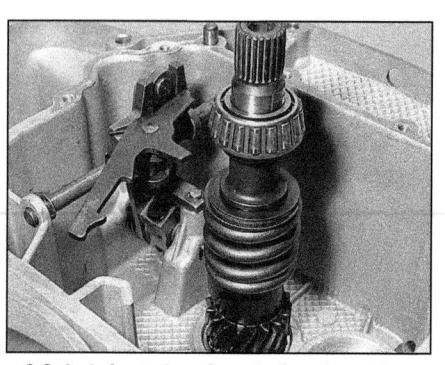

8.6 Lubricate bearings before installing input shaft

5 Fit the spacer and claw arm spring to the claw arm, ensuring that the spacer fits inside the spring loop. Fit the assembly to the claw arm mounting and secure it by refitting the pivot retaining circlip **(see illustration)**. Position the claw arm mounting and refit the guide rod and its circlip to retain it **(see illustrations)**. Tap the gearbox breather sleeve into its orifice, but be careful not to drive it so far in that the black cap rests on the gearbox housing **(see illustration)**. Refit the black plastic cap to the breather sleeve **(see illustration)**.

6 Install the input shaft in its rear bearing; lubricate both bearings with the specified oil **(see illustration)**.
7 Lubricate their bearings, bearing surfaces and all other points of contact, then mesh together the gear pinions of the layshaft and output shaft assemblies and insert the two as a single unit **(see illustration)**. Rock the input shaft away from the layshaft until its bearing is clear of the layshaft gear pinion teeth. Press the layshaft and output shaft into position and straighten the input shaft.
8 Note that if the shaft bearings will not fit easily into the housing locations the housing must be heated evenly, in an oven or similar, to approximately 100°C (212°F) to permit this. If this is found to be necessary first remove all components which might be damaged by the heat and take great care to prevent any risk of personal injury when heating components or when handling heated components.
9 Check that all three shafts are free to rotate, then install the selector forks using the marks or notes made on dismantling to identify each fork and which way it is fitted **(see illustration)**. If no marks were made, proceed as follows:

8.7 Layshaft and output shafts are installed as a single unit – lubricate thoroughly

8.9 Fit selector forks as described in text

Gearbox 4•11

10 The first fork to be refitted is to the output shaft 3rd gear pinion groove; this actually selects 5th gear and is the widest across the claw ends of the three forks **(see illustration)**. It is fitted with its guide pin towards the front of the gearbox housing; this will engage the selector drum rear groove.

11 The next fork selects 3rd and 4th gears and is fitted to the layshaft sliding gear pinion groove; its guide pin will engage the selector drum centre track. It is the narrowest across the claw ends and can be identified by its long neck. It is refitted with its guide pin towards the rear of the gearbox housing.

12 The last fork selects 1st and 2nd gears and is refitted with its guide pin towards the rear of the gearbox housing, to engage the selector drum front groove. Of medium width across the claw ends, it is fitted to the output shaft 4th gear pinion groove.

13 Swing all three forks as far as possible away from the selector drum and refit the separate roller to each fork's guide pin; retain the roller with a dab of grease **(see illustration)**.

14 Fit the five selector pins and the small locating pin to the selector drum front end, refit the selector cam aligning its keyway with the locating pin and insert the drum assembly, pressing back the claw arm to permit this **(see illustrations)**.

15 Rotate the drum until the cam neutral detent recess is approximately in the 12 o'clock position from the drum centre, ie in the neutral position. Swing the forks back into contact with the drum, engaging each fork's guide pin roller in its respective drum groove. Lubricate and refit the selector fork shafts, ensuring that each is pressed fully home in its original location **(see illustration)**.

16 Ensuring that the correct number and thickness of shims are used, refit the output shaft and layshaft shims to their respective bearing housings in the front cover. Press the

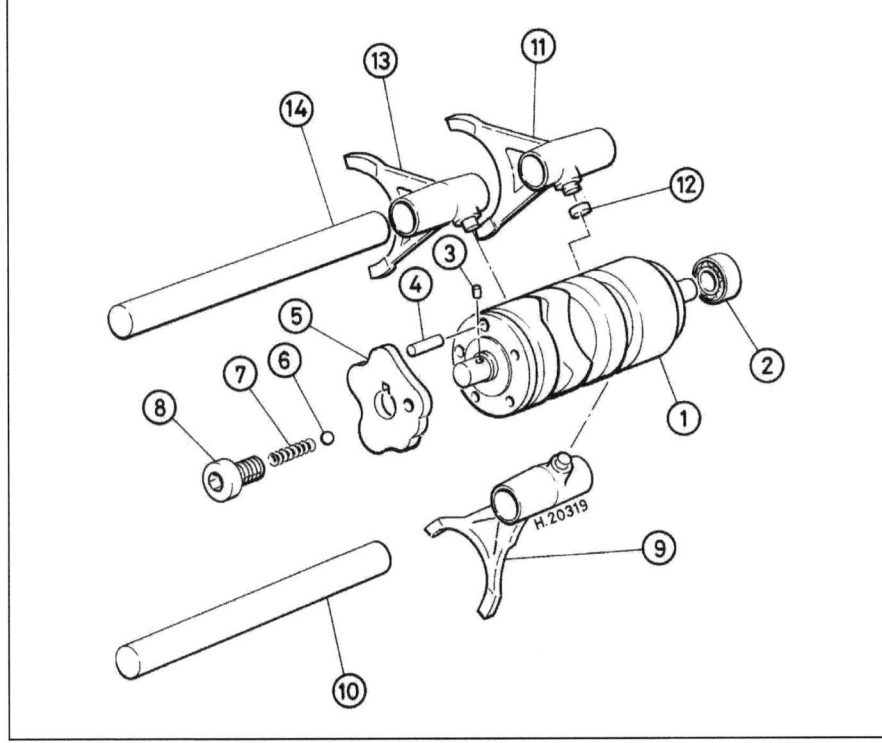

8.10 Selector drum and forks

1 Selector drum
2 Oil seal
3 Locating pin
4 Selector pin – 5 off
5 Selector cam
6 Ball
7 Spring
8 Neutral detent plug
9 3rd/4th gear selector fork
10 Selector fork shaft
11 5th gear selector fork
12 Roller – 3 off
13 1st/2nd gear selector fork
14 Selector fork shaft

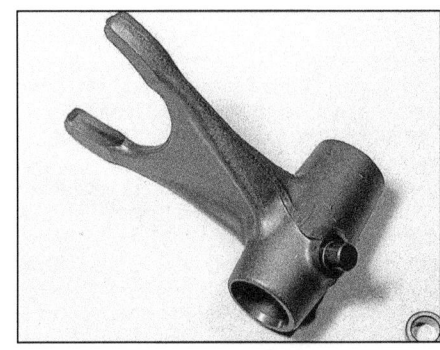

8.13 Do not forget roller fitted to each fork guide pin – use grease to retain while reassembling

8.14a Fit selector pins and locating pin to drum front end . . .

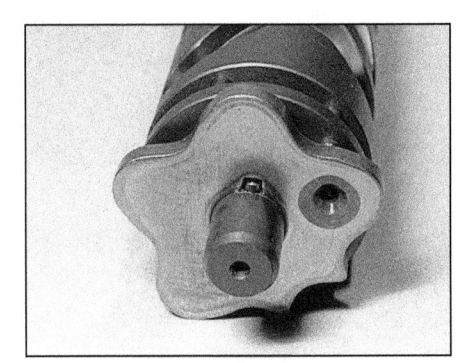

8.14b . . . followed by selector cam – note neutral detent recess

8.14c Press back claw arm to fit selector drum assembly

8.15 Rotate drum to neutral position as shown, align forks and refit fork shafts

4•12 Gearbox

8.16 Unless cover is to be heated to refit, use grease to stick shims into bearing locations

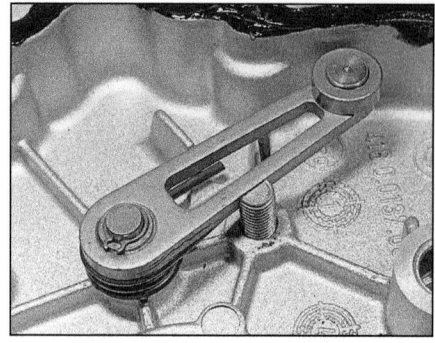

8.17 Note stop fabricated to retain detent arm clear of selector cam

8.18 Check all components are correctly installed before refitting front cover

shims fully into place and use grease to retain them **(see illustration)**.

17 Make up a stop from a suitably-sized rod (a convenient bolt was used for the photograph, with a flat ground on one side to ensure that it would not slip) or similar to hold the detent roller arm clear of the selector drum cam while the front cover is refitted **(see illustration)**. Apply a thin smear of Loctite 573 or similar jointing compound to the degreased mating surfaces. Make a final check that all components have been refitted and that all shafts are free to rotate.

18 BMW recommend that the front cover is heated evenly, in an oven or similar, to approximately 100°C (212°F) to permit refitting. This was found not to be necessary since the cover could be removed and refitted quite easily by hand **(see illustration)**. If it is necessary to heat the cover, take great care to avoid the risk of personal injury when heating components or when handling components that have been heated. Remember also to remove first components such as oil seals which will be damaged by the heat, and to place the shims on the bearings, not in the front cover bores.

19 Press the cover into place, then refit and tighten to the specified torque setting the cover retaining screws. Pull out the roller arm stop; a distinct click should be heard as the arm contacts the cam.

20 Rotating the input shaft, and if necessary the output shaft, check that the shafts rotate smoothly and that all gears can be selected with reasonable ease. If all is well, drift the locking plug into the small orifice drilled next to the detent roller arm pivot **(see illustrations)**.

21 Refit the ball and spring of the neutral detent assembly, apply a few drops of Loctite 242 or a similar thread locking compound to its threads, and refit the neutral detent plug, tightening it to the specified torque wrench setting **(see illustrations)**.

22 Refit any oil seals which have not yet been installed. If removed, install the gear position indicator switch on the gearbox housing rear face; do not overtighten its retaining screws or the switch may crack. Position the switch carefully so that the cutaway section of the selector drum shaft aligns with that of the switch rotor **(see illustration)**.

8.20a Insert locking plug into drilled orifice . . .

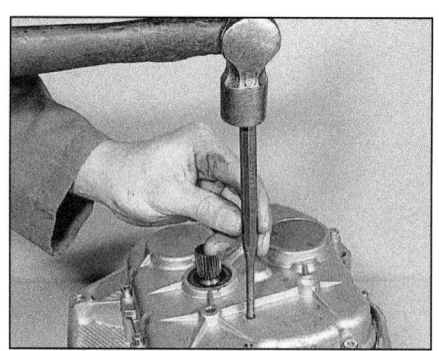

8.20b . . . and secure with a hammer and drift

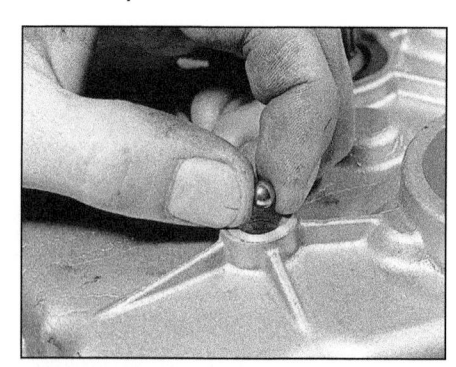

8.21a Refit neutral detent ball – drop into selector cam recess . . .

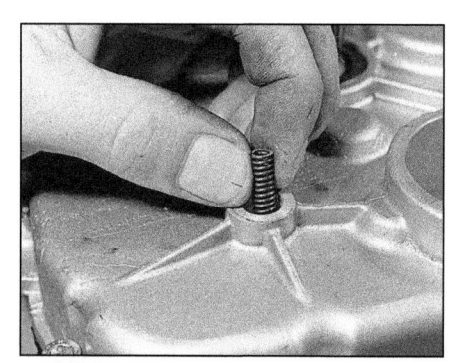

8.21b . . . followed by coil spring . . .

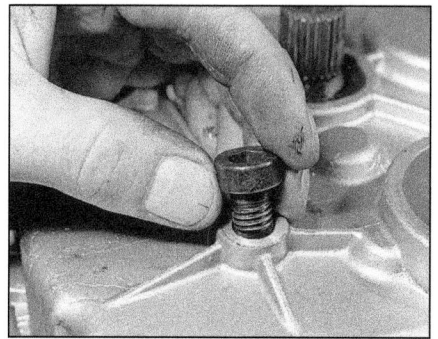

8.21c . . . and plug – secure with thread locking compound

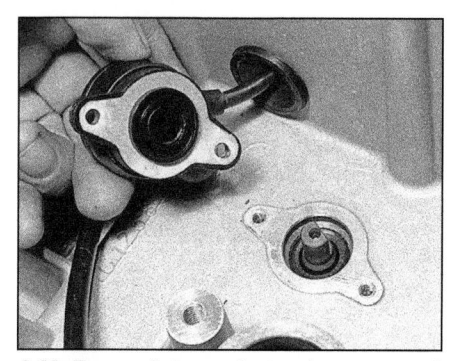

8.22 Ensure flat on selector drum rear end engages with switch rotor when refitting switch

Gearbox 4•13

9 Refitting the gearbox to the frame

1 If the gearbox has just been dismantled make a final check that all components have been refitted and secured correctly, that all shafts are free to rotate and that all gears can be selected with reasonable ease. On 75 models, and 100 models if required, lubricate and install the clutch pushrod. See Chapter 3.

2 Apply a thin coat of the specified lubricant to the splines of the clutch friction plate and the gearbox input shaft, also to the various components of the clutch release mechanism **(see illustration)**. See Chapter 3.

3 If any problems were encountered due to corrosion when separating the gearbox from the bellhousing, thoroughly clean the mating surfaces and dowels with a soft wire brush and apply a thin smear of grease to prevent corrosion in the future. Check that both dowels and the rubber fillet are refitted.

4 Offer up the gearbox to the rear of the engine, aligning the clutch/input shaft splines and the locating dowels. Although there should be no real difficulty in this, some manoeuvring may be required to get the splines to mate correctly; if necessary select top gear and rotate the output shaft back and forth to assist the input shaft in engaging.

5 When the gearbox is correctly installed, refit the six retaining Allen screws, tightening each to their specified torque setting, then refit the two gearbox/frame mounting Allen bolts and tighten them to the appropriate torque wrench settings.

6 Refit the stand assembly, tightening securely its four mounting Allen screws. Lower the centre stand and lower the complete machine until it is securely supported on the stand and front wheel. Refit the starter motor (see Chapter 11) and the clutch release mechanism components (see Chapter 3). Connect the clutch cable and adjust it as described in Chapter 1.

7 Working as described in Chapter 9, refit the swinging arm and final drive shaft, the final drive case and rear brake components and secure the rear suspension unit bottom mounting to the final drive case. Refit the footrest plates, the rear mudguard, the rear wheel and the number plate bracket.

8 Connect the rear brake operating rod (where appropriate), the speedometer impulse transmitter wire, the stop lamp rear switch wire and the gear position indicator switch wire.

9 Refit the exhaust system. See Chapter 6.

10 Refit the ignition HT coil and alternator covers and the battery and coolant expansion tank. Refit the fuel injection control unit and storage tray (see Chapter 6) followed by the seat and side panels.

11 Refill the gearbox with the specified amount and type of oil, then check the level. See Chapter 1.

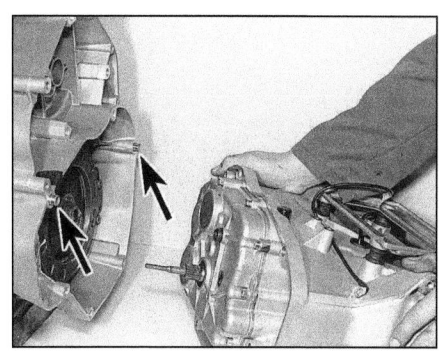

9.2 Lubricate shaft splines and clutch release – note locating dowels projecting from bellhousing rear face

Notes

Chapter 5
Cooling system

Contents

Cooling fan - removal, examination and refitting	10
Cooling system - check	see Chapter 1
Cooling system - draining	2
Cooling system - filling	4
Cooling system - flushing	3
Cooling system electrical components - removal and refitting	11
General description	1
Hoses and connections - removal, refitting and checking for leaks	7
Radiator - removal, cleaning and examination	5
Radiator pressure cap - testing	6
Thermostat - removal and testing	8
Water pump - removal, renovation and refitting	9

Degrees of difficulty

Easy, suitable for novice with little experience	**Fairly easy,** suitable for beginner with some experience	**Fairly difficult,** suitable for competent DIY mechanic	**Difficult,** suitable for experienced DIY mechanic	**Very difficult,** suitable for expert DIY or professional

Specifications

Coolant
Type .... Distilled water with antifreeze
Recommended antifreeze .... BMW-approved good quality long life antifreeze, glycol-based, with corrosion inhibitor, free from nitrides eg:
Fricotin
ICI 007 or 012 antifreeze
Glycoshell P300
Hoechst Genantin VP 1719
BASF Glysantin G41/23

Mixture ratio:
  Standard (down to -28°C/ -18°F) .... 60% water : 40% antifreeze
  Alternative (down to -36°C/ -33°F) .... 50% water : 50% antifreeze
Capacity overall:
  75 models .... Approx 3.00 lit (5.3 Imp pint, 3.2 US qt)
  100 models .... Approx 3.25 lit (5.7 Imp pint, 3.4 US qt)
Capacity of individual components - approximate:
  Radiator - 75 models .... 2.50 lit (4.4 Imp pint, 2.6 US qt)
  Radiator - 100 models .... 2.80 lit (4.9 Imp pint, 3.0 US qt)
  Expansion tank .... 0.40 lit (0.7 Imp pint, 0.4 US qt)

Radiator
Filler cap valve opens at .... 1.00 - 1.15 bar (14.5 - 16.7 psi) - approximately equal to temperature of 120°C (248°F)

Expansion tank
Filler cap valve opens at .... -0.1 bar (-1.5 psi)

5•2 Cooling system

Thermostat
Opens at .... 85°C (185°F)
Fully open at .... 92°C (198°F)

Electrical components
Cooling fan .... Cuts in at 103°C (217°F)
Coolant overheat warning lamp .... Lights at 111°C (232°F)

Torque wrench settings

	Nm	lbf ft
Coolant drain plug	9 ± 1	6.5 ± 0.5
Water pump impeller:		
Early models - 8 mm nut	21 ± 2	15.5 ± 1.5
Late models - 8 mm bolt	33 ± 4	24 ± 3
Oil/water pump assembly mounting screws	7 ± 1	5 ± 0.5
Oil/water pump cover screws	7 ± 1	5 ± 0.5
Coolant pipe stub mounting screws	7 ± 1	5 ± 0.5
Radiator mounting bolt or nut	8 ± 1	6 ± 0.5

1 General description

The cooling system uses a water/antifreeze coolant to carry away excess energy produced in the form of heat. The cylinders are surrounded by a water jacket from which the heated coolant is circulated by thermo-syphonic action in conjunction with a water pump driven from the output shaft front end. The hot coolant passes upwards through the coolant pipe stub and top hose to the radiator which is mounted on the frame downtubes to take advantage of maximum air flow. The coolant then passes across the radiator core where it is cooled by the passing air, through the thermostat and bottom hose and then to the water pump and engine where the cycle is repeated.

A thermostatically-controlled electric fan is fitted behind the radiator to aid cooling. A wax pellet type thermostat is fitted in the system to prevent coolant flow through the radiator when the engine is cold, thereby accelerating the speed at which the engine reaches normal working temperature; coolant is routed instead from the coolant stub through a bypass hose to the thermostat housing and bottom hose.

The complete system is partially sealed and pressurised, the pressure being controlled by a valve contained in the spring loaded radiator cap. By pressurising the coolant to approximately 14.5 psi, the boiling point is raised, preventing premature boiling in adverse conditions. The overflow pipe from the radiator is connected to an expansion tank into which excess coolant is discharged by pressure. The expelled coolant automatically returns to the radiator, to provide the correct level when the engine cools again. A valve in the tank filler cap opens at the required level of outside pressure (relative to that inside the tank) to admit air as necessary.

2 Cooling system - draining

Warning: to avoid the risk of personal injury such as scalding, the cooling system should be drained only when the engine and cooling system are cold. Note also that coolant will attack painted surfaces; wash away any spilled coolant immediately with fresh water.

1 Place the machine on the centre stand so that it rests on level ground.
2 To reach the radiator cap, the fuel tank and the radiator covers or fairing lower sections must be removed. Refer to Chapter 6.
3 If the engine is cold, remove the radiator cap by rotating it in an anti-clockwise direction. If the engine is hot, having just been run, place a thick rag over the cap and turn it **slightly** until all the pressure has been allowed to disperse. A rag must be used to prevent escaping steam from causing scalds to the hand. If the cap were to be removed suddenly, the drop in pressure could allow the water to boil violently and be expelled under pressure from the filler neck. Apart from burning the skin the water/antifreeze mixture will damage paintwork. Where time and circumstances permit it is strongly recommended that a hot engine be allowed to cool before the cap is removed.
4 Place a receptacle below the front of the engine into which the coolant can be drained. The container must be of a capacity greater than the volume of coolant. Unscrew the drain plug underneath the water pump assembly **(see illustration)**. Allow the coolant to drain completely before refitting the drain plug. Note its specified torque setting. The coolant reservoir may be drained by removing it from the machine and tipping out the coolant. If the coolant being drained is to be re-used, ensure that it is drained into a clean non-metallic container.
5 The manufacturer recommends that the coolant be renewed at regular intervals. See Chapter 1.

3 Cooling system - flushing

1 After extended service the cooling system will slowly lose efficiency, due to the build-up of scale, deposits from the water and other foreign matter which will adhere to the internal surfaces of the radiator and water channels. This will be particularly so if distilled water has not been used at all times. Removal of the deposits can be carried out easily, using a suitable flushing agent in the following manner.
2 After allowing the cooling system to drain, replace the drain plug and refill the system with clean water and a quantity of flushing agent. Any proprietary flushing agent in either liquid or dry form may be used, provided that it is recommended for use with aluminium engines. **Never** use a compound suitable for iron engines as it will react violently with the aluminium alloy. The manufacturer of the flushing agent will give instructions as to the quantity to be used.
3 Run the engine for ten minutes at operating temperature and drain the system. Repeat the procedure **twice** and then again using only clean cold water. Finally, refill the system as described in the next section.

2.4 Coolant drain plug is on underside of oil/water pump assembly

Cooling system 5•3

4.5 Refill cooling system at radiator filler after draining...

4.8 ... and top up at expansion tank afterwards

5.2a Disconnect radiator filler and top hoses...

4 Cooling system - filling

1 Before filling the system, always check that the drain plug has been fitted and tightened and that the hose clips are tight.
2 The recommended coolant to be used in the system is made up of 40% corrosion-inhibited ethylene-glycol antifreeze suitable for use in aluminium engines and 60% distilled water; this gives protection against the coolant freezing in temperatures of down to -28°C (-18°F). An alternative mixture ratio of the same ingredients for lower temperatures is listed in the Specifications Section of this Chapter. To give adequate protection against wind chill factor and other variables, the coolant should always be prepared for temperatures -5°C (-9°F) lower than the lowest anticipated.
3 Use only good quality antifreeze of the type specified; never use alcohol-based antifreeze. In view of the small quantities necessary it is recommended that distilled water is used at all times. Against its extra cost can be set the fact that it will keep the system much cleaner and save the time and effort spent flushing the system that would otherwise be necessary. Tap water that is known to be soft, or rainwater caught in a non-metallic container and filtered before use, may be used in cases of real emergency only. Never use hard tap water; the risk of scale building up is too great.
4 So that a reserve is left for subsequent topping-up, make up approximately 3.5 litres (3.7 US qt/6.2 Imp pint) of coolant in a clean container. At the **standard** recommended mixture strength this will mean adding 2.1 litres (2.2 US qt/3.7 Imp pint) of distilled water to 1.4 litres (1.5 US qt/2.5 Imp pint) of antifreeze; do not forget to alter the ratio if lower temperatures are expected.
5 Having checked the system as described in the subsequent Sections of this Chapter, add the new coolant via the radiator filler neck **(see illustration)**. Pour the coolant in slowly to reduce the amount of air which will be trapped; then the level is up to the base of the filler neck, fill the expansion tank to its upper level line. Refit the expansion tank filler cap.
6 Start the engine and allow it to idle until it has warmed up to normal operating temperature, with the temperature gauge needle (where fitted) giving its usual reading; the level in the radiator will drop as the coolant is distributed and the trapped air expelled. Add coolant as necessary. As soon as the thermostat opens, revealed by the sudden steady flow of coolant across the radiator and by a warm top hose, the level will drop again and more air will be expelled in the form of bubbles.
7 All trapped air must be expelled from the system before the radiator cap is refitted. When the level has stabilised for some time with the engine fully warmed up, and there are no more signs of air bubbles appearing, top the level up to the base of the filler neck and refit the radiator cap. Stop the engine, check that the expansion tank is topped-up to its upper level mark and refit the radiator shrouds, fairing components and side panels.
8 When the machine has been ridden for the first time after renewing the coolant and has cooled down, check the level again at the radiator cap to ensure that no further pockets of air have been expelled; top up if necessary **(see illustration)**. At all other times the coolant level should be checked at the expansion tank, as described in *Daily (pre-ride) checks*.

5 Radiator - removal, cleaning and examination

1 Drain the radiator as described in Section 2 of this Chapter. Remove the air intake hose.
2 Disconnect and remove the top, bottom, filler and bypass hoses from the radiator **(see illustrations)**. Remove the radiator top mounting bolt or nut, withdrawing the insulating material (where fitted) to reach it **(see illustration)**.
3 Tilt the radiator forwards, disconnect the fan motor lead at its connector and withdraw the radiator **(see illustrations)**.

5.2b ... followed by bypass and bottom hoses...

5.2c ... then release radiator top mounting bolt or nut

5.3a Tilt radiator forwards on bottom mountings...

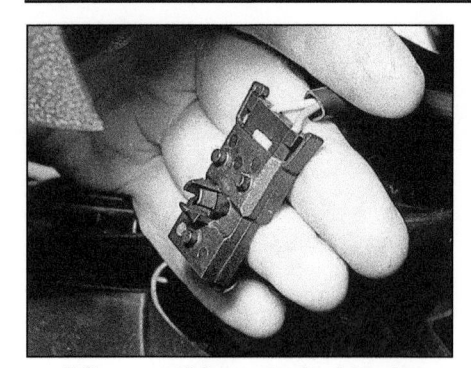

5•4 Cooling system

5.3b ... until fan motor lead can be disconnected

4 Inspect the radiator mounting rubbers for perishing or compaction (see illustration). Renew the rubbers if there is any doubt as to their condition. The radiator may suffer from the effect of vibration if the isolating characteristics of the rubber are reduced.

5 Remove any obstructions from the exterior of the radiator core, using an air line. The conglomeration of moths, flies, and road dust usually collected in the radiator matrix severely reduces the cooling efficiency of the radiator.

6 The interior of the radiator can most easily be cleaned while the radiator is on the motorcycle, using the flushing procedure described in Section 3 of this Chapter. Additional flushing can be carried out by placing a hose in the filler neck and allowing the water to flow through for about ten minutes.

Caution: Under no circumstances should the hose be connected to the filler neck mechanically as any sudden blockage in the radiator outlet would subject the radiator to the full pressure of the mains supply (about 50 psi). The radiator should not be tested to greater than 17 psi.

7 Bent fins can be straightened, if care is exercised, using two screwdrivers. Badly damaged fins cannot be repaired; a new radiator will have to be fitted if bent fins obstruct the air flow more than about 20%.

8 Generally, if the radiator is found to be leaking, repair is impracticable and a new component must be fitted. Very small leaks may sometimes be stopped by the addition of a special sealing agent in the coolant. If an agent of this type is used, follow the manufacturer's instructions very carefully. Soldering, using soft solder, may be effective for caulking large leaks but this is a specialist repair best left to experts.

9 Refitting is a reversal of the removal procedure. Ensure that the radiator is settled securely on its mountings before tightening the mounting bolt and that the electrical lead and all hoses are correctly secured (see illustration).

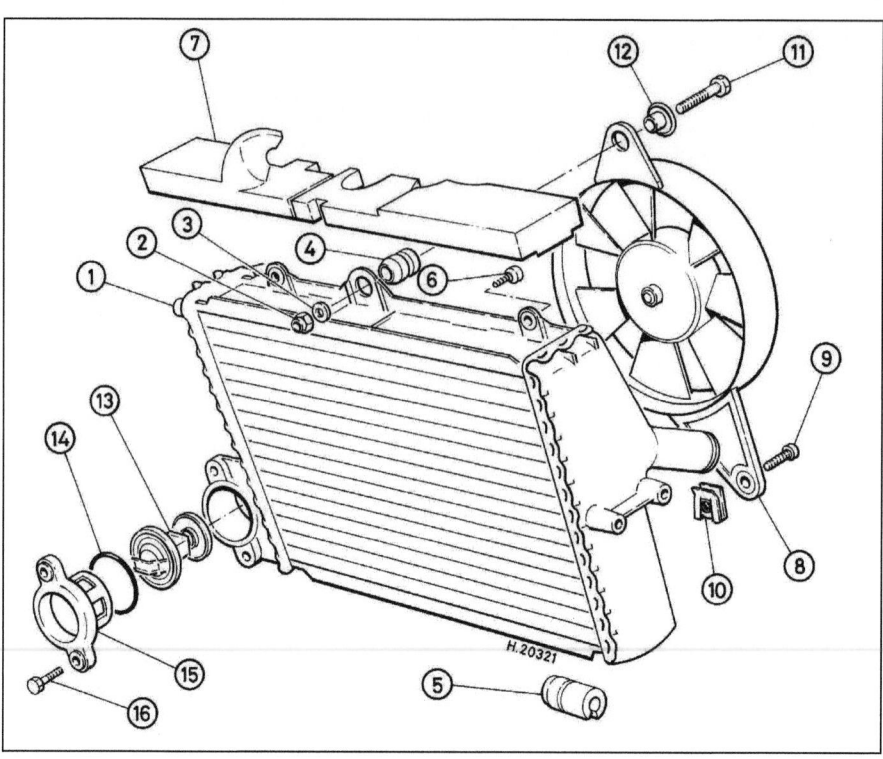

5.4 Radiator and fan

1 Radiator
2 Nut
3 Washer
4 Grommet
5 Mounting rubber – 2 off
6 Damping rubber – 2 off
7 Air deflector plate – K75RT, K100RS, RT, LT
8 Fan
9 Screw – 2 off
10 Nut – 2 off
11 Bolt
12 Spacer – 2 off
13 Thermostat
14 O-ring
15 Cover
16 Bolt – 2 off

6 Radiator pressure cap - testing

1 If the valve or valve spring in the radiator cap becomes defective, the pressure in the cooling system will be reduced, causing boiling over.

2 If the radiator cap is suspect, have it tested by an authorised BMW dealer (see illustration). This job requires specialist equipment and cannot be done at home. The only alternative is to try a new cap since the cap has a screw thread fixing which means that most normal testing equipment cannot be applied to it unless an adapter can be devised.

3 The BMW tool is number 17.0.500 and is connected using a suitable connector/ adapter. A specified pressure is applied, which must be held for at least 6 seconds; above this the cap valve will open. If it sticks or opens too early the complete cap must be renewed. Note that the cap gaskets are available separately and must be renewed if damaged or worn.

4 It should be noted that when tracing an

5.9 Check all hose clamps are tight on refitting

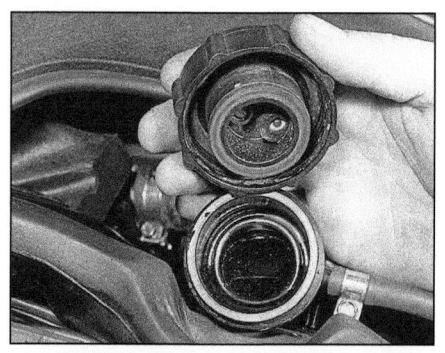

6.2 Radiator filler cap can be tested only using special equipment

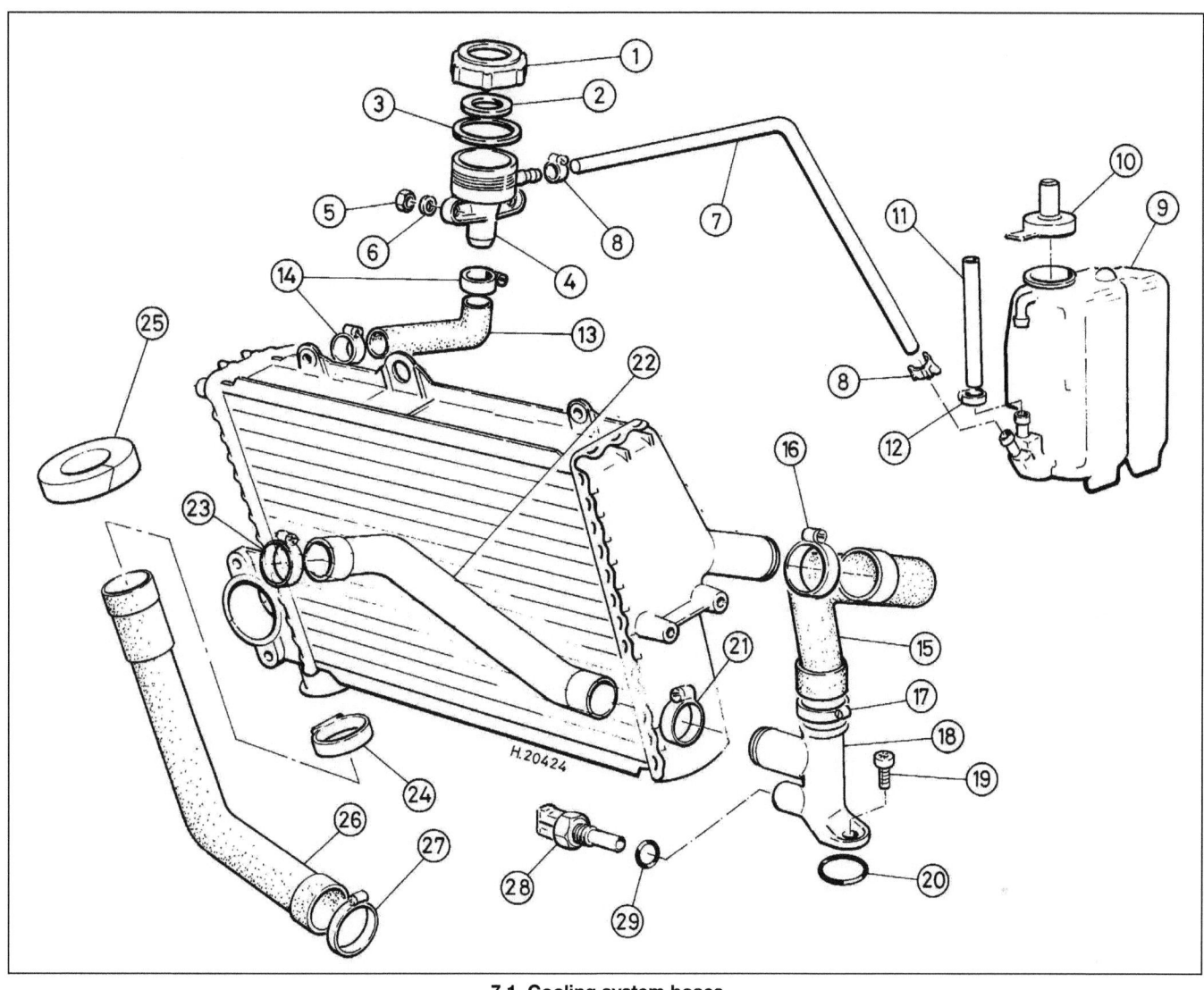

Cooling system 5•5

7.1 Cooling system hoses

1 Radiator filler cap	7 Expansion tank hose	13 Filler hose	19 Screw – 2 off	25 Damping rubber
2 Sealing ring	8 Hose clamp – 2 off	14 Hose clamp – 2 off	20 O-ring	26 Bottom hose
3 Sealing ring	9 Expansion tank	15 Top hose	21 Hose clamp	27 Hose clamp
4 Coolant filler	10 Expansion tank filler cap	16 Hose clamp	22 Bypass hose	28 Temperature sender unit
5 Nut	11 Level tube	17 Hose clamp	23 Hose clamp	
6 Washer	12 Hose clamp	18 Coolant pipe stub	24 Hose clamp	29 Sealing ring

elusive leak the entire cooling system can be pressurised to its normal operating pressure by connecting the test equipment described above to the radiator filler orifice. Remove the radiator cap, check the coolant level, topping it up if necessary, and apply a pressure of no more than 17 psi (1.15 bar) by means of the hand-operated plunger. Any leaks should soon become apparent.

> **HAYNES HiNT** *Coolant leaks can easily be seen by the tell-tale traces of antifreeze left on the components in the immediate area of the leak.*

7 Hoses and connections -
removal, refitting and checking for leaks

1 The radiator is connected to the engine unit by three flexible hoses, there being an additional hose between the coolant pipe stub and the thermostat housing **(see illustration)**. The hoses should be inspected periodically and renewed if any sign of cracking or perishing is discovered. The most likely area for this is around the clips which secure each hose to its unions. Particular attention should be given if regular topping up has become necessary. The cooling system can be considered to be a semi-sealed arrangement, the only normal coolant loss being minute amounts through evaporation in the expansion tank. If significant quantities have vanished, it must be leaking at some point and the source of the leak should be investigated promptly.

2 To disconnect the hoses, use a screwdriver to slacken the clamps then slide them along the hose clear of the union spigot **(see illustration)**. Carefully work the hose off its spigots, noting that it may be necessary to slacken, or remove fully, the radiator mounting bolt to provide room to manoeuvre.

5•6 Cooling system

7.2 Hoses are secured by screw-type clamps at each end

The hoses can be worked off with relative ease when new, or when hot; do not, however attempt to disconnect the system when it is hot as there is a high risk of personal injury through contact with hot components or coolant.

> **Warning: the radiator hose unions are fragile: do not use excessive force when attempting to remove the hoses.**

3 If a hose proves stubborn, try to release it by rotating it on its unions before attempting to work it off. If all else fails, cut the hose with a sharp knife then slit it at each union so that it can be peeled off in two pieces. While expensive, this is preferable to buying a new radiator.

4 Serious leakage will be self-evident, though slight leakage can be more difficult to spot. It is likely that the leak will only be apparent when the engine is running and the system is under pressure, and even then the rate of escape may be such that the hot coolant evaporates as soon as it reaches the atmosphere, although traces of antifreeze should reveal the source of the leak in most cases. If not, it will be necessary to use testing equipment, as described in the previous Section, to pressurise the cooling system when cold, thereby enabling the source of the leak to be pinpointed. To this end it is best to entrust this work to an authorised BMW dealer who will have access to the necessary equipment.

5 In very rare cases the leak may be due to a broken head gasket in which case the coolant may be drawn into the engine and expelled as vapour in the exhaust gases. If this proves to be the case it will be necessary to remove the cylinder head for investigation.

6 Other possible sources of leakage are the O-rings sealing the water pump body/crankcase joint or the joint between the crankcase upper and lower sections, the mechanical seal and the O-ring sealing the coolant stub union. All these should be investigated and any leaks rectified by tightening the retaining screws, where applicable, or by renewing any seals which are worn or damaged **(see illustration)**.

7 On refitting hoses, first slide the clamps on to the hose and then work it on to its respective spigots. **Do not** use lubricant of any type. When the hose is fitted, rotate it to settle it on its spigots and check that the two components being joined are securely fastened so that the hose is correctly fitted before its clamps are slid into position and tightened securely.

7.6 Do not forget coolant stub sealing O-ring when looking for leaks

> **HAYNES HiNT** *The hoses can be softened by soaking them in boiling water before refitting, although care is obviously required to prevent the risk of personal injury when doing this.*

8 Thermostat - removal and testing

1 The thermostat is so designed that it remains in the closed position when it is in a normal cold condition. If the thermostat malfunctions, it will remain closed even when the engine reaches normal working temperature. The flow of coolant will be impeded so that it does not pass through the radiator for cooling and consequently the temperature will rise abnormally, causing boiling over.

2 If the performance of the thermostat is suspect, remove it from the machine as follows and test it for correct operation **(see illustration)**. Remove the fuel tank and drain the coolant as described in Section 2. Remove its two retaining screws and withdraw the thermostat cover, noting how the sealing O-ring is fitted. Withdraw the thermostat. On refitting, note that the sealing O-ring is fitted around the cover inner boss, so that it fits inside the housing when the cover is installed; a smear of grease or similar lubricant will help the O-ring to slide into the housing.

3 Examine the thermostat visually before carrying out tests. If it remains in the open position at room temperature, it should be discarded **(see illustration)**. Suspend the thermostat by a piece of wire in a pan of cold water. Place a thermometer in the water so that the bulb is close to the thermostat. Heat the water, noting when the thermostat opens and the temperature at which the thermostat is fully open. If the performance is different from that specified, the thermostat should be renewed.

4 If the thermostat is faulty it can be removed and the machine used without it as an emergency measure only. Take care when starting the engine from cold as the warm-up will take much longer than usual, and ensure that a new unit is fitted as soon as possible.

9 Water pump - removal, renovation and refitting

1 To prevent leakage of water or oil from the cooling system to the lubrication system and vice versa, two seals are fitted on the pump shaft. The seal on the water pump side is of the mechanical type having a spring loaded annular face which bears against the rear face of the impeller. The second seal, which is mounted behind the mechanical seal, is of the normal 'feathered' lip type. Both seals are a drive fit in the pump body.

2 Where work on the seals is required, the pump must be removed first, as follows.

3 Drain the coolant. See Section 2. Drain the engine oil, as described in Chapter 1. Disconnect the oil pressure switch lead and

8.2 Thermostat is fitted in housing at side of radiator

8.3 Renew thermostat if stuck or faulty

Cooling system 5•7

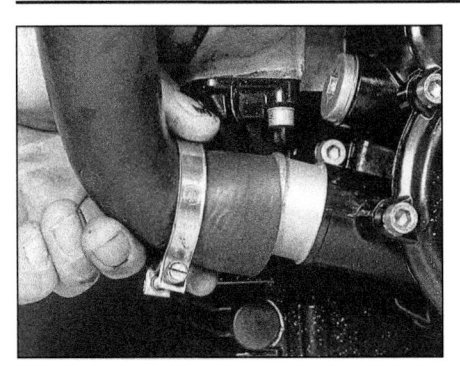

9.3 Remove bottom hose prior to oil/water pump removal

9.4a Remove pump front cover retaining screws ...

9.4b ... to expose pump body mounting screws

remove the radiator bottom hose **(see illustration)**.

4 Remove the pump front cover retaining screws and withdraw the cover then remove the pump body retaining screws and withdraw the pump body; a few gentle taps with a soft-faced mallet should break the joint seal **(see illustrations)**. Note the O-ring sealing the coolant passage between the pump and the crankcase lower section, also the O-ring around the pump drive shaft rear end; both of these should be renewed whenever they are disturbed.

5 Remove the pump drive gear and insert a 6 mm Allen key into the pump shaft rear end. Clamp the key in a vice to hold the pump shaft and unscrew the impeller retaining nut (early models) or bolt (later models) **(see illustration)**. Using a soft-faced mallet, or a hammer and a wooden or soft metal drift, tap the pump shaft out of the impeller, then withdraw the impeller (with spacer - mid 1990-on models) and shaft **(see illustration)**.

6 Taking care not to scratch or damage the pump body, pull or lever the mechanical seal out of its housing and use a slim (5 mm/0.20 in blade width) screwdriver to drive out the rear seal working from the pump's rear face **(see illustration)**.

7 Carefully clean all components and check those of the oil pump for wear; see Chapter 6. Renew both seals whenever they are disturbed, also the O-rings.

8 On reassembly, fit first the rear seal, with its manufacturer's marks or numbers facing forwards, using a hammer and a tubular drift such as a socket spanner which bears only on the seal hard outer edge. Drive the seal in until it seats against its locating shoulder. A smear of grease around its outside edge will help the procedure.

9 The mechanical seal is fitted in the same way, using a 22 mm socket spanner and 1/2 inch drive to drive it in until it seats. However, it must be kept completely free from grease and must be washed in a methylated spirit/water mixture to degrease it before installation.

10 Insert the pump shaft into the rear of the pump body. The mechanical seal centre is a very tight fit on the pump shaft; to refit the shaft rest its rear end against the work surface, apply both thumbs to the mechanical seal centre and press the seal (and pump body) over the shaft end.

11 Fit the spacer on the pump shaft (mid 1990-on models) followed by the impeller. Tighten the impeller retaining nut or bolt to its specified torque setting then refit the pump drive shaft with a new O-ring. Installing an O-ring around the coolant passage **(see illustration)**, apply a thin smear of Three Bond 1207 B sealant to the pump/crankcase mating surfaces and refit the pump ensuring that the drive shaft engages correctly in the output shaft.

12 Rotate the crankshaft to centralise the pump gears while tightening the pump body mounting screws to the specified torque setting (where given). Connect the oil pressure switch lead to the switch terminal and carefully refit the switch cover. Apply a thin smear of Three Bond 1207 B sealant to the mating surfaces and refit the pump front cover. tightening its retaining screws to the specified torque setting, where given.

13 Fill the cooling system again. See Section 4. Refill the engine with oil as described in Chapter 1. Refit all other disturbed components.

14 In the event of seal failure, inter-mixing of oil and coolant in the engine will cause sludge to form. To prevent this, a drain hole is

9.5a Use an Allen key to hold pump shaft when slackening impeller nut or bolt

9.5b Remove impeller to release pump shaft

9.6 Pump mechanical seal is fitted behind impeller

9.11 Always renew O-ring around coolant passage

5•8 Cooling system

provided in the water pump casting between the two seals, which allows any fluid which leaks past either seal to exit through a passage in the front of the sump casting. If oil is visible around this passage the water pump oil seal has failed and should be renewed. However, if coolant is visible this indicates failure of the water pump mechanical seal.

10 Cooling fan - removal, examination and refitting

1 The fan and motor assembly are automatically removed and refitted with the radiator. See Section 5 of this Chapter.
2 If the fan fails to work, connect a fully-charged 12 volt battery directly to the fan motor; for safety's sake this must only be done while the fan assembly is still attached to the radiator (on or off the machine) so that it is still enclosed by its protective shroud. If the fan motor works, the fault is in the thermostatic switch or in the main wiring loom; check for faults as described in Chapter 11.
3 if the fan motor does not work, it must be renewed. Remove the shroud mounting bolts or screws and withdraw the fan from the radiator.
4 If the fan ever comes on with the engine still cold, this is probably due to a poor earth connection between the engine and the frame. Clean the engine/frame bellhousing mounting point as described in Chapter 2, Section 36, also the frame earth point behind the steering head. Both must be cleaned back until metal-to-metal contact is restored to ensure a good earth; apply a thin coat of silicone grease to prevent corrosion and tighten the mounting bolts securely.

11 Cooling system electrical components - removal and refitting

1 Since no test data is available, none of the electrical components can be checked except in the most general terms. See Chapter 11.

Coolant temperature sensor

2 This unit is screwed into the right-hand side of the coolant pipe stub **(see illustration)**; it is therefore necessary to drain the coolant (Section 2) and to remove the radiator (Section 5) to gain access to it. Unplug its connector and unscrew the unit to remove it; apply a smear of sealant to its threads and renew its sealing washer on refitting.
3 The unit is connected directly to the fuel injection control unit and to the temperature sensing switch unit which controls the fan motor and the coolant overheat warning lamp. If it is thought to be faulty it can be tested only by substitution.

Temperature sensing switch unit

4 This unit controls the coolant overheat warning lamp and the fan motor. It is mounted by one or two screws in the electrical components box underneath the rear of the fuel tank **(see illustration)**. If thought to be faulty it can be tested only by substitution.

Coolant overheat warning lamp

5 This is merely a bulb which is renewed if faulty as described in Chapter 11. However, if it should light when the engine is still cold, the fault is most probably due to a poor earth connection between the engine and frame. Clean the bellhousing/frame mounting point as described in Chapter 2, Section 36, also the frame earth point behind the steering head. Both must be cleaned back until metal-to-metal contact is restored to ensure a good earth; apply a thin coat of silicone grease to prevent corrosion and tighten the mounting bolts securely. To overcome this problem the wire thickness from the relay to the earth point was increased on later models. On earlier models a modification was recommended which involved running an additional earth wire from terminal 31 of the relay to the earth point behind the steering head.

11.2 Coolant temperature sensor is mounted in coolant pipe stub

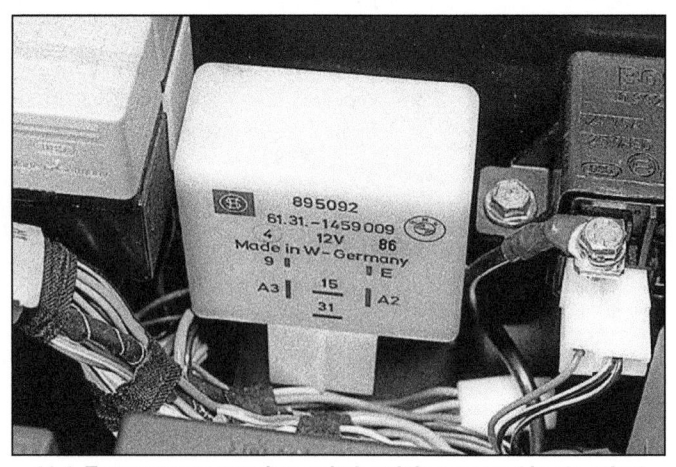

11.4 Temperature sensing switch unit is mounted in electrical components box

Chapter 6
Fuel system and lubrication

Contents

Air filter element - clean	see Chapter 1
Air filter element - renewal	see Chapter 1
Air filter housing - removal and refitting	14
Airflow meter - removal and refitting	15
Compensating for high altitude - US models	20
Exhaust system - removal and refitting	22
Fuel filter - removal and refitting	8
Fuel filter - renewal	see Chapter 1
Fuel gauge sender unit - removal and refitting	7
Fuel pressure - testing	11
Fuel pump - examination and renovation	10
Fuel pump - removal and refitting	9
Fuel rail and injectors - removal, examination and refitting	13
Fuel system - adjustments and checks	18
Fuel system - check	see Chapter 1
Fuel system - fault-finding	4
Fuel system electrical components - removal, examination and refitting	17
Fuel tank - removal and refitting	5
Fuel tank components - general	6
General description	1
Mixture adjustment and checks using an exhaust gas analyser	19
Oil pressure relief valve - general	24
Oil pressure warning lamp - general	26
Oil pump - removal, examination and refitting	23
Oil pump pick-up filter gauze - cleaning	25
Precautions to be observed when servicing the fuel system	2
Pressure regulator - removal, examination and refitting	12
Recommended fuel - general	21
Relieving fuel system pressure	3
Throttle butterfly assembly and plenum chamber - removal and refitting	16

Degrees of difficulty

Easy, suitable for novice with little experience	**Fairly easy,** suitable for beginner with some experience	**Fairly difficult,** suitable for competent DIY mechanic	**Difficult,** suitable for experienced DIY mechanic	**Very difficult,** suitable for expert DIY or professional

Specifications

Fuel tank capacity
100 models
   K100 (1983-87), K100RS, K100RT, K100LT . . . . 22 lit (4.84 Imp gal, 5.81 US gal)
   K100 (1988-on) . . . . 21 lit (4.62 Imp gal, 5.55 US gal)
75 models
   K75, K75C, K75S, K75T . . . . 21 lit (4.62 Imp gal, 5.55 US gal)
   K75RT . . . . 22 lit (4.84 Imp gal, 5.81 US gal)
No reserve supply fitted, low level warning by system of warning lamps - see Chapter 11

6•2 Fuel system and lubrication

Recommended fuel grade - see Section 21 for full information

Early 100 models	Leaded premium*
Later 100 models	Unleaded or leaded regular*
UK 75 models, early US 75 models	Unleaded or leaded premium*
Later US 75 models	Unleaded or leaded regular*

*Premium is defined as:
- Leaded: Premium (super, 4-star) grade petrol (gasoline) to German DIN 51600 standard or equivalent, minimum octane rating 98 Research Method(RM/RON), 88 Motor Method (MM/MON)
- Unleaded: Premium (super, 4-star) grade petrol (gasoline) to German DIN 51607 standard or equivalent, minimum octane rating 95 Research Method (RM/RON), 85 Motor Method (MM/MON)

*Regular is defined as:
- Leaded: Regular (2-star) grade petrol (gasoline) to German DIN 51600 standard or equivalent, minimum octane rating 91 Research Method (RM/RON), 82.5 Motor Method (MM/MON)
- Unleaded: Regular (2-star) grade petrol (gasoline) to German DIN 51607 standard or equivalent, minimum octane rating 91 Research Method (RM/RON), 82.5 Motor Method (MM/MON)

Note: *Information is correct at time of writing - for confirmation of details check with rider's handbook supplied with machine, or with a local BMW dealer or the BMW importer*

Fuel system

Type	Bosch LE-Jetronic
Fuel pump pressure approximate	2.5 bar (36 psi)
Regulator safety valve opens at	4.7 bar (68 psi)
Idle speed	950 ± 50 rpm
Maximum permissible CO value	2.0 - 2.5% (by volume) at idle speed
Injectors shut off at:	
75 models	8905 rpm
100 models	8770 rpm

Engine oil

Quantity:	
At oil change	3.50 lit (6.2 Imp pint, 3.7 US qt)
At oil and filter change	3.75 lit (6.6 Imp pint, 3.9 US qt)
Recommended oil	Good quality HD oil suitable for 4-stroke spark ignition engines, API classification SF, SG or SH
Viscosity	See chart in *Daily (pre-ride) checks*

Engine lubrication system

Relief valve opens at	5.4 bar (78 psi)
Oil pressure warning lamp lights below	0.2 - 0.5 bar (3 - 7 psi)
Filter bypass valve opens at pressure differential of	1.5 bar (22 psi)

Torque wrench settings

	Nm	lbf ft
Intake stub mounting bolts	7 ± 1	5 ± 0.5
Fuel rail mounting bolts	7 ± 1	5 ± 0.5
Pressure regulator mounting nut	25 ± 3	18.5 ± 2
Air filter lower section mounting bolts	21 ± 1	15.5 ± 0.5
Exhaust pipe retaining nuts at cylinder head	21 ± 2	15.5 ± 1.5
Exhaust pipe/silencer clamp bolt	20.5 ± 2	15 ± 1.5
Silencer/footrest mounting bolt	9 ± 1	6.5 ± 0.5
Silencer cover mounting screws	6 ± 1	4.5 ± 0.5
Oil/water pump assembly mounting screws	7 ± 1	5 ± 0.5
Oil/water pump cover screws	7 ± 1	5 ± 0.5
Oil pump pickup mounting screw	7 ± 1	5 ± 0.5
Oil pressure switch	40 ± 5	29.5 ± 4
Oil pressure relief valve plug	35 ± 4	26 ± 3
Oil pan (sump) and filter cover screws	7 ± 1	5 ± 0.5
Engine oil drain plug	32 ± 4	23.5 ± 3
Oil filter - all models:		
1st stage	Lightly oil filter seal, screw on by hand until seal seats on machined surface	
2nd stage	Tighten through 1/2 turn **maximum** (10 - 12 Nm/7.5 - 9 lbf ft)	

Fuel system and lubrication 6•3

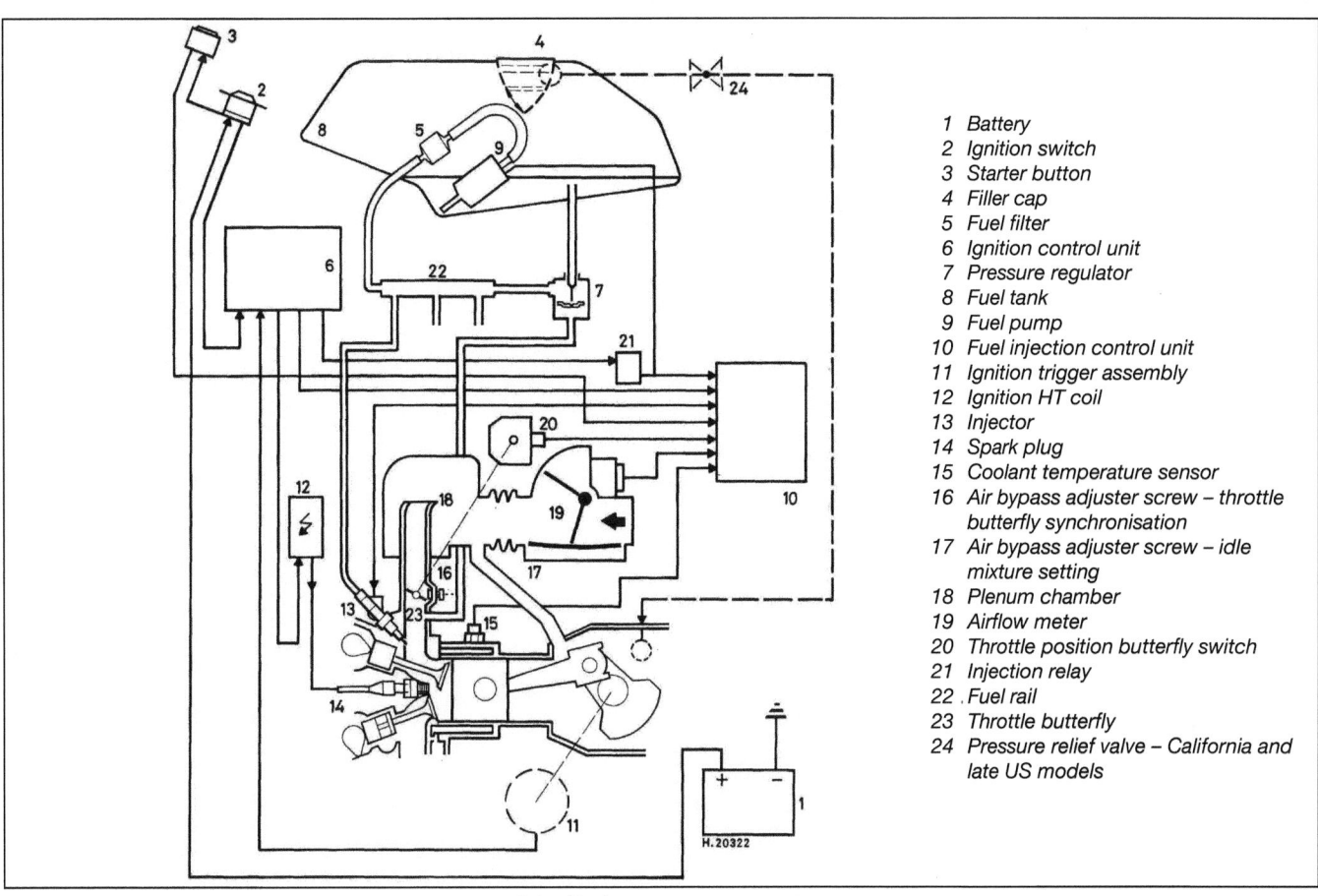

1.1a Fuel system components

1 Battery
2 Ignition switch
3 Starter button
4 Filler cap
5 Fuel filter
6 Ignition control unit
7 Pressure regulator
8 Fuel tank
9 Fuel pump
10 Fuel injection control unit
11 Ignition trigger assembly
12 Ignition HT coil
13 Injector
14 Spark plug
15 Coolant temperature sensor
16 Air bypass adjuster screw – throttle butterfly synchronisation
17 Air bypass adjuster screw – idle mixture setting
18 Plenum chamber
19 Airflow meter
20 Throttle position butterfly switch
21 Injection relay
22 Fuel rail
23 Throttle butterfly
24 Pressure relief valve – California and late US models

1 General description

The Bosch LE-Jetronic fuel injection system is easiest to understand if each of its sub-systems are considered separately. These can be divided into three; the fuel delivery system, the air metering or induction system and the electrical components **(see illustrations)**.

Fuel delivery system

The fuel system starts with the fuel tank in which is housed the electric roller-cell fuel pump. This is protected by a gauze filter on its pick-up side and a full-flow filter on its delivery side. When the ignition is switched on and the starter button operated, the pump supplies fuel to the fuel rail only while the engine is running.

The pressure of fuel is controlled by the vacuum-operated pressure regulator which returns fuel continuously to the tank via a check valve or, on later models, a long stack pipe. Although the regulator relies on induction manifold depression for normal operation, it also incorporates a spring-loaded safety valve.

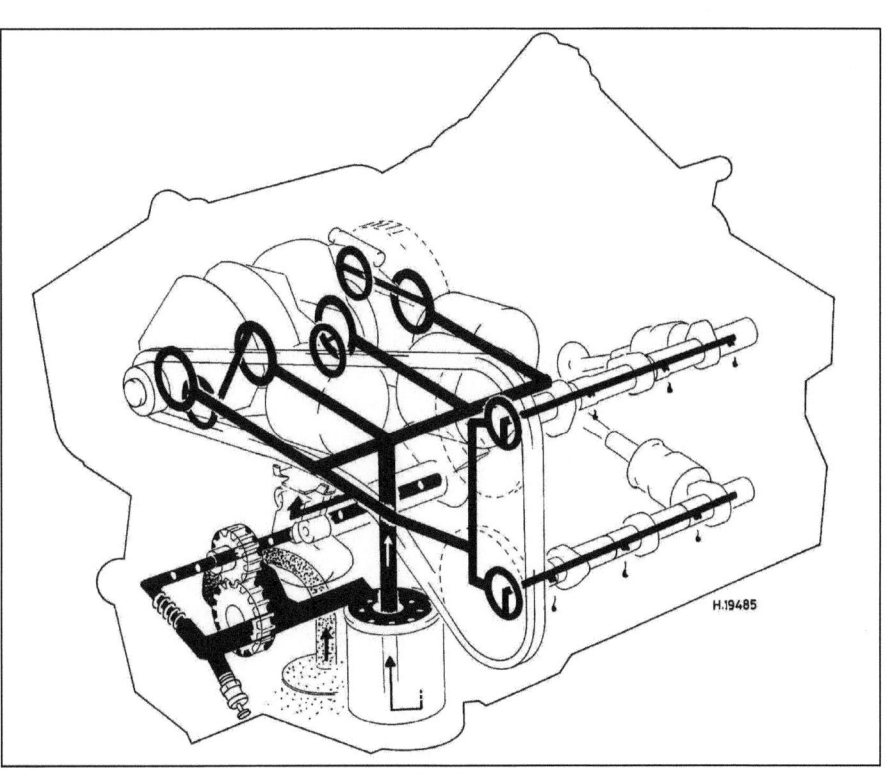

1.1b Lubrication system

6•4 Fuel system and lubrication

The injectors are solenoid-operated and are opened and closed by electrical impulses from the injection control unit; the correct moment is signalled by the ignition control unit based on the information it is receiving from the trigger assembly. Actuating an injector solenoid pulls back a needle valve against spring pressure and allows a controlled amount of fuel to pass from the fuel rail via a small filter, through each injector, and to spray out into the intake port.

Air metering or induction system

The induction system takes cool air from next to the radiator and passes it upwards through the pleated-paper air filter element and into the airflow meter. This device measures the temperature of the incoming air, via a sensor in its intake, and also its volume. The force of the incoming air is used to deflect a sensor flap which converts this movement into voltage by a potentiometer; the information from these two sensors is fed to the injection control unit. The sensor flap is spring-loaded to provide controlled operation and is L-shaped so that pressure variations can be damped out by the movement of the other flap arm in a secondary damping chamber. To permit adjustment of the air/fuel mixture at idle, a bypass duct is fitted into the airflow meter and controlled by a metering screw. By controlling the amount of un-metered air which is allowed to bypass the sensor flap, the screw effectively provides a form of mixture control. From the airflow meter the air passes via a plenum chamber into the intake tracts, in which are situated the throttle butterfly valves which enable the rider to control engine speed via the twistgrip.

To overcome the increased friction of a cold engine, a handlebar-mounted lever is provided which opens the throttle butterflies a small amount to give an increased idle speed when the engine is started from cold. A switch mounted on the end of the throttle shaft provides the injection control unit with information on the throttle position. The throttle bodies incorporate air bypass ducts which are controlled by metering screws to provide a measure of air flow adjustment so that the throttle valves, and therefore their respective cylinders, can be synchronised or balanced.

Electrical components

The heart of the electronic system is the control unit which uses microprocessors to collate information about the volume and temperature of the incoming air (airflow meter), the engine speed (ignition system), the throttle butterfly position (throttle valve switch), and the engine temperature (coolant temperature sensor); it then transmits the appropriate control impulses to the injectors each time an ignition pulse is detected.

The opening time and duration of the injectors can be altered by the control unit to vary the volume of injected fuel and thus vary the air/fuel mixture according to the engine's needs; the surplus of fuel stored in the fuel rail ensures that an adequate supply is always present. To save fuel, the control unit shuts off the injectors when the engine is on the overrun (ie throttle switch in the closed position but ignition system still indicating a high engine speed) until the engine speed has fallen to 2000 rpm or less, when the injectors are reactivated so that the engine does not stall.

The control unit also has two safety functions; the first is to shut off the fuel supply if the ignition is switched on but the engine ceases to run or the ignition system fails, and the second is to shut off the fuel supply if engine speed exceeds a set limit, thus preventing engine damage through excessive speed.

Evaporative Emission Control System

All 1985 on models sold in California and all 1986 on models sold in the other 49 states are fitted with an Evaporative Emission Control System to minimise the escape into the atmosphere of unburned hydrocarbons produced by evaporation.

When the machine is at a standstill, heat from the sun or from the engine causes the fuel in the tank to expand, thus increasing the pressure inside the tank. If this increased pressure exceeds 0.1 bar (1.5 psi) a pressure relief valve in the tank vent hose opens and allows the surplus gases into the crankcase and via the crankcase breather into the induction system and the engine itself; the tank cap is sealed and will not allow vapour to vent into the atmosphere unless a pressure of 0.2 bar (2.9 psi) is exceeded, in which case a safety valve fitted in the cap will open to disperse the surplus pressure.

When the engine is started again, the reduced pressure in the intake tract draws the fuel vapour into the induction system where it is burnt by the engine in the first few seconds of running. An air bleed valve fitted in the fuel tank cap opens at a vacuum of -0.1 bar (-1.5 psi) to admit air and replace the fuel consumed as the engine is running.

Engine lubrication system

The system is a semi dry-sump type in which oil is contained in a reservoir formed by the crankcase lower section, thus minimising the heat build-up and frictional losses that would result from major engine components running submerged in oil.

The gear-type oil pump, mounted in a single assembly with the water pump and driven off the forward end of the engine output shaft; draws oil through a mesh filter set in the pick-up and forces it through a full-flow filter element into a main gallery. From here it is fed to the crankshaft main and big-end bearings and into the camshafts, which are hollow but plugged at their rear ends so that oil is positively supplied to all camshaft bearings and then out on to the lobes and cam followers; a supply is also taken from the camshaft gallery to operate the hydraulic cam chain tensioner. The teeth of the crankshaft/output shaft primary drive gears are lubricated by a supply passed through the output shaft itself. All other components are lubricated by splash, the surplus oil falling down into the crankcase lower section.

Oil pressure is controlled by a plunger-type relief valve set in the pump housing and a bypass valve in the filter ensures that the oil supply is maintained even if the filter is clogged through neglect, to the point where it cannot pass sufficient oil for the engine's needs. If pressure difference exceeds the set amount, the bypass valve opens and allows unfiltered oil to circulate around the engine. A pressure switch set in the pump housing causes a warning lamp to light in the instrument panel if the oil pressure is dangerously low.

2 Precautions to be observed when servicing the fuel system

Warning: Petrol (gasoline) is extremely flammable, particularly when in the form of vapour. Precautions must be taken, as described below, to prevent the risk of fire or explosion when working on any part of the fuel system. Note that gasoline vapour is heavier than air and will collect in poorly ventilated corners of buildings. Avoid getting gasoline in the eyes or mouth and try to avoid skin contact. In case of accidents flush the affected area immediately with copious quantities of water and seek prompt medical advice.

1 Always perform service procedures in a well-ventilated area to prevent the build-up of fumes.
2 Never work in a building containing a gas appliance with a pilot light, or any other form of naked flame. Ensure that there are no naked light bulbs or any sources of flame or sparks nearby.
3 Do not smoke (or allow anyone else to smoke) while in the vicinity of petrol or of components containing petrol. Remember the possible present of petrol vapour from these sources and move well clear before smoking.
4 Check all electrical equipment belonging to the house, garage or workshop where work is being carried on (see the Safety First section of this manual). Remember that certain electrical appliances such as drills, cutters, etc, create sparks in the normal course of operation and must not be used near petrol or any component containing petrol. Again, remember the possible presence of petrol fumes before using electrical equipment.

Fuel system and lubrication 6•5

5 Always mop up any spilt fuel and safely dispose of the shop towel or rag used.
6 Any stored petrol, or petrol that is drained off during servicing work, must be kept in sealed containers that are suitable for holding petrol and clearly marked as such; the containers themselves should be kept in a safe place. Note that this last point applies equally to the fuel tank, if it is removed from the machine; also remember to keep its cap closed at all times.
7 Note that the fuel system consists of the fuel tank, with its cap and related vent hoses, the fuel pump and filters, the fuel feed and return hoses, the fuel rail, the pressure regulator. the injectors and any other related components. On US models, this includes the components of the Evaporative Emission Control System.
8 Most of the above components contain fuel under pressure in normal use; always relieve any residual pressure (Section 3), then wrap a shop towel or clean rag around the joint to prevent fuel spraying out whenever any component is disturbed, and wear suitable eye protection to prevent personal injury.
9 Before working on any part of the fuel system always switch off the ignition at the very least; preferably disconnect the battery (negative terminal first) to prevent the risk of sparks due to short circuits or to improperly-connected components. If test procedures require the use of electricity be careful to check all connections before starting work.
10 Read carefully the Safety First section of this manual before starting work.
11 Owners of machines used in the US, particularly in California, should note that their machines must comply at all times with Federal or State legislation governing the permissible levels of noise and of pollutants such as unburnt hydrocarbons, carbon monoxide, etc., that can be emitted by those machines. All vehicles offered for sale must comply with legislation in force at the date of manufacture and must not subsequently be altered in any way which will affect their emission of noise or of pollutants.
12 In practice this means that adjustments may not be made to any part of the fuel, ignition or exhaust systems by anyone who is not authorised or mechanically qualified to do so, or who does not have the tools, equipment and data necessary to properly carry out the task. Also if any part of these systems is to be renewed it must be replaced only by genuine BMW components or by components which are approved under the relevant legislation, and the machine must never be used with any part of these systems removed, modified or damaged. Owners **must** consult the local enforcement agency (CARB and/or EPA) for full details of local legal requirements **before** attempting any of the servicing procedures described in this Chapter or in the relevant Sections of Chapter 1.

3 Relieving fuel system pressure

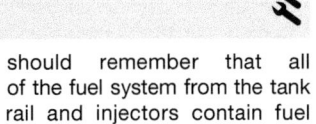

1 Owners should remember that all components of the fuel system from the tank to the fuel rail and injectors contain fuel which is under pressure when the engine is running.
2 The pressure will remain for some time after the engine has been switched off and must be relieved before any of these components is disturbed for servicing work.
3 The first method is simply to exhaust the supply of fuel remaining in the system. Start the engine, remove the right-hand side panel and disconnect the fuel tank wiring connector plug. The pump will then cease to operate and the engine will run only while fuel remains under pressure. Switch off the ignition and re-connect the tank wiring as soon as the engine stops.
4 The second method can be used if the engine has just been switched off. Disconnect the pressure regulator vacuum hose (usually identified by its protective coil spring) from the rearmost throttle body vacuum stub and suck as hard as possible to open the regulator diaphragm. The pressure will then disperse into the fuel tank. Re-connect the vacuum hose.

⚠ *Warning: With both of these methods fuel will still be present in the system components; it will merely no longer be under pressure. Take all suitable precautions (see Section 2) to prevent the risk of fire or of personal injury when working on any part of the fuel system.*

4 Fuel system - fault finding

1 As will be clear from the general description, the fuel injection system is not, to use modern jargon, user-serviceable. While the fuel injection and ignition system are not of the fully-integrated engine management type that is being fitted to some cars and, in prototype form, to one or two motorcycles, they are interconnected to an extent previously unknown in the motorcycling world; this makes accurate fault diagnosis very difficult. Also their components cannot be repaired and due to the lack of any useful information or test data, they cannot easily be tested by the ordinary private owner.
2 This means that emphasis must be more on preventing faults from arising in the first place than on actual remedial repair work. The simplest approach can be summed up as follows:
a) *If the system is working properly, leave it alone.*
b) *Prevention (in the form of preventive maintenance) is better than cure.*
c) *In the event of a fault, take the machine to an expert.*

3 The first of these is obvious, but worth stressing. **Do not attempt** to tune, modify or improve the system in any way. The only maintenance necessary is set out below and in Chapter 1; at all other times the system should not be disturbed.
4 The second is by no means as contradictory as it might first appear - the electronic components themselves are generally very reliable and any faults are usually caused by disruption of the current flow between the various components or by external factors such as excessive heat, vibration or attack by foreign matter or corrosive chemicals. Therefore anything that can be done to ensure that all components receive a stable supply of the correct amount of electrical current, that they are kept clean and properly secured to protect them from excessive heat and/or vibration, and that they are kept free of dirt, corrosion and substances such as water, coolant, brake fluid, battery acid or engine oil which might cause damage, must help to minimise the risk of a fault in the fuel injection system.
5 Preventative measures can be summed up as follows:
a) *Ensure that the battery electrolyte levels are correct and that the terminal connections are clean and securely fastened at all times. If the machine is not used for any length of time, ensure that the battery is given refresher charges to keep it in good condition.*
b) *Working through the relevant wiring diagram to ensure that all components (including individual connectors) are treated, carefully clean back to bare metal all connections and terminals (finishing off with proprietary contact cleaner to remove any grease or oil) then pack them with silicone grease to exclude water and dirt and to prevent corrosion. On reassembly, ensure that, where applicable, the waterproof cover is correctly refitted over each connector plug and that the retaining clip is secured.*
c) *Ensure that all frame earths and earth connections are completely clean and securely fastened. Where wires are connected to the frame earth point, or at the bellhousing/frame mounting joint. ensure that the frame paint is scraped away to provide a clean metal-to-metal joint and that silicone grease or similar is applied to prevent corrosion.*
d) *Ensure that all components are correctly positioned and securely fastened at all times, also that all are as clean and dry as possible.*
e) *All wiring must be correctly routed so that it runs in smooth loops but avoids all possible contact with sharp edges, control cables or components which*

6•6 Fuel system and lubrication

    move or become hot, and must be secured out of harm's way using plastic cable clips or insulating tape. Remember that wires which are too tight or sharply kinked may fail due to the effects of vibration, whilst wires which are too slack may foul other components.
- f) Be careful never to knock, drop, or otherwise mishandle any of the components; all are extremely sensitive and easily damaged. Note that this particularly applies to the injection control unit; always ensure that it is properly secured and that any tools, etc., carried in the storage compartment above it are well wrapped in rag and secured so that they cannot cause vibration by rattling around. BMW specify that tools are to be carried only in the tail compartment; the under seat compartment is for lightweight items only, such as the first-aid box.
- g) If any component is found to be worn or damaged at any time, repair or renew it immediately, before the damage has a chance to affect any other component.
- h) Whenever any part of the induction system (ie air filter, airflow meter, throttle valve assembly, as opposed to the purely electronic components) is disturbed, always ensure that all joints are sealed airtight on reassembly so that there are no air leaks to upset the mixture balance. All soft rubber seals or hoses should be refitted with great care and retaining clips or hose clamps should be correctly positioned and securely fastened; do not overtighten any clamp or there is a grave risk of distorting the components being secured.
- i) Whenever any part of the fuel system (ie fuel feed and return pipes, fuel rail or injectors) is disturbed, always ensure that all joints are securely fastened on reassembly to prevent the possibility of fuel leaks and of the resulting drop in pressure.
- j) Always clean or renew (as applicable) the fuel filters exactly at the intervals specified in Routine maintenance and servicing or earlier, if necessary; the system is extremely vulnerable to the presence of dirt or water and the engine may stop completely if one or more fuel passages become obstructed by particles of foreign matter. Keeping the filters clean is the only way of preventing this, although great care should always be taken not to allow dirt or water into the fuel tank whenever the cap is opened.

6 If a fault does arise, some clue to the reason may be given by its symptoms; if not consider the problem in a logical manner in an attempt to isolate the fault. In the first place check that there is a good quantity of clean fuel in the tank and that the battery is in good condition and fully charged (check that all other electrical systems are working normally as a quick test of battery condition). It should be possible to hear the fuel pump working, if not check the pump circuit fuse. If the pump is working, check that fuel is present under pressure in the fuel rail and that the surplus is returning via the pressure regulator to the tank. Check also that none of the fuel tank vent hoses are blocked by kinks or foreign matter.

7 If the fault occurs only while the engine is running, there is not a great deal that the ordinary owner can do to isolate it. Checking the appearance of the spark plug electrodes will reveal whether the mixture is excessively rich or lean, but the possible causes of either of these conditions are far too many and varied to be checked without the correct test equipment. Check the components of the fuel and induction system (see above) for air or fuel leaks, check the exhaust system for holes or other damage and check the valve clearances and engine compression to ensure that the engine is mechanically sound. As far as is possible, check that the ignition system is in good order.

8 When all other possibilities have been eliminated (as far as the ordinary owner can check them) the fault must be assumed to be in the electronic components of the fuel injection system. At this stage the machine should be taken to a good authorised BMW dealer who has the BMW/Bosch diagnostic unit. This equipment is connected to the machine by a set of adapter leads and should be capable of checking the function of the entire ignition and fuel injection systems; in skilled hands it should be able to trace faults very quickly and easily.

9 Unfortunately there is no alternative to the use of this equipment; while this manual contains all the test data that can be gleaned from BMW's service literature, nothing is available which will allow the checking of the system's components using ordinary equipment. Since all other available data is related specifically to the Bosch diagnostic unit it is of no use to anyone who does not have access to one of these units. **Do not attempt** to test any components using equipment which has its own power source (eg multimeters, ohmmeters, meggers or battery and bulb test circuits) or the applied voltage may destroy one or more of their sensitive circuits.

10 The **only** permissible use for an ordinary tester is to check the wiring loom for damage. Note, however, that all the components of a particular circuit must be disconnected before the wires of that circuit are checked, to avoid any risk of the sort of damage mentioned above. Particular attention should be paid to the various connectors and any earth connections.

11 Taking all the above into account, many owners may well feel that the simplest course of action is to take the machine to an authorised BMW dealer if a fault of any sort is encountered in the fuel injection system. Compared with the time-consuming nature of the various tests and the dangers both to the machine and its owner inherent in some of them, a skilled operator will quickly and safely run through a test sequence on the diagnostic unit to check the entire system and locate any faults, even if this does mean having to pay the labour charge necessary.

5 Fuel tank - removal and refitting

1 Refer to Section 2 of this Chapter for notes on precautions to be observed when servicing any part of the fuel system.
2 Open and raise the dual seat, then remove both side panels. See Chapter 8.
3 On K100 and K75C, K75T and K75 models remove the radiator covers. On K100RS models remove the left-hand knee pad. On K75RT, K100RT and K100LT models remove the left-hand knee pad, storage compartment and compartment holder. See Chapter 8.
4 Relieve any residual fuel system pressure. See Section 3.
5 Remove from its frame clip and disconnect the fuel tank wiring connector plug **(see illustrations)**.
6 On early 100 models remove the single bolt securing the tank rear end to its rubber mounting. On all other models use a pair of pliers to withdraw the flat clip securing each

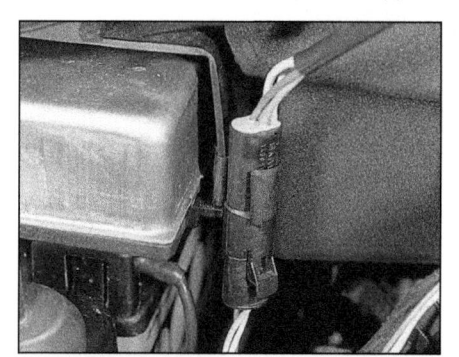

5.5a Remove fuel tank wiring connector from its retaining clip . . .

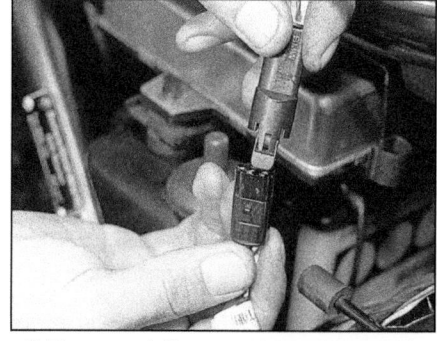

5.5b . . . and disconnect to release tank wiring – ensure catch is fastened correctly on refitting

Fuel system and lubrication 6•7

5.6 Remove clips securing tank rear mountings on later models – early models use single bolt

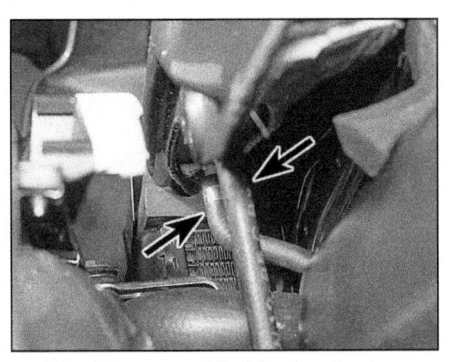

5.7a Disconnect fuel feed and return hoses from unions under tank front left-hand end

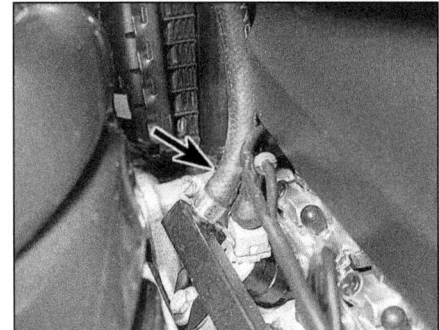

5.7b Note that fuel feed hose can also be disconnected at fuel rail, if required

5.7c Check tank front mounting rubbers and insulating material whenever tank is removed

of the two tank mountings **(see illustration)**. Lift the tank at the rear and disconnect, on early models only, the tank vent and fuel overflow hoses; note carefully where each hose is fitted. Remove the tank wiring lead from the frame tubes.

7 Placing a rag to catch any spilt fuel as described in Section 2, disconnect the fuel feed and return hoses either from underneath the tank front left-hand side or at the fuel rail (feed hose only) **(see illustrations)**. Carefully lift the tank at the rear then pull it backwards to disengage the front mounting rubbers **(see illustration)**. Be very careful not to damage its paintwork, especially on machines with fairings.

8 As soon as the tank is clear of its front mountings, lift it to one side so that the pressure relief hose (US models only, where fitted) can be disconnected and removed. Withdraw the tank, taking care not to spill any fuel (later models only).

9 On refitting, be very careful to connect the various hoses to their correct stubs. On early models the overflow hose is fitted to the stub which passes up to the filter cap recess drain hole, while the vent hose is connected to the stub which exits inside the tank, at the top. The fuel return hose is connected to the front left-hand stub and the feed hose to the rear left-hand stub. On US models the pressure relief hose (where fitted) is connected to the remaining stub. Check carefully that all hose clamps are securely fastened and that all hoses are correctly routed with no kinks or sharp bends.

10 Applying a smear of lubricant to the mountings, manoeuvre the tank into place, connecting the hoses at the appropriate moment. Check that the tank is fully engaged on its front mountings, then lower it into place at the rear. Check carefully that the hoses are not kinked or distorted before fastening the tank rear mountings **(see illustration)**. On late models note that the overflow and vent hoses are connected to a funnel which is clipped to the frame tubes under the tank stubs **(see illustration)**.

11 Ensuring that it is correctly routed, refit the fuel tank wiring lead and connector plug to the frame clip.

12 Check that all hose clamps are securely fastened before starting the engine.

> **HAYNES HiNT** *If the vent hoses are blocked through obstructions or through being kinked or trapped due to careless installation, pressure can build up in the tank to the point where the tank bulges outwards on the left-hand side, fuel sprays out whenever the filler cap is opened and the engine performance is affected. Be very careful to check that all hoses and vent tubes are correctly re-routed whenever the tank is disturbed.*

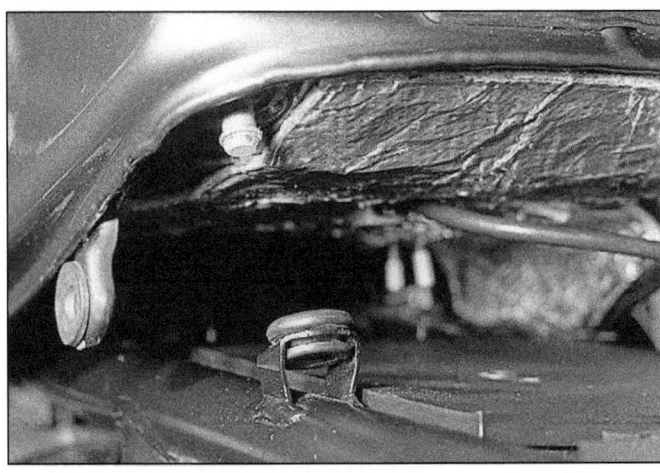

5.10a Lubricate tank mounting rubbers on reassembly

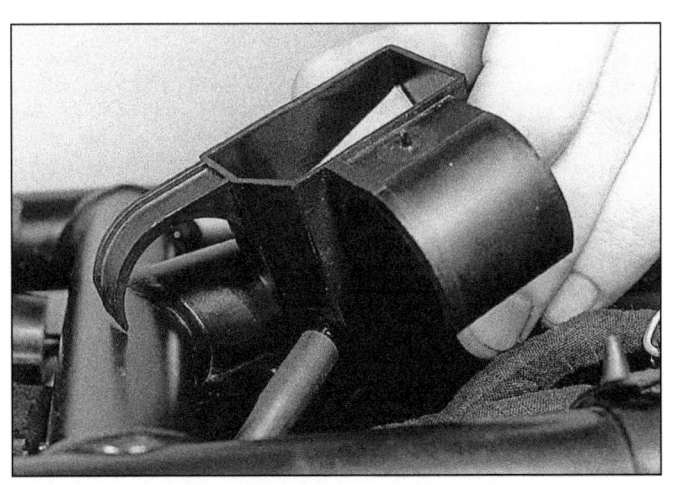

5.10b Check routing of tank hoses – overflow and vent hoses are directed into a funnel on later models

6•8 Fuel system and lubrication

1 Fuel tank
2 Sealing ring
3 Filler cap and insert
4 Screw – 4 off
5 Washer – 4 off
6 Additional seal [1]
7 Gasket
8 Fuel pump
9 Filter gauze
10 Breather tube [1]
11 Negative terminal nut
12 Washer
13 Rubber sleeve
14 Retaining ring
15 Nut – 6 off
16 Spring washer – 6 off
17 Washer – 6 off
18 Pressure hose
19 Clamp – 4 off
20 Fuel filter
21 Pressure hose
22 Positive terminal nut
23 Bolt [2]
24 Mounting rubber [2]
25 Spacer [2]
26 Bolt – 2 off [2]
27 Mounting bracket [2]
28 Nut – 2 off [2]
29 Drain tube [1]
30 Fuel gauge sender unit [1]
31 O-ring [1]
32 Screw – 4 off [1]
33 Fuel return valve [2]
34 Sealing washer [2]
35 Vent tube*
36 Pressure relief valve*
37 Vent tube*
38 Mounting rubber – 2 off
39 Vent funnel [1]
40 Mounting grommet – 2 off [1]
41 Clip – 2 off [1]
42 Fuel gauge sender unit [2]
43 Sealing washer [2]
[1] later models only
[2] early models only
*US models, where fitted

6.1a Fuel tank assembly

6 Fuel tank components - general

Note: *Refer to the warnings given in Section 2 of this Chapter before working on any part of the fuel system.*

Filler cap

1 The tank filler cap is removed by unlocking it, raising the flap and by removing the four screws which retain it to the tank; note the sealing ring between the filler cap insert and the tank **(see illustration)**. Renew the ring if it is damaged or worn in any way, ensuring that the modified type is used.

2 On refitting, the sealing ring must be positioned so that it does not block the overflow hole; do not overtighten the retaining screws or the tank sealing lip will cut into the ring and damage it. Check the operation of the filler cap lock; if stiff, through water penetration or lack of lubrication, lubricate it with CRC5-56 or WD40.

3 Note that the presence of fuel around the filler cap recess is usually due to a faulty cap sealing ring but may also be due to a build-up of pressure as a result of blocked or kinked vent and drain hoses; check that these are clear.

4 The filler cap was modified in late 1984; the original pushbutton release being deleted in favour of a cap which springs up automatically when unlocked. At the same time the sealing lip was raised and a new sealing ring introduced, so that any water that collected in the filler cap recess or was forced into it by a pressure washer, was directed into the drain hole. This component was fitted to all 100 models from that date onwards and to all 75 models. Subsequently an additional gasket was introduced which can be fitted to all later-type caps; the gasket is fitted underneath the cap by removing the three screws which secure the cap lower part to the top. If owners of earlier models encounter persistent problems with water getting into the tank, an authorised BMW dealer will have all the necessary details of the modifications.

5 Note that new locks and replacement keys are available from authorised BMW dealers, also a blank lock which can be coded to match the key already in use on the machine so that only one key is still needed if the lock has to be renewed.

6 On US models fitted with the EEC system, the filler cap assembly incorporates a flap

6.1b Remove retaining screws to release filler cap assembly – check gaskets carefully

Fuel system and lubrication 6•9

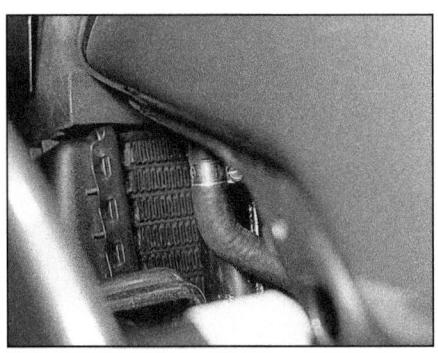

6.9 Check all external hoses regularly for security and condition

which is pushed aside by the pump nozzle on filling the tank but which is deliberately designed to prevent the tank from being filled to the brim. This is to allow room for the expansion of the fuel when warm and to prevent neat fuel from passing into the crankcase via the vent hose; if the engine were started with a quantity of petrol (gasoline) in the crankcase the resulting engine damage could be very severe indeed, also the possible personal injury that might result. **Do not** remove or modify the filler flap in any way.

Internal hoses and pipes

7 Reference to the text and illustration in this Chapter will show the number and layout of the pipes inside the fuel tank. Blow through all vent pipes, drain pipes, etc., to check that all are clear whenever the tank is removed.

8 On very early 100 models low fuel pressure may be due to loose hose connections inside the tank. To check the security of the connections, disconnect the fuel feed hose from the fuel rail and plug it with an 8 mm (0.32 in) rod clamped securely by a hose clamp. Run the starter motor for approximately 15 seconds. by which time the pressure will be at the maximum possible. If the hose connections are intact, they will be serviceable in normal use. If any have given way, renew the hose if split or damaged and secure it with a (smaller) 12 mm clamp. Note that on all connections the hose should be pushed fully on to the metal pipe stub so that the clamps locate securely behind the pipe flared ends. Although the smaller clamps were fitted to all later models, this point should be checked carefully on any machine which loses fuel pressure.

External hoses

9 Note that all fuel feed and return hoses have a petrol (gasoline) resistant inner layer surrounded by a tough outer layer which is designed to give protection against cleaning detergent, salt, etc **(see illustration)**. Since this outer layer is not fuel-proof it the hose clamps are not securely fastened, fuel can work its way between the two layers causing the outer layer to swell and then deteriorate. Always ensure that all hose clamps are securely fastened and that the fuel return valve (where fitted) is securely fastened and that its gasket is not leaking.

Fuel return valve

10 On the original 100 models a spring-loaded ball valve was fitted in the fuel return hose to seal off the passageway whenever the tank was removed. This was found to be annoyingly noisy in operation however, especially from just above idle speed, and so the valve was modified on 1985 models. The modification, which consists of removing the spring, can be carried out as follows on earlier models.

11 Remove the tank, drain the fuel into a suitably-marked container and unscrew the valve. Lever up its top rim and prise out the cover disc, withdraw the spring and refit the cover disc, then carefully peen over the top of the valve to secure the disc again. Refit the valve, ensuring that its gasket is not forgotten and that it is securely fastened. Note that fuel may drip from the valve from now on whenever the tank is removed; the valve lower end should be plugged or capped to prevent this.

12 With the introduction of the K75 S models in mid-1986 the return valve was deleted completely and replaced by a long stack pipe which passes up to the top of the tank; be very careful not to tilt the tank on removal or fuel may be spilt.

Tank insulation

13 Note that under certain weather and traffic conditions it is possible for the temperature in the vicinity of the engine to rise to extremely uncomfortable levels, especially in the case of fully-faired models such as the K75RT, K100 RS, K100 RT and K100 LT.

14 When these machines are ridden in hot weather the heat build-up, apart from being very unpleasant, can cause fuel starvation due to evaporation in the fuel feed hose and fuel rail. Paradoxically US models fitted with the EEC system can suffer from excessive mixture richness since the rate of evaporation inside the tank is so high and all the vapours are sucked into the engine via the crankcase and breather.

15 To effect a cure, BMW lined the underside of all tanks with a layer of reflective insulating material. On the fully-faired 100 models a modification was introduced to improve the flow of air through the fairing. The gaiters are removed and replaced by deflectors which actively scoop cold air into the fairing, the metal fairing inner panels being modified to deflect the hot air away from the rider's legs and outwards through the fairing vents. Also pre-cut knee pads are supplied which are to be glued to the sides of the tank to protect the rider's legs from its heat and a higher output pump is fitted.

Evaporative Emission Control System

16 The system's components and layout are explained in Section 1 of this Chapter. The system requires no maintenance beyond a quick check that the hoses are clear and the valve is working properly whenever the tank is removed.

17 To remove the hose and pressure relief valve the tank should first be withdrawn so that the hose lower end can be released from the union on the crankcase next to the coolant pipe stub. On refitting, note that the arrow on the valve body indicates which way up it is to be fitted.

18 If any part of the system is found to be damaged or faulty, it must be renewed; use only genuine BMW replacement parts.

19 If the machine seems to be running rich, especially when the weather is hot or if the machine is used extensively in heavy traffic, the EEC system may be the cause of the problem; take the machine to an authorised BMW dealer for careful checking. For machines used outside California it may be possible to modify the system, but this must be done only if necessary and in accordance with EPA regulations.

Fuel tank - general

20 Whenever the tank is removed, check that there is no dust or water inside and flush it out if any is found; not only is the fuel system as susceptible as any other to the presence of water but the pump (especially later types) can be seriously damaged if dirt is allowed to enter it.

21 Note that the tank is constructed of aluminium alloy; this makes its repair a task for the expert alone. An authorised BMW dealer should be able to advise you of the nearest person able to undertake such work. Due to the number of internal pipes and passageways, the tank must be flushed out even more carefully than normal before it is taken for repair. Make sure that the repairer is aware of the tank's complex construction so that all breather and vent passages, for example, are kept clear.

7 Fuel gauge sender unit - removal and refitting

Note: *Refer to the warnings given in Section 2 of this Chapter before starting work on any part of the fuel system.*

1 The low fuel level warning lamp system is operated by a float-type level sensor mounted in the base of the fuel tank. Check the system as described in Chapter 11.

2 If the sender unit is to be removed, withdraw the fuel tank and drain the fuel into a suitably-marked container. See Section 5 of this Chapter.

3 Remove the fuel filler cap. See Section 6. Check that the ignition is switched off.

4 Disconnect the fuel pump wires, noting which wire is attached to which pump terminal, then invert the tank on to a layer of clean cloth to protect its paintwork and peel

6•10 Fuel system and lubrication

7.5a Fuel gauge sender unit is mounted in underside of tank – later type shown

7.5b Take care not to bend float arm on later type of sender unit

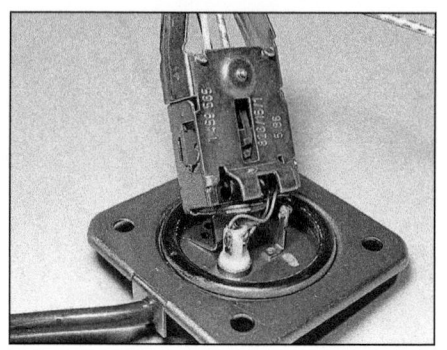

7.7 Always renew seal or O-ring to prevent risk of fuel leaks

back the flap of insulating material which covers the sender unit undersides (later models only).

5 On early models unscrew the gland nut and withdraw the sender unit from its location on the rear of the pump. On later models remove the four retaining screws and withdraw the sender unit, taking care not to bend the float arm **(see illustrations)**.

6 As mentioned in Chapter 11, the sender unit cannot be repaired or adjusted and must be renewed if faulty.

7 On reassembly, always renew the sealing washer or O-ring to prevent leaks and tighten securely the gland nut or mounting screws. Note that the later type of sender unit is refitted with the (smaller thread size) yellow wire on the left-hand side of the tank so that the electrical lead projects to the rear. Be careful to connect the wires correctly to the pump.

8 Fuel filter - removal and refitting

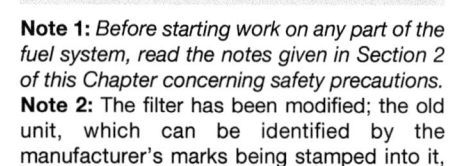

Note 1: *Before starting work on any part of the fuel system, read the notes given in Section 2 of this Chapter concerning safety precautions.*
Note 2: The filter has been modified; the old unit, which can be identified by the manufacturer's marks being stamped into it, was found on occasions to crack around the stamp marks, thus causing a significant loss of pressure and hard starting. The modified component has a thicker housing and can be identified by the manufacturer's marks which are now inked on. Always use the modified component.

1 Unlock and raise the filler cap, then remove it as described in Section 6. Relieve any residual fuel system pressure. See Section 3.
2 Using a long-bladed screwdriver, slacken the clamp securing the filter short hose to the metal pipe, carefully pull the filter assembly off the metal pipe stub and withdraw the filter from the tank; there should be sufficient length in the long filter/pump hose to permit this. Slacken the clamps and withdraw the filter from the hoses. If the clamps are not the smaller (12 mm) type they should be discarded and the modified item fitted.
3 Discard the old filter, disposing of it tidily and safely, then install the new component, using the markings on the filter housing to ensure that the fuel flow direction is correct **(see illustration)**.
4 On refitting, slide the hoses fully on to their metal stubs and slide down the clamps until they are located behind the metal pipe flared ends; tighten the clamps securely.
5 Refit the filler cap. See Section 6. Ensure that its seal is of the modified type (where applicable) and refitted correctly to prevent water from leaking in.

9 Fuel pump - removal and refitting

Note: *Before starting work on any part of the fuel system, read the notes given in Section 2 of this Chapter concerning safety precautions.*

1 Remove the filler cap. See Section 6. Check that the ignition is switched off.
2 Disconnect the fuel pump wires by unscrewing the terminal nuts; although there should be no possibility of confusion since the terminals are of different sizes, note which wire is attached to which terminal. Relieve any residual fuel system pressure, see Section 3.
3 Disconnect the fuel pump/filter hose, slackening the clamp with a long-bladed screwdriver.
4 On later models, disconnect the pump gauze filter breather hose from its stub **(see illustration)**.
5 Squeeze together the nylon ears of the pump retaining ring and withdraw the assembly **(see illustration)**.
6 On refitting, ensure that there is no dirt or water in the fuel tank and that all pump components are absolutely clean. Check that the mesh strainer is securely fastened. If the hose clamps are not the smaller (12 mm) type they should be discarded and the modified items fitted.

8.3 Marks on fuel filter casing show direction of fuel flow – ensure modified type of filter is fitted on renewal

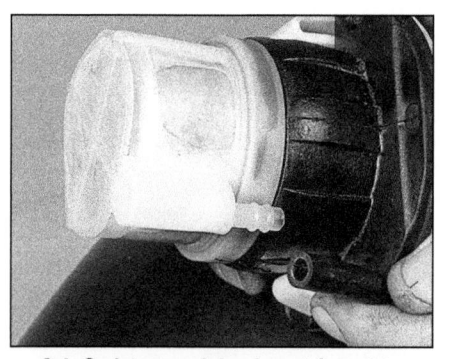

9.4 On later models, do not forget to disconnect pump filter gauze breather hose

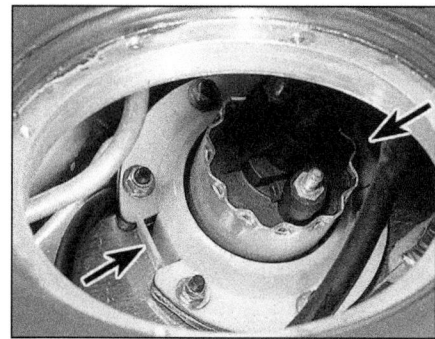

9.5 Squeeze together mounting 'ears' (arrowed) to release pump assembly

Fuel system and lubrication 6•11

7 Fit the pump to its mounting bracket so that the (smaller) positive (+ve) terminal is on the left-hand side, in approximately the 10 - 11 o'clock position. Push the pump firmly into place and check that the retaining ring ears clip into position.
8 Re-connect the mesh filter breather tube (later models only) and the pump/filter hose. Push the hose fully on to its stub and slide down the clamp until it is located behind the stub flared end; tighten the clamp securely.
9 Connect the pump wires to their terminals; the yellow wire must be connected to the smaller positive (+ ve) terminal the black wire to the larger negative (- ve) terminal. Ensure that the terminal nuts are securely fastened.
10 Refit the filler cap.

10 Fuel pump - examination and renovation

1 Note that the pump cannot be dismantled for repair or reconditioning; if it is faulty, or stops working, it must be renewed. The only effective test of the pump's condition is described in Section 11 of this Chapter, but this requires the use of a suitable pressure gauge. Ensure that the working area is absolutely clean when servicing the pump.
2 With the pump removed from the fuel tank, unscrew the nuts which clamp the rubber sleeve to the nylon retaining ring. The retaining ring should have an alignment mark (a small + symbol embossed on it) next to the smaller positive terminal (see illustration); if none can be seen make your own marks before withdrawing the retaining ring and pulling the pump out of the rubber sleeve and mesh filter. Note that while it is, of course, possible merely to pull the filter off the pump lower end, the filter should be removed and refitted with care so that it is not damaged or distorted.
3 Disengage the filter from the sleeve, noting the alignment marks. Check the filter for splits or tears; if any are found or if it is a slack fit on the sleeve, the filter must be renewed. If not, swill it in high flash-point solvent to remove any particles of dirt.
4 Carefully clean all components and check for wear or damage; if any is found the component concerned must be renewed.
5 Note that the pump has been modified; since the introduction of the 75 models (ie all 1986 on models) a pump is fitted which is manufactured to tighter tolerances to ensure that the delivery rate remains correct even at high operating temperatures. This is now supplied as the replacement part for earlier models also. To prevent the formation of vapour bubbles which would otherwise interrupt the fuel supply, the new pump is fitted with a modified mesh filter and rubber sleeve, the filter being fitted with a separate breather hose.
6 While the new pump does ensure greater consistency of fuel supply, its tighter tolerances mean that it is more easily damaged by dirt. To prevent this, take great care to ensure that the pump components are kept as clean as possible at all times. Use only lint free cloths for cleaning purposes and flush out the tank immediately if any dirt or water are noticed inside it at any time.
7 On reassembly, check that all components are absolutely clean, then fit the mesh filter to the rubber sleeve, aligning their marks as shown (see illustration). Fit the retainer ring to the rubber sleeve and tighten the retaining nuts lightly, the ring will fit only the correct way due to the offset studs and mounting ear cut-outs in the rubber sleeve.
8 Lubricate the pump body with a smear of fuel or a very small amount of engine oil, then press it into the rubber sleeve, taking care not to dislodge the mesh filter, until the locating ribs on the pump body snap into the grooves in the rubber sleeve. If the pump is a very tight fit, remove the retainer ring, press the pump into the rubber sleeve and then refit the ring. When the pump is fully in place, rotate it to align the retainer ring mark with the pump positive (+ve) terminal and tighten the retainer ring nuts securely. Make a final check that the mesh filter is fully and securely fixed on the rubber sleeve and that the alignment marks are in line.
9 K75 models from frame number 0 253 816 were fitted with a higher performance fuel pump. In cases where the fuel level in the tank is very low, the pump may exhibit a load noise due to air being drawn in through the pump. This can be cured by re-routing the fuel return hose to the left-hand side of the tank to ensure that the fuel is fed back to the pump area of the tank – see a BMW dealer for details of this modification if problems are experienced.

11 Fuel pressure - testing

Note: *Before starting work on any part of the fuel system, read the notes given in Section 2 of this Chapter concerning safety precautions*
1 The only test of the fuel pump's and pressure regulator's performance is to measure the delivery pressure, as described below. Note however that if the fault occurs under a particular set of circumstances, for example only in very hot weather, these circumstances should be duplicated as closely as is reasonably possible when making the test. First relieve any residual fuel system pressure as described in Section 3.
2 Referring to Section 5 of this Chapter disconnect the fuel feed hose at the fuel rail and connect a suitable pressure gauge between the hose and the rail; BMW's own gauge is available under part number 16 1 500.
3 Start the engine and allow it to idle while taking pressure readings. Since fuel pressure is not related to engine speed there is no point in running the engine any faster unless the fault occurs only at higher speeds or the

10.2 Before removing retaining ring, check for alignment marks with smaller positive terminal (arrowed)

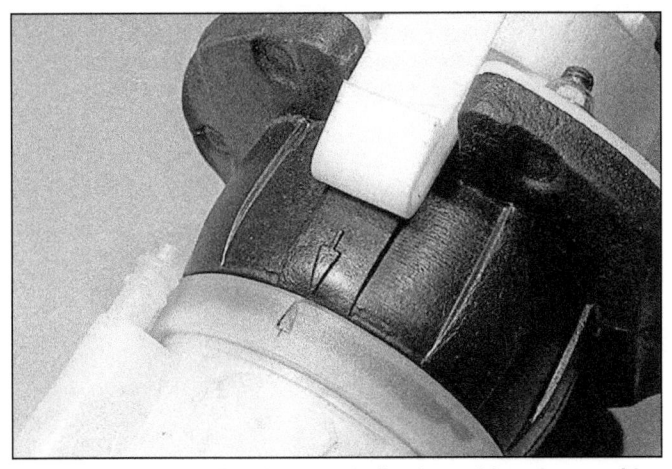

10.7 Ensure mesh filter is securely fixed on rubber sleeve, with arrow marks aligned

6•12 Fuel system and lubrication

12.3 Pressure regulator is mounted on right-hand side of throttle butterfly assembly

13.3 Disconnecting regulator hose from fuel rail rear end

13.4 Disengage wire clip before pulling off each injector connector

pressure regulator performance is to be checked. In the latter case open and close the throttle sharply once or twice to note the effect of the differing intake vacuum pressures on the fuel pressure. If the pressure regulator is faulty, it must be renewed.
4 The pressure reading obtained should be steady at approximately 2.5 bar (36 psi) although some BMW service literature does mention a figure of 2.2 bar (32 psi) at idle speed. If the reading obtained is significantly lower than that specified, check the tank hoses and pipes on the pump delivery side (Section 6), and the fuel filter (Section 8) before renewing the fuel pump as described in Section 9.
5 If the pressure recorded is significantly higher than that specified, the pressure regulator and its vacuum hose should be checked (Section 12). If the pressure exceeds 4.7 bar (68 psi) indicating that the regulator safety valve has stuck, the pressure regulator should be renewed immediately.

12 Pressure regulator - removal, examination and refitting

Note: *Before working on any part of the fuel system, read the notes given in Section 2 of this Chapter concerning safety precautions.*
1 On K75RT, K100RS, K100RT and K100LT models, remove the fairing knee pads, lower side panels and radiator cover. On K75S

models owners may wish to remove the fairing side panels or at least their bottom covers to gain easier working conditions. On all other models, remove the radiator cover panels. See Chapter 8.
2 Remove the complete air filter assembly. See Section 14 of this Chapter. Relieve any residual fuel system pressure. See Section 3.
3 Using a suitable screwdriver to slacken the hose clamps (where fitted) disconnect the fuel rail/pressure regulator hose, the fuel return hose, and the vacuum hose **(see illustration)**.
4 Slacken the nut securing the regulator top to its mounting and withdraw the regulator.
5 On refitting, tighten the nut securely, to the specified torque setting, where available. Connect the fuel return hose (from the tank) to the top union, the fuel rail hose to the side union and the vacuum hose (from the rear throttle body vacuum take off-stub) to the bottom union.
6 Secure the pressure hoses by pushing them fully on to the regulator stubs and sliding each clamp down until it is behind the stub flared end, then tighten the clamp securely. Check carefully for leaks when the engine is started.
7 Examine the regulator carefully; if it is cracked, dented or damaged in any way, it must be renewed. Connect the vacuum hose to the bottom union and suck on the hose end; if there is any sign of leakage, check the hose for splits, tears or damage and renew it if necessary. If the hose is in good condition, the regulator diaphragm must be damaged; if this is the case the regulator must be renewed.

13 Fuel rail and injectors - removal, examination and refitting

Note: *Before starting work on any part of the fuel system, read the notes given in Section 2 of this Chapter concerning safety precautions.*
1 On K75RT, K100RS, K100RT and K100LT models remove the fairing left-hand knee pad and lower side panel. See Chapter 8. Wash any dirt or debris away from the cylinder head.
2 Relieve any residual fuel system pressure. See Section 3.
3 Disconnect the fuel feed hose from the rail front end, and the regulator hose from its rear end **(see illustration)**. Withdraw the injector cover (where fitted).
4 Disconnect the wires from each injector, being careful to disengage the wire clips before pulling off the connector plug **(see illustration)**. Release the wires from any ties securing them to the fuel rail.
5 Remove the two bolts securing the fuel rail, noting the metal washers and rubber mounting at each point, then carefully withdraw the rail from the cylinder head, complete with the injectors **(see illustrations)**. Place a wad of clean rag in each injector port to prevent the entry of dirt.
6 Use a pair of pliers to withdraw the clips securing each injector to the rail **(see illustration)**. Always renew the sealing

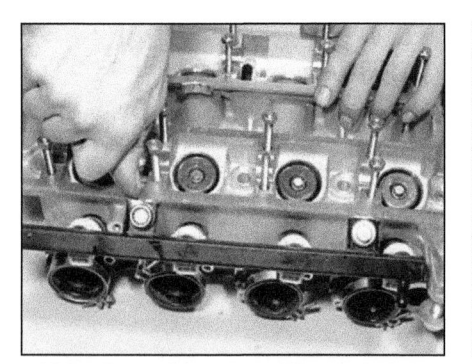

13.5a Fuel rail is secured by two bolts – note rubber mountings

13.5b Removing fuel rail, complete with injectors

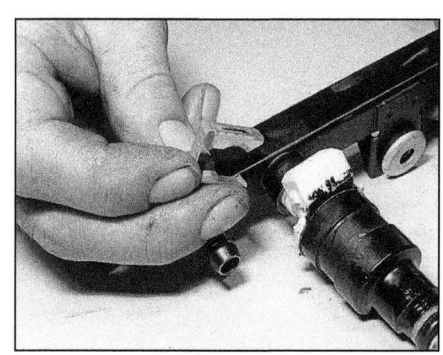

13.6a Withdraw clip to release injectors from fuel rail

Fuel system and lubrication 6•13

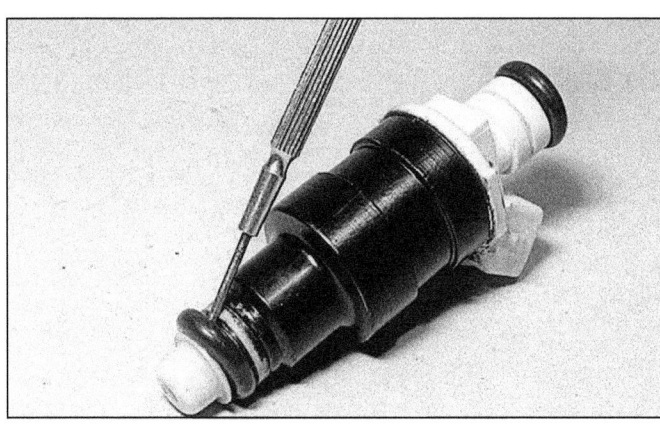

13.6b Be very careful not to damage injector when renewing O-rings

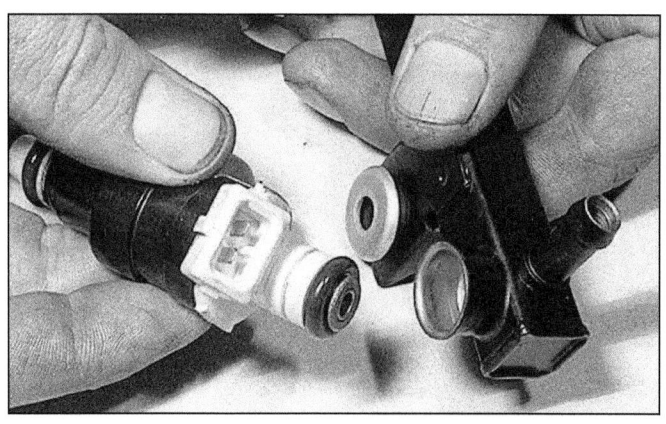

13.8 Always renew sealing O-rings to prevent leaks – do not omit fuel rail mounting spacer

O-rings at each end of the injectors whenever they are disturbed **(see illustration)**.

7 Check that the fuel rail is clean and free from blockages. No information is available to permit the injectors to be tested or serviced; if faulty they must be renewed.

8 On reassembly fit a new O-ring to each end of all injectors and apply a smear of grease to aid refitting **(see illustration)**. Position each injector in the rail cup and secure it with its clip. Check that the metal spacer is in place in each rail mounting grommet.

9 Remove the wads of rag and check that each injector port is completely clean, then refit the fuel rail assembly, guiding the injectors carefully into place. Fit a cupped washer over each side of each rail mounting grommet then refit the mounting bolts and their washers. Do not overtighten the mounting bolts; use the specified torque wrench setting, where available.

10 Arrange the wiring neatly along the fuel rail and refit each connector plug to its respective injector; check that the wire clips lock into place correctly. Secure the wires neatly to the rail with cable ties and refit the injector cover (where fitted).

11 Push the pressure hoses fully on to their stubs at each end of the rail, then slide each clamp down until it is located behind the stub flared end and secure it firmly.

14 Air filter housing - removal and refitting

Note: *The cleaning and renewal of the air filter element are covered in Chapter 1.*

1 On K75RT, K100RS, K100RT and K100LT models, remove the fairing knee pads, radiator cover and lower side panels. On K75S models owners may wish to remove the fairing side panels, or at least their bottom covers, to gain easier access. On all other models, remove the radiator cover panels. See Chapter 8. Removing its top retaining screw (where fitted) withdraw the air intake hose.

2 Although not strictly necessary, the removal of the fuel tank makes work so much easier that it is strongly recommended.

3 Release the three retaining clips which secure the filter assembly top and bottom halves, then withdraw the filter element; note that the single front clip is lifted upwards to release it and that the filter is withdrawn diagonally to the rear.

4 Slacken the clamp which secures the plenum chamber end of the air filter/plenum chamber hose; this is extremely awkward to reach with the fuel tank and/or radiator in place and will require the careful use of a suitable screwdriver **(see illustration)**.

5 With the clamp slackened, pull the air filter top half away from the plenum chamber. Again this is awkward due to the presence of the pieces of insulating material. To enable the filter top half to be completely removed, the airflow meter must be detached so that its connector plug can be unfastened.

6 To remove the airflow meter, unscrew the two retaining screws in the filter top half then invert it and slacken the clamp which secures the air filter end of the connecting hose **(see illustration)**. Withdraw the meter, noting carefully how the wiring is routed, then disengage the wire clip and unplug the meter connector **(see illustrations)**. Pull the meter

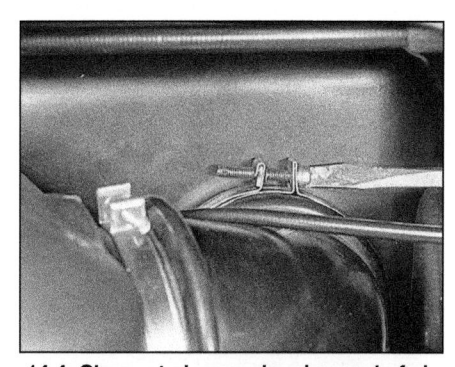

14.4 Clamp at plenum chamber end of air filter/chamber hose is very difficult to reach

14.6a Remove two screws from top of air filter top half . . .

14.6b . . . then slacken hose clamp to release airflow meter

14.6c Disengage wire clip before disconnecting meter plug

14.7a Air filter bottom half is retained by two Allen screws . . .

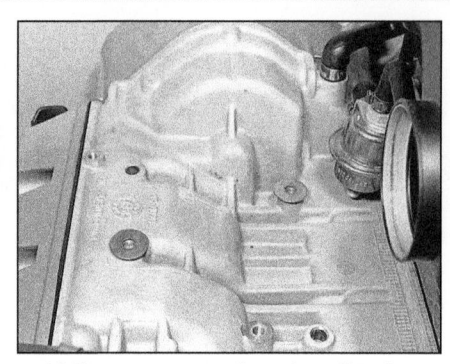

14.7b . . . note metal washers fitted to crankcase mountings – do not omit

lead and sealing grommet through the air filter top half aperture and withdraw the filter top half. Place the airflow meter in a clean secure container where it cannot be damaged.
7 Unscrew the two Allen screws securing the filter bottom half to the crankcase and withdraw it, noting the metal washers on each side of the rubber mounting grommet **(see illustrations)**.
8 On refitting, tighten the filter bottom half retaining Allen screws securely to the specified torque setting, where given.
9 Refit the electrical lead to the air filter top half and plug its connector into the airflow meter. Position the airflow meter in the filter so that the lead is correctly routed, then refit and tighten the meter mounting screws securely. Do not overtighten these screws or the mounting bracket may be cracked; note that it is available as a separate component if it is found to be cracked at any time.
10 Ensuring that the connecting hose is pushed fully into place on the mounting stubs, position and tighten the two clamps securely.
11 Refit the filter element, ensuring that its sealing lips and guide tabs engage fully with those of the filter top and bottom halves, particularly on the filter left-hand side which cannot be seen easily. Note that the side with the Top-Oben marking must be at the rear and the element must be installed so that the arrow points upwards. When the filter is securely positioned so that no unfiltered air can leak past, fasten the retaining clips.
12 Refit the air intake hose and radiator cover panels or fairing components, and the fuel tank (where necessary).
13 Note that the plenum chamber can be removed either by breaking the clips securing it to the throttle butterfly assemblies, which will require new clips and the use of a special tool on reassembly, or by removing it complete with the butterfly assemblies. Refer to Section 16 of this Chapter for details.

15 Airflow meter - removal and refitting

Since the airflow meter is mounted in the top half of the air filter assembly it is removed and refitted as described in Section 14 of this Chapter.

16 Throttle butterfly assembly and plenum chamber - removal and refitting

1 On K75RT, K100RS, K100RT and K100LT models remove the fairing knee pads, radiator cover and lower side panels. On K75S models, owners may wish to remove the fairing side panels, or at least their bottom covers, to gain easier access. On all other models, remove the radiator cover panels. See Chapter 8.
2 Remove the fuel tank. See Section 5.
3 Note that the clips securing the plenum chamber to the throttle butterfly assembly are of a special type which must be broken to remove them and must be renewed, and fastened using a special tool, on refitting. To avoid the need for this it is recommended that the throttle butterfly assembly and plenum chamber are removed as a single unit, as described below.
4 Referring to Section 14 of this Chapter withdraw the air filter housing top half and the filter element; there is no need to separate the airflow meter connection but the connecting hose must be disconnected from the plenum chamber.
5 Slacken its clamp and withdraw the crankcase breather hose from the plenum chamber stub. Note that if its retaining clips are to be broken and renewed, the plenum chamber can now be withdrawn from the machine. On refitting, apply a smear of lubricant to the air filter connecting hose and to the rubber stubs connecting it to the throttle butterfly mouths. Ease the chamber into place, ensuring that the pieces of insulating material are correctly positioned, and settle it fully into place before securing the hose clamps. Note that those fastening the throttle butterfly assembly unions are secured with BMW tool number 13.1.500.
6 Remove the fuel rail and injectors. See Section 13.
7 Slacken their adjuster locknuts and screw in the adjusters to gain the maximum free play in the throttle and choke control cables, then disconnect the cable end nipples from their operating levers and withdraw the outer cables from their brackets **(see illustration)**. Disconnect the throttle position switch at its connector plug, then either unscrew from its mounting bracket or disconnect at the main wiring loom the choke warning lamp switch **(see illustration)**.
8 Slacken the intake stub securing clamps and withdraw the throttle butterfly assembly

16.5 Disconnect crankcase breather hose from plenum chamber stub

16.7a Disconnect throttle and choke control cables

16.7b Disengage wire clip before disconnecting throttle switch plug

Fuel system and lubrication 6•15

16.8a Removing the throttle butterfly assembly and plenum chamber

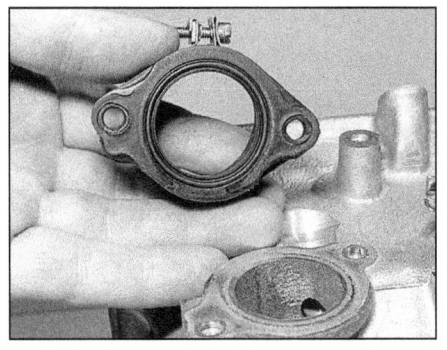

16.8b Check intake stubs for splits or damage – renew if necessary

16.10a Never attempt to dismantle any part of butterfly assembly . . .

and plenum chamber **(see illustration)**. Note how the clamps are positioned to clear the throttle operating mechanism components. Each intake stub is secured by two screws or bolts **(see illustration)**.

9 The pressure regulator, vacuum switch (early 100 models only) and choke warning lamp switch can be removed, if required.

10 **Do not** attempt to dismantle the throttle butterfly assembly further **(see illustration)**, and **never** disturb the screws linking the butterfly operating arms **(see illustration)**. Since the bypass screws provide only a limited adjustment it will not be possible to ensure accurate synchronisation if the butterflies are disturbed; they are set at the factory and can only be renewed as a single assembly.

11 On refitting, apply a thin coat of sealant to the stub mating surfaces and tighten the mounting screws or bolts securely, to the specified torque wrench setting, where given.

12 Refit the throttle butterfly assembly to the stubs and check that the clamp screws are positioned so that they can be secured, but so that they are well clear of any part of the throttle mechanism; operate the mechanism throughout its full travel to check that it is completely clear.

13 Connect (or refit, as applicable) the throttle position switch and choke warning lamp switch.

14 Connect and adjust the throttle and choke control cables.

15 Refit the fuel rail and injectors, then connect the crankcase breather hose to its stub.

16 Refit the air filter element and housing top half, then refit the fuel tank.

17 Check the idle speed setting and the operation of the choke and throttle controls. If necessary, check the synchronisation of the throttle butterfly bypass screws.

18 Refit the radiator cover panels or fairing components as applicable.

17 Fuel system electrical components - removal, examination and refitting

Fuel injection relay

1 This controls the supply of current to the various components of the system and can be tested only by substituting a new component. It is situated in the electrical components box under the rear of the fuel tank and is removed and refitted as described in Chapter 11.

Airflow meter

2 This unit is situated in the top half of the air filter housing. Refer to Section 15 for details of removal and refitting.

3 No information is available to assist the ordinary owner to test this component; in the event of a fault arising the machine should be taken to an authorised BMW dealer or similar

16.10b . . . and do not disturb screws linking butterflies

expert for checking. **Do not** attempt to test it using self-powered test circuits or testing equipment; it may be seriously damaged by the application of incorrect voltages.

4 If the unit is found to be faulty, it must be renewed; note that the mounting bracket is available separately if it has been cracked or otherwise damaged.

5 The air temperature sensor situated in the meter intake is very sensitive and must not be disturbed; it can be renewed only as a part of the meter assembly.

Throttle position switch

6 This component is mounted on the rear end of the throttle butterfly shaft **(see illustration)**. If it is to be removed, on K75RT, K100RT and K100LT models, first detach the fairing left-

17.1 Location of fuel injection relay

17.5 Note air temperature sensor in mouth of airflow meter – do not disturb

17.6 Throttle position switch is situated on rear end of butterfly assembly – note adjusting screws (arrowed)

6•16 Fuel system and lubrication

17.12 Removing fuel injection control unit – withdraw compartment cover as shown . . .

17.13 . . . then disconnect control unit connector plug

hand knee pad to permit adequate working clearance.

7 Disengage the retaining wire clip and unplug the connector, then unscrew the two retaining screws and withdraw the switch.

8 On refitting, position the switch on the butterfly shaft and tighten the retaining screws lightly. Check the throttle cable adjustment and rotate the switch so that a distinct click is heard from it just as the throttle cable slack is taken up and the butterflies begin to open; hold the switch in that position and tighten the retaining screws securely. Refit the connector plug, ensuring that the wire clip locks securely into place.

9 There is no information to assist the ordinary owner in testing this component; in the event of a fault arising the machine should be taken to an authorised BMW dealer for checking. Do not attempt to test it using self-powered test circuits or testing equipment; it may be seriously damaged by the application of incorrect voltages.

10 If the unit is found to be faulty, it must be renewed.

Fuel injection control unit

11 Unlock and raise the seat, then withdraw both side panels. See Chapter 8. Withdraw the cover from the front storage tray, also any items contained in it.

12 Gripping the tab at its front end, pull the black plastic cover sideways out of the control unit storage compartment (see illustration).

13 Inserting a slim-bladed screwdriver through the access hole in the floor of the storage tray, release the locking catch by pressing it to the rear, then unplug the control unit connector plug from the rear end first and pull it out to the side (see illustration).

14 The control unit is secured in its compartment by the rubber mountings on the left-hand side, and by a locking pin on the right-hand side; to extract the locking pin, grip its flattened end with a pair of pliers and pull it upwards (see illustrations). The control unit can be removed from the storage tray while it is in place on the machine, or the two can be removed together and separated, if necessary. Ensure that the rubber mountings are located securely in their grooves on reassembly, and check that the locking catch snaps back into place as the connector plug is refitted.

15 The unit cover is retained by clips around its edge and by the two rubber mountings on the left-hand side. If the unit has become saturated with water it may be permissible to remove the cover to assist in drying out, but at all other times the cover **must not** be disturbed. If the unit is thought to be faulty, take the machine to an authorised BMW dealer for expert attention. Do not undertake any form of testing or repair work with anything other than the BMW test equipment. If the unit is faulty, it must be renewed.

16 The unit is extremely sensitive and must never be knocked, dropped or otherwise mishandled. Note that it can be upset even by tools or similarly heavy objects rattling around in the storage tray; any items carried in the tray should therefore be either very light in weight (as recommended by BMW) with all tools carried in the tail compartment, or they should be well-wrapped in thick cloth so that they cannot move or vibrate when the machine is in motion.

18 Fuel system - adjustments and checks

Fast idle speed (choke) control cable

1 The throttle operating linkage is opened a small amount on starting by the application of a handlebar-mounted control lever. On K75RT, K100RS, K100RT and K100LT models remove the fairing left-hand knee pad to permit access to the components for adjusting.

2 Move the handlebar lever to the first detent position to engage the first stage of operation and check that the idle speed adjusting screw (see below) is raised by the specified distance from its stop, then push the lever fully across to the second position and check that the screw is raised by the specified distance for the second stage setting:

	75 models	100 models
1st stage	1.5 mm (0.06 in)	1.0 mm (0.04 in)
2nd stage	3.5 mm (0.14 in)	2.5 mm (0.10 in)

3 If adjustment is required, slacken the control cable adjuster locknut and rotate the adjuster, as necessary (see illustration). Re-check the setting and tighten the locknut securely. Check that some free play is present between the cable outer and the adjuster when the lever is returned fully to the off position; the usual amount is 0.5 - 1.0 mm (0.02 - 0.04 in).

Idle speed and throttle cable

4 The engine idle speed is adjusted only with the engine fully warmed up to normal

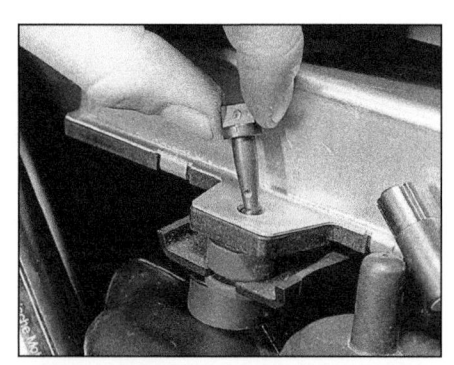

17.14a Control unit is retained by locking pin on right-hand side and by . . .

17.14b . . . rubber mountings on left – these also retain unit cover, but this mounting is incorrectly fastened

18.3 Fast idle speed setting is adjusted at control cable

Fuel system and lubrication 6•17

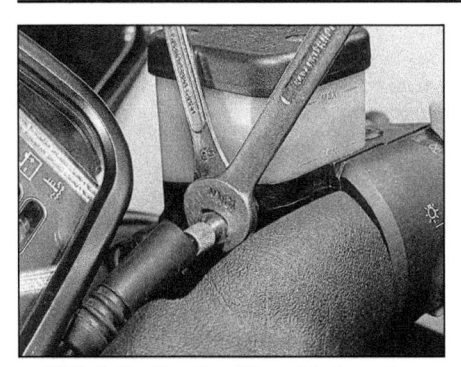

18.8 Adjusting throttle cable free play

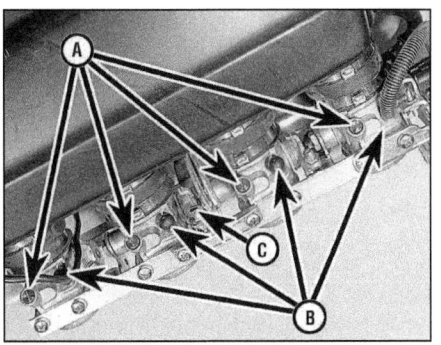

18.16 Throttle butterfly air bypass screws (A); vacuum gauge take-off points (B); idle speed adjusting screw (C)

18.17 Idle speed mixture can only be adjusted at airflow meter bypass screw

operating temperature (minimum coolant temperature of 85°C/185°F).
5 On K75RT, K100RS, K100RT and K100LT models remove the fairing left-hand knee pad and lower side panel (as desired) to gain access to the adjuster screw.
6 Check that free play is present in the throttle cable at all handlebar positions; if not slacken the adjuster and/or re-route the control cable as necessary.
7 With the engine idling at normal operating temperature check the speed recorded by the tachometer (rev-counter). If the speed is outside the specified range turn the idle adjuster screw to correct it; the screw is threaded into an extension of the cable pulley behind number 1 throttle body (75 models) or number 2 throttle body (100 models).
8 When the setting is correct, adjust the throttle cable so that there is 0.5 - 1.0 mm (0.02 - 0.04 in) free play between the cable outer and the abutment at its lower end when the twistgrip is firmly closed; use the adjuster at the twistgrip end to achieve the correct setting, then refit the rubber cover to secure it **(see illustration)**.
9 Finally, slowly open the twistgrip and check that a distinct click can be heard just off the idle position, ie just as all cable free play has been taken up and the throttle butterflies are beginning to open. If no click is heard, either the throttle position switch is incorrectly set (see Section 17) or the idle adjuster screw is tightened too far; in either case check the settings carefully before riding the machine.

Throttle butterfly synchronisation

10 While this task can be carried out using a set of four dial-type vacuum gauges, unless these are of very good quality, with proper glycerine damping, they will not be sufficiently accurate. BMW specify the use of a mercury filled manometer (part number 13.0.700, with adaptors 13.0.702 and 13.0.703) which is much more accurate but more difficult to use.
11 Given these facts, and that synchronisation is likely to be so infrequently required, owners are strongly advised to take their machines to an authorised BMW dealer for this task to be carried out by an expert using the correct equipment. For those owners who have the skill and equipment to carry out such work themselves, proceed as described below.
12 First ensure that the air filter element is clean and/or renewed and that it is securely fastened, also that there are no leaks in the induction system. Check the setting of the choke and throttle cables and that the idle speed is correct (see above). Check that the ignition system (particularly the spark plugs) is in good condition, that the valve clearances are correct and that the exhaust system is sound, with no leaks or damage. If the engine has covered a very high mileage carry out a compression test (see Chapter 2) to ensure that it is in good condition. Note that the engine must be fully warmed up to normal operating temperature (minimum coolant temperature of 85°C/185°F) before the synchronisation is checked. On K75RT, K100RS, K100RT and K100LT models, remove the fairing left-hand knee pad and lower side panel to reach the throttle assembly.
13 Note that this check merely corrects small differences, using the bypass screws, in intake vacuum caused by production tolerances and the different rates of wear of various components. It does not provide sufficient adjustment for synchronisation of the butterflies themselves, which should **never** be disturbed. These are set at the factory using special air flow-measuring equipment; if the butterfly settings are ever disturbed the complete assembly must be renewed.
14 If using equipment other than BMW's own, note that a T-piece adaptor will be required to enable the pressure regulator vacuum hose to remain connected while the test is conducted. The vacuum switch fitted to early 100 models (if still installed) can be disconnected during the test since it becomes effective only above idle speed. The vacuum take-off points are covered by small rubber caps. It was found that the hoses of a high-quality vacuum gauge set could be connected to these take-off points, provided that they were secured by small plastic clips. The pressure regulator was connected using the T-piece from a car windscreen washer system and a short length of tubing.
15 With the engine fully warmed up and the gauges or balancing device securely connected with no air leaks, start the engine and allow it to idle. Where damping adjustment is provided, set it so that the reading flutter is just eliminated but so that it can respond instantly to any small changes in pressure. If aftermarket gauges are being used, it is useful to swap them between different throttle assemblies to ensure that all are producing exactly the same reading; if there is any variation this must be accounted for during adjustment. If any one cylinder is significantly lower than the others, there may be an air leak in the induction system.
16 All gauges (or mercury columns) must show **exactly** the same reading with the engine at idle speed. If adjustment is necessary, it is made by rotating the bypass screw set in the appropriate throttle body **(see illustration)**. Do not disturb the screws and locknuts linking the various throttle butterflies. When all cylinders are giving exactly the same reading, stop the engine and disconnect the equipment.

Idle mixture adjustment

17 The fuel/air mixture ratio can only by adjusted at the airflow meter bypass screw **(see illustration)**, with an exhaust gas analyser being used to measure the level of carbon monoxide (CO) in the exhaust gases. Owners who do not have access to such equipment or the skill to use it should take their machines to an authorised BMW dealer for the work to be carried out. Those owners who have the equipment and wish to carry out the check themselves should proceed as described in Section 19 of this Chapter.

19 Mixture adjustment and checks using an exhaust gas analyser

General

1 The tasks described in this Section all require the use of an exhaust gas analyser (CO meter). Specialised equipment of this sort is normally available only to the better dealers and we would have to advise owners to take their machines to such dealers for servicing or similar work to be carried out. However, exhaust gas analysers have been in widespread use in the car world for some time now and will become more and more commonly available as emission control legislation is tightened. Accordingly, full information is given below for those owners who can gain access to an analyser and who feel that they have the skill and knowledge to use it successfully.

2 There are various types of analysers available; in all cases the manufacturer's instructions should be studied and followed with care. In general, all analysers are fitted with a water trap to remove condensation and filters to protect the unit's delicate internals; these must be cleaned out and the filter elements renewed (where applicable) before each testing session.

3 Switch on the analyser and leave it to run for a few minutes until the indicated CO reading has stabilised at the background level; it may be possible to recalibrate the analyser so that it reads zero at this level, if not, it will be necessary to subtract the background level from the test levels to obtain true readings.

4 If the test results are to be accurate, the engine must be in good mechanical order (check the compression and valve clearances), the exhaust system must be in good condition and free from leaks, the induction system must be free from leaks and the ignition system must be in good condition (eg ignition timing correct and spark plugs renewed or at least clean and correctly gapped). The throttle butterfly synchronisation must have been checked, also the adjusters of the throttle and choke control cables. and the idle speed.

5 Take the machine on a journey of at least 10 minutes duration so that the engine is fully warmed up to normal operating temperature, then check that the choke lever is pressed fully into the 'O' (off, or closed) position.

6 Insert the analyser's probe into the silencer outlet to a depth of approximately 30 cm (1 ft) so that fresh air cannot enter and upset the meter reading, then start the engine and allow it to idle. Secure the probe so that it cannot fall out.

7 Wait a few minutes for the meter reading to stabilise. Note that on US models in particular the reading may indicate quite a high level on starting the engine, due to the action of the Evaporative Emission Control System. The reading can be considered accurate when it has remained steady for one or two minutes.

8 With the analyser producing a steady, true reading of the CO level, proceed as described in the relevant sub-section below; do not forget to make allowance for the background level when taking readings. Note that several seconds may pass before any alteration to the induction system produces a corresponding change in the meter reading; always wait for a few minutes after making any alteration to ensure that the correct reading is obtained. Different meters will respond at varying speeds and levels of sensitivity; some skill and patience will be required to achieve an accurate result.

Idle speed mixture adjustment

9 Connect the test equipment as described above. If the reading obtained is outside the range of 2 ± 0.5% CO, remove the radiator cover panels or fairing right-hand lower side panels (as necessary) and prise out the plug from the top of the front right-hand corner of the air filter housing.

10 Insert a 5 mm Allen-key into the airflow meter bypass screw and rotate it until the setting is correct (see general notes above). Note that the screw should be turned in very small increments at a time; the setting is very sensitive.

11 On completion of adjustment, refit the plug with its index mark pointing to the rear. Check the idle speed and throttle synchronisation before refitting the fairing components or radiator cover panels.

Checking the air filter element

12 The condition of the air filter element can be checked by using the exhaust gas analyser. Connect the equipment and take a reading with the engine running at (no more than) two-thirds of its rated speed. ie approximately 5500 - 5700 rpm, maintain the test speed only for as long as is necessary to obtain a true reading. Stop the engine, remove the air filter element and repeat the test.

13 If the second reading was significantly lower than the first, the element is too choked to be of further use and must be renewed, regardless of its apparent condition.

14 Check that the element is securely refitted when the test is complete.

Checking for induction system air leaks

15 If the idle speed is unstable, or if the engine stalls when the throttles are shut suddenly, first check the ignition timing, the idle mixture setting and the valve clearances. If the fault persists, it may be due to a leak in the induction system.

16 BMW give details of a method of checking for air leaks which involves dropping very small quantities of fuel on to each joint in the system and noting the effect on the CO meter reading. If the reading increases slightly (or the idle speed increases) there is a leak at that point, which must be sealed by tightening the clamp screw or renewing the component, as necessary.

17 Obviously this is an extremely dangerous procedure which requires great care in its execution to avoid any risk of fire. Be especially careful to keep drops of fuel away from electrical components and to wash off all surplus fuel as soon as the test is complete. Owners are advised not to attempt this work themselves but to take the machine to an authorised BMW dealer for the work to be carried out.

20 Compensating for high altitude - US models

1 Machines which are operated for any length of time at altitudes of more than 4000 feet (1200 metres) above sea level must be modified to ensure that the mixture remains correct. This normally involves fitting smaller main jets on carburettor-equipped machines, but on the models covered in this manual an electrical connection is made to the injection control unit.

2 A socket from an extension of the engine wiring loom is clipped to the frame tube behind the left-hand side panel. To adapt the machine for higher altitudes remove the side panel, withdraw the socket cover plug and plug in the correcting adaptor.

3 The adaptor, and the warning label which must be attached to the machine to satisfy EPA requirements are available from authorised BMW dealers. Ensure that the adaptor is removed and the cover plug refitted to the socket when the machine is operated at lower altitudes.

21 Recommended fuel - general

Note: *The information contained in this Section and in the Specifications Section of this Chapter is correct at the time of writing. For updated information, or for more specific details, refer either to the rider's handbook supplied with the machine or to a local BMW dealer or other BMW importer.*

1 At one time choosing the fuel for a machine was a simple task, the main criterion being that of price. However, with the introduction for environmental and health reasons of unleaded fuel and the progressive lowering of permissible levels of lead in leaded fuels, the situation is more complicated. Modern engines are also much more sensitive to the octane rating of the fuel used as they become more and more finely tuned to meet the conflicting demands of the greater performance and economy demanded by the consumer and the reduced pollution levels demanded by legislation. This Section expands on the basic information given in the Specifications Section of this Chapter.

2 First note that all recommendations are the minimum required. Depending on the quality of fuel locally available, on the operating conditions, on its owner's riding style or on its engine's particular characteristics or condition, any motorcycle may perform poorly

Fuel system and lubrication 6•19

on the specified grade of fuel and may require a higher grade to achieve normal performance.

3 Secondly, note that BMW advise against the use of any additives such as upper cylinder lubricants, octane boosters, etc (see Step 6 for exceptions). Owners of machines used in the US should note that pure gasoline only is recommended - fuels containing a percentage of alcohol must not be used since alcohol will cause corrosion in aluminium, brass, rubber and plastic components and can cause severe engine damage. It may also cause bad starting and performance problems such as misfires or erratic idling.

4 Unleaded fuels should be used only as recommended. It is generally believed that the continuous use of unleaded fuels can cause accelerated wear of conventional valve seats, particularly on the exhaust; BMW have therefore fitted toughened exhaust valve seats to all 75 models and to all later 100 models (see below). However, modified engines (100 models only) can be identified only by reference to the frame number (where details are available) or by stripping the cylinder head to check the seats, so great care is required. Note that on suitably-modified engines it is preferable to use unleaded fuel rather than a low-leaded fuel.

5 At any time, if problems such as pinking (knocking) are experienced which could be attributed to poor quality fuel, attempt to solve the problem by changing the fuel before looking for a fault in the machine. First of all check carefully that the octane rating of the fuel used complies with BMW's minimum recommendations (see Specifications) then try higher grades and different types of fuel (eg leaded instead of unleaded) as well as different brands. Sometimes a cure can be effected by changing to a different filling station. If the fault persists, seek the advice of a good BMW dealer. Above all do not resort to unwarranted modifications to the machine; while, for example, it may be considered acceptable practice on many modern machines to retard the ignition timing by a small amount to compensate for reduced octane levels, this **must not** be attempted on the machines described in this Manual due to the difficulty of carrying out the task accurately without the special equipment necessary, and due to the fact that the effect of any such modifications on the machine's ignition and fuel injection systems cannot be checked.

6 Leaded fuel must be used on early 100 models and may be used on all other models. From early in 1985 (from frame numbers UK K100 0 007 291, UK K100RS 0 081 107, UK K100RT 0 024 999 onwards, equivalent US information not available) all engines were fitted with toughened exhaust valve seats. These valve seats. which can be identified by their having a groove 1 mm wide and 0.2 mm deep machined around the inside diameter of the exhaust port side of each seat, are now the only type which will be supplied as replacement parts (or in replacement cylinder heads and engine assemblies) and so may also be found on earlier models. BMW state that unleaded (premium grade) fuel **may** be used, if desired, on these early UK machines, but **only** provided that every third tankful is leaded fuel to protect the valve seats; owners of early US models should seek the advice of a local BMW dealer or the BMW importer for confirmation of this. **Note:** *Should it no longer be possible to obtain leaded fuel, BMW advise that models which have covered at least 30 000 miles (50 000 km) and have been run on leaded fuel will have absorbed enough lead deposits on their exhaust valve seat rings and valve faces to allow the use of unleaded fuel. In such cases, wear-resistant upper cylinder lubricants are permitted – refer to a BMW dealer for details.*

7 Unleaded fuel may be used on all 100 models after the frame numbers given above (US owners must check with their BMW dealer or importer for the necessary information) or on earlier models which are known to have been fitted with the toughened exhaust valve seats, and on all 75 models.

8 Premium-grade fuel must be used on all early 100 models (see details in paragraph 6), on all UK 75 models and on early US 75 models. It may be used also on later 100 and US 75 models.

9 Regular-grade fuel may be used on all later 100 models and later US 75 models. While precise information is not available, and must be checked as described at the beginning of this Section. the changeover dates presumably coincide with the introduction of the modified valve seats on 100 models (see details in paragraph 6) and with the reduction in compression ratio carried out in mid-1986 on US 75 models.

22 Exhaust system - removal and refitting

1 Working evenly on each exhaust pipe in turn, remove the exhaust pipe/cylinder head retaining nuts, then support the front end of the system while the nuts or bolts retaining the silencer to the footrest plate are removed. Withdraw the system and prise out the old gaskets from the exhaust ports; these should be renewed whenever they are disturbed.

2 On refitting, fit the new gaskets to the exhaust ports and stick them in place with grease **(see illustration)**. Carefully clean the threads of all mounting studs, nuts and bolts and apply a high-temperature copper-based anti-seize compound such as Copaslip or Never Seeze to the threads to prevent corrosion. Check that all components are cleaned and in place, particularly the exhaust pipe retainer plates.

3 Fit the system loosely to its rear mountings, then manoeuvre the exhaust pipes into their ports, position the retaining plates and secure them with the nuts **(see illustration)**. Tighten the nuts evenly and progressively to the specified torque wrench setting, then tighten the rear mountings securely **(see illustration)**.

4 The system can be divided into its component parts by slackening the clamp screws or bolts. Note that any component found to be stuck with corrosion should be cleaned carefully and treated with a coat of anti-seize compound on reassembly. The clamps have locating lugs which must be engaged correctly in their recesses on refitting

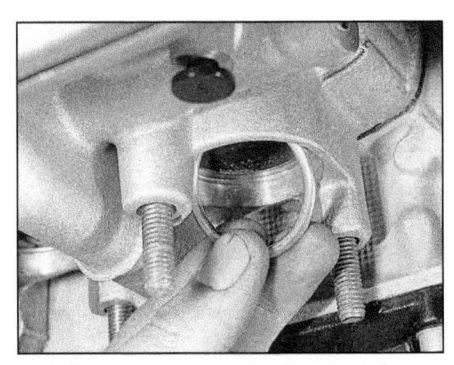

22.2 Always renew all exhaust gaskets whenever they are disturbed

22.3a Assemble system on to its mountings – secure front mountings first . . .

22.3b . . . followed by rear mountings

6•20 Fuel system and lubrication

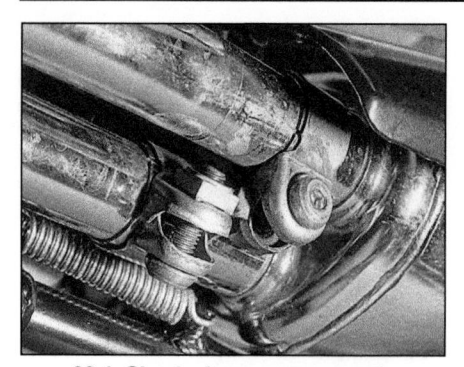

22.4 Check clamps are correctly positioned and securely fastened

so that the clamps do not foul each other or chafe against any other component **(see illustration)**.

5 Check carefully all mounting components and renew any that appear damaged or worn. Note that the silencer mountings were modified on 100 models for 1986 on the simpler mounting used on the 75 models being introduced.

6 Being made of stainless steel the exhaust system should last a considerable length of time. Clean it regularly and inspect it for any signs of damage and seek expert advice if signs of corrosion or deterioration do appear. An authorised BMW dealer may be able to supply suitable cleaning materials and polishes or recommend suitable products.

7 The silencer cover panel is retained by five screws and washers which are fitted into separate nuts set in brackets on the silencer with a cap nut securing a rubber mounting at the front on 100 models. The nut holder on 100 models into which the rubber mounting is screwed can break away as a result of temperature-imposed stresses. If this happens the silencer must be removed and taken to an expert with facilities for welding stainless steel.

8 A new rubber mounting has been introduced to prevent this from happening. Note that the mounting outer end hexagon should be held with an open-ended spanner to prevent it from shearing whenever the cap nut is tightened or slackened, and that the cover panel should not touch the silencer at any point other than its mountings.

9 A further modification has been made to the silencer cover panel retainers on 100 models to stop the cover panel from vibrating, leading to the nut mountings cracking. From late 1988 the cover was retained by six screws with a cap nut on the front rubber mounting, and stronger nut mountings. If fitting this six-hole cover panel to earlier machines, note that it will be necessary to weld an additional nut mounting to the silencer.

23 Oil pump - removal examination and refitting

1 The oil pump is the rear part of a combined oil/water pump assembly which is removed as follows **(see illustration)**:

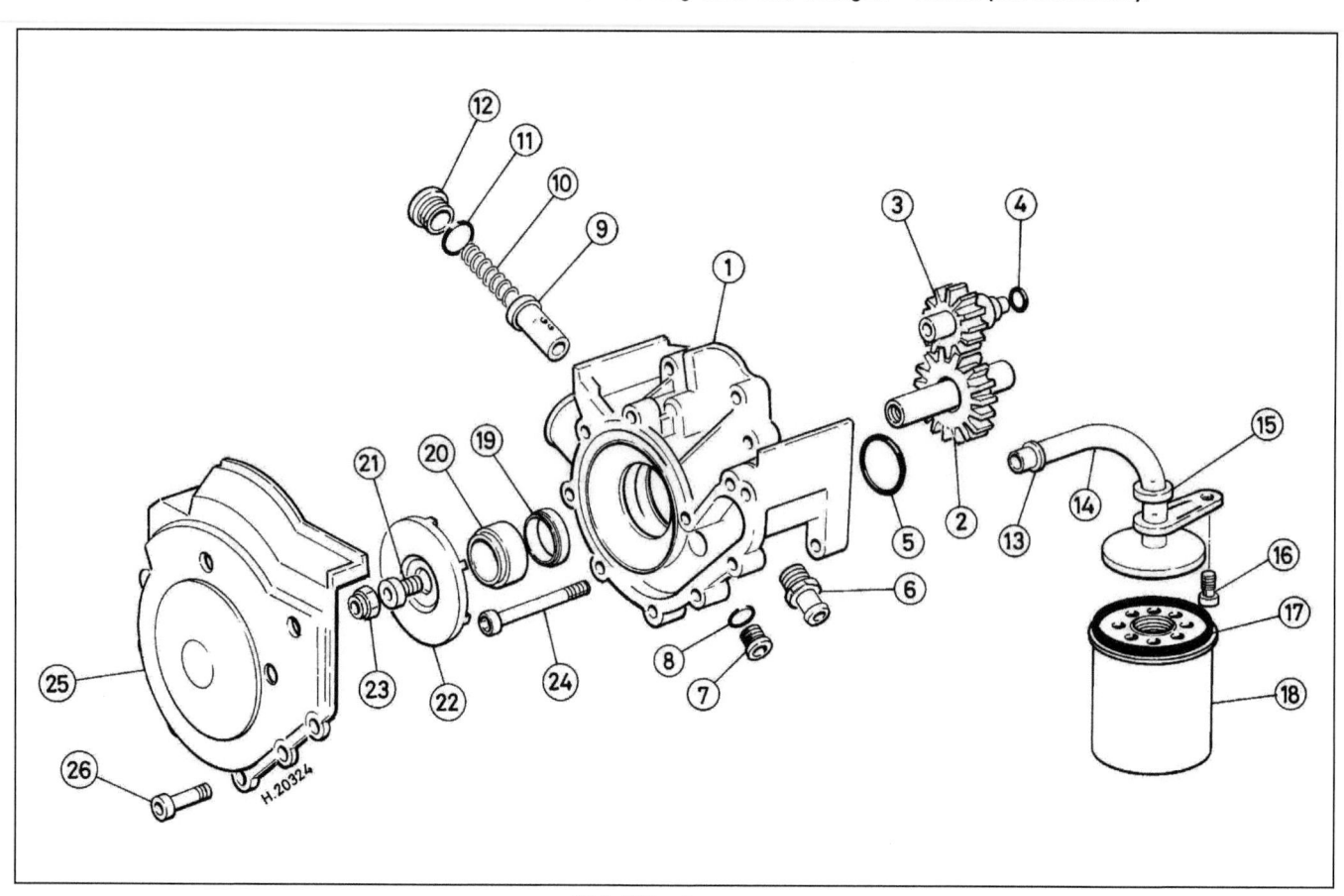

23.1 Oil/water pump

1 Body	8 Sealing washer	14 Oil pump pick-up	21 Bolt – late models
2 Oil pump driven gear	9 Pressure relief valve plunger	15 Grommet – early models	22 Impeller
3 Oil pump drive gear		16 Bolt	23 Nut – early models
4 O-ring	10 Spring	17 Sealing ring	24 Bolt
5 O-ring	11 Sealing washer	18 Oil filter	25 Cover
6 Oil pressure switch	12 Plug	19 Oil seal	26 Screw
7 Coolant drain plug	13 O-ring	20 Mechanical seal	

Fuel system and lubrication 6•21

23.4a Withdraw pump drive shaft

23.4b Water pump must be dismantled to permit removal of pump driven shaft

2 Drain the engine oil as described in Chapter 1 then drain the coolant. See Chapter 5. Disconnect the oil pressure switch lead from the switch and remove the radiator bottom hose.

3 Remove the pump cover retaining screws and withdraw the cover then remove the pump body retaining screws and withdraw the pump body; a few gentle taps with a soft-faced mallet should break the joint seal. Note the O-ring sealing the coolant passage between the pump and the crankcase lower section also the O-ring around the pump drive shaft rear end; both should be renewed whenever they are disturbed.

4 Withdraw the pump drive shaft **(see illustrations)**; if the pump shaft is to be removed or either of the pump seals are to be renewed refer to Chapter 5.

5 Closely examine all gear teeth mating surfaces and the body casting **(see illustration)**; if any component is seen to be worn or damaged in any way it must be renewed. Since there are no service limits specified pump wear cannot be checked by direct measurement; the only possible test of the lubrication system is a test of the operating pressure which will require a pressure gauge and the necessary adaptors.

6 On reassembly, thoroughly clean all components in the pump body, including the pressure relief valve and pressure switch. Blow clear all oilways with compressed air and refit the various components.

7 Fit a new O-ring around the coolant passage and to the pump drive shaft rear end **(see illustration)**. Apply a thin smear of Three Bond 1207 B sealant to the pump/crankcase mating surfaces and refit the pump assembly, ensuring that the drive shaft engages correctly in the output shaft.

8 Rotate the crankshaft to centralise the pump gears while tightening the pump body mounting screws to the specified torque setting (where given). Connect the oil pressure switch lead to the switch terminal and carefully refit the switch cover. Apply a thin smear of Three Bond 1207 B sealant to the mating surfaces and refit the pump front cover, tightening its retaining screws to the specified torque wrench setting, where given.

9 Refill the cooling system (Chapter 5). Replenish the engine with oil as described in Chapter 1, then refit all other disturbed components.

24 Oil pressure relief valve - general

1 The oil pressure relief valve consists of a spring-loaded plunger which is fitted in a bore in the oil pump body.

2 Depending on the tools available it may be possible to remove the valve components with the oil pump installed in which case it will be necessary only to drain the engine oil (see Chapter 1) and to drain the coolant and

23.5 Clean all pump components thoroughly and check for wear

23.7 Do not forget to renew O-rings on refitting oil/water pump assembly

6•22 Fuel system and lubrication

24.3a Unscrew pressure relief valve plug from pump body – note sealing washer

24.3b Withdraw pressure relief valve spring . . .

24.3c . . . and plunger – check carefully for dirt or wear

withdraw the radiator bottom hose (see Chapter 5) before removing the valve. If not remove the oil pump from the machine. See Section 23.

3 Unscrew the valve plug and withdraw the spring and plunger **(see illustration)**. Check both for signs of wear or damage and renew them if necessary; note that the spring should be renewed if there is the slightest doubt about its performance. Polish away any burrs or raised edges from the plunger and check that it is free to slide smoothly but without play in the pump body.

4 On refitting renew its sealing washer and tighten the valve plug to the specified torque wrench setting.

25 Oil pump pick-up filter gauze - cleaning

1 The filter gauze should be cleaned whenever the sump (oil pan) is removed or the engine and/or oil pump are overhauled.
2 Referring to Chapter 1, drain the engine oil and remove the oil filter.
3 Unscrew the retaining bolts around the periphery of the sump (oil pan), tap it with a soft faced mallet to break the seal, and withdraw it **(see illustration)**. Carefully remove all traces of old sealant from both mating surfaces and thoroughly clean the sump (inside and outside). Use a clean, lint-free rag, to wipe down the inside of the crankcase.
4 Remove the retaining Allen screw and manoeuvre the pick-up assembly out of the crankcase **(see illustration)**. Note the sealing O-ring set in a groove in the pipe aperture in the crankcase wall, around the pick-up pipe's upper (oil pump) end; this must be displaced, using a suitable pointed instrument, and renewed whenever it is disturbed. Wash the pick-up thoroughly in a high flash-point solvent and use a soft-bristled brush to scrub away any particles of foreign matter.
5 When the pick-up is completely clean and dry, fit a new O-ring to the groove in the pipe aperture in the crankcase wall and apply a smear of grease to the pipe end **(see**

25.3 Withdraw sump (oil pan) to reach pump pick-up filter gauze

25.4 Pick-up assembly is retained by a single Allen screw

25.5a Note sealing O-ring set in crankcase wall ...

25.5b ... and rubber grommet (early models only) – ensure this is fitted correctly in mounting bracket

26.4 Oil pressure switch is screwed into pump body – ensure it is completely waterproofed

illustration). Carefully refit the pick-up, taking care not to displace the sealing O-ring and ensuring that the rubber grommet (not used on later models) is seated correctly in its bracket **(see illustration)**. Tighten the pick-up retaining screw securely, using the specified torque wrench setting, where given.

6 Degrease the mating surfaces and apply a thin smear of Loctite 574 (early models) or Three Bond 1207 B sealant. Refit the sump (oil pan) and tighten its retaining screws securely to the specified torque wrench setting, working progressively and evenly in a diagonal sequence from the centre outwards.

7 Refit the engine oil drain plug and oil filter, then refill the crankcase with oil as described in Chapter 1.

26 Oil pressure warning lamp - general

1 The oil pressure warning lamp, which comes on when the ignition is switched on, should extinguish at idling speed. It is operated by a switch on the oil pump body.

2 If the lamp flashes, or remains on, check the oil level in the sump and ensure the filter is not clogged. If these are in order, check the electrical system for faults. See Chapter 11. If the lamp comes on when slowing down from high speed, again check the oil level and the filter. If these are OK, the main bearings or big-end bearings may be worn, or the oil pressure relief valve or oil pump may be faulty. Have the oil pressure checked with a gauge. If the pressure is low, overhaul the engine.

3 To remove the switch, peel back the rubber cover and slacken or remove, as necessary, the terminal screw. The oil should be drained before the switch is removed, so that the switch threads can be cleaned properly. Unscrew the switch.

4 On refitting, clean the threads of the switch and the oil pump body, apply a thin coat of sealant, and refit the switch **(see illustration)**. Tighten it carefully to the specified torque wrench setting; do not overtighten it or the switch may be broken and the pump body cracked. Tighten the terminal screw securely, apply a coat of WD40 or similar (see Chapter 11) and refit the rubber cover, ensuring that it seats fully.

Notes

Chapter 7
Ignition system

Contents

General description 1	Ignition timing - adjusting 10
Ignition and engine kill switches - general 9	Ignition trigger assembly - removal and refitting 4
Ignition control unit - removal and refitting 3	Precautions to be observed when checking the ignition system ... 2
Ignition HT coils - removal, refitting and testing 5	Spark plugs - check, adjustment and renewal .... see Chapter 1
Ignition HT leads - general 6	Spark plugs - general 7
Ignition system - fault finding 11	Vacuum switch - general (early 100 models only) 8

Degrees of difficulty

| Easy, suitable for novice with little experience | Fairly easy, suitable for beginner with some experience | Fairly difficult, suitable for competent DIY mechanic | Difficult, suitable for experienced DIY mechanic | Very difficult, suitable for expert DIY or professional |

Specifications

Ignition system
Type	Bosch VZ-51L or VZ-52L
Static ignition timing:	**Crankshaft angle** **Piston position**
US 75 models	4° BTDC 0.10 mm (0.0039 in) BTDC
100 models, UK 75 models	6° BTDC 0.24 mm (0.0095 in) BTDC
Advance starts at	1300 rpm
Advance range:	
US 75 models	26°
100 models, UK 75 models	24°
Maximum advance at	8650 rpm
Retard starts at:	
75 models	8777 rpm
100 models	8650 rpm
Fuel injection shuts off at:	
75 models	8905 rpm
100 models	8770 rpm
Starter motor lockout effective above	711 rpm
Cylinder identification	Numbered consecutively front to rear, Number 1 cylinder at front (cam chain) end
Firing order:	
75 models	3-1-2
100 models	1-3-4-2
Direction of rotation	Anti-clockwise, looking at ignition trigger from front of machine

Ignition HT coil
75 models	
Primary winding resistance	0.8 ohm
Secondary winding resistance	10 K ohm
Suppressor (HT lead connector)	1 K ohm or 0 ohm (marked)
100 models	No resistance values available at time of writing

7•2 Ignition system

Spark plugs
Make	Bosch
Type	X5DC
Gap:	
Standard	0.6 - 0.7 mm (0.024 - 0.028 in)
Service limit	0.8 mm (0.032 in)
Cap resistance	5 K ohm

Torque wrench settings
	Nm	lbf ft
Spark plugs	20 ± 2	15 ± 1.5
Ignition trigger backplate screws	3.5 ± 0.5	2.5 ± 0.5
Ignition trigger cover screws	6 ± 1	4.5 ± 0.5
Ignition HT coil mounting bolts	5 ± 0.5	3.5 ± 0.4

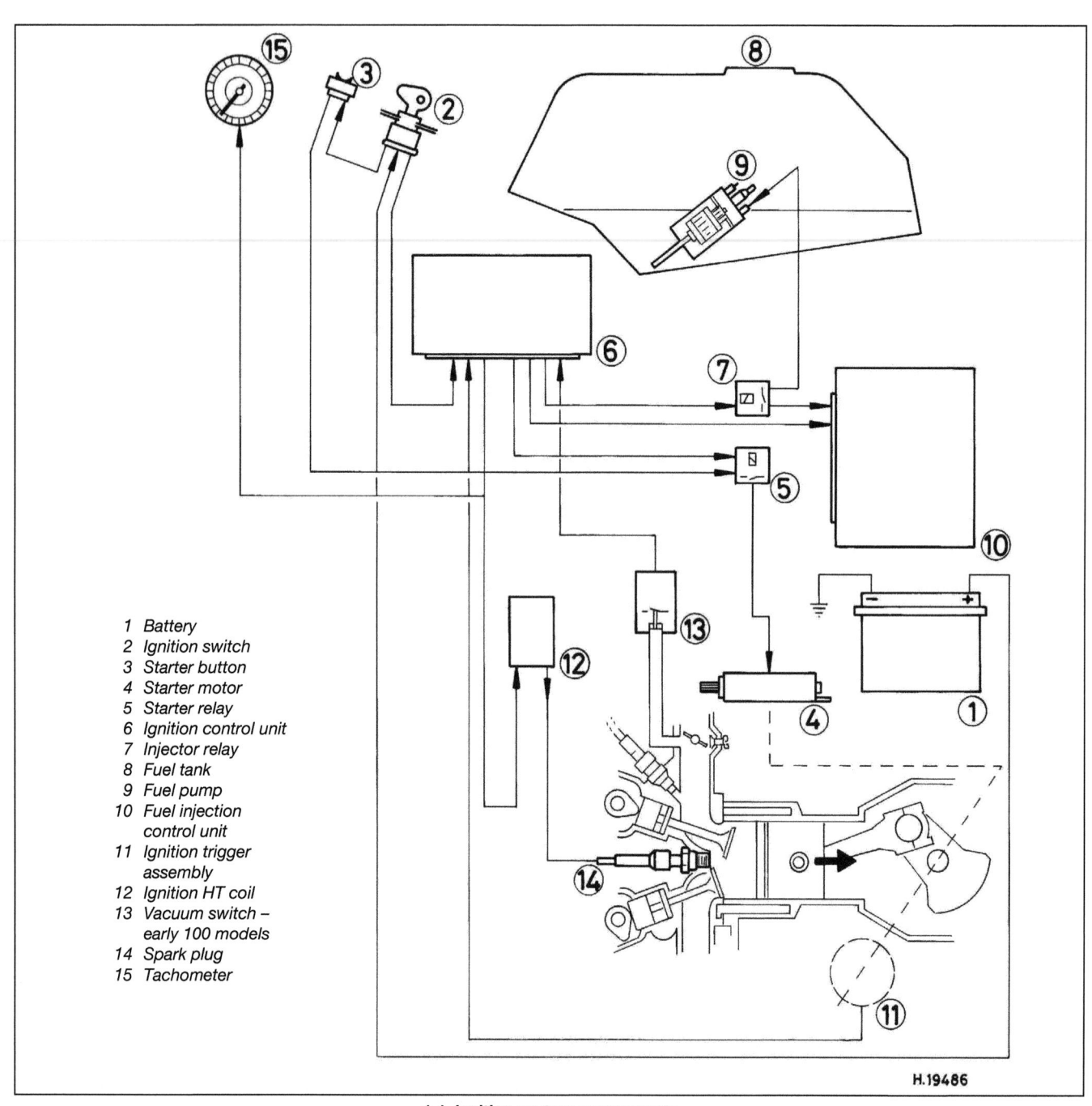

1 Battery
2 Ignition switch
3 Starter button
4 Starter motor
5 Starter relay
6 Ignition control unit
7 Injector relay
8 Fuel tank
9 Fuel pump
10 Fuel injection control unit
11 Ignition trigger assembly
12 Ignition HT coil
13 Vacuum switch – early 100 models
14 Spark plug
15 Tachometer

1.1 Ignition system components

Ignition system 7•3

1 General description

The ignition system is a microprocessor-controlled digital system powered by the battery. The heart of the system is the ignition control unit which receives signals from the trigger assembly mounted on the crankshaft front end and switches off the power supply to the HT coils thus inducing a spark across the spark plug electrodes (see illustration).

The trigger assembly contains two Hall effect transmitters; on 100 models these are equally spaced, one triggering the spark for cylinders 1 and 4 while the other acts for cylinders 2 and 3. On 75 models the transmitters are positioned at 120° and 240° to serve cylinders 1 and 3 respectively; from this the control unit works out the correct firing position for number 2 cylinder. On both models a 'wasted' spark system is used in which the spark plugs fire at every crankshaft revolution.

The impulses transmitted by the trigger assembly are used by the control unit to build up the spark at the HT coils and to advance or retard it according to a pre-programmed curve depending on engine speed and on early 100 models only, intake manifold depression. It also triggers the control pulses for the injectors and prevents engine damage through excessive speed by first retarding the ignition timing at a set speed and then cutting off the injectors when a maximum set engine speed is reached. A lockout circuit prevents the starter motor from being operated if the engine is still turning over.

On early 100 models a vacuum switch fitted to the intake manifold was used to bring in a second advance curve for part-load operation. However this was found to have so little effect in practice that it was omitted from all models from late 1985 on.

2 Precautions to be observed when checking the ignition system

Warning: The very high output of the type of ignition system fitted means that it can be very dangerous or even fatal to touch live components or terminals of any part of the system while it is in operation. Therefore take great care to avoid personal contact with any part of the system while the engine is running, or even when the engine is stopped but the ignition is switched on.

Note: *Owners of machines used in the US, particularly in California, should note the possible legal implications of attempting to service any part of the ignition system before undertaking such work. Refer to Chapter 6, Section 2.*

1 When working on any part of the ignition system, always cut off the power supply either by switching off the ignition key or by disconnecting the battery (negative terminal first). If test procedures require the system to be in operation, take great care to prevent personal contact with any part of the system.
2 Do not attempt to run the engine with the battery disconnected or with its connections made to the wrong terminals; this will destroy the ignition trigger assembly and may damage the alternator and other electrical components.
3 **Never** disconnect or attempt to disconnect the ignition HT leads at the coils or spark plugs while the engine is running; apart from the personal risk described above the coils and control unit would almost certainly be damaged.
4 **Never** attempt to test either the trigger assembly or the control unit using equipment which has its own source (eg multimeters, ohmmeters, meggers, or battery and bulb test circuits); the applied voltage may damage one or more of their sensitive circuits.
5 If the resistance of any other part of the system is to be tested, ensure that the power supply is cut off (see above) and that the wires leading to the trigger assembly or control unit are disconnected. This is to prevent the risk not only of personal injury but also of damage either to the tester or to any of the system's components.

3 Ignition control unit - removal and refitting

1 Remove the fuel tank. See Chapter 6.
2 Observing the precautions noted in Section 2 of this Chapter, peel back the waterproof cap from the rear of the control unit and unplug its connector (see illustration).
3 Remove the mounting nuts and washers and manoeuvre the unit clear of the frame tubes, noting the locating tab which projects into a rubber grommet at the front of the unit.
4 Refitting is the reverse of the above; take great care to ensure that the connection is securely fastened and that the waterproof cover is refitted.
5 Note that all 100 models from early 1985 onwards were fitted with a modified unit which has a strengthened, ribbed cover, and improved sealing arrangements to exclude moisture.

4 Ignition trigger assembly - removal and refitting

1 Remove the fuel tank. See Chapter 6. Where fitted, remove the engine spoiler or belly fairing. Disconnect the trigger assembly wires at the single connector on the frame top tubes, adjacent to the radiator filler.
2 Remove the trigger cover screws from the front of the engine front cover and withdraw the cover and its gasket (see illustration).
3 Carefully punch or scribe a reference mark from the trigger backplate across to the engine front cover so that the backplate can be refitted in its original position (see illustration). Remove the two retaining Allen

3.2 Ignition control unit is mounted just behind the steering head

4.2 Ignition trigger assembly is mounted on engine front cover

4.3 Scribe or punch reference mark before removing backplate so that it can be refitted in same position

7•4 Ignition system

4.4 Ignition rotor is secured to crankshaft flange by three screws

4.5 Timing plate notch aligns with cover pointer at TDC

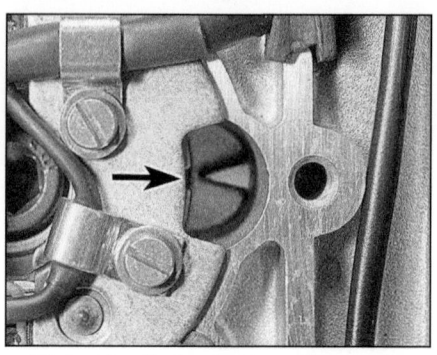

4.6 Ignition timing basic setting can be achieved by aligning cutouts as shown

screws and withdraw the backplate; release the electrical lead from the grommet set in the front cover and from any clamps or ties provided which secure it to the frame.

4 Remove the three screws which secure the ignition rotor and timing plate to the rotor flange and withdraw them, noting the locating pin **(see illustration)**.

5 On reassembly install the timing plate and the ignition rotor noting that they can fit only one way when aligned with the mounting screw holes and locating dowel pin **(see illustration)**. Refit the three retaining screws and tighten them securely.

6 Refit the backplate, align the marks made on dismantling, then refit and tighten the retaining Allen screws. If no marks are available, a basic setting which should allow the engine to run reasonably well can be made by aligning the edges of the cut-out in the backplate exactly with the edges of the cut-out in the housing **(see illustration)**. **It is essential** that the timing is checked properly as soon as possible after the ignition trigger is disturbed.

7 Route the trigger lead up through the sealing grommet and up to the connector securing it to the frame out of harm's way.

8 Refit the ignition trigger cover and gasket, tightening its screws to the specified torque wrench setting (where given).

9 If there is any doubt about the ignition timing setting, take the machine to an authorised BMW dealer as soon as possible to have the timing checked.

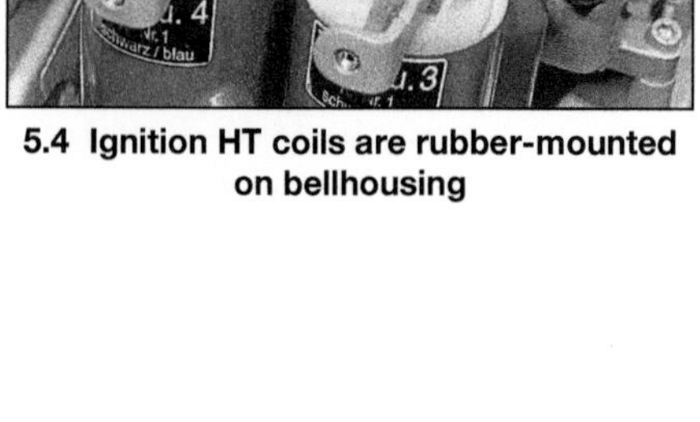

5.4 Ignition HT coils are rubber-mounted on bellhousing

5 Ignition HT coils - removal, refitting and testing

1 Remove the ignition HT coil cover (where fitted) and make a note of the connections before disconnecting the HT leads and the coil wires.

2 On 75 models remove the coil bracket top mounting bolt and swing out the assembly until the bottom mounting bolt can be removed. Withdraw the complete assembly; the individual coils can be unbolted if necessary.

3 On refitting, ensure that there is clean metal-to-metal contact between the coils' centre poles and their mounting bracket, also that the mounting bolts are securely fastened. If there is any doubt about the wire connections, note that the HT lead length will show which coil is connected to which spark plug and that the coil for cylinder number 1 (front) has the black/blue wire, number 2 has the black/red and number 3 (rear) has the black/green wire.

4 On 100 models remove the coil mounting bolts and nuts and withdraw the coils **(see illustration)**. Check that all connections are clean and all mountings securely fastened on reassembly.

5 If there is any doubt about the wire connections note that the front HT coil serves cylinders 1 and 4, 1 being on the outside (left-hand side); the black/blue wire is connected to its terminal 1, the green/yellow wire to its terminal 15 and the brown wire to its (centre) terminal 31. The rear HT coil serves cylinders 2 and 3, 2 being on the outside (left-hand side); apart from the black/red wire being connected to its terminal 1, all other connections are similar to the front coil.

6 The coils can be tested fully only on a spark-gap tester, which means that they must be taken to an authorised BMW dealer or a similar autoelectrical expert who has the necessary equipment if they are thought to be faulty. First of all, however, a suitable meter should be used to check that full battery voltage is available when the ignition is switched on. Connect the meter between the coil terminal 15 and a good earth point to make the test. If no power is found, check back through the system (as far as is possible) to trace the fault.

7 A quick check which will give a reasonable idea of a coil's condition is to measure the resistance of its windings, but this can be applied to 75 models only due to the lack of equivalent data for 100 models. Disconnect the coils completely and connect the meter between terminals 15 and 1 to obtain a reading for the primary winding. To test the secondary winding connect the meter between terminal 15 and the HT lead terminal. In both cases the resistances recorded should be close to those specified; if not the coil is suspect but should be checked very carefully by an expert using the correct equipment before any action is taken.

6 Ignition HT leads - general

1 The HT leads are easily removed by withdrawing the HT coil cover (where fitted) and the spark plug cover. Make a note of the routing of each lead before disconnecting and withdrawing it.

2 On refitting, note that each lead is numbered to identify which cylinder's spark plug it serves. On 75 models the length of the leads will reveal which HT lead is to be connected to which coil; if in doubt note that the HT coil for cylinder number 1 (front) has the black/blue wire, number 2 has the black/red and number 3 (rear) has the black/green wire.

3 On 100 models the front HT coil serves cylinders 1 and 4, 1 being on the outside (left-hand side) terminal, and the rear HT coil serves cylinders 2 and 3, 2 being on the outside (left-hand side).

4 In some cases suppressors are fitted to the HT leads; the resistances of these are usually marked on them as on the spark plug caps. If a fault arises, the HT lead can be quickly and easily detached so that its resistance can be measured. If the resistance reading obtained is significantly different from the value specified the component concerned should be renewed.

5 Always ensure that the leads are correctly

routed to prolong as much as possible their service life and if any are to be renewed at any time it is advisable to use only genuine BMW replacement parts so that the correct resistance values are maintained.

7 Spark plugs - general

1 Refer to Chapter 1 for information on spark plug checks, adjustment and renewal. A colour spark plug condition guide is on the inside rear cover of this manual.
2 Note that if the spark plugs are thought to be faulty they can be tested only by the substitution of new components.

8 Vacuum switch - general (early 100 models only)

1 This unit is to be found on 100 models only that were manufactured before mid-1985; owners should note however, that the switches may well have been removed from, or blanked off on, models built before that date.
2 The switch is a small unit retained by two screws to the right-hand side of the throttle body mounting bracket; a vacuum line joins it to number 1 cylinder vacuum take-off point.
3 The switch's function was to improve economy and part-load running by bringing a second pre-programmed advance curve into operation. However this was found to have so little effect that it was omitted from all later models.
4 If a fault arises which necessitates inspection of the switch, disconnect it and remove it from the throttle body. Insulate its connection and tape the wire back to the loom, then remove the vacuum line and fit a small cap, as on the middle two cylinders, to the vacuum take off point.

9 Ignition and engine kill switches - general

The switches fitted in the ignition system can be tested, after they have been disconnected, by using a meter or other test equipment as described in Chapter 11.

10 Ignition timing - adjusting

Warning: Before starting work refer to Section 2 of this Chapter and take all the necessary precautions to prevent any risk of damage or of personal injury.

1 Setting the ignition timing requires the use not only of a dial gauge with the necessary long adaptors but also a device which will indicate precisely when the trigger assembly sends a pulse to the control unit. BMW recommend a service tool 12.3.650 which is used with a test lead 12.3.651; with this equipment an LED lights when the trigger assembly reaches the firing point. Since it is expensive and not likely to be required very often, this equipment places the task beyond the scope of most owners.
2 Accordingly, owners are advised to take their machine to an authorised BMW dealer for the work to be carried out. For those who have the equipment, proceed as follows.
3 On 75 models the ignition timing is set on number 3 (ie the rearmost) cylinder; on 100 models it is set on number 1 (ie the front) cylinder. Remove the spark plugs (see Chapter 1), install the dial gauge on the appropriate cylinder, and zero it at Top Dead Centre (TDC).
4 Remove the fuel tank. See Chapter 6. Disconnect the trigger assembly wires at the connector on the frame top tubes and connect the test lead and ignition tester. Remove the trigger assembly front cover.
5 Turn the crankshaft backwards (ie clockwise, looking at the ignition trigger) to a point just before the specified firing point then slowly rotate it forwards again until the piston is **exactly** at the specified distance before TDC, whereupon the ignition tester diode should light. If not, slacken the trigger backplate mounting Allen screws and rotate the plate anti-clockwise to retard the timing or clockwise to advance it. When the diode lights at the correct moment, tighten the backplate screws.
6 Repeat the procedure to check that the setting is correct, then disconnect the test equipment and refit all disturbed components.

11 Ignition system - fault finding

1 Although electronic ignition systems are by now familiar equipment to most motorcyclists, the lack of test data on the system fitted to these machines, and its interconnection with the fuel injection system, means that there is very little the ordinary owner can do to test or repair it if a fault should arise.
2 As with the fuel injection system, the emphasis must be more on preventing faults from arising in the first place than on actual remedial repair work. The simplest approach can be summed up as follows:
a) If the system is working properly, leave it alone.
b) Prevention (in the form of preventive maintenance) is better than cure.
c) In the event of a fault, take the machine to an expert.
3 The first of these is obvious, but worth stressing. **Do not** attempt to 'tune', modify or 'improve' the system in any way. The only maintenance necessary is set out below and in Chapter 1; at all other times the system should not be disturbed.
4 The second is by no means as contradictory as it might first appear; the electronic components themselves are generally very reliable and any faults are usually caused by disruption of the current flow between the various components or by external factors such as excessive heat, vibration or attack by foreign matter or corrosive chemicals. Therefore anything that can be done to ensure that all components receive a stable supply of the correct amount of electrical current, that they are kept clean and properly secured to protect them from excessive heat and/or vibration, and that they are kept free of dirt, corrosion and substances such as water, coolant, brake fluid, battery acid or engine oil which might cause damage, must help to minimise the risk of ignition failure.
5 These preventive measures can be summed up as follows:
a) Ensure that the battery electrolyte levels are correct and that the terminal connections are clean and securely fastened at all times. If the machine is not used for any length of time, ensure that the battery is given refresher charges to keep it in good condition.
b) Working through the relevant wiring diagram to ensure that all components (including individual connectors) are treated, carefully clean back to bare metal all connections and terminals (finishing off with proprietary contact cleaner to remove any grease or oil) then pack them with silicone grease to exclude water and dirt and to prevent corrosion. On reassembly ensure that, where applicable, the waterproof cover is correctly refitted over each connector plug and that the retaining clip is secured. The ignition and kill switches should be packed with silicone grease or regularly lubricated with WD40 or similar to protect their terminals.
c) Ensure that all frame earths and earth connections are completely clean and securely fastened. Where wires are connected to the frame earth point, or at the bellhousing/frame mounting joint, ensure that the frame paint is scraped away to provide a clean metal-to-metal joint and that silicone grease or similar is applied to prevent corrosion.
d) Ensure that all components are correctly positioned and securely fastened at all times, also that all are as clean and dry as possible.
e) All wiring must be correctly routed so that it runs in smooth loops but avoids all possible contact with sharp edges, control cables or other moving components and components which became hot in operation. The wiring must

be secured out of harm's way, using plastic cable clips or insulating tape. Remember that wires which are too tight or sharply kinked may fail due to the effects of vibration, but wires which are too slack may foul other components. The HT leads must be routed with particular care to prolong as much as possible their service life, and the spark plug cover should be fitted at all times to protect the plugs, caps and leads from dirt, water and other debris.

f) Be careful never to knock, drop or otherwise mishandle any of the components; all are extremely sensitive and easily damaged.

g) If any component is found to be damaged or faulty at any time, repair or renew it immediately, before the damage has a chance to affect any other component. Note that if the HT coils, suppressors, HT leads or spark plug caps are renewed at any time, only genuine BMW parts must be used to ensure that the replacements are compatible with each other and with the control unit. If non-standard components have to be fitted in emergency, ensure that their resistance values are the same as the genuine items; if incompatible items are fitted the different resistance values may well damage the HT coils or the ignition control unit. Only the specified type and grade of spark plug should be fitted; seek the advice of an authorised BMW dealer or similar expert before making any changes from standard specification. Ensure also that the plugs are regularly serviced and/or removed as described in Chapter 1; wrongly-gapped or worn-out plugs may overload the control unit.

6 If a fault does arise, first read Section 2 concerning the precautions to be taken to prevent personal injury or damage to the machine when carrying out test procedures. To isolate the fault, check through the system in a logical sequence; while different faults may require varying methods, the following sequence of tests should permit the tracing of most faults (as far as the ordinary owner is likely to be able to follow them):

7 Check that the battery is in good condition and fully charged while it is possible, as a quick check. merely to ensure that all the other systems are working normally, it should be remembered that the battery may well be only just able to turn the engine over on the starter motor without having the reserves necessary to power the ignition and fuel injection systems. Therefore in certain circumstances it may be preferable to use a meter to check the battery rather than more rough and ready methods.

8 Check that the ignition and engine kill switches are properly switched on and that both are functioning correctly, also that the load-shedding relay is correctly cutting off the other circuits.

9 If the starter motor will not turn over, check that the fault is not in one of the ignition system-related safety interlock components (refer to the relevant wiring diagram for details).

10 If the starter motor is functioning correctly but the engine will not start, remove the spark plugs, connect each to its cap and lay it on the cylinder head or cylinder head cover. Be careful to place the electrodes as far away as possible from the spark plug apertures and to cover each aperture with a wad of rag or similar to prevent the risk of fire from sparks igniting any fuel/air mixture that may be ejected. Also ensure that the metal body of each spark plug is firmly in contact with the metal of the cylinder head or cover so that the risk of damage to the ignition system is avoided, which might result if one or more of the spark plugs is not correctly earthed during the performance of this test. When the engine is turned over on the starter motor (taking great care to prevent the risk of personal injury, as warned in Section 2), a strong blue spark should appear at regular intervals across the electrodes of each plug.

11 If no spark appears, or if the spark appears thin or yellow, further investigation will be required. First of all, substitute brand new spark plugs of the correct type and grade, then repeat the test to check whether any improvement is obtained. If the fault occurs on one cylinder only, swap the complete HT lead assembly (right angled suppressor/connector, lead, spark plug cap and spark plug) with that of another cylinder to check whether this cures the fault. Note however (on 100 models only) that if cylinders 1 and 4, or 2 and 3, are faulty at the same time the problem is most likely to be in the appropriate HT coil or its connections; this can be checked easily by swapping over the coil connections and repeating the test.

12 All of the HT lead components can be tested as described in Section 6 of this Chapter, but for the purposes of a quick check the various components can be tested by disconnecting them and swapping between cylinders until the faulty item is isolated; it is extremely unlikely that the same fault would cause failure in all three or four of any of these components.

13 If the fault is thought not to be in the HT lead assemblies, check the coils themselves. If all their connections and mountings are secure and there is no visible sign of damage, the power supply can be checked, as described in Section 5; a 12 volt bulb can be substituted if a meter is not available. The only full test for the HT coils that can be carried out by the ordinary owner is described in the same Section, but requires the use of a meter.

14 If the power supply to the coils is not correct, check the ignition and engine kill switches for faults, also the battery and earth connections (see the relevant wiring diagram for details).

15 If the coils are receiving the correct power supply and if there is no apparent fault in the coils themselves or in the HT lead components, the fault must lie in the ignition trigger assembly or in the control unit, or in the wires between them. It is worth checking that the trigger assembly is securely fastened and in the correct position, also that the connections are secure and the wires in good condition. It is permissible for the private owner to use an ordinary multimeter to check the wiring for faults, **provided** that all ignition system or fuel injection system components have been first disconnected. Refer to Section 2.

16 If none of the checks outlined above reveal the cause of the fault, the machine should be taken to an authorised BMW dealer who has the tester/diagnostic unit developed for BMW by Bosch. This equipment is connected to the machine by a set of adaptor leads and should be capable of checking the function of the entire ignition and fuel injection systems; in skilled hands it should be able to trace faults very quickly and easily.

17 Unfortunately there is no real alternative to the use of this equipment; while this manual contains all the relevant test data, nothing additional is available which will allow the checking of the system's components using ordinary equipment. Since all other available data is related specifically to the Bosch diagnostic unit, it is of no use to anyone who does not have access to one of these units. The only other possibility is to test by substitution; since the ignition system has only two major components it is feasible for an ordinary owner to swap first the trigger assembly, and then, if necessary, the control unit, in an attempt to isolate a fault. This is a very inconclusive and unsatisfactory test procedure which of course presupposes that sound components of exactly the correct type are available, either from a friendly BMW dealer or from a friend's machine.

18 Taking all the above into account, many owners may well feel that the simplest course of action is to take the machine to an authorised BMW dealer if a fault of any sort is encountered in the ignition system. Compared with the time-consuming nature of the various tests and the dangers both to the machine and its owner inherent in some of them, the idea must be attractive of having a skilled operator quickly and safely run through a test sequence on the diagnostic unit to check the entire system and locate any faults. even if this does mean having to pay the labour charge necessary.

Chapter 8
Frame and front suspension

Contents

Bodywork - removal and refitting	17	Front forks - removal	2
Fairing - removal and refitting	15	General description	1
Fluidbloc steering damper - general - 75 models	11	Instruments - removal, dismantling and reassembly	20
Footrests - general	13	Luggage - removal and refitting	19
Frame - examination and renovation	12	Mirrors - removal and refitting	18
Front forks - aligning the damping components	7	Seat - removal and refitting	16
Front forks - dismantling	3	Stands and controls - general	14
Front forks - examination and renovation	4	Steering head bearings - check and adjustment	see Chapter 1
Front forks - oil change	see Chapter 1	Steering head bearings - examination and renovation	9
Front forks - reassembly	5	Steering head bearings - refitting	10
Front forks - refitting	6	Steering head bearings - removal	8

Degrees of difficulty

Easy, suitable for novice with little experience	Fairly easy, suitable for beginner with some experience	Fairly difficult, suitable for competent DIY mechanic	Difficult, suitable for experienced DIY mechanic	Very difficult, suitable for expert DIY or professional

Specifications

Front forks – 1985 to 1992 75 models, all 100 models

Type	Fichtel and Sachs
Travel:	
K75S, any model with 'S' suspension	135 mm (5.32 in)
All other models	185 mm (7.28 in)
Stanchion OD	41.325 - 41.350 mm (1.6270 - 1.6280 in)
Lower leg ID	41.400 - 41.439 mm (1.6299 - 1.6315 in)
Stanchion/lower leg clearance	0.050 - 0.114 mm (0.0020 - 0.0045 in)
Stanchion maximum warpage	0.100 mm (0.0039 in)
Stanchion installed height (test length) - from top of stanchion to top machined surface of bottom yoke	180 mm (7.0866 in)
Fork spring free length:	
Top spring - K75S, any model with 'S' suspension	Not available
Main spring - K75S, any model with 'S' suspension	Not available
Main spring - all other models	395 - 401 mm (15.5512 - 15.7874 in)
Main spring wire diameter	4.67 - 4.73 mm (0.1839 - 0.1862 in)
Fork oil capacity - per leg:	
K75S, any model with 'S' suspension	280 ± 10 cc (9.86 ± 0.35 Imp fl oz, 9.47 ± 0.34 US fl oz)
K100, all other 75 models	330 ± 10 cc (11.62 ± 0.35 Imp fl oz, 11.16 ± 0.34 US fl oz)
K100RS, K100RT, K100LT	360 ± 10 cc (12.67 ± 0.35 Imp fl oz, 12.17 ± 0.34 US fl oz)

Front forks – 1985 to 1992 75 models, all 100 models (continued)

Recommended fork oil:
- Aral . . . . 1010 shock absorber oil
- Aral . . . . P3441 shock absorber oil
- Bel-Ray . . . . SAE 5 Fork Oil (with 'Seal Swell')
- BP . . . . Aero Hydraulic
- BP-Olex . . . . HLP 2849
- Castrol . . . . Fork Oil Extra Light
- Castrol . . . . DB Hydraulic Fluid
- Castrol . . . . 1/-318 Shock Absorber Oil
- Castrol . . . . LHM - only for temperatures below 0°C (32°F)
- Castrol . . . . AWH 15
- Esso . . . . Univis 13 Telefork Oil or Comfort
- Golden Spectro . . . . Suspension Fluid Very Light
- Mobil . . . . Aero HFA shock absorber oil
- Mobil . . . . DTE 11 shock absorber oil
- Premium Fork Lubricant . . . . Spectro SAE10 - for competition use only
- Shell . . . . Aero Fluid 4
- Shell . . . . 4001 shock absorber oil
- Wack Chemie . . . . SAE 5 (red) high-performance telescopic fork oil

Front forks - 1993-on K75, K75S, K75RT models

Type	Showa
Travel	135 mm (5.32 in)
Stanchion OD	41.4 mm (1.630 in)
Stanchion maximum warpage	0.1 mm (0.004 in)
Stanchion installed height (test length) from top of stanchion to top machined surface of bottom yoke	180 mm (7.0866 in)
Oil capacity (per leg) - at oil change	410 cc (14.43 Imp fl oz, 13.68 US fl oz)
Oil capacity (per leg) - dry	420 cc (14.78 Imp fl oz, 14.20 US fl oz)
Manufacturer's oil recommendation	Esso Comfort

Torque wrench settings - 75 models

	Nm	lbf ft
Steering stem top bolt - early models	74 ± 5	54.5 ± 4
Steering stem adjuster sleeve - late models	45 ± 3	33 ± 2
Steering stem adjuster sleeve locknut - late models	45 ± 3	33 ± 2
Steering head bearing adjusting knurled circular nut	Tightened until free play is just removed from bearings	
Handlebar clamp bolts	22 ± 2	16 ± 1.5
Handlebar mirror retaining nuts	16 ± 3	12 ± 2
Front forks - 1985-92 models:		
Damper rod Allen screw	20 ± 2	15 ± 1.5
Oil filler plug	15 ± 2	11 ± 1.5
Oil drain plug	9 ± 1	6.5 ± 0.5
Front forks - 1993-on models	Not available	
Fork yoke pinch bolts – Fichtel and Sachs forks:		
Top yoke pinch bolts	21 ± 2	15.5 ± 1.5
Bottom yoke pinch bolt	43 ± 3	32 ± 2
Fork yoke pinch bolts – Showa forks:		
Top yoke pinch bolts	26	19
Bottom yoke pinch bolts (new bolts – see text)	50	37
Fluidbloc retaining screws or bolts	9 ± 1	6.5 ± 0.5
Fork brace/lower leg mounting bolts	21 ± 2	15.5 ± 1.5
Stand mounting bracket/gearbox bolts	41 ± 5	30 ± 4
Centre and side stand pivots	41 ± 5	30 ± 4
Footrest plate/gearbox bolts	15 ± 2	11 ± 1.5
Pillion footrest/footrest plate retaining nuts	29 ± 3	21.5 ± 2
Rear brake pedal pivot	25 ± 3	18.5 ± 2
Fairing mounting bracket/steering head screws or bolts - K75 S	9 ± 1	6.5 ± 0.5

Torque wrench settings - 100 models

	Nm	lbf ft
Steering stem top bolt	74 ± 5	54.5 ± 4
Steering head bearing adjusting knurled circular nut	Tightened until free play is just removed from bearings	
Handlebar clamp bolts	22 ± 2	16 ± 1.5
Fork oil filler plug	15 ± 2	11 ± 1.5
Top yoke pinch bolts	22 ± 1	16 ± 0.5
Bottom yoke pinch bolt	43 ± 3	32 ± 2
Fork brace/lower leg mounting bolts	21 ± 2	15.5 ± 1.5
Damper rod Allen screw	20 ± 2	15 ± 1.5
Fork oil drain plug	9 ± 1	6.5 ± 0.5

Frame and front suspension 8•3

1 General description

The front forks are of the telescopic type with internal coil springs and hydraulic damping and are built for BMW by Fichtel and Sachs or Showa (75 models 1993-on). The original design received a minor modification late in 1984 and a major revision of the damping components in 1986, when the 75 models were introduced. All 75 models and a special edition K100 RS were fitted with an integral fork brace. When the K75 S model was introduced it was fitted with shorter travel forks which were fitted with two springs in each leg and heavily revised damping components. This type of fork, now offered on other models as 'S' type suspension, carries the same damping components as all other current models in its left-hand fork leg but some are omitted from its right-hand leg. The extra spring, coupled with the preload spacers at the bottom of each leg, gives a much stiffer ride than is normal for BMW; these forks must be used only in conjunction with the stiffened K75 S rear suspension unit.

The steering head bearings are of the taper roller type for all models but the top bearing was modified on 75 models early in 1986 to incorporate a more accurate method of adjustment. Also introduced at this time on 75 models was the 'Fluidbloc' steering damper which consists of a stiff rubber bush lubricated with silicone grease and fixed around the steering stem by grub screws passed through the steering head lug; it can be fitted to any earlier 75 model.

The frame is a spine type, constructed of welded steel tubing and incorporating the engine/transmission unit as a stressed member.

2 Front forks - removal

1 It is advisable to prevent any risk of damage to its paintwork by removing the fuel tank. See Chapter 6.
2 On machines fitted with fairings, remove any internal panels (eg the knee pads on K75RT, K100RS, K100RT and K100LT models) that prevent access to the fork yokes, and on K75RT, K100RS, K100RT and K100LT models, remove the fork gaiter retaining screws (where fitted). On models fitted with the handlebar fairing (K75C-type) slacken the clamp screws holding the fairing bracket to the fork stanchions.
3 Remove the front wheel **(see illustration)**. See Chapter 10. Disconnect the second brake caliper from the fork lower leg, place a soft wooden or plastic spacer between the pads of each caliper and tie both calipers loosely to the frame so that both are out of harm's way

2.3 Remove front wheel, both brake calipers and hoses, and front mudguard

and their hoses are not kinked or stretched.
4 Remove its mounting bolts and withdraw the front mudguard and, where fitted, the fork brace.
5 Prise the black plastic cap off the top of each fork leg and slacken fully both fork yoke pinch bolts to release each leg **(see illustrations)**.
6 Unless the yokes have been distorted through excessive overtightening, the fork legs can be pulled easily downwards and out of the yokes.

HAYNES HiNT *If resistance is encountered while removing the fork legs, apply a liberal quantity of penetrating fluid to the fork stanchions where they pass through the yokes, allow time for it to work and then try to rotate the stanchion to break it free of the yoke's grip, before pulling it downwards.*

3 Front forks - dismantling

Fichtel and Sachs forks

1 Always dismantle fork legs separately to avoid the risk of interchanging parts and causing increased wear. Store all components in separate, clearly-marked containers and work on one leg at a time to ensure this.

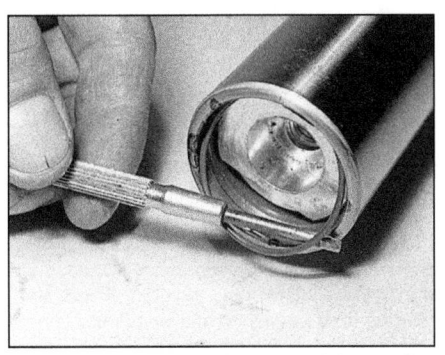

3.4a Push top plug into stanchion until circlip can be withdrawn . . .

2.5a Prise plastic cap off each leg . . .

2.5b . . . then slacken pinch bolts to release fork stanchions

2 Holding the top plug with an open-ended spanner, remove the filler plug then unscrew the drain plug and hold the leg over a suitable container to drain the oil. Pump the leg vigorously to expel as much oil as possible.
3 Using the wheel spindle placed in one of its lugs to prevent rotation, unscrew the damper rod Allen screw from the base of the fork lower leg.
4 Clamp the fork lower leg by the caliper mounting or wheel spindle lugs in a vice equipped with soft jaws to avoid marking the soft alloy, then use a suitable rod to press in the top plug until the retaining circlip is exposed **(see illustration)**. Push the circlip down into the leg on one side only so that it can be gripped with a pair of pliers and withdrawn **(see illustration)**. Allow the spring pressure to push the top plug out of the

3.4b . . . top plug should be pushed out by spring pressure but may require pulling, as shown, if O-ring is a tight fit

8•4 Frame and front suspension

3.9 If damper rod is removed from stanchion, note number and thickness of shims

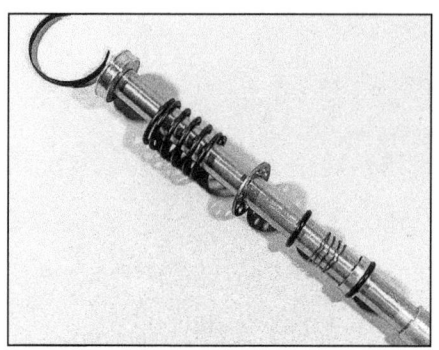

3.10a Do not dismantle damper rod unless necessary – piston must be heated to release locking compound . . .

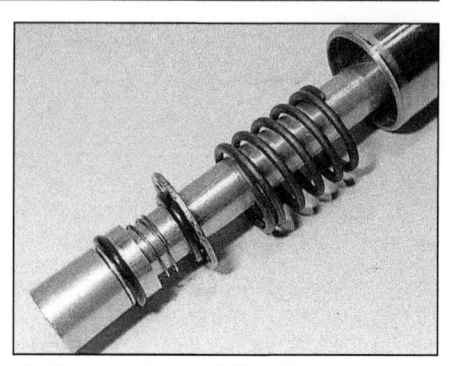

3.10b . . . note carefully which way round components are fitted before removing them

stanchion; in some cases the sealing O-ring may be such a tight fit that the top plug must be extracted using a pair of pliers to grip a bolt screwed into the filler plug thread.

5 Make a very careful note of the order components are removed, and which way round each is fitted. Note that any references to K75S suspension components automatically apply to any model fitted with S type suspension.

6 On all models except the K75S, remove first the white nylon spacer then the fork spring, noting which way round the spring was fitted, also the spring seat at each end. Note that later 100 and 75 (except those fitted with 'S' suspension) models were fitted with two fork springs as opposed to the single spring on earlier models, to minimise spring distortion. In such cases a spring seat will be fitted in each end of the two springs.

7 On K75 S models remove the spacers, followed by the top spring, then the main spring; note carefully which way round each component was fitted.

8 On all models, remove the damper rod Allen screw and pull the fork stanchion assembly out of the lower leg. Owners should note that the rebuilding procedure is quite difficult if the damper components are removed from the stanchion; it is recommended that these components are left undisturbed unless their removal is absolutely necessary.

9 Remove the circlip from the stanchion lower end and note the number and thickness of shims fitted above it (see illustration). Pull the damper assembly carefully out of the stanchion; as the damper piston emerges note which way round the piston ring is fitted. The valve housing can be removed from the lower end of the damper rod and the piston ring can be removed from its groove.

10 If the damper components are to be dismantled, thoroughly clean the rod assembly, removing all traces of oil and dirt and finishing off with a rinse in hot soapy water to remove any flammable solvents. On K75 S models measure the exact overall length of each damper rod from the piston top surface to the rod lower end and record the results. The damper piston is screwed on to the rod upper end and secured at a precise distance by Loctite 638 or 273 thread-locking compound; to release this it must be heated in a gentle flame until the Loctite starts to burn (approximately 250°C/482°F), whereupon the piston can be gripped with a pair of pliers or similar and unscrewed (see illustration). The damper components can then be removed after taking careful note of exactly which way round each is fitted (see illustration).

11 To access the fork oil seals, withdraw the dust excluder from the top of each fork lower leg. On late 1987-on models (and earlier models with modified fork seals) remove the seal retaining circlip. Carefully lever out the seal using only a tool with well-rounded edges to avoid scratching the seal housing; place a piece of wood across the top of the leg to act as a pivot and prevent damage to the leg itself. If a seal is very difficult to remove, pour boiling water over its upper end, taking care to prevent the risk of personal injury.

12 On K75S models once the seals are removed the spacers can be tipped out of the fork lower legs; note which way round each is fitted.

Showa forks

13 Remove the plastic cap from the top of the stanchion. With the fork leg in an upright position, hold the top plug steady whilst the oil filler plug is unscrewed from the centre of the top plug. Unscrew the oil drain screw from the rear of the lower leg and allow the fork oil to drain into a container; pump the leg to expel the oil fully.

14 Release the dust excluder from the top of the lower leg and slide it up and off the stanchion. Using a small flat-bladed screwdriver, lever the oil seal retaining circlip out of its groove in the lower leg.

15 Clamp the lower leg between a vice with well padded jaws, and unscrew the damper rod bolt from the base of the lower leg. Note that compressing the stanchion in the leg will apply spring pressure to the damper rod head, holding it steady whilst the bolt is slackened. Remove the lower leg from the vice.

16 It is now necessary to separate the stanchion and lower leg by pulling the two apart with a slide-hammer action. This will serve to dislodge the oil seal, backing washer and outer bush from the lower leg. Once released, invert the lower leg to tip out the damper rod seat.

17 To dismantle the damper components, press the top plug down into the stanchion whilst its retaining circlip is dislodged from the groove and removed. Slowly release pressure on the top plug and allow spring pressure to push it out of the stanchion. Invert the stanchion and withdraw the long spacer, spring seat, fork spring, damper rod and rebound spring.

4 Front forks - examination and renovation

Fichtel and Sachs forks

1 If the forks have been damaged in an accident, it is essential to inspect both fork yokes, the stanchions and the lower legs, for distortion and hairline cracks. Distorted components must be renewed, do not attempt to straighten them.

2 Stanchions may be checked for straightness by rolling them along a flat surface.

3 Check the fork bottom yoke by clamping the steering stem horizontally in a vice with soft jaws. Fit the stanchions to the yoke, with the upper ends projecting the specified test length beyond the top machined face of the yoke.

4 Take a sight across two straightedges laid across the extreme ends of the stanchions. Check for parallelism by measuring between the stanchions at each end, at right angles. Fit the top yoke and check that the steering stem and both stanchions fit into it without any apparent strain.

5 The fork lower legs are not bushed; the stanchions bear directly in the alloy casting. If the lower legs are worn or scored they must be renewed. Permissible clearance is given in the Specifications Section of this Chapter.

Frame and front suspension 8•5

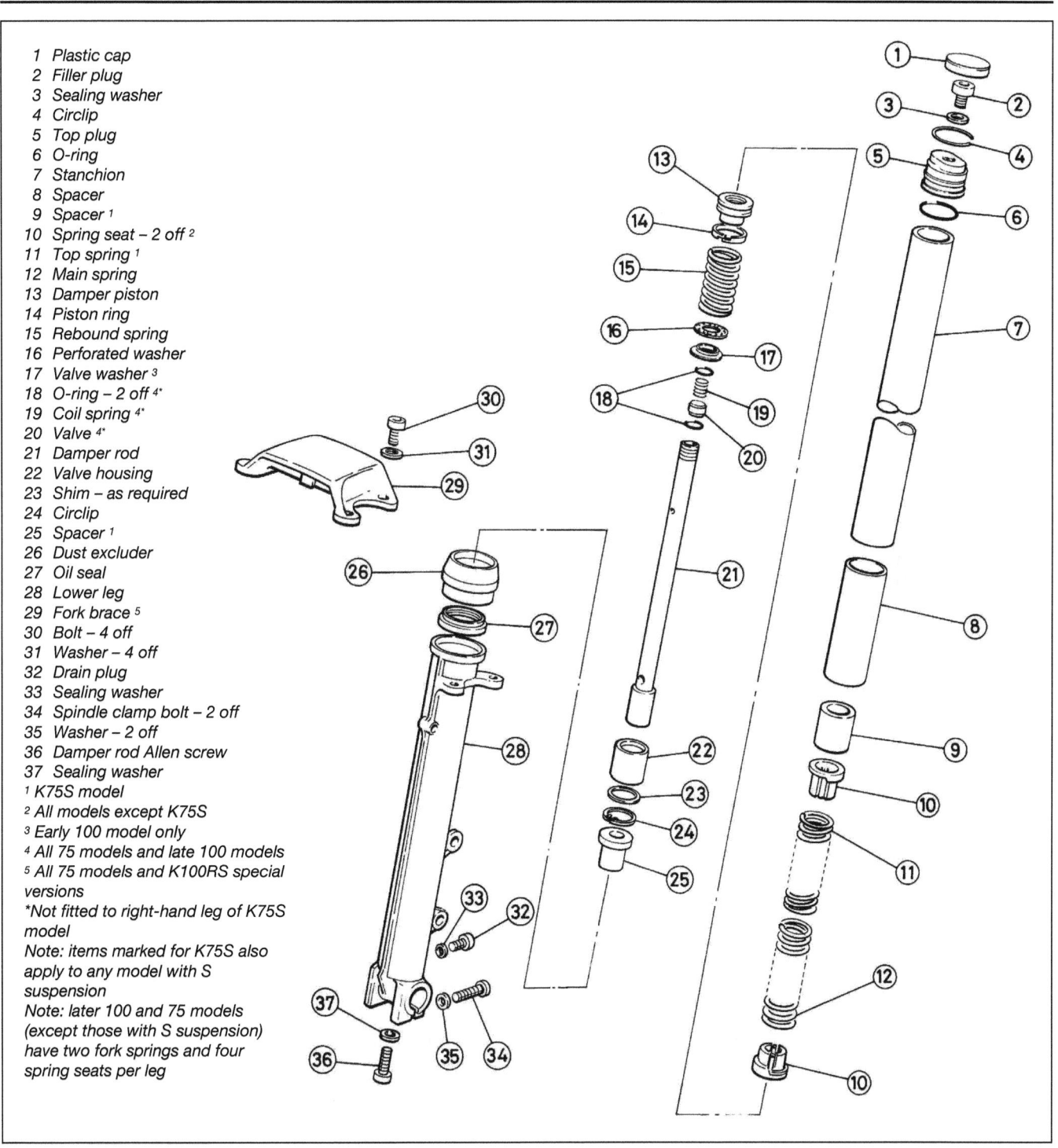

1 Plastic cap
2 Filler plug
3 Sealing washer
4 Circlip
5 Top plug
6 O-ring
7 Stanchion
8 Spacer
9 Spacer [1]
10 Spring seat – 2 off [2]
11 Top spring [1]
12 Main spring
13 Damper piston
14 Piston ring
15 Rebound spring
16 Perforated washer
17 Valve washer [3]
18 O-ring – 2 off [4]
19 Coil spring [4]
20 Valve [4]
21 Damper rod
22 Valve housing
23 Shim – as required
24 Circlip
25 Spacer [1]
26 Dust excluder
27 Oil seal
28 Lower leg
29 Fork brace [5]
30 Bolt – 4 off
31 Washer – 4 off
32 Drain plug
33 Sealing washer
34 Spindle clamp bolt – 2 off
35 Washer – 2 off
36 Damper rod Allen screw
37 Sealing washer
[1] K75S model
[2] All models except K75S
[3] Early 100 model only
[4] All 75 models and late 100 models
[5] All 75 models and K100RS special versions
*Not fitted to right-hand leg of K75S model
Note: items marked for K75S also apply to any model with S suspension
Note: later 100 and 75 models (except those with S suspension) have two fork springs and four spring seats per leg

4.6 Front forks - Fichtel and Sachs

6 The oil seals should be renewed whenever they are disturbed, as should all sealing O-rings and washers. Check carefully the condition of each damper rod piston ring and renew it if there is any doubt about its condition. Where fitted, check the dust excluder and fork gaiters for signs of wear or damage and renew them if necessary **(see illustration).**

7 Measure the spring free lengths; if either has settled to less than the specified length, where available, both springs must be renewed.

8 Thoroughly clean all components and dry them ready for reassembly.

Showa forks

9 Clean all components thoroughly and inspect for signs of wear as described for the Fichtel and Sachs forks, referring also to the specifications at the beginning of this Chapter.

10 Any wear should be taken by the bush on the bottom end of the stanchion and the bush which resides in the top of the lower leg; examine the working surfaces of both for visible damage. The stanchion bush is split for ease of removal and fitting; if it requires

8•6 Frame and front suspension

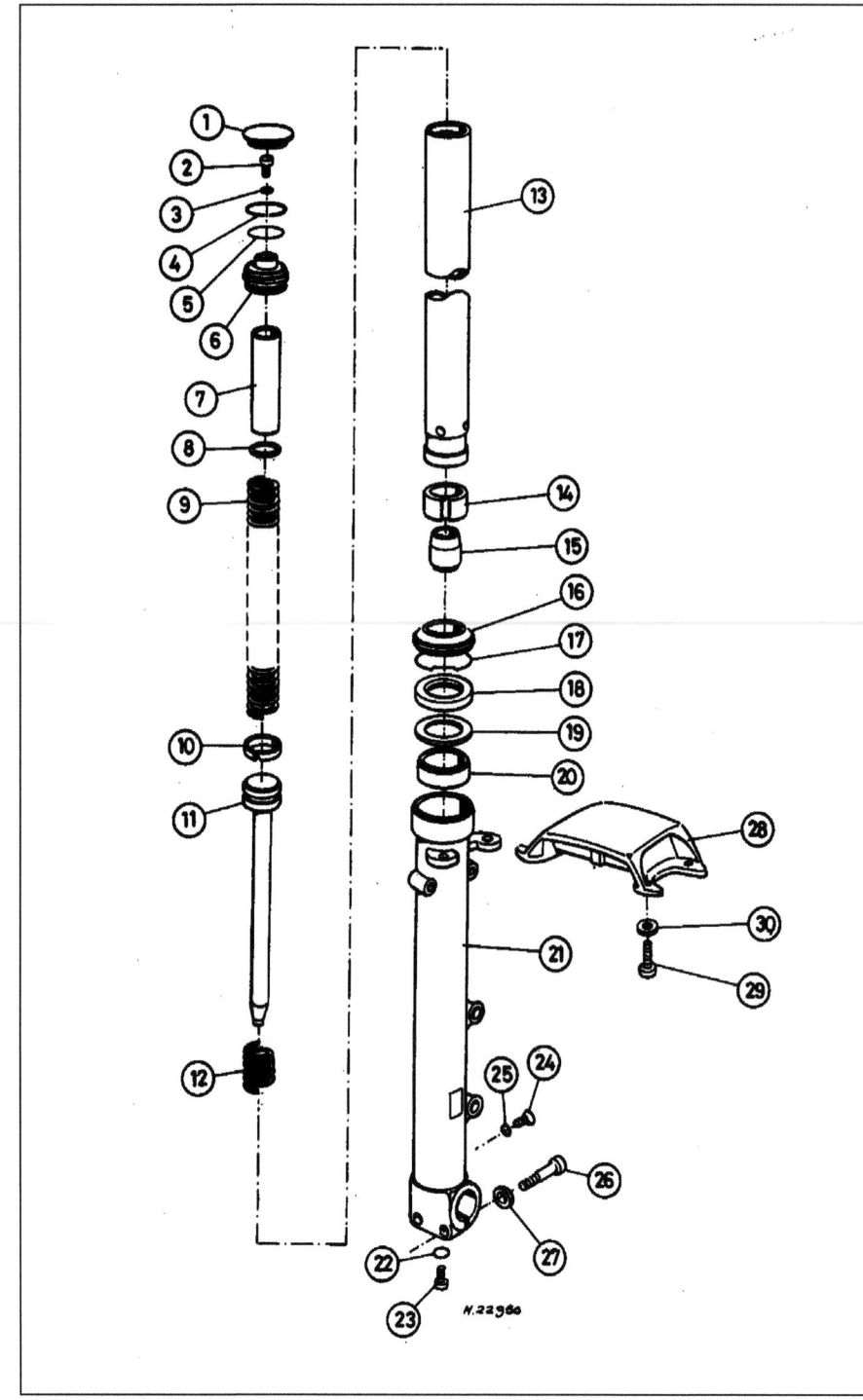

4.10 Front forks - Showa

1 Plastic cap
2 Oil filler plug
3 O-ring
4 Circlip
5 O-ring
6 Top plug
7 Spacer
8 Spring seat
9 Fork spring
10 Damper rod ring
11 Damper rod
12 Rebound spring
13 Stanchion
14 Stanchion bush
15 Damper rod seat
16 Dust excluder
17 Circlip
18 Oil seal
19 Backing washer
20 Lower leg bush
21 Lower leg
22 Sealing washer
23 Damper rod Allen screw
24 Oil drain screw
25 Sealing washer
26 Spindle clamp bolt – 2 off
27 Washer
28 Fork brace
29 Bolt – 4 off
30 Washer – 4 off

renewal gently prise its ends apart sufficient to withdraw it from the stanchion end and apply the same caution when installing the new component **(see illustration)**.

5 Front forks - reassembly

Fichtel and Sachs forks

1 On K75S models refit the spacers to the fork lower legs, ensuring that they are the correct way up.

2 On all models refit the fork seals. Check that each housing is free from burrs or raised edges, then smear grease over the seal's outside edge and tap it squarely into its housing until it is **just** flush with the top of the fork lower leg. **Do not** attempt to drive it in any further as this will merely distort the seal and promote leaks. Use a hammer and a tubular drift such as a socket spanner which bears only on the seal's hard outer edge to tap the seal into place. **Note:** *From late 1987 a modified fork seal with an extra dust seal lip was fitted. A wire circlip retains the seal in the lower leg. Note that when refitting the dust excluder the manufacturer recommends that its groove be packed with Gleitmo 805 or Shell Retinax A grease. The modified oil seal can be fitted to all earlier machines, although it is also necessary to fit a spacer washer to prevent the dust excluder coming into direct contact with the oil seal's lip.*

3 If the damper rod assembly was disturbed, it must be rebuilt following the accompanying photographs and illustrations to ensure that all components are correctly refitted. Note particularly that the valve fitted at the bottom of the rod on later models has an O-ring around it which should be on the lower side of the valve.

4 When the damper assembly is complete, the piston must be refitted to retain the components; make a final check that all are refitted and degrease the piston and rod threads. Apply a single drop of Loctite 638 or 273 thread-locking compound and screw the piston on to the rod until the rod's overall length (from the top of the piston to the bottom of the rod's lower end) is 258 ± 0.5 mm (10.16 ± 0.02 in). Note that a specified figure is not available for K75S models; these must be rebuilt to the length noted on dismantling. When the piston is correctly set, either dry the Loctite with a hot-air blower or leave it to cure for 24 hours at room temperature.

5 Fit the damper piston ring to the piston groove so that its notched end is downwards then wrap a sheet of thin (the metal in the illustration is 0.35 mm/0.014 in thick) metal or stiff plastic around the piston and ring to hold the ring securely in its groove and to act as a guide to lead it into the stanchion bore.

Frame and front suspension 8•7

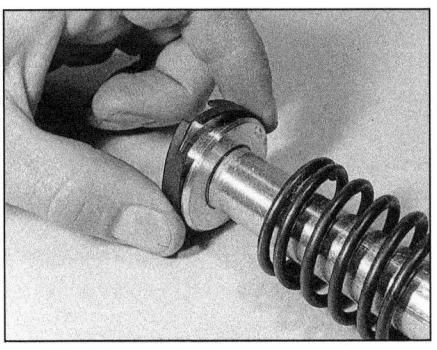

5.5a Wrap piston ring around piston groove ...

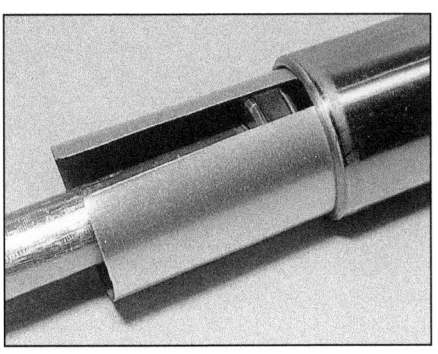

5.5b ... and use fabricated guide to ensure assembly is inserted into stanchion without damage

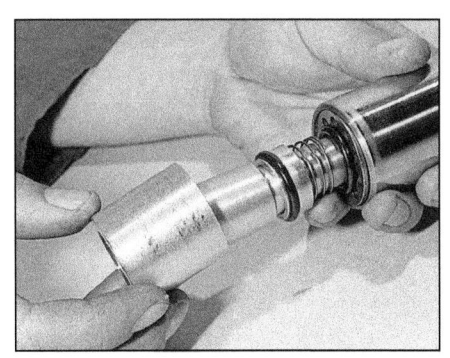

5.6a Fit valve housing over damper rod lower end ...

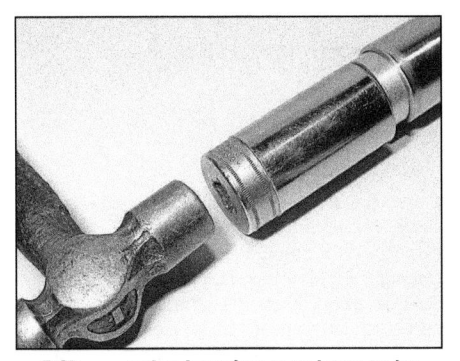

5.6b ... valve housing may have to be tapped gently into stanchion

5.6c Clearance between valve housing and circlip must be eliminated using shims

5.7a Lubricate all components before refitting stanchion assembly to lower leg

Withdraw the guide and push the damper rod into the stanchion **(see illustrations)**.

6 Fit the valve housing over the rod lower end and insert it into the bottom of the stanchion **(see illustrations)**. The housing is retained by a circlip but the clearance between them must be eliminated by careful shimming to prevent an annoying rattle **(see illustration)**. Shims are available in thicknesses of 0.1 and 0.3 mm (0.004 and 0.012 in) for early 100 models but can only be used in conjunction with a modified circlip which was subsequently fitted to all other models. For later models shims are available in thicknesses of 1.6, 1.7, 1.8, 1.9 and 2.0 mm (0.063, 0.067, 0.071, 0.074 and 0.079 in).

7 Smear the stanchion assembly with oil and insert it into the fork lower leg, using the spring(s) to stop the damper rod from disappearing inside the stanchion **(see illustration)**. Refit the damper rod Allen screw and its sealing washer. Either pass a slim wooden dowel, with a coarse taper ground on one end, down inside the stanchion to bear against the damper piston or refit the spring(s) and spacer(s) and use these to apply sufficient pressure to stop the damper rod from rotating. Tighten the damper rod Allen screw to the specified torque wrench setting, where given **(see illustration)**. Refit the drain plug and tighten it to its specified torque setting. Check the condition of the dust excluder, particularly its sealing lip; if this is in anything other than perfect condition it should be renewed. Note that the lips on some dust excluders have been found to be chamfered at the point of contact with the stanchion, leading to leakage and the ingress of dirt. Smear the sealing lips and internal groove of the dust excluder with grease (BMW specify Gleitmo 805 or Shell Retinax A) and refit the dust excluder **(see illustration)**.

8 If required, the fork oil can be added at this stage rather than risk wasting any in trying to pour it through the rather small filler hole. Refit the fork spring(s) ensuring that the spring seats (where fitted) are correctly installed and that the springs are refitted the correct way up **(see illustration)**. Refit the spacer(s) and

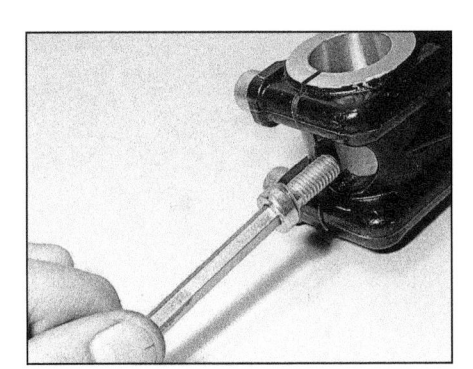

5.7b Prevent damper rod from rotating while Allen screw is fastened

5.7c Refit dust seal to top of lower leg – do not forget gaiter (where fitted)

5.8a Ensure springs are refitted original way up – do not omit spring seats, if fitted

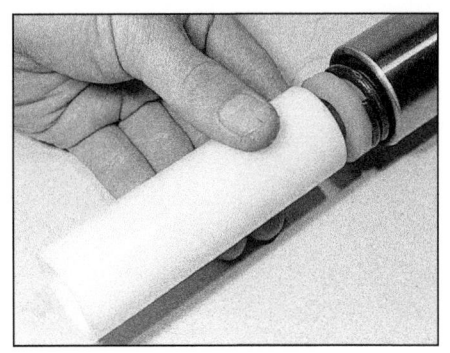

8•8 Frame and front suspension

5.8b Refit fork spring spacer . . .

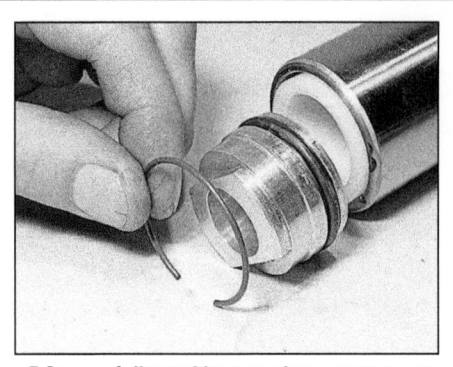

5.8c . . . followed by top plug – note new sealing O-ring

5.9 Push top plug into stanchion until circlip can be refitted

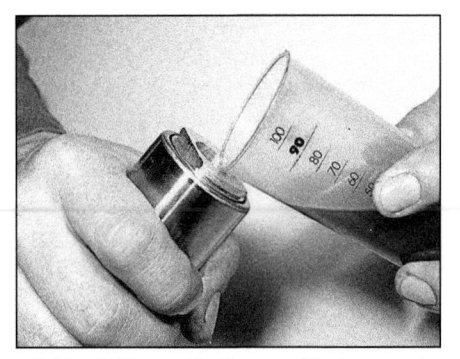

5.10a Add exactly the specified amount and type of oil to each fork leg

5.10b Hold top plug as shown while tightening filler plug – fork leg should be fully extended

6 Front forks - refitting

Refitting

1 Use fine abrasive paper to polish away any burrs, raised edges or deposits of corrosion from the fork stanchions and from the yokes through which they must fit. Smear a light coat of grease over the stanchion upper end and slide the legs into place **(see illustration)**. On 75 models with Showa forks, lubricate the top and bottom yoke fork pinch bolt threads with engine oil – see Step 6 for details of modified bolts.

2 Lightly tighten the pinch bolts so that the legs are just held in the yokes, then check that the tops of the stanchions are flush with the top of the top yoke. Slide the wheel spindle through the spindle lugs to ensure that the fork legs are correctly aligned, then tighten first the top yoke pinch bolts to their specified torque setting, followed by the bottom yoke pinch bolts which must also be tightened to their specified setting **(see illustration)**. Refit the black plastic cap to the top of each leg.

3 Refit the fork brace (if fitted) and the front mudguard, followed by the front wheel and the brake calipers.

4 When the front mudguard and wheel have been refitted, push the machine off its stand, apply the front brake and pump the forks up

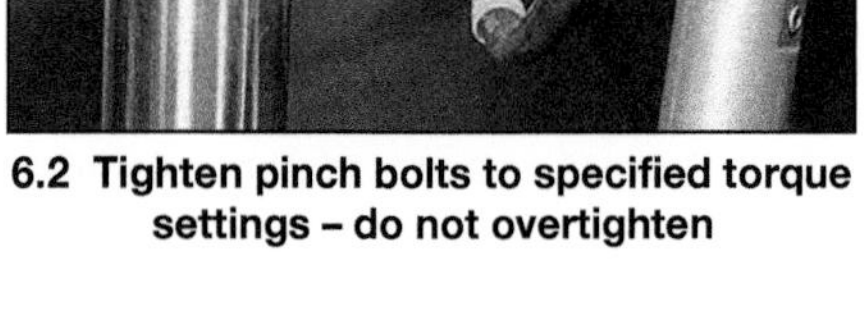

install the fork top plug with a new O-ring **(see illustrations)**.

9 Push the plug into the stanchion, fit the retaining circlip to its groove and allow the spring pressure to push the plug back up against the circlip.

10 Fill the fork leg with exactly the specified amount of the correct type of oil, as described in Chapter 1 **(see illustration)**, then check that the fork leg is fully extended before refitting the filler plug; the forks are designed with the cushioning effect of the trapped air in mind. Hold the top plug with an open-ended spanner and tighten the filler plug to the specified torque setting **(see illustration)**.

Showa forks

9 Install the rebound spring on the damper rod and insert into the stanchion, allowing the rod end to extend from the stanchion base. Fit the fork spring (closer-wound coils at top), spring seat, spacer and top plug, pressing the top plug down the stanchion until its retaining circlip can be safely installed in the groove.

10 Fit the damper rod seat to the exposed end of the rod and insert the assembly into the lower leg, having first applied a smear of fork oil to the bush surface. Using a new sealing washer, fit the damper rod Allen screw through the lower leg base to secure the damper rod and tighten it securely.

11 Apply a smear of fork oil to the lower leg bush then slide it over the stanchion and down into its housing in the lower leg. The bush is an interference fit and will require driving into place with a short length of tubing which is sufficiently large in internal diameter to fit over the stanchion, yet no wider than the lower leg housing. With the bush in position, fit the backing washer and oil seal, again using the tubing to press the seal squarely into position. Install the circlip in its groove and fit the dust excluder. Apply Shell Retinax A grease to the excluder's internal cavity to prevent the ingress of dirt into the oil seal.

12 Using a new sealing washer, install the oil drain plug. Fill the leg with the specified quantity and type of oil via the filler hole in the top plug, then install the filler plug. Refit the plastic cap.

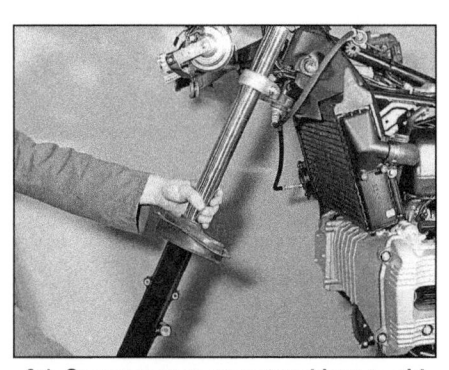

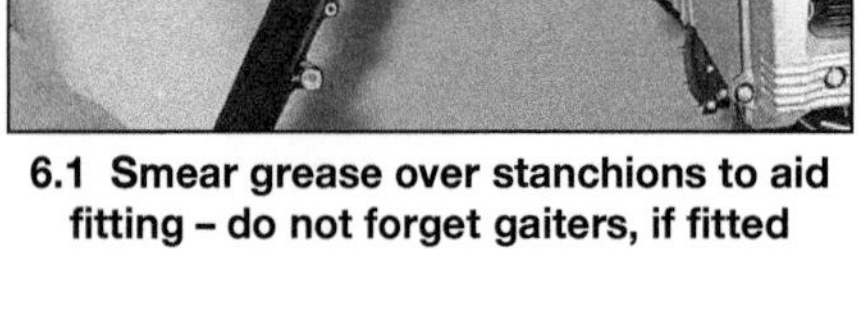

6.1 Smear grease over stanchions to aid fitting – do not forget gaiters, if fitted

6.2 Tighten pinch bolts to specified torque settings – do not overtighten

Frame and front suspension

and down to align the legs and their mountings. Working from the top downwards tighten all fasteners to their specified torque settings, where available.

5 Check that all controls are correctly adjusted, that all components are securely fastened and that the suspension works smoothly before using the machine.

Modifications

6 On all 75 models with Showa forks, it may be found that the fork stanchions move upwards in the fork yokes in use – this is particularly relevant on K75RT models with ABS. To prevent this, BMW advise that the threads of the top and bottom yoke pinch bolts are lubricated with engine oil before being secured to the revised torque settings given in the Specifications at the beginning of this Chapter.

7 The black-finished lower yoke bolts should be replaced with higher tensile bolts (10.9), identified by their aluminium coloured finish, and stronger washers used under the bolt heads.

7 Front forks - aligning the damping components

1 Due to their long travel and relatively complex construction, these forks can be noisy in operation or, especially after they have been disturbed, they can become stiff in operation. While the standard procedure described in Sections 5 and 6 of this Chapter is sufficient in most cases, to remedy this, on occasion a stiff or noisy fork can be cured only by the more elaborate procedure described below. Note that the procedure starts with the premise that the stanchions are in place on the machine, with the damper rods fitted, and that the lower legs are attached loosely by the damper rod Allen screws; the mudguard. front wheel and fork brace (if fitted) must be removed.

2 Push each lower leg sharply upwards until it is heard to make contact, then rotate it two or three times around the stanchion to centre the damper rods before tightening the damper rod Allen screw to the specified torque setting (where given); use the spring or a wooden dowel to prevent the damper rod from rotating. Check that the lower leg still slides smoothly and easily and rotates without stiffness; if necessary slacken the Allen screw and repeat the procedure until results are satisfactory.

3 If a fork brace is fitted, install it but tighten the bolts only lightly then refit the wheel spindle and clamp it on one side only. Push both lower legs upwards simultaneously until contact is heard again then tighten the fork brace mounting bolts evenly and in a diagonal sequence to the specified torque setting; tighten also the second pair of spindle clamp bolts to the specified torque setting.

4 Pump the lower leg assembly up and down several times to check for any signs of stiffness or distortion, then check that the wheel spindle can be easily removed and refitted. If any stiffness or difficulty is found, check the fork components for distortion.

5 Refit the oil drain plugs, the front mudguard, the front wheel and the brake components then fill each leg with the specified quantity and type of fork oil and refit the fork springs and spacers.

6 Raise the front wheel from the ground and support the machine with a wooden box or similar under the crankcase so that the forks are fully extended. Refit the top plugs and oil filler plugs, then lower the machine to the ground and check the fork action.

7 Note that some stiffness will be inevitable in a freshly-rebuilt fork and a running-in period of 600 miles (1000 km) will probably prove necessary before the fork operates with absolute smoothness.

8 Steering head bearings - removal

1 Owners of machines with fairings are strongly advised to remove the fairing components to prevent any risk of damage.

2 Remove the fuel tank. See Chapter 6.

3 Remove the front fork legs. See Section 2 of this Chapter.

4 Carefully prise out the ignition switch surround and disengage the switch from the handlebar panel with a small screwdriver, then remove the panel mounting screws and withdraw the panel (see illustrations).

5 On K75, K75 C, K75T and K100 models remove the headlamp surround/handlebar fairing, then remove its two fixing bolts and withdraw the headlamp unit, disconnecting the electrical leads to release it. Disconnect the horn wires, slacken the horn mounting bolts and remove the single screw securing the connector plug cover to the underside of the instrument panel. Withdraw the cover and unplug the connectors, then unscrew four Allen screws or hexagon-headed bolts securing the housing rear cover to the fork yokes. Withdraw the rear cover complete with the instrument panel, manoeuvring the panel clear of the bottom mounting bracket.

6 Where the brake hose passes up through the steering head, disconnect the brake hose at the unions on the steering stem upper end and either plug the hose or wrap it tightly in a plastic bag or similar so that brake fluid cannot leak out (see illustration). Unscrew the plastic nut (early 75 models and all 100 models) or release the retainer (later 75 models) at the top of the steering stem and pull the brake pipe down through the steering head, taking care not to splash brake fluid. On models, where the brake hose is routed outside of the steering head, there is no need to disconnect the hydraulic hose, although removal of any hose guides or union mountings will be necessary.

7 Remove the handlebar clamp bolts and bring the handlebars to the rear, clear of the steering head area, ensuring that all cables and wiring are out of the way. The fork yokes should now be completely clear and ready for removal.

8 On all 100 models and early 75 models unscrew the steering stem top bolt, tap the top yoke upwards off the steering stem using only a soft-faced mallet, unscrew the circular adjusting nut and pull the bottom yoke downwards out of the steering head; it may

8.4a Prise off switch surround to release ignition switch from handlebar cover . . .

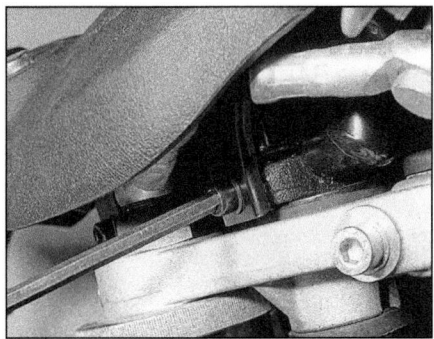

8.4b . . . then remove panel mounting screws and withdraw panel

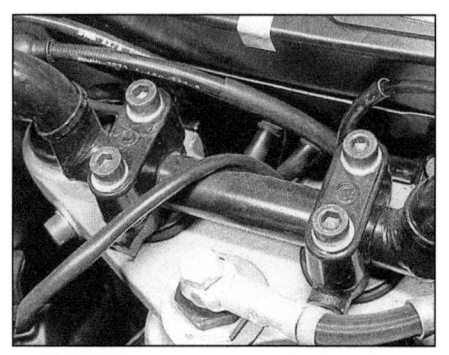

8.6 Brake hose must be disconnected before fork top yoke can be removed

8•10 Frame and front suspension

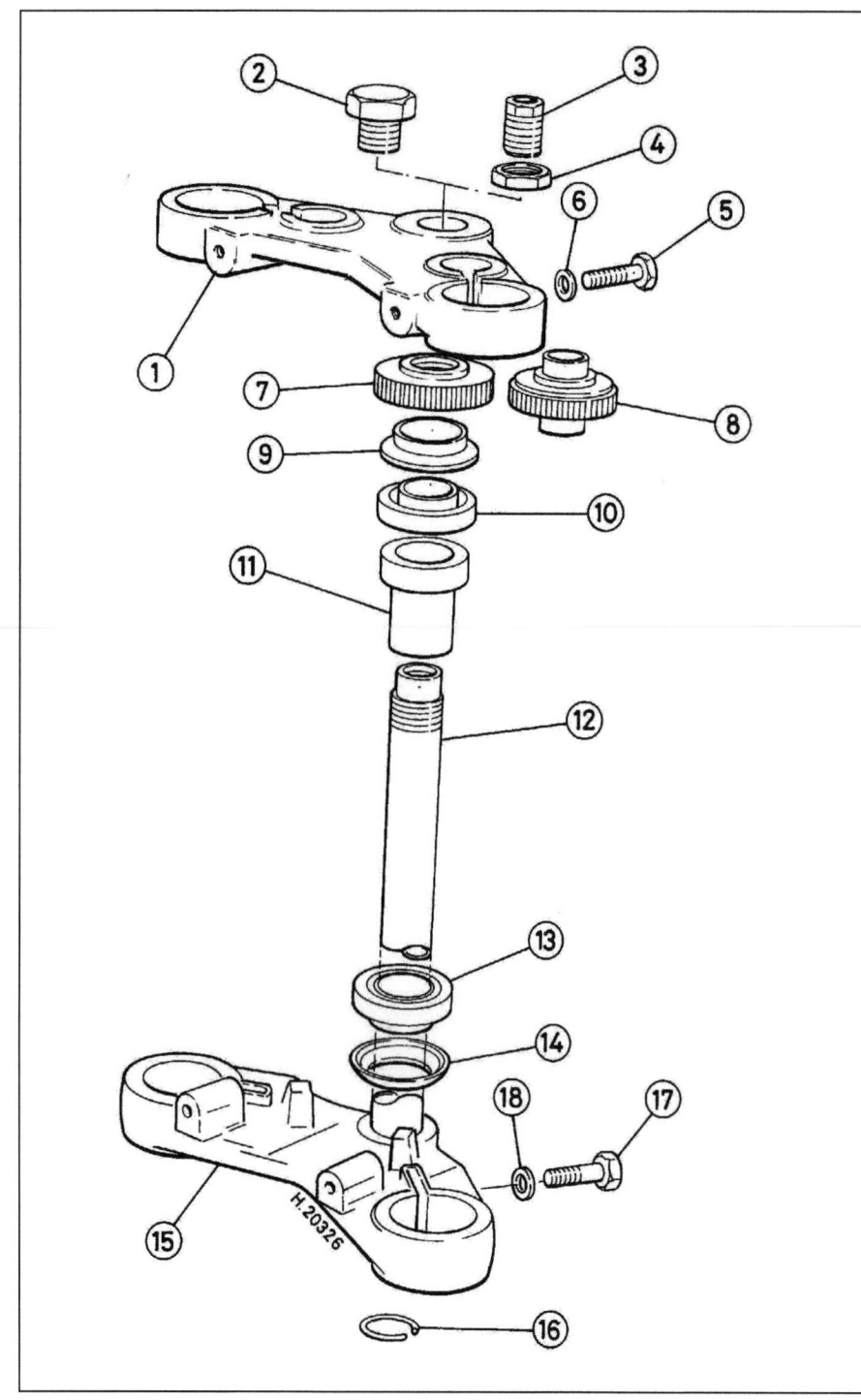

be necessary to use a soft-faced mallet to tap the steering stem down through the bearings. Withdraw the top bearing (see illustration).

9 On all 75 models, particularly early K75 C models which have been subsequently fitted with a 'Fluidbloc' damper (identified by the two bolt heads protruding from the steering head lug) wipe all traces of grease away from the steering stem and wrap a thin layer of insulating tape around the threads to prevent them damaging the damper rubber as they pass through it.

10 On later 75 models unscrew the locking sleeve locknut and tap the fork top yoke upwards off the steering stem, then slacken the locking sleeve and unscrew the bearing adjuster nut while pulling the bottom yoke downwards out of the steering stem. The top bearing must be driven off the adjuster nut using a hammer and a pin punch passed through the holes in the nut top cover.

11 The bearing outer races can only be extracted using a slide hammer or similar puller which has an internally-expanding adaptor of the necessary size.

12 To remove the bottom bearing on models with Fichtel and Sachs forks, thoroughly clean the whole steering stem and mark its installed position in the bottom yoke next to the slot for the steering lock. Heat the assembly to 120 - 130°C (248 - 266°F) and drive or press the steering stem downwards through the bottom yoke until the bearing is released.

13 Before the yoke cools down, use a 30 mm (1.2 in) drift to tap the stem back into its previously marked position; the circlip should locate against the yoke underside.

14 To remove the bottom bearing on models with Showa forks, drive the stem down through the yoke by approximately 5 mm, then drive it back into its original position; this will create sufficient clearance to gain purchase on the back of the bearing with a suitable puller and withdraw it from the stem.

9 Steering head bearings - examination and renovation

1 Clean and examine the outer bearing tracks whilst in the steering head. Since the forks rotate through only a small angle, the commonest damage to the bearings is brinelling. This is indenting of the roller tracks by the rollers, generally due to maladjustment. It can be felt when turning the forks, by the steering seeming to 'index' in one position.

2 Check the rollers and their cages for signs of wear or damage and renew the complete bearing if in doubt about its condition.

3 Always renew any dust seals or other sealing components to prevent the entry of dirt.

8.8 Steering head assembly

1 Top yoke
2 Steering stem top bolt [1]
3 Locking sleeve [2]
4 Locknut [2]
5 Bolt – 2 off
6 Washer – 2 off
7 Bearing adjuster nut [1]
8 Bearing adjuster nut [2]
9 Dust seal – where fitted [2]
10 Taper roller bearing
11 Fluidbloc steering damper [2]
12 Steering stem
13 Taper roller bearing
14 Dust seal – where fitted
15 Bottom yoke
16 Circlip
17 Bolt – 2 off
18 Washer – 2 off

[1] All models except late 75
[2] Late 75 models only

10 Steering head bearings - refitting

1 To refit the bearing outer races assemble a drawbolt consisting of a pair of thick steel washers which are large enough to fit over the end of the steering head lug, a bolt long enough to pass through the head lug, both washers and one outer race, and a large nut.
2 Ensuring that it is square to its housing in the steering head lug draw the bottom bearing outer race into the head lug until it seats fully. Do not forget to fit the Fluidbloc (where fitted) before repeating the procedure to refit the top bearing outer race.
3 Both inner races must be heated to 80°C (176°F) to refit them. To fit the lower bearing inner race a tubular drift must be found that will fit over the steering stem and yet bear only against the bearing inner race itself, not touching the rollers or cages. Refit the dust seal (where fitted) heat the bearing and drop it over the steering stem (ensuring that it is the correct way up) then tap it firmly down on to the bottom yoke; there must be no clearance between the bearing and the yoke.
4 The top bearing is fitted in a similar manner to the adjuster nut; again there must be no clearance between the bearing and the nut top cover.
5 Thoroughly grease all bearings after they have cooled, but be careful to keep grease away from the 'Fluidbloc' (where fitted). On all 75 models, particularly K75 C models which have subsequently been fitted with a Fluidbloc, wrap a thin layer of tape around its threads before refitting the steering stem.
6 On early 75 models and all 100 models check that the bottom bearing is greased and refit the bottom yoke to the steering head. Remove the tape (if applicable). Heat the top bearing to 80°C (176°F) and drop it over the stem upper end. Tap it into place and refit the circular adjuster nut. Allow the bearing to cool, pack it with grease, if necessary, and tighten the nut hard to preload the bearings then slacken it fully and re-tighten it until all free play is **just** eliminated.
7 On later 75 models check that the bearings are greased and carefully refit the bottom yoke to the steering head. Refit the circular adjuster nut with the top bearing and locking sleeve. Again tighten the adjuster nut hard to preload the bearings, then slacken it fully and retighten it until all free play is just eliminated.
8 On all models refit the top yoke, followed by the top bolt (early 75 models and all 100 models) or locknut (late 75 models); do not tighten them until adjustment is complete.
9 Refit the handlebars, ensuring that the punch mark is aligned on the inside of the left-hand clamp, between the joint faces of the two clamps.
10 On models where the brake pipe passes up through the steering head, refit the brake pipe to the steering head, fasten the plastic nut or retainer to secure it and connect the master cylinder brake hose again, using new sealing washers. Refill the brake system with fresh fluid, check that the spacers are in place between the brake pads, and bleed the brake system until normal lever pressure is restored. If the handlebars are kept on full left lock, the master cylinder will be the highest point in the system which will aid this procedure. Be very careful to check that the brakes are working correctly before taking the machine out on the road. On models where the brake pipe is routed clear of the steering head, secure the brake hose with any guides or union retaining bolts.
11 Refit the front forks, mudguard and fork brace. See Sections 6 and 7 of this Chapter. Refit the front wheel as described in Chapter 10.
12 Adjust the steering head bearings as described in Chapter 1, then refit all disturbed fairing or headlamp housing components, the handlebar panel and ignition switch and the fuel tank.
13 Check that the front brakes, the suspension, the steering and all controls work properly and are adjusted correctly before taking the machine out on the road. All fasteners should be securely tightened to their respective torque wrench settings, if available.

11 Fluidbloc steering damper - general (75 models)

1 This component is fitted as standard to all 75 models from the end of 1985 onwards; it can also be fitted to any earlier K75 C model.
2 It consists of a firm rubber bush set in the steering head lug and retained by two tapered screws or bolts which are of exactly the required length to penetrate the soft surface of the damper without tearing it and so cannot be swapped between models.
3 The carefully shaped pattern on the damper's inside diameter, coupled with the use of the specified heavy silicone grease, gives sufficient friction to damp any fork movement greater than 1 degree side to side.
4 The unit requires no maintenance since the grease specified is a longlife lubricant. If the steering head bearings are to be adjusted at any time remove the tapered screws or bolts so that the damper no longer exerts any damping effect which would otherwise give a false setting, and always take great care to protect the damper from other types of grease and from any damage when overhauling the steering head bearings.
5 It will be necessary to remove the steering head bearings to remove or refit a Fluidbloc damper. If installing a new damper mark a line on its larger diameter at a point 7 mm (0.28 in) below its top edge **(see illustration)**. Fill the recesses with the specified Silicone Grease 300 Heavy and press the damper into the steering head until the mark appears in the tapped holes; refit and tighten to the specified torque setting the tapered retaining screws or bolts.

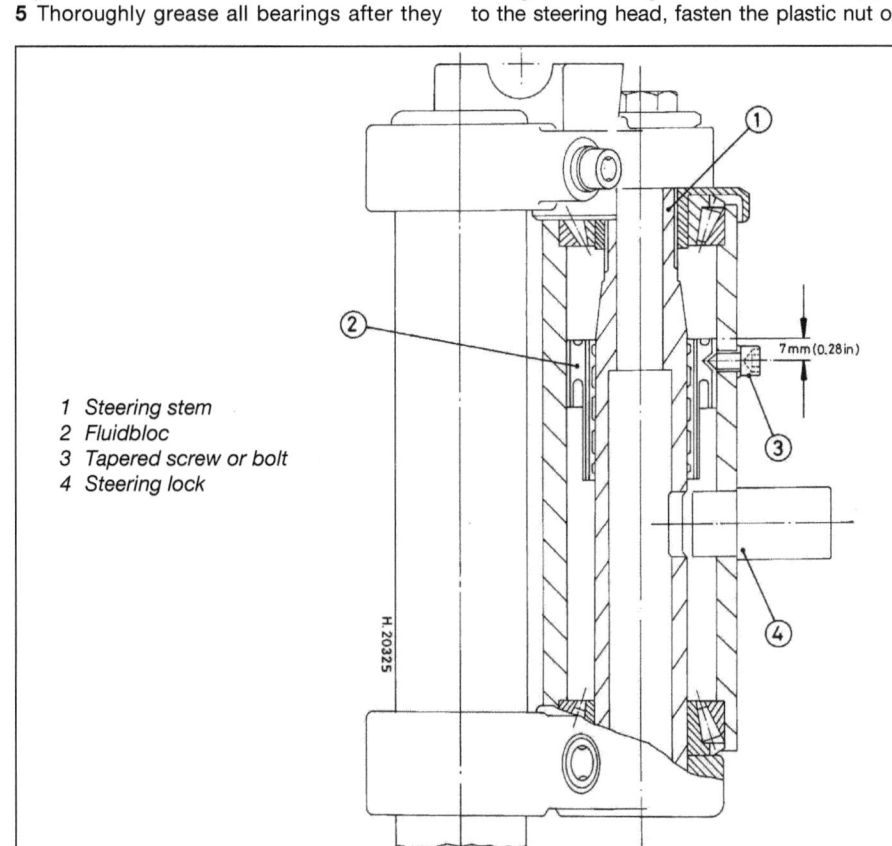

1 Steering stem
2 Fluidbloc
3 Tapered screw or bolt
4 Steering lock

11.5 Fluidbloc steering damper installation

12 Frame - examination and renovation

1 The frame is unlikely to require attention unless accident damage has occurred. In some cases, renewal of the frame is the only satisfactory remedy if the frame is badly out of alignment. Only a few frame specialists have the jigs and mandrels necessary for resetting the frame to the required standard of accuracy, and even then there is no easy means of assessing to what extent the frame may have been over-stressed. Note that BMW specifically advise against straightening or repairing components such as frames, fork stanchions and wheels because of the real danger of a fatigue fracture appearing subsequently.
2 After the machine has covered a considerable mileage, it is advisable to examine the frame closely for signs of cracking or splitting at the welded joints. Rust corrosion can also cause weakness at these joints. Minor damage can be repaired by welding or brazing depending on the extent and nature of the damage.
3 Remember that a frame which is out of alignment will cause handling problems and may even promote 'speed wobbles'. If misalignment is suspected, as a result of an accident, it will be necessary to strip the machine completely so that the frame can be checked, and if necessary, renewed.
4 BMW specifically advise against fitting a sidecar or a trailer to any of the machines described in this Manual. Note that they also advise against fitting RS- or RT-type fairings to K100 models (with rigid engine front mountings) because of the risk of vibration damage. Check with an authorised BMW dealer for details.

13 Footrests - general

1 The footrests are pivoted, the rider's is being spring-loaded on large alloy plates bolted to the gearbox housing (see illustration). On the early 100 models the plates were rubber mounted but since they were found to promote vibration they were replaced for the 1986 models by the 75 (rigidly-mounted) type. A modified version which can be fitted to early models was introduced in the US during 1985.
2 The footrests require no attention save a quick check at intervals that they are securely fastened and that the pivots are unworn; apply a few drops of lubricant at regular intervals to each bearing surface. Check regularly that all components are undamaged. If any are found to be damaged, cracked or broken they must be renewed unless an expert alloy welder can be found.
3 The footrests can be removed and refitted as major assemblies; it is merely necessary to unscrew the three bolts securing each plate to the gearbox housing to release them, although the rear brake components must be disconnected or removed to release the right-hand plate. On refitting, tighten the bolts to their specified torque setting, where given.

14 Stands and controls - general

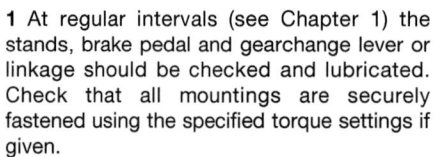

1 At regular intervals (see Chapter 1) the stands, brake pedal and gearchange lever or linkage should be checked and lubricated. Check that all mountings are securely fastened using the specified torque settings if given.
2 If necessary, dismantle the assembly so that all pivot points and bearing surfaces can be cleaned and greased. Return springs, where fitted, must be in good condition with no trace of fatigue and must be securely mounted.
3 If accident damage is to be repaired, check that the component is not cracked or broken. Such damage may be repaired by welding if the pieces are taken to an expert but since this will destroy the finish renewal is the most satisfactory course of action. If a component is bent it can be straightened after heating the affected area to a dull cherry red with a blowlamp or welding torch. Again the finish will be destroyed but painted surfaces can be repainted easily, while chromed surfaces can only be replated.
4 Periodically inspect the reinforcement plate between the centre stand and footbar for cracking around the welded area. In isolated cases cracks were discovered on early 100 models and as a result a modified centre stand was introduced for later machines. If in any doubt about the stand's condition seek the advice of an authorised BMW dealer. Note that all 75 models are fitted with the later-design centre stand.
5 A redesigned and strengthened centre stand bracket was fitted to all models from March 1991. It will be found that the stand pivot bush housings are drilled to accept grease nipples, and on certain models the grease nipples may actually be fitted. The side stand pivot is similarly drilled to accept a grease nipple.

15 Fairing - removal and refitting

K75 - headlamp surround

1 The headlamp surround is retained by two screws at the bottom rear, one on each side, by two screws into the instrument panel/rear cover and by a screw on each side next to the headlamp shell mountings.
2 Remove the screws, withdraw the surround, and disconnect the turn signal lamp wires. Refitting is the reverse of the removal procedure. If the rear cover is to be removed, refer to Section 8.

K75C, K75T, K100 - headlamp surround

3 The headlamp surround is retained by four screws which pass forwards from the rear cover; one at the top and one at the bottom, next to each fork yoke.
4 Remove the four screws, lift the surround forwards and disconnect the turn signal wires to release it. Refitting is the reverse of the removal procedure.
5 Once the surround has been removed the top panel can be unclipped and the turn signal lamp assemblies removed; each is retained by a single screw or bolt from inside the surround. If the rear cover is to be removed, refer to Section 8.

K75C - handlebar fairing

6 This unit is listed as an optional extra for the K100 model and may be found on some K75 T versions.
7 Working from the rear of the unit, use an Allen key or a screwdriver, as necessary, to remove the screw which is threaded into the rear of each turn signal lamp assembly, then remove the four screws (two on each side) which secure the fairing to the fork stanchion brackets. Lift the fairing forwards, disconnect the turn signal lamp wires and withdraw it.
8 If required, remove the two clamp screws securing each bracket to the fork stanchions and withdraw the brackets. If the rear cover is to be removed, refer to Section 8.
9 Refitting is the reverse of the removal procedure.
10 Note that the windscreen is attached to the fairing by six rivets which require the use of a special tool to fit.

K75T - windscreen

11 This unit is listed as an optional extra and may be found on K75 C and K100 models.
12 The screen itself is mounted at four points. Remove the four cap nuts and their

13.1 Footrests are mounted on alloy plates bolted to gearbox housing

plain washers and carefully withdraw the screen, noting the rubber grommet fitted on each side of all four mounting points, also the two bushes at each of the bottom mountings.

13 On refitting, ensure that all mounting rubbers are correctly placed on each side of the screen so that it is completely rubber-mounted. Refit the plain washers and nuts; tighten the nuts securely but do not overtighten them or the mountings will be distorted and the screen may crack.

14 The screen mountings are clamped to the fork stanchions, just under the top yoke, giving a small amount of adjustment for height.

K75S - fairing

15 Remove its four mounting screws and withdraw the windscreen. Working from in front of the radiator cover, remove its four mounting screws (two on each side) and carefully withdraw the cover; the mesh panel is retained by seven small screws and can now be removed if required. Unscrew the single mounting screw from in front of the brake hose union.

16 Remove the single screw retaining each turn signal lamp assembly, withdraw the assemblies and disconnect their wiring to release them.

17 Working from underneath the bottom rear edge of each main side panel, remove the single screw securing each bottom cover to its respective side panel and withdraw the bottom cover to expose the side panel mounting bolt. Move to the top of each side panel and remove the single retaining screw from inside each turn signal lamp housing and the two screws passing down into each side panel from the top centre panel (peel back the windscreen gaskets, if necessary), then move downwards along the panel's upper edge and remove the screw securing each one to the fairing inner cover. Remove each side panel's mounting bolt and withdraw both side panels.

18 The top centre panel is now retained by a single bolt and a small screw on each side; remove the two bolts (noting the arrangement of the rubber mountings) and the two screws and withdraw the panel, then disconnect the headlamp, parking lamp and horn wires to release it. If required, the two retaining screws can be removed from the headlamp mounting to separate the centre panel.

19 Remove the single retaining screw, withdraw the connector block cover from underneath the instrument panel and unplug the two connector blocks. Remove the four retaining screws and withdraw the instrument panel, noting the mounting components, then disengage the wiring leads from the inner cover clips.

20 Noting how the wiring and control cables are routed on each side of its mountings, remove its two mounting screws and remove the small cover from the front of the top yoke. Withdraw the fairing inner cover from around the fork stanchions, slackening the mounting bracket fasteners. if necessary. If required, the mounting bracket can be removed, but note that of its four mounting bolts the two top ones are the tapered screws or bolts which secure the Fluidbloc; ensure that these are correctly refitted.

21 On refitting, do not tighten the mounting bracket screws or bolts until the fairing inner cover is in place, then tighten all four to the specified torque setting. Ensure that the wiring and control cables are correctly routed before refitting the small cover to the top yoke, and clip the electrical leads into place on the inner cover once the instruments have been refitted.

22 Assemble the centre panel and headlamp assembly and refit the two retaining screws. Fit the panel and headlamp as a single unit and connect their wires to the bulbs and horn; check that the centre panel/fairing mounting bracket mounting grommet is correctly refitted before pressing the shouldered bush through it from the inside outwards and refitting the bolt and washer.

23 If working alone, fit one side panel and tighten its four retaining screws and one mounting bolt lightly, then refit the second panel and ensure that the two mate correctly at all points of contact with each other or with the other panels before tightening all fasteners on both panels. Do not forget the single screw at the joint in front of the brake hose union. Refit the side panel bottom cover, the radiator cover, the turn signal lamp assemblies and the windscreen.

K75S - engine spoiler/belly fairing

24 A similarly-mounted version of this component is listed as an optional extra for other 75 models.

25 Remove from under the bottom edge of the fairing radiator cover the single mounting screw, noting the metal and rubber washers. Remove the two screws from underneath the front of the belly fairing, noting the plastic shouldered sleeves pressed into the rubber mounting grommets. Carefully move the belly fairing forwards and downwards to disengage it from the tongue of the rear mounting. Refitting is the reverse of the removal procedure.

26 The belly fairing's front mounting consists of a large bracket bolted to the sump or crankcase casting, and its rear mounting is bolted to the centre stand mounting bracket; the rear mounting's height is adjusted using shims which must be refitted correctly if the mounting is disturbed or the line of the fairing against the engine will be spoiled. If any shims are omitted, the fairing may contact the engine castings, thus damaging the paintwork and causing an annoying rattle.

27 If the belly fairing is to be dismantled, remove the four mounting screws and withdraw the mesh panel, then remove the rear mounting socket and unscrew the screws which secure the two halves along their mating surface. On refitting, use strips of draught-proofing tape, if necessary, to prevent the mesh panel from rattling against the inside of the fairing.

K100RS - fairing

28 Remove the single retaining screw at the bottom rear edge of each lower side panel **(see illustration)** and the two screws at the top edge of each knee pad, then withdraw the knee pads, noting the clip at the bend in the middle of each pad **(see illustration)**.

29 Remove the six screws which secure each fork leg gaiter to the underside of the fairing and push the gaiters up inside **(see illustration)**.

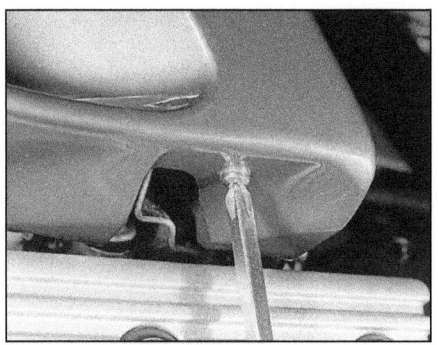

15.28a K100RS fairing removal – knee pads are retained by single screw at bottom . . .

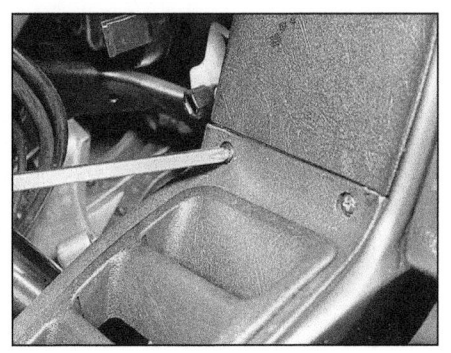

15.28b . . . and by two screws at upper edge – note clip at middle bend

15.29 Remove screws securing each gaiter to fairing

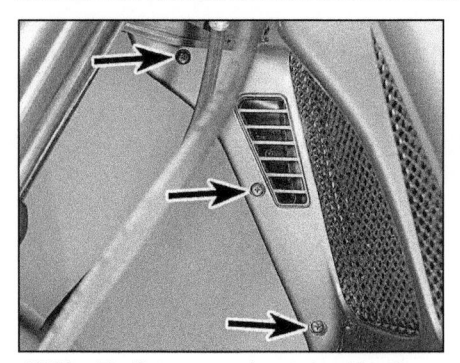

8•14 Frame and front suspension

15.30a Radiator cover is retained by three screws (arrowed) to each lower side panel ...

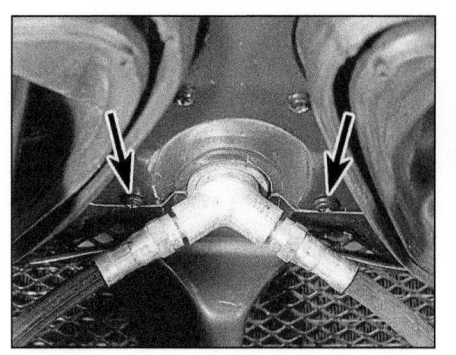

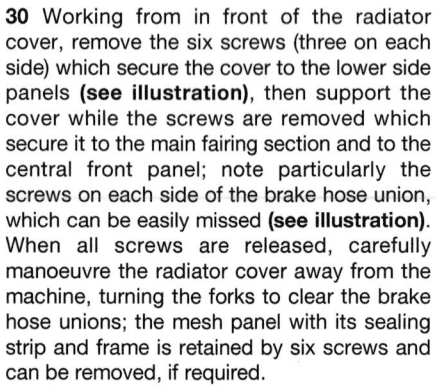

15.30b ... do not forget two screws next to brake hose union when removing radiator cover

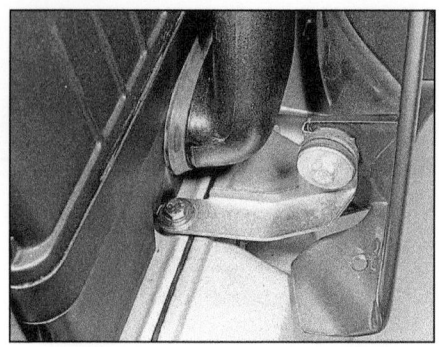

15.31a Lower side panels are each retained by single bottom mounting bolt ...

30 Working from in front of the radiator cover, remove the six screws (three on each side) which secure the cover to the lower side panels **(see illustration)**, then support the cover while the screws are removed which secure it to the main fairing section and to the central front panel; note particularly the screws on each side of the brake hose union, which can be easily missed **(see illustration)**. When all screws are released, carefully manoeuvre the radiator cover away from the machine, turning the forks to clear the brake hose unions; the mesh panel with its sealing strip and frame is retained by six screws and can be removed, if required.

31 To remove each of the lower side panels, unscrew the single bottom mounting bolt and the four small screws along the top edge **(see illustrations)**; be careful to support each panel while removing the fasteners and to remove it carefully once all have been unscrewed.

32 Remove the mirrors. To gain adequate working space inside the fairing remove the covers and panels. The small covers fitted between the top of the knee pads and the horizontal centre panel can be lifted up gently and unclipped from the centre panel **(see illustrations)**. The covers over the windscreen mountings are each retained by a countersunk screw at their middle and a cheese-head screw at the top **(see illustrations)**; remove the two screws and unclip each cover from the front of the centre panel. The centre panel itself is retained by a screw at each front corner; removing the cover with the fairing installed is a difficult operation but if required it can be left loosely in place so that it can be moved when necessary.

33 Remove the metal inner panels which are each retained by one screw at the bottom rear, one screw next to the mirror mounting and one screw at the panel front mounting **(see illustrations)**.

34 Slacken the horn mounting nuts and pivot the horns away from the guide channels, then remove from outside the fairing, the guide

15.31b ... and by four screws along top edge

15.32a Unclip small panels from horizontal centre panel

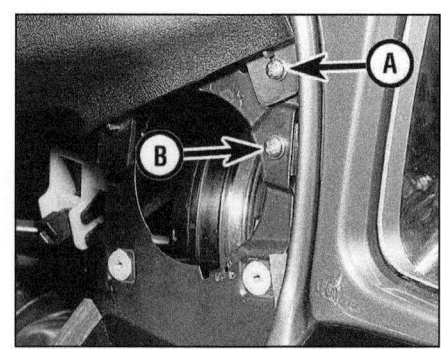

15.32b Screw A retains horizontal centre panel, screw B retains metal inner panel

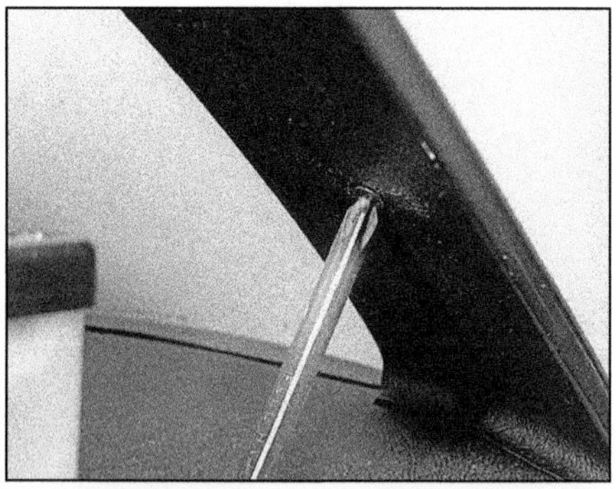

15.32c Windscreen mounting covers are each retained by countersunk screw at centre ...

15.32d ... and by standard screw at upper end

15.33a With screw next to mirror mounting removed, unscrew front mounting ...

Frame and front suspension 8•15

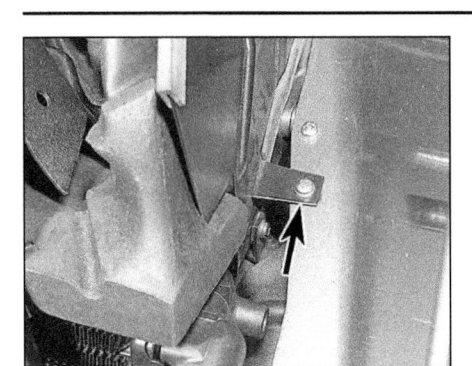

15.33b ... and bottom rear mounting screws (arrowed) to remove each metal inner panel

15.34a Slacken horn mountings and pivot horns backwards ...

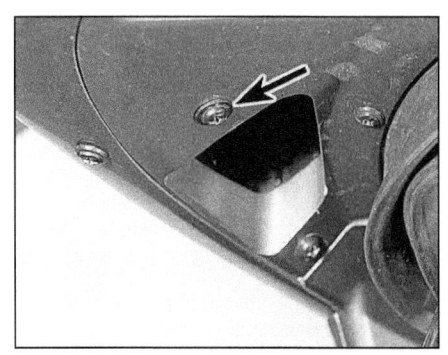

15.34b ... then remove guide channel retaining screw (arrowed) ...

channel retaining screw and withdraw each channel **(see illustrations)**. Disconnect the headlamp and parking lamp wires.

35 The main fairing section should now be retained by two bolts (to frame-mounted brackets) at the lower side panel mating surface and by four nuts or bolts to the fairing mounting bracket at the front. Engage the aid of an assistant to help support the fairing as it is removed.

36 Unscrew the two rear mounting nuts and remove the bolts, noting the arrangement of the mounting rubber grommets and metal washers, then ensure that the assistant is supporting the fairing as the front mounting nuts or bolts are removed **(see illustrations)**. Withdraw the fairing.

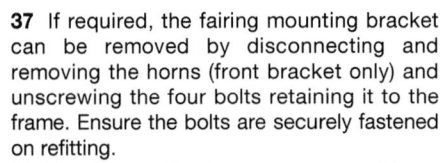

37 If required, the fairing mounting bracket can be removed by disconnecting and removing the horns (front bracket only) and unscrewing the four bolts retaining it to the frame. Ensure the bolts are securely fastened on refitting.

38 To remove the headlamp assembly or windscreen, remove first the adjustable spoiler, then remove the windscreen mounting screws and withdraw the screen **(see illustrations)**. Remove the three headlamp assembly mounting screws and withdraw the assembly, noting the sealing grommet around its outer edge **(see illustration)**. The central front panel can be removed from the fairing underside by unscrewing the remaining mounting screws **(see illustration)**.

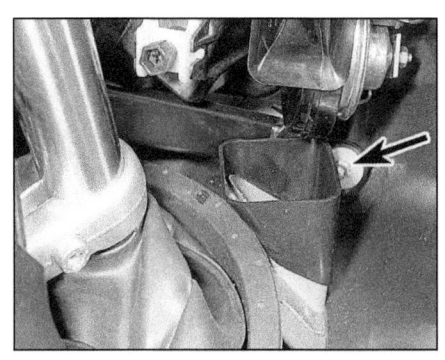

15.34c ... and withdraw horn guide channels to expose main fairing lower front mountings (arrowed)

15.36a To remove main fairing remove rear mounting nuts and bolts ...

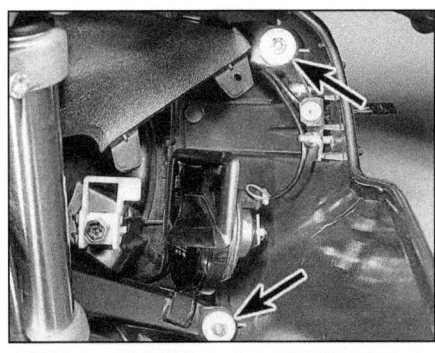

15.36b ... then front upper and lower nuts or bolts (arrowed)

15.38a Dismantle spoiler assembly, noting angled spacers ...

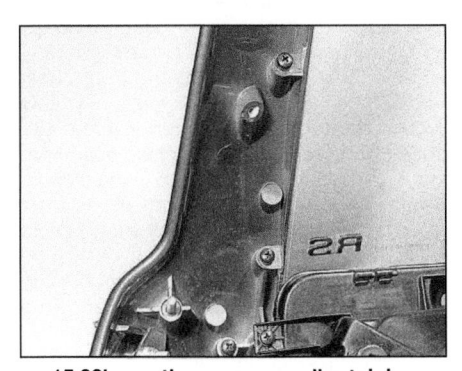

15.38b ... then unscrew all retaining screws to remove windscreen

15.38c Headlamp assembly is retained by three screws (arrowed)

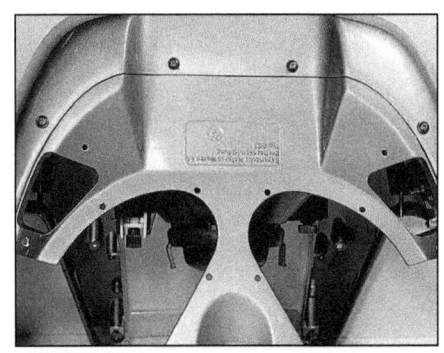

15.38d Fairing central front panel can be removed if required

39 On reassembly, place the sealing grommet on the headlamp outer edge, refit it to the fairing and tighten securely the mounting screws. Refit the windscreen and ensure that its bottom edge seats correctly on the grommet before refitting only the bottom four mounting screws. Do not overtighten the screws, or those of the spoiler which should be fitted next; the screen or spoiler may be cracked. Ensure that the spoiler angled spacers are positioned so that it can be adjusted through its full travel. Refit the central front panel if disturbed.

40 Push the gaiters to the top of the stanchions with their curved edges outwards, hold the horizontal centre panel roughly in place under the instruments and refit the fairing, ensuring that the recess in the central front panel engages around the rubber collar fitted to the brake hose union. Engage the fairing on its mountings and refit all mounting nuts or bolts, ensuring that the rubber grommets are correctly placed so that the fairing is isolated from the frame. Check the fit of the central front panel around the brake hose union, connect the headlamp and parking lamp leads to the bulbs and check that the horizontal centre panel is correctly fitted underneath the instruments then tighten securely the fairing mounting nuts and/or bolts. Check that both fork gaiter mounting flanges are pushed inside the fairing and aligned with it.

41 The remainder of the reassembly procedure is the reverse of that followed on dismantling, noting the following points. Do not forget to position the horns so that their mouths are over the horn channels, then tighten their retaining nuts securely and refit the channel retaining screws. Fit the metal inner panels next, followed by the windscreen mounting covers, which share the windscreen top mounting screws (as well as the countersunk screws) and clip into the horizontal centre panel at their bottom edges. Refit the centre panel mounting screws, followed by the small cover fitted next to each mirror mounting. Refit the mirrors, not forgetting to connect the turn signal lamp wires.

42 Be very careful not to scratch or damage any component as the lower side panels are refitted and the radiator cover installed; it is best to refit these as a single operation and to tighten the retaining screws by just enough to hold each panel until all are correctly aligned. Be careful to align the air intake hose front end with the aperture in the radiator cover, or the machine's performance will be noticeably reduced and ensure that the radiator cover is engaged correctly on the brake hose union. Refit the gaiter mounting screws and the knee pads and make a final check that all components are correctly installed and secured **(see illustration)**.

43 An engine spoiler is fitted as standard on a number of K100RS Special Edition models. Alternatively it can be obtained as an optional extra.

44 The spoiler is retained to a bracket mounted on the engine sump. Remove the four Allen screws, two on each side, to allow the spoiler to be withdrawn, leaving its mounting bracket in place. On refitting be careful not to overtighten the screws. If removal of the mounting bracket is required remove the two Allen screws from the left-hand side, lower the bracket slightly and disengage it from the two studs on the right-hand side. On reassembly ensure that any mounting rubbers and washers are refitted in their original locations.

K75RT, K100RT, K100LT fairing

45 Remove the single retaining screw at the bottom rear edge of each knee pad and the two screws securing the storage compartment to its upper edge (it will be necessary to unlock and open the compartment to reach the screws). Withdraw the knee pads, noting the clip at the bend in the middle of each pad.

46 Remove the remaining four retaining screws and withdraw each storage compartment. Remove the fuel tank, as described in Chapter 6.

47 Remove the six screws which secure each fork leg gaiter to the underside of the fairing and push the gaiter up inside. Note that some models may have had air scoops substituted for the gaiters, in which case their removal is not necessary.

48 Checking carefully that all screws are removed, withdraw the radiator cover and the central front panel set in the underside of the main fairing section. Work around the outer edge of each panel to ensure that all screws are removed, then carefully withdraw each in turn, taking care not to scratch or damage the paintwork and turning the forks to clear the brake hose union. The mesh panel with its sealing strip and frame can be released from the radiator cover, if required, by removing the retaining screws.

49 With the knee pads, storage compartments and radiator cover removed, withdraw the lower side panels by removing the three screws securing each panel's top edge to the main fairing section (noting that this will also release the metal inner panels) then unscrewing the two mounting bolts. Note

15.42 Do not forget to secure spoiler on reassembly – do not overtighten screws

carefully the arrangement of the mounting rubber grommets and metal washers.

50 Slacken evenly the windscreen retaining screws working from the outside inwards, noting the cap nut retaining each upper mounting and the shouldered bushes pressed into the captive nuts at the four front retaining screws. Withdraw the windscreen and the inner fairing panels.

51 Disconnect the wires to the headlamp, parking lamp and turn signal lamps. The main fairing section should now be retained only by two bolts (to frame-mounted brackets) at the lower side panel mating surface and by four nuts or bolts to the fairing mounting bracket at the front. Engage the aid of an assistant to help support the fairing as it is removed.

52 Noting the arrangement of the mounting rubber grommets and metal washers, unscrew the two rear mounting nuts and remove the bolts, then remove the front mounting nuts or bolts and withdraw the fairing.

53 If required, the fairing mounting brackets can be removed by disconnecting and removing the horns (front bracket only) and unscrewing the retaining bolts. Ensure the bolts are securely fastened once the brackets have been re-aligned on refitting. The headlamp is retained by three screws and can be removed, if required; ensure the sealing grommet is correctly installed around its outer edge on refitting.

54 Refitting the fairing is the reverse of the removal procedure, noting the following points. If gaiters are fitted to the fork legs, push them to the top of each stanchion with the curved edges outwards. Engage the fairing on its mountings and refit the nuts or bolts and metal washers, ensuring that the rubber grommets are correctly placed so that the fairing is isolated from the frame. If the mounting brackets were disturbed, ensure that all components are correctly aligned before tightening the mounting nuts and/or bolts. Check that the horn mouths are aligned over the horn channels and connect the headlamp, parking lamp and turn signal lamp wires again.

55 Be careful not to scratch or damage any component as the lower panels are refitted; it is best to refit these as a single operation and to tighten the retaining screws by just enough to hold each panel until all are correctly aligned. Ensure that the central front panel and radiator cover are engaged correctly around the rubber collar fitted to the brake hose union and that the air intake hose front end is aligned with the aperture in the radiator cover. If the hose is distorted against the radiator cover, the machine's air supply could be severely restricted.

56 Where fitted, refit the fork gaiter mounting screws, then refit the storage compartments and knee pads. When refitting the windscreen, be careful to install the shouldered bushes in the four front mounting nuts and to tighten the screws securely,

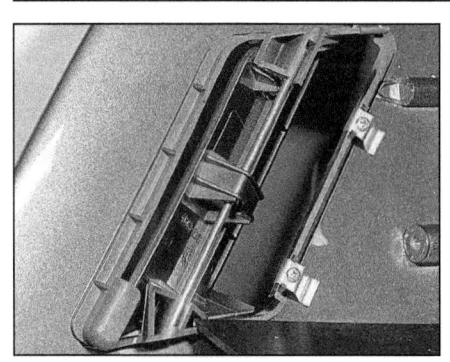

Frame and front suspension 8•17

15.59 Fairing air intake flap mechanism – later LT model

working from the front centre outwards and upwards. Do not overtighten the screws or the screen will crack. The spoiler on early models is retained by clear plastic fasteners which were later modified. Check with an authorised BMW dealer for details.

57 Make a final check that all disturbed components have been correctly installed and secured.

58 Note that different riders and passengers will experience different levels of noise from behind full fairings, particularly wind roar and buffeting. Windscreens of varying heights, some electronically controlled, are available RT and LT fairings, and for some early models, modified spoilers. Check with an authorised BMW dealer for details.

59 Additional cooling for the rider is provided by fresh air intake apertures in each side of the fairing main sections on 1989 and later K100LT and early K75RT models **(see illustration)**. the air outlet is via a grille near the rider's knees. The fresh air intakes can be opened by pushing gently on the rear of the intake covers.

K100 - fairing installation

60 At the time of writing BMW advise against the fitting of RS or RT type fairings to standard K100 models because of the risk of vibration damage. Owners wishing to fit full fairings to these machines should check with an authorised BMW dealer for details of suitable after-market equipment.

16 Seat – removal and refitting

Standard seat - all models except K75 and K100

1 Remove the side panels, then unlock and raise the seat.
2 Remove the circlips from the front (early models only) and rear seat hinges and from the supporting arm pivot, withdraw the pivot pins and lift the seat away **(see illustrations)**; on later models it must be moved forwards to disengage the hinge from the front mounting.
3 The mounting bracket and hinges may be removed, if necessary, by unscrewing the mounting nuts or bolts **(see illustration)**.
4 Note that if the seat mountings are disturbed, the length of the latch pin may require adjustment; this is made by slackening the locknut and screwing the pin in or out until the seat locks correctly when it is bearing fully on the frame.
5 Seat covers are available as separate items but the fitting of a seat cover is a task for the expert upholsterer only.

Low seat and cushioned insert - K75 and K100 models

6 The low seat fitted as standard on these models dispenses with the plastic side panels fitted to all other models. Instead, a cushioned insert is fitted between the seat and fuel tank.
7 To remove the seat unlock the seat lock, operate the seat catch then lift the seat at the front end and pull forwards to remove. On refitting, locate the two rear seat hooks and latch the front hook with the operating catch. Inspect the joint between the seat catch and the operating rod. Instances have occurred of the rod becoming detached from the catch, and as a result on later models the rod is grooved to accept two spring nuts. Note that it should be possible to modify earlier models if this problem occurs.
8 The insert or tank cushion can be released by removing the Allen-headed bolt which retains it to the rear of the fuel tank and pulling the insert rearwards. Be careful to disengage the two hooks on the insert rear sections from the frame tubes during removal. When refitting ensure that the channels on its inner face locate correctly with the tabs on each side of the fuel tank. Hook the rear edges around the frame rails and refit the retaining bolt and washer, having first checked that the damping rubber is in place.
9 Note that for access to the battery or fuel injection control unit, the seat and insert must first be removed, together with the seat catch bracket. The bracket is secured by four Allen screws and locates on two pins in the frame top tubes.

17 Bodywork – removal and refitting

Front mudguard

1 On 100 models without a fork brace the mudguard is retained by four Allen bolts or screws. Remove the bolts or screws and carefully withdraw the mudguard, noting the metal brackets which retain the nuts.
2 On all 75 models, and 100 models fitted with a fork brace, the mudguard is in two pieces, joined by the brace. Fold down the cover at the rear of the brace, remove the longitudinal Allen screw, then unscrew the lateral Allen screws securing the mudguard section to the fork lower legs; note carefully the location of the spacers between the fork lower legs and the mudguard, also the rubber grommets which protect the brake hoses.
3 Taking care not to distort the brake pipes, withdraw the mudguard rear section followed by the front section. The fork brace can then be unbolted, if required.
4 On refitting, take great care to ensure that all mounting components, particularly any spacers, are refitted correctly, so that the fork legs are not distorted as the mudguard mountings are tightened. Ensure that the brake hoses are correctly routed and secured by the clamps, guides or grommets provided. Note that on the one-piece design mudguard, the manufacturer recommends that a few drops of Loctite 242 or a similar thread-

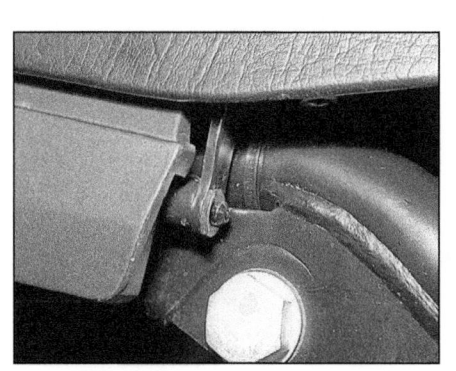

16.2a Remove circlips from seat hinges . . .

16.2b . . . and from supporting arm to release seat

16.3 Seat mounting bracket may be unbolted if required

8•18 Frame and front suspension

locking compound, be applied to the Allen bolt or screw threads before assembly.

Rear mudguard

5 Unlock and raise the seat; remove the tail storage compartment cover and slacken the nuts (either a wingnut or an ordinary nut covered by a cap) on the compartment floor. From underneath the tail lamp assembly, on the outside of the machine remove the two screws and withdraw the number plate bracket.
6 To remove the rear mudguard front section unscrew the two nuts in the storage compartment followed by the two nuts at the front mounting bracket. Withdraw both brackets, noting the arrangement of the mounting rubbers, pull the mudguard downwards at the rear and disengage it from the locating pins and rubber bushes set in the gearbox housing.
7 Refitting is the reverse of the above. Ensure that the mudguard is settled correctly and fully on its mountings before tightening the retaining nuts.

Radiator cover panels - K75, K75C, K75T, K100

K75 models

8 On 75 models very carefully prise each panel's upper rear corner out of the rubber mounting grommet in the fuel tank, then pull it forwards until it is clear of the front mounting prongs and withdraw the panel assembly downwards and to the side.
9 If required, the mesh panel can be removed from inside the panel and the two securing nuts and bolts can be removed to separate the panel halves.

K100 models

10 On 1983-1987 K100 models, working from the front of the radiator cover, remove the three screws retaining the left-hand side cover, then very carefully pull the cover out of the rubber mounting grommet in the fuel tank and withdraw it. Pull the right-hand side cover out of its rubber mounting grommet and withdraw it, complete with the cover front panel. Note the mounting buffers bolted to each side of the radiator. The mesh panel can be removed, if required, from inside the cover by unscrewing the retaining screws and withdrawing the frame, sealing strip and the mesh panel.
11 A different radiator cover is fitted to all 1988-on K100 models. To remove either side cover, pull the cover out of its grommet in the fuel tank and disengage the front mounting hook. The central grille is retained by a single screw on its bottom edge and by hooks at the top.

> **HAYNES HINT** On all models refitting is considerably eased if the rubber grommets are coated with a film of rubber lubricant or even moistened with water.

Side panels

12 On all models note that the side panels are fragile and will crack easily if wrenched off their mountings; exercise care at all times and note that refitting is eased if the rubber grommets are first coated with a film of rubber lubricant or even moistened with water.
13 On 75 models carefully pull each panel outwards at the bottom to release the clip, swing it downwards away from the fuel tank mounting, and slide it to the front to release the rear locating pin.
14 Note that if the spring clip is loose, the side panels may work loose and drop off. Check first that the fuel tank is fully seated in its rear mountings and that the bottom mounting pins on the frame are not bent. Check that the spring clip is installed so that its retaining lug is seated correctly in the opening provided. If necessary, bend the spring clip (taking care not to damage the panel) or the frame mounting pin, so that the spring clip grips securely. Check that the protective moulding is in place along each tank bottom seam before refitting the panels.
15 On early (1984 and 1985 models, identified by the panel's angled bottom rear edge) 100 models carefully pull the panels outwards at the top front and rear corners to disengage them from their mounting grommets, then slide them gently to the rear to release them from the bottom mounting prongs.
16 On later (1986-on models, identified by the panel's straight bottom rear edge) 100 models carefully pull each panel outwards at its top front corner to disengage it from its mounting grommet, then swing it downwards just enough to release the bottom mounting hook and slide it to the front to release the rear locating pin **(see illustrations)**.

Tail unit

17 Unlock and raise the seat and remove the tail storage compartment cover. Remove the tail lamp assembly, the seat and the rear mudguard. Remove the seat rear pivot mounting bracket and disconnect the rear turn signal lamp wires.
18 Unscrew the mounting screws and nuts and withdraw the tail unit. The pillion grab handles can be unbolted from inside the storage compartment, each is retained by a nut and a bolt.

Engine protection bars

19 Some models are fitted as standard with engine protection bars. Note that these cannot be fitted to machines with engine spoilers (belly fairings) and if they are to be fitted to K75RT, K100 RS, K100 RT or K100 LT models, the fairing lower side panels must be provided with cut-outs to permit the bars to be fitted. Any authorised BMW dealer should be able to provide the templates required to position the holes accurately.
20 Genuine BMW bars are rubber-mounted to absorb shocks without passing them

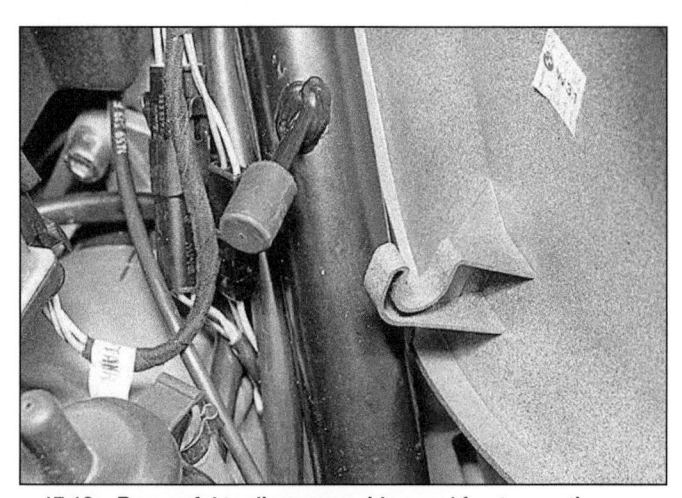

17.16a Be careful to disengage side panel front mountings as described . . .

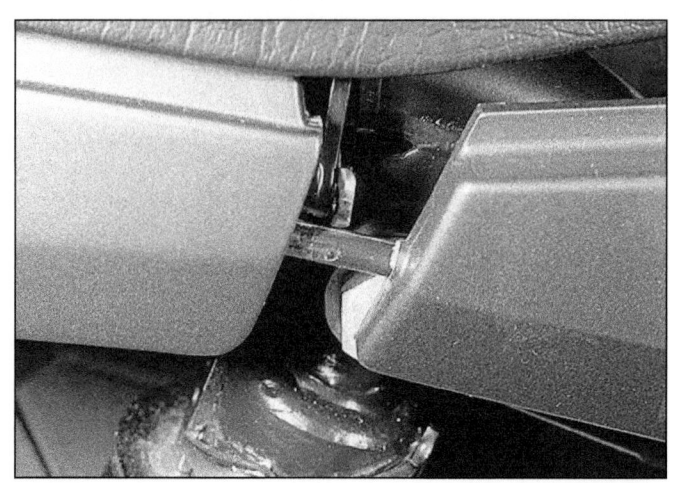

17.16b . . . then move panel forwards to disengage rear mounting

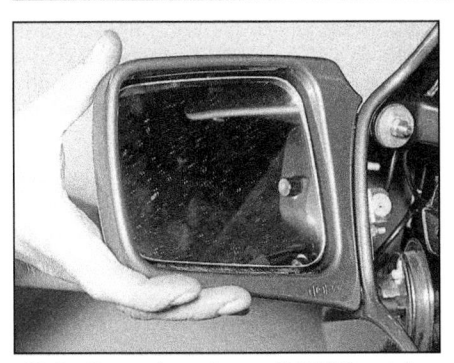

Frame and front suspension 8•19

18.3a Removing mirrors, K100RS – strike sharply upwards . . .

18.3b . . . to unclip mirror from mountings

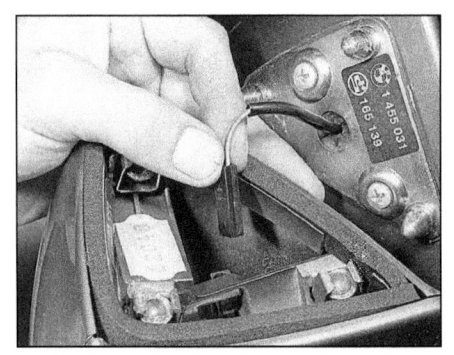

18.3c Do not forget to connect turn signal lamp wire on refitting

directly to the frame or to the engine castings; this is preferable to the usual after-market type which is bolted rigidly to the engine and frame and can cause severe damage to the crankcase lower section or sump castings in even the most minor incident.

21 A large mounting plate is bolted to the (normally blanked-off) mounting points on each side of the crankcase lower section or sump (oil pan) castings. Bonded to or screwed into these plates are mounting points for the bar lower ends. At the top the standard engine mounting bolts are replaced by extended sleeve bolts into which are screwed rubber mountings. The outer end of each mounting is fitted into the bar upper end and secured by a nut; a blanking plug is fitted over the nut for the sake of appearance.

18 Mirrors -
removal and refitting

1 The mirrors fitted to standard models are mounted on stalks which are fastened to the handlebar lever assemblies by nuts and washers, each nut being covered by a cap. if damaged or faulty, they must be renewed as complete assemblies.

2 On K75RT, K100RS, K100RT and K100LT models the mirrors are attached to the fairing by mountings which are designed to break off on impact to minimise damage.

3 To remove the mirrors, hold each one firmly next to the fairing and strike sharply upwards with the palm of the other hand on the outside end of the fairing **(see illustrations)**. This requires a considerable amount of force, so great care is required to ensure that no damage is done. Once one mounting has released the mirror can be manoeuvred off the remaining two. On K100RS models disconnect the turn signal lamp wires, and withdraw the unit **(see illustration)**.

4 If they are cracked or damaged, the glasses of these mirrors can be renewed individually. Each is fixed by a ball and socket joint which is hinged to provide adjustment in the vertical and horizontal planes. Insert a lever, behind the glass, pad the edge of the mirror with a cloth to protect its finish and lever the glass out of its socket. Considerable force is again required, quite enough to break the mirror glass, so take great care not to damage the mirror housing. Apply a suitable lubricant to aid refitting.

19 Luggage -
removal and refitting

Panniers

1 The panniers are locked by a single catch to a cast alloy frame which is bolted between the footrest plates and the rear frame rails. All components are available as separate replacement parts, if required. The same panniers are available as optional extras for all models not fitted with them as standard.

Top box

2 The top box is attached to the rack on top of the tail compartment by an adaptor plate and is locked in place by a single locking plug which is rotated to engage or disengage the adaptor plate.

3 As with the panniers, all components are available as replacement parts and the assembly is available as an optional extra for any model not fitted with them as standard. Where a rack is not fitted as standard, it must be fitted with the topbox; it is retained by four bolts.

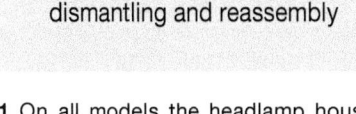

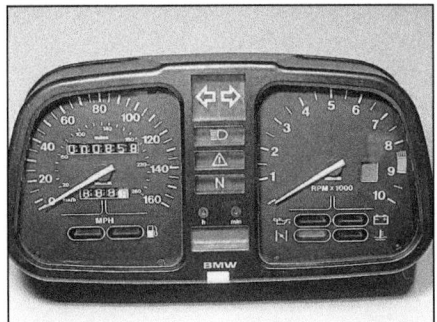

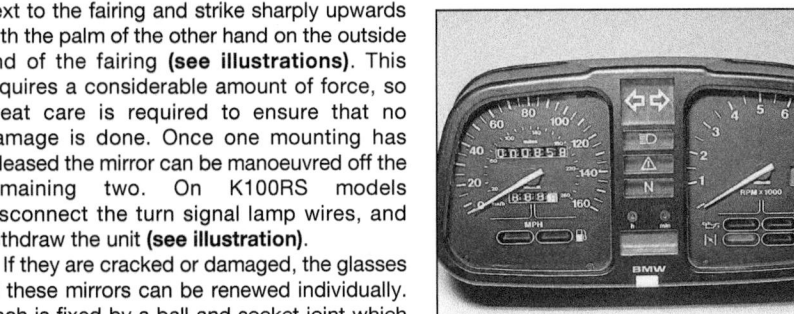

20.3 Instrument panel is very delicate – handle carefully

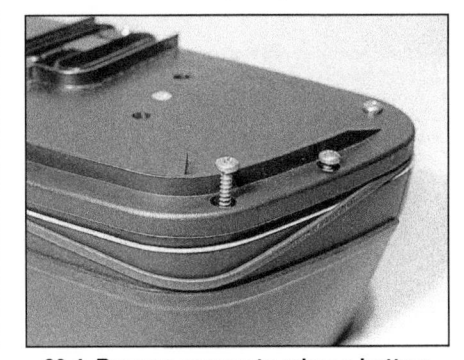

20 Instruments - removal, dismantling and reassembly

1 On all models the headlamp housing or handlebar fairing, the headlamp assembly or the fairing (as appropriate) must be either removed or partially dismantled to gain access to the instrument panel mountings. Refer to Section 15 for full details.

2 With the panel mountings exposed, remove its single retaining screw and withdraw the connector plug cover, then unplug both connector blocks.

3 Remove the four mounting screws or bolts and withdraw the panel assembly **(see illustration)**. Note: *Check the panel rubber mountings very carefully and renew them if there is the least sign of wear or damage. The instruments are sensitive and will be damaged if subjected to excessive vibration levels.* If the panel mountings are altered for any reason (such as fitting aftermarket fairings to standard models) great care must be taken to mount the panel correctly so that it is insulated from vibration.

4 To dismantle the assembly, invert it on a completely clean work surface and remove the screws around the periphery (there are seven on early 100 models, nine on all 75 models and 1986 on 100 models) **(see illustration)**. Withdraw the bottom cover and examine the sealing ring; this must be

20.4 Remove screws to release bottom cover – note sealing ring

8•20 Frame and front suspension

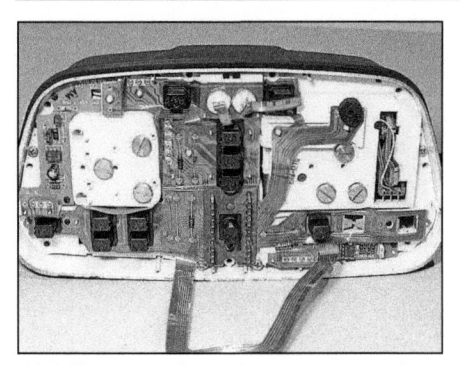

20.5 Removal of panel bottom cover gives access to panel bulb holders

renewed if it is damaged in the slightest way to prevent moisture from entering.

5 All instrument illuminating and warning lamp bulbs may be removed at this stage, if required **(see illustration)**. Being very careful not to damage any component, especially the connector pins, use a pair of pliers to extract the bulb holder; the bulb is of the capless type which is pulled easily out of the holder. Ensure that the wire filaments are correctly inserted on refitting. Note that certain bulbs have a cap fitted over their envelopes; these must be replaced on the new bulb.

6 The printed circuit board is retained by two small black-finished screws, each immediately next to the instrument illuminating lamp bulb holder in the bottom left and right corners (looking at the unit as it is inverted on the bench), and by two larger plated screws at the bottom edge of the connector plug pins. Remove these screws and **very carefully** use a small screwdriver to prise the board up at all contact plug points, ie top left above the tachometer and bottom left, top right above the speedometer and at the bottom, just to the right of the connector plug pin. **Do not** use force; if the contact pins will not release easily take the assembly to an authorised BMW dealer to be dismantled by an expert. With the pins released, withdraw the board.

7 Using a small screwdriver to release the locking catches, front pair first and then the rear pair, lift the clock (where fitted) out to the top. Disengage the locking catches and lift out the warning lamp bulb holder frame.

8 The fuel gauge circuit board is secured in the panel top left corner (looking at the unit as it is inverted on the bench) by two small screws (with either plated slotted heads or black-finished cross-heads). Remove the screws and carefully prise the circuit board off its connector pins.

9 Remove its two large, plated cross-head retaining screws and withdraw the tachometer assembly. Carefully lever off the needle, remove the retaining screws and withdraw the dial then turn the unit round, remove the two retaining screws and withdraw the gear indicator circuit board to one side, noting the spacer.

10 The speedometer circuit board is secured by two small screws (with either plated slotted heads or black-finished cross-heads) below the speedometer assembly. Remove the screws and carefully prise the circuit board off its connector pins.

11 Pull out as far as possible the speedometer trip reset button and remove the two retaining screws to release the unit.

12 On reassembly, all components must be scrupulously clean and dry. Do not overtighten any mounting screws or use force to fit components, but ensure that all are correctly fastened and that all connector pins are fully seated. To rebuild the assembly, follow exactly the reverse of the removal procedure.

13 If renewal of the instrument panel is required ensure that the modified unit is purchased. Improvements were made to the assembly during 1987, mainly to alleviate sealing problems, but also to cure instrument failure due to vibration; refer to an authorised BMW dealer for details of the later type unit.

14 From 1989 the instrument panel was further modified, the most significant improvement being to prevent misting of the instrument face. A Gore-Tex membrane, inserted between the housing and bottom cover, allows ventilation of the housing and also prevents the entry of moisture. As a means of identification, models fitted with the later instrument panel will have two three-segment ventilation holes in the panel bottom cover.

Chapter 9
Final drive and rear suspension

Contents

Final drive - examination and renovation	3	General description	1
Final drive - refitting	4	Nivomat suspension unit - general	10
Final drive - removal	2	Rear suspension unit - adjustments, removal and examination	9
Final drive case - oil change	see Chapter 1	Swinging arm - examination and renovation	6
Final drive case - oil level check	see Chapter 1	Swinging arm and drive shaft - refitting	8
Final drive shaft splines - greasing	see Chapter 1	Swinging arm and drive shaft - removal	5
Final drive shaft - examination and renovation	7	Swinging arm pivot bearings - check	see Chapter 1

Degrees of difficulty

Easy, suitable for novice with little experience	**Fairly easy,** suitable for beginner with some experience	**Fairly difficult,** suitable for competent DIY mechanic	**Difficult,** suitable for experienced DIY mechanic	**Very difficult,** suitable for expert DIY or professional

Specifications

Final drive

Reduction ratio: **Standard**   **Optional**

	Standard	Optional
K75S	3.20 : 1 (32/10T)	3.09 : 1 (34/11T)
All other 75 models	3.20 : 1 (32/10T)	3.36 : 1 (37/11T)
K100RS	2.82 : 1 (31/11T)	2.91 : 1 (32/11T)
All other 100 models	2.91 : 1 (32/11T)	3.00 : 1 (33/11T)

Tooth backlash .... 0.070 - 0.160 mm (0.0028 - 0.0063 in)
Crownwheel taper roller bearing preload:
   Tolerance .... 0.050 - 0.100 mm (0.0020 - 0.0039 in)
   Approximate equivalent, expressed in friction values .... 600 - 1600 N (134.89 - 359.69 lbf)

Final drive lubrication

Recommended oil .... Good quality hypoid gear oil of API class GL-5 or to specification MIL-L-2105 B or C

Viscosity:
   Above 5°C (41°F) .... SAE 90
   Below 5°C (41°F) .... SAE 80
   Alternatively .... SAE 80W90
Capacity .... 260 cc (0.46 Imp pint, 0.28 US qt)

Rear suspension

Travel .... 110 mm (4.33 in)
Spring free length:
   K75S .... Not available
   All other 75 models .... 271 - 277 mm (10.6693 - 10.9055 in)
   100 models - except K100LT .... 265 - 269 mm (10.4331 - 10.5905 in)
Spring wire diameter:
   75 models .... 9.00 mm (0.3543 in)
   100 models - except K100LT .... 9.86 mm (0.3882 in)

9•2 Final drive and rear suspension

Torque wrench settings	Nm	lbf ft
Swinging arm fixed pivot stub retaining screws	9 ± 1	6.5 ± 0.5
Swinging arm adjustable pivot stub	7.5 ± 0.5	5.4 ± 0.4
Swinging arm adjustable pivot stub locknut	41 ± 3	30 ± 2
Final drive case/swinging arm bolts	40 ± 3	29 ± 25
Suspension unit mountings	51 ± 6	37.5 ± 4
Final drive pinion retaining nut	200 ± 20	148 ± 15
Drive pinion assembly/drive case retaining threaded ring	118 ± 12	87 ± 9
Final drive case cover screws or bolts	21 ± 2	15.5 ± 1.5
Speedometer impulse transmitter retaining screw	2.5 ± 0.5	1.8 ± 0.4
Final drive case oil filler plug	20 ± 2	15 ± 1.5
Final drive case oil drain plug	25 ± 3	18.5 ± 2

1 General description

From the gearbox output shaft the drive is transmitted by another shaft to the final drive assembly. The shaft consists of two tubular metal components bonded together by a rubber sleeve to form a single assembly, with a universal joint at the front to permit the shaft to move with the rear suspension, and splined couplings at both ends to allow for the alteration in effective length as the suspension moves through its travel.

The final drive assembly consists of the drive pinion which rotates on a combined ball and roller bearing and the crownwheel which rotates on a taper roller bearing at its right-hand end and a ball journal bearing at its left-hand end; since the rear wheel is bolted directly to a flange on the crownwheel left-hand end, these crownwheel bearings also serve as the rear wheel bearings. A castellated ring on the crownwheel right-hand end serves as the rotor for the speedometer impulse transmitter which is mounted on the final drive housing.

The rear suspension is by an hydraulically-damped coil spring suspension unit acting on a single-sided swinging arm; the arm is a single large aluminium alloy casting which pivots on taper roller bearings that are set on stubs screwed into the rear of the gearbox housing. The final drive shaft rotates inside the swinging arm and the final drive housing is bolted to its rear end.

The K75S model, and any other machine fitted with 'S' suspension, is fitted with a suspension unit that is stiffened to match the front forks. The K100LT model is fitted with Boge Nivomat self-levelling suspension at the rear; this is described in detail in Section 10 of this Chapter and is listed as an optional extra for other models in the range.

2 Final drive - removal

1 Remove the rear wheel. See Chapter 10.
2 Remove the single retaining screw and carefully prise the speedometer impulse transmitter out of the housing (see illustration). If the final drive is to be dismantled, drain the oil as described in *Routine maintenance and servicing*; if not, remember to store it upright to prevent any loss of oil and to keep the transmitter orifice plugged with clean rag to prevent the entry of dirt. Remove the transmitter wire from the guide provided.
3 If the final drive is to be dismantled, on machines with disc rear brakes apply the rear brake firmly to prevent rotation and unscrew the disc mounting screws; on machines with drum rear brakes remove the brake shoes and the operating lever and camshaft. Whether the final drive is to be dismantled or not, on machines with disc rear brakes remove the brake caliper and press the brake pipe grommet sideways out of the locating clamp; on machines with drum rear brakes disconnect the brake operating rod (see illustrations).
4 Remove the suspension unit bottom mounting nut and washer then slacken the top mounting nut and bolt. **Note:** *To prevent the risk of damage to the swinging arm or gearbox housing castings or the sealing gaiter, support the swinging arm in its normal working position, ie no more than 349 mm (13.7 in) below the suspension unit top mounting.* Either place a block of wood or similar under the arm or use a strong strap passed around the arm and the frame seat tubes to hold it at the required height. **Never** allow the swinging arm to drop suddenly and sharply. With the arm correctly supported, remove the suspension unit from its bottom mounting.

2.2 Speedometer impulse transmitter is retained by a single screw

2.3a Remove brake components if final drive is to be dismantled

2.3b Rear brake caliper is retained by two Allen bolts

2.3c Withdraw brake hose/pipe from swinging arm clamp

Final drive and rear suspension 9•3

5 Unscrew the four mounting bolts and withdraw the final drive housing from the swinging arm rear end; if necessary use a soft-faced mallet to tap the housing backwards off the locating dowels. If any sign of rust or water is detected check carefully the sealing gaiter and any other possible points of entry.

3 Final drive - examination and renovation

1 Dismantling the final drive is beyond the scope of the majority of amateur mechanics **(see illustration)**. Wear or damage will be indicated by a high pitched whine. Backlash between the crownwheel and pinion may be assessed by holding the wheel flange firmly and rotating the pinion shaft in both directions. Any lateral play in the crownwheel can only be checked with the assembly installed in the machine, by pulling and pushing the rear wheel.

2 If any wear or damage is found or suspected, take the unit to an authorised BMW dealer for reconditioning.

3 The only task which can be undertaken by the private owner is the removal of the cover to renew a faulty crownwheel oil seal or to attend to the speedometer impulse transmitter rotor **(see illustration)**.

4 If this is to be undertaken, drain the oil from

3.1 Do not attempt to disturb final drive pinion assembly

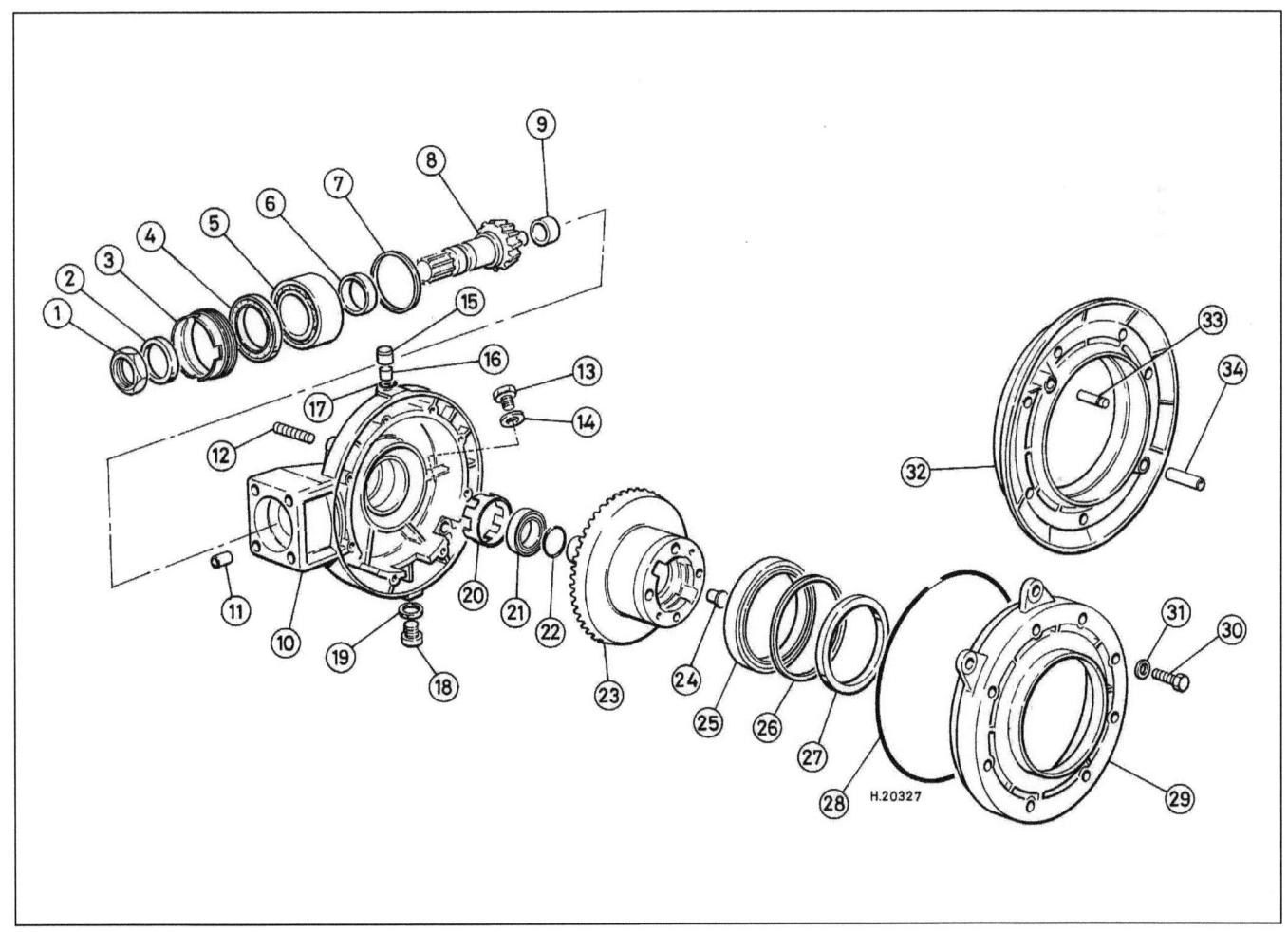

3.3 Final drive assembly

1	Nut	10	Housing	19	Sealing washer	28	O-ring
2	Compression ring	11	Dowel – 2 off	20	Speedometer rotor	29	Housing cover [1]
3	Threaded ring	12	Stud	21	Taper roller bearing	30	Bolt – 8 off
4	Oil seal	13	Filler plug	22	Shim	31	Washer – 8 off
5	Bearing	14	Sealing washer	23	Crownwheel	32	Housing cover [2]
6	Thrust ring	15	Breather cap	24	Plug	33	Brake shoe pivot [2]
7	Shim	16	Sleeve	25	Ball bearing	34	Camshaft sleeve [2]
8	Drive pinion	17	O-ring	26	Shim	[1]	Disc brake models
9	Needle roller bearing	18	Drain plug	27	Oil seal	[2]	Drum brake models

3.4a Disc rear brake models only – make reference marks to ensure correct reassembly ...

3.4b ... before removing final drive case cover

3.5a Crownwheel, bearing and speedometer rotor will be removed with cover ...

the unit and mark the cover and housing across the joint face so that it can be correctly refitted on disc rear brake models **(see illustration)**; on drum rear brake models use a stepped drift of suitable size to tap the brake camshaft sleeve out of the cover to the housing right-hand side. Working progressively and evenly in a diagonal sequence remove the cover retaining bolts or Allen screws and withdraw the cover, applying a few firm taps from a soft-faced mallet to break the seal **(see illustration)**.

5 The crownwheel should be removed with the cover; since the shims are fitted between the taper roller bearing inner race and the crownwheel, or between the ball bearing and cover, they will not be disturbed at this stage **(see illustrations)**.

6 First check that the speedometer rotor is firmly fixed on the crownwheel end and that it is undamaged; this applies mainly to early 100 models since the fit of these two components was improved on all 75 models and later 100 models. If it is to be renewed, the taper roller bearing inner race must be extracted first, using a knife-edged bearing puller; take careful note of any shims found and ensure that they are fitted in exactly their original positions on reassembly. If the rotor is loose but the mating surfaces are undamaged, all components should be thoroughly degreased and all traces of oil deposits or corrosion polished away. Apply a few drops of Loctite 638 or RC/620 (62040) adhesive to the contact faces and tap the rotor onto the crownwheel with a soft-faced mallet. When the rotor is seated fully against the crownwheel shoulder, leave the assembly for four hours so that the adhesive can cure. This can be speeded up to 30 - 40 minutes by heating the crownwheel and rotor to 120°C (248°F).

7 If the oil seal is to be renewed, tap out the crownwheel and bearing; BMW recommend that the cover be heated to approximately 80°C (176°F) to permit this. The ball bearing should stay on the crownwheel, in which case the shim behind it should be refitted exactly the same way round. The seal itself can then be driven out and the new seal fitted with a smear of grease around its outer edge. Fit the new seal by hand as far as possible, ensuring it remains square to its housing, then tap it into place using a hammer and a tubular drift which bears only on the seal hard outer edge. If a sufficiently large drift cannot be found, use either a soft-faced mallet with great care, tapping the seal evenly and squarely into its housing until it is flush with the cover, or take the assembly to an authorised BMW dealer to be rebuilt with the correct service tools.

8 On very early (1984 models only) UK K100 models check that the breather is clear by removing the breather cap and inserting a length of wire into the breather passage. If the wire enters by more than 22 mm (0.9 in), down to 30 mm (1.2 in) approximately, the passage is clear and the wire can be removed and the cap refitted. If the wire cannot be inserted as far as this, the passage is blocked and must be cleared by the careful use of a 7.5 mm (0.3 in) diameter drill bit. With the breather cap and final drive housing cover removed, drill downwards to the outer annular cavity, taking great care not to damage the thin walls of the breather passage. Be very careful to clean away all traces of swarf and other debris. Note - This only proved necessary on very early models after which the breather was checked at the factory. It is also very unlikely that any machine has survived unmodified.

9 Later 100 models were fitted with a modified type of breather incorporating an O-ring around the breather base and a cap with a 3 mm (0.12 in) hole drilled in it; note that the hole must face to the rear. This modification was to further seal the breather against the entry of water and is fitted as standard to all 75 models. If water is found in the final drive oil on early 100 models, take the machine to an authorised BMW dealer for checking.

10 On reassembly, grease the seal lips and do not forget the shim as the crownwheel is fitted to the cover. Fit a new O-ring to the cover groove and grease it, then place the cover assembly on the final drive housing and align the marks made on removal (disc brake models) or the brake camshaft passages (drum brake models) before tapping the cover into place; ensure that the O-ring is not damaged or disturbed **(see illustrations)**. Working progressively and evenly in a

3.5b ... and must be tapped out if seal is to be renewed

3.10a Thoroughly clean housing mating surfaces on reassembly ...

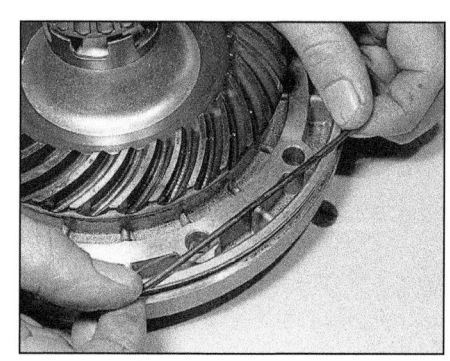

3.10b ... and always renew sealing O-ring

Final drive and rear suspension 9•5

4.3a Rotate crownwheel flange to align shaft and drive pinion splines on refitting

4.3b Tighten bolts to specified torque setting

diagonal sequence tighten the cover retaining bolts or Allen screws to the specified torque wrench setting. Use the stepped drift to tap the brake camshaft sleeve back into place in the cover (drum brake models only).

4 Final drive - refitting

1 Before refitting the final drive assembly check the swinging arm gaiter is securely fixed and undamaged (especially if signs of water were noted in the swinging arm). Apply a coat of the specified lubricant (see Chapter 1) to the drive shaft splines and check that the swinging arm is securely supported at the normal working position.
2 Especially on early 100 models, but on any model which has been fitted with a new or different final drive housing or swinging arm, measure the depth of the tapped holes in the final drive housing into which are screwed the retaining bolts; they must be at least 17.5 mm (0.7 in) deep, measured from the joint face. The manufacturing limits of the swinging arm mounting flange thickness were increased and to ensure that the thread length remained sufficient the final drive housing holes were drilled and tapped deeper; longer bolts 45 mm instead of 40 mm were also used. The early swinging arm and final drive housing are identified by the external horizontal cast rib which is 3.5 mm (0.14 in) wide; on modified castings it is 10 mm (0.40 in) wide. To ensure that the bolts are long enough to clamp the housing threads securely but without bottoming in their tapped holes, select bolts as follows. If a modified final drive housing is fitted to either type of swinging arm, bolts 45 mm long must be used, also if an unmodified final drive housing is fitted to a modified swinging arm; note however that in this latter case the 40 mm bolts must be used if the longer bolts bottom in the tapped holes. Obviously if two unmodified (early type) castings are being installed, the 40 mm bolts are required.
3 If water was found in the swinging arm apply a thin coat of sealant to the mating surfaces and check that the two locating dowels are securely fixed in the final drive housing surface. Refit the housing, aligning the drive pinion splines with those of the drive shaft rear end, then push the housing firmly into place **(see illustration)**. Refit and tighten the retaining bolts to the specified torque setting **(see illustration)**.
4 Refit the rear suspension unit to its bottom mounting and tighten the mounting nuts and bolts to the specified torque setting. Remove the swinging arm support.
5 Refit the rear brake components and rear wheel, as described in the relevant Sections of Chapter 10.
6 Press the speedometer impulse transmitter into the final drive housing, ensuring that it does not contact the rotor and that the sealing O-ring is coated with the specified oil to prevent any risk of damage. Fasten the retaining screw and secure the transmitter lead in the guide provided.
7 Where necessary, fill the housing with oil as described in *Routine maintenance and servicing*, then check the oil level. Make a final check that all disturbed components are correctly refitted and fully secured, that the brake is correctly adjusted and working properly and that the rear suspension is working properly. Check also that the rear wheel is free to rotate smoothly and easily before taking the machine out on the road.

5 Swinging arm and drive shaft - removal

1 Remove the final drive housing. See Section 2 of this Chapter.
2 Remove the exhaust silencer mounting nuts and unscrew its mounting Allen screws or bolts to withdraw the left-hand footrest plate. Similarly, remove the right-hand footrest plate complete with the rear brake components **(see illustration)**; if care is taken there is no need to dismantle the rear brake at all. On machines with disc rear brakes note that the fluid reservoir is secured to the battery carrier by a single bolt or nut **(see illustration)**.
3 Disconnect the clutch cable from the operating lever and withdraw it from the gearbox housing.
4 On the left-hand side of the gearbox

5.2a Remove both footrest plates to reach swinging arm pivots

5.2b Disc rear brake models only – fluid reservoir is secured by single bolt to battery carrier

9•6 Final drive and rear suspension

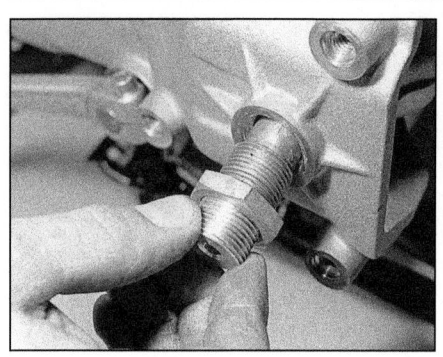

5.4 Unscrew swinging arm adjustable pivot stub . . .

5.5 . . . and remove fixed pivot stub to release swinging arm

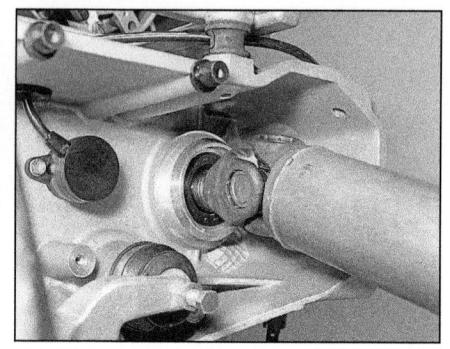

5.7 Disengage circlip to release drive shaft from gearbox output shaft

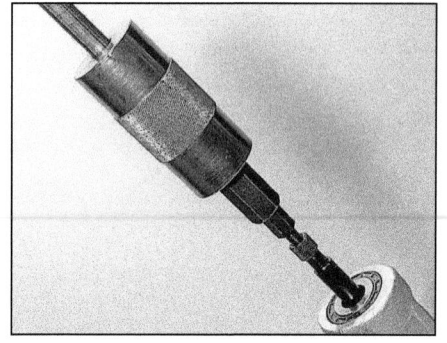

6.1 Slide-hammer with internally-expanding attachment is required to remove pivot bearings

housing slacken the large locknut and unscrew the swinging arm adjustable pivot stub **(see illustration)**.

5 On the gearbox right-hand side remove its three retaining Allen screws and carefully prise out the swinging arm fixed pivot stub **(see illustration)**; if it proves stubborn, screw a suitably sized bolt into its centre thread and use a large pair of pliers to draw it out, rotating it to break the seal.

6 With both pivot stubs removed, withdraw the swinging arm.

7 Using a small screwdriver to ease the circlip at its front end over the gearbox output shaft splines **(see illustration)**, pull the drive shaft sharply backwards to remove it.

6 Swinging arm - examination and renovation

1 The swinging arm pivot bearings incorporate seals and must be removed using a slide-hammer with the appropriate internally expanding attachment **(see illustration)**.

2 Thoroughly clean all components, removing all traces of dirt, foreign matter and old grease from the bearings and from the swinging arm casting **(see illustration)**.

3 Check all components for signs of wear or damage, particularly the bearing outer and inner races, the rollers themselves and the

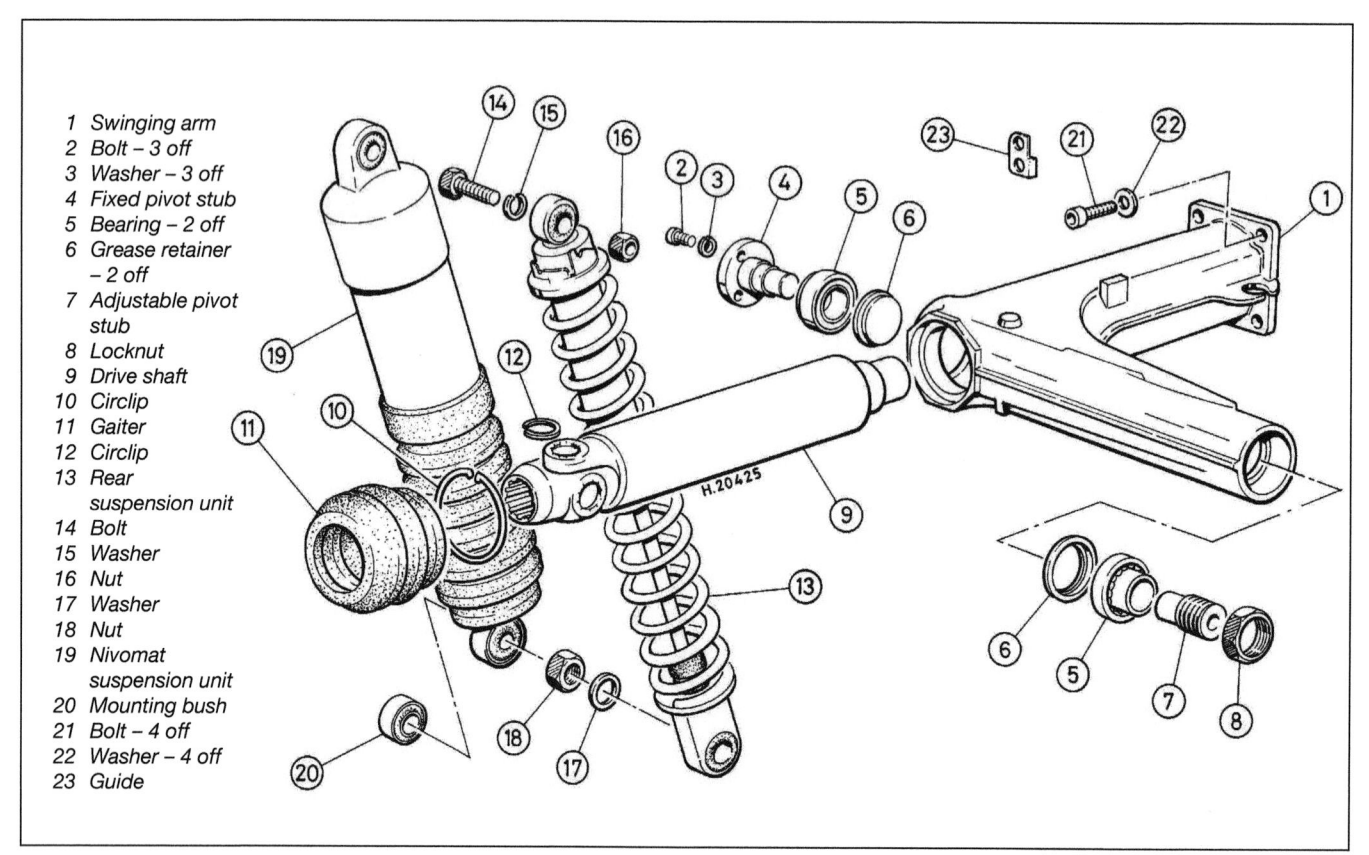

1 Swinging arm
2 Bolt – 3 off
3 Washer – 3 off
4 Fixed pivot stub
5 Bearing – 2 off
6 Grease retainer – 2 off
7 Adjustable pivot stub
8 Locknut
9 Drive shaft
10 Circlip
11 Gaiter
12 Circlip
13 Rear suspension unit
14 Bolt
15 Washer
16 Nut
17 Washer
18 Nut
19 Nivomat suspension unit
20 Mounting bush
21 Bolt – 4 off
22 Washer – 4 off
23 Guide

6.2 Swinging arm and driveshaft

Final drive and rear suspension 9•7

6.4 Slide-hammer with internally-expanding attachment is required to remove bearing outer races – note grease retainer behind outer race

6.5 Pack bearings with specified grease on refitting

bearing cage. Any component which is damaged or worn must be renewed.

4 The bearing outer races must be extracted using a slide-hammer with the appropriate internally-expanding attachment. The grease retainer on the swinging arm right-hand side can be tapped out from the inside **(see illustration)**, if required, by passing a drift through the drive shaft aperture; the left-hand side retainer can then be tapped out from behind, passing a drift through the swinging arm cross tube.

5 On reassembly, the pivot bearing outer races can be tapped into place (after the grease retainers have been refitted) using a hammer and a tubular drift such as a socket spanner which bears only on the bearing outer edge. Tap each outer race into place until it seats on its locating shoulder. Pack the bearing inner races liberally with the specified grease and fit them to the swinging arm **(see illustration)**.

6 Examine closely the condition of the sealing gaiter at the swinging arm front end; this must be renewed if it is split, torn, has deteriorated or is damaged in any way. To remove it, pull it out of the shaft, then remove the retaining circlip from inside it. On early 100 models the gaiter can be replaced by the modified type (with an additional internal front sealing lip to exclude water) fitted to all 75 models and to all later 100 models.

7 On refitting the gaiter, ensure that it is installed the correct way round, with the internal sealing lip at the front and the end with the internal circlip groove at the rear, inside the swinging arm. Refitting is eased if the gaiter's inside and outside sealing surfaces are coated with the lubricant specified for the final drive splined joints (see *Routine maintenance and servicing*). Refit the large circlip to the gaiter groove with its open end aligned with the rib on the swinging arm cross tube.

7 Final drive shaft - examination and renovation

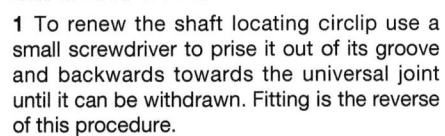

1 To renew the shaft locating circlip use a small screwdriver to prise it out of its groove and backwards towards the universal joint until it can be withdrawn. Fitting is the reverse of this procedure.

2 Holding the shaft front end in a vice with padded jaws, feel for free play in the universal joint bearings by pulling it backwards and forwards and twisting it to and fro in its normal direction of rotation.

3 If any free play is found in the joint, or if any other sign of wear or damage is detected, the shaft must be renewed as a complete assembly. Check with particular care the shaft splines and the bonded rubber section.

8 Swinging arm and drive shaft - refitting

1 Apply a coat of the specified lubricant to the splines of the gearbox output shaft, to the splines at each end of the drive shaft and to the inside of the swinging arm rubber gaiter. Check that the swinging arm bearings are refitted and fully packed with clean grease and that their respective circlips are refitted inside the rubber gaiter and inside the drive shaft front end. Apply a coat of anti-seize compound such as Copaslip or Never Seeze to the swinging arm pivot stubs.

2 Note that the swinging arm must not be refitted with the drive shaft in place; the rubber gaiter cannot be correctly refitted to the gearbox if this is attempted.

3 With the gaiter and bearings in place, fit the swinging arm to the rear of the gearbox housing and manoeuvre it to and fro until the gaiter sealing lips have snapped into place on the gearbox flange **(see illustration)**; pull the swinging arm gently backwards to check that the gaiter is fully in place.

4 Refit the fixed pivot stub to the gearbox housing and pivot bearing, then refit and tighten securely the three retaining Allen screws to the specified torque wrench setting, if available **(see illustration)**.

5 Screw into the gearbox housing and left-hand pivot bearing the adjustable pivot stub. Tighten the stub as hard as possible by hand only, using an ordinary Allen key to preload

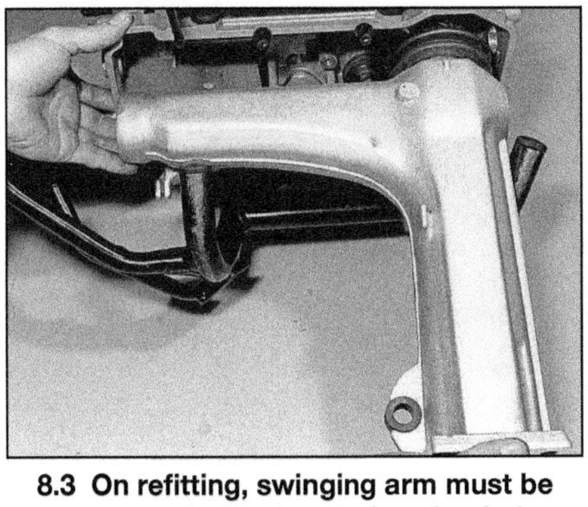

8.3 On refitting, swinging arm must be installed before drive shaft – check that sealing gaiter is securely fastened

8.4 Refit fixed pivot stub and tighten screws securely

9•8 Final drive and rear suspension

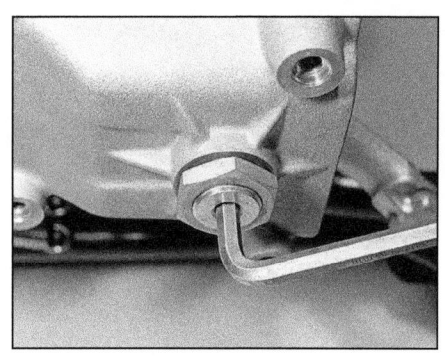

8.5a Refit adjustable pivot stub and tighten as hard as possible by hand to preload bearings

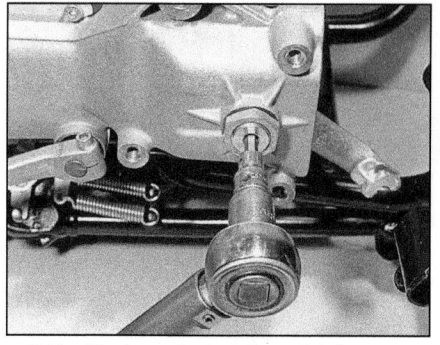

8.5b Slacken pivot stub and tighten to specified torque setting

8.5c Tighten pivot stub locknut securely, to specified torque setting if possible

the bearings **(see illustration)**, then slacken it fully and tighten it to the specified torque setting **(see illustration)**. Hold the stub in that position while the locknut is tightened securely, also to the specified torque wrench setting, if possible **(see illustration)**. Check that the swinging arm moves smoothly and easily throughout its full travel with no free play being discernible.

6 Checking that its splines are properly lubricated, insert the drive shaft into the swinging arm and move it forwards until the front end engages with the gearbox output shaft. Push the shaft on to the output shaft splines until the locating circlip is heard to snap into its groove; pull the shaft gently backwards to check its security.

7 Connect the clutch cable to the operating lever and adjust the release mechanism as described in Chapter 1.

8 Refit the footrest plates, tightening their mounting bolts and the exhaust silencer mounting nuts to the specified torque wrench settings, where available. Refit the brake components that were disturbed to withdraw the footrest.

9 Refit the final drive housing as described in Section 4 of this Chapter.

9 Rear suspension unit - adjustment, removal and examination

1 The two-way hydraulically damped suspension unit may be adjusted to three spring load settings. Adjustment is effected by using a C-spanner to rotate the adjusting collar at the top of the unit to the desired setting; the normal setting for solo riding is at the top, and the stiffest setting for maximum loads is with the collar engaged on the lowest position.

2 Since the unit is sealed, unless any obvious damage is found such as oil leaks around the damper rod or if the unit's body is dented, the unit can only be checked by assessing its performance.

3 With the machine standing on its wheels press down on the rear and release sharply; the suspension should compress smoothly and return smoothly to the at rest position. If any signs of jerkiness is noted, or if any undue noises are heard the unit must be renewed. The most effective test, however, is to ride the machine. If it is taken to a person who is familiar with the type, he or she should be able immediately to spot a suspension fault to which the regular rider has become accustomed. If there is any evidence of faulty handling or cornering due to worn rear suspension, the unit must be renewed as soon as possible.

4 *Note: Before removing the suspension unit ensure that the swinging arm is supported by a block of wood or similar or by a strong strap passed around the swinging arm and frame tubes. If the swinging arm is secured in approximately its normal working position, ie not more than 349 mm (13.7 in) below the suspension unit, the risk of damage to the sealing gaiter or to the gearbox housing or swinging arm castings will be avoided.* **Never allow the swinging arm to drop suddenly and sharply.**

5 With the swinging arm supported, remove the suspension unit bottom mounting nut and top mounting bolt and withdraw the unit. On refitting, ensure that the mounting bolt and nuts are fastened to the specified torque wrench settings and that the unit is installed with the spring adjusting collar at the top **(see illustrations)**.

6 As stated above, the unit can only be renewed if faulty; repairs are not possible

9.5a Suspension unit is installed with spring preload collar uppermost . . .

9.5b . . . both mountings must be fastened to specified torque wrench settings

since replacement parts are not available and the unit itself is sealed. The only exception to this are the unit mounting bushes which can be removed using a drawbolt arrangement or a vice and suitably sized socket spanners. During 1988 a strengthened rear suspension unit lower mounting eye was introduced for models produced between late 1985 and early 1987, as a result of cracks appearing in the eye in some cases. The strengthened eye has 4 mm/0.16 in of material (previously 2.5 mm/0.10 in) surrounding the steel/rubber mounting bush. An authorised BMW dealer will have full details of the modification.

7 If the unit is to be stored for a long time, always keep it upright, except for K75S models and others with 'S' suspension, where the unit should be stored with the damper rod upwards; in all cases this is to prevent the seals from drying out.

10 Nivomat suspension unit - general

1 Nivomat suspension, developed in conjunction with the manufacturers, Boge, requires no adjustment or maintenance and is self-adjusting to provide the same ride height, ground clearance, suspension travel and performance for all loads up to the maximum permissible and at all speeds. Spring preload (or its equivalent) and damping action are adjusted automatically to be relatively soft during low speed solo use and become progressively harder as the need arises.

2 The unit functions as follows **(see illustration)**: the pump rod is resiliently mounted to the top of the unit, the piston rod being attached to the bottom. As the suspension moves, the relative movement of these two components causes oil to be sucked from the low-pressure chamber via passages to the pump intake valve, from where it is forced through the pump check valve into the high-pressure chamber. This pressurises the gas, which is kept separate by a rubber diaphragm, increases the pressure in the unit's working parts and increases the spring preload to raise the machine to a pre-determined ride height. When this has been reached, a valve opens to allow the oil to flow through the unit back to the low-pressure chamber. Damping action is provided by the pumping action itself, in addition to the spring-loaded damper valves. Note that if the load limit is exceeded, a safety valve prevents excessive pressure from building up; this means that the full ride height will not be reached.

3 It is important to remember that the ride height and suspension travel will not reach their full values until the unit has pumped itself up. Therefore if the first few miles of a journey are on a completely smooth road, the rear suspension may not be ready to take a sudden bump. Also if the load is suddenly altered, ie the rider takes all his weight on his legs when stopped at a traffic light, if a pillion passenger mounts or dismounts, or if luggage is added or removed, the rear suspension will take a little while to adjust itself to the new requirements. This is not a fault, merely a function of the system's design and should not cause problems once the rider is familiar with it.

4 To test the unit, place a load on the rear of the machine, sufficient to noticeably compress the suspension, then with the machine stationary, but on its wheels, press down on its rear end (20 to 25 strokes of approximately 15 - 20 mm (1/2 - 3/4 in). The unit should be seen to pump itself up to the normal ride height.

⚠ *Warning: do not attempt to dismantle the unit or to alter its performance. Do not touch the two screws in the unit body. If any fault is suspected in the rear suspension performance take the machine to a BMW dealer for attention. Note that a light film of oil on the damper piston rod does not necessarily indicate a fault, although any serious oil leakage will obviously warrant instant attention by a BMW dealer.*

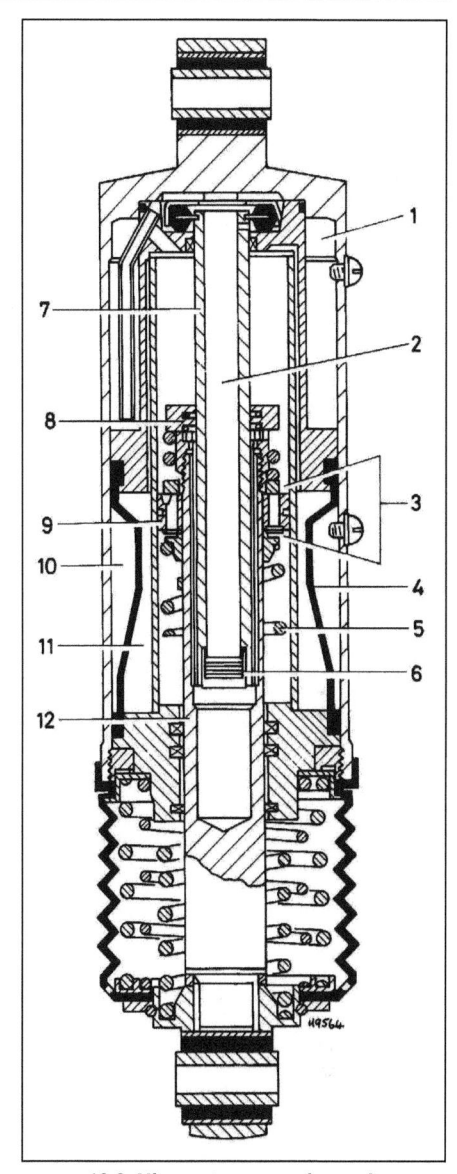

10.2 Nivomat suspension unit

1 Low pressure chamber
2 Ride height control passage
3 Damper spring loaded valves
4 Rubber diaphragm
5 Rebound spring
6 Pump intake valve
7 Hollow pump rod
8 Pump check valve
9 Damper piston
10 Gas (high pressure)
11 High pressure chamber
12 Piston rod

9•10 Final drive and rear suspension

Notes

Chapter 10
Wheels, brakes and tyres

Contents

ABS - bleeding and fluid renewal	18
ABS - check and overhaul	see Chapter 1
ABS - control unit location	15
ABS - general description	11
ABS - modifications	19
ABS - testing	17
ABS - warnings	12
ABS pressure modulators - removal and refitting	14
ABS relays - location	16
ABS wheel speed sensors - removal and refitting	13
Bleeding the hydraulic brake system	9
Brake pads - wear check and renewal	see Chapter 1
Brake fluid - renewal	see Chapter 1
Caliper - removal, examination and refitting	6
Front brake master cylinder - removal, examination and refitting	7
Front wheel - removal and refitting	2
General description	1
Hydraulic brake overhaul - general	5
Rear disc brake master cylinder - removal, examination and refitting	8
Rear drum brake - check and adjustment	see Chapter 1
Rear drum brake - examination and renovation (K75, K75T, K75C)	10
Rear wheel - removal and refitting	3
Tyres - general information and fitting	20
Tyres - pressure check and wear	see Daily (pre-ride) checks
Wheel bearings - removal, examination and refitting	4
Wheels and wheel bearings - check	see Chapter 1

Degrees of difficulty

Easy, suitable for novice with little experience	Fairly easy, suitable for beginner with some experience	Fairly difficult, suitable for competent DIY mechanic	Difficult, suitable for experienced DIY mechanic	Very difficult, suitable for expert DIY or professional

Specifications

Wheels

Size:
	Front	Rear
K75C, K75T, 1987-89 K75	MTH 2.50 x 18E	MTH 2.75 x 18E also 2.75 x 17
K75RT, 1990-on K75	MTH 2.50 x 18E	MTH 2.75 x 17
1986-90 K75S, all 100 models	MTH 2.50 x 18E	MTH 2.75 x 17E also 3.00 x 17
1991-on K75S (with 3-spoke design wheel)	MTH 2.50 x 18E	MTH 3.00 x 17

Rim maximum runout - radial and axial .... 0.50 mm (0.0197 in)
Wheel bearing size (front) .... 6005 25 mm x 47 mm x 12 mm

Brakes

Type:
	Front	Rear
K75, K75C, K75T	Twin hydraulic discs	SLS drum - rod operated
K75S, K75RT, all 100 models	Twin hydraulic discs	Single hydraulic disc

Disc brakes - front and rear

Disc diameter .... 285 mm (11.22 in)
Disc thickness:
   Standard .... 4.300 - 4.400 mm (0.1693 - 0.1732 in)
   Service limit .... 3.556 mm (0.1400 in)
Disc maximum warpage .... 0.200 mm (0.0079 in)
Brake pad friction material thickness:
   Standard - approximate .... 5.0 mm (0.1969 in)
   Service limit .... 1.5 mm (0.0591 in)
Front master cylinder piston OD .... 13 mm (0.5118 in)
Rear master cylinder piston OD:
   Up to late 1988 .... 13 mm (0.5118 in)
   From late 1988 .... 12 mm (0.4724 in)
Caliper piston OD .... 38 mm (1.4961 in)
Recommended brake fluid .... DOT 4 - eg ATE 'SL'

Drum brake
Drum ID:
  Standard .... 200.00 mm (7.8740 in)
  Maximum .... 201.16 mm (7.9197 in)
Brake shoe friction material minimum thickness .... 1.5 mm (0.0591 in)

ABS components
Controlled minimum speed .... 2.5 mph (4.0 kph)
Power rating of system - whilst riding 0.6A
Wheel speed sensor clearance .... 0.35 - 0.65 mm (0.0138 - 0.0256 in)

Tyres
Note: *check with BMW importer/dealer for currently approved makes and types of tyre*

Size:	Front	Rear
K75C, K75T, 1987-89 K75	100/90 - 18 56 H, also 100/90 H 18	120/90 - 18 65 H, also 120/90 H 18
1990-on K75	100/90 x 18 56 H	130/90 x 17 68 V
K75RT	100/90 x 18 56 V	130/90 x 17 68 V
K75S, all 100 models	100/90 V 18. also 100/90 x 18 56 V	130/90 V 17, also 130/90 x 17 68 V
Radial tyres - 100 models*	100/90 VR 18	140/80 VR 17

Pressures and tread depth .... see Daily (pre-ride) checks

Radial tyres are only recommended for certain 100 models - check with BMW importer/dealer. Radial tyres must be used on both wheels. See Section 20 for clearance details.

Torque wrench settings

	Nm	lbf ft
Front wheel spindle retaining collar Allen screw	33 ± 4	24 ± 3
Front wheel spindle clamp bolts	14 ± 2	10 ± 1.5
Rear wheel mounting bolts	105 ± 4	77.5 ± 3
Front brake disc mountings	29 ± 3	21.5 ± 2
Rear brake disc mounting screws	21 ± 2	15.5 ± 1.5
Brake caliper mounting bolts	32 ± 2	23.5 ± 1.5
Brake pipe retaining plastic nut at steering head - early 75 models, all 100 models	10 ± 1	7.5 ± 0.5
All brake hose or pipe unions	7 ± 1	5 ± 0.5
Brake caliper bleed nipples	7 ± 1	5 ± 0.5

1 General description

The wheels are one-piece cast alloy components with a rim configuration suitable for the tubeless tyres fitted to all models. Note that not only should the tyres always be of the specified size and speed and/or load rating for the wheel to which they are fitted, but that they should also always be of the same make and type from the selection approved by BMW. **Do not** fit any make or type of tyre that is **not** approved by BMW; the BMW importer or an authorised BMW dealer will be able to provide details of the current list.

The front brakes are of the hydraulically-operated twin disc type. The application of the handlebar lever moves the piston in the Magura master cylinder assembly producing an equivalent increase in pressure transmitted by the hydraulic fluid to all parts of the system. The Brembo brake caliper bodies are bolted rigidly to each fork lower leg and contain a separate aluminium alloy piston in each body half. The pistons are arranged facing towards each other on each side of each disc, so that the increase in pressure, magnified by the difference in piston sizes, causes each piston to move towards the disc, pressing the brake pad friction material against the disc surface. Given that none of the components are stuck with dirt or corrosion, exactly the same clamping force should be applied to each disc to slow the wheel. Each piston is surrounded by a fluid seal and a smaller dust seal to exclude any dirt or moisture. As the piston moves outwards the fluid seal distorts and, on release of brake pressure, springs back into shape, thus retracting the piston with it to prevent brake drag. As the pad friction material wears, the piston moves through the fluid seal to compensate for this wear, more fluid entering the system from the master cylinder reservoir to increase the system's capacity accordingly.

The rear brake fitted to K75S and to all 100 models uses a Brembo-built master cylinder/fluid reservoir assembly operated by the rear brake pedal and mounted on the rear of the right-hand footrest plate. It acts on a single brake disc bolted to the final drive crownwheel flange via a Brembo caliper, in all other respects it is similar to the front brake system. Note that while early 1984 100 models were fitted with drilled rear brake discs, all later models are fitted with undrilled components.

Other 75 models are fitted with a rod-operated drum rear brake in which two shoes, with friction material bonded to their outer surfaces, are forced outwards against the inside of a drum, mounted in the rear wheel casting, by the rotation of a camshaft. On release of pedal pressure, the shoes are pulled clear of the drum by heavy return springs. Since only one cam is fitted, the brake is only of the single leading shoe type.

The BMW FAG-Kuggelfischer anti-lock braking system (ABS) was available for the 100 models from 1988 and for the 75 models from 1990. Refer to Section 11 or a full description of ABS.

Wheels, brakes and tyres 10•3

2.1 Before removing the wheel, note tyre fitting mark and use to determine direction of installation

2.3 One caliper, possibly both, must be removed before the wheel can be withdrawn

2.4 Unscrew spindle retaining Allen screw and withdraw retainer to release spindle

2 Front wheel - removal and refitting

1 Place the machine on its centre stand and wedge a wooden block or similar under the sump so that the front wheel is clear of the ground. Make a note of the tyre rotation arrow (or mark the wheel itself) to ensure that the wheel is refitted the original way round **(see illustration)**.

2 During wheel removal make a careful note of any washers and spacers fitted; these must be refitted in their original locations. Also wedge a piece of wood between the brake pads; do not apply the brake lever. It will be necessary to remove at least one brake caliper to permit wheel removal; depending on the type and make of front tyre fitted it may prove necessary to remove both.

3 To remove either caliper, first unscrew the brake hose/pipe clamp at the top of the fork lower leg (on models with two-piece mudguards it may well prove quicker to remove the mudguard rear section), then remove the two caliper mounting bolts and withdraw the caliper, wedging a spacer such as a clean piece of wood between its pads **(see illustration)**.

4 Unscrew the Allen screw which secures the spindle retaining collar on the right-hand side and withdraw it with the collar **(see illustration)**. Slacken the spindle clamp bolts, insert a tommy-bar into the spindle and pull out the spindle with a twisting motion. Note the two spacers.

5 On refitting, grease the spindle to prevent corrosion and reverse the removal procedure. The wider of the two spacers fits against the hub left-hand side **(see illustrations)**. Hold the spindle with the tommy-bar and tighten the Allen screw to the specified torque setting. Refit the caliper(s), if removed, and tighten the mounting bolts securely, to the specified torque wrench setting.

6 When the wheel has been refitted, tighten the spindle Allen screw to its specified torque setting **(see illustration)**, then push the machine off its stand and apply the front brake (having refitted the calipers, where applicable). Pump the forks up and down several times to align the fork lower legs on the spindle, then raise the machine on to its centre stand and tighten the spindle clamps to their specified torque settings **(see illustration)**. Apply the brake lever repeatedly to bring the pads back into contact with the discs.

7 Check that the brake and front forks operate correctly, that the wheel is free to rotate easily, and that all disturbed fasteners are correctly tightened before riding the machine. If ABS is fitted, the sensor air gap should be checked, as described in Chapter 1.

3 Rear wheel - removal and refitting

1 Place the machine on its centre stand so that it is supported securely with the rear wheel clear of the ground. Unlock and raise the seat then remove the tail storage compartment lid.

2 Slacken the two nuts (either wingnuts or ordinary nuts with plastic caps) on the floor of the storage compartment and remove (working from outside the rear of the tail unit) the two screws from underneath the tail lamp assembly. Withdraw the number plate

2.5a Note that wider spacer is on hub left-hand side . . .

2.5b . . . narrower spacer on hub right-hand side

2.6a Tighten spindle retainer Allen screw to specified torque setting and align fork legs on spindle . . .

2.6b . . . before tightening spindle clamp bolts to specified torque setting

10•4 Wheels, brakes and tyres

3.2 On machines with disc rear brakes prise off hub cover

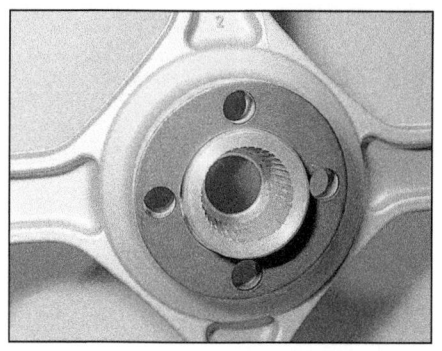

3.4 Mating surfaces must be absolutely clean on refitting – do not forget metal washer (where fitted)

3.5a Ensure conical spacers are refitted correctly . . .

3.5b . . . before tightening wheel bolts to specified torque setting

bracket. On machines with disc rear brakes, prise off the wheel hub cover **(see illustration)**.

3 Either select top gear or apply the rear brake to prevent wheel rotation, then unscrew the mounting bolts, noting their conical spacers. Withdraw the wheel, noting the large metal washer fitted on disc brake models. On drum brake models, it may be necessary to slacken off the brake adjusting nut to release the wheel.

4 On refitting, check that the mating surfaces of the wheel and the final drive mounting flange are completely clean and free from grease **(see illustration)**, also the mounting bolts and their threads. On machines with disc rear brakes, do not forget to refit the large metal washer. Note also that the bolts are not interchangeable between models; drum brake models have bolts 55 mm long (indicated by the number 55 marked on the bolt heads) and disc brake models have bolts 60 mm long (indicated by the number 60 marked on the bolt heads).

5 Fit the rear wheel and mounting bolts. Ensure that the conical spacers under the bolt heads engage correctly with the wheel tapered surfaces **(see illustration)**. Tighten the mountings securely using a torque wrench or the machine's own tools **(see illustration)**. With its own tubular extension the wheel nut spanner provided will need only normal hand pressure to tighten the mounting to approximately the correct torque setting. Check the tightness of the mountings with a torque wrench as soon as possible.

6 Refit the wheel hub cover (disc rear brakes only) **(see illustration)**; on the 1991-on K75S note that the locating tab on the cover must engage the cutout in the wheel **(see illustration)**. Refit the number plate bracket. Where appropriate, check the adjustment of the rear brake. See Chapter 1.

7 On machines with drum rear brakes, if the rear brake feels spongy or imprecise in operation at any time, but particularly after the rear wheel has been disturbed the shoes will probably need to be centralised on the drum. Slacken the wheel mounting bolts, spin the wheel and apply the brake hard. Maintain full pressure while the mounting bolts are tightened to the specified torque wrench setting. Re-check the brake adjustment.

8 If ABS is fitted, the sensor air gap should be checked, as described in Chapter 1.

4 Wheel bearings - removal, examination and refitting

1 Check the bearings for wear as described in Chapter 1.

Front wheel

2 Remove the wheel from the machine. See Section 2.

3 Note that BMW recommend that the wheel is heated to approximately 100°C (212°F) to install the wheel bearings. If this is to be done the brake discs, balance weights, tyre and valve should be removed first, as described in

3.6a Do not forget to refit the hub cover

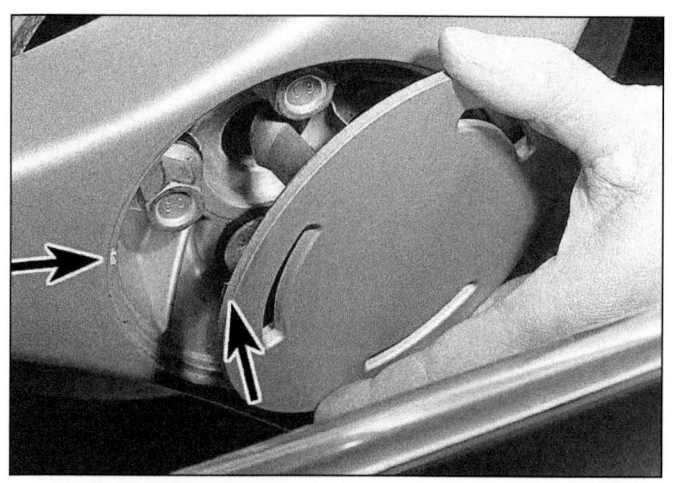

3.6b On 1991-on K75S models engage tab with cut-out in hub when refitting rear wheel cover

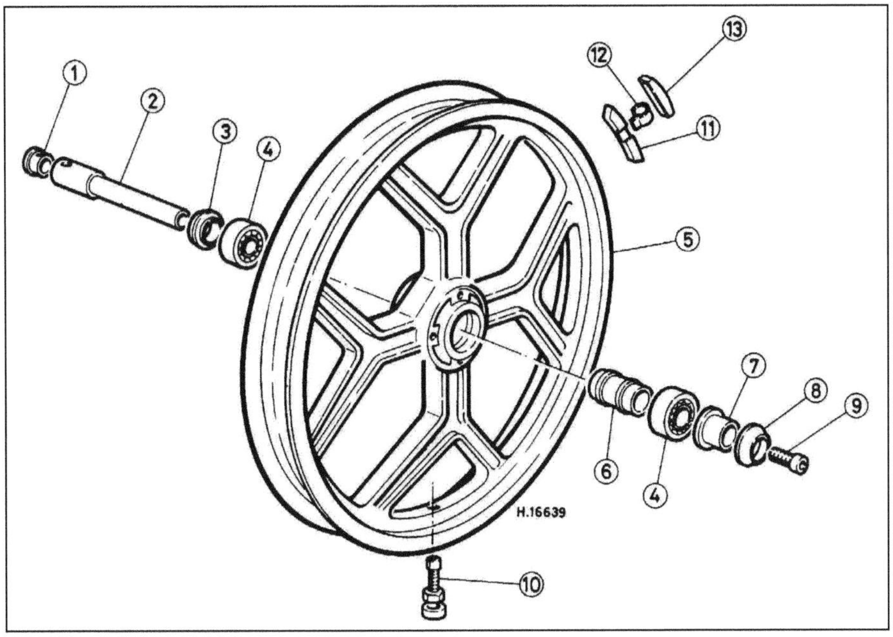

Wheels, brakes and tyres 10•5

4.5 Front wheel - all models except 1991-on K75S

1 Spindle cap
2 Spindle
3 Spacer
4 Ball bearing
5 Wheel
6 Spacer
7 Spacer
8 Retaining collar
9 Allen screw
10 Tyre valve
11 Balance weight*
12 Clip*
13 Balance weight – later type

*early 100 models only

the relevant Sections of this Chapter, to prevent damage to them.

4 On 1991-on K75S models, remove the circlip retaining the left-hand bearing in the hub.

5 Due to the tight fit of the central spacer, the bearings can only be removed using a slide-hammer or other puller with the correct internally-expanding adaptor. With the bearings removed, wash them in a high flash-point solvent and check them for wear or damage **(see illustration)**. If any signs of wear or damage is discovered, if free play was found at the wheel rim, or if either bearing rotates roughly, both must be renewed. Pack the bearings with grease before reassembly.

6 On reassembly, BMW recommend that the hub is heated to 100°C (212°F); heating such a large component evenly will prove very difficult and must be done with great care. The simplest course may well prove to be stripping the wheel (see paragraph 3 above) and placing it in a large container, then slowly pouring boiling water over it, avoiding splashes. Take great care to avoid any risk of personal injury or of component damage when heating components or when handling components that have been heated.

7 Fit the first bearing into the heated hub with its sealed surface outwards and tap it firmly into place against its locating shoulder with a hammer and a tubular drift such as a socket spanner which bears only on the bearing outer race **(see illustrations)**. Invert the wheel, check that both bearings are fully packed with the specified grease and refit the central spacer **(see illustration)**, followed by the remaining bearing, which is fitted as described above. Note that if the bearing outer races are a loose fit in the hub, Loctite 638 should be applied at the joint between the outer race and wheel hub. Take care to thoroughly degrease the hub and bearing outer surfaces. On 1991-on K75S models, refit the circlip to retain the left-hand bearing in the hub.

8 Refit the valve, tyre, balance weights and discs (if disturbed) and check that the wheel rotates freely and easily on the spindle before refitting.

Rear wheel

9 Note that the rear wheel is bolted to the flange of the final drive crownwheel and therefore has no bearings of its own. If play is detected at the wheel rim this can only be due (assuming the mounting bolts are securely fastened) to worn bearings in the final drive assembly. Since the overhaul of this is beyond the scope of this manual and of most owners, the machines should be taken to an authorised BMW dealer for attention.

5 Hydraulic brake overhaul - general

1 Before starting work on any component of a hydraulic brake system, note the following:
2 Caliper overhaul should be preceded by removing the pads, as described in Chapter 1.
3 Check carefully with a BMW dealer exactly what replacement parts are available to recondition the components; there is no point in attempting to dismantle an assembly if lack of pistons and seals means that it cannot be repaired. On the front brakes, both calipers should be always overhauled together to preserve brake performance.

Warning: Remember that brake fluid is an excellent paint stripper and will also attack plastic components. If any is spilt, wash it off as soon as possible with fresh water. Use only new fluid from a freshly-opened sealed container as it is hygroscopic, which means that it absorbs water from the air. This eventually lowers the fluid's boiling point to an unsafe degree; fluid should never be re-used.

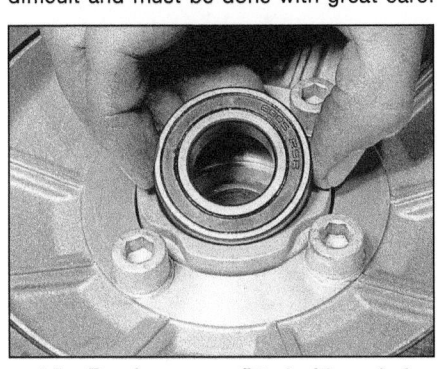

4.7a Bearings are refitted with sealed surfaces outwards . . .

4.7b . . . and are tapped down to locating shoulder as shown

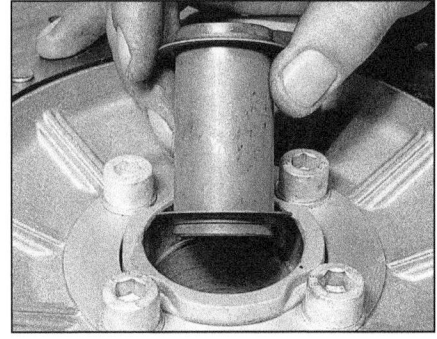

4.7c Do not forget to refit central spacer before second bearing is installed

10•6 Wheels, brakes and tyres

5.4a Front brake discs are secured by four bolts and nuts

5.4b Rear brake disc is secured by countersunk screws – fasten to specified torque setting

4 The brake discs can be checked for warpage by clamping a dial gauge to the fork leg or final drive housing; if run-out exceeds the maximum limit specified, the disc(s) should be renewed. If they are worn at any point to less than the minimum specified thickness, or if they become scored for any reason, braking efficiency will be impaired. The discs should then be renewed; they are held on by bolts, which pass through the front wheel hub, secured by nuts **(see illustration)**. On refitting, ensure that these are tightened to the specified torque wrench setting. The rear brake disc is fastened to the final drive crownwheel flange by two countersunk screws which are treated with thread locking compound **(see illustration)**. They were found to be tight enough to distort noticeably under the pressure required to slacken them; owners would be wise to have new replacements on hand in case similar problems are encountered. Be careful to degrease and clean the mating surfaces and before refitting the disc, also the tapped holes in the crownwheel flange. Tighten the retaining screws to the specified torque wrench setting.

5 Examine the flexible hoses for cracks or scuffing and the metal pipes for cracks or corrosion. At the first sign of damage, they must be renewed. First drain the system. Unscrew the unions at each end of the hose and remove the hose, releasing it from any clamps or guides. After fitting a new hose, tighten it securely, re-fill the hydraulic system with new, clean fluid, and bleed the brake as described in Section 9 of this Chapter.

6 The front brake flexible hose passes directly from the pressure modulator to the right-hand caliper on ABS-equipped models. The hose terminates in a union on the mudguard or fork mounting and then via a short metal pipe to the caliper. A metal link pipe connects the calipers and is routed on top of the mudguard on 100 models and early 75 models **(see illustration)**, and beneath it on 1993-on 75 models. In all cases, if the pipe is disturbed ensure that any guides or clamps are correctly arranged so that the pipe is well clear of moving parts **(see illustration)**.

7 Check all unions for tightness. The hoses and brake pipes must not rub on an adjacent part.

8 If fluid leaks around the brake pads, the caliper seals are faulty. The handlebar lever will feel 'spongy'. Complete failure of the brakes, although there is pressure at the handlebar lever, may indicate a seized piston. In either case, the unit must be removed for servicing.

6 Caliper - removal, examination and refitting

1 The caliper assemblies are identical in design and construction whether fitted to the front or to the rear brake. In both cases, it will be necessary to remove the caliper from the fork lower leg or from the final drive housing as appropriate. Each caliper is retained by two bolts.

2 The caliper units should be removed for overhaul if there has been any evidence of

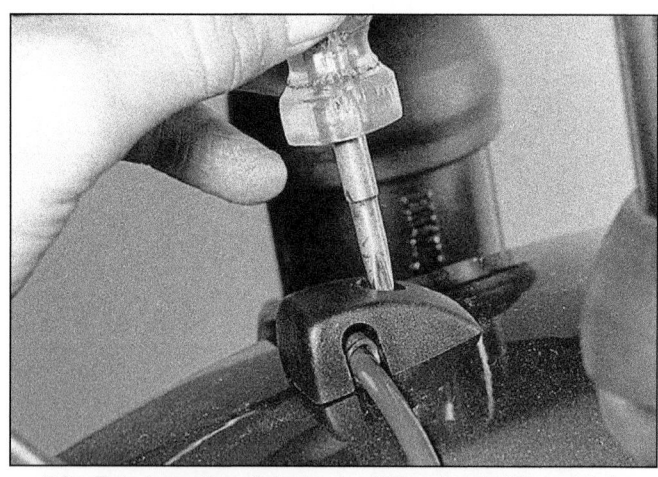

5.6a Exterior caliper link pipe on 100 and early 75 models is secured to mudguard top surface

5.6b On 1993-on 75 models ensure that correct use is made of the pipe guide brackets

Wheels, brakes and tyres 10•7

1 Caliper assembly
2 Bolt
3 Seal kit
4 Washer
5 Brake pads
6 Cover
7 Bleed nipple
8 Dust cap
9 Pad retaining pins and spring

6.4 Brake caliper

weeping from the seals. Note that seals can sometimes leak enough to admit air to the system without allowing the fluid to leak out. Whatever the case, immediate investigation is warranted. Start by disconnecting the brake pipe at the caliper gland nut and block the open pipe end with a suitable wooden or rubber plug. This will prevent the ingress of contaminants and the loss of hydraulic fluid.

3 Take great care during the dismantling and reassembly sequences, that no hydraulic fluid is allowed to come into contact with any painted or plastic parts. It will quickly destroy both of these surfaces, and if accidentally splashed, should be washed off immediately. Remove the plastic caliper cover and the pads as described in .

4 Remove the two socket screws which retain the caliper halves, to give access to each piston assembly **(see illustration)**. Remove the dust seal and withdraw the piston and seals from each side. If the pistons are difficult to extract, wrap the caliper in thick rag and apply compressed air to the fluid passage to force the pistons out. Examine all the components carefully. The seals should be renewed as a matter of course. The working surface of the piston should be highly polished with no scores or corroded areas. If these are evident, the piston must be renewed or it will rapidly destroy the new seals. **Note:** *The pistons fitted to 1989-on models have phenolic resin inserts to prevent the brake fluid from overheating and the piston seal material has been changed to a highly heat resistant silicone rubber - this modification was made at the same time as a move to sintered metal brake pads.* The caliper bores are least likely to exhibit signs of wear or corrosion damage but if such evidence is present, it will necessitate renewal of the caliper body as a unit.

5 The component parts should be cleaned thoroughly with new brake fluid prior to reassembly. On no account use petrol (gasoline) or paraffin (kerosene) as these will ruin the seals. Reassemble, by reversing the dismantling sequence, ensuring that all parts are kept clinically clean. Lubricate the seal and piston with hydraulic fluid prior to fitting them to the caliper. Make sure that the brake pipe is fitted correctly. Before using the machine, bleed the brake system. See Section 9.

7 Front brake master cylinder - removal, examination and refitting

1 To dismantle the system, attach clear tubing to the bleed nipple of each of the brake calipers, open the nipples by one full turn, and apply the front brake lever repeatedly to expel all the fluid. When no more fluid can be seen issuing from the nipples, tighten down each one. Slacken and remove the single screw which retains the twistgrip top cover, then remove the cover and disconnect the throttle cable. Unscrew the single clamping screw and withdraw carefully the right-hand switch cluster from the rear of the twistgrip assembly.

2 Note that the master cylinder and fluid reservoir can be detached from the main handlebar unit by removing the two small Allen screws. Or the entire unit can be removed from the handlebars by disconnecting the stop lamp front switch wire and the brake hose, by removing the handlebar end weight (where fitted) and slackening the single clamp screw.

3 Disconnect the brake hose either at the master cylinder end or (after removing the handlebar panel) at the union above the steering head. In either case place clean rags or similar around the area of the union to prevent brake fluid splashing on to any other components, particularly those that are painted or made of plastic.

4 With the master cylinder assembly disconnected and removed from the handlebar unit, remove the retaining screws and withdraw the reservoir cap with its gasket (fitted on early 100 models only) and

10•8 Wheels, brakes and tyres

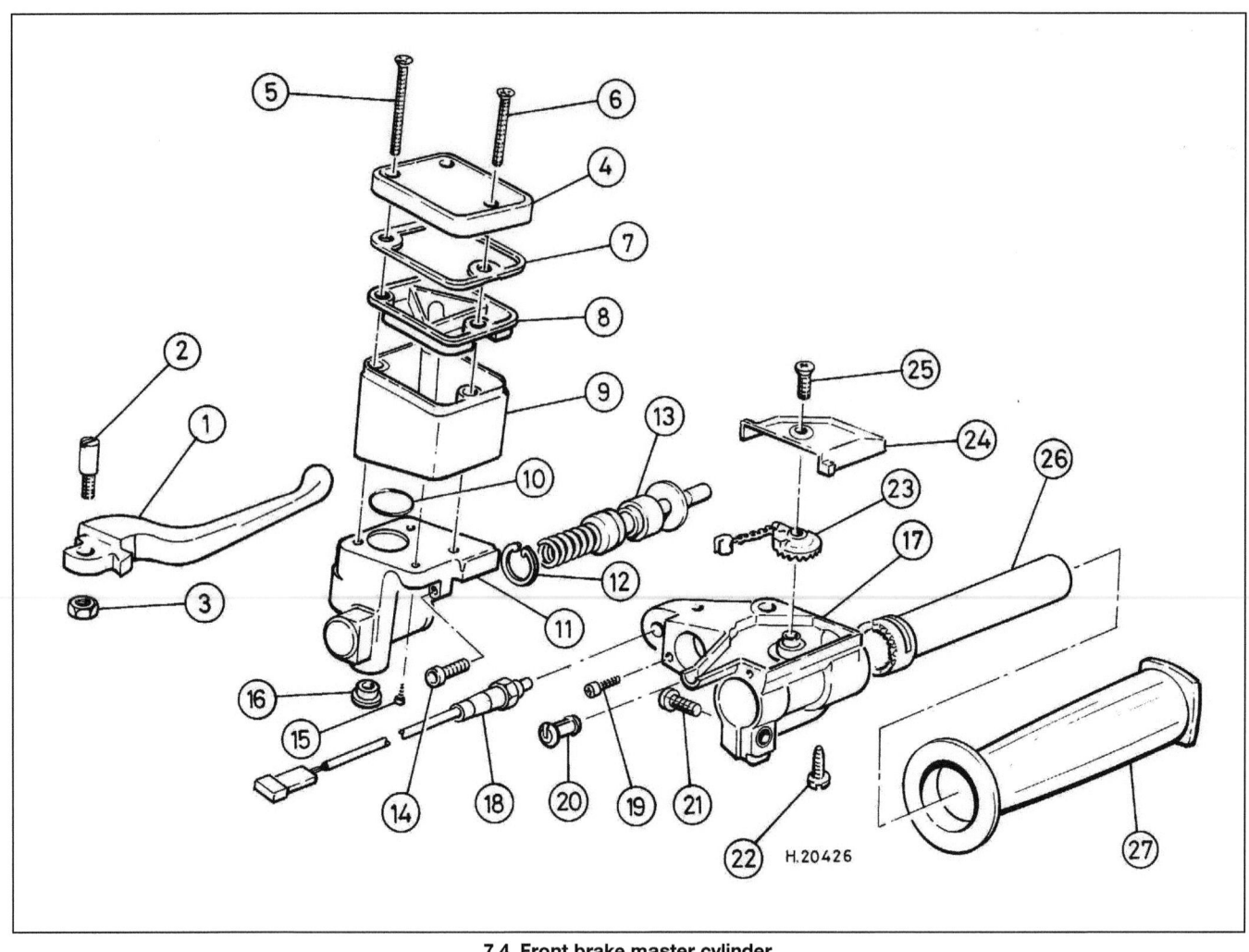

7.4 Front brake master cylinder

1 Brake lever	8 Rubber diaphragm	15 Screw	22 Locking bolt – 100 models only
2 Pivot bolt	9 Fluid reservoir	16 Plug	23 Throttle cable pulley
3 Nut	10 O-ring	17 Throttle twistgrip unit	24 Twistgrip top cover
4 Reservoir cap	11 Master cylinder	18 Brake stop lamp switch	25 Screw
5 Screw – 2 off	12 Circlip	19 Screw	26 Twistgrip inner sleeve
6 Screw	13 Piston assembly	20 Cable support	27 Twistgrip rubber
7 Gasket (where fitted)	14 Allen screw	21 Screw	

diaphragm **(see illustration)**. If necessary, the reservoir body can be separated from the master cylinder by removing the single retaining screw and pulling off the reservoir with a twisting motion as if unscrewing it. The sealing O-ring fitted to the reservoir joint must be renewed whenever it is disturbed, regardless of its apparent condition.

5 Using a suitable sharp-pointed instrument, prise out the circlip from the master cylinder right-hand end, then pull out the piston assembly and return spring. Examine all the components closely, renewing any that are found to be worn or in any way damaged. Remember that it is essential that the master cylinder is maintained at peak efficiency if the brakes are to be in a safe and usable condition.

6 When purchasing new components note that the reservoir cover has been modified twice on early 100 models to improve its sealing properties; the second modification included the omission of the cover gasket, which applies to all 75 models. Additionally the diaphragm material was changed on later models and a groove was cut in one of the cover screw locations to allow venting of the diaphragm. The piston assembly was also modified on early 100 models; only use the modified type of piston (identified by its dark grey coating as opposed to the earlier golden yellow finish) which is fitted as standard to all 75 models.

7 Carefully clean and lubricate all components prior to reassembly, using only clean hydraulic fluid. Reassembly is the reverse of the dismantling procedure described above, remembering that the use of new seals is recommended at all applicable joints and brake hose unions. Refill the system and remove all traces of air bubbles by bleeding as described in Section 9, then wash off any surplus brake fluid using copious quantities of fresh water and check for any fluid leaks which may subsequently appear.

8 Remember to check that the throttle cable is adjusted correctly and functioning properly, that any disturbed electrical circuits are operating correctly, that all the nuts and bolts are securely fastened, and that the brakes themselves are operating correctly and efficiently before the machine is taken out on the road.

Wheels, brakes and tyres 10•9

8.2 Rear brake master cylinder

1 Master cylinder	7 Dust cover	13 Rubber diaphragm	19 Washer – 2 off	25 Nut
2 Bolt – 2 off	8 Adjusting screw	14 Mounting bracket	20 Bracket	26 Pivot bolt
3 Brake hose	9 Clamp – 2 off	15 Grommet	21 Return spring	27 Inner sleeve
4 Brake pipe	10 Fluid hose	16 Bolt	22 Bush – 2 off	28 Bush
5 Spring	11 Reservoir cap	17 Washer	23 Brake pedal	29 Washer
6 Piston assembly	12 Fluid reservoir	18 Nut – 2 off	24 Bolt	30 Nut

8 Rear disc brake master cylinder - removal, examination and refitting

Removal

1 To remove the master cylinder, attach a clear plastic tube to the caliper bleed nipple, open the bleed nipple by one full turn, and drain the fluid from the system by operating the brake pedal until no more fluid can be seen issuing from the nipple.

2 While the right-hand footrest plate is still attached to the gearbox housing, slacken the locknut securing the master cylinder adjuster to the brake pedal, the brake pedal pivot nut and bolt and the two screws securing the master cylinder to the footrest plate (see illustration).

3 Withdraw the right-hand side panel and remove the single bolt or nut which secures the fluid reservoir to the battery carrier. Disconnect the fluid reservoir/master cylinder pipe at the hose clamp on the master cylinder top and withdraw the fluid reservoir.

4 Remove its retaining Allen screws or bolts and withdraw the footrest plate, then unscrew the retaining nut and dismantle the brake pedal pivot. Unscrew the pedal from the adjuster, if required, otherwise peel off the rubber dust cover from the front of the master cylinder and withdraw the pedal and adjuster.

5 Disconnect the brake hose at either end, then remove the master cylinder retaining screws and withdraw the cylinder assembly.

Examination

6 With the dust cover removed, clean the master cylinder and look carefully for the fastener which secures the piston components. A circlip is usually fitted which can be removed with circlip pliers or prised out with a sharply-pointed instrument, depending on the type used. If the piston components cannot be extracted easily, take the assembly to an authorised BMW dealer and seek expert advice. Note however, particularly on very early K100 and K100RS models, that if the master cylinder components are sticking or appear badly corroded, the complete assembly should be renewed. Unless the cylinder bore is in perfect condition, merely renewing the piston seals will not provide a safe long term repair; if there is the slightest doubt about any of the components of a brake system they should be renewed for safety's sake.

7 Carefully examine the seals and piston, renewing them if there is the slightest doubt about their condition, although the seals should be renewed as a matter of course whenever they are disturbed. If the slightest trace of damage is found in the master cylinder bore, the master cylinder should be renewed as a complete assembly.

8 From late 1988 the rear brake master cylinder piston diameter was reduced to 12 mm (0.4724 in), identification being by either the letters 'ABS' or a spot of green paint on the master cylinder body. Note that it is important when reassembling the master cylinder components or adjusting the brake light switch, to set the specified clearance of 0 - 0.2 mm between the end of the adjuster and the piston; if the piston is pushed in too far there is a danger of the flow of brake fluid from the reservoir being restricted. After setting the correct clearance, tighten the locknut and check the brake light switch setting; the brake light should come on at the same time as the rear brake pads come into operation. If necessary, use the adjuster which bears on the switch contact tab to alter the setting. If adjustment has been necessary, subsequently recheck the master cylinder clearance.

9 The rear master cylinder reservoir, previously sited above the right-hand footrest plate, has been moved out of sight under the side panel on all models from 1988 (see illustration). On K75 and K100 models, the reservoir is partially hidden by the cushioned insert. Although necessary on ABS equipped machines in order to accommodate the pressure modulators, this modification has been made to all K models.

Refitting

10 Carefully clean each component and lubricate it with clean hydraulic fluid, then reassemble and refit the assembly following the reverse of the above instructions. To prevent water which leaks past the rubber dust cover from causing corrosion to form around the piston front end, pack the recess at the front of the master cylinder outside with silicone grease or a similar waterproofing agent which will not attack the rubber seals. Refit the dust cover. Pack the brake pedal pivot components with the specified grease (see Chapter 1) on reassembly.

11 Refill the system with clean brake fluid and bleed it, as described in Section 9 to remove all traces of air. Wash off all surplus hydraulic fluid and check that the brake operates correctly and efficiently before using the machine on the road.

13 When refitting the brake pedal note that its height can be adjusted via the threaded adjuster and locknut, but check always that there is free play (which is measured most easily at the pedal tip) between the end of the adjuster and the piston. While BMW do not specify the required free play, there should be a very small amount discernible at all times or severe brake drag will result.

9 Bleeding the hydraulic brake system

Note: *Refer to Section 18 for additional information relating to ABS-equipped models.*

1 The method of bleeding a brake system of air as described below applies equally to either the front brake or to a rear brake of the hydraulically actuated type.

2 If the brake action becomes spongy, or if any part of the hydraulic system is disturbed, it is necessary to bleed the system in order to remove all traces of air. The procedure is best carried out by two people.

3 Check the fluid level in the reservoir and top up with new fluid of the specified type, if required. Keep the reservoir at least half full during the bleeding procedure; if the level is allowed to fall too far air will enter the system requiring that the procedure be started again from scratch. Refit the cap onto the reservoir to prevent the ingress of dust or the ejection of a spout of fluid.

4 Remove the dust cap from the caliper bleed nipple and clean the area with a rag. Place a clean glass jar below the caliper and connect a pipe from the bleed nipple to the jar (see illustration). A clear plastic tube should be used so that the air bubbles can be more easily seen. When working on the front brakes it may well prove necessary to connect both nipples at the same time and to operate them simultaneously. Pour enough clean hydraulic fluid into the jar(s) to immerse the end of the pipe; ensure that the pipe end remains submerged (to stop air returning into the system whenever the pressure is released) throughout the operation.

5 If parts of the system have been renewed, so that it must first be filled, open the bleed nipple about one turn and pump the brake lever until fluid starts to issue from the clear tube. Tighten the bleed nipple and then continue the normal bleeding operation as described below. Keep a close check on the reservoir level whilst the system is being filled.

6 Apply the brake as firmly as possible and hold it in this position against the fluid pressure. If the brake feels spongy it may be necessary to pump it rapidly a number of times until pressure is built up. With pressure applied, loosen the bleed nipple about half a turn. Tighten the nipple as soon as the brake lever or pedal has reached its full travel and then release. Repeat this operation until no more air bubbles are expelled with the fluid into the glass jar. When this condition is reached, the air bleeding operation should be complete, resulting in a firm feel to the brake lever or pedal. If sponginess is still evident, continue the bleeding operation; it may be that an air bubble trapped at the top of the system has yet to work down through the caliper.

7 The description above is an outline of what can be a very time-consuming operation; great care and patience should be exercised at all times. When working on the front brakes note that if the forks are held on full left lock the master cylinder becomes the highest point in the system; this may help to clear a bubble. On the rear brake the caliper can be dismounted and hung from the frame seat tubes (with a spacer wedged between its pads and care taken not to distort or damage the brake hose and pipe) to achieve a similar result. Note also that at approximately half the lever or pedal travel air bubbles can escape from the system back into the fluid reservoir; repeated, gentle applications of the lever or pedal to this point may well release a quantity of air.

8 In particularly stubborn cases bubbles may be released by tapping the brake pipes and hoses lightly or by topping up the reservoir and operating the brake rapidly (without splashing fluid or allowing air into the system) until the reservoir is nearly empty, to flush the system through. In some cases the only answer is to remove as much air as possible and then to leave the machine overnight (ensuring that the system is fully sealed against the entry of dirt or moisture by refitting the reservoir cap or cover and tightening the bleed nipples) so that the remaining air will build up into one bigger bubble at the top of the system.

8.9 Rear brake master cylinder reservoir location - 1988-on models

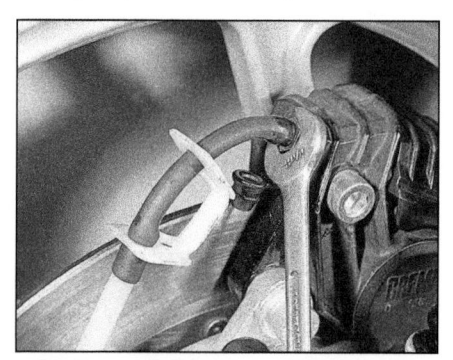

9.4 Be careful not to overtighten bleed nipples – use specified torque setting, where available

Wheels, brakes and tyres 10•11

HAYNES HiNT *A spongy brake can also be caused by fluid that has not been renewed at the required annual interval and has badly deteriorated, by defective brake hoses, by defective master cylinder or caliper seals or by a caliper piston that it sticking due to corrosion. All these points should be checked carefully if the brake remains spongy after thorough bleeding.*

9 **Do not** confuse excessive lever or pedal travel with a spongy feel; if the brake discs are excessively warped, for example, or if the calipers or discs are not securely fastened, the brake pads and caliper pistons will be knocked back away from the disc as the wheel rotates. This will cause a marked increase in lever or pedal travel before normal pressure is achieved; when riding the difference may not be noticed. Disc runout should be checked carefully (see Section 5), as should the security of the brake system component mountings.

10 When all traces of air have been removed from the system, top up the reservoir and refit the diaphragm and cap or cover. Check the entire system for leaks, and check also that the brake system in general is functioning efficiently before using the machine on the road.

11 Brake fluid drained from the system will almost certainly be contaminated, either by foreign matter or more commonly by the absorption of water from the air. All hydraulic fluids are hygroscopic, that is, they are capable of drawing water from the atmosphere, and thereby degrading their specifications. In view of this, and the relative cheapness of the fluid, old fluid should always be discarded.

12 Great care should be taken not to spill hydraulic fluid on any painted cycle parts; it is a very effective paint stripper. Also, the plastic glasses in the instrument heads, and most other plastic parts, will be damaged by contact with the fluid.

10 Rear drum brake - examination and renovation (K75, K75C, K75T)

1 Adjust the rear brake (when necessary) and check the remaining thickness of brake shoe friction material as described in Chapter 1.

2 If the brake is to be overhauled, first remove the rear wheel. See Section 3.

3 Before starting work, use a vacuum cleaner to remove all traces of loose dust, or at least wipe away all traces of dust using a rag well soaked in high flash-point solvent.

⚠ **Warning: The brake shoe friction material may contain asbestos which is toxic and especially dangerous when inhaled as loose dust particles, Refer to the warnings given in the Safety First section of this manual.**

4 Unscrew the adjuster nut to release the brake rod. If required, the pedal pivot can be dismantled after the pivot bolt retaining nut has been unscrewed from behind the footrest plate. The pivot bush and sleeve can be checked for wear and renewed if necessary.

5 Make note of the brake shoe positions as a guide to refitting (upper and lower shoes differ). Withdraw the retaining circlip from the brake shoe pivot and withdraw the brake shoes as a single unit, folding them inwards to form a 'V' to release spring pressure **(see illustration)**.

6 To ensure that the camshaft is correctly refitted, use a hammer and a punch to mark the shaft at the gap in the operating lever. Remove the operating lever pinch bolt, noting how the wear indicator plate is fitted to the

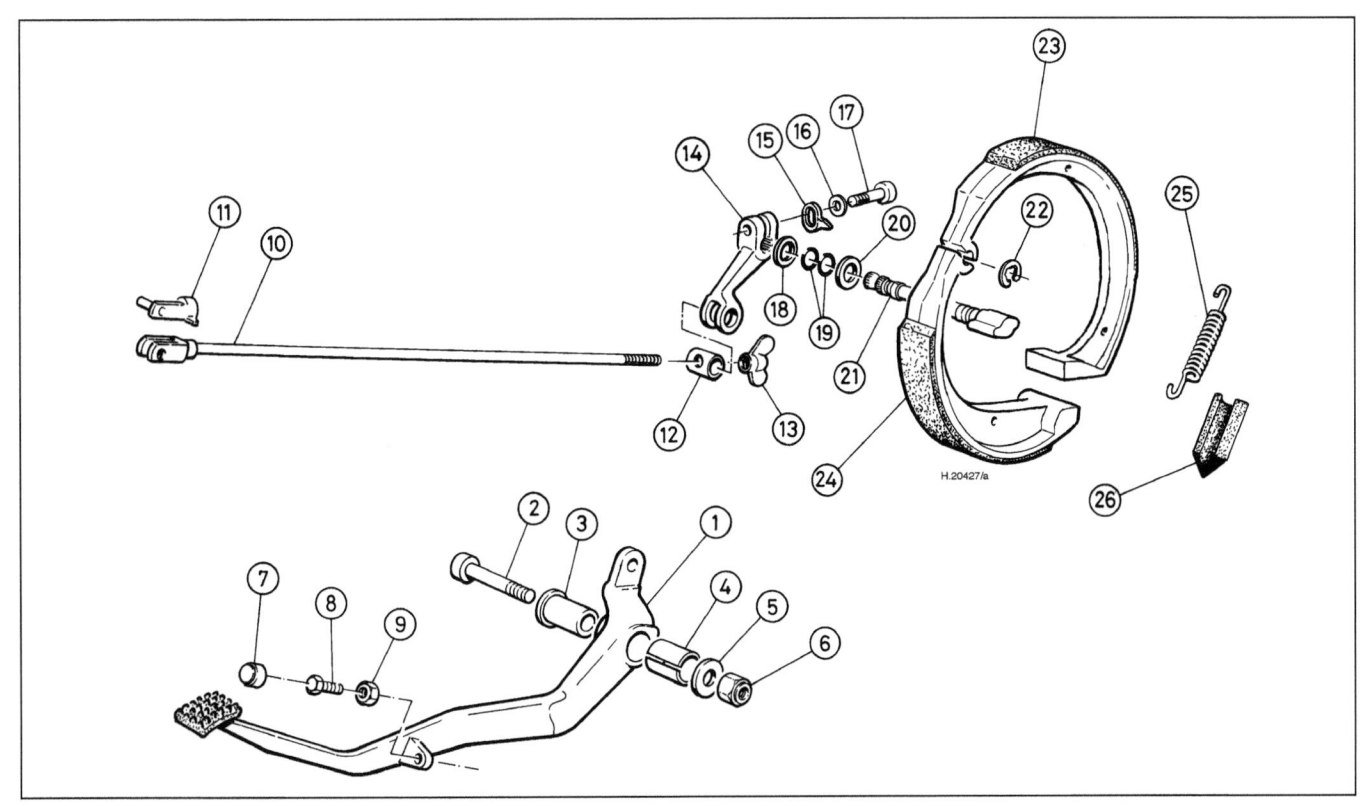

10.5 Rear drum brake

1 Brake pedal	7 Cap	13 Adjuster nut	17 Pinch bolt	22 Circlip
2 Pivot bolt	8 Bolt	14 Operating lever	18 Sealing washer	23 Upper brake shoe
3 Inner sleeve	9 Nut	15 Wear indicator pointer	19 O-ring – 2 off	24 Lower brake shoe
4 Bush	10 Brake rod	16 Washer	20 Metal washer	25 Return spring – 2 off
5 Washer	11 Retaining pin		21 Camshaft	26 Rubber damper
6 Nut	12 Trunnion			

10•12 Wheels, brakes and tyres

11.1 ABS electrical circuit diagram

lever, then carefully prise the lever off the camshaft splines. Tap out the camshaft to the left, noting the sealing washer at its right-hand end the two O-rings, and the flat washer at its left-hand end.

7 If the brake shoe friction material is damaged, fouled with grease or oil, or worn at any point to a thickness of 1.5 mm (0.06 in) or less, the shoes must be renewed. If the friction material is still serviceable, clean the shoes thoroughly using a soft wire brush that is free from oil or grease and remove any areas of glazing using emery cloth. Check carefully that the shoe ends are smooth and unworn.

8 Examine the return springs with great care and renew them if there is the slightest doubt about their condition or if they show signs of stretching, fatigue, or wear. Later models will have a rubber damper fitted around the rearmost (camshaft side) return spring to prevent any risk of the spring vibrating to the point of breaking, a problem which also produces severe brake squeal. If a machine is found without a rubber damper, one should be fitted on reassembly; since two different types of damper are available, the brake shoes must be taken to an authorised BMW dealer for the correct type to be identified. Note that BMW also recommend that both return springs must be renewed whenever an unmodified machine is found.

9 Clean thoroughly and check for wear or damage to the brake drum interior and the final drive housing (noting the warning above about dust particles), the brake shoe fixed pivot and the camshaft and operating lever components. If any component is found to be faulty it must be renewed. Check particularly the camshaft and pivot bearing surfaces and the fit of the camshaft in its passage through the final drive housing. The camshaft sealing O-rings should be renewed whenever they are disturbed. If any sign of oil leakage is found the defective seal must be found and renewed. See Chapter 9.

10 Examine the drum surface. Scrape off any deposits of dirt, brake dust or rust and wipe the surface with a rag soaked in high flash-point solvent. If the necessary equipment is available, measure the drum's inside diameter at several points to check for ovality; none should be discernible. If the drum is heavily scored it can be reclaimed only by skimming on a lathe, a task which can be undertaken only by an expert who has the necessary equipment. If the drum is worn at any point to the specified service limit or beyond, or if skimming will enlarge it to a similar degree, the rear wheel must be renewed.

11 On reassembly, fit the new camshaft sealing O-rings to their grooves and apply a coat of the specified grease to the bearing surfaces of the camshaft and its passage and to the fixed pivot. Refit the camshaft with its flat washer on its left-hand end; ensure that it is well greased, that the O-rings are not disturbed and that the sealing washer is pressed into place on its right-hand end. Rotate the camshaft so that the alignment mark made on removal is uppermost, then tap the operating lever onto its splines so that the mark aligns with the lever split. If the shoes are to be renewed, do not refit the pinch bolt yet.

12 Identify the upper and lower brake shoe **(see illustration 10.5)**. Hook the return springs on to the shoes from left to right, ie so that the springs are on the left-hand (wheel) side of the shoes. Apply a thin smear of grease to the shoe ends, fold them together and refit them to the fixed pivot and camshaft. Check that the shoes are securely and correctly positioned then wipe off all surplus grease and refit the retaining circlip to the fixed pivot. Fit the rubber damper to the rearmost (camshaft side) return spring so that the damper flat rear face touches the brake shoes and cam, and its chamfered side face is towards the wheel. Refit the rear wheel.

13 If the original shoes have been refitted, install the wear indicator plate and operating lever exactly as they were removed, adjust the rear brake and check that the brake operates correctly and that the rear wheel is free to rotate smoothly and easily.

14 If new shoes have been fitted, first check that the brake pedal height setting is correct (see Chapter 1) and connect the brake rod to the operating lever so that the angle between them is less than 90° when the brake is correctly adjusted and fully applied. See Chapter 1 for details of this procedure, which may involve the repositioning of the operating lever on the camshaft splines.

15 When the operating mechanism is correctly set and adjusted, position the wear indicator plate pointer to align with the upper (Maximum) wear limit line on the final drive housing when the brake is fully applied. Hold the indicator plate steady while tightening securely the operating lever pinch bolt, do not disturb the plate after this without first marking its exact position on the operating lever. Check the rear brake adjustment and that the brake works correctly, also that the rear wheel is free to rotate smoothly and easily.

11 ABS - general description

1 Sensors mounted on both wheels continually monitor the individual wheel speeds, picking up this information from the 100-tooth impulse gears **(see illustration)**. This information is then fed to the control unit, situated in the tail fairing.

2 If either sensor indicates that a wheel is about to lock, the control unit will activate the appropriate pressure modulator, situated just above the rider's footrests. The pressure modulator will respond immediately by reducing hydraulic pressure to the caliper, until there is no danger of the wheel locking. This process will be repeated up to seven times a second whilst brake pressure is applied at the lever or pedal. Due to the fitting of a valve the reflow of brake fluid is prevented, alleviating lever or pedal pulsation experienced on many automobile systems.

3 Note that when monitoring the rear wheel speed, which will obviously be affected by reduction in throttle and gear changing, the system closely compares this with the front wheel speed so that it cannot be misinterpreted as braking action.

4 The electronic control unit automatically carries out a checking function, which checks the sensors, pressure modulators and system voltage. In the event of a fault this is brought to the attention of the rider by the flashing of the two warning lights in the instrument panel, indicating that ABS is no longer operative and that the rider must rely on normal braking. A cancel switch marked (ABS) and situated in the handlebar panel allows the rider to turn the two warning lights to the permanently on state, as opposed to the distracting flashing state. The system will automatically re-run the warning procedure at ten minute intervals until the system is checked out and repaired by an authorised BMW dealer.

5 Another system checks ABS prior to riding. Once the ignition is switched on the ABS light, situated at the bottom of the speedometer, will flash on and off **(see illustration)**. At the same time the warning light (which doubles as the tail lamp warning light), situated in the central column will illuminate until the brake lever and pedal have been operated, at which point it will also flash on and off. As the machine begins to move (above 2.5 mph/4.0 kmh) and the system's checking operation is complete both lights should extinguish.

6 Note that the ABS will not operate if the ignition is switched off or at speeds less than 2.5 mph/4.0 kmh.

12 ABS - warnings

1 When working on ABS **always** first disconnect the battery at its negative lead. Note that it is essential that the ignition switch

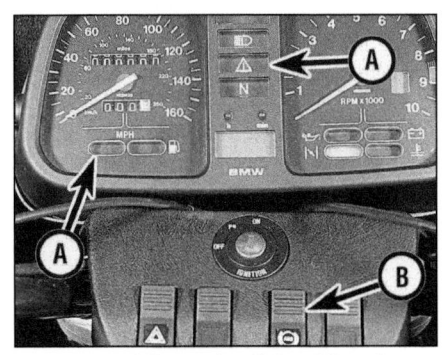

11.5 ABS warning lights (A) and cancel switch (B)

10•14 Wheels, brakes and tyres

13.1a Remove two Torx screws . . .

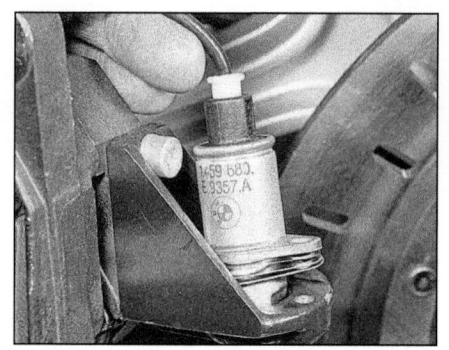

13.1b . . . and lift sensor and any shims out of holder

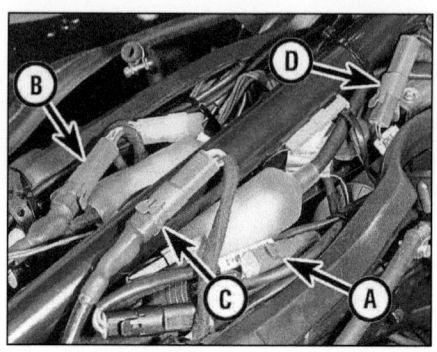

13.2a Front sensor connector (A) Pressure modulator front (B) and rear (C) connectors Cancel switch connector (D)

is in the Off position prior to disconnecting the battery, otherwise a fault will be indicated in the ABS control unit's memory.

2 The manufacturer specifically warns against the use of a pressure washer, steam cleaner or even a powerful hose. The operating pressure of such machines is high enough to force a mixture of water and dirt past seals on electronic components could well render the system inoperative. Similarly the use of aggressive cleaning solutions are also not recommended.

3 If the installation of high-powered electromagnetic equipment is intended, it is advised that you first seek the advice of an authorised BMW dealer, since its use may well interfere with the operation of the ABS control unit. Overloading the motorcycle with electrical accessories may well upset the voltage supply to the ABS also; it is therefore advised that you refer to an authorised BMW dealer before fitting extra electrical equipment. Note that BMW advise against the use of the onboard power socket for battery charging purposes, since it may well cause a voltage fluctuation which will in turn indicate a fault in the ABS memory.

4 Due to the important safety factor and the test equipment needed to carry out fault diagnosis on ABS it is recommended that any faults are referred to an authorised BMW dealer. At the very least, any work carried out on the machine should be checked by the dealer.

13 ABS wheel speed sensors - removal and refitting

Note: *disconnect the battery (negative lead first) before working on the ABS system.*

1 The sensor locates in a holder mounted on the caliper body. Two Torx screws retain the sensor in its holder, which when removed will allow the sensor to be pulled free **(see illustrations)**. Note that due to the limited working space available it is recommended that the caliper be detached from the fork leg and manoeuvred clear of the disc for better access; remember to support the caliper once removed to prevent strain on the hydraulic hose.

2 The front sensor wiring can be disconnected at the connector under the fuel tank which joins it to the ABS circuit **(see illustration)**. The rear sensor wiring connector will be found alongside the frame right-hand top tube, in the vicinity of the master cylinder reservoir **(see illustration)**. Note that both wiring connectors are coloured blue for easy identification. The wiring will also require detaching from any ties fitted.

3 Prior to refitting, clean any dust particles off the sensor tip and ensure that the impulse gear teeth are clean. Tighten its retaining screws securely. Ensure that all electrical connections are remade correctly and secure the wiring with cable ties.

4 Refit the brake caliper, noting that of the two retaining Allen bolts the one with the flanged head should be positioned at the top (front caliper) or front (rear caliper) **(see illustration)**. Make sure that the brake pipe/hose is properly routed and secured by any clamps or guides **(see illustration)**. Note that the distance between the sensor tip and the impulse gear is critical for the correct operation of the system. Apart from checking this gap periodically it must be checked whenever the wheel or brake caliper is disturbed. Refer to Chapter 1 for details.

14 ABS pressure modulators - removal and refitting

Note: *disconnect the battery (negative lead first) before working on the ABS system.*

1 Each pressure modulator can be considered a sealed unit, no replacement parts being available **(see illustration)**. Note that the right-hand unit controls the rear brake and the left-hand unit controls the front brake.

2 If removal is required, disconnect the hydraulic hose or pipe unions at its rear end and drain the fluid into a suitable container. Have ready a supply of clean rag to mop up any spilt brake fluid before it has chance to

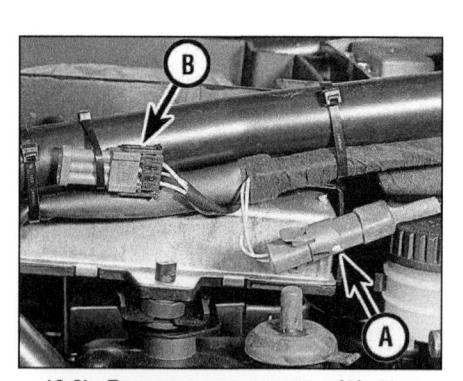

13.2b Rear sensor connector (A). Also diagnostic tester socket (B)

13.4a On refitting ensure caliper bolts are fitted in correct location

13.4b Secure hose guide bracket (where applicable)

Wheels, brakes and tyres 10•15

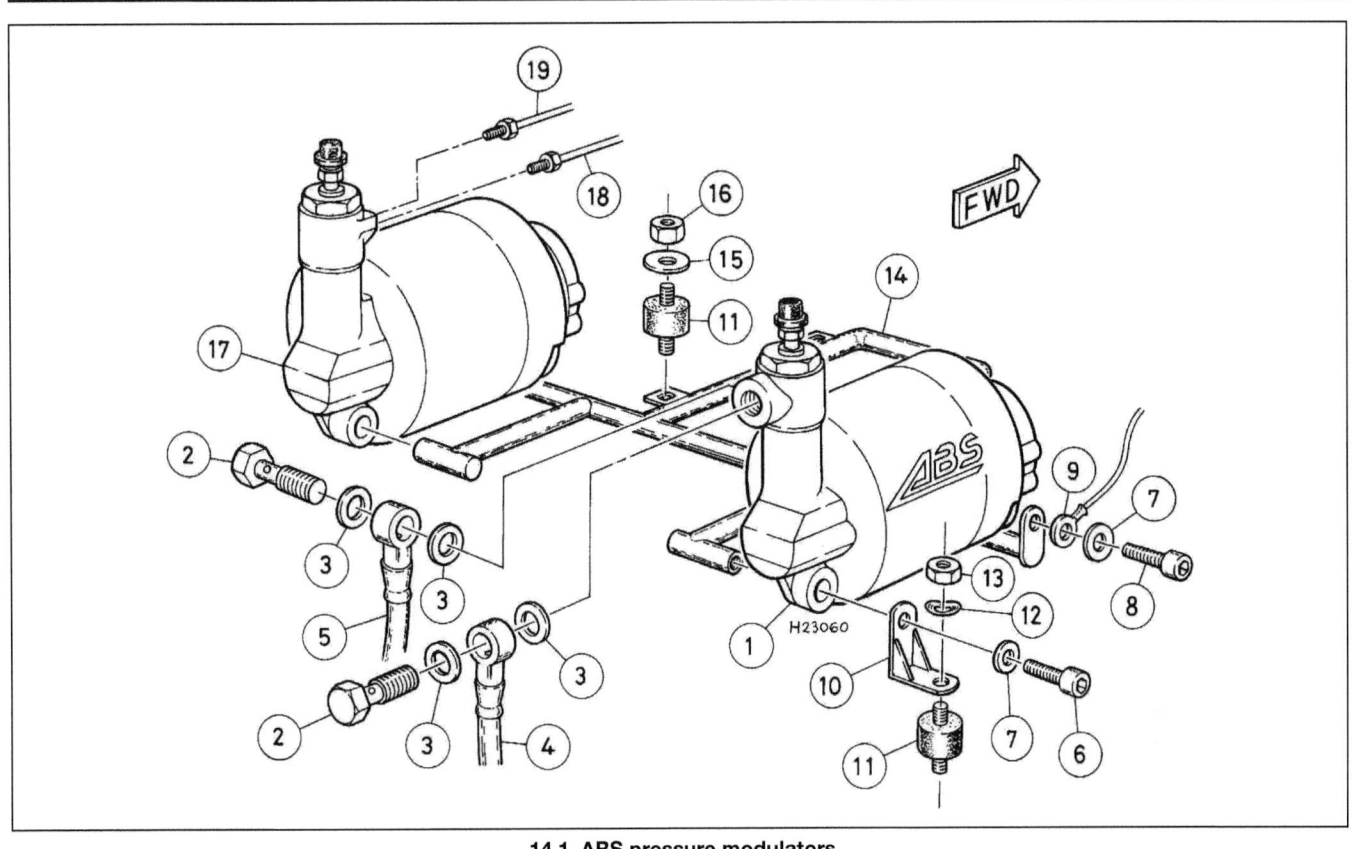

14.1 ABS pressure modulators

1 Rear brake modulator
2 Union bolt – 2 off
3 Sealing washer – 4 off
4 Hose to rear master cylinder
5 Hose to rear caliper
6 Allen screw – 2 off
7 Washer – 4 off
8 Allen screw – 2 off
9 Earth lead – 2 off
10 Rear bracket – 2 off
11 Rubber mounting – 6 off
12 Lock washer – 2 off
13 Nut – 2 off
14 Mounting bracket
15 Washer – 4 off
16 Nut – 4 off
17 Front brake modulator
18 Pipe to front master cylinder
19 Pipe to front caliper

damage the machine's paintwork, and plug each hose end to prevent further fluid leakage or the ingress of dirt. Disconnect the electrical wires at the wiring connector, located under the fuel tank, see photo 13.2a. Note that the connectors are coloured blue for easy identification. Remove the two Allen screws and lift the unit away. Note that the pressure modulators are fairly heavy, each unit weighing 3.8 kg (8.4 lb). Whilst removed, check the condition of the mounting bracket rubbers; if signs of deterioration are evident these should be renewed. Check the hydraulic hoses for cracking and abrasion and renew them if necessary.

3 On reassembly fit and tighten securely the retaining screws, not forgetting the earth leads on the front mountings **(see illustration)**. Remake the electrical connectors in their original positions and reconnect the hydraulic hoses, using new sealing washers on each side of the union **(see illustrations)**. Connect the brake hoses correctly, some models may be colour-coded for easy reconnection, but if not note that the hose from the master cylinder goes to the upper union and the caliper hose goes to the lower union. Ensure that the hydraulic hoses are routed clear of all moving components; secure the hose which runs from the modulator to the master cylinder with a cable tie around the modulator rear mounting bracket.

4 The system should then be bled as described in Section 18 and the system operation checked.

14.3a Pressure modulator earth lead is secured to footrest bracket

14.3b Front pressure modulator pipe connections

14.3c Rear pressure modulator hose connections

10•16 Wheels, brakes and tyres

15.2a Remove two screws to free control unit carrier

15.2b Unclip main connector to release control unit

15 ABS - control unit location

Note: *disconnect the battery (negative lead first) before working on the ABS system.*

1 The control unit is housed in the tail unit, and is set in a polystyrene holder to protect it from vibration. No maintenance to the unit is necessary but be especially careful not to damage the unit by the careless insertion of tools or other items in the storage compartment below.

2 Note that the control unit terminals are marked from 1 to 25, and will correspond with the information given in the accompanying ABS circuit diagram. To gain access to the unit, raise the seat and remove the tail unit compartment cover. Remove the two screws retaining the carrier and lower the unit to permit its removal **(see illustration)**. The wiring connector plug can be unclipped to free the unit **(see illustration)**. Note that the connector is designed to prevent it being incorrectly reconnected.

16 ABS relays - location

Note: *disconnect the battery (negative lead first) before working on the ABS system.*

The two ABS relays are housed in the electrical components box described in Chapter 11, Section 18. The ABS system relay and warning light relay are a push fit in their connecting plugs **(see illustration)**.

17 ABS - testing

Testing of the ABS components is not possible using conventional workshop equipment since the test data available is only obtainable by using the BMW diagnostic tester. Similarly only this tester is capable of reading out and then erasing the control unit's fault memory should the system indicate a fault. It therefore follows that the complete machine should be taken to an authorised BMW dealer if a fault is either suspected or brought to the rider's attention by the ABS warning system. The machine is equipped with a blue coloured connection plug for the diagnostic tester, located alongside the frame right-hand top tube, under the seat (see photo 13.2b).

18 ABS - bleeding and fluid renewal

In addition to the bleed nipples fitted to each brake caliper, the pressure modulators have a bleed nipple at the highest point on their castings, near the hose unions. Bleeding can be carried out as described in Section 9, noting that the pressure modulator should be bled first, followed by the caliper. If it proves impossible to remove trapped air from the hydraulic circuit using the conventional procedure, use of the BMW pressure bleeding equipment may be necessary.

19 ABS - modifications

1 The first machines equipped with ABS had part of their fuel injection relay rendered non-operational to overcome early problems with the ABS system causing fuel cut-off. On later models, however, a modified fuel injection control unit was fitted to correct the fault and allowed the full use of the fuel injection relay with ABS. In the UK the modified unit was introduced from the following frame nos:

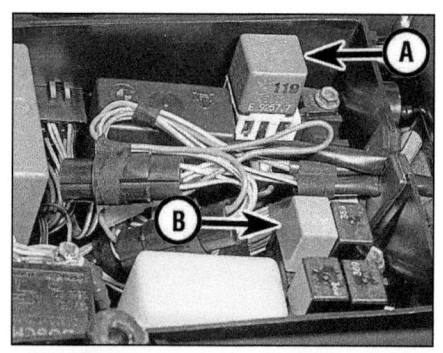

K100	6 308 763
K100RS	0 147 188
K100RT	0 096 800
K100LT	0 173 750

On all models the later unit can be identified by its green plate as opposed to the black plate on earlier models.

2 When fitting the modified fuel injection control unit to earlier models, to enable correct operation of the fuel injection relay it will be necessary to connect the white/black wire from the throttle butterfly position switch to terminal 2 of the fuel injection control unit. The switch must then be adjusted as described in Chapter 3, Section 17.

3 To ensure that the flow volume of the ABS system does not exceed the maximum limit on all early models it is important that if the brake lever, master cylinder or throttle twistgrip unit require renewal that the three components are renewed as a set, never singly. On later models the primary piston has been redesigned to prevent the fluid flow exceeding the maximum limit. Also an adjustment screw was built into the butt end of the brake lever **(see illustration)**. The modified assembly can be identified by the production code no 846, stamped on the underside of the master cylinder, next to the ABS stamp.

4 To set up the correct brake adjustment, screw in the Allen screw until all free play between the lever and piston end is taken up. Then turn the screw a further 360° to arrive at the correct setting. The piston will then be so positioned to prevent the flow volume exceeding the maximum limit.

20 Tyres - general information and fitting

General information

1 The cast wheels are designed to take tubeless tyres only. The fitting of tubed tyres or an inner tube inside a tubeless tyre is not recommended.

16.1 ABS relay locations – system relay (A) and warning light relay (B)

19.3 Front brake lever adjustment screw location – later models

Wheels, brakes and tyres 10•17

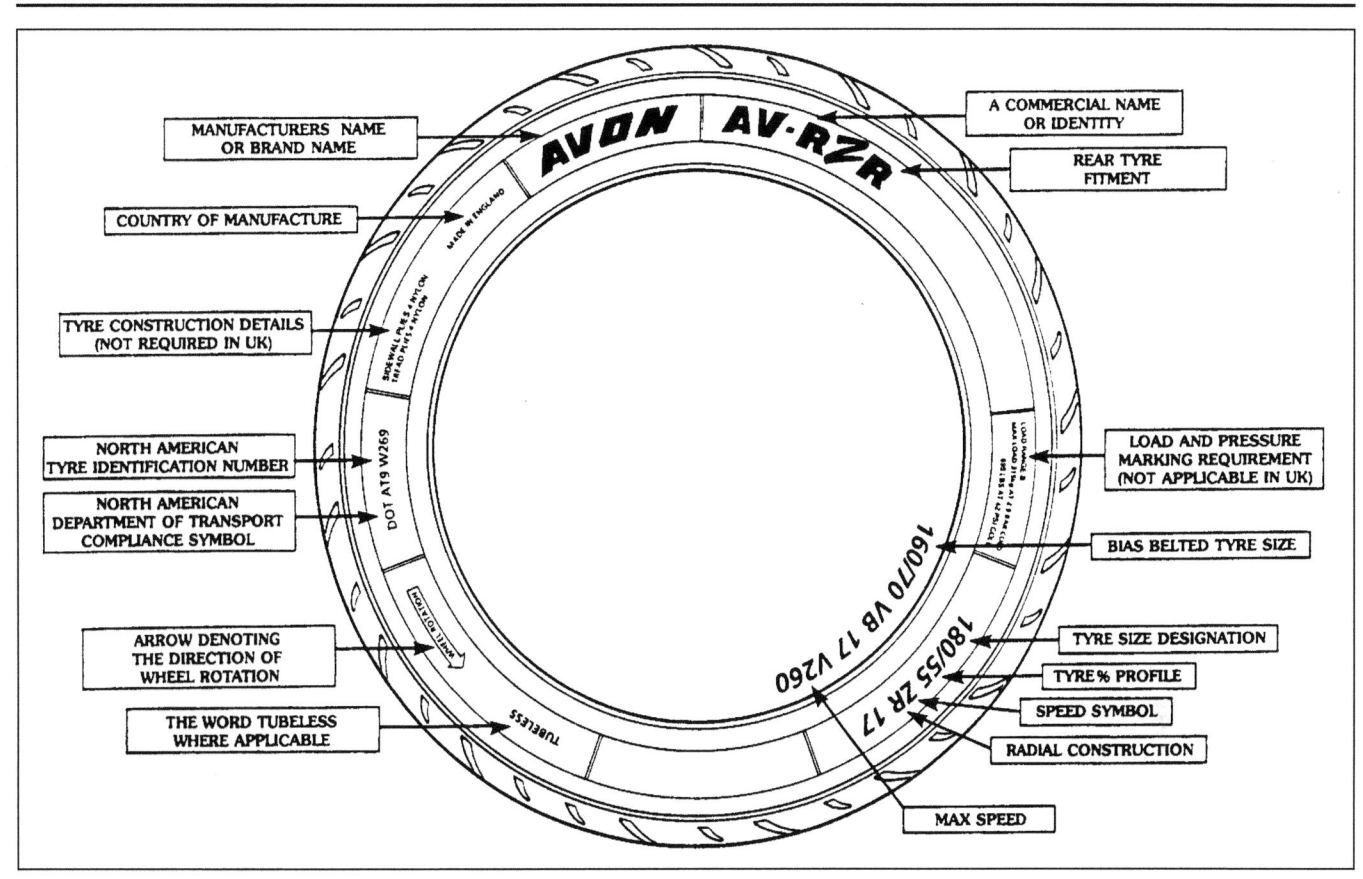

20.3 Common tyre sidewall markings

2 Refer to the *Daily (pre-ride) checks* at the beginning of this manual for tyre maintenance.

Fitting new tyres

3 Note that not only should the tyres always be of the specified size and speed and/or load rating for the wheel to which they are fitted, but that they should always be of the same make and type from the selection approved by BMW **(see illustration)**. **Do not** fit any make or type of tyre that is **not** approved by BMW; the BMW importer or an authorised BMW dealer will be able to provide details of the current list.

4 If radial tyres are fitted to 100 models, it may be found that in the case of the rear wheel, there is insufficient clearance between the tyre and swinging arm, causing rapid wear of the tyre. To overcome this problem, a 3 mm (0.12 in) thick washer is available to replace the 2 mm (0.08 in) washer fitted between the rear wheel and final drive unit; refer to a BMW dealer for details.

5 It is recommended that tyres are fitted by a motorcycle tyre specialist rather than attempted in the home workshop. This is particularly relevant in the case of tubeless tyres because the force required to break the seal between the wheel rim and tyre bead is substantial, and is usually beyond the capabilities of an individual working with normal tyre levers. Additionally, the specialist will be able to balance the wheels after tyre fitting.

6 BMW Note that not only should the tyres always be of the specified size and speed and/or load rating for the wheel to which they are fitted, but that they should also always be of the same make and type from the selection approved by BMW. **Do not** fit any make or type of tyre that is **not** approved by BMW; the BMW importer or an authorised BMW dealer will be able to provide details of the current list.

7 BMW provide an emergency repair kit for tubeless tyres as part of the machine's toolkit. This can be used, following the instructions provided, to repair holes up to 4 mm (0.16 in) in diameter, but note that a repaired tyre should not be ridden above 37 mph (60 km/h) or for more than 250 miles (400 km). The kit is an emergency repair only; the tyre should be renewed as a safety precaution as soon as possible.

Notes

Chapter 11
Electrical system

Contents

Alternator - checking the output	5	General description	1
Alternator - general	4	Horn - location and adjustment	20
Alternator - overhaul	7	Oil pressure warning lamp circuit - testing	12
Alternator - removal and refitting	6	Radio - general	21
Battery - check	see Chapter 1	Relays - location and renewal	18
Battery - examination and maintenance	3	Speedometer impulse transmitter - clean	see Chapter 1
Bulbs - renewal	22	Starter motor - overhaul	10
Cold start (choke) device indicator - general	15	Starter motor - removal and refitting	9
Coolant overheat warning lamp circuit - testing	13	Starter system - checks	11
Electrical system - general information and preliminary checks	2	Switches - general	17
Fuel level gauge circuit - testing	14	Tail lamp bulb monitoring device - general	16
Fuses - general	8	Turn signal relay - location and testing	19

Degrees of difficulty

Easy, suitable for novice with little experience	Fairly easy, suitable for beginner with some experience	Fairly difficult, suitable for competent DIY mechanic	Difficult, suitable for experienced DIY mechanic	Very difficult, suitable for expert DIY or professional

Specifications

Electrical system
Voltage	12V
Earth (ground)	Negative (-)

Battery
Manufacturer	BMW - Mareg
Capacity:	
Standard - models up to 1986	20 Ah
Standard - models from 1987 on	25 Ah
Optional - all models	30 Ah (may be fitted to K100LT as standard)
Electrolyte specific gravity	1.280 @ 20°C (68°F)

Alternator
Type	Bosch 0.120.339.546. G1 - 14V 33A 27
Rated output	460W / 14V 33Ah
Reduction ratio	1.5 : 1
Maximum speed	12,300 rpm
Voltage regulator	Bosch 1.197.311.001. EL 14V 4C
Charge starts at	950 ± 50 rpm
Regulated voltage	13.7 - 14.5 volts
Stator winding resistance - across phase outputs	0.28 ohm ± 10% @ 60°C (140°F)
Resistance between slip rings - exciter winding	4.0 ohm ± 10% @ 60°C (140°F)
Stator/rotor air gap	0.22 mm (0.0087 in)
Rotor maximum runout at claw poles	0.05 mm (0.0020 in)
Slip ring maximum runout	0.03 mm (0.0012 in)
Slip ring OD:	
Standard	27.8 mm (1.0945 in)
Service limit	26.8 mm (1.0551 in)
Brush projection:	
Standard	10 mm (0.3937 in)
Service limit	5 mm (0.1969 in)

11•2 Electrical system

Starter motor
Type	Nippon Denso 028000 - 8990
Power	0.7kW (1 hp)
Reduction ratio - overall	27:1
Lockout effective above	711 rpm
Brush length - see text:	
Standard - approximate	12 mm (0.4724 in)
Service limit	50% of new length

Fuses
1 Instrument cluster, stop and tail lamps	7.5A
2 Parking lamp	7.5A
3 Turn signals, clock	15A
4 Power socket - where fitted	15A
5 Optional extra equipment - where fitted	15A
6 Fuel pump	7.5A
7 Horns, radiator fan	15A

Bulbs
Headlamp	12V, 60/55W
Parking lamps	12V, 4W
Tail lamp	12V, 10W
Stop lamp	12V, 21W
Turn signal lamps	12V, 21W
Turn signal warning lamps	12V, 4W
All other warning and instrument illuminating lamps	12V, 3W

Torque wrench settings
	Nm	lbf ft
Alternator shock absorber body retaining nut	45 ± 6	32.5 ± 4
Alternator mounting bolts	22 ± 3	16 ± 2
Starter motor mounting bolts	7 ± 1	5 ± 0.5

1 General description

The electrical system is powered by a three-phase 12 volt alternator driven from the rear end of the auxiliary drive shaft via a cush-type shock absorber with rubber blocks to damp out shock loads. The alternator is a self-contained unit which includes the diode pack to rectify the output and an electronic voltage regulator, mounted in the brush holder, to control the output which is used to maintain battery charge.

The starter motor drives through a series of reduction gears and a one-way clutch mounted on the auxiliary drive shaft.

Apart from a few components fitted to the more lavishly-equipped models, all models share basically the same electrical system; refer for details to the relevant wiring diagram at the back of this Manual.

2 Electrical system - general information and preliminary checks

1 In the event of an electrical system fault, always check the physical condition of the wiring and connectors before attempting any of the test procedure described here and in subsequent Sections. Look for chafed, trapped or broken electrical leads and repair or renew these as necessary. Leads which have broken internally are not easily spotted, but may be checked using a multimeter or a simple battery and bulb circuit as a continuity tester. The various multi-pin connectors are generally trouble-free but may corrode if exposed to water. Clean them carefully, scraping off any surface deposits, and pack with silicone grease during assembly to avoid recurrent problems. The same technique can be applied to the handlebar switches.
2 A sound, fully charged battery is essential to the normal operation of the system. There is no point in attempting to locate a fault if the battery is partly discharged or worn out. Check battery condition and recharge or renew the battery before proceeding further.
3 Many of the test procedures described in this Chapter require that voltages or resistances be checked. This necessitates the use of some form of test equipment such as a simple and inexpensive multimeter of the type sold by electronics or motor accessory shops.
4 If you doubt your ability to check the electrical system entrust the work to an authorised BMW dealer. In any event have your findings double checked before consigning expensive components to the scrap bin.
5 Note that on these machines many puzzling electrical faults can be caused by poor earths between the engine/transmission unit and the frame, particularly at the bellhousing/frame mounting bracket and the main frame earth. Clean the mating surfaces back to bare metal at these points, scraping away the frame paint, where necessary, and apply a thin coat of silicone grease or similar to prevent corrosion before bolting up the components again.

> **HAYNES HiNT** *Refer to Fault Finding Equipment in the Reference section for information on the use of electrical test meters.*

3 Battery - examination and maintenance

1 Details of the regular checks needed to maintain the battery in good condition are given in Chapter 1, together with instructions on removal and refitting and general battery care. Batteries can be dangerous if mishandled; read carefully the 'Safety First' section at the front of this Manual before starting work, and always wear overalls or old clothing in case of accidental acid spillage. If acid is ever allowed to splash into your eyes or on to your skin, flush it away with copious quantities of fresh water and seek medical advice immediately.
2 When new, the battery is filled with an electrolyte of dilute sulphuric acid having a specific gravity of 1.280 at 20°C (68°F). Subsequent evaporation, which occurs in normal use, can be compensated for by topping up with distilled or demineralised water only. Never use tap water as a

Electrical system 11•3

> **HAYNES HiNT** *Apply a thin coat of petroleum jelly to the battery connections to slow corrosion.*

substitute and do not add fresh electrolyte unless spillage has occurred.

3 The state of charge of a battery can be checked using an hydrometer.

4 The normal charge rate for a battery is 1/10 of its rated capacity, thus for a 14 ampere hour unit charging should take place at 1.4 amp. Exceeding this figure can cause the battery to overheat, buckling the plates and rendering it useless. Few owners will have access to an expensive current controlled charger, so if a normal domestic charger is used check that after a possible initial peak, the charge rate falls to a safe level. If the battery becomes hot during charging **stop**. Further charging will cause damage. Note that cell caps should be loosened and vents unobstructed during charging to avoid a build-up of pressure and risk of explosion.

5 After charging top up with distilled water as required, then check the specific gravity and battery voltage. Specific gravity should be above 1.270 and a sound, fully charged battery will produce around 13 - 14 volts. If the recharged battery discharges rapidly if left disconnected, it is likely that an internal short caused by physical damage or sulphation has occurred. A new battery will be required. A sound item will tend to lose its charge at about 1% per day.

> **HAYNES HiNT** *Refer to Fault Finding Equipment in the Reference section for information on how to check battery voltage and specific gravity.*

6 If the battery is completely flat due to the motorcycle not having been ridden for some time, initial charging may indicate that the battery is faulty. The manufacturer recommends that in this case the battery receives a full charge at the correct rate and time before condemning it as scrap.

4 Alternator - general

To avoid damage to the alternator semiconductors, and indeed to many other components, the following precautions should be observed:
a) Do not disconnect the battery or the alternator whilst the engine is running.
b) Do not allow the engine to turn the alternator when the latter is not connected.
c) Do not test for output from the alternator by 'flashing' the output lead to earth.
d) Do not use a battery charger of more than 12 volts output, even as a starting aid.
e) Disconnect the battery and the alternator before carrying out electric arc welding on the vehicle.
f) Always observe correct battery polarity.

5 Alternator - checking the output

1 The charge warning lamp should light when the ignition is switched on and should remain lit as the engine is started, but should go out as soon as the engine speed increases significantly above idle. If this is not the case, first check the bulb itself and the connections to the instrument panel. Note that the lamp is connected directly to the alternator via the smaller, blue, wire which appears at the alternator connector plug, from the D + terminal. Note also that a faulty charge warning lamp operation is usually (but not always) caused by faulty brushes; a lot of time may be saved if these are checked first. See Section 7.

2 If the fault persists, remove both side panels to expose the battery terminals. Check that the battery and alternator connections are securely fastened and that the battery is fully charged.

3 Accurate assessment of alternator output requires special equipment and a degree of skill. A rough idea of whether output is adequate can be gained by using a voltmeter (range 0 to 15 or 0 to 20 volts) as follows.

4 Connect the voltmeter across the battery terminals. Switch on the lights (UK models only) and note the voltage reading: it should be between 12 and 13 volts.

5 Start the engine and run it at a fast idle (approx 1500 rpm). Read the voltmeter it should indicate 13 to 14 volts.

6 With the engine still running at a fast idle, switch on as many electrical consumers as possible (lights, stop lamp, turn signals and any accessories). The voltage at the battery should be maintained at 13 to 14 volts. Increase the engine speed slightly if necessary to keep the voltage up.

7 If alternator output is low or zero, check the brushes, as described in Section 7. If the brushes are in good condition the alternator requires attention.

8 Occasionally the condition may arise where the alternator output is excessive. Clues to this condition are constantly blowing bulbs; brightness of lights varying considerably with engine speed; overheating of alternator and battery, possibly with steam or fumes coming from the battery. This condition is almost certainly due to a defective voltage regulator, but expert advice should be sought.

9 Note that the alternator voltage regulator can be renewed without removing the alternator from the machine. The procedure is part of brush renewal (Section 7).

6 Alternator - removal and refitting

1 Remove both side panels and the alternator cover **(see illustration)**.

2 Remove the fuel injection control unit and storage tray. See Chapter 6. Remove the battery, as described in Chapter 1.

3 Disconnect the connector plug from the alternator rear end **(see illustration)**, then remove the three mounting bolts and pull the unit backwards out of the bellhousing **(see illustrations)**.

4 If required, the shock absorber outer body and the cooling fan can be withdrawn from

6.1 Alternator cover is retained by two Allen screws

6.3a Disconnect the alternator connector plug . . .

6.3b . . . unscrew the three mounting bolts . . .

11•4 Electrical system

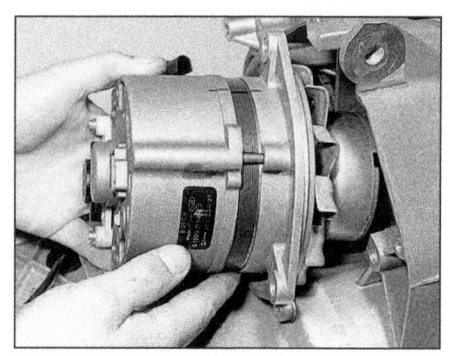

6.3c ... and pull the alternator away from the drive

6.4 Unscrew retaining nut to release shock absorber body and fan

6.5a On reassembly refit cooling fan and Woodruff key

6.5b Tighten retaining nut to specified torque setting

6.6 Fit shock absorber rubbers as shown and lubricate to aid refitting

the alternator shaft **(see illustration)**. Clamping the body or fan as securely but as lightly as possible in a vice to prevent rotation, unscrew the retaining nut and withdraw the body and fan with the locating Woodruff key.

5 On reassembly, refit the locating key **(see illustration)**, then the fan and shock absorber body, aligning their keyways with the key. Fit the retaining nut and washer, lock the fan or body as firmly as possible without damaging them, then tighten the nut to its specified torque setting **(see illustration)**.

6 Refit the rubber blocks to the shock absorber body and apply a smear of lubricant to them to ease refitting as the alternator is placed on the drive flange **(see illustration)**. Tighten its mounting bolts securely to the specified torque setting where given.

7 Refit the connector plug to the alternator rear end then refit all other disturbed components.

7 Alternator - overhaul

1 Owners should note that since the alternator is a slightly modified version of a unit that can be found on many modern cars, particularly European models, most auto-electrical specialists will be familiar with it **(see illustration)**.

2 This means that it may be economically more sensible to take the unit to a specialist for overhaul than to attempt repairs; certainly an auto-electrical specialist will be able to test very quickly and thoroughly an alternator that is thought to be suspect, even if he cannot obtain the necessary replacement parts from his usual sources. Note also that the manufacturers, Bosch, have their own network of service agents. Owners should investigate the economics of all possibilities

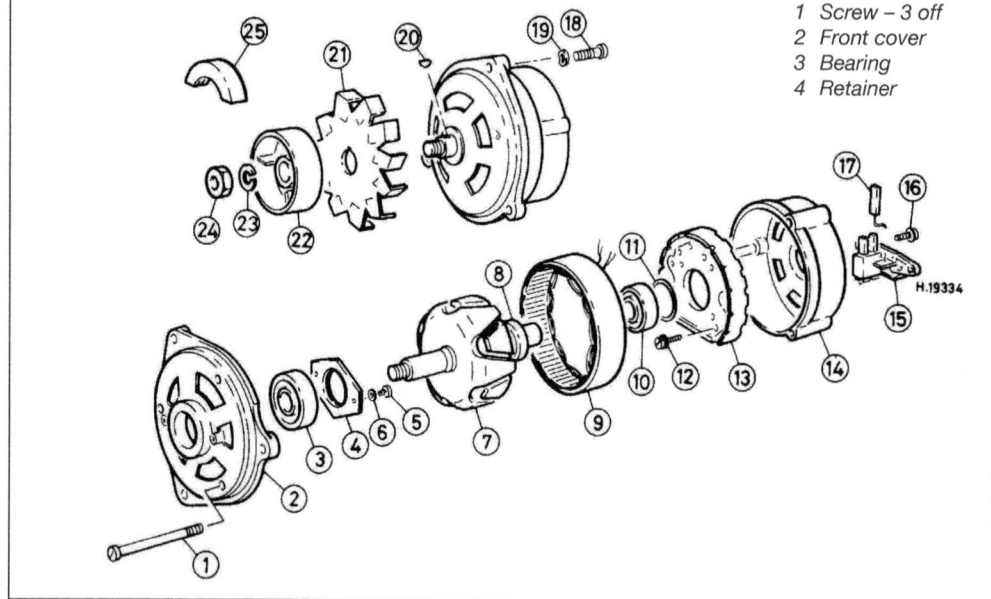

1 Screw – 3 off	5 Screw – 2 off
2 Front cover	6 Washer – 2 off
3 Bearing	7 Rotor
4 Retainer	8 Slip ring
	9 Stator
	10 Bearing
	11 O-ring
	12 Screw – 4 off
	13 Rectifier
	14 Rear cover
	15 Voltage regulator/brush holder
	16 Bolt – 2 off
	17 Brush – 2 off
	18 Screw 3 off
	19 Washer – 3 off
	20 Locating key
	21 Cooling fan
	22 Shock absorber body
	23 Spring washer
	24 Nut
	25 Shock absorber rubber – 3 off

7.1 Alternator

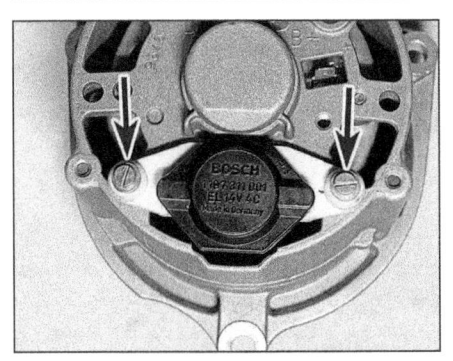

Electrical system 11•5

7.4a Remove retaining screws (arrowed) . . .

7.4b . . . and withdraw voltage regulator/brush carrier to check brushes

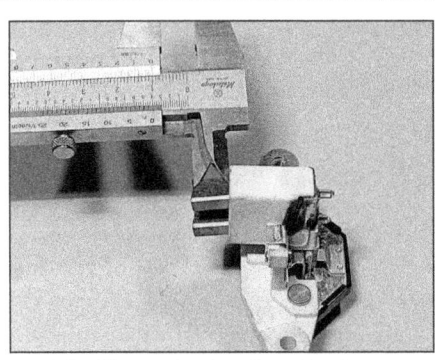

7.5a Measuring brush projection to determine brush wear

before starting work, and should ascertain whether exchange units are available before purchasing expensive replacement parts.

3 The alternator brushes can be inspected or renewed without removing the alternator from the machine, but disconnect the battery negative lead first.

4 From the rear of the alternator remove the two screws which secure the voltage regulator/brush carrier assembly **(see illustration)**. Withdraw the assembly **(see illustration)**.

5 Measure the length of each brush projecting from the carrier **(see illustration)**. If they are worn down to, or below, the minimum projection specified the old brushes will have to be unsoldered and new ones soldered into place. Some skill with a soldering iron will be required; excess heat from the soldering iron could damage the voltage regulator **(see illustration)**. When fitted, the new brushes must move freely in their holders; ensure that solder does not run down the brush leads. If the original brushes are still serviceable, check that they are both free to move easily in their carrier and that their ends bear fully on the slip rings.

6 While the brush holder is removed, take the opportunity to clean the slip rings with a cloth soaked in high flash-paint solvent. If badly marked, use a piece of fine glass paper.

7 To dismantle the unit remove the brush carrier/voltage regulator as described above, and the shock absorber body and fan as described in Section 6. Mark the unit across the mating surfaces of the front housing, the stator windings and the rear cover so that all can be aligned correctly on reassembly **(see illustration)**. Remove the three retaining screws and withdraw the rear cover far enough to permit removal of the four small screws which secure the diode plate to the cover inside **(see illustrations)**.

8 Test the diode plate using a battery and bulb test circuit or an ohmmeter or multimeter set to the resistance scale **(see illustration)**. When testing rectifier assemblies the important consideration is that each diode must allow current to flow in one direction only, ie current should flow or little resistance should be measured in one direction but when the tester probes are reversed no current should flow or much heavier resistance should be measured. Test between the diode plate surround (or alternator rear cover) and

7.5b When fitting new brushes, great care is required when using soldering iron

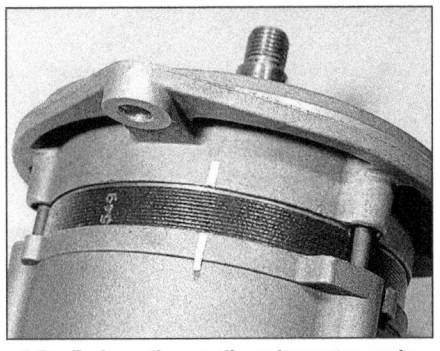

7.7a Before dismantling alternator make reference marks to ensure correct reassembly

7.7b Remove three long screws from front cover to dismantle alternator

7.7c Remove four screws from inside alternator (arrowed) . . .

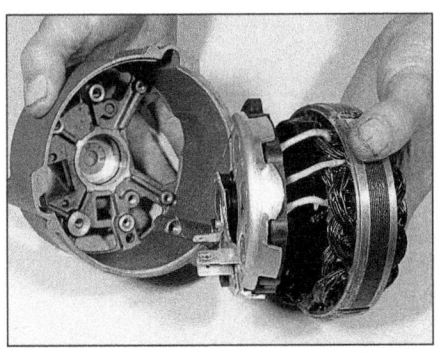

7.7d . . . so that rear cover can be detached from stator and diode plate

7.8 Diode plate and stator can be tested as described

11•6 Electrical system

each stator winding end in turn, then between the B + terminal and each winding end, finally between the D + terminal and each winding end. If current flows in both directions or in neither during any of these tests, that diode is faulty and the plate assembly must be renewed. This means unsoldering the connections between the stator and the diode plate; take great care to ensure that the connections are properly re-made on reassembly.

9 Test the stator windings by measuring the resistance between each pair of phase outputs. If the readings obtained differ significantly from that specified, the stator is faulty and must be renewed. If its connections are first unsoldered, the stator can also be checked for short circuits to earth, testing between each wire end and the stator body; the coil windings should be completely insulated from the body.

10 The rotor need only be removed from its front bearing and the front housing if necessary; this task may require the use of a press. Check the rotor exciter winding by measuring the resistance across the slip rings; the reading obtained should be close to that specified. If the slip rings are worn, scored or distorted, they can be trued up by skimming in a lathe, provided that this does not reduce their outside diameter to less than the minimum specified.

11 Check the rotor by testing for continuity between both slip rings in turn and each of the rotor steel claw poles; applying up to 80 volts ac, there should be no continuity, ie infinite resistance. If the rotor or bearings are to be renewed, use a bearing puller to draw off the rear bearing and a hammer and a tubular drift which bears only on its inner race to refit the bearing. Once its retainer plate has been withdrawn, the front bearing can be removed and refitted using a hammer and a tubular drift which bears only on its outer race. Ensure the bearing is square in its housing.

12 On reassembly, fit the front bearing and fasten securely the retainer plate screws, then press the rotor shaft into the bearing. When soldering the stator connections use the bare minimum of solder possible to achieve a good joint and ensure that the wires are clear of the rotor. Do not forget to align the marks made on removal across the stator, the front housing and the rear cover when reassembling. Tighten securely the retaining screws but do not overtighten them.

8.2 Fuses are of spade type – always carry spares of correct type and rating

8 Fuses - general

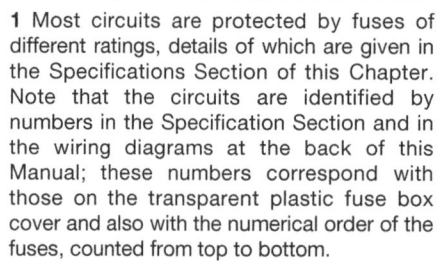

1 Most circuits are protected by fuses of different ratings, details of which are given in the Specifications Section of this Chapter. Note that the circuits are identified by numbers in the Specification Section and in the wiring diagrams at the back of this Manual; these numbers correspond with those on the transparent plastic fuse box cover and also with the numerical order of the fuses, counted from top to bottom.

2 The fuse box is located behind the left-hand side panel, on the side of the electrical components box underneath the fuel tank **(see illustration)**. Remove the side panel, unclip the transparent plastic cover and pull out the faulty fuse.

3 Blown fuses can be recognised easily by the melted metal strip **(see illustration)**; each is clearly marked with its rating and must be replaced only by a fuse of the same rating. **Never** put in a fuse of higher rating or bridge the terminals with any other substitute, however temporary; serious damage may be done to the circuit components, or a fire may start. Always carry a supply of spare fuses of each rating on the machine.

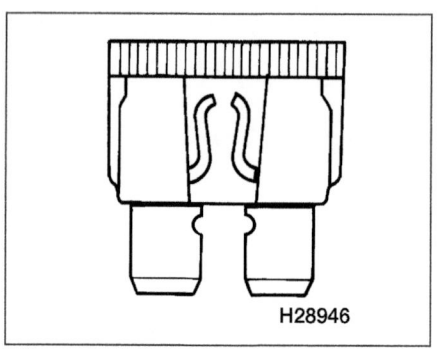

8.3 A blown fuse can be identified by its melted metal strip

4 While an isolated fault may occasionally blow a fuse and never occur again, such cases are rare and generally due to faulty connections, although fuses do sometimes blow due to old age or similar factors. However, if the fuse for any circuit blows repeatedly, a more serious fault is indicated which must be traced and remedied as soon as possible.

> **HAYNES HINT** *Corrosion of the fuse ends and fuse block terminals may occur and cause poor fuse contact. If this happens, remove the corrosion with a wire brush or emery paper, then spray the fuse end and terminals with electrical contact cleaner.*

9 Starter motor - removal and refitting

1 Remove both side panels.
2 Remove the fuel injection control unit and storage tray. See Chapter 6. Remove the battery as described in Chapter 1.
3 Disconnect the starter motor lead **(see illustration)**, remove the two retaining screws **(see illustration)** and withdraw the motor, manoeuvring it out to the rear **(see illustration)**.
4 Reassembly is the reverse of the removal procedure.

9.3a Disconnect battery before disturbing starter motor connection

9.3b Unscrew two retaining screws to release starter motor

9.3c Renew sealing O-ring to prevent oil leaks

Electrical system 11•7

10.1 Mark motor covers and body before dismantling to ensure correct reassembly

10.2 Remove two long screws to release motor front cover

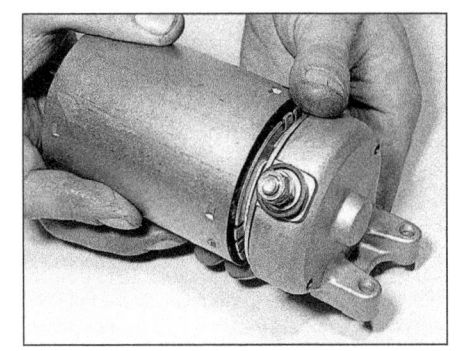

10.3a Be careful not to damage brushes when removing and refitting rear cover . . .

10 Starter motor - overhaul

1 First mark the front and rear ends of the motor body and the end covers so that all can be refitted in their original locations **(see illustration)**.
2 Remove the two long retaining screws and withdraw the motor front cover noting the sealing O-rings around its locating boss and its mating surface. check carefully that no shims are fitted **(see illustration)**.
3 Carefully withdraw the motor rear cover; as the brushes slide off the end of the commutator they should be heard to extend under spring pressure **(see illustration)**. Withdraw the rear cover and brush holder plate as a single unit, noting the presence and number of any shims fitted to the armature shaft **(see illustration)**.
4 Carefully ease the springs out of the brush holders to release the brushes then lift off the brush holder plate **(see illustration)**. Push the armature out of the motor body. Unscrew the terminal retaining nut, withdraw the metal and insulating washers and the O-ring, then remove the field coil brush assembly. The plastic insulator can be removed if necessary.
5 Measure the length of each brush; they are worn out if reduced to half their original length or less **(see illustration)**. BMW do not specify the original length, so this can be determined only by measuring the length of new components in a BMW dealer's stock. As a guide, the brushes fitted to the machine featured in the accompanying photographs measured 12 mm (0.47 in) long, which would give a minimum length of 6 mm (0.24 in). Whenever new brushes are fitted, measure their length and note for future reference the minimum length derived from this. Note that one brush is soldered to the motor terminal and must be renewed with the terminal, while the other brush is crimped to the brush holder plate; this also must be renewed as a single assembly **(see illustration)**.
6 Check that the springs exert firm pressure on the brushes, that the brushes are not chipped or damaged and that they bear fully on the commutator; check also that each brush is free to slide easily in its holder. The springs are not available separately and will be renewed with the holder plate.
7 Clean the commutator segments with a rag soaked in methylated spirits and inspect each one for scoring or discoloration. If any pair of segments is discoloured, a shorted armature winding is indicated. The manufacturer supplies no information regarding skimming and re-cutting the armature in the event of serious scoring or burning, and so by implication suggests that a new armature is the only solution. It is suggested, however, that the advice of a vehicle electrical specialist is sought first; professional help may work out a lot cheaper.
8 The cleaning of the commutator segments with abrasive paper is not recommended due to the risk of particles becoming embedded in

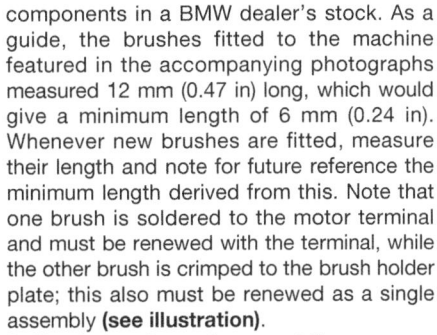

10.3b . . . and note presence of any shims fitted to armature shaft

the soft segments. It is suggested, therefore, that an ink eraser be used to burnish the segments and remove any surface oxide deposits before installing the brushes.
9 Using a multimeter set on the resistance scale, check the continuity between pairs of segments, noting that anything other than a very low resistance indicates a partially or completely open circuit. Next check the armature insulation by checking for continuity between the armature core and each segment, Anything other than infinite resistance indicates an internal failure.
10 Check the field coil brush by testing for continuity between it and the terminal; no resistance should be encountered. Check also that the terminal is completely insulated from the motor body. Finally, check that continuity (ie little or no resistance) exists between the

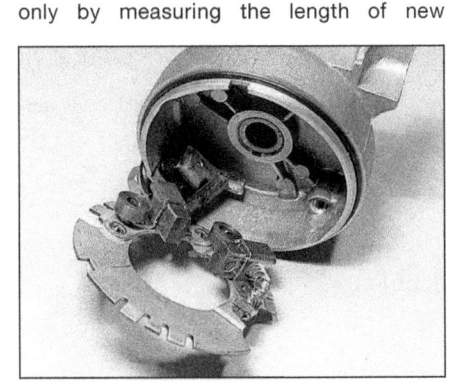

10.4 Dismantle terminal assembly to release brush holder from rear cover

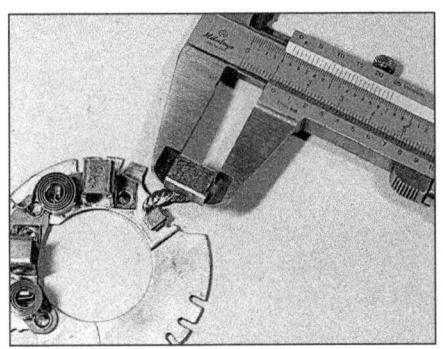

10.5a Measuring brush free length

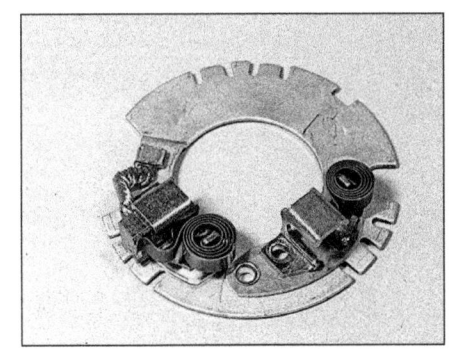

10.5b Note method of wedging brush in retracted position with spring end

11•8 Electrical system

field coils, then that each coil is completely insulated from the motor body. If continuity is found between the field coils and the body there is a breakdown in insulation which means that the complete assembly must be renewed.

11 If oil is found in the starter motor, the seal pressed into the front cover is faulty and must be renewed **(see illustration)**. Check the bearing at each end of the armature by reassembling the motor and feeling for free play. Spin the front bearing and check for signs of roughness, wear, or other damage. The bearing must be renewed if at all worn, but note that neither this nor the seal are available separately; the apparent solution is to purchase a new starter motor assembly. To avoid unnecessary expense, an automotive parts supplier or specialist bearing supplier may be able to find suitable replacements. Ensure that all relevant dimensions and seal or bearing markings are noted so that the correct items can be selected; if necessary take the motor assembly to provide a pattern.

12 The front bearing can be removed using a knife-edged bearing puller and is refitted using a hammer and a tubular drift such as a socket spanner which bears only on the inner race. Ensure that the armature is fully supported. The oil seal can be levered out of the front cover and a new component can be tapped evenly and squarely into place. The bearing in the rear cover cannot be removed without risk of damage and so should be renewed as part of the cover, if necessary.

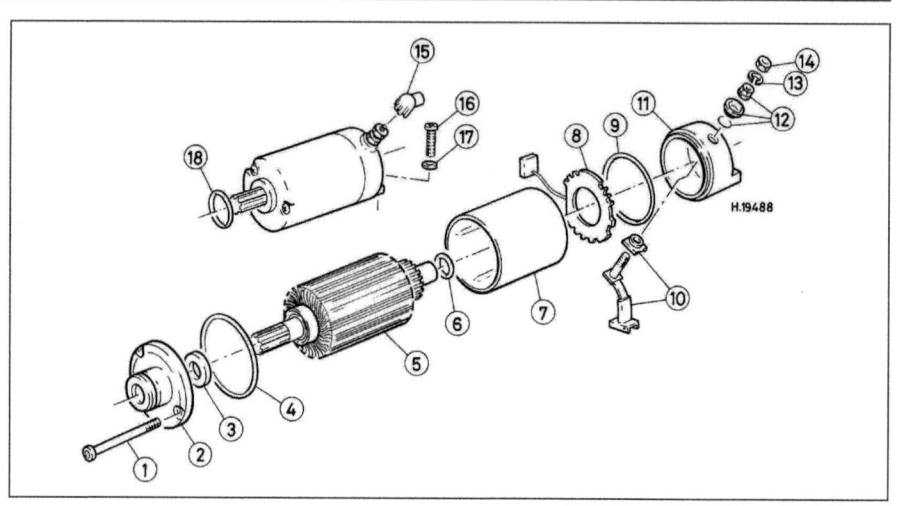

11 Starter system - checks

Starter relay

1 In the event of a starter malfunction, always check first that the battery is fully charged. A partly discharged battery may be able to provide enough power for the lighting circuit, but not the very heavy current required for starting the engine.

2 Remove the fuel tank and note the location of the starter relay **(see illustration)**. This is mounted in the electrical components box and can be identified by the two heavy duty cables connected to two of its four terminals. Switch on the ignition and press the starter button. If the relay is operating a distinct click will be heard as the internal solenoid closes the starter lead contact. A silent relay can be assumed to be defunct.

3 Disconnect the heavy duty starter lead at the motor terminal and connect a 12 volt test bulb between it and a sound earth point. Operate the starter switch again. If the bulb lights, the motor is being supplied with power and should be removed for overhaul.

4 To test the relay itself, disconnect all cables and wires and check that there is continuity across the relay battery and starter motor cable terminals when a fully-charged 12 volt battery is connected to the relay switch

10.11 Starter motor

1 Screw – 2 off	6 Shim – as required	11 Rear cover	14 Nut
2 Front cover	7 Motor body	12 Terminal insulating	15 Cap
3 Oil seal	8 Brush holder	assembly	16 Bolt – 2 off
4 O-ring	9 O-ring	13 Washer (where	17 Washer – 2 off
5 Armature	10 Brush assembly	fitted)	18 O-ring

terminals. If this is not the case, the relay is faulty and must be renewed.

5 If the relay is working properly, but not receiving any power, check back through the circuit, there may be a fault in the clutch interlock switch, the gear position indicator switch or in the diode between them. Test each as described below.

Gear position indicator switch

6 This switch is secured to the rear of the gearbox housing, fitted over the end of the selector drum. Depending on the position of the selector drum, the switch either lights the neutral warning lamp in the instrument panel or causes the number of the gear selected to appear in an LCD unit set in the panel. If the switch is faulty, it must be renewed, but check first that the apparent fault is not due to slack switch mounting screws, or to poor connections.

Clutch interlock switch

7 A small plunger-type switch is incorporated in the clutch lever, serving to prevent operation of the starter circuit when any gear has been selected, unless the clutch lever is held in. Check that there is continuity across the switch terminals only when it is extended (clutch lever applied). If defective, it must be renewed, as there is no satisfactory means of repair. The switch can be unscrewed and disconnected, when required.

Interlock circuit diode

8 A small diode unit is fitted in the interlock circuit to ensure that the clutch switch can override the neutral switch, ie so that the machine can be started in gear when the clutch lever is pulled in. The diode is a small component mounted in the instrument panel components.

9 To test the diode, check that there is current flowing one way only, in the direction indicated in the relevant wiring diagram. If current flows in both directions, or in neither, the unit is faulty but cannot be renewed individually.

Load-shedding relay

10 This component is also to be found in the electrical component box under the rear of the fuel tank **(see illustration)**. Its function is to

11.2 Starter relay is mounted in electrical components box

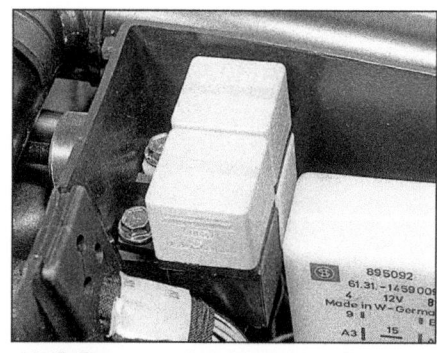

11.10 Do not confuse horn relay with load-shedding relay – use wire colours to identify

cut off the power supply to all non-essential circuits that may be in use whenever the starter button is pressed, so that full battery voltage is available. If it is faulty the relay must be renewed.

Starter button

11 This is incorporated with the engine kill button in the handlebar right-hand switch cluster. Although repairs are not likely to be successful in the long term, if the switch proves faulty at any time there is nothing to be lost by attempting to dismantle it for cleaning and possible repairs. See the general notes in Section 17.

12 Oil pressure warning lamp circuit - testing

1 This circuit consists of a simple pressure switch mounted on the oil pump body **(see illustration)** which lights a warning lamp in the instrument panel whenever the ignition is switched on; as soon as the oil pressure rises above a certain point, the lamp should go out.
2 If the lamp fails to light, first check the bulb and renew it if blown. If not, disconnect the switch wire and earth it briefly to the crankcase; the lamp should light. If it does not light, the switch is faulty and must be renewed.
3 If the lamp lights while the engine is running, declutch and stop the engine immediately; serious engine damage may be done if the engine is run with a faulty oil supply. Check first the level of oil in the crankcase and top up if necessary; if this does not cure the problem, the lubrication system must be checked further. If the warning lamp circuit is thought to be faulty, the switch can be tested only by the substitution of a new component.
4 Note however that the light may stay on or flicker due to corrosion at the switch terminal caused by an improperly-fitted switch cover. To cure this, thoroughly clean the switch connections and terminal, then apply a liberal quantity of water dispersant lubricant such as WD40 or CRC556. On refitting, ensure that the wire protective sleeve fits well inside the switch cover and that the cover itself is correctly installed to seal the switch. If corrosion has penetrated to the internal contacts, the switch must be renewed.

13 Coolant overheat warning lamp circuit - testing

1 This circuit consists of the switch, screwed into the coolant pipe stub on the cylinder head, which controls the operation of the coolant overheat warning lamp, mounted in the instrument panel, and the fan motor, mounted on the back of the radiator, through the temperature sensing switch unit, mounted in the electrical components box under the rear of the fuel tank.
2 Although detailed information is not available, if the fan and coolant warning lamp do not cut in at the specified temperature, the switch can be considered faulty. The only certain test, however, is to try a new component and to note its effect on performance.
3 The fan motor is tested as described in Chapter 5. If the circuit is still faulty, the temperature sensing switch unit must be considered at fault and tested by substitution.
4 Note that this circuit is one of those that can suffer from a poor earth contact at the frame earth and the bellhousing/frame mounting bracket. If the fan and warning lamp operate when the engine is still cold, the earths must be cleaned carefully to ensure good contact. Refer to Section 2 of this Chapter or to Chapter 2 or 4 for details. To overcome this problem the wire thickness from the relay to the earth point was increased on later models. On earlier models a modification was recommended which involved running an additional earth wire from terminal 31 of the relay to the earth point behind the steering head.

14 Fuel level gauge circuit - testing

1 This circuit comprises the float-type sender unit mounted in the base of the tank and the warning lamp(s) in the instrument panel.
2 Early 100 models were fitted with two warning lamps; an orange lamp which lit when approximately 7 litres were left in the tank and a red lamp which lit at 4 litres. All 75 models and 1986-on 100 models are fitted with a single orange lamp which lights at 5 litres. A different type of sender unit is fitted to these models so that a conventional fuel gauge can be fitted; a gauge is listed as an optional extra for all later models.
3 If any of the lamps fail to light, check the bulbs first, then the connections and wiring back to the sender unit. Open the tank filler cap and use a long piece of wire to check that the sender unit float arm is free to move smoothly throughout its full travel. If any fault is discovered, the sender unit must be renewed.
4 If the unit is merely inaccurate, there is little that the owner can do other than to drain the tank and pour in measured quantities of fuel until the lamp(s) go out; in this way the warning system may still prove to be of use.

15 Cold start (choke) device indicator - general

1 A plunger-type switch is screwed into the throttle body mounting bracket **(see illustration)** so that it illuminates a warning lamp in the instrument panel whenever the cold start lever (choke) is applied.
2 If the lamp fails to light, first check the bulb, then use a multimeter or similar to ensure that the switch is operating correctly. If not, check that the switch is securely mounted and fastened before renewing it.

16 Tail lamp bulb monitoring device - general

1 This component is mounted in the electrical component box underneath the rear of the fuel tank **(see illustration)**.

12.1 Oil pressure switch is mounted on oil pump body – ensure switch is waterproofed

15.1 Cold start device warning lamp is actuated by switch in throttle butterfly assembly

16.1 Tail lamp bulb monitor must be renewed if faulty

11•10 Electrical system

2 Its function is to illuminate a warning lamp set in the instrument panel if either of the bulbs in the rear lamp fails to light irrespective of whether this failure is caused by a defective bulb or a wiring fault.

3 When the ignition and the lights (UK models only) are switched on, the warning lamp should light and remain on until the brakes are applied; if it then goes out the rear lights are working properly. If the lamp stays on, there is a fault in one of the lights; on UK models if the warning lamp lights when the lights are switched off, the fault must be in the stop lamp circuit. The operation of the circuit can be checked quickly by removing one of the bulbs; the warning lamp should light.

4 If there is any doubt as to the correct operation of the system any faults can be eliminated as follows. Check the correct operation of the stop lamp bulb and the warning lamp bulb. Remove any corrosion that has built up in the bulbholders. By following the wiring diagram trace all the relevant wires, checking for continuity. Make sure all wiring connectors are free from corrosion and are fitted correctly. If the unit continues to malfunction it must be assumed that the fault lies within the unit, which is a sealed component and must be renewed.

17 Switches - general

General

1 While the switches should give little trouble, they can be tested using a multimeter set to the resistance function or a battery and bulb test circuit. Using the information given in the wiring diagrams at the end of this Manual, check that full continuity exists in all switch positions and between the relevant pairs of wires. When checking a particular circuit follow a logical sequence to eliminate the switch concerned.

2 As a simple precaution always disconnect the battery (negative lead first) before removing any of the switches, to prevent the possibility of a short circuit. Most troubles are caused by dirty contacts, which can be cleaned, but in the event of the breakage of some internal part, it will be necessary to renew the complete switch **(see illustration)**.

3 Note that handlebar switches are secured by a single screw to the rear of the handlebar lever clamp or twistgrip assembly on all models **(see illustration)**.

4 When replacing the switch, ensure that it seats correctly in its housing. If necessary, chamfer the spigots of new switches slightly to achieve this.

5 On all models, note that if a switch is found to be faulty it can only be renewed There is little to lose, therefore, by attempting

17.2a Front brake stop lamp switch is screwed into place

to dismantle and repair it although whether this is successful or not depends entirely on the owner's skill and the nature of the fault.

6 Owners of early 100 models should note that their machines should have separate earth wires from the handlebar switch assemblies which must be reconnected always whenever the switches have been disturbed. If these wires are not reconnected, the switches may earth via the throttle control cable, causing the inner wire to heat up and melt the outer cable then causing a stiff throttle and the possible risk of loss of control.

> **HAYNES HINT**
> Note that the regular application of a water dispersant lubricant, such as CRC5-56 or WD40, will greatly extend switch life.

Modifications

7 The front brake stop lamp switch, rear brake stop lamp switch (K75C), clutch interlock switch and cold start (choke) device switch were modified on later models. The modified switch is more resistant to the ingress of water or dirt, and the resulting arcing across the contacts.

8 Removal and refitting procedures remain unchanged, although when fitting the new

17.2b Rear stop lamp switch location - early models

switch to either of the handlebar levers check first that the lever recess is large enough so that the switch plunger makes contact squarely and not on one edge, causing it to bend or break in use; if necessary open out the recess until the plunger operation is correct. If fitting the new switch to the rear brake of a K75C model, a cap, obtainable through BMW dealers, must be fitted over the head of the brake pedal stop screw. In all cases take care not to overtighten the switch when fitting. It is recommended that a drop of Loctite 242 or a similar thread-locking compound be applied to the threads and that the switch is tightened by hand, the maximum torque setting being 5 Nm (3.5 lbf ft).

9 A new rear brake stop lamp switch was fitted during 1986 together with a modified right-hand footrest plate. The switch is noticeably different from the plunger type switch fitted to earlier models and is fitted on the inside of the footrest bracket.

10 To remove the switch, disconnect its wiring connector and release its wiring from the ties on the frame. Remove the pressure modulator rear mounting bolt, the two pannier support bracket bolts and the three footrest bolts, then pivot the bracket downwards. The switch is held by a single screw to the reverse side of the bracket **(see illustration)**.

11 On refitting, position the switch so that its mounting plate rests against the rib cast in the footrest bracket and so that there is a small gap between the contact tab and the footrest bracket

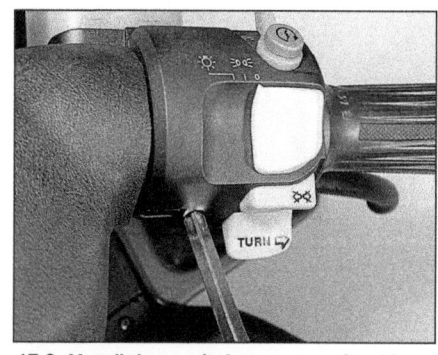

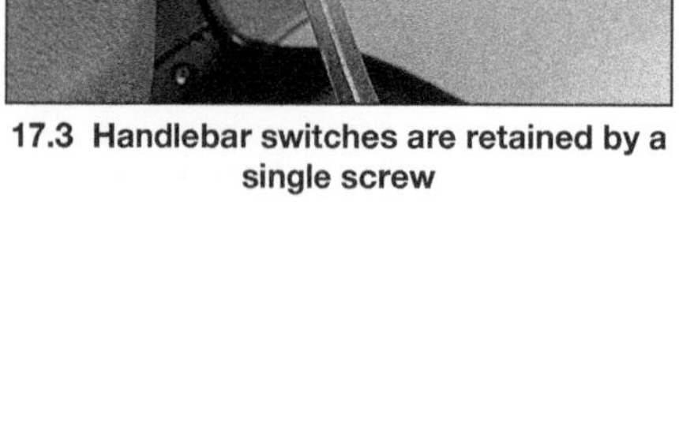

17.3 Handlebar switches are retained by a single screw

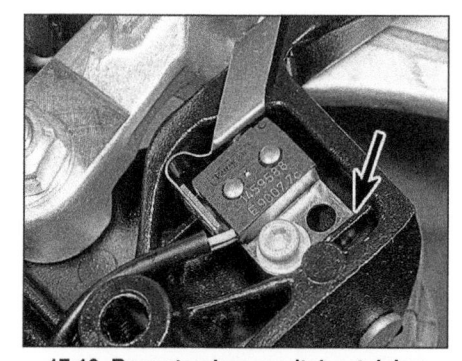

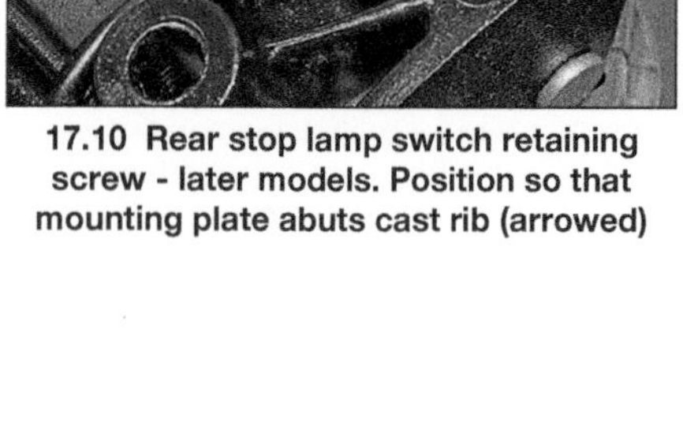

17.10 Rear stop lamp switch retaining screw - later models. Position so that mounting plate abuts cast rib (arrowed)

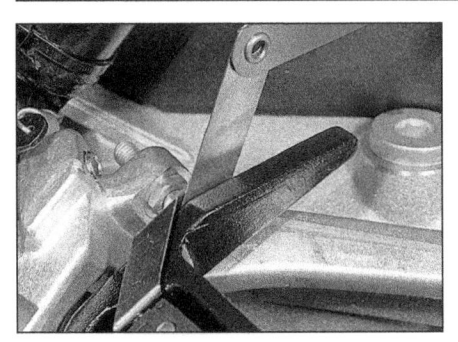

Electrical system 11•11

17.11 Slight gap should be evident between switch contact tab and footrest bracket

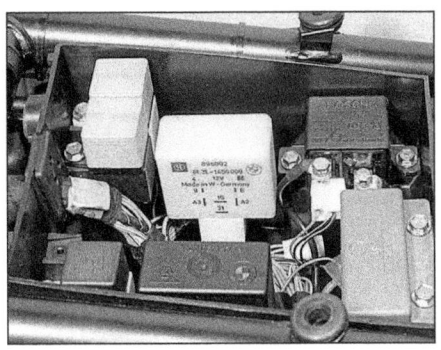

18.1 Relays are mounted in electrical components box, under rear of fuel tank

19.1 Remove mounting bolts to release turn signal relay

(see illustration). Check that the switch is heard to click as the brake pedal is operated then apply a drop of Loctite 242 or similar thread locking compound to the retaining screw threads and tighten the screw to a maximum torque of 5 Nm (3.5 lbf ft). Do not omit the rear pressure modulator earth lead on the footrest bracket top bolt. After reassembly, check that the brake light comes on at the same time as the rear brake pads contact the disc, making any adjustment of the switch setting using the adjuster which bears on the switch contact tab. Tighten the locknut on completion of adjustment. It is then important to subsequently check the rear master cylinder clearance as described in Chapter 10, Section 8.

18 Relays - location and renewal

1 The various relays are mounted in the electrical components box under the fuel tank (see illustration). In some cases (usually early models only) the wires have separate connectors, but usually the relays are pressed into a connecting plug.
2 If a relay which has individual wires leading to it is removed at any time, make a written note as each wire is removed, showing which colour wire should be connected to each terminal (the numbers are stamped into the relay itself). Use the colours of the wires shown in the diagrams at the back of this Manual to identify each relay.
3 If a relay is suspected of being faulty, it must be renewed: repairs are not possible.

19 Turn signal relay - location and testing

1 The turn signal relay is the larger unit mounted by two bolts in the electrical components box under the rear of the fuel tank (see illustration).
2 If the turn signal lamps cease to function correctly, there may be any one of several possible faults responsible which should be checked before the relay is suspected. First check that the lamps are correctly mounted and that all the earth connections are clean and tight. Check that the bulbs are of the correct wattage and that corrosion has not developed on the bulbs or in their holders. Any such corrosion must be thoroughly cleaned off to ensure proper bulb contact. Also check that the turn signal switches are functioning correctly and that the wiring is in good order. Finally ensure that the battery is fully charged.
3 Faults in any one or more of the above items will produce symptoms for which the turn signal relay may be blamed unfairly. If the fault persists even after the preliminary checks have been made, the relay must be at fault. Unfortunately the only practical method of testing the relay is to substitute a known good one. if the fault is then cured, the relay is proven faulty and must be renewed.
4 Note that the relay has a self-cancelling circuit which is connected to the speedometer so that the turn signals cancel automatically after a distance of 210 metres (689 feet) has been traversed or a period of 10 seconds at above 31 mph (50 kmh) has elapsed. If this circuit fails, the relay unit must be renewed.

20 Horn - location and adjustment

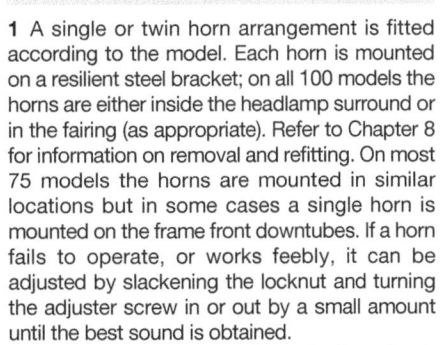

1 A single or twin horn arrangement is fitted according to the model. Each horn is mounted on a resilient steel bracket; on all 100 models the horns are either inside the headlamp surround or in the fairing (as appropriate). Refer to Chapter 8 for information on removal and refitting. On most 75 models the horns are mounted in similar locations but in some cases a single horn is mounted on the frame front downtubes. If a horn fails to operate, or works feebly, it can be adjusted by slackening the locknut and turning the adjuster screw in or out by a small amount until the best sound is obtained.
2 If the horn fails to work at all, first check that power is reaching it by disconnecting the wires. Substitute a 12 volt bulb, switch on the ignition and press the horn button. If the bulb lights, the circuit is proved good and the horn is at fault, if the bulb does not light, there is a fault in the circuit which must be found and rectified. Check the relay first.

3 To test the horn itself, connect a fully-charged 12 volt battery directly to the horn. If it does not sound, a gentle tap on the outside may free the internal contacts. If this fails, the horn must be renewed as repairs are not possible, but there is little to be lost by attempting to dismantle the horn and repair it; Fiamm horns for example can be dismantled and their contacts can be cleaned quite easily.

21 Radio - general

These models are sold usually with either a complete radio installation included or at least the fitting kit comprising the aerial, wiring, waterproof loudspeakers and the necessary suppressors. Since a number of different units can be found, specific instructions cannot be given in this Manual. Owners should refer for information to the selling dealer or to agents of the radio manufacturer. A full wiring diagram showing all modified or additional components should be included with the fitting kit when purchased.

22 Bulbs - renewal

Headlamp and parking lamp
1 **Note:** The headlamp bulb fitted to all models is the standard H4 pattern which is connected to the wiring loom by a three-pin plug and

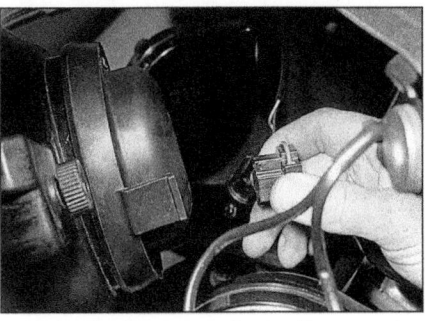

22.1a Unplug connector to disconnect headlamp bulb wiring

11•12 Electrical system

22.1b Bulb is located by offset tangs – never touch glass envelope

22.6a Headlamp bulb renewal, K100RS – remove rubber cover . . .

which is located in the headlamp reflector by the three protruding tangs **(see illustrations)**. These tangs are offset so that the bulb will fit correctly only one way. Never touch the glass envelope of these bulbs; any dirt or greasy or acidic deposits will etch the glass and shorten the bulb's life. Ensure that the bulb is clean and dry before switching on the light.

> **HAYNES HiNT** *If the headlamp bulb glass is touched inadvertently it should be wiped clean with a soft cloth soaked with a solvent such as methylated spirit.*

2 On K75 models the rim and reflector unit must be removed from the headlamp shell to reach the bulb. Check carefully around the rim and remove any retaining screws, then gently unclip the rim from the shell and withdraw it. Withdraw the connector plug, peel back the rubber cover and unclip the bulb from the back of the reflector. To remove the parking lamp bulb withdraw the bulb holder from the back of the reflector then press the bulb into the holder and turn it anti-clockwise to release it. Refitting is the reverse of the removal procedure ensuring that the headlamp rim is securely fastened.
3 On K75C, K75T and K100 models withdraw the windscreen and the headlamp surround or handlebar fairing as appropriate. Refer to Chapter 8. Remove its two mounting bolts and lift forwards the headlamp unit, disengaging the adjuster screw from its bracket. Turn the parking lamp bulb holder anticlockwise to release it from the reflector, then press the bulb into the holder and turn it anti-clockwise to release it from the holder. To remove the headlamp bulb unplug the connector, peel off the rubber cover and rotate the locking ring anti-clockwise to release the bulb.
4 Reassembly is the reverse of the removal procedure, but when refitting the headlamp unit be careful to engage the adjuster screw nut in its bracket and to align the triangular marks on the headlamp unit brackets with those of the rear cover mounting brackets so that the unit is correctly aligned in the vertical plane before its mounting bolts are tightened.
5 On K75S models reach forward inside the fairing to pull the parking lamp bulb holder out of the reflector right-hand side; the bulb is a standard bayonet fitting in its holder and is removed as described in paragraph 3 above. To remove the headlamp bulb unplug the connector, peel back the rubber cover and release the retaining wire clip to release the bulb. Refitting is the reverse of the removal procedure.
6 On K100RS models refer to the relevant Section of Chapter 8 and remove the fairing kneepads and the small panels above them; it may also be necessary to release the horizontal centre panel from its mountings under the instruments to gain access to the headlamp unit. Bulb removal and refitting is as described in paragraph 3 above **(see illustrations)**.
7 On K75RT, K100RT and K100LT models no dismantling is necessary; it is possible to reach forwards inside the fairing to remove the bulbs as described in paragraph 3 above.

Headlamp - beam alignment

8 On all models the headlamp beam alignment should be set with the rider, and pillion passenger if one is regularly carried, seated normally; the machine should be standing on its wheels with the tyre pressures and rear suspension correctly set for the load carried. On K100RS, K100RT and K100LT models set the vertical aim three-position lever to its top position so that the headlamp beam is at maximum height **(see illustration)**; this then gives two additional settings to compensate for increased loads.
9 The headlamp beam should be adjusted vertically (and horizontally, where possible) to comply with local legislation.
10 On K75 models only, vertical adjustment is possible, by slackening the headlamp mounting bolts and tilting the unit. On K75C, K75T and K100 models a knurled plastic adjusting screw is fitted to the bottom left-hand corner of the headlamp unit to provide vertical adjustment. On K75S models two knurled plastic adjusting screws are fitted; that in the bottom left-hand corner of the headlamp unit adjusts vertical aim, while that in the top right-hand corner adjusts horizontal aim. On K100RS, K100RT and K100LT models vertical aim is adjusted by a knurled plastic screw in the centre of the three-position lever, on the right-hand side of the unit and horizontal aim is adjusted by a knurled plastic screw in the top left-hand corner of the unit. Except for K100RS models, where it may prove necessary to remove the fairing knee pads and other panels (see above), the adjusters are easily reached by hand from behind the headlamp assembly **(see illustrations)**.
11 Check the headlamp beam height requirements of local traffic laws and regulations. For UK owners, refer to MOT Test Checks in the Reference section of this manual.

Stop and tail lamp

12 Unlock and raise the seat, then remove the tail storage compartment cover and unscrew the two knurled plastic nuts or screws inside the compartment rear wall

22.6b . . . and disengage locking ring to release headlamp bulb

22.6c Parking lamp bulb is a bayonet fit in bulb holder

22.8 Headlamp beam adjustment, K100RS – knurled screw provides basic vertical setting, white lever provides alteration to suit loads

Electrical system 11•13

22.10a Single knurled screw provides horizontal adjustment

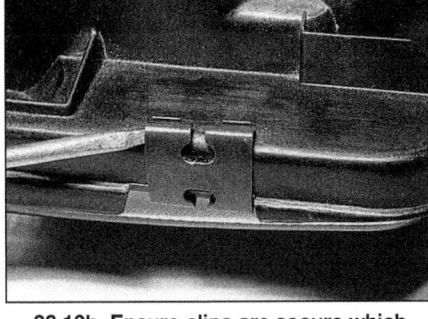

22.10b Ensure clips are secure which fasten headlamp assembly

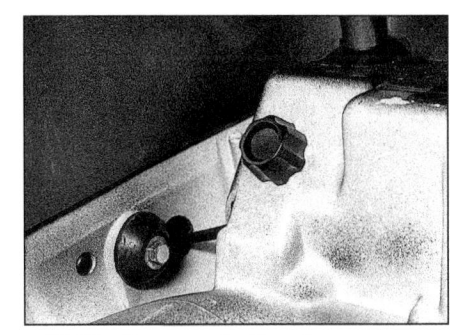

22.12a Remove plastic nuts or screws inside tail compartment . . .

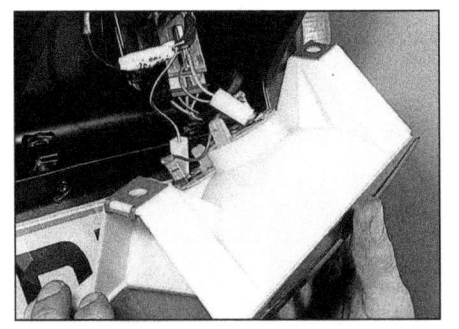

22.12b . . . to release tail lamp assembly

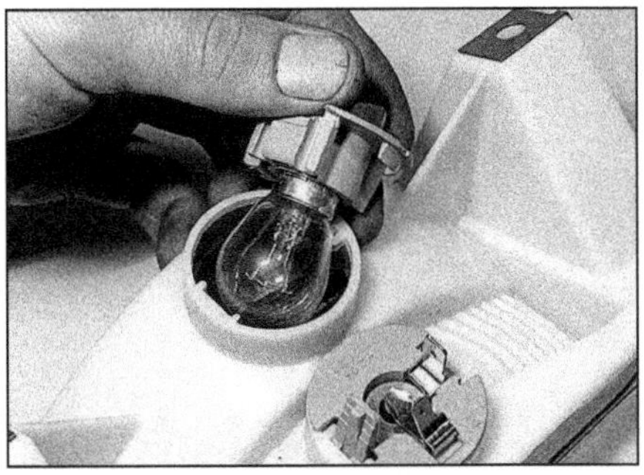

22.13 Disengage bulb holder plastic clip as shown to remove bulb assemblies

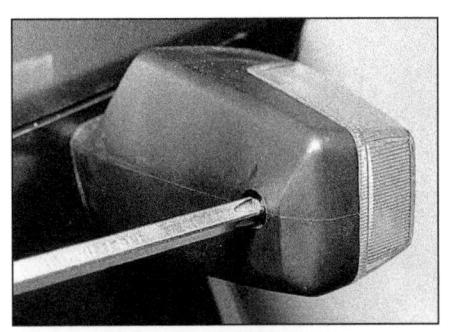

22.14a Except for fairing mounted lamp, remove single retaining screw . . .

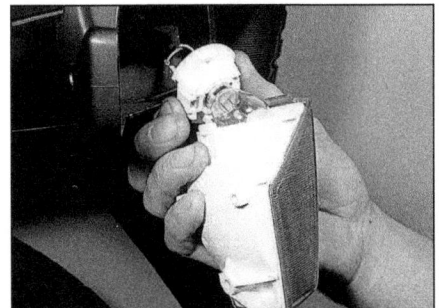

22.14b . . . to release lens assembly and expose bulb holder

22.16a K100RS – remove single lens retaining screw from front lamp assembly

22.16b Bulbs are of bayonet type – press in and twist anti-clockwise to release

22.18 Instrument panel bulbs are capless type – do not damage wire tails on refitting

which retain the rear lamp unit (**see illustrations**).

13 Withdraw the unit and remove either bulb by pressing inwards the bulb holder plastic clip and pulling it out of the unit (**see illustration**). Both bulbs are a standard bayonet fitting and are removed by pressing them into the holder and turning them anticlockwise to release them. Refitting is the reverse of the removal procedure.

Turn signal lamps

14 With the exception of the front turn signal assemblies incorporated in fairings as described below, the turn signal lamps are retained by a single screw which passes through the back of each unit's body and into the lens assembly. Remove the retaining screw, withdraw the lens assembly then remove the bulb holder and bulb exactly as described in paragraph 13 above (**see illustrations**); the bulb holders are identical to those used in the rear lamp assembly. Do not overtighten the screw on refitting.

15 On K75S front turn signal lamps remove the single screw which retains the assembly to the fairing, withdraw the assembly and turn the bulb holder anti-clockwise to release it. The bulb is a standard bayonet fitting and is removed as described in paragraph 13 above. Do not overtighten the screw or the lens will crack.

16 On K100RS front turn signal lamps remove the single screw which retains the lens and withdraw the lens (**see illustration**). Remove the bulb as described in paragraph 13 above (**see illustration**). On reassembly take care not to overtighten the retaining screw or the lens will be cracked.

17 On K75RT, K100RT and K100LT front turn signal lamps, position the front forks as necessary to permit access, then reach forward inside the fairing until the bulb holder can be twisted anti-clockwise to release it and pulled out. The bulb is the standard bayonet type which is removed and refitted as described in paragraph 13 above.

Instrument panel bulbs

18 Refer to the relevant Section of Chapter 8 for details of removing the instrument panel from the machine and dismantling it far enough to reach the bulbs (**see illustration**).

11•14 Wiring diagrams

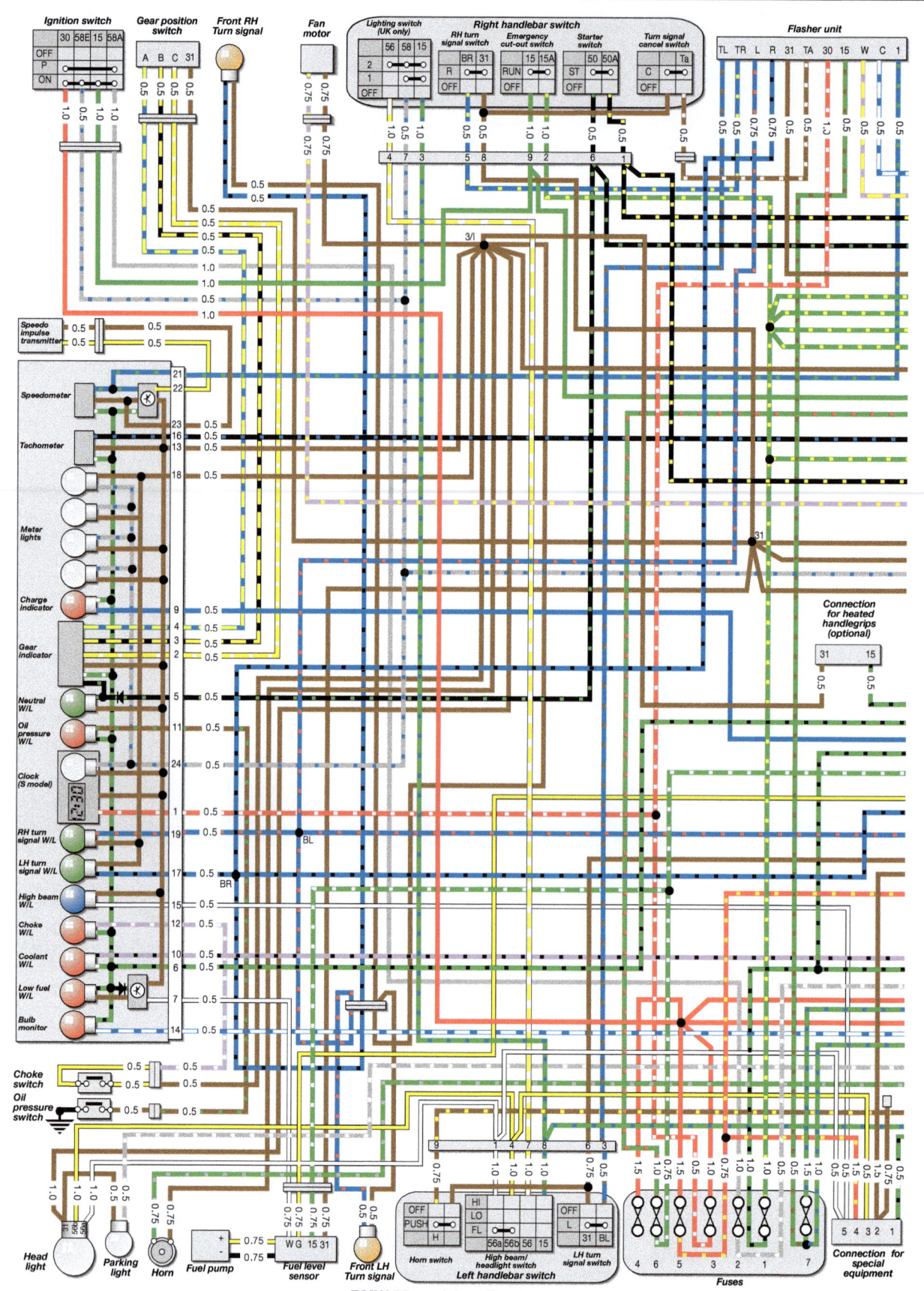

BMW 75 models - diagram 1a

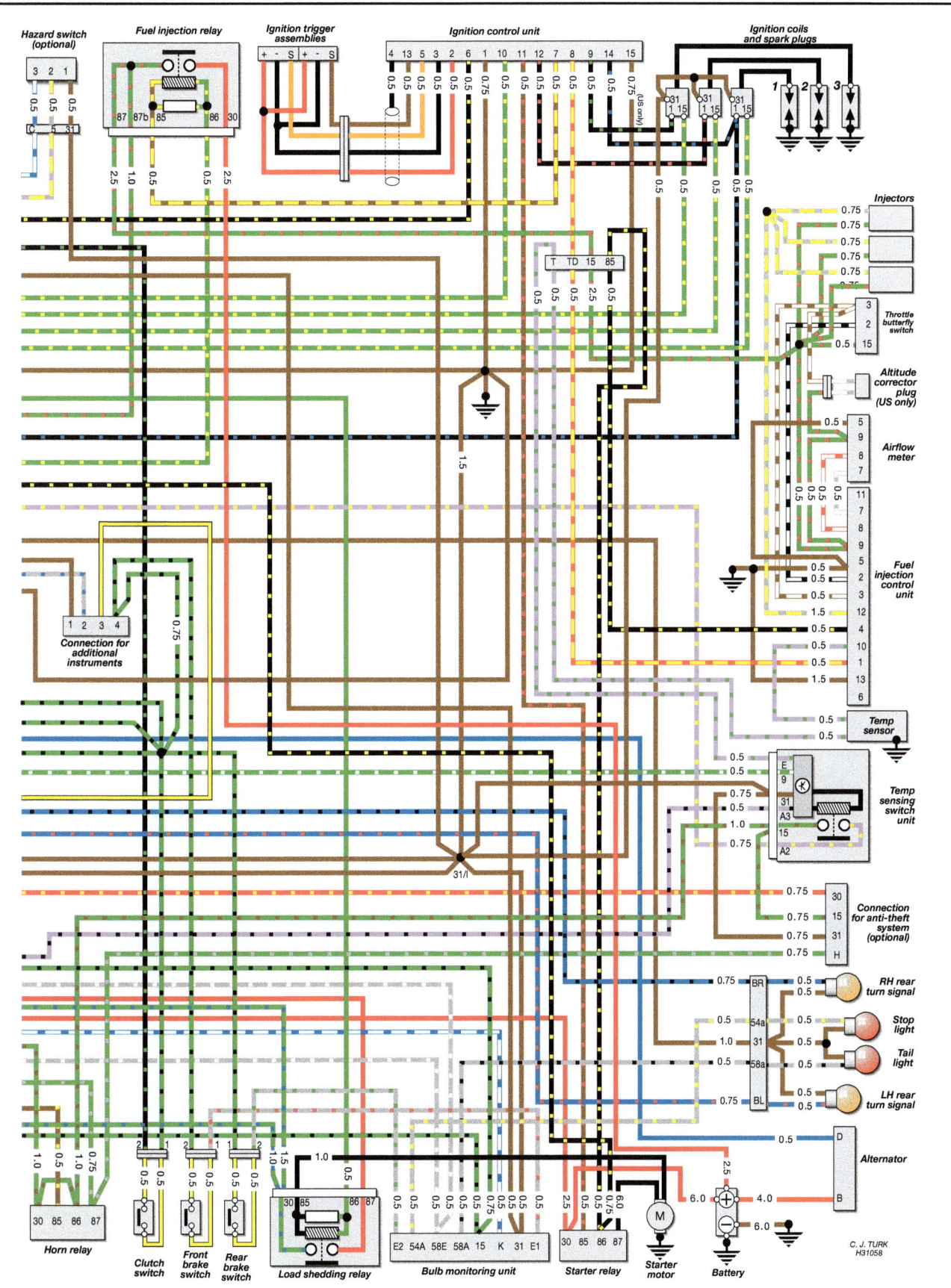

Wiring diagrams 11•15

BMW 75 models - diagram 1b

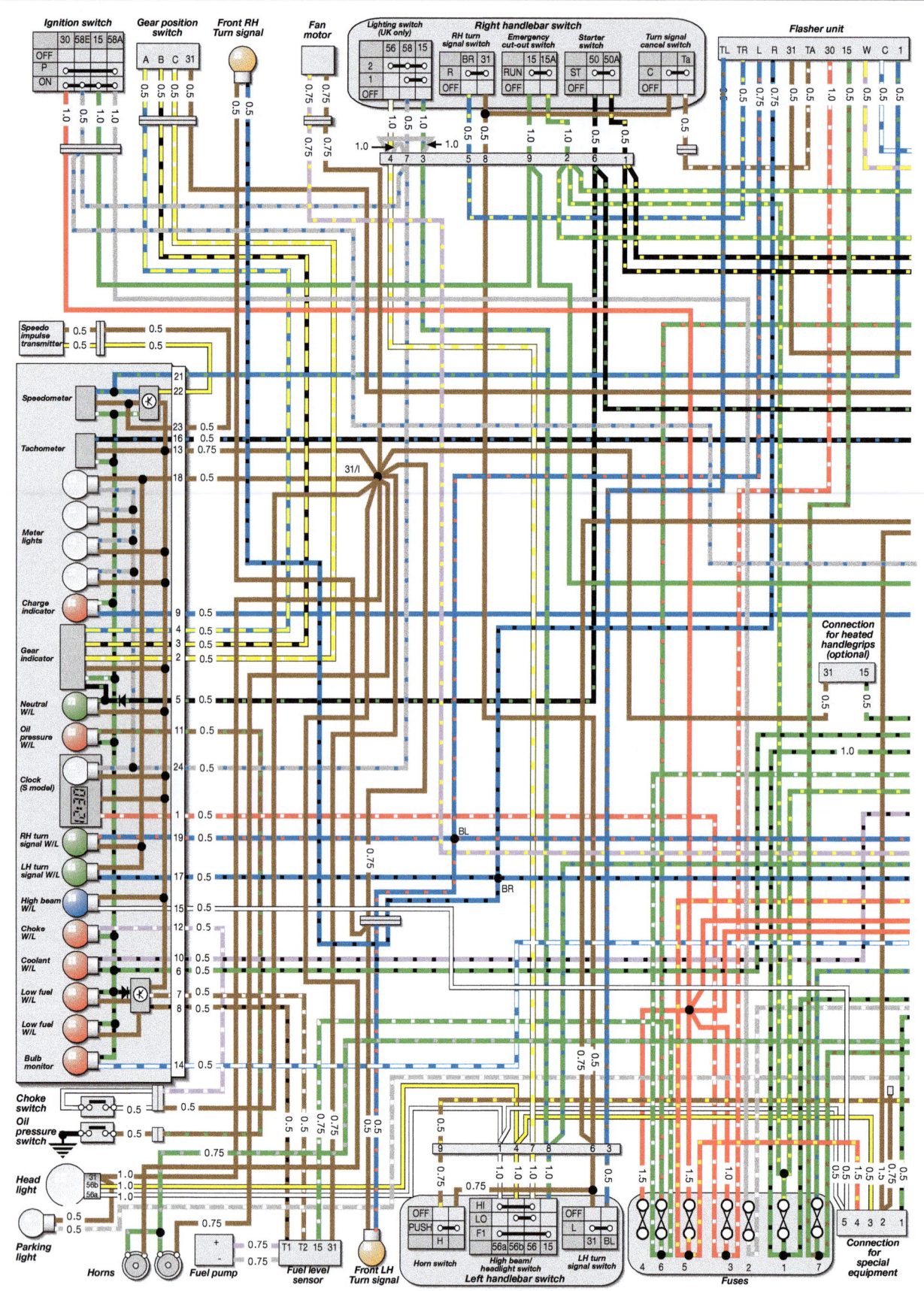

11•16 Wiring diagrams

BMW early K100 models - diagram 2a

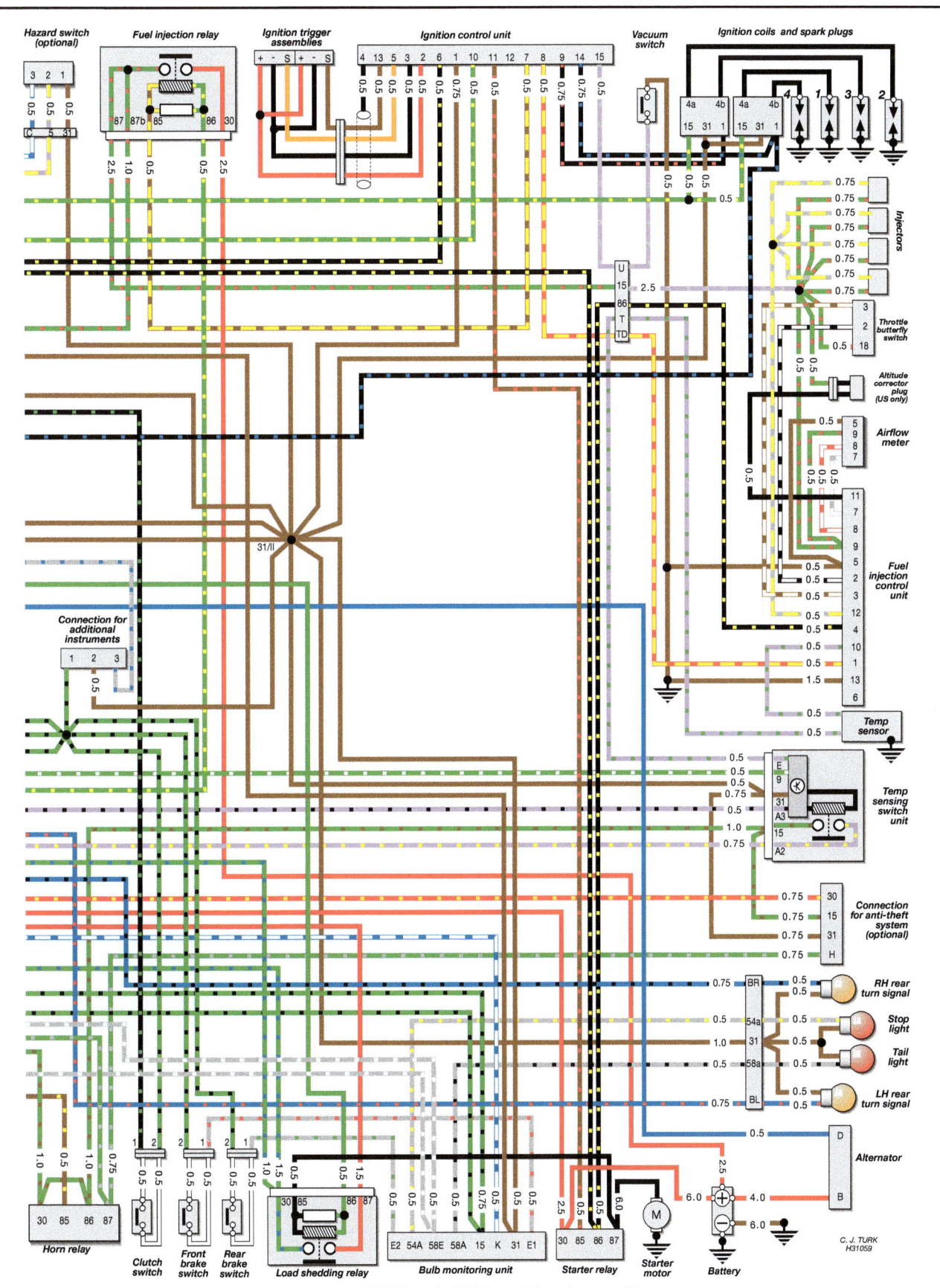

Wiring diagrams 11•17

BMW early K100 models - diagram 2b

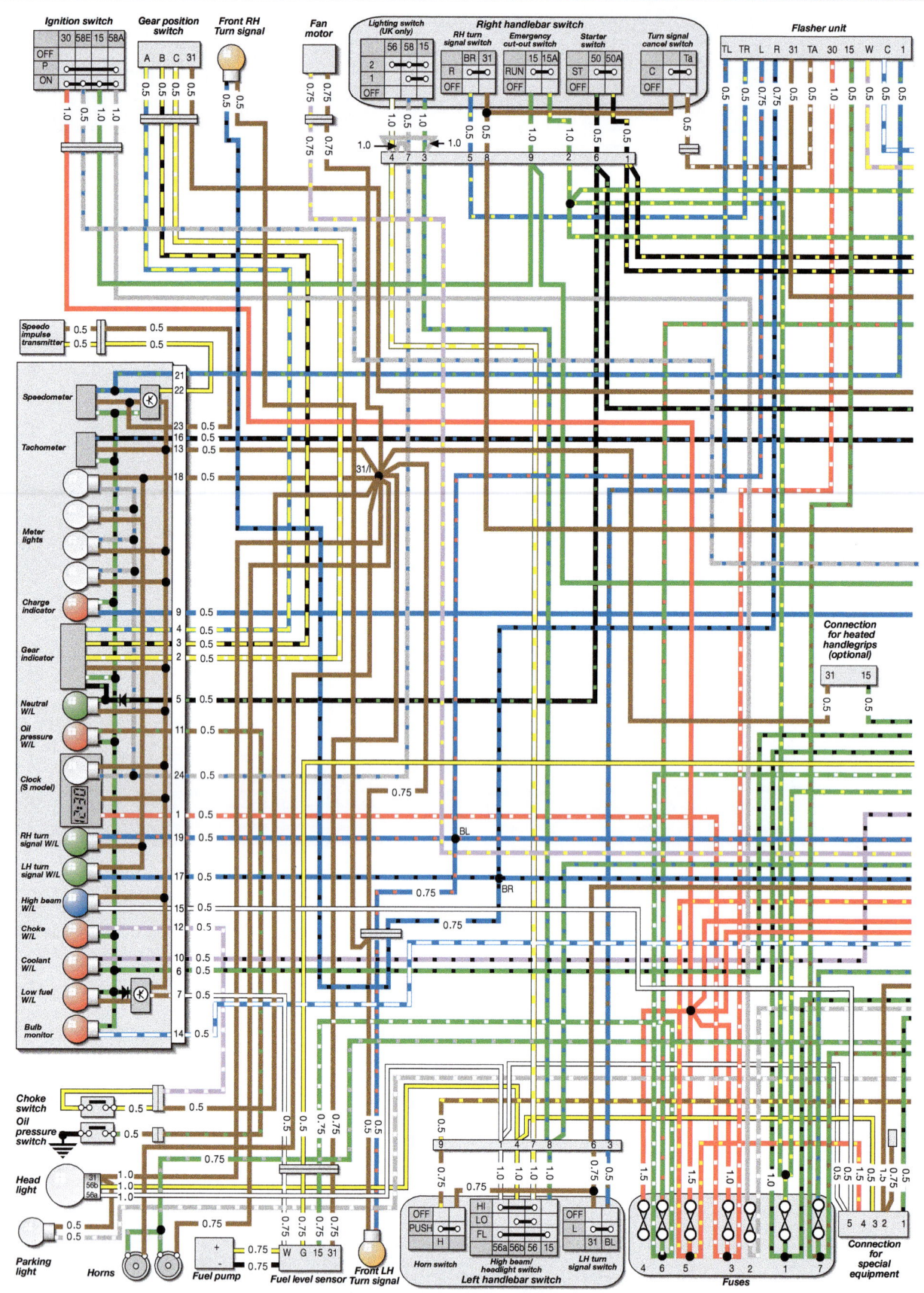

11•18 Wiring diagrams

BMW late K100 models - diagram 3a

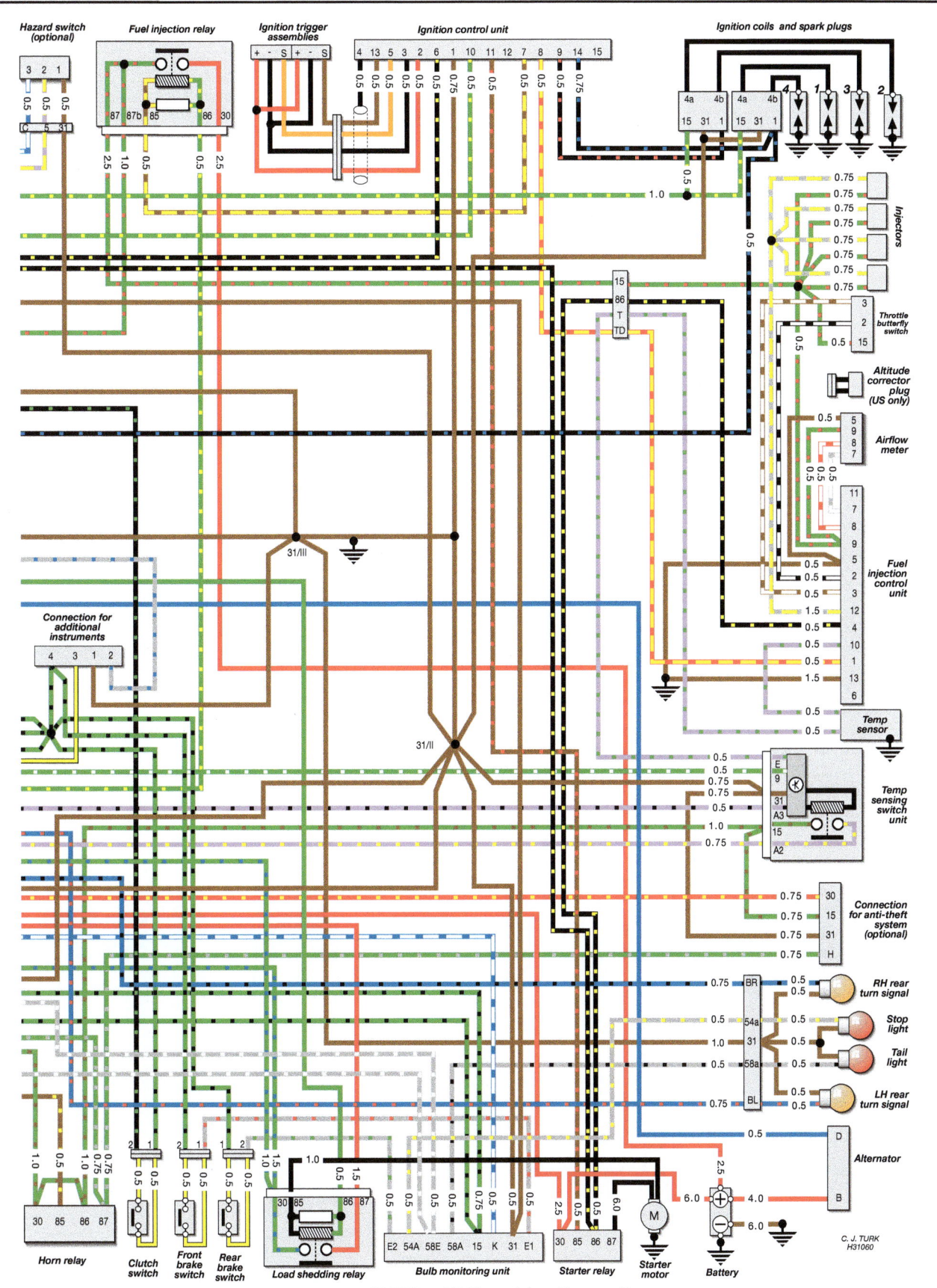

Wiring diagrams 11•19

BMW late K100 models - diagram 3b

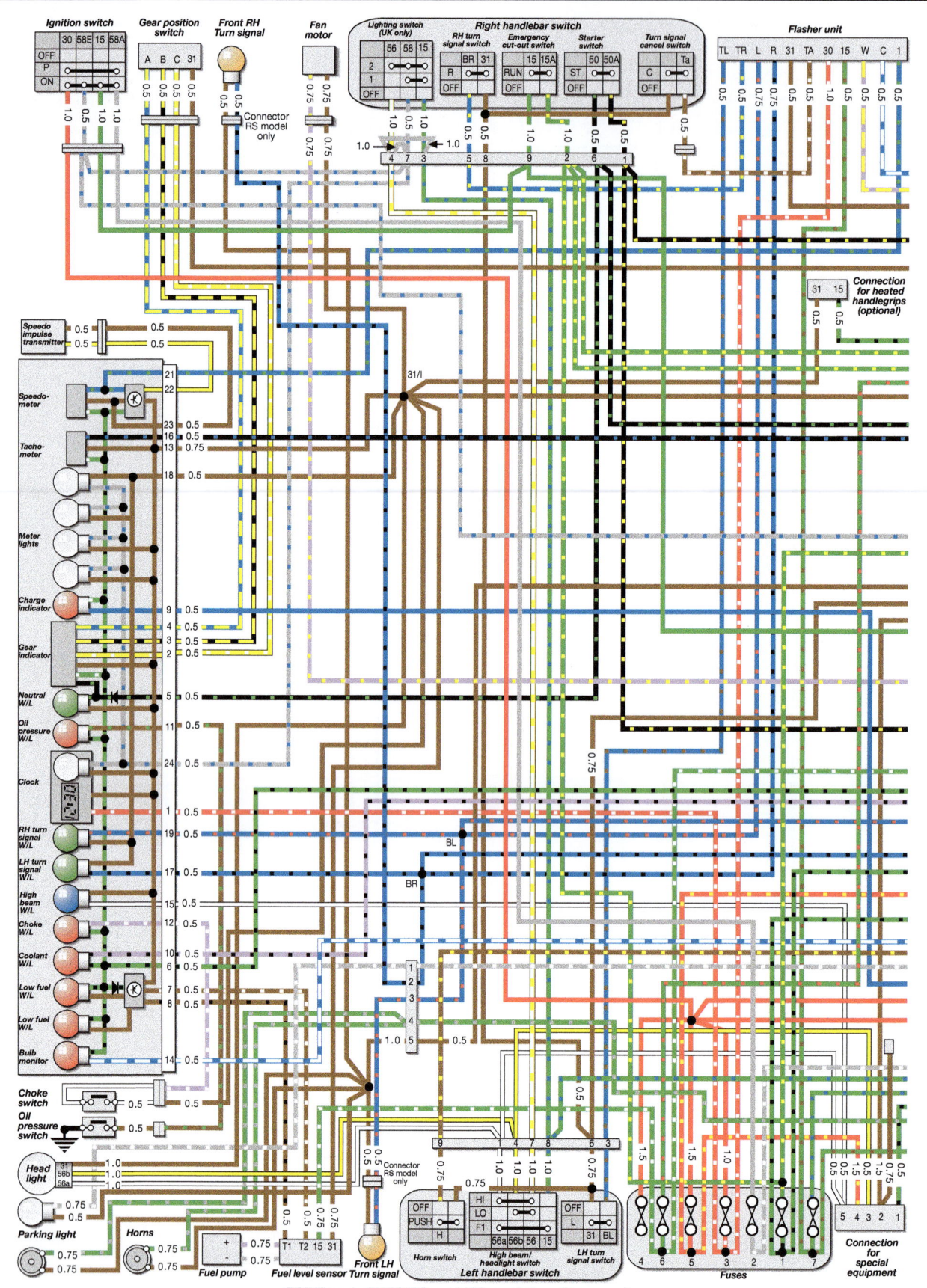

11•20 Wiring diagrams

BMW early K100 RS and RT models – diagram 4a

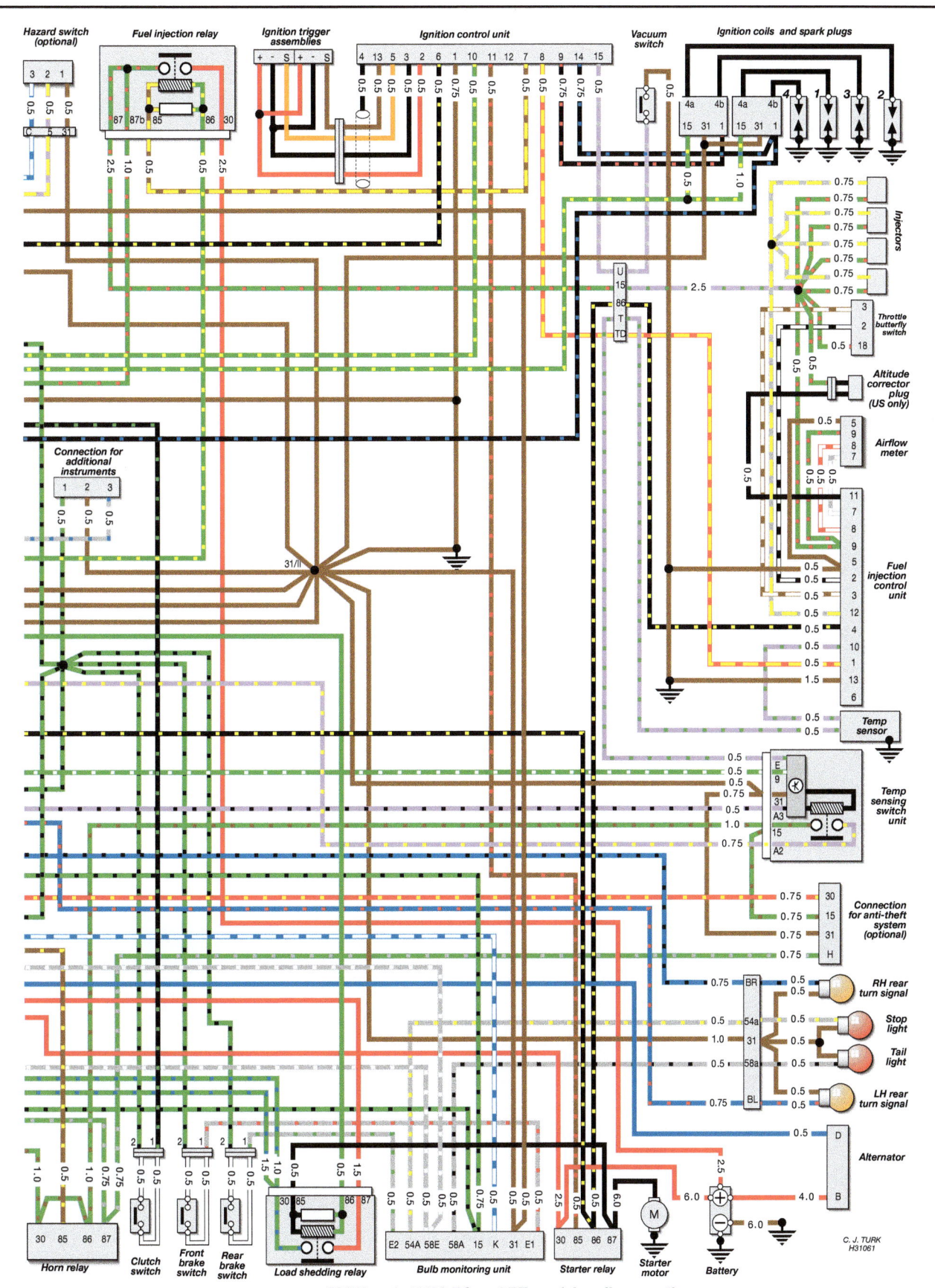

Wiring diagrams 11•21

BMW early K100 RS and RT models - diagram 4b

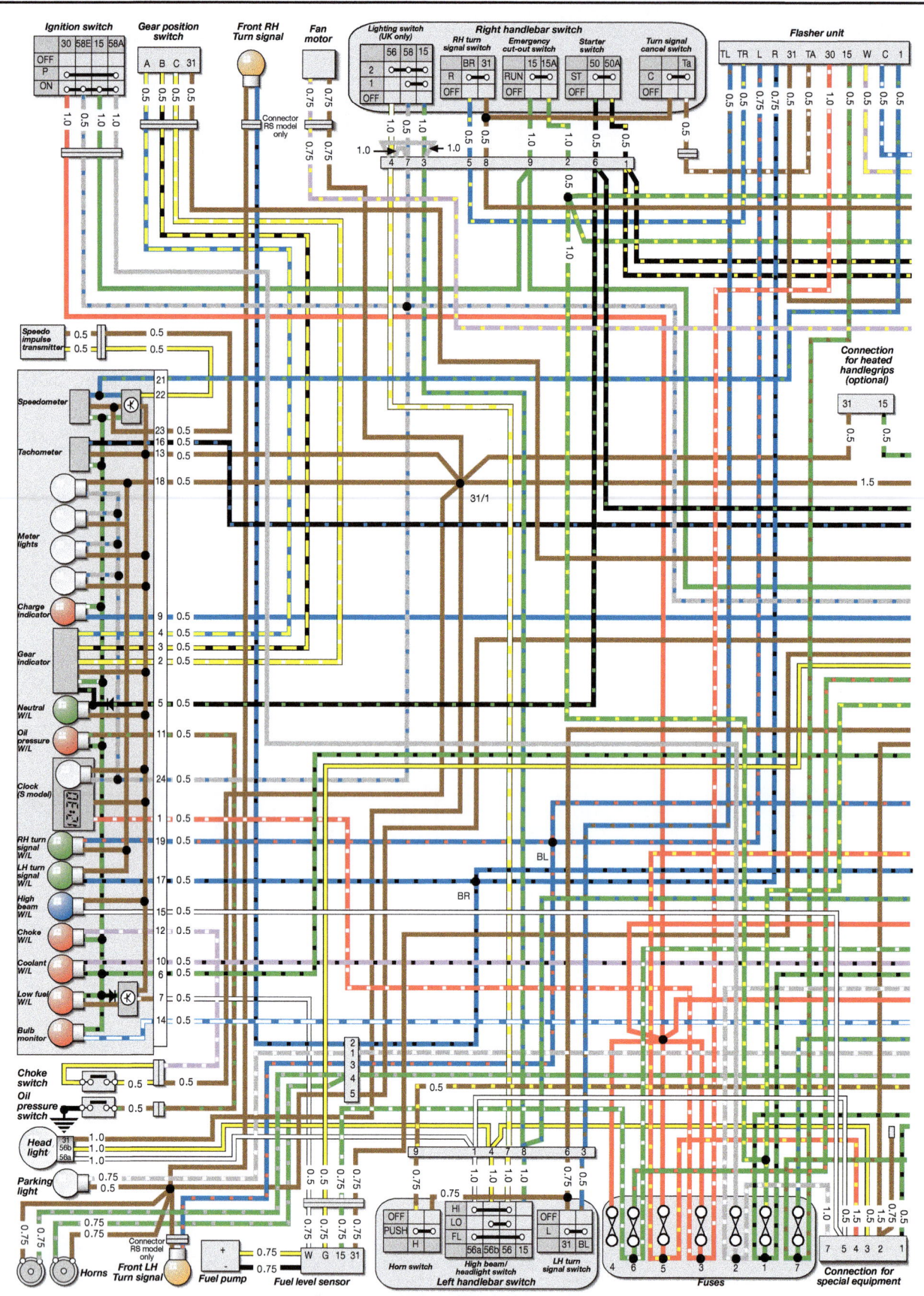

11•22 Wiring diagrams

BMW late K100 RS and RT models - diagram 5a

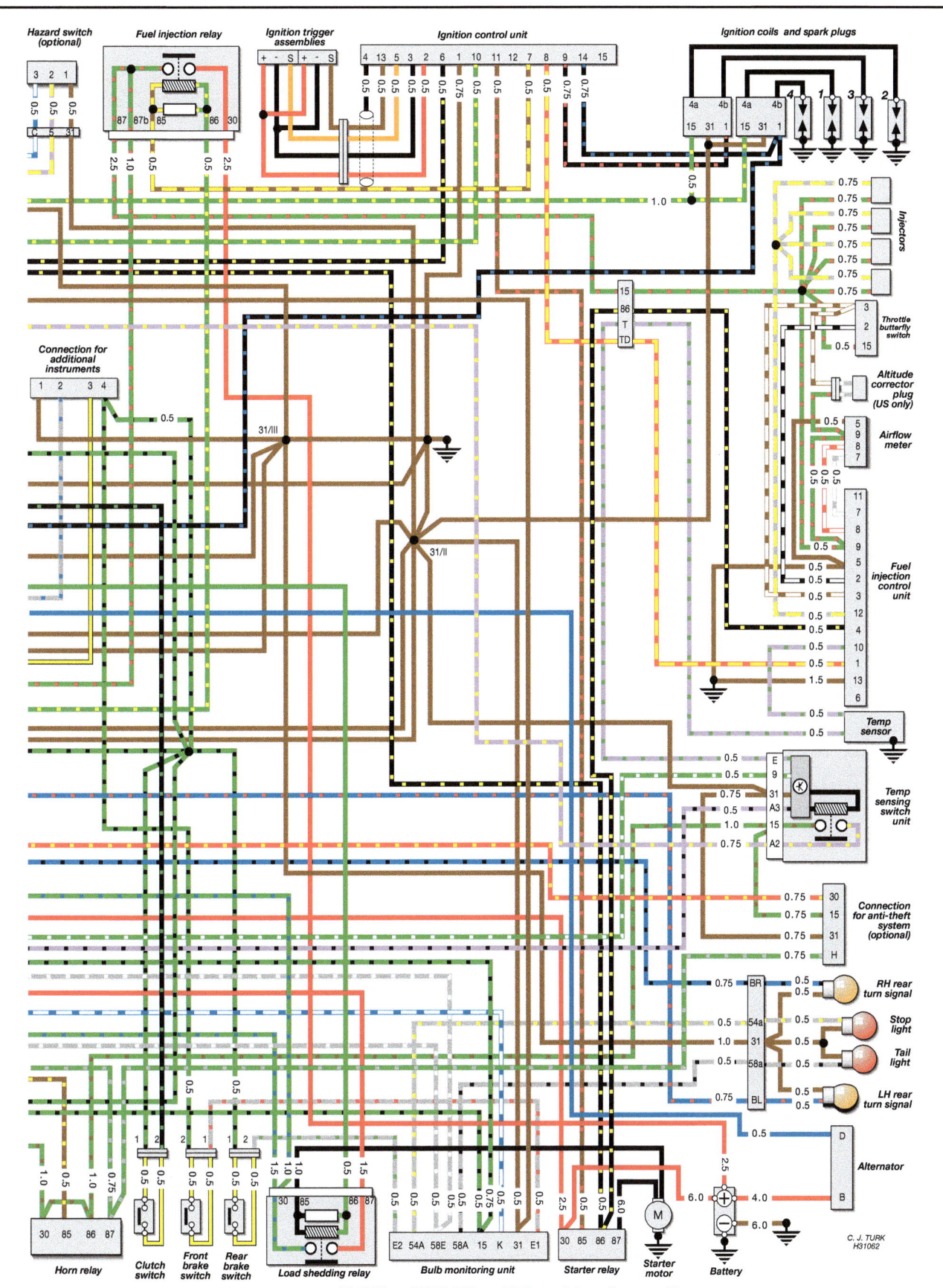

Wiring diagrams 11•23

BMW late K100 RS and RT models - diagram 5b

Notes

Reference REF•1

Dimensions and Weights	REF•1	Storage	REF•27
Tools and Workshop Tips	REF•2	Fault Finding	REF•30
Conversion Factors	REF•20	Fault Finding Equipment	REF•39
Motorcycle Chemicals and Lubricants	REF•21	Technical Terms Explained	REF•43
MOT Test Checks	REF•22	Index	REF•47

Dimensions and Weights

Overall width
K75S .... 810 mm (31.9 in)
K75RT .... 916 mm (36.0 in)
All other 75 models .... 900 mm (35.4 in)
K100 .... 960 mm (37.8 in)
K100RS .... 800 mm (31.5 in)
K100RT, K100LT .... 920 mm (36.2 in)

Overall height
K75, K75T .... Not available
K75C .... 1300 mm (51.2 in)
K75S .... 1340 mm (52.7 in)
K100 .... 1155 mm (45.5 in)
K100RS .... 1271 mm (50.0 in)
K75RT, K100RT, K100LT .... 1460 mm (57.5 in)

Seat height - unladen
Low seat models .... 760 mm (29.9 in)
All other models .... 810 mm (31.9 in)

Overall length
.... 2220 mm (87.4 in)

Wheelbase - with rider weighing 165 lb (75 kg) seated
.... 1511 mm (59.5 in)

Ground clearance - with rider weighing 165 lb (75 kg) seated
.... 150 mm (5.9 in)

Kerb weight - machine with full fuel tank, tools etc
K75T .... Not available
K75, K75C .... 503 lb (228 kg)
K75S .... 518 lb (235 kg)
K75RT .... 569 lb (258 kg)
K100 .... 527 lb (239 kg)
K100RS .... 558 lb (253 kg)
K100RT .... 580 lb (263 kg)
K100LT .... 624 lb (283 kg)

Gross weight limit - total of machine, passenger(s) and luggage
75 models, early 100 models .... 992 lb (450 kg)
Late 100 models (including all K100LT) .... 1058 lb (480 kg)
Note: *100 models only - refer to machine's handbook, to the plate riveted to the frame, and/or label under seat for precise details. The weight limit was altered early in 1985 but a higher limit may be used **only** if the maximum axle loads of 441 lb/200 kg (front) and 694 lb/315 kg (rear) are not exceeded and that suitable tyres (see Chapter 10 Specifications) are used. If in doubt, check with a BMW dealer or the importer.*

REF•2 Tools and Workshop Tips

Buying tools

A toolkit is a fundamental requirement for servicing and repairing a motorcycle. Although there will be an initial expense in building up enough tools for servicing, this will soon be offset by the savings made by doing the job yourself. As experience and confidence grow, additional tools can be added to enable the repair and overhaul of the motorcycle. Many of the specialist tools are expensive and not often used so it may be preferable to hire them, or for a group of friends or motorcycle club to join in the purchase.

As a rule, it is better to buy more expensive, good quality tools. Cheaper tools are likely to wear out faster and need to be renewed more often, nullifying the original saving.

> **Warning: To avoid the risk of a poor quality tool breaking in use, causing injury or damage to the component being worked on, always aim to purchase tools which meet the relevant national safety standards.**

The following lists of tools do not represent the manufacturer's service tools, but serve as a guide to help the owner decide which tools are needed for this level of work. In addition, items such as an electric drill, hacksaw, files, soldering iron and a workbench equipped with a vice, may be needed. Although not classed as tools, a selection of bolts, screws, nuts, washers and pieces of tubing always come in useful.

For more information about tools, refer to the Haynes *Motorcycle Workshop Practice TechBook* (Bk. No. 3470).

Manufacturer's service tools

Inevitably certain tasks require the use of a service tool. Where possible an alternative tool or method of approach is recommended, but sometimes there is no option if personal injury or damage to the component is to be avoided. Where required, service tools are referred to in the relevant procedure.

Service tools can usually only be purchased from a motorcycle dealer and are identified by a part number. Some of the commonly-used tools, such as rotor pullers, are available in aftermarket form from mail-order motorcycle tool and accessory suppliers.

Maintenance and minor repair tools

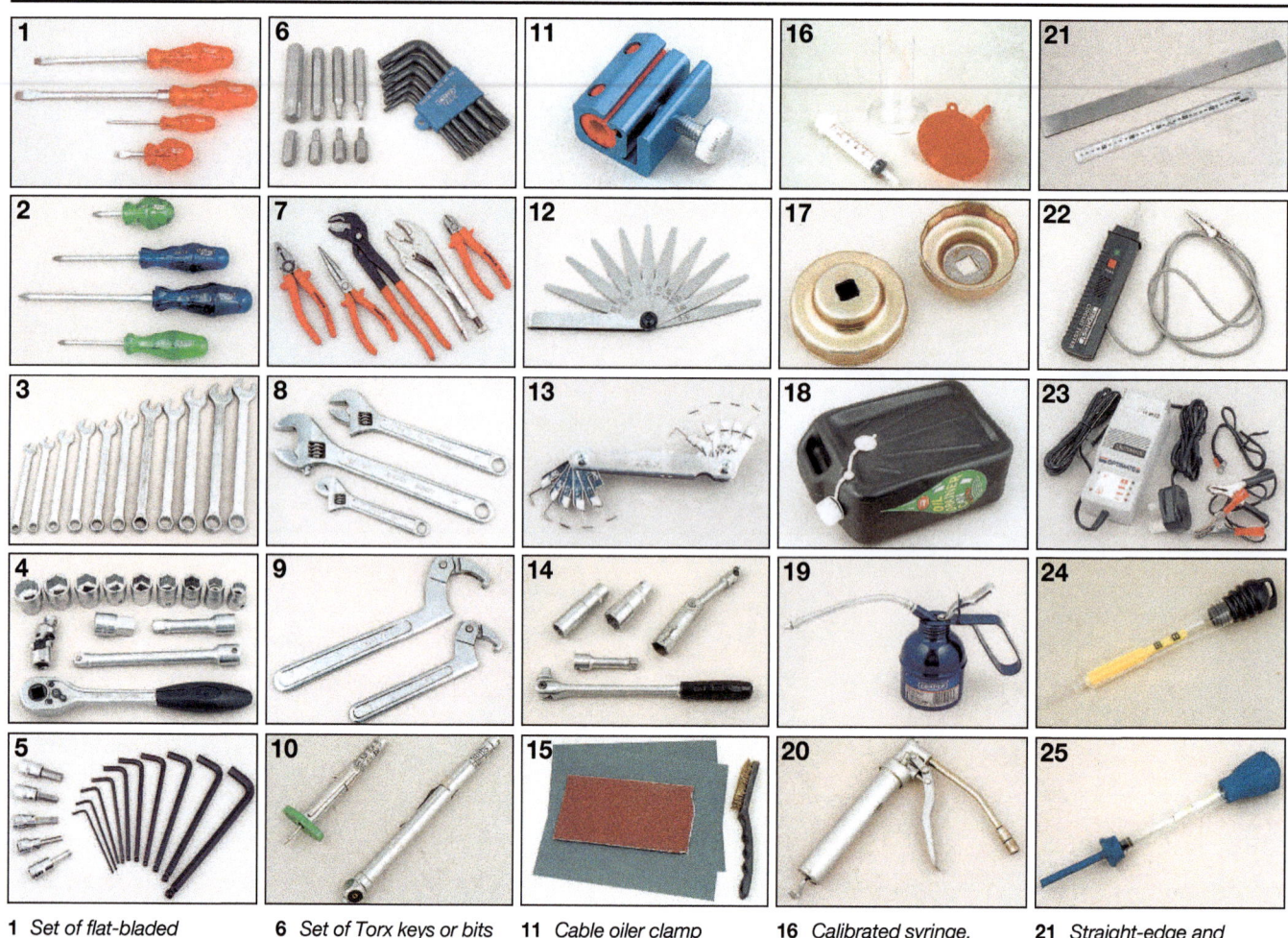

1. Set of flat-bladed screwdrivers
2. Set of Phillips head screwdrivers
3. Combination open-end and ring spanners
4. Socket set (3/8 inch or 1/2 inch drive)
5. Set of Allen keys or bits
6. Set of Torx keys or bits
7. Pliers, cutters and self-locking grips (Mole grips)
8. Adjustable spanners
9. C-spanners
10. Tread depth gauge and tyre pressure gauge
11. Cable oiler clamp
12. Feeler gauges
13. Spark plug gap measuring tool
14. Spark plug spanner or deep plug sockets
15. Wire brush and emery paper
16. Calibrated syringe, measuring vessel and funnel
17. Oil filter adapters
18. Oil drainer can or tray
19. Pump type oil can
20. Grease gun
21. Straight-edge and steel rule
22. Continuity tester
23. Battery charger
24. Hydrometer (for battery specific gravity check)
25. Anti-freeze tester (for liquid-cooled engines)

Tools and Workshop Tips REF•3

Repair and overhaul tools

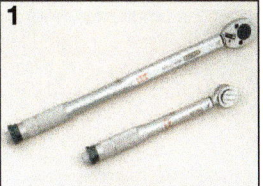

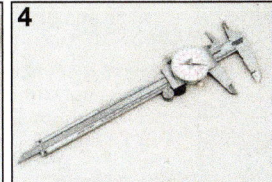

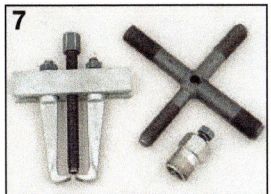

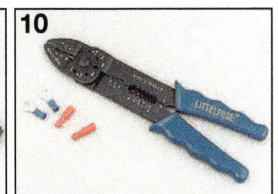

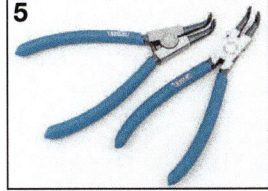

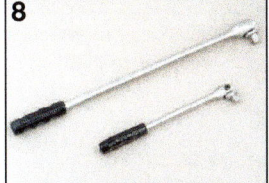

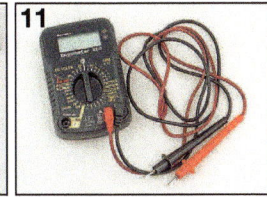

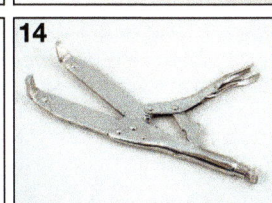

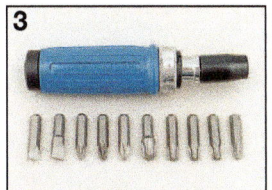

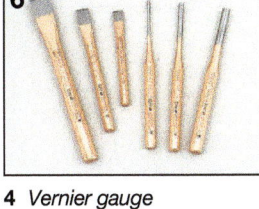

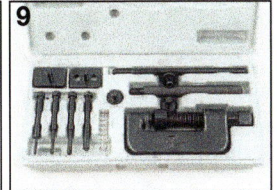

1. Torque wrench (small and mid-ranges)
2. Conventional, plastic or soft-faced hammers
3. Impact driver set
4. Vernier gauge
5. Circlip pliers (internal and external, or combination)
6. Set of cold chisels and punches
7. Selection of pullers
8. Breaker bars
9. Chain breaking/riveting tool set
10. Wire stripper and crimper tool
11. Multimeter (measures amps, volts and ohms)
12. Stroboscope (for dynamic timing checks)
13. Hose clamp (wingnut type shown)
14. Clutch holding tool
15. One-man brake/clutch bleeder kit

Specialist tools

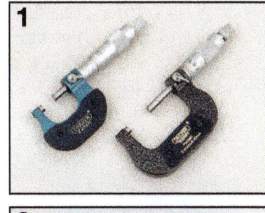

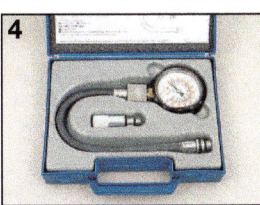

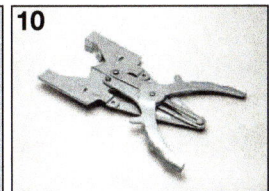

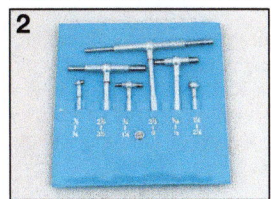

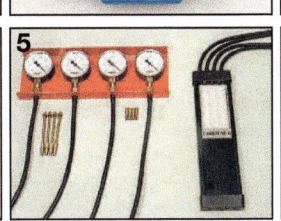

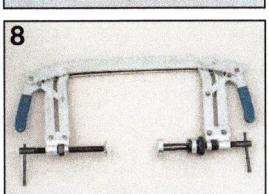

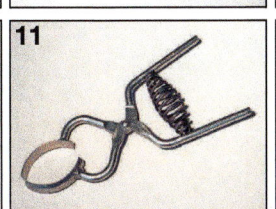

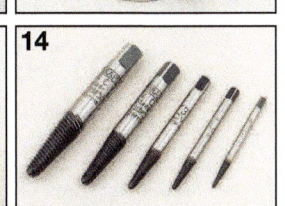

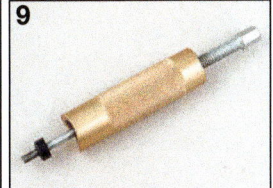

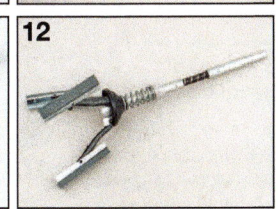

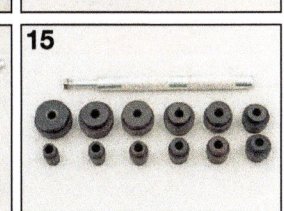

1. Micrometers (external type)
2. Telescoping gauges
3. Dial gauge
4. Cylinder compression gauge
5. Vacuum gauges (left) or manometer (right)
6. Oil pressure gauge
7. Plastigauge kit
8. Valve spring compressor (4-stroke engines)
9. Piston pin drawbolt tool
10. Piston ring removal and installation tool
11. Piston ring clamp
12. Cylinder bore hone (stone type shown)
13. Stud extractor
14. Screw extractor set
15. Bearing driver set

REF•4 Tools and Workshop Tips

1 Workshop equipment and facilities

The workbench

● Work is made much easier by raising the bike up on a ramp - components are much more accessible if raised to waist level. The hydraulic or pneumatic types seen in the dealer's workshop are a sound investment if you undertake a lot of repairs or overhauls **(see illustration 1.1)**.

1.1 Hydraulic motorcycle ramp

● If raised off ground level, the bike must be supported on the ramp to avoid it falling. Most ramps incorporate a front wheel locating clamp which can be adjusted to suit different diameter wheels. When tightening the clamp, take care not to mark the wheel rim or damage the tyre - use wood blocks on each side to prevent this.

● Secure the bike to the ramp using tie-downs **(see illustration 1.2)**. If the bike has only a sidestand, and hence leans at a dangerous angle when raised, support the bike on an auxiliary stand.

1.2 Tie-downs are used around the passenger footrests to secure the bike

● Auxiliary (paddock) stands are widely available from mail order companies or motorcycle dealers and attach either to the wheel axle or swingarm pivot **(see illustration 1.3)**. If the motorcycle has a centrestand, you can support it under the crankcase to prevent it toppling whilst either wheel is removed **(see illustration 1.4)**.

1.3 This auxiliary stand attaches to the swingarm pivot

1.4 Always use a block of wood between the engine and jack head when supporting the engine in this way

Fumes and fire

● Refer to the Safety first! page at the beginning of the manual for full details. Make sure your workshop is equipped with a fire extinguisher suitable for fuel-related fires (Class B fire - flammable liquids) - it is not sufficient to have a water-filled extinguisher.

● Always ensure adequate ventilation is available. Unless an exhaust gas extraction system is available for use, ensure that the engine is run outside of the workshop.

● If working on the fuel system, make sure the workshop is ventilated to avoid a build-up of fumes. This applies equally to fume build-up when charging a battery. Do not smoke or allow anyone else to smoke in the workshop.

Fluids

● If you need to drain fuel from the tank, store it in an approved container marked as suitable for the storage of petrol (gasoline) **(see illustration 1.5)**. Do not store fuel in glass jars or bottles.

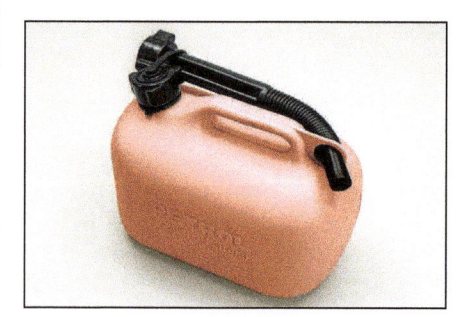

1.5 Use an approved can only for storing petrol (gasoline)

● Use proprietary engine degreasers or solvents which have a high flash-point, such as paraffin (kerosene), for cleaning off oil, grease and dirt - never use petrol (gasoline) for cleaning. Wear rubber gloves when handling solvent and engine degreaser. The fumes from certain solvents can be dangerous - always work in a well-ventilated area.

Dust, eye and hand protection

● Protect your lungs from inhalation of dust particles by wearing a filtering mask over the nose and mouth. Many frictional materials still contain asbestos which is dangerous to your health. Protect your eyes from spouts of liquid and sprung components by wearing a pair of protective goggles **(see illustration 1.6)**.

1.6 A fire extinguisher, goggles, mask and protective gloves should be at hand in the workshop

● Protect your hands from contact with solvents, fuel and oils by wearing rubber gloves. Alternatively apply a barrier cream to your hands before starting work. If handling hot components or fluids, wear suitable gloves to protect your hands from scalding and burns.

What to do with old fluids

● Old cleaning solvent, fuel, coolant and oils should not be poured down domestic drains or onto the ground. Package the fluid up in old oil containers, label it accordingly, and take it to a garage or disposal facility. Contact your local authority for location of such sites or ring the oil care hotline.

Note: It is antisocial and illegal to dump oil down the drain. To find the location of your local oil recycling bank, call this number free.

OIL CARE
OIL BANK LINE
0800 66 33 66

In the USA, note that any oil supplier must accept used oil for recycling.

Tools and Workshop Tips   REF•5

2 Fasteners -
screws, bolts and nuts

Fastener types and applications

Bolts and screws

● Fastener head types are either of hexagonal, Torx or splined design, with internal and external versions of each type **(see illustrations 2.1 and 2.2)**; splined head fasteners are not in common use on motorcycles. The conventional slotted or Phillips head design is used for certain screws. Bolt or screw length is always measured from the underside of the head to the end of the item **(see illustration 2.11)**.

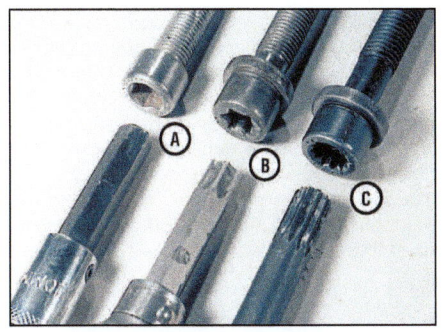

2.1 Internal hexagon/Allen (A), Torx (B) and splined (C) fasteners, with corresponding bits

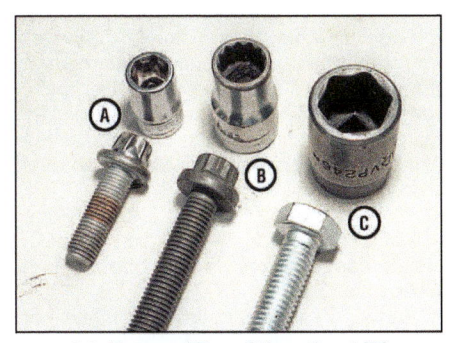

2.2 External Torx (A), splined (B) and hexagon (C) fasteners, with corresponding sockets

● Certain fasteners on the motorcycle have a tensile marking on their heads, the higher the marking the stronger the fastener. High tensile fasteners generally carry a 10 or higher marking. Never replace a high tensile fastener with one of a lower tensile strength.

Washers (see illustration 2.3)

● Plain washers are used between a fastener head and a component to prevent damage to the component or to spread the load when torque is applied. Plain washers can also be used as spacers or shims in certain assemblies. Copper or aluminium plain washers are often used as sealing washers on drain plugs.

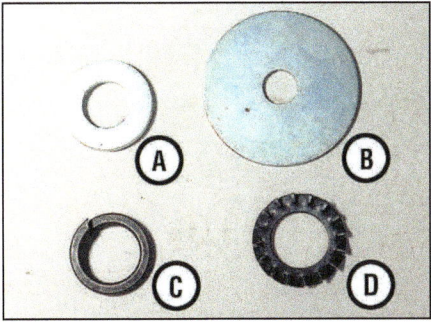

2.3 Plain washer (A), penny washer (B), spring washer (C) and serrated washer (D)

● The split-ring spring washer works by applying axial tension between the fastener head and component. If flattened, it is fatigued and must be renewed. If a plain (flat) washer is used on the fastener, position the spring washer between the fastener and the plain washer.

● Serrated star type washers dig into the fastener and component faces, preventing loosening. They are often used on electrical earth (ground) connections to the frame.

● Cone type washers (sometimes called Belleville) are conical and when tightened apply axial tension between the fastener head and component. They must be installed with the dished side against the component and often carry an OUTSIDE marking on their outer face. If flattened, they are fatigued and must be renewed.

● Tab washers are used to lock plain nuts or bolts on a shaft. A portion of the tab washer is bent up hard against one flat of the nut or bolt to prevent it loosening. Due to the tab washer being deformed in use, a new tab washer should be used every time it is disturbed.

● Wave washers are used to take up endfloat on a shaft. They provide light springing and prevent excessive side-to-side play of a component. Can be found on rocker arm shafts.

Nuts and split pins

● Conventional plain nuts are usually six-sided **(see illustration 2.4)**. They are sized by thread diameter and pitch. High tensile nuts carry a number on one end to denote their tensile strength.

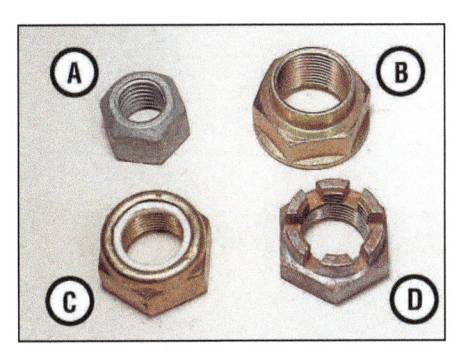

2.4 Plain nut (A), shouldered locknut (B), nylon insert nut (C) and castellated nut (D)

● Self-locking nuts either have a nylon insert, or two spring metal tabs, or a shoulder which is staked into a groove in the shaft - their advantage over conventional plain nuts is a resistance to loosening due to vibration. The nylon insert type can be used a number of times, but must be renewed when the friction of the nylon insert is reduced, ie when the nut spins freely on the shaft. The spring tab type can be reused unless the tabs are damaged. The shouldered type must be renewed every time it is disturbed.

● Split pins (cotter pins) are used to lock a castellated nut to a shaft or to prevent slackening of a plain nut. Common applications are wheel axles and brake torque arms. Because the split pin arms are deformed to lock around the nut a new split pin must always be used on installation - always fit the correct size split pin which will fit snugly in the shaft hole. Make sure the split pin arms are correctly located around the nut **(see illustrations 2.5 and 2.6)**.

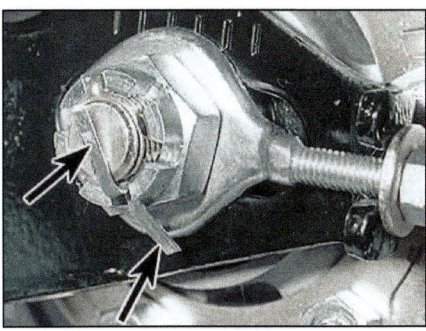

2.5 Bend split pin (cotter pin) arms as shown (arrows) to secure a castellated nut

2.6 Bend split pin (cotter pin) arms as shown to secure a plain nut

Caution: If the castellated nut slots do not align with the shaft hole after tightening to the torque setting, tighten the nut until the next slot aligns with the hole - never slacken the nut to align its slot.

● R-pins (shaped like the letter R), or slip pins as they are sometimes called, are sprung and can be reused if they are otherwise in good condition. Always install R-pins with their closed end facing forwards **(see illustration 2.7)**.

Tools and Workshop Tips

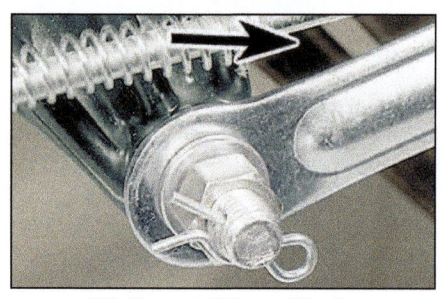

2.7 Correct fitting of R-pin. Arrow indicates forward direction

Circlips (see illustration 2.8)

• Circlips (sometimes called snap-rings) are used to retain components on a shaft or in a housing and have corresponding external or internal ears to permit removal. Parallel-sided (machined) circlips can be installed either way round in their groove, whereas stamped circlips (which have a chamfered edge on one face) must be installed with the chamfer facing away from the direction of thrust load **(see illustration 2.9)**.

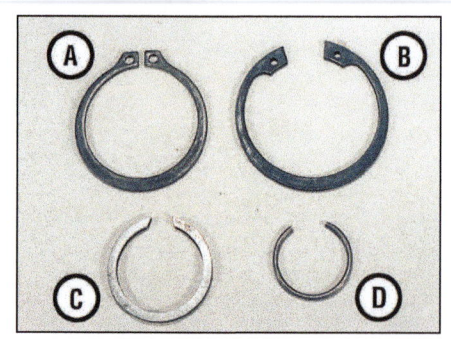

2.8 External stamped circlip (A), internal stamped circlip (B), machined circlip (C) and wire circlip (D)

• Always use circlip pliers to remove and install circlips; expand or compress them just enough to remove them. After installation, rotate the circlip in its groove to ensure it is securely seated. If installing a circlip on a splined shaft, always align its opening with a shaft channel to ensure the circlip ends are well supported and unlikely to catch **(see illustration 2.10)**.

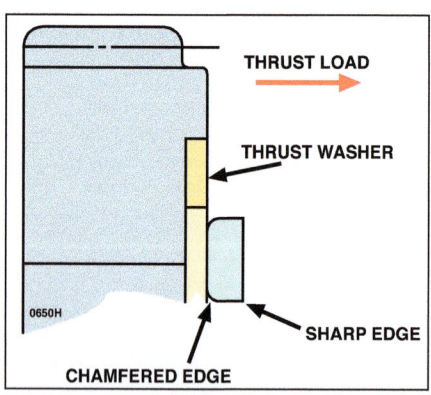

2.9 Correct fitting of a stamped circlip

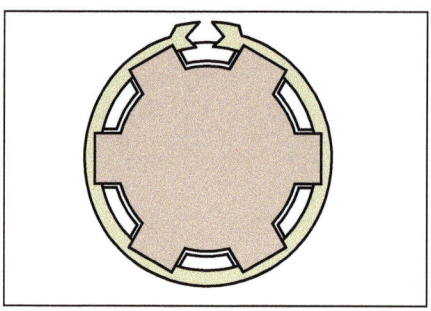

2.10 Align circlip opening with shaft channel

• Circlips can wear due to the thrust of components and become loose in their grooves, with the subsequent danger of becoming dislodged in operation. For this reason, renewal is advised every time a circlip is disturbed.

• Wire circlips are commonly used as piston pin retaining clips. If a removal tang is provided, long-nosed pliers can be used to dislodge them, otherwise careful use of a small flat-bladed screwdriver is necessary. Wire circlips should be renewed every time they are disturbed.

Thread diameter and pitch

• Diameter of a male thread (screw, bolt or stud) is the outside diameter of the threaded portion **(see illustration 2.11)**. Most motorcycle manufacturers use the ISO (International Standards Organisation) metric system expressed in millimetres, eg M6 refers to a 6 mm diameter thread. Sizing is the same for nuts, except that the thread diameter is measured across the valleys of the nut.

• Pitch is the distance between the peaks of the thread **(see illustration 2.11)**. It is expressed in millimetres, thus a common bolt size may be expressed as 6.0 x 1.0 mm (6 mm thread diameter and 1 mm pitch). Generally pitch increases in proportion to thread diameter, although there are always exceptions.

• Thread diameter and pitch are related for conventional fastener applications and the accompanying table can be used as a guide. Additionally, the AF (Across Flats), spanner or socket size dimension of the bolt or nut **(see illustration 2.11)** is linked to thread and pitch specification. Thread pitch can be measured with a thread gauge **(see illustration 2.12)**.

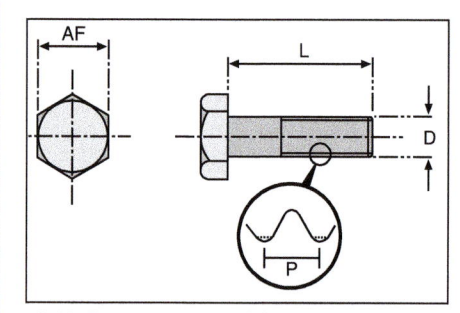

2.11 Fastener length (L), thread diameter (D), thread pitch (P) and head size (AF)

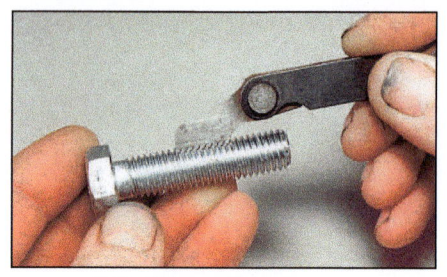

2.12 Using a thread gauge to measure pitch

AF size	Thread diameter x pitch (mm)
8 mm	M5 x 0.8
8 mm	M6 x 1.0
10 mm	M6 x 1.0
12 mm	M8 x 1.25
14 mm	M10 x 1.25
17 mm	M12 x 1.25

• The threads of most fasteners are of the right-hand type, ie they are turned clockwise to tighten and anti-clockwise to loosen. The reverse situation applies to left-hand thread fasteners, which are turned anti-clockwise to tighten and clockwise to loosen. Left-hand threads are used where rotation of a component might loosen a conventional right-hand thread fastener.

Seized fasteners

• Corrosion of external fasteners due to water or reaction between two dissimilar metals can occur over a period of time. It will build up sooner in wet conditions or in countries where salt is used on the roads during the winter. If a fastener is severely corroded it is likely that normal methods of removal will fail and result in its head being ruined. When you attempt removal, the fastener thread should be heard to crack free and unscrew easily - if it doesn't, stop there before damaging something.

• A smart tap on the head of the fastener will often succeed in breaking free corrosion which has occurred in the threads **(see illustration 2.13)**.

• An aerosol penetrating fluid (such as WD-40) applied the night beforehand may work its way down into the thread and ease removal. Depending on the location, you may be able to make up a Plasticine well around the fastener head and fill it with penetrating fluid.

2.13 A sharp tap on the head of a fastener will often break free a corroded thread

Tools and Workshop Tips REF•7

• If you are working on an engine internal component, corrosion will most likely not be a problem due to the well lubricated environment. However, components can be very tight and an impact driver is a useful tool in freeing them **(see illustration 2.14)**.

2.14 Using an impact driver to free a fastener

• Where corrosion has occurred between dissimilar metals (eg steel and aluminium alloy), the application of heat to the fastener head will create a disproportionate expansion rate between the two metals and break the seizure caused by the corrosion. Whether heat can be applied depends on the location of the fastener - any surrounding components likely to be damaged must first be removed **(see illustration 2.15)**. Heat can be applied using a paint stripper heat gun or clothes iron, or by immersing the component in boiling water - wear protective gloves to prevent scalding or burns to the hands.

2.15 Using heat to free a seized fastener

• As a last resort, it is possible to use a hammer and cold chisel to work the fastener head unscrewed **(see illustration 2.16)**. This will damage the fastener, but more importantly extreme care must be taken not to damage the surrounding component.

Caution: Remember that the component being secured is generally of more value than the bolt, nut or screw - when the fastener is freed, do not unscrew it with force, instead work the fastener back and forth when resistance is felt to prevent thread damage.

2.16 Using a hammer and chisel to free a seized fastener

Broken fasteners and damaged heads

• If the shank of a broken bolt or screw is accessible you can grip it with self-locking grips. The knurled wheel type stud extractor tool or self-gripping stud puller tool is particularly useful for removing the long studs which screw into the cylinder mouth surface of the crankcase or bolts and screws from which the head has broken off **(see illustration 2.17)**. Studs can also be removed by locking two nuts together on the threaded end of the stud and using a spanner on the lower nut **(see illustration 2.18)**.

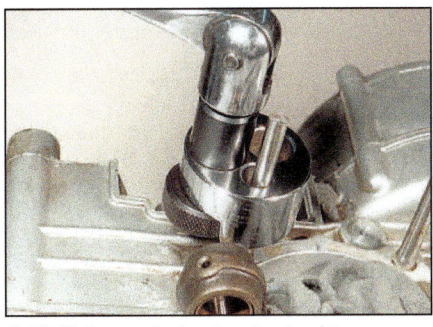

2.17 Using a stud extractor tool to remove a broken crankcase stud

2.18 Two nuts can be locked together to unscrew a stud from a component

• A bolt or screw which has broken off below or level with the casing must be extracted using a screw extractor set. Centre punch the fastener to centralise the drill bit, then drill a hole in the fastener **(see illustration 2.19)**. Select a drill bit which is approximately half to three-quarters the diameter of the fastener and drill to a depth which will accommodate the extractor. Use the largest size extractor possible, but avoid leaving too small a wall thickness otherwise the extractor will merely force the fastener walls outwards wedging it in the casing thread.

2.19 When using a screw extractor, first drill a hole in the fastener . . .

• If a spiral type extractor is used, thread it anti-clockwise into the fastener. As it is screwed in, it will grip the fastener and unscrew it from the casing **(see illustration 2.20)**.

2.20 . . . then thread the extractor anti-clockwise into the fastener

• If a taper type extractor is used, tap it into the fastener so that it is firmly wedged in place. Unscrew the extractor (anti-clockwise) to draw the fastener out.

⚠️ **Warning: Stud extractors are very hard and may break off in the fastener if care is not taken - ask an engineer about spark erosion if this happens.**

• Alternatively, the broken bolt/screw can be drilled out and the hole retapped for an oversize bolt/screw or a diamond-section thread insert. It is essential that the drilling is carried out squarely and to the correct depth, otherwise the casing may be ruined - if in doubt, entrust the work to an engineer.

• Bolts and nuts with rounded corners cause the correct size spanner or socket to slip when force is applied. Of the types of spanner/socket available always use a six-point type rather than an eight or twelve-point type - better grip

REF•8 Tools and Workshop Tips

2.21 Comparison of surface drive ring spanner (left) with 12-point type (right)

is obtained. Surface drive spanners grip the middle of the hex flats, rather than the corners, and are thus good in cases of damaged heads **(see illustration 2.21)**.

- Slotted-head or Phillips-head screws are often damaged by the use of the wrong size screwdriver. Allen-head and Torx-head screws are much less likely to sustain damage. If enough of the screw head is exposed you can use a hacksaw to cut a slot in its head and then use a conventional flat-bladed screwdriver to remove it. Alternatively use a hammer and cold chisel to tap the head of the fastener around to slacken it. Always replace damaged fasteners with new ones, preferably Torx or Allen-head type.

> **HAYNES HINT**
>
> *A dab of valve grinding compound between the screw head and screwdriver tip will often give a good grip.*

Thread repair

- Threads (particularly those in aluminium alloy components) can be damaged by overtightening, being assembled with dirt in the threads, or from a component working loose and vibrating. Eventually the thread will fail completely, and it will be impossible to tighten the fastener.
- If a thread is damaged or clogged with old locking compound it can be renovated with a thread repair tool (thread chaser) **(see illustrations 2.22 and 2.23)**; special thread

2.22 A thread repair tool being used to correct an internal thread

2.23 A thread repair tool being used to correct an external thread

chasers are available for spark plug hole threads. The tool will not cut a new thread, but clean and true the original thread. Make sure that you use the correct diameter and pitch tool. Similarly, external threads can be cleaned up with a die or a thread restorer file **(see illustration 2.24)**.

2.24 Using a thread restorer file

- It is possible to drill out the old thread and retap the component to the next thread size. This will work where there is enough surrounding material and a new bolt or screw can be obtained. Sometimes, however, this is not possible - such as where the bolt/screw passes through another component which must also be suitably modified, also in cases where a spark plug or oil drain plug cannot be obtained in a larger diameter thread size.
- The diamond-section thread insert (often known by its popular trade name of Heli-Coil) is a simple and effective method of renewing the thread and retaining the original size. A kit can be purchased which contains the tap, insert and installing tool **(see illustration 2.25)**. Drill out the damaged thread with the size drill specified **(see illustration 2.26)**. Carefully retap the thread **(see illustration 2.27)**. Install the

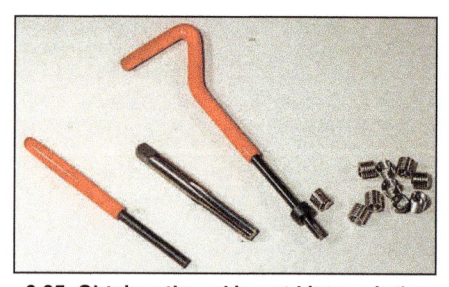

2.25 Obtain a thread insert kit to suit the thread diameter and pitch required

2.26 To install a thread insert, first drill out the original thread . . .

2.27 . . . tap a new thread . . .

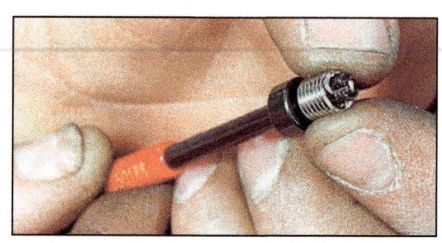

2.28 . . . fit insert on the installing tool . . .

2.29 . . . and thread into the component . . .

2.30 . . . break off the tang when complete

insert on the installing tool and thread it slowly into place using a light downward pressure **(see illustrations 2.28 and 2.29)**. When positioned between a 1/4 and 1/2 turn below the surface withdraw the installing tool and use the break-off tool to press down on the tang, breaking it off **(see illustration 2.30)**.

- There are epoxy thread repair kits on the market which can rebuild stripped internal threads, although this repair should not be used on high load-bearing components.

Tools and Workshop Tips REF•9

Thread locking and sealing compounds

● Locking compounds are used in locations where the fastener is prone to loosening due to vibration or on important safety-related items which might cause loss of control of the motorcycle if they fail. It is also used where important fasteners cannot be secured by other means such as lockwashers or split pins.

● Before applying locking compound, make sure that the threads (internal and external) are clean and dry with all old compound removed. Select a compound to suit the component being secured - a non-permanent general locking and sealing type is suitable for most applications, but a high strength type is needed for permanent fixing of studs in castings. Apply a drop or two of the compound to the first few threads of the fastener, then thread it into place and tighten to the specified torque. Do not apply excessive thread locking compound otherwise the thread may be damaged on subsequent removal.

● Certain fasteners are impregnated with a dry film type coating of locking compound on their threads. Always renew this type of fastener if disturbed.

● Anti-seize compounds, such as copper-based greases, can be applied to protect threads from seizure due to extreme heat and corrosion. A common instance is spark plug threads and exhaust system fasteners.

3 Measuring tools and gauges

Feeler gauges

● Feeler gauges (or blades) are used for measuring small gaps and clearances **(see illustration 3.1)**. They can also be used to measure endfloat (sideplay) of a component on a shaft where access is not possible with a dial gauge.

● Feeler gauge sets should be treated with care and not bent or damaged. They are etched with their size on one face. Keep them clean and very lightly oiled to prevent corrosion build-up.

3.1 Feeler gauges are used for measuring small gaps and clearances - thickness is marked on one face of gauge

● When measuring a clearance, select a gauge which is a light sliding fit between the two components. You may need to use two gauges together to measure the clearance accurately.

Micrometers

● A micrometer is a precision tool capable of measuring to 0.01 or 0.001 of a millimetre. It should always be stored in its case and not in the general toolbox. It must be kept clean and never dropped, otherwise its frame or measuring anvils could be distorted resulting in inaccurate readings.

● External micrometers are used for measuring outside diameters of components and have many more applications than internal micrometers. Micrometers are available in different size ranges, eg 0 to 25 mm, 25 to 50 mm, and upwards in 25 mm steps; some large micrometers have interchangeable anvils to allow a range of measurements to be taken. Generally the largest precision measurement you are likely to take on a motorcycle is the piston diameter.

● Internal micrometers (or bore micrometers) are used for measuring inside diameters, such as valve guides and cylinder bores. Telescoping gauges and small hole gauges are used in conjunction with an external micrometer, whereas the more expensive internal micrometers have their own measuring device.

External micrometer

Note: *The conventional analogue type instrument is described. Although much easier to read, digital micrometers are considerably more expensive.*

● Always check the calibration of the micrometer before use. With the anvils closed (0 to 25 mm type) or set over a test gauge (for

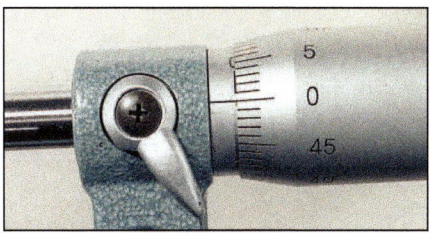

3.2 Check micrometer calibration before use

the larger types) the scale should read zero **(see illustration 3.2)**; make sure that the anvils (and test piece) are clean first. Any discrepancy can be adjusted by referring to the instructions supplied with the tool. Remember that the micrometer is a precision measuring tool - don't force the anvils closed, use the ratchet (4) on the end of the micrometer to close it. In this way, a measured force is always applied.

● To use, first make sure that the item being measured is clean. Place the anvil of the micrometer (1) against the item and use the thimble (2) to bring the spindle (3) lightly into contact with the other side of the item **(see illustration 3.3)**. Don't tighten the thimble down because this will damage the micrometer - instead use the ratchet (4) on the end of the micrometer. The ratchet mechanism applies a measured force preventing damage to the instrument.

● The micrometer is read by referring to the linear scale on the sleeve and the annular scale on the thimble. Read off the sleeve first to obtain the base measurement, then add the fine measurement from the thimble to obtain the overall reading. The linear scale on the sleeve represents the measuring range of the micrometer (eg 0 to 25 mm). The annular scale

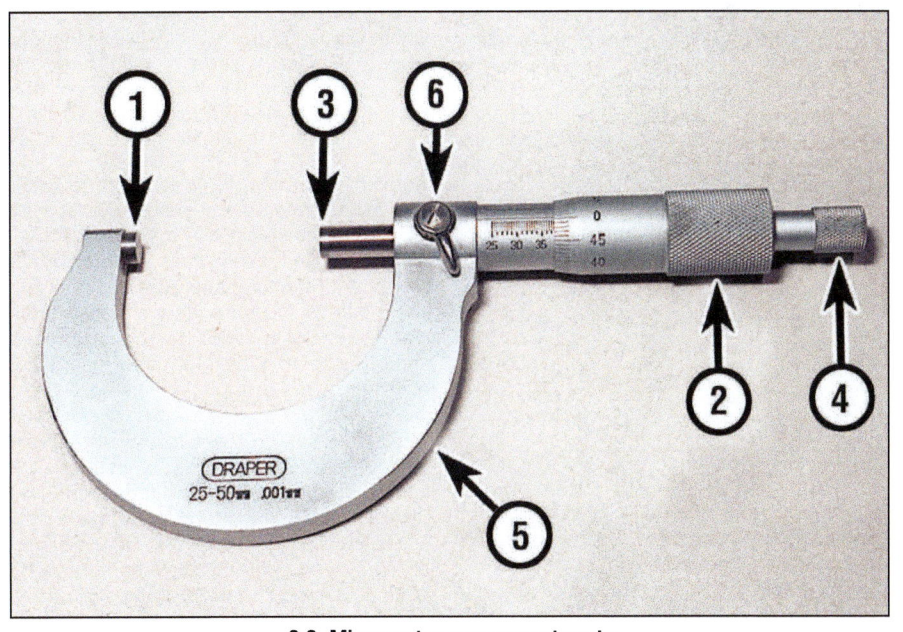

3.3 Micrometer component parts

1 Anvil	3 Spindle	5 Frame
2 Thimble	4 Ratchet	6 Locking lever

REF•10 Tools and Workshop Tips

on the thimble will be in graduations of 0.01 mm (or as marked on the frame) - one full revolution of the thimble will move 0.5 mm on the linear scale. Take the reading where the datum line on the sleeve intersects the thimble's scale. Always position the eye directly above the scale otherwise an inaccurate reading will result.

In the example shown the item measures 2.95 mm **(see illustration 3.4)**:

Linear scale	2.00 mm
Linear scale	0.50 mm
Annular scale	0.45 mm
Total figure	**2.95 mm**

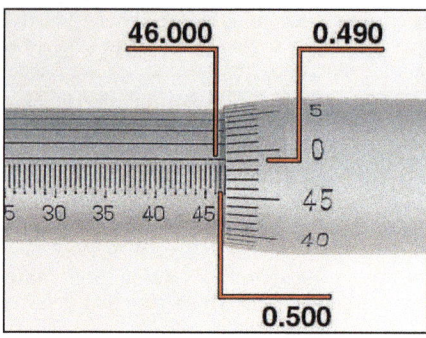

3.5 Micrometer reading of 46.99 mm on linear and annular scales...

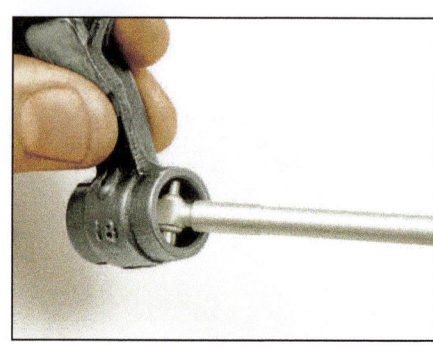

3.7 Expand the telescoping gauge in the bore, lock its position...

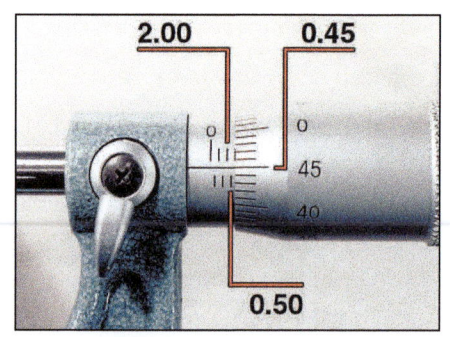

3.4 Micrometer reading of 2.95 mm

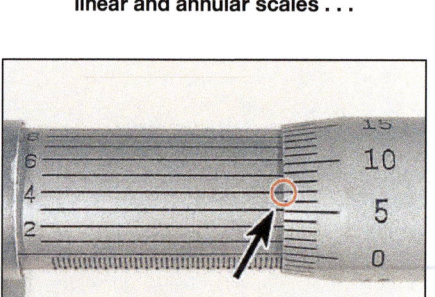

3.6 ...and 0.004 mm on vernier scale

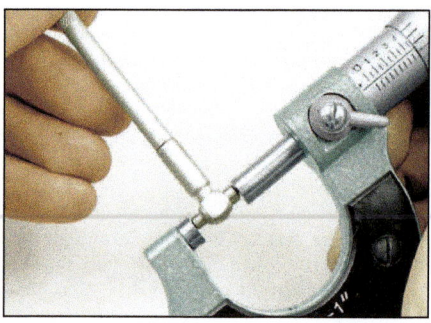

3.8 ...then measure the gauge with a micrometer

Most micrometers have a locking lever (6) on the frame to hold the setting in place, allowing the item to be removed from the micrometer.
• Some micrometers have a vernier scale on their sleeve, providing an even finer measurement to be taken, in 0.001 increments of a millimetre. Take the sleeve and thimble measurement as described above, then check which graduation on the vernier scale aligns with that of the annular scale on the thimble **Note:** *The eye must be perpendicular to the scale when taking the vernier reading - if necessary rotate the body of the micrometer to ensure this.* Multiply the vernier scale figure by 0.001 and add it to the base and fine measurement figures.

In the example shown the item measures 46.994 mm **(see illustrations 3.5 and 3.6)**:

Linear scale (base)	46.000 mm
Linear scale (base)	00.500 mm
Annular scale (fine)	00.490 mm
Vernier scale	00.004 mm
Total figure	**46.994 mm**

Internal micrometer

• Internal micrometers are available for measuring bore diameters, but are expensive and unlikely to be available for home use. It is suggested that a set of telescoping gauges and small hole gauges, both of which must be used with an external micrometer, will suffice for taking internal measurements on a motorcycle.
• Telescoping gauges can be used to measure internal diameters of components. Select a gauge with the correct size range, make sure its ends are clean and insert it into the bore. Expand the gauge, then lock its position and withdraw it from the bore **(see illustration 3.7)**. Measure across the gauge ends with a micrometer **(see illustration 3.8)**.
• Very small diameter bores (such as valve guides) are measured with a small hole gauge. Once adjusted to a slip-fit inside the component, its position is locked and the gauge withdrawn for measurement with a micrometer **(see illustrations 3.9 and 3.10)**.

Vernier caliper

Note: *The conventional linear and dial gauge type instruments are described. Digital types are easier to read, but are far more expensive.*
• The vernier caliper does not provide the precision of a micrometer, but is versatile in being able to measure internal and external diameters. Some types also incorporate a depth gauge. It is ideal for measuring clutch plate friction material and spring free lengths.
• To use the conventional linear scale vernier, slacken off the vernier clamp screws (1) and set its jaws over (2), or inside (3), the item to be measured **(see illustration 3.11)**. Slide the jaw into contact, using the thumbwheel (4) for fine movement of the sliding scale (5) then tighten the clamp screws (1). Read off the main scale (6) where the zero on the sliding scale (5) intersects it, taking the whole number to the left of the zero; this provides the base measurement. View along the sliding scale and select the division which

3.9 Expand the small hole gauge in the bore, lock its position...

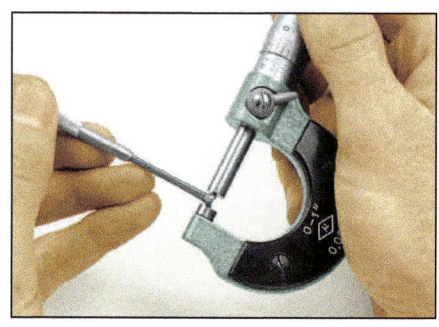

3.10 ...then measure the gauge with a micrometer

lines up exactly with any of the divisions on the main scale, noting that the divisions usually represents 0.02 of a millimetre. Add this fine measurement to the base measurement to obtain the total reading.

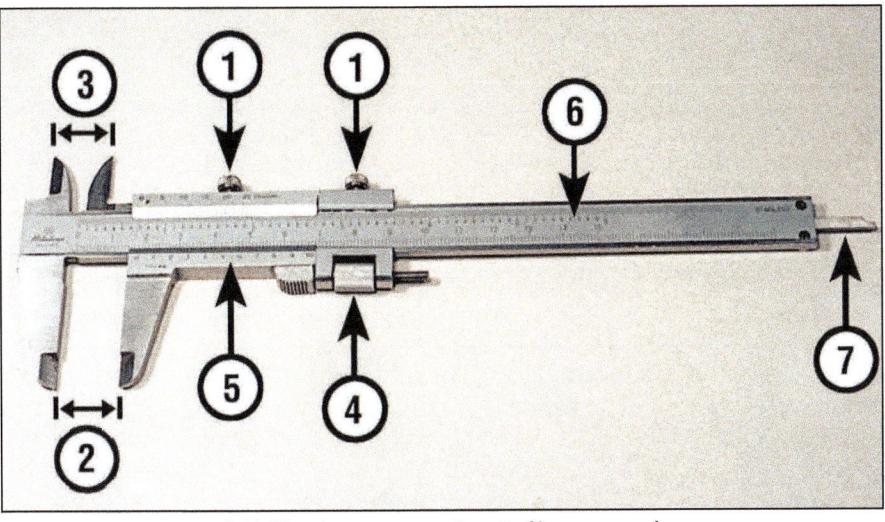

Tools and Workshop Tips REF•11

3.11 Vernier component parts (linear gauge)

1 Clamp screws
2 External jaws
3 Internal jaws
4 Thumbwheel
5 Sliding scale
6 Main scale
7 Depth gauge

In the example shown the item measures 55.92 mm **(see illustration 3.12)**:

Base measurement	55.00 mm
Fine measurement	00.92 mm
Total figure	**55.92 mm**

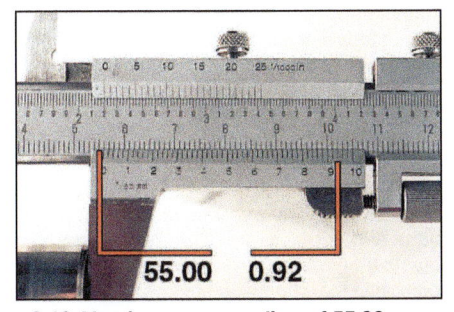

3.12 Vernier gauge reading of 55.92 mm

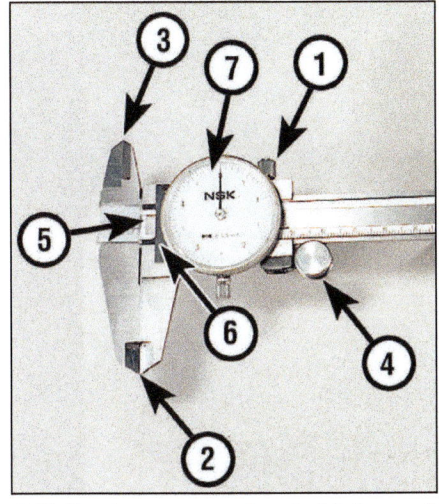

● Some vernier calipers are equipped with a dial gauge for fine measurement. Before use, check that the jaws are clean, then close them fully and check that the dial gauge reads zero. If necessary adjust the gauge ring accordingly. Slacken the vernier clamp screw (1) and set its jaws over (2), or inside (3), the item to be measured **(see illustration 3.13)**. Slide the jaws into contact, using the thumbwheel (4) for fine movement. Read off the main scale (5) where the edge of the sliding scale (6) intersects it, taking the whole number to the left of the zero; this provides the base measurement. Read off the needle position on the dial gauge (7) scale to provide the fine measurement; each division represents 0.05 of a millimetre. Add this fine measurement to the base measurement to obtain the total reading.

In the example shown the item measures 55.95 mm **(see illustration 3.14)**:

Base measurement	55.00 mm
Fine measurement	00.95 mm
Total figure	**55.95 mm**

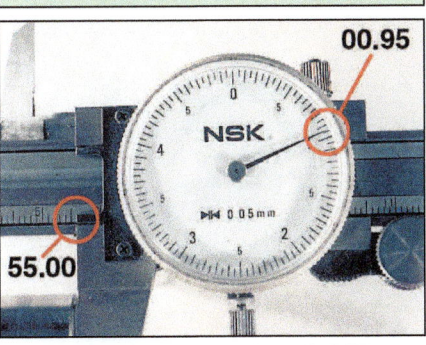

3.13 Vernier component parts (dial gauge)

1 Clamp screw
2 External jaws
3 Internal jaws
4 Thumbwheel
5 Main scale
6 Sliding scale
7 Dial gauge

3.14 Vernier gauge reading of 55.95 mm

Plastigauge

● Plastigauge is a plastic material which can be compressed between two surfaces to measure the oil clearance between them. The width of the compressed Plastigauge is measured against a calibrated scale to determine the clearance.

● Common uses of Plastigauge are for measuring the clearance between crankshaft journal and main bearing inserts, between crankshaft journal and big-end bearing inserts, and between camshaft and bearing surfaces. The following example describes big-end oil clearance measurement.

● Handle the Plastigauge material carefully to prevent distortion. Using a sharp knife, cut a length which corresponds with the width of the bearing being measured and place it carefully across the journal so that it is parallel with the shaft **(see illustration 3.15)**. Carefully install both bearing shells and the connecting rod. Without rotating the rod on the journal tighten its bolts or nuts (as applicable) to the specified torque. The connecting rod and bearings are then disassembled and the crushed Plastigauge examined.

3.15 Plastigauge placed across shaft journal

● Using the scale provided in the Plastigauge kit, measure the width of the material to determine the oil clearance **(see illustration 3.16)**. Always remove all traces of Plastigauge after use using your fingernails.

Caution: Arriving at the correct clearance demands that the assembly is torqued correctly, according to the settings and sequence (where applicable) provided by the motorcycle manufacturer.

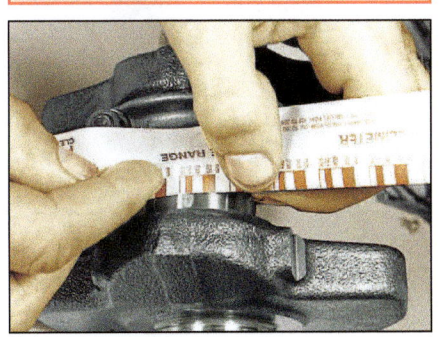

3.16 Measuring the width of the crushed Plastigauge

REF•12 Tools and Workshop Tips

Dial gauge or DTI (Dial Test Indicator)

● A dial gauge can be used to accurately measure small amounts of movement. Typical uses are measuring shaft runout or shaft endfloat (sideplay) and setting piston position for ignition timing on two-strokes. A dial gauge set usually comes with a range of different probes and adapters and mounting equipment.

● The gauge needle must point to zero when at rest. Rotate the ring around its periphery to zero the gauge.

● Check that the gauge is capable of reading the extent of movement in the work. Most gauges have a small dial set in the face which records whole millimetres of movement as well as the fine scale around the face periphery which is calibrated in 0.01 mm divisions. Read off the small dial first to obtain the base measurement, then add the measurement from the fine scale to obtain the total reading.

In the example shown the gauge reads 1.48 mm (see illustration 3.17):

Base measurement	1.00 mm
Fine measurement	0.48 mm
Total figure	**1.48 mm**

3.17 Dial gauge reading of 1.48 mm

● If measuring shaft runout, the shaft must be supported in vee-blocks and the gauge mounted on a stand perpendicular to the shaft. Rest the tip of the gauge against the centre of the shaft and rotate the shaft slowly whilst watching the gauge reading (see illustration 3.18). Take several measurements along the length of the shaft and record the maximum gauge reading as the amount of runout in the shaft. **Note:** *The reading obtained will be total runout at that point - some manufacturers specify that the runout figure is halved to compare with their specified runout limit.*

● Endfloat (sideplay) measurement requires that the gauge is mounted securely to the surrounding component with its probe touching the end of the shaft. Using hand pressure, push and pull on the shaft noting the maximum endfloat recorded on the gauge (see illustration 3.19).

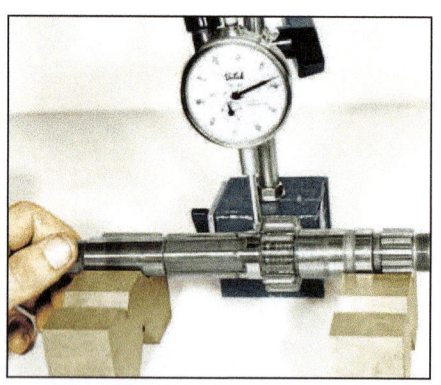

3.18 Using a dial gauge to measure shaft runout

3.19 Using a dial gauge to measure shaft endfloat

● A dial gauge with suitable adapters can be used to determine piston position BTDC on two-stroke engines for the purposes of ignition timing. The gauge, adapter and suitable length probe are installed in the place of the spark plug and the gauge zeroed at TDC. If the piston position is specified as 1.14 mm BTDC, rotate the engine back to 2.00 mm BTDC, then slowly forwards to 1.14 mm BTDC.

Cylinder compression gauges

● A compression gauge is used for measuring cylinder compression. Either the rubber-cone type or the threaded adapter type can be used. The latter is preferred to ensure a perfect seal against the cylinder head. A 0 to 300 psi (0 to 20 Bar) type gauge (for petrol/gasoline engines) will be suitable for motorcycles.

● The spark plug is removed and the gauge either held hard against the cylinder head (cone type) or the gauge adapter screwed into the cylinder head (threaded type) (see illustration 3.20). Cylinder compression is measured with the engine turning over, but not running - carry out the compression test as described in *Fault Finding Equipment*. The gauge will hold the reading until manually released.

3.20 Using a rubber-cone type cylinder compression gauge

Oil pressure gauge

● An oil pressure gauge is used for measuring engine oil pressure. Most gauges come with a set of adapters to fit the thread of the take-off point (see illustration 3.21). If the take-off point specified by the motorcycle manufacturer is an external oil pipe union, make sure that the specified replacement union is used to prevent oil starvation.

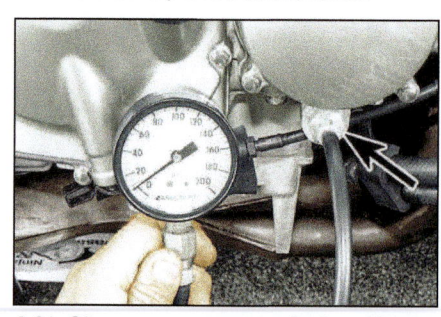

3.21 Oil pressure gauge and take-off point adapter (arrow)

● Oil pressure is measured with the engine running (at a specific rpm) and often the manufacturer will specify pressure limits for a cold and hot engine.

Straight-edge and surface plate

● If checking the gasket face of a component for warpage, place a steel rule or precision straight-edge across the gasket face and measure any gap between the straight-edge and component with feeler gauges (see illustration 3.22). Check diagonally across the component and between mounting holes (see illustration 3.23).

3.22 Use a straight-edge and feeler gauges to check for warpage

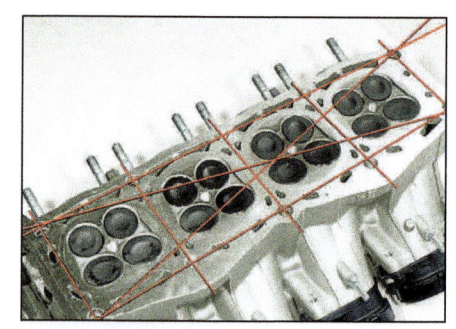

3.23 Check for warpage in these directions

Tools and Workshop Tips   REF•13

- Checking individual components for warpage, such as clutch plain (metal) plates, requires a perfectly flat plate or piece or plate glass and feeler gauges.

4 Torque and leverage

What is torque?

- Torque describes the twisting force about a shaft. The amount of torque applied is determined by the distance from the centre of the shaft to the end of the lever and the amount of force being applied to the end of the lever; distance multiplied by force equals torque.
- The manufacturer applies a measured torque to a bolt or nut to ensure that it will not slacken in use and to hold two components securely together without movement in the joint. The actual torque setting depends on the thread size, bolt or nut material and the composition of the components being held.
- Too little torque may cause the fastener to loosen due to vibration, whereas too much torque will distort the joint faces of the component or cause the fastener to shear off. Always stick to the specified torque setting.

Using a torque wrench

- Check the calibration of the torque wrench and make sure it has a suitable range for the job. Torque wrenches are available in Nm (Newton-metres), kgf m (kilograms-force metre), lbf ft (pounds-feet), lbf in (inch-pounds). Do not confuse lbf ft with lbf in.
- Adjust the tool to the desired torque on the scale (see illustration 4.1). If your torque wrench is not calibrated in the units specified, carefully convert the figure (see Conversion Factors). A manufacturer sometimes gives a torque setting as a range (8 to 10 Nm) rather than a single figure - in this case set the tool midway between the two settings. The same torque may be expressed as 9 Nm ± 1 Nm. Some torque wrenches have a method of locking the setting so that it isn't inadvertently altered during use.

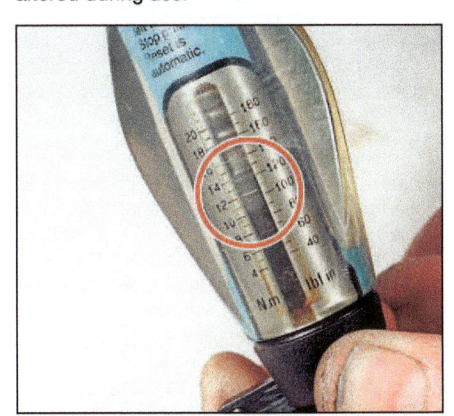

- Install the bolts/nuts in their correct location and secure them lightly. Their threads must be clean and free of any old locking compound. Unless specified the threads and flange should be dry - oiled threads are necessary in certain circumstances and the manufacturer will take this into account in the specified torque figure. Similarly, the manufacturer may also specify the application of thread-locking compound.
- Tighten the fasteners in the specified sequence until the torque wrench clicks, indicating that the torque setting has been reached. Apply the torque again to double-check the setting. Where different thread diameter fasteners secure the component, as a rule tighten the larger diameter ones first.
- When the torque wrench has been finished with, release the lock (where applicable) and fully back off its setting to zero - do not leave the torque wrench tensioned. Also, do not use a torque wrench for slackening a fastener.

Angle-tightening

- Manufacturers often specify a figure in degrees for final tightening of a fastener. This usually follows tightening to a specific torque setting.
- A degree disc can be set and attached to the socket (see illustration 4.2) or a protractor can be used to mark the angle of movement on the bolt/nut head and the surrounding casting (see illustration 4.3).

4.2 Angle tightening can be accomplished with a torque-angle gauge ...

4.3 ... or by marking the angle on the surrounding component

4.1 Set the torque wrench index mark to the setting required, in this case 12 Nm

Loosening sequences

- Where more than one bolt/nut secures a component, loosen each fastener evenly a little at a time. In this way, not all the stress of the joint is held by one fastener and the components are not likely to distort.
- If a tightening sequence is provided, work in the REVERSE of this, but if not, work from the outside in, in a criss-cross sequence (see illustration 4.4).

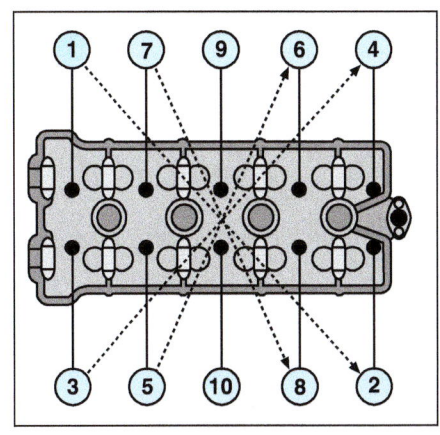

4.4 When slackening, work from the outside inwards

Tightening sequences

- If a component is held by more than one fastener it is important that the retaining bolts/nuts are tightened evenly to prevent uneven stress build-up and distortion of sealing faces. This is especially important on high-compression joints such as the cylinder head.
- A sequence is usually provided by the manufacturer, either in a diagram or actually marked in the casting. If not, always start in the centre and work outwards in a criss-cross pattern (see illustration 4.5). Start off by securing all bolts/nuts finger-tight, then set the torque wrench and tighten each fastener by a small amount in sequence until the final torque is reached. By following this practice,

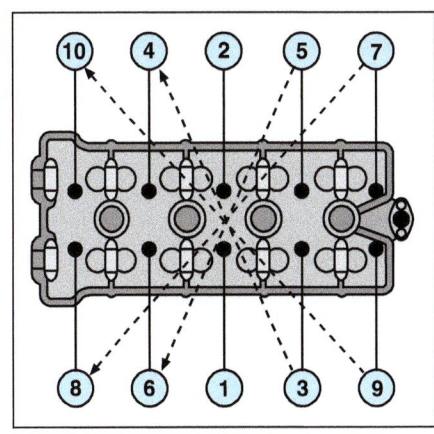

4.5 When tightening, work from the inside outwards

REF•14 Tools and Workshop Tips

the joint will be held evenly and will not be distorted. Important joints, such as the cylinder head and big-end fasteners often have two- or three-stage torque settings.

Applying leverage

● Use tools at the correct angle. Position a socket wrench or spanner on the bolt/nut so that you pull it towards you when loosening. If this can't be done, push the spanner without curling your fingers around it **(see illustration 4.6)** - the spanner may slip or the fastener loosen suddenly, resulting in your fingers being crushed against a component.

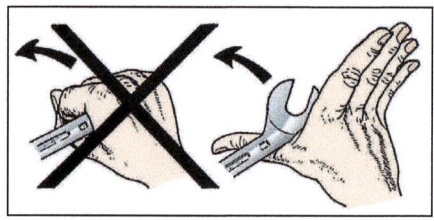

4.6 If you can't pull on the spanner to loosen a fastener, push with your hand open

● Additional leverage is gained by extending the length of the lever. The best way to do this is to use a breaker bar instead of the regular length tool, or to slip a length of tubing over the end of the spanner or socket wrench.
● If additional leverage will not work, the fastener head is either damaged or firmly corroded in place (see *Fasteners*).

5 Bearings

Bearing removal and installation

Drivers and sockets

● Before removing a bearing, always inspect the casing to see which way it must be driven out - some casings will have retaining plates or a cast step. Also check for any identifying markings on the bearing and if installed to a certain depth, measure this at this stage. Some roller bearings are sealed on one side - take note of the original fitted position.
● Bearings can be driven out of a casing using a bearing driver tool (with the correct size head) or a socket of the correct diameter. Select the driver head or socket so that it contacts the outer race of the bearing, not the balls/rollers or inner race. Always support the casing around the bearing housing with wood blocks, otherwise there is a risk of fracture. The bearing is driven out with a few blows on the driver or socket from a heavy mallet. Unless access is severely restricted (as with wheel bearings), a pin-punch is not recommended unless it is moved around the bearing to keep it square in its housing.

● The same equipment can be used to install bearings. Make sure the bearing housing is supported on wood blocks and line up the bearing in its housing. Fit the bearing as noted on removal - generally they are installed with their marked side facing outwards. Tap the bearing squarely into its housing using a driver or socket which bears only on the bearing's outer race - contact with the bearing balls/rollers or inner race will destroy it **(see illustrations 5.1 and 5.2)**.
● Check that the bearing inner race and balls/rollers rotate freely.

5.1 Using a bearing driver against the bearing's outer race

5.2 Using a large socket against the bearing's outer race

Pullers and slide-hammers

● Where a bearing is pressed on a shaft a puller will be required to extract it **(see illustration 5.3)**. Make sure that the puller clamp or legs fit securely behind the bearing and are unlikely to slip out. If pulling a bearing

5.3 This bearing puller clamps behind the bearing and pressure is applied to the shaft end to draw the bearing off

off a gear shaft for example, you may have to locate the puller behind a gear pinion if there is no access to the race and draw the gear pinion off the shaft as well **(see illustration 5.4)**.

Caution: Ensure that the puller's centre bolt locates securely against the end of the shaft and will not slip when pressure is applied. Also ensure that puller does not damage the shaft end.

5.4 Where no access is available to the rear of the bearing, it is sometimes possible to draw off the adjacent component

● Operate the puller so that its centre bolt exerts pressure on the shaft end and draws the bearing off the shaft.
● When installing the bearing on the shaft, tap only on the bearing's inner race - contact with the balls/rollers or outer race with destroy the bearing. Use a socket or length of tubing as a drift which fits over the shaft end **(see illustration 5.5)**.

5.5 When installing a bearing on a shaft use a piece of tubing which bears only on the bearing's inner race

● Where a bearing locates in a blind hole in a casing, it cannot be driven or pulled out as described above. A slide-hammer with knife-edged bearing puller attachment will be required. The puller attachment passes through the bearing and when tightened expands to fit firmly behind the bearing **(see illustration 5.6)**. By operating the slide-hammer part of the tool the bearing is jarred out of its housing **(see illustration 5.7)**.
● It is possible, if the bearing is of reasonable weight, for it to drop out of its housing if the casing is heated as described opposite. If this

Tools and Workshop Tips REF•15

5.6 Expand the bearing puller so that it locks behind the bearing . . .

5.7 . . . attach the slide hammer to the bearing puller

method is attempted, first prepare a work surface which will enable the casing to be tapped face down to help dislodge the bearing - a wood surface is ideal since it will not damage the casing's gasket surface. Wearing protective gloves, tap the heated casing several times against the work surface to dislodge the bearing under its own weight **(see illustration 5.8)**.

5.8 Tapping a casing face down on wood blocks can often dislodge a bearing

- Bearings can be installed in blind holes using the driver or socket method described above.

Drawbolts

- Where a bearing or bush is set in the eye of a component, such as a suspension linkage arm or connecting rod small-end, removal by drift may damage the component. Furthermore, a rubber bushing in a shock absorber eye cannot successfully be driven out of position. If access is available to a engineering press, the task is straightforward. If not, a drawbolt can be fabricated to extract the bearing or bush.

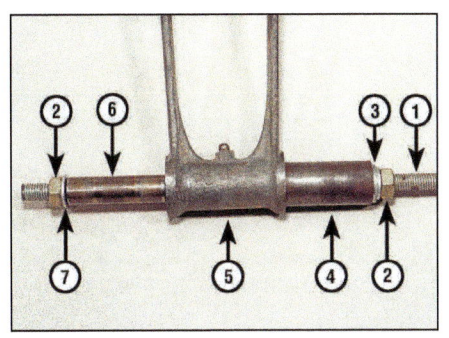

5.9 Drawbolt component parts assembled on a suspension arm

1. Bolt or length of threaded bar
2. Nuts
3. Washer (external diameter greater than tubing internal diameter)
4. Tubing (internal diameter sufficient to accommodate bearing)
5. Suspension arm with bearing
6. Tubing (external diameter slightly smaller than bearing)
7. Washer (external diameter slightly smaller than bearing)

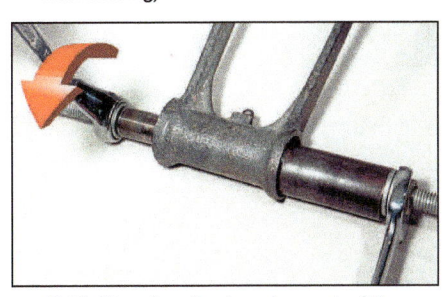

5.10 Drawing the bearing out of the suspension arm

- To extract the bearing/bush you will need a long bolt with nut (or piece of threaded bar with two nuts), a piece of tubing which has an internal diameter larger than the bearing/bush, another piece of tubing which has an external diameter slightly smaller than the bearing/bush, and a selection of washers **(see illustrations 5.9 and 5.10)**. Note that the pieces of tubing must be of the same length, or longer, than the bearing/bush.
- The same kit (without the pieces of tubing) can be used to draw the new bearing/bush back into place **(see illustration 5.11)**.

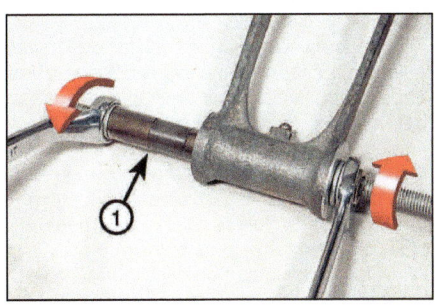

5.11 Installing a new bearing (1) in the suspension arm

Temperature change

- If the bearing's outer race is a tight fit in the casing, the aluminium casing can be heated to release its grip on the bearing. Aluminium will expand at a greater rate than the steel bearing outer race. There are several ways to do this, but avoid any localised extreme heat (such as a blow torch) - aluminium alloy has a low melting point.
- Approved methods of heating a casing are using a domestic oven (heated to 100°C) or immersing the casing in boiling water **(see illustration 5.12)**. Low temperature range localised heat sources such as a paint stripper heat gun or clothes iron can also be used **(see illustration 5.13)**. Alternatively, soak a rag in boiling water, wring it out and wrap it around the bearing housing.

> ⚠️ **Warning:** *All of these methods require care in use to prevent scalding and burns to the hands. Wear protective gloves when handling hot components.*

5.12 A casing can be immersed in a sink of boiling water to aid bearing removal

5.13 Using a localised heat source to aid bearing removal

- If heating the whole casing note that plastic components, such as the neutral switch, may suffer - remove them beforehand.
- After heating, remove the bearing as described above. You may find that the expansion is sufficient for the bearing to fall out of the casing under its own weight or with a light tap on the driver or socket.
- If necessary, the casing can be heated to aid bearing installation, and this is sometimes the recommended procedure if the motorcycle manufacturer has designed the housing and bearing fit with this intention.

REF•16 Tools and Workshop Tips

● Installation of bearings can be eased by placing them in a freezer the night before installation. The steel bearing will contract slightly, allowing easy insertion in its housing. This is often useful when installing steering head outer races in the frame.

Bearing types and markings

● Plain shell bearings, ball bearings, needle roller bearings and tapered roller bearings will all be found on motorcycles **(see illustrations 5.14 and 5.15)**. The ball and roller types are usually caged between an inner and outer race, but uncaged variations may be found.

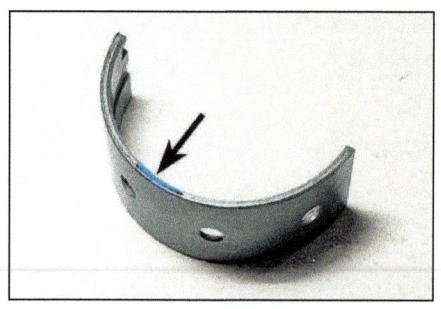

5.14 Shell bearings are either plain or grooved. They are usually identified by colour code (arrow)

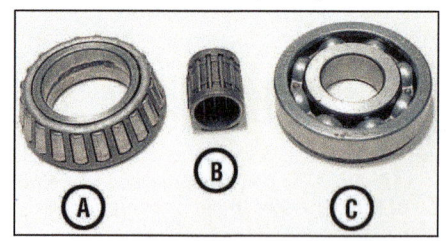

5.15 Tapered roller bearing (A), needle roller bearing (B) and ball journal bearing (C)

● Shell bearings (often called inserts) are usually found at the crankshaft main and connecting rod big-end where they are good at coping with high loads. They are made of a phosphor-bronze material and are impregnated with self-lubricating properties.
● Ball bearings and needle roller bearings consist of a steel inner and outer race with the balls or rollers between the races. They require constant lubrication by oil or grease and are good at coping with axial loads. Taper roller bearings consist of rollers set in a tapered cage set on the inner race; the outer race is separate. They are good at coping with axial loads and prevent movement along the shaft - a typical application is in the steering head.
● Bearing manufacturers produce bearings to ISO size standards and stamp one face of the bearing to indicate its internal and external diameter, load capacity and type **(see illustration 5.16)**.
● Metal bushes are usually of phosphor-bronze material. Rubber bushes are used in suspension mounting eyes. Fibre bushes have also been used in suspension pivots.

5.16 Typical bearing marking

Bearing fault finding

● If a bearing outer race has spun in its housing, the housing material will be damaged. You can use a bearing locking compound to bond the outer race in place if damage is not too severe.
● Shell bearings will fail due to damage of their working surface, as a result of lack of lubrication, corrosion or abrasive particles in the oil **(see illustration 5.17)**. Small particles of dirt in the oil may embed in the bearing material whereas larger particles will score the bearing and shaft journal. If a number of short journeys are made, insufficient heat will be generated to drive off condensation which has built up on the bearings.

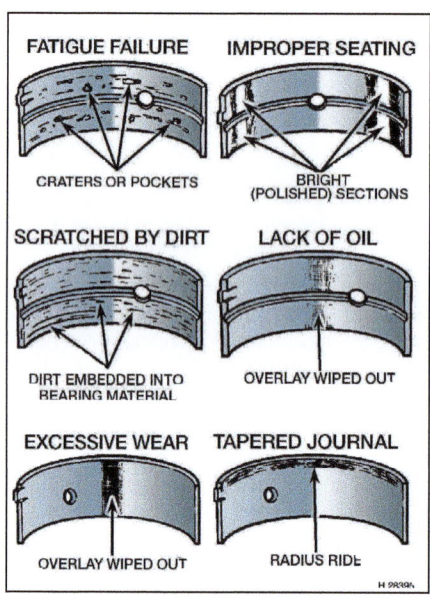

5.17 Typical bearing failures

● Ball and roller bearings will fail due to lack of lubrication or damage to the balls or rollers. Tapered-roller bearings can be damaged by overloading them. Unless the bearing is sealed on both sides, wash it in paraffin (kerosene) to remove all old grease then allow it to dry. Make a visual inspection looking to dented balls or rollers, damaged cages and worn or pitted races **(see illustration 5.18)**.
● A ball bearing can be checked for wear by listening to it when spun. Apply a film of light oil to the bearing and hold it close to the ear - hold the outer race with one hand and spin the inner race with the other hand **(see illustration 5.19)**. The bearing should be almost silent when spun; if it grates or rattles it is worn.

5.18 Example of ball journal bearing with damaged balls and cages

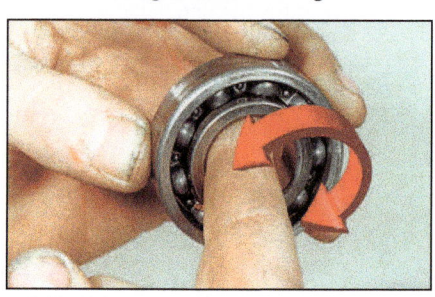

5.19 Hold outer race and listen to inner race when spun

6 Oil seals

Oil seal removal and installation

● Oil seals should be renewed every time a component is dismantled. This is because the seal lips will become set to the sealing surface and will not necessarily reseal.
● Oil seals can be prised out of position using a large flat-bladed screwdriver **(see illustration 6.1)**. In the case of crankcase seals, check first that the seal is not lipped on the inside, preventing its removal with the crankcases joined.

6.1 Prise out oil seals with a large flat-bladed screwdriver

● New seals are usually installed with their marked face (containing the seal reference code) outwards and the spring side towards the fluid being retained. In certain cases, such as a two-stroke engine crankshaft seal, a double lipped seal may be used due to there being fluid or gas on each side of the joint.

Tools and Workshop Tips

- Use a bearing driver or socket which bears only on the outer hard edge of the seal to install it in the casing - tapping on the inner edge will damage the sealing lip.

Oil seal types and markings

- Oil seals are usually of the single-lipped type. Double-lipped seals are found where a liquid or gas is on both sides of the joint.
- Oil seals can harden and lose their sealing ability if the motorcycle has been in storage for a long period - renewal is the only solution.
- Oil seal manufacturers also conform to the ISO markings for seal size - these are moulded into the outer face of the seal (see illustration 6.2).

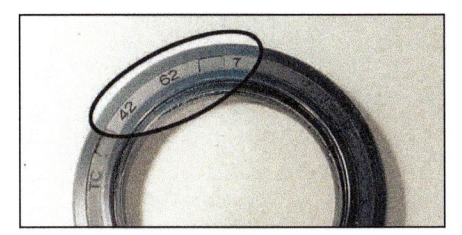

6.2 These oil seal markings indicate inside diameter, outside diameter and seal thickness

7 Gaskets and sealants

Types of gasket and sealant

- Gaskets are used to seal the mating surfaces between components and keep lubricants, fluids, vacuum or pressure contained within the assembly. Aluminium gaskets are sometimes found at the cylinder joints, but most gaskets are paper-based. If the mating surfaces of the components being joined are undamaged the gasket can be installed dry, although a dab of sealant or grease will be useful to hold it in place during assembly.
- RTV (Room Temperature Vulcanising) silicone rubber sealants cure when exposed to moisture in the atmosphere. These sealants are good at filling pits or irregular gasket faces, but will tend to be forced out of the joint under very high torque. They can be used to replace a paper gasket, but first make sure that the width of the paper gasket is not essential to the shimming of internal components. RTV sealants should not be used on components containing petrol (gasoline).
- Non-hardening, semi-hardening and hard setting liquid gasket compounds can be used with a gasket or between a metal-to-metal joint. Select the sealant to suit the application: universal non-hardening sealant can be used on virtually all joints; semi-hardening on joint faces which are rough or damaged; hard setting sealant on joints which require a permanent bond and are subjected to high temperature and pressure. **Note:** *Check first if the paper gasket has a bead of sealant impregnated in its surface before applying additional sealant.*

- When choosing a sealant, make sure it is suitable for the application, particularly if being applied in a high-temperature area or in the vicinity of fuel. Certain manufacturers produce sealants in either clear, silver or black colours to match the finish of the engine. This has a particular application on motorcycles where much of the engine is exposed.
- Do not over-apply sealant. That which is squeezed out on the outside of the joint can be wiped off, whereas an excess of sealant on the inside can break off and clog oilways.

Breaking a sealed joint

- Age, heat, pressure and the use of hard setting sealant can cause two components to stick together so tightly that they are difficult to separate using finger pressure alone. Do not resort to using levers unless there is a pry point provided for this purpose (see illustration 7.1) or else the gasket surfaces will be damaged.
- Use a soft-faced hammer (see illustration 7.2) or a wood block and conventional hammer to strike the component near the mating surface. Avoid hammering against cast extremities since they may break off. If this method fails, try using a wood wedge between the two components.

Caution: If the joint will not separate, double-check that you have removed all the fasteners.

7.1 If a pry point is provided, apply gently pressure with a flat-bladed screwdriver

7.2 Tap around the joint with a soft-faced mallet if necessary - don't strike cooling fins

Removal of old gasket and sealant

- Paper gaskets will most likely come away complete, leaving only a few traces stuck on

HAYNES HINT

Most components have one or two hollow locating dowels between the two gasket faces. If a dowel cannot be removed, do not resort to gripping it with pliers - it will almost certainly be distorted. Install a close-fitting socket or Phillips screwdriver into the dowel and then grip the outer edge of the dowel to free it.

the sealing faces of the components. It is imperative that all traces are removed to ensure correct sealing of the new gasket.

- Very carefully scrape all traces of gasket away making sure that the sealing surfaces are not gouged or scored by the scraper (see illustrations 7.3, 7.4 and 7.5). Stubborn deposits can be removed by spraying with an aerosol gasket remover. Final preparation of

7.3 Paper gaskets can be scraped off with a gasket scraper tool . . .

7.4 . . . a knife blade . . .

7.5 . . . or a household scraper

REF•18 Tools and Workshop Tips

7.6 Fine abrasive paper is wrapped around a flat file to clean up the gasket face

7.7 A kitchen scourer can be used on stubborn deposits

8.1 Tighten the chain breaker to push the pin out of the link . . .

8.2 . . . withdraw the pin, remove the tool . . .

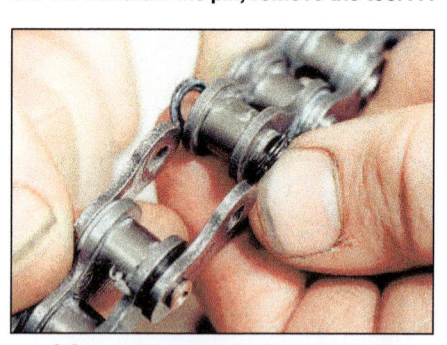

8.3 . . . and separate the chain link

8.4 Insert the new soft link, with O-rings, through the chain ends . . .

8.5 . . . install the O-rings over the pin ends . . .

8.6 . . . followed by the sideplate

8.7 Push the sideplate into position using a clamp

the gasket surface can be made with very fine abrasive paper or a plastic kitchen scourer **(see illustrations 7.6 and 7.7)**.
● Old sealant can be scraped or peeled off components, depending on the type originally used. Note that gasket removal compounds are available to avoid scraping the components clean; make sure the gasket remover suits the type of sealant used.

8 Chains

Breaking and joining final drive chains

● Drive chains for all but small bikes are continuous and do not have a clip-type connecting link. The chain must be broken using a chain breaker tool and the new chain securely riveted together using a new soft rivet-type link. Never use a clip-type connecting link instead of a rivet-type link, except in an emergency. Various chain breaking and riveting tools are available, either as separate tools or combined as illustrated in the accompanying photographs - read the instructions supplied with the tool carefully.

> **Warning: The need to rivet the new link pins correctly cannot be overstressed - loss of control of the motorcycle is very likely to result if the chain breaks in use.**

● Rotate the chain and look for the soft link. The soft link pins look like they have been deeply centre-punched instead of peened over like all the other pins **(see illustration 8.9)** and its sideplate may be a different colour. Position the soft link midway between the sprockets and assemble the chain breaker tool over one of the soft link pins **(see illustration 8.1)**. Operate the tool to push the pin out through the chain **(see illustration 8.2)**. On an O-ring chain, remove the O-rings **(see illustration 8.3)**. Carry out the same procedure on the other soft link pin.

> **Caution: Certain soft link pins (particularly on the larger chains) may require their ends to be filed or ground off before they can be pressed out using the tool.**

● Check that you have the correct size and strength (standard or heavy duty) new soft link - do not reuse the old link. Look for the size marking on the chain sideplates **(see illustration 8.10)**.
● Position the chain ends so that they are engaged over the rear sprocket. On an O-ring chain, install a new O-ring over each pin of the link and insert the link through the two chain ends **(see illustration 8.4)**. Install a new O-ring over the end of each pin, followed by the sideplate (with the chain manufacturer's marking facing outwards) **(see illustrations 8.5 and 8.6)**. On an unsealed chain, insert the link through the two chain ends, then install the sideplate with the chain manufacturer's marking facing outwards.
● Note that it may not be possible to install the sideplate using finger pressure alone. If using a joining tool, assemble it so that the plates of the tool clamp the link and press the sideplate over the pins **(see illustration 8.7)**. Otherwise, use two small sockets placed over

Tools and Workshop Tips   REF•19

8.8 Assemble the chain riveting tool over one pin at a time and tighten it fully

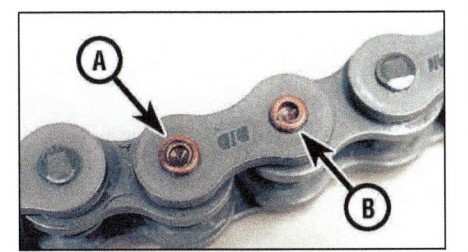

8.9 Pin end correctly riveted (A), pin end unriveted (B)

the rivet ends and two pieces of the wood between a G-clamp. Operate the clamp to press the sideplate over the pins.
● Assemble the joining tool over one pin (following the maker's instructions) and tighten the tool down to spread the pin end securely **(see illustrations 8.8 and 8.9)**. Do the same on the other pin.

> **Warning:** Check that the pin ends are secure and that there is no danger of the sideplate coming loose. If the pin ends are cracked the soft link must be renewed.

Final drive chain sizing

● Chains are sized using a three digit number, followed by a suffix to denote the chain type **(see illustration 8.10)**. Chain type is either standard or heavy duty (thicker sideplates), and also unsealed or O-ring/X-ring type.
● The first digit of the number relates to the pitch of the chain, ie the distance from the centre of one pin to the centre of the next pin **(see illustration 8.11)**. Pitch is expressed in eighths of an inch, as follows:

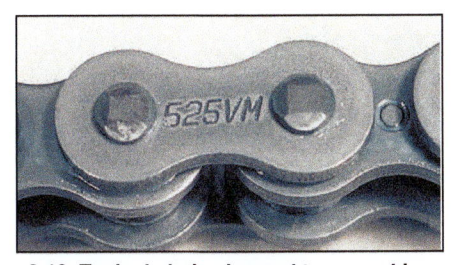

8.10 Typical chain size and type marking

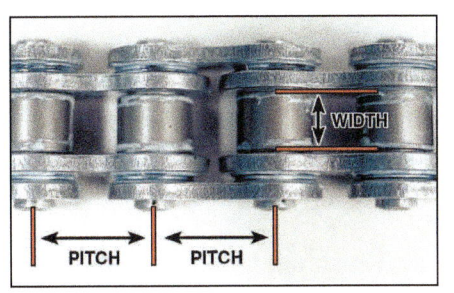

8.11 Chain dimensions

Sizes commencing with a 4 (eg 428) have a pitch of 1/2 inch (12.7 mm)

Sizes commencing with a 5 (eg 520) have a pitch of 5/8 inch (15.9 mm)

Sizes commencing with a 6 (eg 630) have a pitch of 3/4 inch (19.1 mm)

● The second and third digits of the chain size relate to the width of the rollers, again in imperial units, eg the 525 shown has 5/16 inch (7.94 mm) rollers **(see illustration 8.11)**.

9 Hoses

Clamping to prevent flow

● Small-bore flexible hoses can be clamped to prevent fluid flow whilst a component is worked on. Whichever method is used, ensure that the hose material is not permanently distorted or damaged by the clamp.
a) A brake hose clamp available from auto accessory shops **(see illustration 9.1)**.
b) A wingnut type hose clamp **(see illustration 9.2)**.
c) Two sockets placed each side of the hose and held with straight-jawed self-locking grips **(see illustration 9.3)**.
d) Thick card each side of the hose held between straight-jawed self-locking grips **(see illustration 9.4)**.

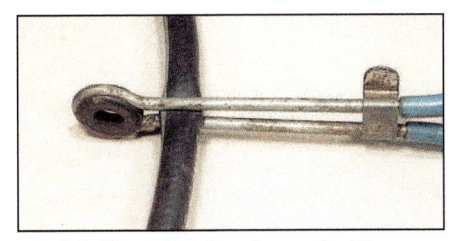

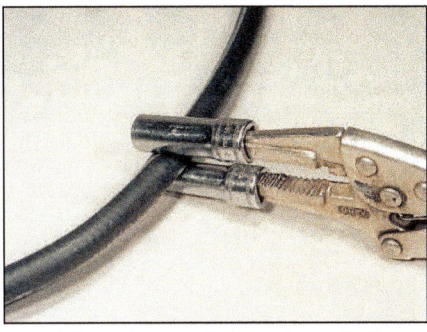

9.1 Hoses can be clamped with an automotive brake hose clamp . . .

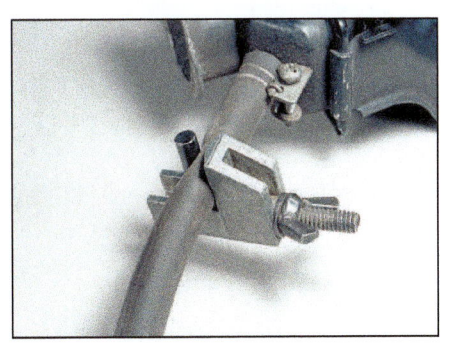

9.2 . . . a wingnut type hose clamp . . .

9.3 . . . two sockets and a pair of self-locking grips . . .

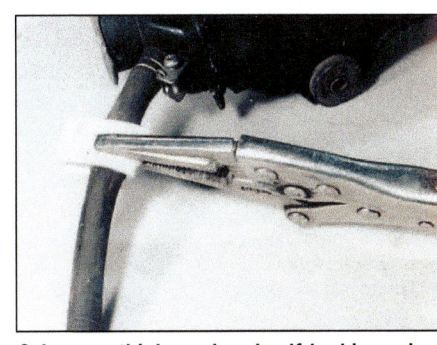

9.4 . . . or thick card and self-locking grips

Freeing and fitting hoses

● Always make sure the hose clamp is moved well clear of the hose end. Grip the hose with your hand and rotate it whilst pulling it off the union. If the hose has hardened due to age and will not move, slit it with a sharp knife and peel its ends off the union **(see illustration 9.5)**.
● Resist the temptation to use grease or soap on the unions to aid installation; although it helps the hose slip over the union it will equally aid the escape of fluid from the joint. It is preferable to soften the hose ends in hot water and wet the inside surface of the hose with water or a fluid which will evaporate.

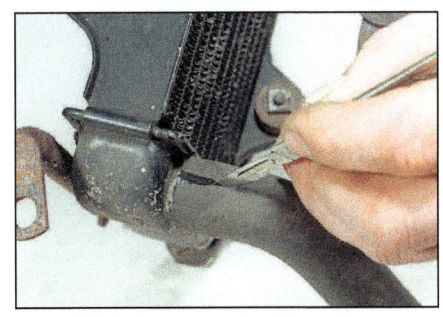

9.5 Cutting a coolant hose free with a sharp knife

Conversion Factors

Length (distance)

Inches (in)	x 25.4	= Millimetres (mm)	x 0.0394	=	Inches (in)
Feet (ft)	x 0.305	= Metres (m)	x 3.281	=	Feet (ft)
Miles	x 1.609	= Kilometres (km)	x 0.621	=	Miles

Volume (capacity)

Cubic inches (cu in; in³)	x 16.387	= Cubic centimetres (cc; cm³)	x 0.061	=	Cubic inches (cu in; in³)
Imperial pints (Imp pt)	x 0.568	= Litres (l)	x 1.76	=	Imperial pints (Imp pt)
Imperial quarts (Imp qt)	x 1.137	= Litres (l)	x 0.88	=	Imperial quarts (Imp qt)
Imperial quarts (Imp qt)	x 1.201	= US quarts (US qt)	x 0.833	=	Imperial quarts (Imp qt)
US quarts (US qt)	x 0.946	= Litres (l)	x 1.057	=	US quarts (US qt)
Imperial gallons (Imp gal)	x 4.546	= Litres (l)	x 0.22	=	Imperial gallons (Imp gal)
Imperial gallons (Imp gal)	x 1.201	= US gallons (US gal)	x 0.833	=	Imperial gallons (Imp gal)
US gallons (US gal)	x 3.785	= Litres (l)	x 0.264	=	US gallons (US gal)

Mass (weight)

Ounces (oz)	x 28.35	= Grams (g)	x 0.035	=	Ounces (oz)
Pounds (lb)	x 0.454	= Kilograms (kg)	x 2.205	=	Pounds (lb)

Force

Ounces-force (ozf; oz)	x 0.278	= Newtons (N)	x 3.6	=	Ounces-force (ozf; oz)
Pounds-force (lbf; lb)	x 4.448	= Newtons (N)	x 0.225	=	Pounds-force (lbf; lb)
Newtons (N)	x 0.1	= Kilograms-force (kgf; kg)	x 9.81	=	Newtons (N)

Pressure

Pounds-force per square inch (psi; lbf/in²; lb/in²)	x 0.070	= Kilograms-force per square centimetre (kgf/cm²; kg/cm²)	x 14.223	=	Pounds-force per square inch (psi; lbf/in²; lb/in²)
Pounds-force per square inch (psi; lbf/in²; lb/in²)	x 0.068	= Atmospheres (atm)	x 14.696	=	Pounds-force per square inch (psi; lbf/in²; lb/in²)
Pounds-force per square inch (psi; lbf/in²; lb/in²)	x 0.069	= Bars	x 14.5	=	Pounds-force per square inch (psi; lbf/in²; lb/in²)
Pounds-force per square inch (psi; lbf/in²; lb/in²)	x 6.895	= Kilopascals (kPa)	x 0.145	=	Pounds-force per square inch (psi; lbf/in²; lb/in²)
Kilopascals (kPa)	x 0.01	= Kilograms-force per square centimetre (kgf/cm²; kg/cm²)	x 98.1	=	Kilopascals (kPa)
Millibar (mbar)	x 100	= Pascals (Pa)	x 0.01	=	Millibar (mbar)
Millibar (mbar)	x 0.0145	= Pounds-force per square inch (psi; lbf/in²; lb/in²)	x 68.947	=	Millibar (mbar)
Millibar (mbar)	x 0.75	= Millimetres of mercury (mmHg)	x 1.333	=	Millibar (mbar)
Millibar (mbar)	x 0.401	= Inches of water (inH$_2$O)	x 2.491	=	Millibar (mbar)
Millimetres of mercury (mmHg)	x 0.535	= Inches of water (inH$_2$O)	x 1.868	=	Millimetres of mercury (mmHg)
Inches of water (inH$_2$O)	x 0.036	= Pounds-force per square inch (psi; lbf/in²; lb/in²)	x 27.68	=	Inches of water (inH$_2$O)

Torque (moment of force)

Pounds-force inches (lbf in; lb in)	x 1.152	= Kilograms-force centimetre (kgf cm; kg cm)	x 0.868	=	Pounds-force inches (lbf in; lb in)
Pounds-force inches (lbf in; lb in)	x 0.113	= Newton metres (Nm)	x 8.85	=	Pounds-force inches (lbf in; lb in)
Pounds-force inches (lbf in; lb in)	x 0.083	= Pounds-force feet (lbf ft; lb ft)	x 12	=	Pounds-force inches (lbf in; lb in)
Pounds-force feet (lbf ft; lb ft)	x 0.138	= Kilograms-force metres (kgf m; kg m)	x 7.233	=	Pounds-force feet (lbf ft; lb ft)
Pounds-force feet (lbf ft; lb ft)	x 1.356	= Newton metres (Nm)	x 0.738	=	Pounds-force feet (lbf ft; lb ft)
Newton metres (Nm)	x 0.102	= Kilograms-force metres (kgf m; kg m)	x 9.804	=	Newton metres (Nm)

Power

Horsepower (hp)	x 745.7	= Watts (W)	x 0.0013	=	Horsepower (hp)

Velocity (speed)

Miles per hour (miles/hr; mph)	x 1.609	= Kilometres per hour (km/hr; kph)	x 0.621	=	Miles per hour (miles/hr; mph)

Fuel consumption*

Miles per gallon (mpg)	x 0.354	= Kilometres per litre (km/l)	x 2.825	=	Miles per gallon (mpg)

Temperature

Degrees Fahrenheit = (°C x 1.8) + 32   Degrees Celsius (Degrees Centigrade; °C) = (°F - 32) x 0.56

It is common practice to convert from miles per gallon (mpg) to litres/100 kilometres (l/100km), where mpg x l/100 km = 282

Motorcycle chemicals and lubricants

A number of chemicals and lubricants are available for use in motorcycle maintenance and repair. They include a wide variety of products ranging from cleaning solvents and degreasers to lubricants and protective sprays for rubber, plastic and vinyl.

- **Contact point/spark plug cleaner** is a solvent used to clean oily film and dirt from points, grime from electrical connectors and oil deposits from spark plugs. It is oil free and leaves no residue. It can also be used to remove gum and varnish from carburettor jets and other orifices.

- **Carburettor cleaner** is similar to contact point/spark plug cleaner but it usually has a stronger solvent and may leave a slight oily reside. It is not recommended for cleaning electrical components or connections.

- **Brake system cleaner** is used to remove grease or brake fluid from brake system components (where clean surfaces are absolutely necessary and petroleum-based solvents cannot be used); it also leaves no residue.

- **Silicone-based lubricants** are used to protect rubber parts such as hoses and grommets, and are used as lubricants for hinges and locks.

- **Multi-purpose grease** is an all purpose lubricant used wherever grease is more practical than a liquid lubricant such as oil. Some multi-purpose grease is coloured white and specially formulated to be more resistant to water than ordinary grease.

- **Gear oil** (sometimes called gear lube) is a specially designed oil used in transmissions and final drive units, as well as other areas where high friction, high temperature lubrication is required. It is available in a number of viscosities (weights) for various applications.

- **Motor oil**, of course, is the lubricant specially formulated for use in the engine. It normally contains a wide variety of additives to prevent corrosion and reduce foaming and wear. Motor oil comes in various weights (viscosity ratings) of from 5 to 80. The recommended weight of the oil depends on the seasonal temperature and the demands on the engine. Light oil is used in cold climates and under light load conditions; heavy oil is used in hot climates and where high loads are encountered. Multi-viscosity oils are designed to have characteristics of both light and heavy oils and are available in a number of weights from 5W-20 to 20W-50.

- **Petrol additives** perform several functions, depending on their chemical makeup. They usually contain solvents that help dissolve gum and varnish that build up on carburettor and inlet parts. They also serve to break down carbon deposits that form on the inside surfaces of the combustion chambers. Some additives contain upper cylinder lubricants for valves and piston rings.

- **Brake and clutch fluid** is a specially formulated hydraulic fluid that can withstand the heat and pressure encountered in brake/clutch systems. Care must be taken that this fluid does not come in contact with painted surfaces or plastics. An opened container should always be resealed to prevent contamination by water or dirt.

- **Chain lubricants** are formulated especially for use on motorcycle final drive chains. A good chain lube should adhere well and have good penetrating qualities to be effective as a lubricant inside the chain and on the side plates, pins and rollers. Most chain lubes are either the foaming type or quick drying type and are usually marketed as sprays. Take care to use a lubricant marked as being suitable for O-ring chains.

- **Degreasers** are heavy duty solvents used to remove grease and grime that may accumulate on engine and frame components. They can be sprayed or brushed on and, depending on the type, are rinsed with either water or solvent.

- **Solvents** are used alone or in combination with degreasers to clean parts and assemblies during repair and overhaul. The home mechanic should use only solvents that are non-flammable and that do not produce irritating fumes.

- **Gasket sealing compounds** may be used in conjunction with gaskets, to improve their sealing capabilities, or alone, to seal metal-to-metal joints. Many gasket sealers can withstand extreme heat, some are impervious to petrol and lubricants, while others are capable of filling and sealing large cavities. Depending on the intended use, gasket sealers either dry hard or stay relatively soft and pliable. They are usually applied by hand, with a brush, or are sprayed on the gasket sealing surfaces.

- **Thread locking compound** is an adhesive locking compound that prevents threaded fasteners from loosening because of vibration. It is available in a variety of types for different applications.

- **Moisture dispersants** are usually sprays that can be used to dry out electrical components such as the fuse block and wiring connectors. Some types can also be used as treatment for rubber and as a lubricant for hinges, cables and locks.

- **Waxes and polishes** are used to help protect painted and plated surfaces from the weather. Different types of paint may require the use of different types of wax polish. Some polishes utilise a chemical or abrasive cleaner to help remove the top layer of oxidised (dull) paint on older vehicles. In recent years, many non-wax polishes (that contain a wide variety of chemicals such as polymers and silicones) have been introduced. These non-wax polishes are usually easier to apply and last longer than conventional waxes and polishes.

REF•22 MOT Test Checks

About the MOT Test

In the UK, all vehicles more than three years old are subject to an annual test to ensure that they meet minimum safety requirements. A current test certificate must be issued before a machine can be used on public roads, and is required before a road fund licence can be issued. Riding without a current test certificate will also invalidate your insurance.

For most owners, the MOT test is an annual cause for anxiety, and this is largely due to owners not being sure what needs to be checked prior to submitting the motorcycle for testing. The simple answer is that a fully roadworthy motorcycle will have no difficulty in passing the test.

This is a guide to getting your motorcycle through the MOT test. Obviously it will not be possible to examine the motorcycle to the same standard as the professional MOT tester, particularly in view of the equipment required for some of the checks. However, working through the following procedures will enable you to identify any problem areas before submitting the motorcycle for the test.

It has only been possible to summarise the test requirements here, based on the regulations in force at the time of printing. Test standards are becoming increasingly stringent, although there are some exemptions for older vehicles. More information about the MOT test can be obtained from the TSO publications, *How Safe is your Motorcycle* and *The MOT Inspection Manual for Motorcycle Testing*.

Many of the checks require that one of the wheels is raised off the ground. If the motorcycle doesn't have a centre stand, note that an auxiliary stand will be required. Additionally, the help of an assistant may prove useful.

Certain exceptions apply to machines under 50 cc, machines without a lighting system, and Classic bikes - if in doubt about any of the requirements listed below seek confirmation from an MOT tester prior to submitting the motorcycle for the test.

Check that the frame number is clearly visible.

> **HAYNES HINT** *If a component is in borderline condition, the tester has discretion in deciding whether to pass or fail it. If the motorcycle presented is clean and evidently well cared for, the tester may be more inclined to pass a borderline component than if the motorcycle is scruffy and apparently neglected.*

Electrical System

Lights, turn signals, horn and reflector

✔ With the ignition on, check the operation of the following electrical components. **Note:** *The electrical components on certain small-capacity machines are powered by the generator, requiring that the engine is run for this check.*

a) *Headlight and tail light. Check that both illuminate in the low and high beam switch positions.*
b) *Position lights. Check that the front position (or sidelight) and tail light illuminate in this switch position.*
c) *Turn signals. Check that all flash at the correct rate, and that the warning light(s) function correctly. Check that the turn signal switch works correctly.*
d) *Hazard warning system (where fitted). Check that all four turn signals flash in this switch position.*
e) *Brake stop light. Check that the light comes on when the front and rear brakes are independently applied. Models first used on or after 1st April 1986 must have a brake light switch on each brake.*
f) *Horn. Check that the sound is continuous and of reasonable volume.*

✔ Check that there is a red reflector on the rear of the machine, either mounted separately or as part of the tail light lens.

✔ Check the condition of the headlight, tail light and turn signal lenses.

Headlight beam height

✔ The MOT tester will perform a headlight beam height check using specialised beam setting equipment **(see illustration 1)**. This equipment will not be available to the home mechanic, but if you suspect that the headlight is incorrectly set or may have been maladjusted in the past, you can perform a rough test as follows.

✔ Position the bike in a straight line facing a brick wall. The bike must be off its stand, upright and with a rider seated. Measure the height from the ground to the centre of the headlight and mark a horizontal line on the wall at this height. Position the motorcycle 3.8 metres from the wall and draw a vertical line up the wall central to the centreline of the motorcycle. Switch to dipped beam and check that the beam pattern falls slightly lower than the horizontal line and to the left of the vertical line **(see illustration 2)**.

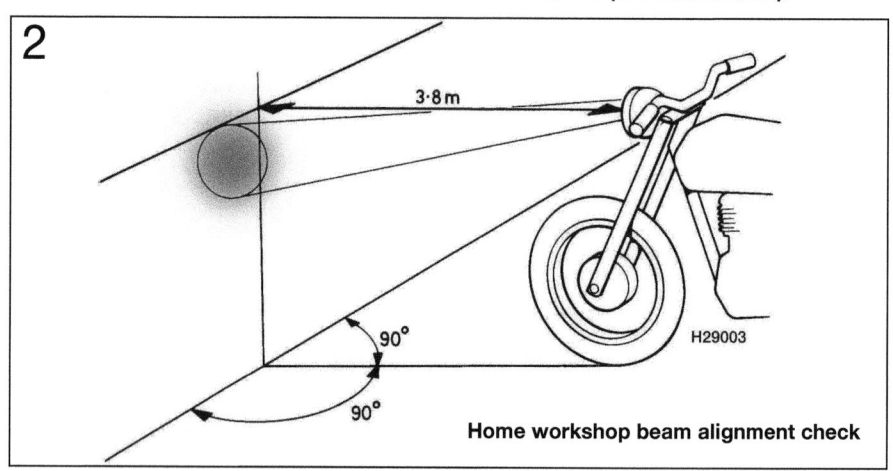

1

Headlight beam height checking equipment

2

Home workshop beam alignment check

MOT Test Checks REF•23

Exhaust System and Final Drive

Exhaust

✔ Check that the exhaust mountings are secure and that the system does not foul any of the rear suspension components.
✔ Start the motorcycle. When the revs are increased, check that the exhaust is neither holed nor leaking from any of its joints. On a linked system, check that the collector box is not leaking due to corrosion.

✔ Note that the exhaust decibel level ("loudness" of the exhaust) is assessed at the discretion of the tester. If the motorcycle was first used on or after 1st January 1985 the silencer must carry the BSAU 193 stamp, or a marking relating to its make and model, or be of OE (original equipment) manufacture. If the silencer is marked NOT FOR ROAD USE, RACING USE ONLY or similar, it will fail the MOT.

Final drive

✔ On chain or belt drive machines, check that the chain/belt is in good condition and does not have excessive slack. Also check that the sprocket is securely mounted on the rear wheel hub. Check that the chain/belt guard is in place.
✔ On shaft drive bikes, check for oil leaking from the drive unit and fouling the rear tyre.

Steering and Suspension

Steering

✔ With the front wheel raised off the ground, rotate the steering from lock to lock. The handlebar or switches must not contact the fuel tank or be close enough to trap the rider's hand. Problems can be caused by damaged lock stops on the lower yoke and frame, or by the fitting of non-standard handlebars.
✔ When performing the lock to lock check, also ensure that the steering moves freely without drag or notchiness. Steering movement can be impaired by poorly routed cables, or by overtight head bearings or worn bearings. The tester will perform a check of the steering head bearing lower race by mounting the front wheel on a surface plate, then performing a lock to lock check with the weight of the machine on the lower bearing (see illustration 3).
✔ Grasp the fork sliders (lower legs) and attempt to push and pull on the forks (see illustration 4). Any play in the steering head bearings will be felt. Note that in extreme cases, wear of the front fork bushes can be misinterpreted for head bearing play.
✔ Check that the handlebars are securely mounted.
✔ Check that the handlebar grip rubbers are secure. They should by bonded to the bar left end and to the throttle cable pulley on the right end.

Front wheel mounted on a surface plate for steering head bearing lower race check

Front suspension

✔ With the motorcycle off the stand, hold the front brake on and pump the front forks up and down (see illustration 5). Check that they are adequately damped.

Checking the steering head bearings for freeplay

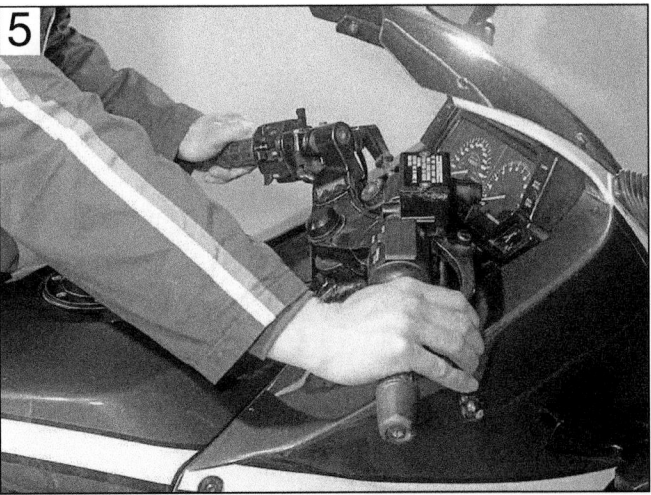

Hold the front brake on and pump the front forks up and down to check operation

REF•24 MOT Test Checks

Inspect the area around the fork dust seal for oil leakage (arrow)

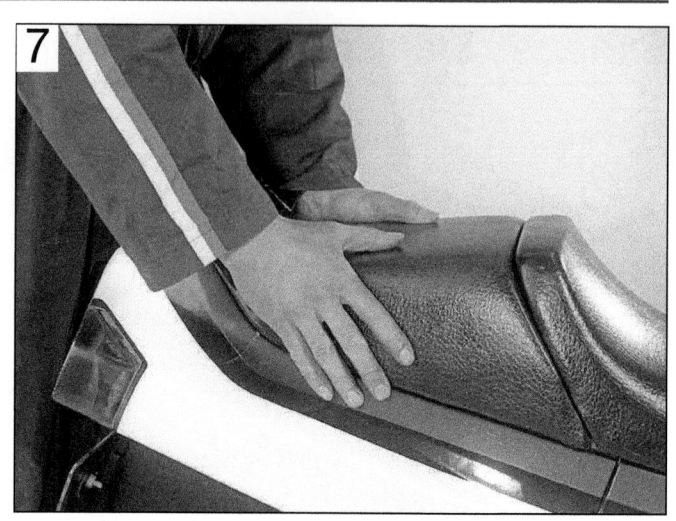

Bounce the rear of the motorcycle to check rear suspension operation

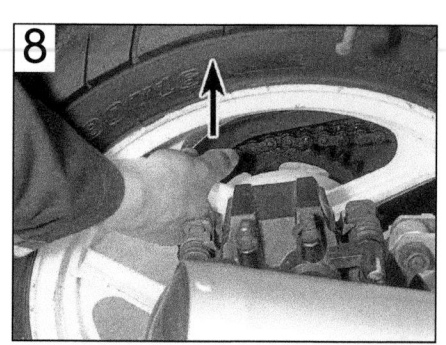

Checking for rear suspension linkage play

✔ Inspect the area above and around the front fork oil seals **(see illustration 6)**. There should be no sign of oil on the fork tube (stanchion) nor leaking down the slider (lower leg). On models so equipped, check that there is no oil leaking from the anti-dive units.

✔ On models with swingarm front suspension, check that there is no freeplay in the linkage when moved from side to side.

Rear suspension

✔ With the motorcycle off the stand and an assistant supporting the motorcycle by its handlebars, bounce the rear suspension **(see illustration 7)**. Check that the suspension components do not foul on any of the cycle parts and check that the shock absorber(s) provide adequate damping.

✔ Visually inspect the shock absorber(s) and check that there is no sign of oil leakage from its damper. This is somewhat restricted on certain single shock models due to the location of the shock absorber.

✔ With the rear wheel raised off the ground, grasp the wheel at the highest point and attempt to pull it up **(see illustration 8)**. Any play in the swingarm pivot or suspension linkage bearings will be felt as movement. **Note:** *Do not confuse play with actual suspension movement.* Failure to lubricate suspension linkage bearings can lead to bearing failure **(see illustration 9)**.

✔ With the rear wheel raised off the ground, grasp the swingarm ends and attempt to move the swingarm from side to side and forwards and backwards - any play indicates wear of the swingarm pivot bearings **(see illustration 10)**.

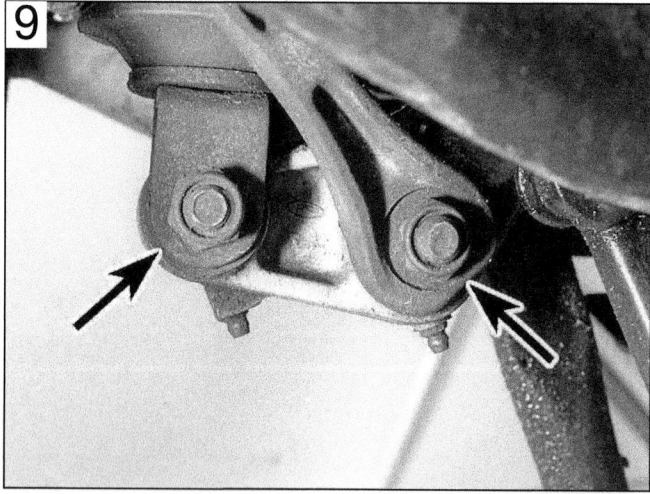

Worn suspension linkage pivots (arrows) are usually the cause of play in the rear suspension

Grasp the swingarm at the ends to check for play in its pivot bearings

MOT Test Checks   REF•25

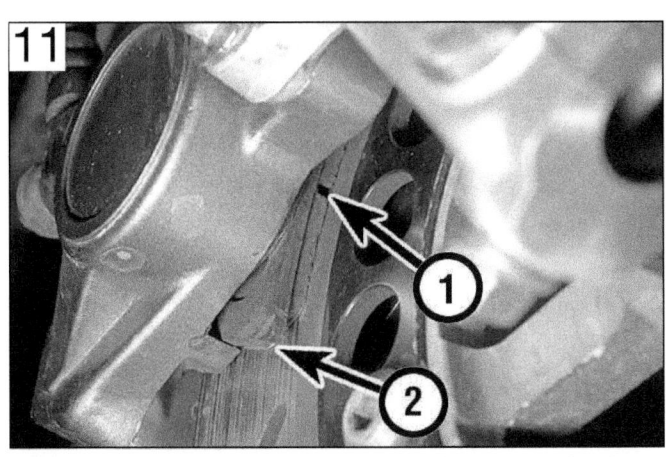

Brake pad wear can usually be viewed without removing the caliper. Most pads have wear indicator grooves (1) and some also have indicator tangs (2)

On drum brakes, check the angle of the operating lever with the brake fully applied. Most drum brakes have a wear indicator pointer and scale.

Brakes, Wheels and Tyres

Brakes

✔ With the wheel raised off the ground, apply the brake then free it off, and check that the wheel is about to revolve freely without brake drag.

✔ On disc brakes, examine the disc itself. Check that it is securely mounted and not cracked.

✔ On disc brakes, view the pad material through the caliper mouth and check that the pads are not worn down beyond the limit **(see illustration 11)**.

✔ On drum brakes, check that when the brake is applied the angle between the operating lever and cable or rod is not too great **(see illustration 12)**. Check also that the operating lever doesn't foul any other components.

✔ On disc brakes, examine the flexible hoses from top to bottom. Have an assistant hold the brake on so that the fluid in the hose is under pressure, and check that there is no sign of fluid leakage, bulges or cracking. If there are any metal brake pipes or unions, check that these are free from corrosion and damage. Where a brake-linked anti-dive system is fitted, check the hoses to the anti-dive in a similar manner.

✔ Check that the rear brake torque arm is secure and that its fasteners are secured by self-locking nuts or castellated nuts with split-pins or R-pins **(see illustration 13)**.

✔ On models with ABS, check that the self-check warning light in the instrument panel works.

✔ The MOT tester will perform a test of the motorcycle's braking efficiency based on a calculation of rider and motorcycle weight. Although this cannot be carried out at home, you can at least ensure that the braking systems are properly maintained. For hydraulic disc brakes, check the fluid level, lever/pedal feel (bleed of air if its spongy) and pad material. For drum brakes, check adjustment, cable or rod operation and shoe lining thickness.

Wheels and tyres

✔ Check the wheel condition. Cast wheels should be free from cracks and if of the built-up design, all fasteners should be secure. Spoked wheels should be checked for broken, corroded, loose or bent spokes.

✔ With the wheel raised off the ground, spin the wheel and visually check that the tyre and wheel run true. Check that the tyre does not foul the suspension or mudguards.

✔ With the wheel raised off the ground, grasp the wheel and attempt to move it about the axle (spindle) **(see illustration 14)**. Any play felt here indicates wheel bearing failure.

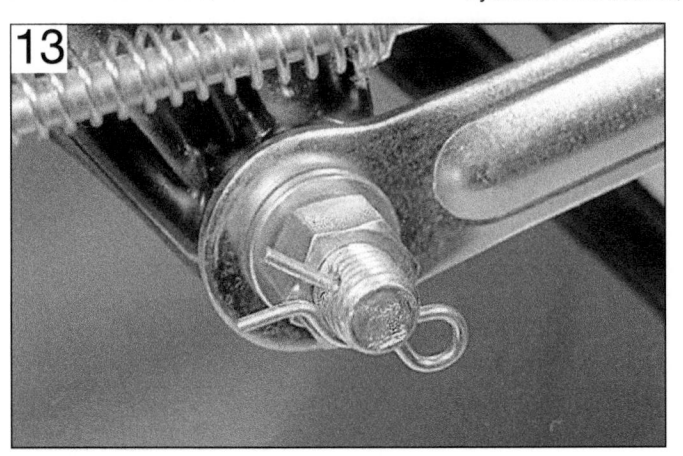

Brake torque arm must be properly secured at both ends

Check for wheel bearing play by trying to move the wheel about the axle (spindle)

REF•26 MOT Test Checks

Checking the tyre tread depth

Tyre direction of rotation arrow can be found on tyre sidewall

Castellated type wheel axle (spindle) nut must be secured by a split pin or R-pin

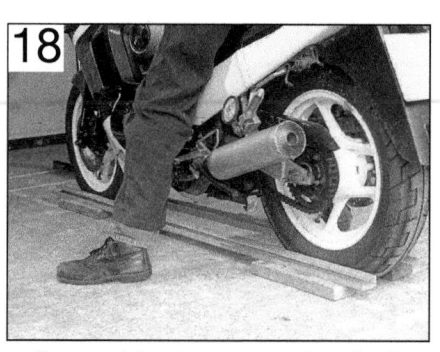

Two straightedges are used to check wheel alignment

✔ Check the tyre tread depth, tread condition and sidewall condition **(see illustration 15)**.
✔ Check the tyre type. Front and rear tyre types must be compatible and be suitable for road use. Tyres marked NOT FOR ROAD USE, COMPETITION USE ONLY or similar, will fail the MOT.

✔ If the tyre sidewall carries a direction of rotation arrow, this must be pointing in the direction of normal wheel rotation **(see illustration 16)**.
✔ Check that the wheel axle (spindle) nuts (where applicable) are properly secured. A self-locking nut or castellated nut with a split-pin or R-pin can be used **(see illustration 17)**.
✔ Wheel alignment is checked with the motorcycle off the stand and a rider seated. With the front wheel pointing straight ahead, two perfectly straight lengths of metal or wood and placed against the sidewalls of both tyres **(see illustration 18)**. The gap each side of the front tyre must be equidistant on both sides. Incorrect wheel alignment may be due to a cocked rear wheel (often as the result of poor chain adjustment) or in extreme cases, a bent frame.

General checks and condition

✔ Check the security of all major fasteners, bodypanels, seat, fairings (where fitted) and mudguards.

✔ Check that the rider and pillion footrests, handlebar levers and brake pedal are securely mounted.

✔ Check for corrosion on the frame or any load-bearing components. If severe, this may affect the structure, particularly under stress.

Sidecars

A motorcycle fitted with a sidecar requires additional checks relating to the stability of the machine and security of attachment and swivel joints, plus specific wheel alignment (toe-in) requirements. Additionally, tyre and lighting requirements differ from conventional motorcycle use. Owners are advised to check MOT test requirements with an official test centre.

Storage REF•27

Preparing for storage

Before you start

If repairs or an overhaul is needed, see that this is carried out now rather than left until you want to ride the bike again.

Give the bike a good wash and scrub all dirt from its underside. Make sure the bike dries completely before preparing for storage.

Engine

● Remove the spark plug(s) and lubricate the cylinder bores with approximately a teaspoon of motor oil using a spout-type oil can **(see illustration 1)**. Reinstall the spark plug(s). Crank the engine over a couple of times to coat the piston rings and bores with oil. If the bike has a kickstart, use this to turn the engine over. If not, flick the kill switch to the OFF position and crank the engine over on the starter **(see illustration 2)**. If the nature on the ignition system prevents the starter operating with the kill switch in the OFF position, remove the spark plugs and fit them back in their caps; ensure that the plugs are earthed (grounded) against the cylinder head when the starter is operated **(see illustration 3)**.

⚠ **Warning: It is important that the plugs are earthed (grounded) away from the spark plug holes otherwise there is a risk of atomised fuel from the cylinders igniting.**

HAYNES HINT: *On a single cylinder four-stroke engine, you can seal the combustion chamber completely by positioning the piston at TDC on the compression stroke.*

● Drain the carburettor(s) otherwise there is a risk of jets becoming blocked by gum deposits from the fuel **(see illustration 4)**.

● If the bike is going into long-term storage, consider adding a fuel stabiliser to the fuel in the tank. If the tank is drained completely, corrosion of its internal surfaces may occur if left unprotected for a long period. The tank can be treated with a rust preventative especially for this purpose. Alternatively, remove the tank and pour half a litre of motor oil into it, install the filler cap and shake the tank to coat its internals with oil before draining off the excess. The same effect can also be achieved by spraying WD40 or a similar water-dispersant around the inside of the tank via its flexible nozzle.

● Make sure the cooling system contains the correct mix of antifreeze. Antifreeze also contains important corrosion inhibitors.

● The air intakes and exhaust can be sealed off by covering or plugging the openings. Ensure that you do not seal in any condensation; run the engine until it is hot,

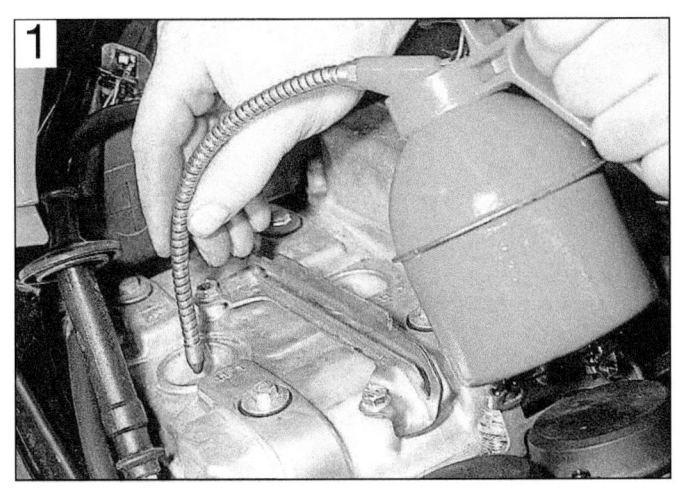

1 Squirt a drop of motor oil into each cylinder

2 Flick the kill switch to OFF . . .

3 . . . and ensure that the metal bodies of the plugs (arrows) are earthed against the cylinder head

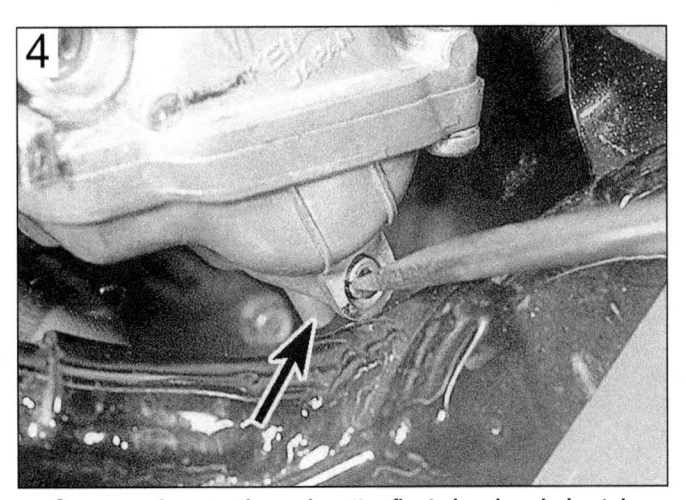

4 Connect a hose to the carburettor float chamber drain stub (arrow) and unscrew the drain screw

REF•28 Storage

Exhausts can be sealed off with a plastic bag

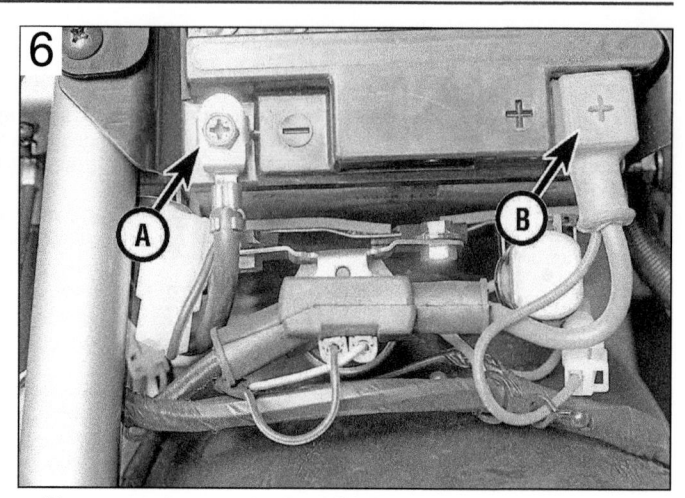

Disconnect the negative lead (A) first, followed by the positive lead (B)

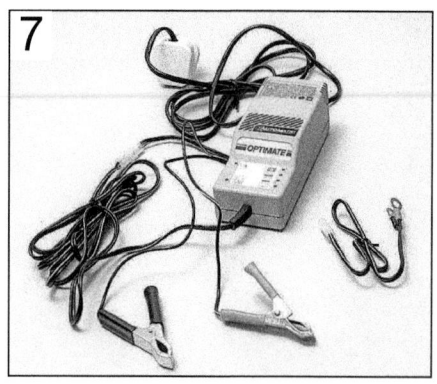

Use a suitable battery charger - this kit also assess battery condition

then switch off and allow to cool. Tape a piece of thick plastic over the silencer end(s) **(see illustration 5)**. Note that some advocate pouring a tablespoon of motor oil into the silencer(s) before sealing them off.

Battery

● Remove it from the bike - in extreme cases of cold the battery may freeze and crack its case **(see illustration 6)**.

● Check the electrolyte level and top up if necessary (conventional refillable batteries). Clean the terminals.
● Store the battery off the motorcycle and away from any sources of fire. Position a wooden block under the battery if it is to sit on the ground.
● Give the battery a trickle charge for a few hours every month **(see illustration 7)**.

Tyres

● Place the bike on its centrestand or an auxiliary stand which will support the motorcycle in an upright position. Position wood blocks under the tyres to keep them off the ground and to provide insulation from damp. If the bike is being put into long-term storage, ideally both tyres should be off the ground; not only will this protect the tyres, but will also ensure that no load is placed on the steering head or wheel bearings.
● Deflate each tyre by 5 to 10 psi, no more or the beads may unseat from the rim, making subsequent inflation difficult on tubeless tyres.

Pivots and controls

● Lubricate all lever, pedal, stand and footrest pivot points. If grease nipples are fitted to the rear suspension components, apply lubricant to the pivots.
● Lubricate all control cables.

Cycle components

● Apply a wax protectant to all painted and plastic components. Wipe off any excess, but don't polish to a shine. Where fitted, clean the screen with soap and water.
● Coat metal parts with Vaseline (petroleum jelly). When applying this to the fork tubes, do not compress the forks otherwise the seals will rot from contact with the Vaseline.
● Apply a vinyl cleaner to the seat.

Storage conditions

● Aim to store the bike in a shed or garage which does not leak and is free from damp.
● Drape an old blanket or bedspread over the bike to protect it from dust and direct contact with sunlight (which will fade paint). This also hides the bike from prying eyes. Beware of tight-fitting plastic covers which may allow condensation to form and settle on the bike.

Getting back on the road

Engine and transmission

● Change the oil and replace the oil filter. If this was done prior to storage, check that the oil hasn't emulsified - a thick whitish substance which occurs through condensation.
● Remove the spark plugs. Using a spout-type oil can, squirt a few drops of oil into the cylinder(s). This will provide initial lubrication as the piston rings and bores comes back into contact. Service the spark plugs, or fit new ones, and install them in the engine.

● Check that the clutch isn't stuck on. The plates can stick together if left standing for some time, preventing clutch operation. Engage a gear and try rocking the bike back and forth with the clutch lever held against the handlebar. If this doesn't work on cable-operated clutches, hold the clutch lever back against the handlebar with a strong elastic band or cable tie for a couple of hours **(see illustration 8)**.
● If the air intakes or silencer end(s) were blocked off, remove the bung or cover used.
● If the fuel tank was coated with a rust

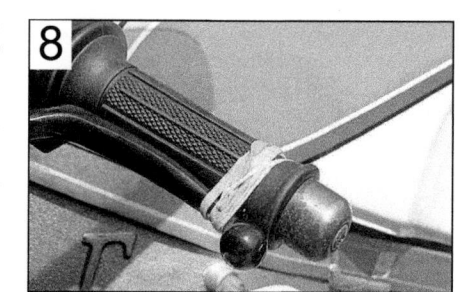

Hold clutch lever back against the handlebar with elastic bands or a cable tie

preventative, oil or a stabiliser added to the fuel, drain and flush the tank and dispose of the fuel sensibly. If no action was taken with the fuel tank prior to storage, it is advised that the old fuel is disposed of since it will go off over a period of time. Refill the fuel tank with fresh fuel.

Frame and running gear

- Oil all pivot points and cables.
- Check the tyre pressures. They will definitely need inflating if pressures were reduced for storage.
- Lubricate the final drive chain (where applicable).
- Remove any protective coating applied to the fork tubes (stanchions) since this may well destroy the fork seals. If the fork tubes weren't protected and have picked up rust spots, remove them with very fine abrasive paper and refinish with metal polish.
- Check that both brakes operate correctly. Apply each brake hard and check that it's not possible to move the motorcycle forwards, then check that the brake frees off again once released. Brake caliper pistons can stick due to corrosion around the piston head, or on the sliding caliper types, due to corrosion of the slider pins. If the brake doesn't free after repeated operation, take the caliper off for examination. Similarly drum brakes can stick due to a seized operating cam, cable or rod linkage.
- If the motorcycle has been in long-term storage, renew the brake fluid and clutch fluid (where applicable).
- Depending on where the bike has been stored, the wiring, cables and hoses may have been nibbled by rodents. Make a visual check and investigate disturbed wiring loom tape.

Battery

- If the battery has been previously removal and given top up charges it can simply be reconnected. Remember to connect the positive cable first and the negative cable last.
- On conventional refillable batteries, if the battery has not received any attention, remove it from the motorcycle and check its electrolyte level. Top up if necessary then charge the battery. If the battery fails to hold a charge and a visual checks show heavy white sulphation of the plates, the battery is probably defective and must be renewed. This is particularly likely if the battery is old. Confirm battery condition with a specific gravity check.
- On sealed (MF) batteries, if the battery has not received any attention, remove it from the motorcycle and charge it according to the information on the battery case - if the battery fails to hold a charge it must be renewed.

Starting procedure

- If a kickstart is fitted, turn the engine over a couple of times with the ignition OFF to distribute oil around the engine. If no kickstart is fitted, flick the engine kill switch OFF and the ignition ON and crank the engine over a couple of times to work oil around the upper cylinder components. If the nature of the ignition system is such that the starter won't work with the kill switch OFF, remove the spark plugs, fit them back into their caps and earth (ground) their bodies on the cylinder head. Reinstall the spark plugs afterwards.
- Switch the kill switch to RUN, operate the choke and start the engine. If the engine won't start don't continue cranking the engine - not only will this flatten the battery, but the starter motor will overheat. Switch the ignition off and try again later. If the engine refuses to start, go through the fault finding procedures in this manual. **Note:** *If the bike has been in storage for a long time, old fuel or a carburettor blockage may be the problem. Gum deposits in carburettors can block jets - if a carburettor cleaner doesn't prove successful the carburettors must be dismantled for cleaning.*
- Once the engine has started, check that the lights, turn signals and horn work properly.
- Treat the bike gently for the first ride and check all fluid levels on completion. Settle the bike back into the maintenance schedule.

REF•30 Fault Finding

This Section provides an easy reference-guide to the more common faults that are likely to afflict your machine. Obviously, the opportunities are almost limitless for faults to occur as a result of obscure failures, and to try and cover all eventualities would require a book. Indeed, a number have been written on the subject.

Successful troubleshooting is not a mysterious 'black art' but the application of a bit of knowledge combined with a systematic and logical approach to the problem. Approach any troubleshooting by first accurately identifying the symptom and then checking through the list of possible causes, starting with the simplest or most obvious and progressing in stages to the most complex.

Take nothing for granted, but above all apply liberal quantities of common sense.

The main symptom of a fault is given in the text as a major heading below which are listed the various systems or areas which may contain the fault. Details of each possible cause for a fault and the remedial action to be taken are given, in brief, in the paragraphs below each heading. Further information should be sought in the relevant Chapter.

Note: *If a fault is thought to lie in the fuel or ignition systems, the simplest solution may well be to take the machine immediately to an authorised BMW dealer for attention. Refer to Chapter 6 or 6 as appropriate, but always check all other possible causes first, eg a misfire can also be caused by dirty fuel. Items such as dragging brakes or underinflated tyres should not be overlooked.*

1 Starter motor problems
- [ ] Starter motor not rotating
- [ ] Starter motor rotates but engine does not turn over
- [ ] Starter motor and clutch function but engine will not turn over

2 Engine does not start when turned over
- [ ] No fuel flow to carburettor
- [ ] Fuel not reaching cylinder
- [ ] Engine flooding
- [ ] No spark at plug
- [ ] Weak spark at plug
- [ ] Compression low

3 Engine stalls after starting
- [ ] General causes

4 Poor running at idle and low speed
- [ ] Weak spark at plug or erratic firing
- [ ] Fuel/air mixture incorrect
- [ ] Compression low

5 Acceleration poor
- [ ] General causes

6 Poor running or lack of power at high speeds
- [ ] Weak spark at plug or erratic firing
- [ ] Fuel/air mixture incorrect
- [ ] Compression low

7 Knocking or pinking
- [ ] General causes

8 Overheating
- [ ] Firing incorrect
- [ ] Fuel/air mixture incorrect
- [ ] Lubrication inadequate
- [ ] Miscellaneous causes

9 Clutch operating problems
- [ ] Clutch slip
- [ ] Clutch drag

10 Gear selection problems
- [ ] Gear lever does not return
- [ ] Gear selection difficult or impossible
- [ ] Jumping out of gear
- [ ] Overselection

11 Abnormal engine noise
- [ ] Knocking or pinking
- [ ] Piston slap or rattling from cylinder
- [ ] Valve noise or tapping from cylinder head
- [ ] Other noises

12 Abnormal transmission noise
- [ ] Clutch noise
- [ ] Transmission noise

13 Exhaust smokes excessively
- [ ] White/blue smoke (caused by oil burning)
- [ ] Black smoke (caused by over-rich mixture)

14 Oil pressure indicator lamp goes on
- [ ] Engine lubrication system failure
- [ ] Electrical system failure

15 Poor handling or roadholding
- [ ] Directional instability
- [ ] Steering bias to left or right
- [ ] Handlebar vibrates or oscillates
- [ ] Poor front fork performance
- [ ] Front fork judder when braking
- [ ] Poor rear suspension performance

16 Abnormal frame and suspension noise
- [ ] Front end noise
- [ ] Rear suspension noise

17 Brake problems
- [ ] Brakes are spongy or ineffective - disc brakes
- [ ] Brakes drag - disc brakes
- [ ] Brake lever or pedal pulsates in operation - disc brakes
- [ ] Disc brake noise
- [ ] Brakes are spongy or ineffective - drum brakes
- [ ] Brake drag - drum brakes
- [ ] Brake lever or pedal pulsates in operation - drum brakes
- [ ] Drum brake noise
- [ ] Brake induced fork judder

18 Electrical problems
- [ ] Battery dead or weak
- [ ] Battery overcharged
- [ ] Total electrical failure
- [ ] Circuit failure
- [ ] Bulbs blowing repeatedly

Fault Finding REF•31

1 Starter motor problems

Starter motor not rotating
- [ ] Engine stop switch off.
- [ ] Fuse blown. Check fuse number 1 located behind the left-hand side panel.
- [ ] Battery voltage low. Switching on the headlamp and operating the horn will give a good indication of the charge level. If necessary recharge the battery from an external source.
- [ ] Load-shedding relay faulty. If the ancillary circuits are not cut off when the starter motor is operating the current drain may be sufficient to prevent the motor from rotating. Renew the relay.
- [ ] Neutral gear not selected.
- [ ] Faulty neutral indicator switch or clutch interlock switch. Check the switch wiring and switches for correct operation.
- [ ] Ignition switch defective. Check switch for continuity and connections for security.
- [ ] Engine stop switch defective. Check switch for continuity in 'Run' position. Fault will be caused by broken, wet or corroded switch contacts. Clean or renew as necessary.
- [ ] Starter button switch faulty. Check continuity of switch. Faults as for engine stop switch.
- [ ] Starter relay faulty. If the switch is functioning correctly a pronounced click should be heard when the starter button is depressed. This presupposes that current is flowing to the solenoid when the button is depressed.
- [ ] Wiring open or shorted. Check first that the battery terminal connections are tight and corrosion free. Follow this by checking that all wiring connections are dry, tight and corrosion free. Check also for frayed or broken wiring. Occasionally a wire may become trapped between two, moving components, particularly in the vicinity of the steering head, leading to breakage of the internal core but leaving the softer but more resilient outer cover intact. This can cause mysterious intermittent or total power loss.
- [ ] Starter motor defective. A badly worn starter motor may cause high current drain from a battery without the motor rotating. If current is found to be reaching the motor, after checking the starter button and starter relay, suspect a damaged motor. The motor should be removed for inspection.

Starter motor rotates but engine does not turn over
- [ ] Starter motor clutch defective. Suspect jammed or worn engagement rollers, plungers and springs (early 100 models) or locking sprags (all other models). Note particularly that clutch may be rendered inoperable by build-up of oily sludge, in which case stripping and flushing out is required. Modified components may be available to effect a more permanent solution. Refer to Chapter 2 for more details.
- [ ] Damaged starter motor drive train. Inspect and renew components where necessary. Failure in this area is unlikely.

Starter motor and clutch function but engine will not turn over
- [ ] Engine seized. Seizure of the engine is always a result of damage to internal components due to lubrication failure, or component breakage resulting from abuse, neglect or old age. A seizing or partially seized component may go un-noticed until the engine has cooled down and an attempt is made to restart the engine. Suspect first seizure of the valves, valve gear and the pistons. Instantaneous seizure whilst the engine is running indicates component breakage. In either case major dismantling and inspection will be required.

2 Engine does not start when turned over

No fuel flow to engine
- [ ] No fuel or insufficient fuel in tank.
- [ ] Fuel pump faulty. Check first fuse number 6, located behind the left-hand side panel, then fuel injection relay before suspecting pump. Refer to Chapter 6 and/or 10.
- [ ] Tank filler cap air vent obstructed. Usually caused by dirt or water. Clean the vent orifice.
- [ ] Fuel filter blocked. Blockage may be due to accumulation of rust or paint flakes from the tank's inner surface or of foreign matter from contaminated fuel. Renew the filter and clean the pump gauze strainer. Look also for water droplets in the fuel.
- [ ] Fuel line blocked. Blockage of the fuel line is more likely to result from a kink in the line rather than the accumulation of debris.

Fuel not reaching cylinder
- [ ] If fuel is present under pressure in the rail but not reaching the intake port then either the injector is blocked or faulty of there is a fault in the fuel or ignition system components. Take the machine to an authorised BMW dealer for testing.

Engine flooding
- [ ] Flooding of the engine itself can be caused only by dirt jamming an injector open. Renew the injector and clean out the fuel system.
- [ ] An excessively rich mixture can only be caused by a fault in the fuel injection control unit, although it is possible for a faulty temperature sensor to cause the control unit to carry on feeding a rich mixture to the engine when it is fully warmed up.

No spark at plug
- [ ] Ignition switch not on.
- [ ] Engine stop switch off.
- [ ] Fuse blown. Check fuse for ignition circuit. See wiring diagram.
- [ ] Battery voltage low. The current draw required by a starter motor is sufficiently high that an under-charged battery may not have enough spare capacity to provide power for the ignition circuit during starting.
- [ ] Load shedding relay faulty, causing same symptoms as above. Renew the relay.
- [ ] Starter motor inefficient. A starter motor with worn brushes and a worn or dirty commutator will draw excessive amounts of current causing power starvation in the ignition system. Starter motor overhaul will be required.
- [ ] Spark plug failure. Clean the spark plugs thoroughly and reset the electrode gaps. Refer to the spark plug section in *Routine maintenance and servicing*. If a spark plug shorts internally or has sustained visible damage to the electrodes, core or ceramic insulator it should be renewed. On rare occasions a plug that appears to spark vigorously will fail to do so when refitted to the engine and subjected to the compression pressure in the cylinder.
- [ ] Spark plug cap or high tension (HT) lead faulty. Check condition and security. Replace if deterioration is evident.
- [ ] Spark plug cap loose. Check that the spark plug caps fit securely over the plug and, where fitted, the screwed terminal on the plug ends are secure.
- [ ] Shorting due to moisture. Certain parts of the ignition system are susceptible to shorting when the machine is ridden or parked in wet weather. Check particularly the area from the spark plug cap back to the ignition coil. A water dispersant spray may be used to dry out waterlogged components. Recurrence of the problem can be prevented by using an ignition sealant spray after drying out and cleaning.

REF•32 Fault Finding

2 Engine does not start when turned over (continued)

- ☐ Ignition or stop switch shorted. May be caused by water, corrosion or wear. Water dispersant and contact cleaning sprays may be used. If this fails to overcome the problem dismantling and visual inspection of the switches will be required.
- ☐ Shorting or open circuit in wiring. Failure in any wire connecting any of the ignition components will cause ignition malfunction. Check also that all connections are clean, dry and tight.
- ☐ Ignition coil failure. Check the coil, referring to Chapter 7.

Weak spark at plug
- ☐ Feeble sparking at the plug may be caused by any of the faults mentioned in 'No spark at plug' other than the first three. Check first the spark plug, this being the most likely culprit.

Compression low
- ☐ Spark plug loose. This will be self-evident on inspection, and may be accompanied by a hissing noise when the engine is turned over. Remove the plugs and check that the threads in the cylinder head are not damaged. Check also that the plug sealing washers are in good condition.
- ☐ Cylinder head gasket leaking. This condition is often accompanied by a high pitched squeak from around the cylinder head and oil loss, and may be caused by insufficiently tightened cylinder head fasteners, a warped cylinder head or mechanical failure of the gasket material. Re-torqueing the fasteners to the correct specification may seal the leak in some instances but if damage has occurred this course of action will provide, at best, only a temporary cure.
- ☐ Valve not seating correctly. The failure of a valve to seat may be caused by insufficient valve clearance, pitting of the valve seat or face, carbon deposits on the valve seat or seizure of the valve stem or valve gear components. Valve spring breakage will also prevent correct valve closure. The valve clearances should be checked first and then, if these are found to be in order, further dismantling will be required to inspect the relevant components for failure.
- ☐ Cylinder, piston and ring wear. Compression pressure will be lost if any of these components are badly worn. Wear in one component is invariably accompanied by wear in another. A top end overhaul will be required.
- ☐ Piston rings sticking or broken. Sticking of the piston rings may be caused by seizure due to lack of lubrication or heating as a result of poor carburation or incorrect fuel type. Gumming of the rings may result from lack of use, or carbon deposits in the ring grooves. Broken rings result from over-revving, overheating or general wear. In either case a top-end overhaul will be required.

3 Engine stalls after starting

General causes
- ☐ Fuel system fault. See Chapter 6.
- ☐ Ignition malfunction. See Section 2, 'Weak spark at plug'.
- ☐ Fuel contamination. Clean the filter and, where water is in evidence, drain and flush the fuel tank.
- ☐ Intake air leak. Check for security of the hose connections, and for cracks or splits in the hoses.
- ☐ Air filter blocked or omitted. A blocked filter will cause an over-rich mixture; the omission of a filter will cause an excessively weak mixture. Both conditions will affect the mixture ratio adversely. Clean or renew the filter as necessary.
- ☐ Fuel filler cap air vent blocked. Usually caused by dirt or water. Clean the vent orifice.

4 Poor running at idle and low speed

Weak spark at plug or erratic firing
- ☐ Battery voltage low. In certain conditions low battery charge, especially when coupled with a badly sulphated battery, may result in misfiring. If the battery is in good general condition it should be recharged; an old battery suffering from sulphated plates should be renewed.
- ☐ Spark plugs fouled, faulty or incorrectly adjusted. See Section 2 'No spark at plug' or refer to *Routine maintenance and servicing*.
- ☐ Spark plug caps or high tension leads shorting. Check the condition of both these items ensuring that they are in good condition and dry and that the caps are fitted correctly.
- ☐ Spark plug type incorrect. Fit plugs of correct type and heat range as given in Specifications. In certain conditions a plug of hotter or colder type may be required for normal running.
- ☐ Ignition timing incorrect. Check the ignition timing.
- ☐ Faulty ignition coil. Partial failure of the coil internal insulation will diminish the performance of the coil. No repair is possible, a new component must be fitted.
- ☐ Ignition system fault. Refer to Chapter 7.

Fuel/air mixture incorrect
- ☐ Intake air leak. See Section 3.
- ☐ Mixture strength incorrect. Adjust idle mixture strength using airflow meter bypass screw.
- ☐ Fuel system fault. Refer to Chapter 6.
- ☐ Air cleaner clogged or omitted. Clean or fit air cleaner element as necessary. Check also that the element and air filter cover are correctly seated.
- ☐ Fuel tank air vent obstructed. Obstruction usually caused by dirt or water. Clean vent orifice.
- ☐ Valve clearance incorrect. Check, and if necessary, adjust, the clearances.

Compression low
- ☐ See Section 2.

5 Acceleration poor

General causes
- ☐ All items as for previous Section.
- ☐ Fuel system fault. Refer to Chapter 6, checking particularly the airflow meter and throttle butterfly assembly.
- ☐ Brakes binding. Usually caused by maladjustment or partial seizure of the operating mechanism due to poor maintenance. Check brake adjustment (where applicable). A bent wheel spindle or warped brake disc can produce similar symptoms.

Fault Finding REF•33

6 Poor running or lack of power at high speeds

Weak spark at plug or erratic firing
- [ ] All items as for Section 4.
- [ ] HT lead insulation failure. Insulation failure of an HT lead and spark plug cap due to old age or damage can cause shorting when the engine is driven hard. This condition may be less noticeable, or not noticeable at all at lower engine speeds.

Fuel/air mixture incorrect
- [ ] All items as for Section 4, with the exception of reason 2.

Compression low
- [ ] See Section 2.

7 Knocking or pinking

General causes
- [ ] Carbon build-up in combustion chamber. After high mileages have been covered a large accumulation of carbon may occur. This may glow red hot and cause premature ignition of the fuel/air mixture, in advance of normal firing by the spark plug. Cylinder head removal will be required to allow inspection and cleaning.
- [ ] Fuel incorrect. A low grade fuel, or one of poor quality may result in compression induced detonation of the fuel resulting in knocking and pinking noises. Old fuel can cause similar problems. A too highly leaded fuel will reduce detonation but will accelerate deposit formation in the combustion chamber and may lead to early pre-ignition as described in item 1. Refer to fuel recommendation given in Chapter 6.
- [ ] Spark plug heat range incorrect. Uncontrolled pre-ignition can result from the use of a spark plug the heat range of which is too hot.
- [ ] Weak mixture. Overheating of the engine due to a weak mixture can result in pre-ignition occurring where it would not occur when engine temperature was within normal limits.

8 Overheating

Firing incorrect
- [ ] Spark plug fouled, defective or maladjusted. See Section 2 'No spark at plug'.
- [ ] Spark plug type incorrect. Refer to the Specifications and ensure that the correct plug type is fitted.
- [ ] Incorrect ignition timing. Timing that is far too much advanced or far too much retarded will cause overheating. Check the ignition timing is correct.

Fuel/air mixture incorrect
- [ ] Idle speed mixture strength incorrect. Adjust airflow meter bypass.
- [ ] Air filter badly fitted or omitted. Check that the filter element is in place and that it and the air filter box cover are sealing correctly. Any leaks will cause a weak mixture.
- [ ] Induction air leaks. Check the security of the hose connections, and for cracks and splits in the hoses.
- [ ] Fuel level too low. See Section 2 'Fuel not reaching cylinder'.
- [ ] Fuel tank filler cap air vent obstructed. Clear blockage.

Lubrication inadequate
- [ ] Engine oil too low. Not only does the oil serve as a lubricant by preventing friction between moving components, but it also acts as a coolant. Check the oil level and replenish.
- [ ] Engine oil overworked. The lubricating properties of oil are lost slowly during use as a result of changes resulting from heat and also contamination. Always change the oil at the recommended interval.
- [ ] Engine oil of incorrect viscosity or poor quality. Always use the recommended viscosity and type of oil.
- [ ] Oil filter and filter by-pass valve blocked. Renew filter.

Miscellaneous causes
- [ ] Radiator fins clogged, or other cooling system fault. Refer to Chapter 5.

9 Clutch operating problems

Clutch slip
- [ ] No clutch lever play. Adjust clutch according to the procedure in *Routine maintenance and servicing*.
- [ ] Clutch plate worn or warped. Overhaul clutch assembly, replacing plate if necessary. See Chapter 3.
- [ ] Pressure or cover plates worn or warped. Overhaul clutch assembly, replacing plates if necessary. See Chapter 3.
- [ ] Clutch spring broken or worn. An old or heat-damaged (from slipping clutch) spring should be replaced with a new one.
- [ ] Clutch inner cable snagging. Caused by a frayed cable or kinked outer cable. Replace the cable with a new one. Repair of a frayed cable is not advised.
- [ ] Clutch release mechanism defective. Worn or damaged parts in the clutch release mechanism could include the pushrod, thrust bearing or piston. Replace parts as necessary.
- [ ] Oil leaking on to clutch plate. Dismantle clutch (Chapter 3) renew clutch plate, wash off all traces of oil and trace source of leak. If the leak is from the engine, see Chapter 2, if from the gearbox, see Chapter 4.

Clutch drag
- [ ] Clutch lever play excessive. Adjust release mechanism. See *Routine maintenance and servicing*.
- [ ] Clutch plates warped or damaged. This will cause a drag on the clutch, causing the machine to creep. Overhaul clutch assembly (Chapter 3).
- [ ] Clutch release mechanism defective. Worn or damaged release mechanism parts can stick and fail to provide leverage. Overhaul clutch release mechanism (Chapter 3).
- [ ] Engine output shaft not properly located. Endfloat will permit movement of the clutch housing which may cause clutch drag. See Chapter 2.
- [ ] Loose clutch housing nut. See above. Tighten as described in Chapter 3.

REF•34 Fault Finding

10 Gear selection problems

Gear lever does not return
☐ Weak or broken spring. Renew the spring.
☐ Gearchange shaft bent or seized. Distortion of the gearchange shaft often occurs if the machine is dropped heavily on the gear lever. Provided that damage is not severe straightening of the shaft is permissible.

Gear selection difficult or impossible
☐ Clutch not disengaging fully. See Section 9 'Clutch drag'.
☐ Gearchange shaft bent. This often occurs if the machine is dropped heavily on the gear lever. Straightening of the shaft is permissible if the damage is not too great.
☐ Gearchange arms or pins worn or damaged. Wear or breakage of any of these items may cause difficulty in selecting one or more gears. Overhaul the selector mechanism
☐ Selector claw arm spring broken. Renew spring.
☐ Gearchange drum detent cam or plunger damage. Failure, rather than wear, of these items may jam the drum thereby preventing gearchanging. The damaged items must be renewed.
☐ Selector forks bent or seized. This can be caused by dropping the machine heavily on the gearchange lever or as a result of lack of lubrication. Though rare, bending of a shaft can result from a missed gearchange or false selection at high speed.
☐ Selector fork end and pin wear. Pronounced wear of these items and the grooves in the gearchange drum can lead to imprecise selection and, eventually, no selection. Renewal of the worn components will be required.
☐ Structural failure. Failure of any one component of the selector rod and change mechanism will result in improper or fouled gear selection.

Jumping out of gear
☐ Detent plunger assembly worn or damaged. Wear of the plunger and the cam with which it locates and breakage of the detent spring can cause imprecise gear selection resulting in jumping out of gear. Renew the damaged components.
☐ Gear pinion dogs worn or damaged. Rounding off the dog edges and the mating recesses in adjacent pinions can lead to jumping out of gear when under load. The gears should be inspected and renewed. Attempting to reprofile the dogs is not recommended.
☐ Selector forks, gearchange drum and pinion grooves worn. Extreme wear of these interconnected items can occur after high mileages especially when lubrication has been neglected. The worn components must be renewed.
☐ Gear pinions, bushes and shafts worn. Renew the worn components.
☐ Bent gearchange shaft. Often caused by dropping the machine on the gear lever.
☐ Gear pinion tooth broken. Chipped teeth are unlikely to cause jumping out of gear once the gear has been selected fully; a tooth which is completely broken off, however, may cause problems in this respect and in any event will cause transmission noise.

Overselection
☐ Claw arm spring weak or broken. Renew the spring.
☐ Detent plunger worn or broken. Renew the damaged items.
☐ Detent roller arm spring worn or broken. Renew the spring.
☐ Selector claw arm ends worn. Repairs can be made by welding and reprofiling with a file.
☐ Selector limiter claw components worn or damaged. Renew the damaged items.

11 Abnormal engine noise

Knocking or pinking
☐ See Section 7.

Piston slap or rattling from cylinder
☐ Cylinder bore/piston clearance excessive. Resulting from wear or partial seizure. This condition can often be heard as a high, rapid tapping noise when the engine is under little or no load, particularly when power is just beginning to be applied. Either fit new pistons or renew the cylinder block.
☐ Connecting rod bent. This can be caused by over-revving, trying to start a very badly flooded engine (resulting in a hydraulic lock in the cylinder) or by earlier mechanical failure such as a dropped valve. Attempts at straightening a bent connecting rod from a high performance engine are not recommended. Careful inspection of the crankshaft should be made before renewing the damaged connecting rod.
☐ Gudgeon pin, piston boss bore or small-end bearing wear or seizure. Excess clearance or partial seizure between normal moving parts of these items can cause continuous or intermittent tapping noises. Rapid wear or seizure is caused by lubrication starvation resulting from an insufficient engine oil level or oilway blockage.
☐ Piston rings worn, broken or sticking. Renew the rings after careful inspection of the piston and bore.

Valve noise or tapping from the cylinder head
☐ Valve clearance incorrect. Adjust the clearances with the engine cold.
☐ Valve spring broken or weak. Renew the spring set.
☐ Camshaft or cylinder head worn or damaged. The camshaft lobes are the most highly stressed of all components in the engine and are subject to high wear if lubrication becomes inadequate. The bearing surfaces on the camshaft and cylinder head are also sensitive to a lack of lubrication. Lubrication failure due to blocked oilways can occur, but neglect of oil changes and of topping-up is the usual cause.
☐ Worn camshaft drive components. A rustling noise or light tapping can be emitted by a worn cam chain or worn sprockets and chain. If uncorrected, subsequent cam chain breakage may cause extensive damage. The worn components must be renewed before wear becomes too far advanced.

Other noises
☐ Big-end bearing wear. A pronounced knock from within the crankcase which worsens rapidly is indicative of big-end bearing failure as a result of extreme normal wear or lubrication failure. Remedial action in the form of a bottom end overhaul should be taken; continuing to run the engine will lead to further damage including the possibility of connecting rod breakage.
☐ Main bearing failure. Extreme normal wear or failure of the main bearings is characteristically accompanied by a rumble from the crankcase and vibration felt through the frame and footrests. Renew the worn bearings and carry out a very careful examination of the crankshaft.
☐ Crankshaft excessively out of true. A bent crank may result from over-revving or damage from an upper cylinder component or gearbox failure. Damage can also result from dropping the machine on the right-hand side. Straightening of the crankshaft is not possible in normal circumstances; a replacement item should be fitted.
☐ Engine mounting loose. Tighten all the engine mounting nuts and bolts.

Fault Finding REF•35

11 Abnormal engine noise (continued)

- ☐ Cylinder head gasket leaking. The noise most often associated with a leaking head gasket is a high pitched squeaking, although any other noise consistent with gas being forced out under pressure from a small orifice can also be emitted. Gasket leakage is often accompanied by oil seepage from around the mating joint or from the cylinder head holding down bolts and nuts. Leakage into the cam chain tunnel or oil return passages will increase crankcase pressure and may cause oil leakage at joints and oil seals. Also, oil contamination will be accelerated. Leakage results from insufficient or uneven tightening of the cylinder head fasteners, or from random mechanical failure. Retightening to the correct torque figure will, at best, only provide a temporary cure. The gasket should be renewed at the earliest opportunity.
- ☐ Exhaust system leakage. Popping or crackling in the exhaust system, particularly when it occurs with the engine on the overrun, indicates a poor joint either at the cylinder port or at the exhaust pipe/silencer connection. Failure of the gasket or looseness of the clamp should be looked for.

12 Abnormal transmission noise

Clutch noise
- ☐ Clutch plate centre splines worn. Renew the clutch plate and examine closely the gearbox input shaft.
- ☐ Loose clutch housing nut or cover plate bolts. Retighten securely. See Chapter 3.

Transmission noise
- ☐ Bearing or bushes worn or damaged. Renew the affected components.
- ☐ Gear pinions worn or chipped. Renew the gear pinions.
- ☐ Metal chips jammed in gear teeth. This can occur when pieces of metal from any failed component are picked up by a meshing pinion. The condition will lead to rapid bearing wear or early gear failure.
- ☐ Oil level too low. Top up immediately to prevent damage to gearbox.
- ☐ Gearchange mechanism worn or damaged. Wear or failure of certain items in the selection and change components can induce mis-selection of gears (see Section 10) where incipient engagement of more than one gear set is promoted. Remedial action, by the overhaul of the gearbox, should be taken without delay.

13 Exhaust smokes excessively

White/blue smoke (caused by oil burning)
- ☐ Cloud of smoke released upon starting, especially if machine has been parked on side stand or if engine is still warm. This appears to be a characteristic possessed by all K-series BMWs to a greater or lesser extent, but should reduce considerably as the pistons and rings bed in. Provided little or no oil is used, there is nothing that can be done about this, other than to use the centre stand at all times. If oil consumption is significant, or increases suddenly, a full engine strip will be required to investigate the cause.
- ☐ Piston rings worn or broken. Breakage or wear of any ring, but particularly an oil control ring, will allow engine oil past the piston into the combustion chamber. Overhaul the cylinder block and pistons.
- ☐ Cylinder block cracked, worn or scored. These conditions may be caused by overheating, lack of lubrication, component failure or advanced normal wear. The cylinder block should be renewed.
- ☐ Valve oil seal damaged or worn. This can occur as a result of valve guide failure or old age. The emission of smoke is likely to occur when the throttle is closed rapidly after acceleration, for instance, when changing gear. Renew the valve oil seals and, if necessary, the valve guides.
- ☐ Valve guides worn. See the preceding reason.
- ☐ Engine oil level too high. This increases the crankcase pressure and allows oil to be forced past the piston rings. Often accompanied by seepage of oil at joints and oil seals.
- ☐ Cylinder head gasket blown between cam chain tunnel or oil return passage. Renew the cylinder head gasket.
- ☐ Abnormal crankcase pressure. This may be caused by blocked breather passages or hoses causing back-pressure at high engine revolutions.

Black smoke (caused by over-rich mixture)
- ☐ All items as for Section 2 'Engine flooding'.

14 Oil pressure indicator lamp goes on

Engine lubrication system failure
- ☐ Engine oil defective. Oil pump shaft or locating pin sheared off from ingesting debris or seizing from lack of lubrication (low oil level).
- ☐ Engine oil screen clogged. Change oil and filter and service pick-up screen. See Routine maintenance and servicing and/or Chapter 6.
- ☐ Engine oil level too low. Inspect for leak or other problem causing low oil level and add recommended lubricant. See Daily (pre-ride) checks.
- ☐ Engine oil viscosity too low. Very old, thin oil, or an improper weight of oil used in engine. Change to correct lubricant.
- ☐ Camshaft or journals worn. High wear causing drop in oil pressure. Replace cam and/or head. Abnormal wear could be caused by oil starvation at high rpm from low oil level, improper oil weight or type.
- ☐ Crankshaft and/or bearings worn. Same problems as reason 5. Overhaul lower end (Chapter 2).
- ☐ Relief valve stuck open. This causes the oil to be dumped back into the sump. Repair or replace. (See Chapter 6.)

Electrical system failure
- ☐ Oil pressure switch defective. Check switch according to the procedures in Chapter 11. Replace if defective.
- ☐ Oil pressure indicator lamp wiring system defective. Check for pinched, shorted, disconnected or damaged wiring (Chapter 11).

15 Poor handling or roadholding

Directional instability

- [ ] Steering head bearing adjustment too tight. This will cause rolling or weaving at low speeds. Re-adjust the bearings.
- [ ] Steering head bearings worn or damaged. Correct adjustment of the bearing will prove impossible to achieve if wear or damage has occurred. Inconsistent handling will occur including rolling or weaving at low speed and poor directional control at indeterminate higher speeds. The steering head bearing should be dismantled for inspection and renewed if required. Lubrication should also be carried out.
- [ ] Bearing races pitted or dented. Impact damage caused, perhaps, by an accident or riding over a pot-hole can cause indentation of the bearing, usually in one position. This should be noted as notchiness when the handlebars are turned. Renew and lubricate the bearings.
- [ ] Steering stem bent. This will occur only if the machine is subjected to a high impact such as hitting a curb or a pot-hole. The lower yoke/stem should be renewed; do not attempt to straighten the stem.
- [ ] Front or rear tyre pressures too low.
- [ ] Front or rear tyre worn. General instability, high speed wobbles and skipping over white lines indicates that tyre renewal may be required. Tyre induced problems, in some machine/tyre combinations, can occur even when the tyre in question is by no means fully worn.
- [ ] Swinging arm bearings worn. Difficulty in holding line, particularly when cornering or when changing power settings indicates wear in the swinging arm bearings. The swinging arm should be removed from the machine and the bearings renewed if adjustment does not cure the fault.
- [ ] Swinging arm flexing. The symptoms given in the preceding reason will also occur if the swinging arm fork flexes badly. This can be caused by structural weakness as a result of corrosion, fatigue or impact damage.
- [ ] Wheel bearings worn. Renew the worn bearings.
- [ ] Tyres unsuitable for machine. Not all available tyres will suit the characteristics of the frame and suspension, indeed, some tyres or tyre combinations may cause a transformation in the handling characteristics. If handling problems occur immediately after changing to a new tyre type or make, revert to the original tyres to see whether an improvement can be noted. In some instances a change to what are, in fact, suitable tyres may give rise to handling deficiencies. In this case a thorough check should be made of all frame and suspension items which affect stability.

Steering bias to left or right

- [ ] Wheels out of alignment. This can be caused by impact damage to the frame, swinging arm, wheel spindle or front forks. Although occasionally a result of material failure or corrosion it is usually as a result of a crash.
- [ ] Front forks twisted in the fork yokes. A light impact, for instance with a pot-hole or low curb, can twist the fork legs in the yokes without causing structural damage to the fork legs or the yokes themselves. Re-alignment can be made by loosening the yoke pinch bolts, wheel spindle and mudguard bolts. Re-align the wheel with the handlebars and tighten the bolts working upwards from the wheel spindle. This action should be carried out only when there is no chance that structural damage has occurred.

Handlebar vibrates or oscillates

- [ ] Tyres worn or out of balance. Either condition, particularly in the front tyre, will promote shaking of the fork assembly and thus the handlebars. A sudden onset of shaking can result if a balance weight is displaced during use.
- [ ] Tyres badly positioned on the wheel rims. A moulded line on each wall of a tyre is provided to allow visual verification that the tyre is correctly positioned on the rim. A check can be made by rotating the tyre; any misalignment will be immediately obvious.
- [ ] Wheel rims warped or damaged. Inspect the wheels for runout as described in Routine maintenance and servicing.
- [ ] Swinging arm bearings worn. Renew the bearings.
- [ ] Wheel bearings worn. Renew the bearings.
- [ ] Steering head bearings incorrectly adjusted. Vibration is more likely to result from bearings which are too loose rather than too tight. Re-adjust the bearings.
- [ ] Loose fork component fasteners. Loose nuts and bolts holding the fork legs, wheel spindle, mudguards or steering stem can promote shaking at the handlebars. Fasteners on running gear such as the forks and suspension should be check tightened occasionally to prevent dangerous looseness of components occurring.
- [ ] Engine mounting bolts loose. Tighten all fasteners.

Poor front fork performance

- [ ] Damping fluid level incorrect. If the fluid level is too low poor suspension control will occur resulting in a general impairment of roadholding and early loss of tyre adhesion when cornering and braking. Too much oil is unlikely to change the fork characteristics unless severe overfilling occurs when the fork action will become stiffer and oil seal failure may occur.
- [ ] Damping oil viscosity incorrect. The damping action of the fork is directly related to the viscosity of the damping oil. The lighter the oil used, the less will be the damping action imparted. For general use, use the recommended type of oil, changing to a slightly higher or heavier oil only when a change in damping characteristic is required. Overworked oil, or oil contaminated with water which has found its way past the seals, should be renewed to restore the correct damping performance and to prevent bottoming of the forks.
- [ ] Damping components worn or corroded. Advanced normal wear of the fork internals is unlikely to occur until a very high mileage has been covered. Continual use of the machine with damaged oil seals which allows the ingress of water, or neglect, will lead to rapid corrosion and wear. Dismantle the forks for inspection and overhaul. See Chapter 8.
- [ ] Weak fork springs. Progressive fatigue of the fork springs, resulting in a reduced spring free length, will occur after extensive use. This condition will promote excessive fork dive under braking, and in its advanced form will reduce the at-rest extended length of the forks and thus the fork geometry. Renewal of the springs as a pair is the only satisfactory course of action.
- [ ] Bent stanchions or corroded stanchions. Both conditions will prevent correct telescoping of the fork legs, and in an advanced state can cause sticking of the fork in one position. In a mild form corrosion will cause stiction of the fork thereby increasing the time the suspension takes to react to an uneven road surface. Bent fork stanchions should be attended to immediately because they indicate that impact damage has occurred, and there is a danger that the forks will fail with disastrous consequences.

Front fork judder when braking (see also Section 17)

- [ ] Wear between the fork stanchions and the fork legs. Renewal of the affected components is required.
- [ ] Slack steering head bearings. Re-adjust the bearings.
- [ ] Warped brake disc. If irregular braking action occurs fork judder can be induced in what are normally serviceable forks. Renew the damaged brake components.

Poor rear suspension performance

- [ ] Rear suspension unit damper worn out or leaking. The damping performance of most rear suspension units falls off with age. This is a gradual process, and thus may not be immediately obvious. Indications of poor damping include hopping of the rear end when cornering or braking, and a general loss of positive stability. See Chapter 9.
- [ ] Weak rear spring. If the suspension unit spring fatigues it will promote excessive pitching of the machine and reduce the ground clearance when cornering.
- [ ] Swinging arm flexing or bearings worn. See 'Directional instability' and 'Steering bias to left or right'.
- [ ] Bent suspension unit damper rod. This is likely to occur only if the machine is dropped or if seizure of the piston occurs.

Fault Finding REF•37

16 Abnormal frame and suspension noise

Front end noise
- [ ] Oil level low or too thin. This can cause a 'spurting' sound and is usually accompanied by irregular fork action.
- [ ] Spring weak or broken. Makes a clicking or scraping sound. Fork oil will have a lot of metal particles in it.
- [ ] Steering head bearings loose or damaged. Clicks when braking. Check, adjust or replace.
- [ ] Fork yokes loose. Make sure all fork yoke pinch bolts are tight.
- [ ] Fork stanchion bent. Good possibility if machine has been dropped. Repair or replace tube.

Rear suspension noise
- [ ] Fluid level too low. Leakage of a suspension unit, usually evident by oil on the outer surface, can cause a spurting noise. The suspension unit should be renewed.
- [ ] Defective rear suspension unit with internal damage. Renew the suspension unit.

17 Brake problems

Brakes are spongy or ineffective - disc brakes
- [ ] Air in brake circuit. This is only likely to happen in service due to neglect in checking the fluid level or because a leak has developed. The problem should be identified and the brake system bled of air.
- [ ] Pad worn. Check the pad wear and renew the pads if necessary.
- [ ] Contaminated pads. Cleaning pads which have been contaminated with oil, grease or brake fluid is unlikely to prove successful; the pads should be renewed.
- [ ] Pads glazed. This is usually caused by overheating. The surface of the pads may be roughened using glass-paper or a fine file.
- [ ] Brake fluid deterioration. A brake which on initial operation is firm but rapidly becomes spongy in use may be failing due to water contamination of the fluid. The fluid should be drained and then the system refilled and bled.
- [ ] Master cylinder seal failure. Wear or damage of master cylinder internal parts will prevent pressurisation of the brake fluid. Overhaul the master cylinder unit.
- [ ] Caliper seal failure. This will almost certainly be obvious by loss of fluid, a lowering of fluid in the master cylinder reservoir and contamination of the brake pads and caliper. Overhaul the caliper assembly.
- [ ] Brake pedal improperly adjusted. Adjust the clearance between the pedal and master cylinder to take up lost motion, as recommended in Chapter 10.

Brakes drag - disc brakes
- [ ] Disc warped. The disc must be renewed.
- [ ] Caliper piston, caliper or pads corroded. The brake caliper assembly is vulnerable to corrosion due to water and dirt, and unless cleaned at regular intervals and lubricated in the recommended manner, will become sticky in operation.
- [ ] Piston seal deteriorated. The seal is designed to return the piston in the caliper to the retracted position when the brake is released. Wear or old age can affect this function. The caliper should be overhauled if this occurs.
- [ ] Brake pad damaged. Pad material separating from the backing plate due to wear or faulty manufacture. Renew the pads. Faulty installation of a pad also will cause dragging.
- [ ] Wheel spindle bent. The spindle may be straightened if no structural damage has occurred.
- [ ] Brake lever or pedal not returning. Check that the lever or pedal works smoothly throughout its operating range and does not snag on any adjacent cycle parts. Lubricate the pivot if necessary.
- [ ] Twisted caliper support bracket. This is likely to occur only after impact in an accident. Renew the caliper assembly.

Brake lever/pedal pulsates in operation - disc brakes
- [ ] Disc warped or irregularly worn. The disc must be renewed.
- [ ] Wheel spindle bent. The spindle may be straightened provided no structural damage has occurred.

Disc brake noise
- [ ] Brake squeal. Squealing can be caused by dust on the pads, usually in combination with glazed pads, or other contamination from oil, grease, brake fluid or corrosion. Persistent squealing which cannot be traced to any of the normal causes can often be cured by applying a thin layer of high temperature silicone grease to the rear of the pads. Make absolutely certain that no grease is allowed to contaminate the braking surface of the pads.
- [ ] Glazed pads. This is usually caused by high temperatures or contamination. The pad surfaces may be roughened using glass-paper or a fine file. If this approach does not effect a cure the pads should be renewed.
- [ ] Pad material incompatible. BMW state that some non-genuine brake pads are made of poor quality friction materials which cause excessive squeal; these should be avoided.
- [ ] Pad material. Friction material designed to cope with extreme temperatures may squeal at lower speeds, ie town use.
- [ ] Disc warped. This can cause a chattering, clicking or intermittent squeal and is usually accompanied by a pulsating brake lever or pedal or uneven braking. The disc must be renewed.
- [ ] Brake pads fitted incorrectly. Inspect the pads for correct installation and security.

Brakes are spongy or ineffective - drum brakes
- [ ] Worn brake linings. Determine lining wear using the external brake wear indicator on the brake backplate, or by removing the wheel and withdrawing the brake backplate. Renew the shoes as a pair if the linings are worn below the minimum thickness.
- [ ] Worn brake camshaft. Wear between the camshaft and the bearing surface will reduce brake feel and reduce operating efficiency. Renewal of one or both items will be required to rectify the fault.
- [ ] Worn brake cam and shoe ends. Renew the worn components.
- [ ] Linings contaminated with dust or grease. Any accumulations of dust should be cleaned from the brake assembly and drum using a petrol dampened cloth. Do not blow or brush off the dust because it is asbestos based and thus harmful if inhaled. Light contamination from grease can be removed from the surface of the brake linings using a solvent; attempts at removing heavier contamination are less likely to be successful because some of the lubricant will have been absorbed by the lining material which will severely reduce the braking performance.
- [ ] Brake components not centralised on wheel. See Chapter 10.
- [ ] Angle between operating lever and brake rod incorrect. See *Routine maintenance and servicing*.

Brake drag - drum brakes
- [ ] Incorrect adjustment. Re-adjust the brake operating mechanism.
- [ ] Drum warped or oval. This can result from overheating or impact. The condition is difficult to correct, although if slight ovality only occurs, skimming the surface of the brake drum can provide a cure. This is work for a specialist engineer. Renewal of the complete wheel is normally the only satisfactory solution.
- [ ] Weak brake shoe return springs. This will prevent the brake shoes from pulling away from the drum surface once the brake is released. The springs should be renewed.
- [ ] Brake camshaft, lever pivot or cable poorly lubricated. Failure to attend to regular lubrication of these areas will increase operating resistance which, when compounded, may cause tardy operation and poor release movement.

17 Brake problems (continued)

Brake pedal pulsates in operation - drum brakes
- [ ] Drum warped or oval. This can result from overheating or impact. This condition is difficult to correct, although if slight ovality only occurs skimming the surface of the drum can provide a cure. This is work for a specialist engineer. Renewal of the wheel is normally the only satisfactory solution.

Drum brake noise
- [ ] Drum warped or oval. This can cause intermittent rubbing of the brake linings against the drum. See the preceding reason.
- [ ] Brake linings glazed. This condition, usually accompanied by heavy lining dust contamination, often induces brake squeal. The surface of the linings may be roughened using glass-paper or a fine file.
- [ ] Return springs vibrating. See Chapter 10.

Brake induced fork judder
- [ ] Worn front fork stanchions and legs, or worn or badly adjusted steering head bearings. These conditions, combined with uneven or pulsating braking as described in 'Brake lever or pedal pulsates in operation - disc brakes' will induce more or less judder when the brakes are applied, dependent on the degree of wear and poor brake operation. Attention should be given to both areas of malfunction. See the relevant Section.

18 Electrical problems

Battery dead or weak
- [ ] Battery faulty. Battery life should not be expected to exceed 3 to 4 years. Complete or intermittent failure may be due to a broken terminal. Lack of electrolyte will prevent the battery maintaining charge.
- [ ] Battery leads making poor contact. Remove the battery leads and clean them and the terminals, removing all traces of corrosion. Reconnect leads and apply a coating of petroleum jelly to the terminals.
- [ ] Load excessive. If additional items increase the total electrical load above the maximum alternator output, the battery will fail to maintain full charge. Reduce the load to suit the capacity.
- [ ] Alternator failure.

Battery overcharged
- [ ] Alternator faulty. Overcharging is indicated if the battery becomes hot or it is noticed that the electrolyte level falls repeatedly between checks. In extreme cases the battery will boil causing corrosive gases and electrolyte to be emitted through the vent pipes.
- [ ] Battery wrongly matched to the electrical circuit. Ensure that the specified battery is fitted to the machine.

Total electrical failure
- [ ] Fuse blown. Check the main fuse. If a fault has occurred, it must be rectified before a new fuse is fitted.
- [ ] Battery faulty. See 'Battery dead or weak'.
- [ ] Earth failure. Check that the frame main earth strap from the battery is securely affixed to the frame and is making a good contact.
- [ ] Ignition switch or power circuit failure. Check for current flow to the ignition switch. Check the ignition switch for continuity.

Circuit failure
- [ ] Cable failure. Refer to the machine's wiring diagram and check the circuit for continuity. Open circuits are a result of loose or corroded connections, either at terminals or in-line connectors, or because of broken wires. Occasionally, the core of a wire will break without there being any apparent damage to the outer plastic cover.
- [ ] Switch failure. All switches may be checked for continuity in each switch position. Switch failure may be a result of mechanical breakage, corrosion or water.
- [ ] Fuse blown. Refer to the wiring diagram to check whether or not a circuit fuse is fitted. Replace the fuse, if blown, only after the fault has been identified and rectified.

Bulbs blowing repeatedly
- [ ] Vibration failure. This is often an inherent fault related to the natural vibration characteristics of the engine and frame and is, thus, difficult to resolve. Modifications of the lamp mounting, to change the damping characteristics may help.
- [ ] Intermittent earth. Repeated failure of one bulb, particularly where the bulb is fed directly from the generator, indicates that a poor earth exists somewhere in the circuit. Check that a good contact is available at each earthing point in the circuit.
- [ ] Reduced voltage. Where a quartz-halogen bulb is fitted the voltage to the bulb should be maintained or early failure of the bulb will occur. Do not overload the system with additional electrical equipment in excess of the system's power capacity and ensure that all circuit connections are maintained clean and tight.

Fault Finding Equipment   REF•39

Checking engine compression

● Low compression will result in exhaust smoke, heavy oil consumption, poor starting and poor performance. A compression test will provide useful information about an engine's condition and if performed regularly, can give warning of trouble before any other symptoms become apparent.
● A compression gauge will be required, along with an adapter to suit the spark plug hole thread size. Note that the screw-in type gauge/adapter set up is preferable to the rubber cone type.
● Before carrying out the test, first check the valve clearances as described in Chapter 1.

1 Run the engine until it reaches normal operating temperature, then stop it and remove the spark plug(s), taking care not to scald your hands on the hot components.
2 Install the gauge adapter and compression gauge in No. 1 cylinder spark plug hole **(see illustration 1)**.

Screw the compression gauge adapter into the spark plug hole, then screw the gauge into the adapter

3 On kickstart-equipped motorcycles, make sure the ignition switch is OFF, then open the throttle fully and kick the engine over a couple of times until the gauge reading stabilises.
4 On motorcycles with electric start only, the procedure will differ depending on the nature of the ignition system. Flick the engine kill switch (engine stop switch) to OFF and turn the ignition switch ON; open the throttle fully and crank the engine over on the starter motor for a couple of revolutions until the gauge reading stabilises. If the starter will not operate with the kill switch OFF, turn the ignition switch OFF and refer to the next paragraph.
5 Install the spark plugs back into their suppressor caps and arrange the plug electrodes so that their metal bodies are earthed (grounded) against the cylinder head; this is essential to prevent damage to the ignition system as the engine is spun over **(see illustration 2)**. Position the plugs well

All spark plugs must be earthed (grounded) against the cylinder head

away from the plug holes otherwise there is a risk of atomised fuel escaping from the combustion chambers and igniting. As a safety precaution, cover the top of the valve cover with rag. Now turn the ignition switch ON and kill switch ON, open the throttle fully and crank the engine over on the starter motor for a couple of revolutions until the gauge reading stabilises.
6 After one or two revolutions the pressure should build up to a maximum figure and then stabilise. Take a note of this reading and on multi-cylinder engines repeat the test on the remaining cylinders.
7 The correct pressures are given in Chapter 2 Specifications. If the results fall within the specified range and on multi-cylinder engines all are relatively equal, the engine is in good condition. If there is a marked difference between the readings, or if the readings are lower than specified, inspection of the top-end components will be required.
8 Low compression pressure may be due to worn cylinder bores, pistons or rings, failure of the cylinder head gasket, worn valve seals, or poor valve seating.
9 To distinguish between cylinder/piston wear and valve leakage, pour a small quantity of oil into the bore to temporarily seal the piston rings, then repeat the compression tests **(see illustration 3)**. If the readings show

Bores can be temporarily sealed with a squirt of motor oil

a noticeable increase in pressure this confirms that the cylinder bore, piston, or rings are worn. If, however, no change is indicated, the cylinder head gasket or valves should be examined.
10 High compression pressure indicates excessive carbon build-up in the combustion chamber and on the piston crown. If this is the case the cylinder head should be removed and the deposits removed. Note that excessive carbon build-up is less likely with the used on modern fuels.

Checking battery open-circuit voltage

⚠ *Warning: The gases produced by the battery are explosive - never smoke or create any sparks in the vicinity of the battery. Never allow the electrolyte to contact your skin or clothing - if it does, wash it off and seek immediate medical attention.*

REF•40 Fault Finding Equipment

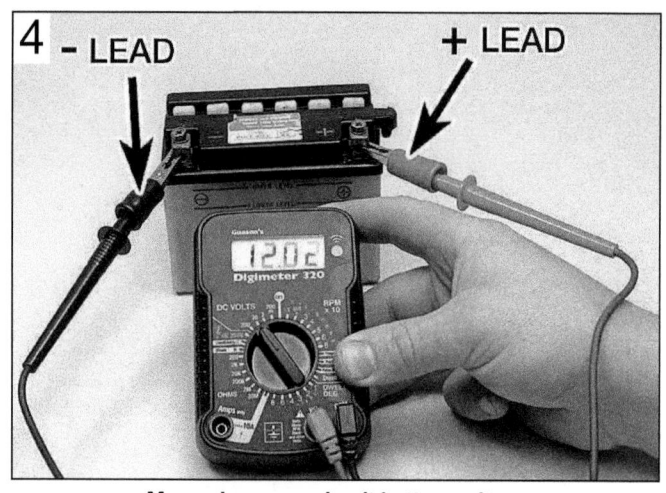

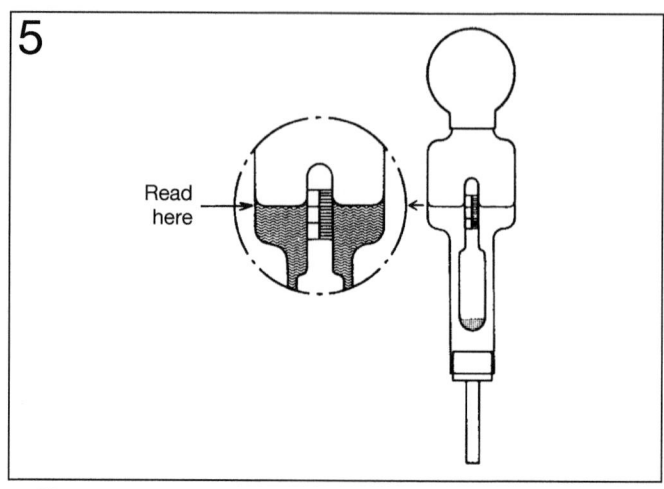

Measuring open-circuit battery voltage

Float-type hydrometer for measuring battery specific gravity

- Before any electrical fault is investigated the battery should be checked.
- You'll need a dc voltmeter or multimeter to check battery voltage. Check that the leads are inserted in the correct terminals on the meter, red lead to positive (+ve), black lead to negative (-ve). Incorrect connections can damage the meter.
- A sound fully-charged 12 volt battery should produce between 12.3 and 12.6 volts across its terminals (12.8 volts for a maintenance-free battery). On machines with a 6 volt battery, voltage should be between 6.1 and 6.3 volts.

1 Set a multimeter to the 0 to 20 volts dc range and connect its probes across the battery terminals. Connect the meter's positive (+ve) probe, usually red, to the battery positive (+ve) terminal, followed by the meter's negative (-ve) probe, usually black, to the battery negative terminal (-ve) **(see illustration 4)**.

2 If battery voltage is low (below 10 volts on a 12 volt battery or below 4 volts on a six volt battery), charge the battery and test the voltage again. If the battery repeatedly goes flat, investigate the motorcycle's charging system.

Checking battery specific gravity (SG)

⚠️ *Warning: The gases produced by the battery are explosive - never smoke or create any sparks in the vicinity of the battery. Never allow the electrolyte to contact your skin or clothing - if it does, wash it off and seek immediate medical attention.*

- The specific gravity check gives an indication of a battery's state of charge.
- A hydrometer is used for measuring specific gravity. Make sure you purchase one which has a small enough hose to insert in the aperture of a motorcycle battery.
- Specific gravity is simply a measure of the electrolyte's density compared with that of water. Water has an SG of 1.000 and fully-charged battery electrolyte is about 26% heavier, at 1.260.
- Specific gravity checks are not possible on maintenance-free batteries. Testing the open-circuit voltage is the only means of determining their state of charge.

1 To measure SG, remove the battery from the motorcycle and remove the first cell cap. Draw

Digital multimeter can be used for all electrical tests

Battery-powered continuity tester

some electrolyte into the hydrometer and note the reading **(see illustration 5)**. Return the electrolyte to the cell and install the cap.

2 The reading should be in the region of 1.260 to 1.280. If SG is below 1.200 the battery needs charging. Note that SG will vary with temperature; it should be measured at 20°C (68°F). Add 0.007 to the reading for every 10°C above 20°C, and subtract 0.007 from the reading for every 10°C below 20°C. Add 0.004 to the reading for every 10°F above 68°F, and subtract 0.004 from the reading for every 10°F below 68°F.

3 When the check is complete, rinse the hydrometer thoroughly with clean water.

Checking for continuity

- The term continuity describes the uninterrupted flow of electricity through an electrical circuit. A continuity check will determine whether an **open-circuit** situation exists.
- Continuity can be checked with an ohmmeter, multimeter, continuity tester or battery and bulb test circuit **(see illustrations 6, 7 and 8)**.

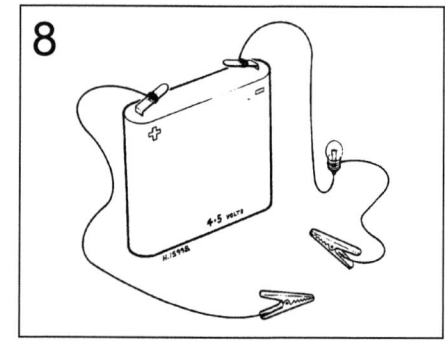

Battery and bulb test circuit

Fault Finding Equipment REF•41

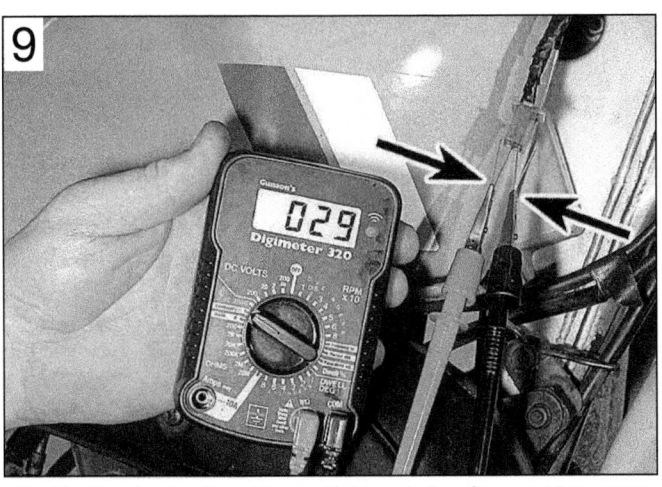

Continuity check of front brake light switch using a meter - note split pins used to access connector terminals

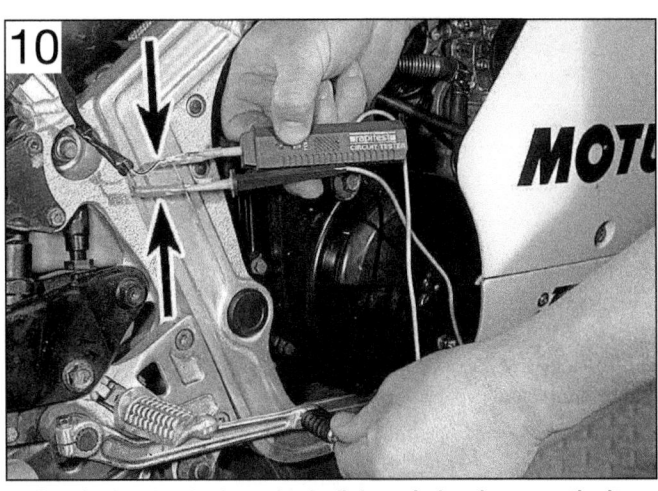

Continuity check of rear brake light switch using a continuity tester

- All of these instruments are self-powered by a battery, therefore the checks are made with the ignition OFF.
- As a safety precaution, always disconnect the battery negative (-ve) lead before making checks, particularly if ignition switch checks are being made.
- If using a meter, select the appropriate ohms scale and check that the meter reads infinity (∞). Touch the meter probes together and check that meter reads zero; where necessary adjust the meter so that it reads zero.
- After using a meter, always switch it OFF to conserve its battery.

Switch checks

1 If a switch is at fault, trace its wiring up to the wiring connectors. Separate the wire connectors and inspect them for security and condition. A build-up of dirt or corrosion here will most likely be the cause of the problem - clean up and apply a water dispersant such as WD40.

2 If using a test meter, set the meter to the ohms x 10 scale and connect its probes across the wires from the switch (see illustration 9). Simple ON/OFF type switches, such as brake light switches, only have two wires whereas combination switches, like the ignition switch, have many internal links. Study the wiring diagram to ensure that you are connecting across the correct pair of wires. Continuity (low or no measurable resistance - 0 ohms) should be indicated with the switch ON and no continuity (high resistance) with it OFF.

3 Note that the polarity of the test probes doesn't matter for continuity checks, although care should be taken to follow specific test procedures if a diode or solid-state component is being checked.

4 A continuity tester or battery and bulb circuit can be used in the same way. Connect its probes as described above (see illustration 10). The light should come on to indicate continuity in the ON switch position, but should extinguish in the OFF position.

Wiring checks

- Many electrical faults are caused by damaged wiring, often due to incorrect routing or chaffing on frame components.
- Loose, wet or corroded wire connectors can also be the cause of electrical problems, especially in exposed locations.

1 A continuity check can be made on a single length of wire by disconnecting it at each end and connecting a meter or continuity tester across both ends of the wire (see illustration 11).

2 Continuity (low or no resistance - 0 ohms) should be indicated if the wire is good. If no continuity (high resistance) is shown, suspect a broken wire.

Checking for voltage

- A voltage check can determine whether current is reaching a component.
- Voltage can be checked with a dc voltmeter, multimeter set on the dc volts scale, test light or buzzer (see illustrations 12 and 13). A meter has the advantage of being able to measure actual voltage.
- When using a meter, check that its leads are inserted in the correct terminals on the meter, red to positive (+ve), black to negative (-ve). Incorrect connections can damage the meter.
- A voltmeter (or multimeter set to the dc volts scale) should always be connected in parallel (across the load). Connecting it in series will destroy the meter.
- Voltage checks are made with the ignition ON.

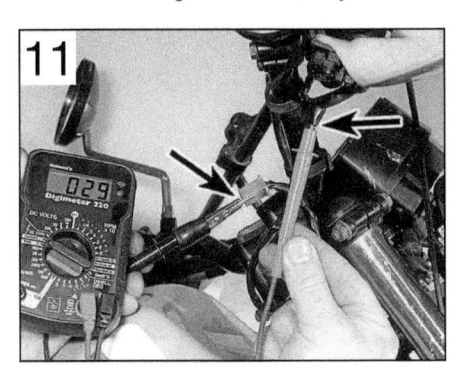

Continuity check of front brake light switch sub-harness

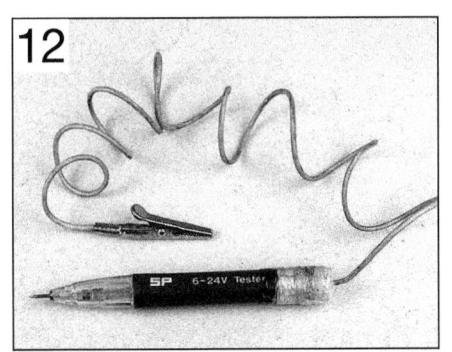

A simple test light can be used for voltage checks

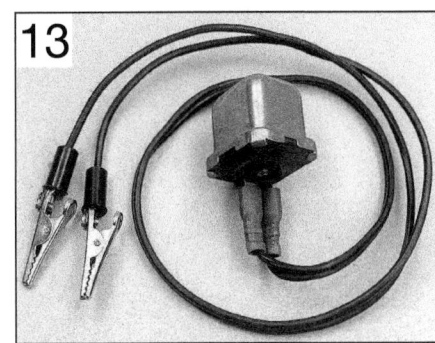

A buzzer is useful for voltage checks

REF•42 Fault Finding Equipment

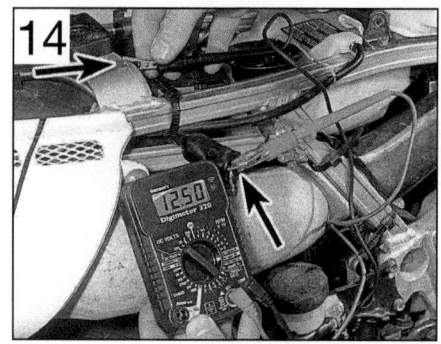

Checking for voltage at the rear brake light power supply wire using a meter . . .

1 First identify the relevant wiring circuit by referring to the wiring diagram at the end of this manual. If other electrical components share the same power supply (ie are fed from the same fuse), take note whether they are working correctly - this is useful information in deciding where to start checking the circuit.

2 If using a meter, check first that the meter leads are plugged into the correct terminals on the meter (see above). Set the meter to the dc volts function, at a range suitable for the battery voltage. Connect the meter red probe (+ve) to the power supply wire and the black probe to a good metal earth (ground) on the motorcycle's frame or directly to the battery negative (-ve) terminal **(see illustration 14)**. Battery voltage should be shown on the meter

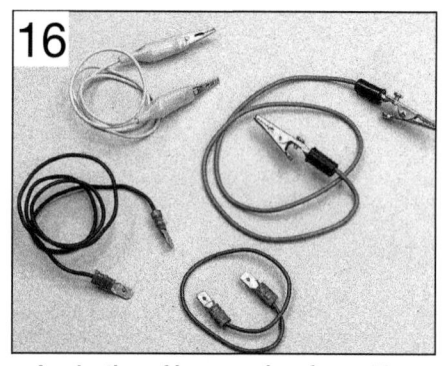

A selection of jumper wires for making earth (ground) checks

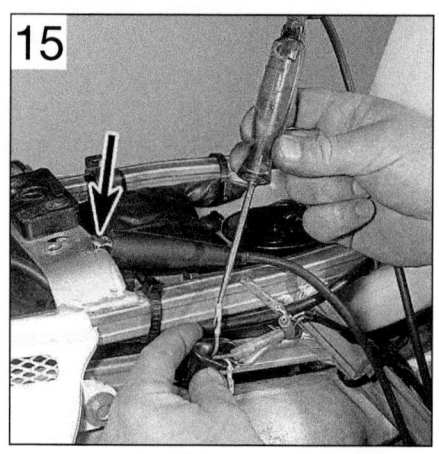

. . . or a test light - note the earth connection to the frame (arrow)

with the ignition switched ON.

3 If using a test light or buzzer, connect its positive (+ve) probe to the power supply terminal and its negative (-ve) probe to a good earth (ground) on the motorcycle's frame or directly to the battery negative (-ve) terminal **(see illustration 15)**. With the ignition ON, the test light should illuminate or the buzzer sound.

4 If no voltage is indicated, work back towards the fuse continuing to check for voltage. When you reach a point where there is voltage, you know the problem lies between that point and your last check point.

Checking the earth (ground)

● Earth connections are made either directly to the engine or frame (such as sensors, neutral switch etc. which only have a positive feed) or by a separate wire into the earth circuit of the wiring harness. Alternatively a short earth wire is sometimes run directly from the component to the motorcycle's frame.
● Corrosion is often the cause of a poor earth connection.
● If total failure is experienced, check the security of the main earth lead from the negative (-ve) terminal of the battery and also the main earth (ground) point on the wiring harness. If corroded, dismantle the connection and clean all surfaces back to bare metal.

1 To check the earth on a component, use an insulated jumper wire to temporarily bypass its earth connection **(see illustration 16)**. Connect one end of the jumper wire between the earth terminal or metal body of the component and the other end to the motorcycle's frame.

2 If the circuit works with the jumper wire installed, the original earth circuit is faulty. Check the wiring for open-circuits or poor connections. Clean up direct earth connections, removing all traces of corrosion and remake the joint. Apply petroleum jelly to the joint to prevent future corrosion.

Tracing a short-circuit

● A short-circuit occurs where current shorts to earth (ground) bypassing the circuit components. This usually results in a blown fuse.

● A short-circuit is most likely to occur where the insulation has worn through due to wiring chafing on a component, allowing a direct path to earth (ground) on the frame.

1 Remove any bodypanels necessary to access the circuit wiring.

2 Check that all electrical switches in the circuit are OFF, then remove the circuit fuse and connect a test light, buzzer or voltmeter (set to the dc scale) across the fuse terminals. No voltage should be shown.

3 Move the wiring from side to side whilst observing the test light or meter. When the test light comes on, buzzer sounds or meter shows voltage, you have found the cause of the short. It will usually shown up as damaged or burned insulation.

4 Note that the same test can be performed on each component in the circuit, even the switch.

Technical Terms Explained

A

ABS (Anti-lock braking system) A system, usually electronically controlled, that senses incipient wheel lockup during braking and relieves hydraulic pressure at wheel which is about to skid.
Aftermarket Components suitable for the motorcycle, but not produced by the motorcycle manufacturer.
Allen key A hexagonal wrench which fits into a recessed hexagonal hole.
Alternating current (ac) Current produced by an alternator. Requires converting to direct current by a rectifier for charging purposes.
Alternator Converts mechanical energy from the engine into electrical energy to charge the battery and power the electrical system.
Ampere (amp) A unit of measurement for the flow of electrical current. Current = Volts ÷ Ohms.
Ampere-hour (Ah) Measure of battery capacity.
Angle-tightening A torque expressed in degrees. Often follows a conventional tightening torque for cylinder head or main bearing fasteners **(see illustration)**.

Angle-tightening cylinder head bolts

Antifreeze A substance (usually ethylene glycol) mixed with water, and added to the cooling system, to prevent freezing of the coolant in winter. Antifreeze also contains chemicals to inhibit corrosion and the formation of rust and other deposits that would tend to clog the radiator and coolant passages and reduce cooling efficiency.
Anti-dive System attached to the fork lower leg (slider) to prevent fork dive when braking hard.
Anti-seize compound A coating that reduces the risk of seizing on fasteners that are subjected to high temperatures, such as exhaust clamp bolts and nuts.
API American Petroleum Institute. A quality standard for 4-stroke motor oils.
Asbestos A natural fibrous mineral with great heat resistance, commonly used in the composition of brake friction materials. Asbestos is a health hazard and the dust created by brake systems should never be inhaled or ingested.
ATF Automatic Transmission Fluid. Often used in front forks.
ATU Automatic Timing Unit. Mechanical device for advancing the ignition timing on early engines.
ATV All Terrain Vehicle. Often called a Quad.
Axial play Side-to-side movement.
Axle A shaft on which a wheel revolves. Also known as a spindle.

B

Backlash The amount of movement between meshed components when one component is held still. Usually applies to gear teeth.
Ball bearing A bearing consisting of a hardened inner and outer race with hardened steel balls between the two races.
Bearings Used between two working surfaces to prevent wear of the components and a build-up of heat. Four types of bearing are commonly used on motorcycles: plain shell bearings, ball bearings, tapered roller bearings and needle roller bearings.
Bevel gears Used to turn the drive through 90°. Typical applications are shaft final drive and camshaft drive **(see illustration)**.

Bevel gears are used to turn the drive through 90°

BHP Brake Horsepower. The British measurement for engine power output. Power output is now usually expressed in kilowatts (kW).
Bias-belted tyre Similar construction to radial tyre, but with outer belt running at an angle to the wheel rim.
Big-end bearing The bearing in the end of the connecting rod that's attached to the crankshaft.
Bleeding The process of removing air from an hydraulic system via a bleed nipple or bleed screw.
Bottom-end A description of an engine's crankcase components and all components contained there-in.
BTDC Before Top Dead Centre in terms of piston position. Ignition timing is often expressed in terms of degrees or millimetres BTDC.
Bush A cylindrical metal or rubber component used between two moving parts.
Burr Rough edge left on a component after machining or as a result of excessive wear.

C

Cam chain The chain which takes drive from the crankshaft to the camshaft(s).
Canister The main component in an evaporative emission control system (California market only); contains activated charcoal granules to trap vapours from the fuel system rather than allowing them to vent to the atmosphere.
Castellated Resembling the parapets along the top of a castle wall. For example, a castellated wheel axle or spindle nut.
Catalytic converter A device in the exhaust system of some machines which converts certain pollutants in the exhaust gases into less harmful substances.
Charging system Description of the components which charge the battery, ie the alternator, rectifier and regulator.
Circlip A ring-shaped clip used to prevent endwise movement of cylindrical parts and shafts. An internal circlip is installed in a groove in a housing; an external circlip fits into a groove on the outside of a cylindrical piece such as a shaft. Also known as a snap-ring.
Clearance The amount of space between two parts. For example, between a piston and a cylinder, between a bearing and a journal, etc.
Coil spring A spiral of elastic steel found in various sizes throughout a vehicle, for example as a springing medium in the suspension and in the valve train.
Compression Reduction in volume, and increase in pressure and temperature, of a gas, caused by squeezing it into a smaller space.
Compression damping Controls the speed the suspension compresses when hitting a bump.
Compression ratio The relationship between cylinder volume when the piston is at top dead centre and cylinder volume when the piston is at bottom dead centre.
Continuity The uninterrupted path in the flow of electricity. Little or no measurable resistance.
Continuity tester Self-powered bleeper or test light which indicates continuity.
Cp Candlepower. Bulb rating commonly found on US motorcycles.
Crossply tyre Tyre plies arranged in a criss-cross pattern. Usually four or six plies used, hence 4PR or 6PR in tyre size codes.
Cush drive Rubber damper segments fitted between the rear wheel and final drive sprocket to absorb transmission shocks **(see illustration)**.

Cush drive rubbers dampen out transmission shocks

D

Degree disc Calibrated disc for measuring piston position. Expressed in degrees.
Dial gauge Clock-type gauge with adapters for measuring runout and piston position. Expressed in mm or inches.
Diaphragm The rubber membrane in a master cylinder or carburettor which seals the upper chamber.
Diaphragm spring A single sprung plate often used in clutches.
Direct current (dc) Current produced by a dc generator.

Technical Terms Explained

Decarbonisation The process of removing carbon deposits - typically from the combustion chamber, valves and exhaust port/system.

Detonation Destructive and damaging explosion of fuel/air mixture in combustion chamber instead of controlled burning.

Diode An electrical valve which only allows current to flow in one direction. Commonly used in rectifiers and starter interlock systems.

Disc valve (or rotary valve) A induction system used on some two-stroke engines.

Double-overhead camshaft (DOHC) An engine that uses two overhead camshafts, one for the intake valves and one for the exhaust valves.

Drivebelt A toothed belt used to transmit drive to the rear wheel on some motorcycles. A drivebelt has also been used to drive the camshafts. Drivebelts are usually made of Kevlar.

Driveshaft Any shaft used to transmit motion. Commonly used when referring to the final driveshaft on shaft drive motorcycles.

E

Earth return The return path of an electrical circuit, utilising the motorcycle's frame.

ECU (Electronic Control Unit) A computer which controls (for instance) an ignition system, or an anti-lock braking system.

EGO Exhaust Gas Oxygen sensor. Sometimes called a Lambda sensor.

Electrolyte The fluid in a lead-acid battery.

EMS (Engine Management System) A computer controlled system which manages the fuel injection and the ignition systems in an integrated fashion.

Endfloat The amount of lengthways movement between two parts. As applied to a crankshaft, the distance that the crankshaft can move side-to-side in the crankcase.

Endless chain A chain having no joining link. Common use for cam chains and final drive chains.

EP (Extreme Pressure) Oil type used in locations where high loads are applied, such as between gear teeth.

Evaporative emission control system Describes a charcoal filled canister which stores fuel vapours from the tank rather than allowing them to vent to the atmosphere. Usually only fitted to California models and referred to as an EVAP system.

Expansion chamber Section of two-stroke engine exhaust system so designed to improve engine efficiency and boost power.

F

Feeler blade or gauge A thin strip or blade of hardened steel, ground to an exact thickness, used to check or measure clearances between parts.

Final drive Description of the drive from the transmission to the rear wheel. Usually by chain or shaft, but sometimes by belt.

Firing order The order in which the engine cylinders fire, or deliver their power strokes, beginning with the number one cylinder.

Flooding Term used to describe a high fuel level in the carburettor float chambers, leading to fuel overflow. Also refers to excess fuel in the combustion chamber due to incorrect starting technique.

Free length The no-load state of a component when measured. Clutch, valve and fork spring lengths are measured at rest, without any preload.

Freeplay The amount of travel before any action takes place. The looseness in a linkage, or an assembly of parts, between the initial application of force and actual movement. For example, the distance the rear brake pedal moves before the rear brake is actuated.

Fuel injection The fuel/air mixture is metered electronically and directed into the engine intake ports (indirect injection) or into the cylinders (direct injection). Sensors supply information on engine speed and conditions.

Fuel/air mixture The charge of fuel and air going into the engine. See **Stoichiometric ratio**.

Fuse An electrical device which protects a circuit against accidental overload. The typical fuse contains a soft piece of metal which is calibrated to melt at a predetermined current flow (expressed as amps) and break the circuit.

G

Gap The distance the spark must travel in jumping from the centre electrode to the side electrode in a spark plug. Also refers to the distance between the ignition rotor and the pickup coil in an electronic ignition system.

Gasket Any thin, soft material - usually cork, cardboard, asbestos or soft metal - installed between two metal surfaces to ensure a good seal. For instance, the cylinder head gasket seals the joint between the block and the cylinder head.

Gauge An instrument panel display used to monitor engine conditions. A gauge with a movable pointer on a dial or a fixed scale is an analogue gauge. A gauge with a numerical readout is called a digital gauge.

Gear ratios The drive ratio of a pair of gears in a gearbox, calculated on their number of teeth.

Glaze-busting see **Honing**

Grinding Process for renovating the valve face and valve seat contact area in the cylinder head.

Gudgeon pin The shaft which connects the connecting rod small-end with the piston. Often called a piston pin or wrist pin.

H

Helical gears Gear teeth are slightly curved and produce less gear noise that straight-cut gears. Often used for primary drives.

Installing a Helicoil thread insert in a cylinder head

Helicoil A thread insert repair system. Commonly used as a repair for stripped spark plug threads (see illustration).

Honing A process used to break down the glaze on a cylinder bore (also called glaze-busting). Can also be carried out to roughen a rebored cylinder to aid ring bedding-in.

HT (High Tension) Description of the electrical circuit from the secondary winding of the ignition coil to the spark plug.

Hydraulic A liquid filled system used to transmit pressure from one component to another. Common uses on motorcycles are brakes and clutches.

Hydrometer An instrument for measuring the specific gravity of a lead-acid battery.

Hygroscopic Water absorbing. In motorcycle applications, braking efficiency will be reduced if DOT 3 or 4 hydraulic fluid absorbs water from the air - care must be taken to keep new brake fluid in tightly sealed containers.

I

lbf ft Pounds-force feet. An imperial unit of torque. Sometimes written as ft-lbs.

lbf in Pound-force inch. An imperial unit of torque, applied to components where a very low torque is required. Sometimes written as in-lbs.

IC Abbreviation for Integrated Circuit.

Ignition advance Means of increasing the timing of the spark at higher engine speeds. Done by mechanical means (ATU) on early engines or electronically by the ignition control unit on later engines.

Ignition timing The moment at which the spark plug fires, expressed in the number of crankshaft degrees before the piston reaches the top of its stroke, or in the number of millimetres before the piston reaches the top of its stroke.

Infinity (∞) Description of an open-circuit electrical state, where no continuity exists.

Inverted forks (upside down forks) The sliders or lower legs are held in the yokes and the fork tubes or stanchions are connected to the wheel axle (spindle). Less unsprung weight and stiffer construction than conventional forks.

J

JASO Quality standard for 2-stroke oils.

Joule The unit of electrical energy.

Journal The bearing surface of a shaft.

K

Kickstart Mechanical means of turning the engine over for starting purposes. Only usually fitted to mopeds, small capacity motorcycles and off-road motorcycles.

Kill switch Handebar-mounted switch for emergency ignition cut-out. Cuts the ignition circuit on all models, and additionally prevent starter motor operation on others.

km Symbol for kilometre.

kmh Abbreviation for kilometres per hour.

L

Lambda (λ) sensor A sensor fitted in the exhaust system to measure the exhaust gas oxygen content (excess air factor).

Technical Terms Explained REF•45

Lapping see **Grinding**.
LCD Abbreviation for Liquid Crystal Display.
LED Abbreviation for Light Emitting Diode.
Liner A steel cylinder liner inserted in a aluminium alloy cylinder block.
Locknut A nut used to lock an adjustment nut, or other threaded component, in place.
Lockstops The lugs on the lower triple clamp (yoke) which abut those on the frame, preventing handlebar-to-fuel tank contact.
Lockwasher A form of washer designed to prevent an attaching nut from working loose.
LT Low Tension Description of the electrical circuit from the power supply to the primary winding of the ignition coil.

M

Main bearings The bearings between the crankshaft and crankcase.
Maintenance-free (MF) battery A sealed battery which cannot be topped up.
Manometer Mercury-filled calibrated tubes used to measure intake tract vacuum. Used to synchronise carburettors on multi-cylinder engines.
Micrometer A precision measuring instrument that measures component outside diameters **(see illustration)**.

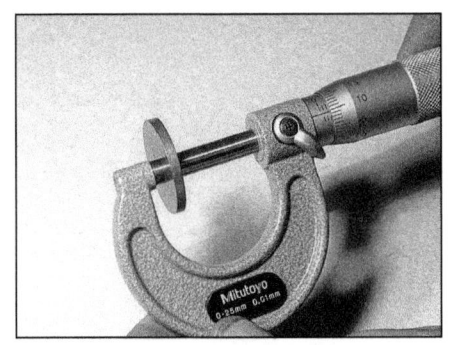

Tappet shims are measured with a micrometer

MON (Motor Octane Number) A measure of a fuel's resistance to knock.
Monograde oil An oil with a single viscosity, eg SAE80W.
Monoshock A single suspension unit linking the swingarm or suspension linkage to the frame.
mph Abbreviation for miles per hour.
Multigrade oil Having a wide viscosity range (eg 10W40). The W stands for Winter, thus the viscosity ranges from SAE10 when cold to SAE40 when hot.
Multimeter An electrical test instrument with the capability to measure voltage, current and resistance. Some meters also incorporate a continuity tester and buzzer.

N

Needle roller bearing Inner race of caged needle rollers and hardened outer race. Examples of uncaged needle rollers can be found on some engines. Commonly used in rear suspension applications and in two-stroke engines.
Nm Newton metres.
NOx Oxides of Nitrogen. A common toxic pollutant emitted by petrol engines at higher temperatures.

O

Octane The measure of a fuel's resistance to knock.
OE (Original Equipment) Relates to components fitted to a motorcycle as standard or replacement parts supplied by the motorcycle manufacturer.
Ohm The unit of electrical resistance. Ohms = Volts ÷ Current.
Ohmmeter An instrument for measuring electrical resistance.
Oil cooler System for diverting engine oil outside of the engine to a radiator for cooling purposes.
Oil injection A system of two-stroke engine lubrication where oil is pump-fed to the engine in accordance with throttle position.
Open-circuit An electrical condition where there is a break in the flow of electricity - no continuity (high resistance).
O-ring A type of sealing ring made of a special rubber-like material; in use, the O-ring is compressed into a groove to provide the sealing action.
Oversize (OS) Term used for piston and ring size options fitted to a rebored cylinder.
Overhead cam (sohc) engine An engine with single camshaft located on top of the cylinder head.
Overhead valve (ohv) engine An engine with the valves located in the cylinder head, but with the camshaft located in the engine block or crankcase.
Oxygen sensor A device installed in the exhaust system which senses the oxygen content in the exhaust and converts this information into an electric current. Also called a Lambda sensor.

P

Plastigauge A thin strip of plastic thread, available in different sizes, used for measuring clearances. For example, a strip of Plastigauge is laid across a bearing journal. The parts are assembled and dismantled; the width of the crushed strip indicates the clearance between journal and bearing.
Polarity Either negative or positive earth (ground), determined by which battery lead is connected to the frame (earth return). Modern motorcycles are usually negative earth.
Pre-ignition A situation where the fuel/air mixture ignites before the spark plug fires. Often due to a hot spot in the combustion chamber caused by carbon build-up. Engine has a tendency to 'run-on'.
Pre-load (suspension) The amount a spring is compressed when in the unloaded state. Preload can be applied by gas, spacer or mechanical adjuster.
Premix The method of engine lubrication on older two-stroke engines. Engine oil is mixed with the petrol in the fuel tank in a specific ratio. The fuel/oil mix is sometimes referred to as "petroil".
Primary drive Description of the drive from the crankshaft to the clutch. Usually by gear or chain.
PS Pfedestärke - a German interpretation of BHP.
PSI Pounds-force per square inch. Imperial measurement of tyre pressure and cylinder pressure measurement.
PTFE Polytetrafluroethylene. A low friction substance.
Pulse secondary air injection system A process of promoting the burning of excess fuel present in the exhaust gases by routing fresh air into the exhaust ports.

Q

Quartz halogen bulb Tungsten filament surrounded by a halogen gas. Typically used for the headlight **(see illustration)**.

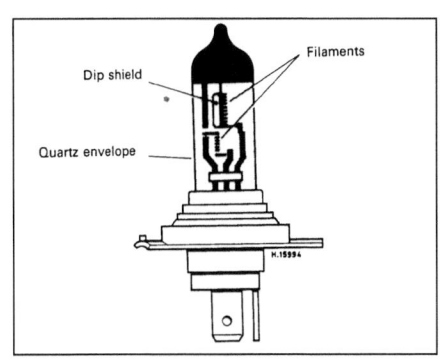

Quartz halogen headlight bulb construction

R

Rack-and-pinion A pinion gear on the end of a shaft that mates with a rack (think of a geared wheel opened up and laid flat). Sometimes used in clutch operating systems.
Radial play Up and down movement about a shaft.
Radial ply tyres Tyre plies run across the tyre (from bead to bead) and around the circumference of the tyre. Less resistant to tread distortion than other tyre types.
Radiator A liquid-to-air heat transfer device designed to reduce the temperature of the coolant in a liquid cooled engine.
Rake A feature of steering geometry - the angle of the steering head in relation to the vertical **(see illustration)**.

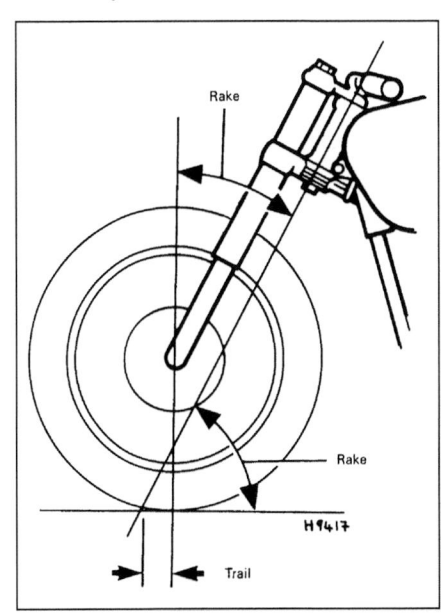

Steering geometry

REF•46 Technical Terms Explained

Rebore Providing a new working surface to the cylinder bore by boring out the old surface. Necessitates the use of oversize piston and rings.
Rebound damping A means of controlling the oscillation of a suspension unit spring after it has been compressed. Resists the spring's natural tendency to bounce back after being compressed.
Rectifier Device for converting the ac output of an alternator into dc for battery charging.
Reed valve An induction system commonly used on two-stroke engines.
Regulator Device for maintaining the charging voltage from the generator or alternator within a specified range.
Relay A electrical device used to switch heavy current on and off by using a low current auxiliary circuit.
Resistance Measured in ohms. An electrical component's ability to pass electrical current.
RON (Research Octane Number) A measure of a fuel's resistance to knock.
rpm revolutions per minute.
Runout The amount of wobble (in-and-out movement) of a wheel or shaft as it's rotated. The amount a shaft rotates 'out-of-true'. The out-of-round condition of a rotating part.

S

SAE (Society of Automotive Engineers) A standard for the viscosity of a fluid.
Sealant A liquid or paste used to prevent leakage at a joint. Sometimes used in conjunction with a gasket.
Service limit Term for the point where a component is no longer useable and must be renewed.
Shaft drive A method of transmitting drive from the transmission to the rear wheel.
Shell bearings Plain bearings consisting of two shell halves. Most often used as big-end and main bearings in a four-stroke engine. Often called bearing inserts.
Shim Thin spacer, commonly used to adjust the clearance or relative positions between two parts. For example, shims inserted into or under tappets or followers to control valve clearances. Clearance is adjusted by changing the thickness of the shim.
Short-circuit An electrical condition where current shorts to earth (ground) bypassing the circuit components.
Skimming Process to correct warpage or repair a damaged surface, eg on brake discs or drums.
Slide-hammer A special puller that screws into or hooks onto a component such as a shaft or bearing; a heavy sliding handle on the shaft bottoms against the end of the shaft to knock the component free.
Small-end bearing The bearing in the upper end of the connecting rod at its joint with the gudgeon pin.
Spalling Damage to camshaft lobes or bearing journals shown as pitting of the working surface.
Specific gravity (SG) The state of charge of the electrolyte in a lead-acid battery. A measure of the electrolyte's density compared with water.
Straight-cut gears Common type gear used on gearbox shafts and for oil pump and water pump drives.
Stanchion The inner sliding part of the front forks, held by the yokes. Often called a fork tube.

Stoichiometric ratio The optimum chemical air/fuel ratio for a petrol engine, said to be 14.7 parts of air to 1 part of fuel.
Sulphuric acid The liquid (electrolyte) used in a lead-acid battery. Poisonous and extremely corrosive.
Surface grinding (lapping) Process to correct a warped gasket face, commonly used on cylinder heads.

T

Tapered-roller bearing Tapered inner race of caged needle rollers and separate tapered outer race. Examples of taper roller bearings can be found on steering heads.
Tappet A cylindrical component which transmits motion from the cam to the valve stem, either directly or via a pushrod and rocker arm. Also called a cam follower.
TCS Traction Control System. An electronically-controlled system which senses wheel spin and reduces engine speed accordingly.
TDC Top Dead Centre denotes that the piston is at its highest point in the cylinder.
Thread-locking compound Solution applied to fastener threads to prevent slackening. Select type to suit application.
Thrust washer A washer positioned between two moving components on a shaft. For example, between gear pinions on gearshaft.
Timing chain See **Cam Chain**.
Timing light Stroboscopic lamp for carrying out ignition timing checks with the engine running.
Top-end A description of an engine's cylinder block, head and valve gear components.
Torque Turning or twisting force about a shaft.
Torque setting A prescribed tightness specified by the motorcycle manufacturer to ensure that the bolt or nut is secured correctly. Undertightening can result in the bolt or nut coming loose or a surface not being sealed. Overtightening can result in stripped threads, distortion or damage to the component being retained.
Torx key A six-point wrench.
Tracer A stripe of a second colour applied to a wire insulator to distinguish that wire from another one with the same colour insulator. For example, Br/W is often used to denote a brown insulator with a white tracer.
Trail A feature of steering geometry. Distance from the steering head axis to the tyre's central contact point.
Triple clamps The cast components which extend from the steering head and support the fork stanchions or tubes. Often called fork yokes.
Turbocharger A centrifugal device, driven by exhaust gases, that pressurises the intake air. Normally used to increase the power output from a given engine displacement.
TWI Abbreviation for Tyre Wear Indicator. Indicates the location of the tread depth indicator bars on tyres.

U

Universal joint or U-joint (UJ) A double-pivoted connection for transmitting power from a driving to a driven shaft through an angle. Typically found in shaft drive assemblies.
Unsprung weight Anything not supported by the bike's suspension (ie the wheel, tyres, brakes, final drive and bottom (moving) part of the suspension).

V

Vacuum gauges Clock-type gauges for measuring intake tract vacuum. Used for carburettor synchronisation on multi-cylinder engines.
Valve A device through which the flow of liquid, gas or vacuum may be stopped, started or regulated by a moveable part that opens, shuts or partially obstructs one or more ports or passageways. The intake and exhaust valves in the cylinder head are of the poppet type.
Valve clearance The clearance between the valve tip (the end of the valve stem) and the rocker arm or tappet/follower. The valve clearance is measured when the valve is closed. The correct clearance is important - if too small the valve won't close fully and will burn out, whereas if too large noisy operation will result.
Valve lift The amount a valve is lifted off its seat by the camshaft lobe.
Valve timing The exact setting for the opening and closing of the valves in relation to piston position.
Vernier caliper A precision measuring instrument that measures inside and outside dimensions. Not quite as accurate as a micrometer, but more convenient.
VIN Vehicle Identification Number. Term for the bike's engine and frame numbers.
Viscosity The thickness of a liquid or its resistance to flow.
Volt A unit for expressing electrical "pressure" in a circuit. Volts = current x ohms.

W

Water pump A mechanically-driven device for moving coolant around the engine.
Watt A unit for expressing electrical power. Watts = volts x current.
Wear limit see **Service limit**
Wet liner A liquid-cooled engine design where the pistons run in liners which are directly surrounded by coolant **(see illustration)**.

Wet liner arrangement

Wheelbase Distance from the centre of the front wheel to the centre of the rear wheel.
Wiring harness or loom Describes the electrical wires running the length of the motorcycle and enclosed in tape or plastic sheathing. Wiring coming off the main harness is usually referred to as a sub harness.
Woodruff key A key of semi-circular or square section used to locate a gear to a shaft. Often used to locate the alternator rotor on the crankshaft.
Wrist pin Another name for gudgeon or piston pin.

Index

Note: *References throughout this index relate to Chapter•page number*

A

ABS - 10•13, 10•14, 10•16
   check - 0•12, 1•8
Air filter
   element - 1•12, 1•14
   housing - 6•13
Airflow meter - 6•14
Alternator - 11•3, 11•4
Antifreeze - 0•12, 1•2
Auxiliary driveshaft - 2•8, 2•25, 2•34

B

Battery - 11•2
   check - 1•12
   open-circuit voltage - REF•39
   specific gravity - REF•40
Bearings - REF•14
   engine - 2•14, 2•15, 2•20, 2•21, 2•27
   gearbox - 4•4
   steering head - 1•17, 8•9, 8•10, 8•11
   swinging arm pivot - 1•18
   wheel - 1•17, 10•4
Bellhousing - 2•8, 2•34
Big-end bearings - 2•20
Bleeding the brakes - 10•10
Bodywork - 8•17
Brake fluid - 0•11, 1•2, 1•16
Brake pads - 1•15
Brake problems - REF•37
Brakes - 10•1 et seq
   bleeding - 10•10
   caliper - 10•6
   check and adjustment - 1•17
   drum - 10•11
   master cylinder - 10•7, 10•9
   overhaul - 10•5
   pads - 1•15
Bulbs - 11•11

C

Caliper - 10•6
Cam chain - 2•9
Camshaft - 2•9, 2•15, 2•32
   drive mechanism - 2•15
Capacity - 1•2
Cases - 2•15
Chains - REF•18
Chemicals - REF•21
Clutch - 3•1 et seq
   check and adjustment - 1•14
   dismantling - 3•3
   examination and renovation - 3•4
   problems - REF•33
   reassembly - 3•4
   release mechanism - 3•6
   removal - 3•3
Cold start (choke) device indicator - 11•9
Component locations - 1•4

Compression test - 2•5, REF•39
Connecting rods - 2•11, 2•20, 2•30
Continuity - REF•40
Controls - 0•12, 8•12
   lubrication - 1•8
Conversion factors - REF•20
Coolant - 0•12, 1•2
   overheat warning lamp circuit - 11•9
   pump - 5•6
Cooling fan - 5•8
Cooling system - 5•1 et seq
   check - 1•14
   draining and flushing - 5•2
   electrical components - 5•8
   filling - 5•3
   hoses and connections - 5•5
Covers - 2•8, 2•15, 2•35
Crankcase lower section - 2•12, 2•28
Crankshaft - 2•13, 2•21, 2•28
Cylinder block - 2•19
Cylinder head - 2•10, 2•16, 2•31

D

Daily (pre-ride) checks - 0•10
Dimensions - REF•1
Dismantling the engine - 2•5, 2•7
Draining the cooling system - 5•2
Drive shaft - 9•5, 9•7
Drum - 10•11

Index

E

Earth - REF•42
Electrical problems - REF•38
Electrical system - 11•1 et seq
Engine - 2•1 et seq
   ancillary components - 2•36
   auxiliary driveshaft - 2•8, 2•25, 2•34
   bearings - 2•14, 2•15, 2•20, 2•21, 2•27, REF•14
   bellhousing - 2•8, 2•34
   big-end bearings - 2•20
   camshaft drive mechanism - 2•15
   camshafts - 2•9, 2•15, 2•32
   cases - 2•15
   compression test - 2•5, REF•39
   connecting rods - 2•11, 2•20, 2•30
   covers - 2•8, 2•15, 2•35
   crankcase lower section - 2•12, 2•28
   crankshaft - 2•13, 2•21, 2•28
   cylinder block - 2•19
   cylinder head - 2•10, 2•16, 2•31
   dismantling - 2•5, 2•7
   doesn't start - REF•31
   examination and renovation - 2•14
   fault finding - REF•30
   kill switches - 7•5
   noise - REF•34
   oil - 0•10, 1•2, 1•6
   oil filter - 1•6
   oil seals - 2•14, 2•15, 2•27, REF•16
   output/balancer shaft - 2•12, 2•23, 2•28
   piston rings - 2•19
   pistons - 2•11, 2•19, 2•30
   reassembly - 2•26
   refitting - 2•37
   removal - 2•6
   starter clutch - 2•25
   valve timing - 2•32
   valves - 2•17
Exhaust system - 6•19

F

Fairing - 8•12
Fasteners - REF•5
Fault finding - REF•30
   equipment - REF•39
   fuel system - 6•5
   ignition system - 7•5
Filling the cooling system - 5•3
Final drive - 9•1 et seq
   examination and renovation - 9•3
   oil - 1•2, 1•8, 1•13
   refitting - 9•5
   removal - 9•2
   shaft - 9•7
   shaft splines - 1•18
Fluidbloc steering damper - 8•11
Fluids - 1•2, REF•21
Flushing the cooling system - 5•2
Footrests - 8•12
Forks - 8•3, 8•4, 8•6, 8•8, 8•9
   oil - 1•2, 1•14
Frame - 8•1 et seq
   examination - 8•12
   noise - REF•37

Front forks - 8•3
   oil change - 1•2, 1•14
Front suspension - 8•1 et seq
Front wheel - 10•3
Fuel check - 0•12
Fuel filter - 1•18, 6•10
Fuel gauge sender unit - 6•9
Fuel injectors - 6•12
Fuel level gauge circuit - 11•9
Fuel pump - 6•10, 6•11
Fuel rail - 6•12
Fuel system - 6•1 et seq
   adjustment - 6•16
   check - 1•15
   compensating for high altitude - 6•18
   electrical components - 6•15
   fault finding - 6•5
   mixture adjustment - 6•17
   plenum chamber - 6•14
   pressure - 6•5, 6•11
   pressure regulator - 6•12
   recommended fuel - 6•18
   throttle butterfly assembly - 6•14
Fuel tank - 6•6, 6•8
Fuses - 11•6

G

Gaskets - REF•17
Gauges - REF•9
Gear selection problems - REF•34
Gearbox - 4•1 et seq
   bearings - 4•4
   dismantling - 4•3
   examination and renovation - 4•6
   noise - REF•35
   oil - 1•2, 1•7, 1•13
   reassembly - 4•8
   refitting - 4•13
   removal - 4•2
   seals - 4•4
   shafts - 4•5, 4•8

H

Horn - 11•11
Hoses - REF•19
Hydraulic fluid - 0•11, 1•2, 1•16

I

Identification numbers - 0•8
Ignition - 7•1 et seq
   control unit - 7•3
   fault finding - 7•5
   HT coils - 7•4
   HT leads - 7•4
   switches - 7•5
   timing - 7•5
   trigger assembly - 7•3
Injectors - 6•12
Instruments - 8•19
Introduction - 0•4

L

Legal checks - 0•12
Leverage - REF•13
Lighting check - 0•12
Lubricants - 1•2, REF•21
Luggage - 8•19

M

Main bearings - 2•21
Maintenance schedule - 1•3
Master cylinder - 10•7, 10•9
Measuring tools - REF•9
Mirrors - 8•19
Mixture adjustment - 6•17
MOT - REF•22

N

Nivomat suspension unit - 9•9

O

Oil, engine - 0•10, 1•2, 1•6
Oil, final drive - 1•2, 1•8, 1•13
Oil, forks - 1•2, 1•14
Oil, gearbox - 1•2, 1•7, 1•13
Oil filter - 1•6
Oil pressure relief valve - 6•21
Oil pressure warning lamp - 6•23, REF•35
   circuit - 11•9
Oil pump - 6•20
   pick-up filter gauze - 6•22
Oil seals - 2•14, 2•15, 2•27, 4•4, REF•16
Outer covers - 2•8, 2•15, 2•35
Output/balancer shaft - 2•12, 2•23, 2•28
Overheating - REF•33

P

Pads - 1•15
Pistons - 2•11, 2•19, 2•30
Plenum chamber - 6•14
Poor handling or roadholding - REF•36
Poor running - REF•32, REF•33
Pre-ride checks - 0•10
Pressure regulator - 6•12
Pressures, tyres - 0•13
Punctures - 10•17

R

Radiator - 5•3
   pressure cap - 5•4
Radio - 11•11
Rear suspension - 9•1 et seq
   unit - 9•8
Rear wheel - 10•3
Reassembling the engine - 2•26
Recommended fuel - 6•18

Index

Reference - REF•1 et seq
Refitting the engine to the frame - 2•37
Relays - 11•11
Relieving the fuel system pressure - 6•5
Removing the engine from the frame - 2•6
Routine maintenance and servicing - 1•1 et seq

S

Safety checks - 0•12
Safety first - 0•9
Sealants - REF•17
Seals - 2•14, 2•15, 2•27, 4•4, REF•16
Seat - 8•17
Servicing see Routine maintenance
Servicing specifications - 1•2
Shafts - 4•5
 endfloat and preload - 4•8
Short-circuit - REF•42
Spare parts - 0•8
Spark plugs - 1•11, 1•15, 7•5
Speedometer impulse transmitter - 1•14
Stands - 8•12
 pivots lubrication - 1•8
Starter clutch - 2•25

Starter motor - 11•7
 problems - REF•31
Starting and running the rebuilt engine - 2•39
Starting problems - REF•31
Starting system checks - 11•8
Steering - 0•12
 damper - 8•11
 head bearings - 1•17, 8•9, 8•10, 8•11
Storage - REF•27
Suspension - 8•1 et seq, 9•1 et seq
 check - 0•12
Swinging arm - 9•5, 9•6, 9•7
 pivot bearings - 1•18
Switches - 7•5, 11•10

T

Tail lamp bulb monitoring device - 11•9
Taking the rebuilt engine on the road - 2•39
Technical terms explained - REF•43
Thermostat - 5•6
Throttle butterfly assembly - 6•14
Tools - REF•2
Torque - REF•13
Transmission see gearbox

Turn signal relay - 11•11
Tyres - 10•1 et seq
 check and pressures - 0•13
 fitting - 10•16

V

Vacuum switch - 7•5
Valve clearances - 1•9, 1•18
Valve timing - 2•32
Valves - 2•17
Voltage - REF•41

W

Water pump - 5•6
Weights - REF•1
Wheels - 10•1 et seq
 bearings - 1•17, 10•4
 changing - 10•17
 check - 1•17
Wiring diagrams - 11•14 et seq
Workshop
 equipment and facilities - REF•4
 tips - REF•2

Notes

Haynes Motorcycle Manuals – The Complete List

Title		Book No
APRILIA RS50 (99 – 06) & RS125 (93 – 06)		4298
Aprilia RSV1000 Mille (98 – 03)	♦	4255
Aprilia SR50		4755
BMW 2-valve Twins (70 -96)	♦	0249
BMW F650	♦	4761
BMW K100 & 75 2-valve models (83 - 96)	♦	1373
BMW F800 (F650) Twins (06 – 10)	♦	4872
BMW R850, 1100 & 1150 4-valve Twins (93 – 06)	♦	3466
BMW R1200 (04 – 09)	♦	4598
BMW R1200 dohc Twins (10 – 12)	♦	4925
BSA Bantam (48 – 71)		0117
BSA Unit Singles (58 – 72)		0127
BSA Pre-unit Singles (54 – 61)		0326
BSA A7 & A10 Twins (47 – 62)		0121
BSA A50 & A65 Twins (62 – 73)		0155
CHINESE, Taiwanese & Korean Scooters		4768
Chinese, Taiwanese & Korean 125cc motorcyles		4781
Pulse/Pioneer Adrenaline, Sinnis Apache, Superbyke RMR (07 – 14)	◇♦	5750
DUCATI 600, 620, 750 & 900 2-valve V-twins (91 – 05)	♦	3290
Ducati Mk III & Desmo singles (69 – 76)	◇	0445
Ducati 748, 916 & 996 4-valve V-twins (94 – 01)	♦	3756
GILERA Runner, DNA, Ice & SKP/Stalker (97 – 11)		4163
HARLEY-DAVIDSON Sportsters (70 – 10)	♦	2534
Harley-Davidson Shovelhead & Evolution Big Twins (70 -99)	♦	2536
Harley-Davidson Twin Cam 88, 96 & 103 models (99 – 10)	♦	2478
HONDA NB, ND, NP & NS50 Melody (81 -85)	◇	0622
Honda NE/NB50 Vision & SA50 Vision Met-in (85-95)	◇	1278
Honda MB, MBX, MT & MTX50 (80 – 93)		0731
Honda C50, C70 & C90 (67 – 03)		0324
Honda XR50/70/80/100R & CRF50/70/80/100F (85 – 07)		2218
Honda XL/XR 80, 100, 125, 185 & 200 2-valve models (78 – 87)		0566
Honda H100 & H100S Singles (80 – 92)	◇	0734
Honda 125 Scooters (00 – 09)		4873
Honda ANF125 Innova Scooters (03 -12)	♦	4926
Honda CB/CD125T & CM125C Twins (77 – 88)	◇	0571
Honda CBF125 (09 – 14)	♦	5540
Honda CG125 (76 – 07)	◇	0433
Honda NS125 (86 – 93)	◇	3056
Honda CBR125R (04 – 10)		4620
Honda CBR125R, CBR250R & CRF250L/M (11 – 14)	♦	5919
Honda MBX/MTX125 & MTX200 (83 – 93)	◇	1132
Honda XL125V & VT125C (99 – 11)		4899
Honda CD/CM185 200T & CM250C 2-valve Twins (77 – 85)		0572
Honda CMX250 Rebel & CB250 Nighthawk Twins (85 – 09)	◇	2756
Honda XL/XR 250 & 500 (78 – 84)		0567
Honda XR250L, XR250R & XR400R (86 – 04)		2219
Honda CB250 & CB400N Super Dreams (78 – 84)	◇	0540
Honda CR Motocross Bikes (86 – 07)		2222
Honda CRF250 & CRF450 (02 – 06)		2630
Honda CBR400RR Fours (88 – 99)	◇♦	3552
Honda VFR400 (NC30) & RVF400 (NC35) V-Fours (89 – 98)	◇♦	3496
Honda CB500 (93 – 02) & CBF500 (03 – 08)	◇	3753
Honda CB400 & CB550 Fours (73 – 77)		0262
Honda CX/GL500 & 650 V-Twins (78 – 86)		0442
Honda CBX550 Four (82 – 86)	◇	0940
Honda XL600R & XR600R (83 – 08)	♦	2183
Honda XL600/650V Transalp & XRV750 Africa Twin (87 – 07)	♦	3919
Honda CB600 Hornet, CBF600 & CBR600F (07 – 12)	♦	5572
Honda CBR600F1 & 1000F Fours (87 – 96)	♦	1730
Honda CBR600F2 & F3 Fours (91 – 98)	♦	2070
Honda CBR600F4 (99 – 06)	♦	3911
Honda CB600F Hornet & CBF600 (98 – 06)	◇♦	3915
Honda CBR600RR (03 – 06)	♦	4590
Honda CBR600RR (07 -12)	♦	4795
Honda CB650 sohc Fours (78 – 84)		0665
Honda NTV600 Revere, NTV650 & NT650V Deauville (88 – 05)	◇♦	3243
Honda Shadow VT600 & 750 (USA) (88 – 09)		2312
Honda NT700V Deauville & XL700V Transalp (06 -13)	♦	5541
Honda CB750 sohc Four (69 – 79)		0131
Honda V45/65 Sabre & Magna (82 – 88)		0820
Honda VFR750 & 700 V-Fours (86 – 97)	♦	2101
Honda VFR800 V-Fours (97 – 01)	♦	3703
Honda VFR800 V-Tec V-Fours (02 – 09)	♦	4196
Honda CB750 & CB900 dohc Fours (78 – 84)		0535
Honda CBF1000 (06 -10) & CB1000R (08 – 11)	♦	4927
Honda VTR1000 Firestorm, Super Hawk & XL1000V Varadero (97 – 08)	♦	3744
Honda CBR900RR Fireblade (92 – 99)	♦	2161
Honda CBR900RR Fireblade (00 – 03)	♦	4060
Honda CBR1000RR Fireblade (04 – 07)	♦	4604
Honda CBR1000RR Fireblade (08 – 13)	♦	5688
Honda CBR1100XX Super Blackbird (97 – 07)	♦	3901
Honda ST1100 Pan European V-Fours (90 – 02)	♦	3384
Honda ST1300 Pan European (02 -11)	♦	4908
Honda Shadow VT1100 (USA) (85 – 07)		2313

Title		Book No
Honda GL1000 Gold Wing (75 – 79)		0309
Honda GL1100 Gold Wing (79 – 81)		0669
Honda Gold Wing 1200 (USA) (84 - 87)		2199
Honda Gold Wing 1500 (USA) (88 – 00)		2225
Honda Goldwing GL1800	♦	2787
KAWASAKI AE/AR 50 & 80 (81 – 95)		1007
Kawasaki KC, KE & KH100 (75 – 99)		1371
Kawasaki KMX125 & 200 (86 – 02)	◇	3046
Kawasaki 250, 350 & 400 Triples (72 – 79)		0134
Kawasaki 400 & 440 Twins (74 – 81)		0281
Kawasaki 400, 500 & 550 Fours (79 – 91)		0910
Kawasaki EN450 & 500 Twins (Ltd/Vulcan) (85 – 07)		2053
Kawasaki ER-6F & ER-6N (06 -10)	♦	4874
Kawasaki EX500 (GPZ500S) & ER500 (ER-5) (87 – 08)	♦	2052
Kawasaki ZX600 (ZZ-R600 & Ninja ZX-6) (90 – 06)	♦	2146
Kawasaki ZX-6R Ninja Fours (95 – 02)	♦	3451
Kawasaki ZX-6R (03 – 06)	♦	4742
Kawasaki ZX600 (GPZ600R, GPX600R, Ninja 600R & RX) & ZX750 (GPX750R, Ninja 750R) (85 – 97)	♦	1780
Kawasaki 650 Four (76 – 78)		0373
Kawasaki Vulcan 700/750 & 800 (85 – 04)	♦	2457
Kawasaki Vulcan 1500 & 1600 (87 – 08)	♦	4913
Kawasaki 750 Air-cooled Fours		0574
Kawasaki ZR550 & 750 Zephyr Fours (90 – 97)	♦	3382
Kawasaki Z750 & Z1000 (03 – 08)	♦	4762
Kawasaki ZX750 (Ninja ZX-7 & ZXR750) Fours (89 – 96)	♦	2054
Kawasaki Ninja ZX-7R & ZX-9R (94 – 04)	♦	3721
Kawasaki 900 & 1000 Fours (73 – 77)		0222
Kawasaki ZX900, 1000 & 1100 Liquid-cooled Fours (83 – 97)	♦	1681
Kawasaki ZX-10R (04 – 10)	♦	5542
KTM EXC Enduro & SX Motocross (00 – 07)	♦	4629
LAMBRETTA Scooters (58 – 00)	♦	5573
MOTO GUZZI 750, 850 & 1000 V-Twins (74 – 78)		0339
MZ ETZ models (81 – 95)	◇	1680
NORTON 500, 600, 650 & 750 Twins (57 – 70)		0187
Norton Commando (68 – 77)		0125
PEUGEOT Speedfight, Trekker & Vivacity Scooters (96 – 08)	◇	3920
Peugeot V-Clic, Speedfight 3, Vivacity 3, Kisbee & Tweet (08 – 14)	◇♦	5751
PIAGGIO (Vespa) Scooters (91 – 09)	◇	3492
SUZUKI GT, ZR & TS50 (77 – 90)	◇	0799
Suzuki TS50X (84 – 00)	◇	1599
Suzuki 100, 125, 185 & 250 Air-cooled Trail bikes (79 – 89)		0797
Suzuki GP100 & 125 Singles (78 – 93)	◇	0576
Suzuki GS, GN, GZ & DR125 Singles (82 – 05)	◇	0888
Suzuki Burgman 250 & 400 (98 – 11)	♦	4909
Suzuki GSX-R600/750 (06 – 09)	♦	4790
Suzuki 250 & 350 Twins (68 – 78)		0120
Suzuki GT250X7, GT200X5 & SB200 Twins (78 – 83)	◇	0469
Suzuki DR-Z400 (00 – 10)	♦	2933
Suzuki GS/GSX250, 400 & 450 Twins (79 – 85)		0736
Suzuki GS500 Twin (89 – 08)	♦	3238
Suzuki GS550 (77 – 82) & GS750 Fours (76 – 79)		0363
Suzuki GS/GSX550 4-valve Fours (83 – 88)		1133
Suzuki SV650 & SV650S (99 – 08)	♦	3912
Suzuki DL650 V-Strom & SFV650 Gladius (04 – 13)	♦	5643
Suzuki GSX-R600 & 750 (96 – 00)	♦	3553
Suzuki GSX-R600 (01 – 03), GSX-R750 (00 – 03) & GSX-R1000 (01 – 02)	♦	3986
Suzuki GSX-R600/750 (04 – 05) & GSX-R1000 (03 – 06)	♦	4382
Suzuki GSF600, 650 & 1200 Bandit Fours (95 – 06)	♦	3367
Suzuki Intruder, Marauder, Volusia & Boulevard (85 – 09)	♦	2618
Suzuki GS850 Fours (78 – 88)		0536
Suzuki GS1000 Four (77 – 79)		0484
Suzuki GSX-R750, GSX-R1100 (85 – 92) GSX600F, GSX750F, GSX1100F (Katana) Fours (88 – 96)	♦	2055
Suzuki GSX600/750F & GSX750 (98 – 02)	♦	3987
Suzuki GS/GSX1000, 1100 & 1150 4-valve Fours (79 – 88)		0737
Suzuki TL1000S/R & DL V-Strom (97 – 04)	♦	4083
Suzuki GSF650/1250 Bandit & GSX650/1250F (07 – 14)	♦	4798
Suzuki GSX1300R Hayabusa (99 – 14)	♦	4184
Suzuki GSX1400 (02 – 08)	♦	4758
TRIUMPH Tiger Cub & Terrier (52 – 68)		0414
Triumph 350 & 500 Unit Twins (58 – 73)		0137
Triumph Pre-Unit Twins (47 – 62)		0251
Triumph 650 & 750 2-valve Unit Twins (63 – 83)		0122
Triumph 675 (06 – 10)	♦	4876
Triumph Tiger 800 (10 – 14)	♦	5752
Triumph 1050 Sprint, Speed Triple & Tiger (05 -13)	♦	4796
Triumph Trident & BSA Rocket 3 (69 – 75)		0136
Triumph Bonneville (01 – 12)	♦	4364
Triumph Daytona, Speed Triple, Sprint & Tiger (97 – 05)	♦	3755
Triumph Triples & Fours (carburetor engines) (91 – 04)	♦	2162
VESPA P/PX125, 150 & 200 Scooters (78 – 12)		0707
Vespa GTS125, 250 & 300 (05 – 10)		4898
Vespa Scooters (59 – 78)		0126

Title		Book No
YAMAHA DT50 & 80 Trail Bikes (78 – 95)	◇	0800
Yamaha T50 & 80 Townmate (83 – 95)	◇	1247
Yamaha YB100 Singles (73 – 91)	◇	0474
Yamaha RS/RXS 100 & 125 Singles (74 – 95)		0331
Yamaha RD & DT125LC (82 – 87)	◇	0887
Yamaha TZR125 (87 – 93) & DT125R (88 – 07)	◇	1655
Yamaha TY50, 80, 125 & 175 (74 – 84)	◇	0464
Yamaha XT & SR125 (82 – 03)	◇	1021
Yamaha YBR125 & XT125R/X (05 – 13)		4797
Yamaha YZF-R125 (08 – 11)	♦	5543
Yamaha Trail Bikes (81 – 03)		2350
Yamaha 2-stroke Motocross Bikes (86 – 06)		2662
Yamaha YZ & WR 4-stroke Motorcross Bikes (98 – 08)		2689
Yamaha 250 & 350 Twins (70 – 79)		0040
Yamaha XS250, 360 & 400 sohc Twins (75 – 84)		0378
Yamaha RD250 & 350LC Twins (80 – 82)		0803
Yamaha RD350 YPVS Twins (83 – 95)		1158
Yamaha RD400 Twin (75 – 79)		0333
Yamaha XT, TT & SR500 Singles (75 – 83)		0342
Yamaha XZ550 Vision V-Twins (82 – 85)		0821
Yamaha FJ, FX, XY & YX600 Radian (84 – 92)		2100
Yamaha XT660 & MT-03 (04 – 11)	♦	4910
Yamaha XJ600S (Diversion, Seca II) & XJ600N Fours (92 – 03)	♦	2145
Yamaha XJ6 & FZ6R (09 – 15)	♦	5889
Yamaha YZF600R Thundercat & FZS600 Fazer (96 – 03)	♦	3702
Yamaha FZ-6 Fazer (04 – 08)	♦	4751
Yamaha YZF-R6 (99 – 02)	♦	3900
Yamaha YZF-R6 (03 – 05)	♦	4601
Yamaha YZF-R6 (06 – 13)	♦	5544
Yamaha 650 Twins (70 – 83)		0341
Yamaha XJ650 & 750 Fours (80 – 84)		0738
Yamaha XS750 & 850 Triples (76 – 85)		0340
Yamaha TDM850, TRX850 & XTZ750 (89 – 99)	◇♦	3450
Yamaha YZF750R & YZF1000R Thunderace (93 – 00)	♦	3720
Yamaha FZR600, 750 & 1000 Fours (87 – 96)	♦	2056
Yamaha XV (Virago) V-Twins (81 – 03)	♦	0802
Yamaha XVS650 & 1100 Drag Star/V-Star (97 – 05)	♦	4195
Yamaha XJ900F Fours (83 – 94)	♦	3239
Yamaha XJ900S Diversion (94 – 01)	♦	3739
Yamaha YZF-R1 (98 – 03)	♦	3754
Yamaha YZF-R1 (04 – 06)	♦	4605
Yamaha FZS1000 Fazer (01 – 05)	♦	4287
Yamaha FJ1100 & 1200 Fours (84 – 96)	♦	2057
Yamaha FJR1300 (01 – 13)	♦	5607
Yamaha XJR1200 & 1300 (95 – 06)	♦	3981
Yamaha V-Max (85 – 03)	♦	4072
ATVs		
Honda ATC 70, 90, 110, 185 & 200 (71 – on)		0565
Honda Rancher, Recon & TRX250EX ATVs		2553
Honda TRX300 Shaft Drive ATVs (88 – 00)		2125
Honda Foreman (95 – 11)		2465
Honda TRX300EX, TRX400EX & TRX450R/ER ATVs (93 – 06)		2318
Kawasaki Bayou 220/250/300 & Prairie 300 ATVs (86 – 03)		2351
Polaris ATVs (85 – 97)		2302
Polaris ATVs (98 – 07)		2508
Suzuki/Kawasaki/Artic Cat ATVs (03 – 09)		2910
Yamaha YFS200 Blaster ATV (88 – 06)		2317
Yamaha YFM350 & YFM400 (ER & Big Bear) ATVs (87 – 09)		2126
Yamaha YFZ450 & YFZ450R (04 – 10)		2899
Yamaha Banshee and Warrior ATVs (87 – 10)		2314
Yamaha Kodiak and Grizzly ATVs (93 – 05)		2567
ATV Basics		10450
SCOOTERS		
Twist and Go (automatic transmission) Scooters Service and Repair Manual	◇	4082
TECHBOOK SERIES		
Motorcycle Basics Techbook (2nd edition)		3515
Motorcycle Electrical Techbook (3rd edition)		3471
Motorcycle Fuel Systems Techbook		3514
Motorcycle Maintenance Techbook		4071
Motorcycle Modifying		4272
Motorcycle Workshop Practice Techbook (2nd edition)		3470

◇ = not available in the USA ♦ = Superbike

The manuals on this page are available through good motorcycle dealers and accessory shops.
In case of difficulty, contact: **Haynes Publishing**
(UK) **+44 1963 442030** (USA) **+1 805 498 6703**
(SV) **+46 18 124016**
(Australia/New Zealand) **+61 2 8713 1400**

MCL 07.05.15

Preserving Our Motoring Heritage

The Model J Duesenberg Derham Tourster. Only eight of these magnificent cars were ever built – this is the only example to be found outside the United States of America

Almost every car you've ever loved, loathed or desired is gathered under one roof at the Haynes Motor Museum. Over 300 immaculately presented cars and motorbikes represent every aspect of our motoring heritage, from elegant reminders of bygone days, such as the superb Model J Duesenberg to curiosities like the bug-eyed BMW Isetta. There are also many old friends and flames. Perhaps you remember the 1959 Ford Popular that you did your courting in? The magnificent 'Red Collection' is a spectacle of classic sports cars including AC, Alfa Romeo, Austin Healey, Ferrari, Lamborghini, Maserati, MG, Riley, Porsche and Triumph.

A Perfect Day Out

Each and every vehicle at the Haynes Motor Museum has played its part in the history and culture of Motoring. Today, they make a wonderful spectacle and a great day out for all the family. Bring the kids, bring Mum and Dad, but above all bring your camera to capture those golden memories for ever. You will also find an impressive array of motoring memorabilia, a comfortable 70 seat video cinema and one of the most extensive transport book shops in Britain. The Pit Stop Cafe serves everything from a cup of tea to wholesome, home-made meals or, if you prefer, you can enjoy the large picnic area nestled in the beautiful rural surroundings of Somerset.

John Haynes O.B.E., Founder and Chairman of the museum at the wheel of a Haynes Light 12.

The 1936 490cc sohc-engined International Norton – well known for its racing success

The Museum is situated on the A359 Yeovil to Frome road at Sparkford, just off the A303 in Somerset. It is about 40 miles south of Bristol, and 25 minutes drive from the M5 intersection at Taunton.
Open 9.30am - 5.30pm (10.00am - 4.00pm Winter) 7 days a week, *except Christmas Day, Boxing Day and New Years Day*
Special rates available for schools, coach parties and outings Charitable Trust No. 292048